A LION HANDBOOK

The History of Christianity

Organizing Editor
DR TIM DOWLEY

Consulting Editors

JOHN H.Y. BRIGGS
Senior Lecturer in History
University of Keele
Staffordshire, England

DR ROBERT LINDER
Professor of History
Kansas State University
Manhattan, Kansas, USA

DAVID F. WRIGHT
Senior Lecturer in Ecclesiastical History
University of Edinburgh
Scotland

Designed by Tony Cantale Graphics

A LION HANDBOOK

The History of Christianity

Published by
Lion Publishing plc
Sandy Lane West, Oxford, England
www.lion-publishing.co.uk
ISBN 0 7459 1625 2 (hb)
ISBN 0 7459 3690 3 (pb)

First edition 1977
Revised edition 1990
10 9 8 7 6 5 4
Paperback edition 1996
10 9 8 7 6 5 4 3

A catalogue record for this book is available
from the British Library

Printed and bound in Singapore

PREFACE

Nearly two thousand years ago Jesus of Nazareth was put to death on a cross in an obscure corner of the Roman Empire. Today, world-wide faith in the risen Christ has grown as never before, not just in the so-called Christian West but in the new centres of Christianity in Africa, South-East Asia and South America.

How has the belief of a handful of persecuted and frightened people in Jerusalem expanded into a faith capable of 'turning the world upside-down'? How has it outlived the mighty Roman Empire—and outlasted the more recent empires of the last century? How did the Christian churches, denominations, movements, doctrines and beliefs we know today come into being? How has the faith been passed on from generation to generation, and from country to country? These are some of the questions we attempt to answer in this book.

To write the full story of the rise of the Christian faith in one volume is an almost impossible task. But we have at least tried to tackle it. We have called on the expertise of many contributors to help open up the subject. We have involved writers from many countries throughout the world, and drawn on wide resources for photographs, illustrations and charts.

Our aim has been to draw a rounded picture of the world-wide development of Christianity, focussing on the key movements, the outstanding Christian leaders, crucial turning-points, revolutionary breakthroughs. The compression necessary to a book of this length offers the prospect of exciting new perspectives across the centuries, a bird's-eye view of two thousand years of Christianity.

Is it objective history? Yes—if we mean that it is written by experts, well-informed on their subjects and abreast of modern views. Yes—if we mean that it claims to be accurate, scholarly and balanced. But no history can be detached. It is also written by scholars who are themselves Christians. They write with a sympathetic understanding which breathes life into their accounts. They are committed both to Christianity and to the unhindered pursuit of truth. They have not disguised or avoided the darker, the depressing or the disgraceful sides of the varied story of Christianity. But they can offer the bonus of insights into the people and movements they describe.

The story is an exciting one. We have tried not to over-simplify difficult questions. Wherever possible we have presented material visually and graphically, to give a 'feel' for the period concerned, to see the wood as well as the trees. We have had in mind those who may come new to the subject, excited by the discoveries, gripped by the unfolding story, wanting an account which is not so superficial as to be unsatisfying, but which wears its learning lightly; concerned not so much with academic theories as with real people and the real issues. We have tried to let the facts speak for themselves.

This new revised edition has kept to the aims of the original book. We have redesigned and re-arranged material to make things clearer and easier to follow. We have taken the opportunity to update, though surprisingly little material was 'dated', and to bring the story up-to-the-minute for a new decade. As the book was being prepared, revolutionary change was taking place in Eastern Europe – change in which the Christian church has played a major role.

It is the hope of editors and contributors alike that this Handbook in its new form will open up the story of the Christian faith to a whole new generation of readers.

CONTENTS

SECTION 4
A CHRISTIAN SOCIETY 600–1500

SECTION 5
REFORM 1500–1650

SECTION 6
REASON, REVIVAL AND REVOLUTION 1650–1789

SECTION 7
CITIES AND EMPIRES 1789–1914

SECTION 8
PRESENT AND FUTURE

CONTRIBUTORS

DR JOHN S. ANDREWS, formerly Sub Librarian, University of Lancaster, England. *Hymns and church music; Hymns and church music after 1800.*

CANON JAMES ATKINSON, Director of the Centre for Reformation Studies, University of Sheffield, England. *Reform; Thomas Cranmer.*

DR SHERMAN B. BARNES, formerly Professor of History, Kent State University, Kent, Ohio, USA. *Time and progress; Kenneth Latourette.*

DR D.W. BEBBINGTON, Lecturer in History, University of Stirling, Scotland. *C.H. Spurgeon; William Carey; William Wilberforce.*

DR PAUL M. BECHTEL, Professor of English, Wheaton College, Illinois, USA. *Fyodor Dostoevsky; Leo Tolstoy; Blaise Pascal; Alexander Solzhenitsyn.*

DR JANETTE BOHI, Professor of History, University of Wisconsin, Whitewater, Wisconsin, USA. *A crusade among equals.*

JOHN H. Y. BRIGGS, Senior Lecturer in History, University of Keele, Staffordshire, England. *God, time and history; Weighing up the evidence; The English Baptists; The first industrial nation; The Salvation Army; Present and future..*

DR COLIN BROWN, Professor of Systematic Theology and Associate Dean for Advanced Theological Studies, Fuller Theological Seminary, Pasadena, California, USA. *Anselm; Scholasticism; Reason and unreason; A world come of age; Friedrich Schleiermacher.*

THE REV. COLIN BUCHANAN, Bishop of Woolwich, England. *The sacraments are developed; Organizing for unity.*

DR JOHN CLARE, City of London School, London, England. *The Crusades; The Cathars.*

DR ROBERT G. CLOUSE, Professor of History, Indiana State University, Terre Haute, Indiana, USA. *Columba; Patrick; Boethius; Flowering: the Western church; Francis of Assisi; Thomas Aquinas; Savonarola; John of the Cross.*

DR L.W. COWIE, formerly Senior Lecturer in History, Whitelands College, London, England. *The first English missions.*

DR JAMES A. DE JONG, President and Professor of Historical Theology, Calvin Theological Seminary, Grand Rapids, Michigan, USA. *Expansion World-wide.*

DR WALTER DELIUS, Professor of Church History, Theological Faculty, Berlin, Germany. *Alcuin.*

DR BRUCE A. DEMAREST, Professor of Systematic Theology, Denver Seminary, Denver, Colorado, USA. *Jerome; Interpreting the Bible.*

DR WAYNE A. DETZLER, Associate European Director, Greater Europe Mission. *Europe in Revolt; Pope Pius IX; The Bible Societies.*

THE REV. DR JOHN P. DONNELLY, Associate Professor of History, Marquette University, Milwaukee, Wisconsin, USA. *Gasparo Contarini; The Jesuits; Pope John XXIII.*

DR JAMES D.G. DUNN, Department of Theology, Durham University, Durham, England. *Pentecostalism and the Charismatic Movement.*

H.L. ELLISON. *The Christian church and the Jews.*

DR EVERETT FERGUSON, Professor of Church History, Abilene Christian University, Texas, USA. *Irenaeus; Origen; Tertullian; Athanasius; John Chrysostom.*

DR RONALD C. FINUCANE, Chairman, Department of History, Benedictine College, Atchison, Kansas, USA. *Medieval monasticism in the West; Persecution and Inquisition; The Waldensians; An age of unrest.*

THE REV. SHIN FUNAKI, Japan Bible Seminary, Tokyo, Japan. *Toyohiko Kagawa.*

DR HARLIE KAY GALLATIN, Professor of History, Southwest Baptist University, Bolivar, Missouri, USA. *The Eastern church.*

DR W. WARD GASQUE, E. Marshall Sheppard Professor of Biblical Studies, Regent College, Vancouver, Canada. *The Church Expands: Jerusalem to Rome; The challenge to faith.*

DR COLIN HEMER. *Archaeological light on earliest Christianity; Justin Martyr.*

CANON MICHAEL M. HENNELL, Manchester Cathedral, Manchester, England. *The Evangelicals; The Oxford Movement; Cardinal Newman.*

WALTER HOOPER, Literary Advisor to the Estate of C.S. Lewis. *C.S. Lewis.*

THOMAS HOWARD, Chairman of the Department of English, St John's Seminary, Brighton, Massachusetts, USA. *Christianity and the arts.*

DR LARRY W. HURTADO, Professor of Religion, University of Manitoba, Winnipeg, Manitoba, Canada. *How the New Testament has come down to us.*

DR FRIEDRICH WILHELM KANTZENBACH, Professor of History of Church and Christian Doctrine, University of Saarland, West Germany. *Albert Schweitzer.*

DR ALAN KREIDER, Warden, The London Mennonite Centre, London, England. *John Foxe; Christians and war; The Anabaptists.*

A.N.S. LANE, Lecturer in Christian Doctrine, London Bible College, Northwood, England. *A flood of Bibles; William Tyndale and the English Bible.*

DR ROBERT D. LINDER, Professor of History, Kansas State University, Manhattan, USA. *Peter Abelard; The Catholic Reformation.*

DR ANDREAS LINDT, Professor of Modern Church History, University of Berne, Switzerland. *John Calvin* (abridged and translated).

DR H. DERMOT MCDONALD, formerly Vice-Principal and Senior Lecturer, History of Doctrine and Philosophy of Religion, London Bible College, Northwood, England. *Marcion; Basil the Great; Nestorius; Cyril of Alexandria; William of Ockham.*

DR PHILIP M. J. MCNAIR, Professor and Head of Department in Italian, University of Birmingham, England. *Seeds of Renewal.*

DR CAROLINE T. MARSHALL, Professor of History, Madison College, Harrisonburg, Virginia, USA. *Bernard of Clairvaux; Thomas Becket; Popular religion; Jan Hus; Teresa of Avila.*

DR RALPH P. MARTIN, Professor of New Testament, Fuller Theological Seminary, Pasadena, USA. *How the first Christians worshipped.*

DR JAMES R. MOORE, Arts Faculty, The Open University, Milton Keynes, England. *The rise of modern science; The reasonableness of Christianity.*

DR JAMES I. PACKER, Regent College, Vancouver, Canada. *The faith of the Protestants; Ignatius of Loyola.*

DR C. RENÉ PADILLA, Ediçiones Certeza, Buenos Aires, Argentina. *How many theologies?; An age of liberation; Helder Camara.*

DR RICHARD PIERARD, Professor of History, Indiana State University, Terre Haute, Indiana, USA. *An age of ideology; Billy Graham.*

ARTHUR O. ROBERTS, Professor at large, George Fox College, Newberg, Oregon, USA. *George Fox and the Quakers.*

DR WESLEY A. ROBERTS, Pastor, Peoples Baptist Church of Boston, 134 Camden Street, Boston, Massachusetts, USA. *Martin Luther King, Jr.*

DR H.R. ROOKMAAKER. *Art and the spirit.*

DR HARRY ROSENBERG, Professor of History, Colorado State University, Fort Collins, Colorado, USA. *Bede; The West in Crisis; Gregory the Great; Pope Innocent III.*

DR HAROLD ROWDON, former Lecturer, London Bible College; General Editor and International Secretary of Partnership, a network of independent churches. *The Brethren; Hudson Taylor.*

THE REV. W.J. ROXBOROGH, Presbyterian Church of New Zealand. *Thomas Chalmers.*

HOWARD SAINSBURY, Senior Lecturer in Education, Edge Hill College of Higher Education, Ormskirk, England. *Jonathan Edwards.*

DR ROBERT V. SCHNUCKER, Professor of History and Religion, North East Missouri State University, Kirksville, Missouri, USA. *Huldreich Zwingli; Theodore Beza.*

DR HENRY R. SEFTON, Master of Christ's College, Aberdeen and Lecturer in Church History, University of Aberdeen, Scotland. *Buildings and belief; Building for worship; Cathedrals and their builders.*

DR IAN SELLERS, Honorary Lecturer in Church History, University of Manchester, England. *George Whitefield; Howell Harris; The Unitarians.*

THE REV. MICHAEL A. SMITH, Minister of Golcar Baptist Church, Huddersfield, Yorkshire, England. *Worship and the Christian year; Josephus; Eusebius; Peter; Paul; Novatianists; Ignatius of Antioch; Spreading the good news; Clement of Rome; Ambrose of Milan; Leo the Great; Christian ascetics and monks.*

DR KEITH L. SPRUNGER, Professor of History, Bethel College, North Newton, Kansas, USA. *Puritans and Separatists.*

DR PAUL D. STEEVES, Assistant Professor of History, Stetson University, DeLand, Florida, USA. *The Paulicians and the Bogomils; The Orthodox church in Eastern Europe and Russia; The Russian Church.*

DR ROBERT STUPPERICH, Professor of Church History, University of Munster, Germany. *Martin Luther; Philip Melanchthon; Martin Bucer.*

DR ANTHONY C. THISELTON, Principal, St John's College, Durham, England. *An age of anxiety.*

THE REV. DEREK TIDBALL, Senior Minister of Mutley Baptist Church, Plymouth, England. Formerly Director of Studies, London Bible College. *D.L. Moody.*

DR RICHARD A. TODD, Associate Professor of History, Wichita State University, Wichita, Kansas, USA. *Constantine and the Christian Empire; The fall of the Roman Empire; Clergy, bishops and pope.*

ANDREW F. WALLS, Director of the Centre of the Study of Christianity in the Non-Western World, University of Edinburgh, Scotland. *Outposts of Empire; Societies for mission; David Livingstone; Samuel Adjai Crowther; African independent churches.*

THE REV. DR A. SKEVINGTON WOOD, Principal, Cliff College, Calver, England. *Awakening; John and Charles Wesley; The Methodists; Count von Zinzendorf.*

CANON R.W.F. WOOTTON. *Translating the Bible.*

DAVID F. WRIGHT, Senior Lecturer in Ecclesiastical History, University of Edinburgh, Scotland. *The Montanists; Cyprian and North Africa; What the first Christians believed; Councils and creeds; The church in North Africa; Augustine of Hippo; The Donatists in North Africa; Pseudo-Dionysius the Areopagite; Cassiodorus.*

DR EDWIN YAMAUCHI, Professor of History, Miami University, Oxford, Ohio, USA. *The religion of the Romans; Manichaeans; The Gnostics.*

DR JOHN HOWARD YODER, Departments of Theology, University of Notre Dame, South Blend, Indiana, USA and Associated Mennonite Biblical Seminaries, Elkhart, Indiana, USA. *Christians and war; The Anabaptists.*

DR RUTH ZERNER, Associate Professor of History, City University of New York, USA. *Dietrich Bonhoeffer.*

SECTION 1
GOD AND HISTORY

THE CHRISTIAN CENTURIES

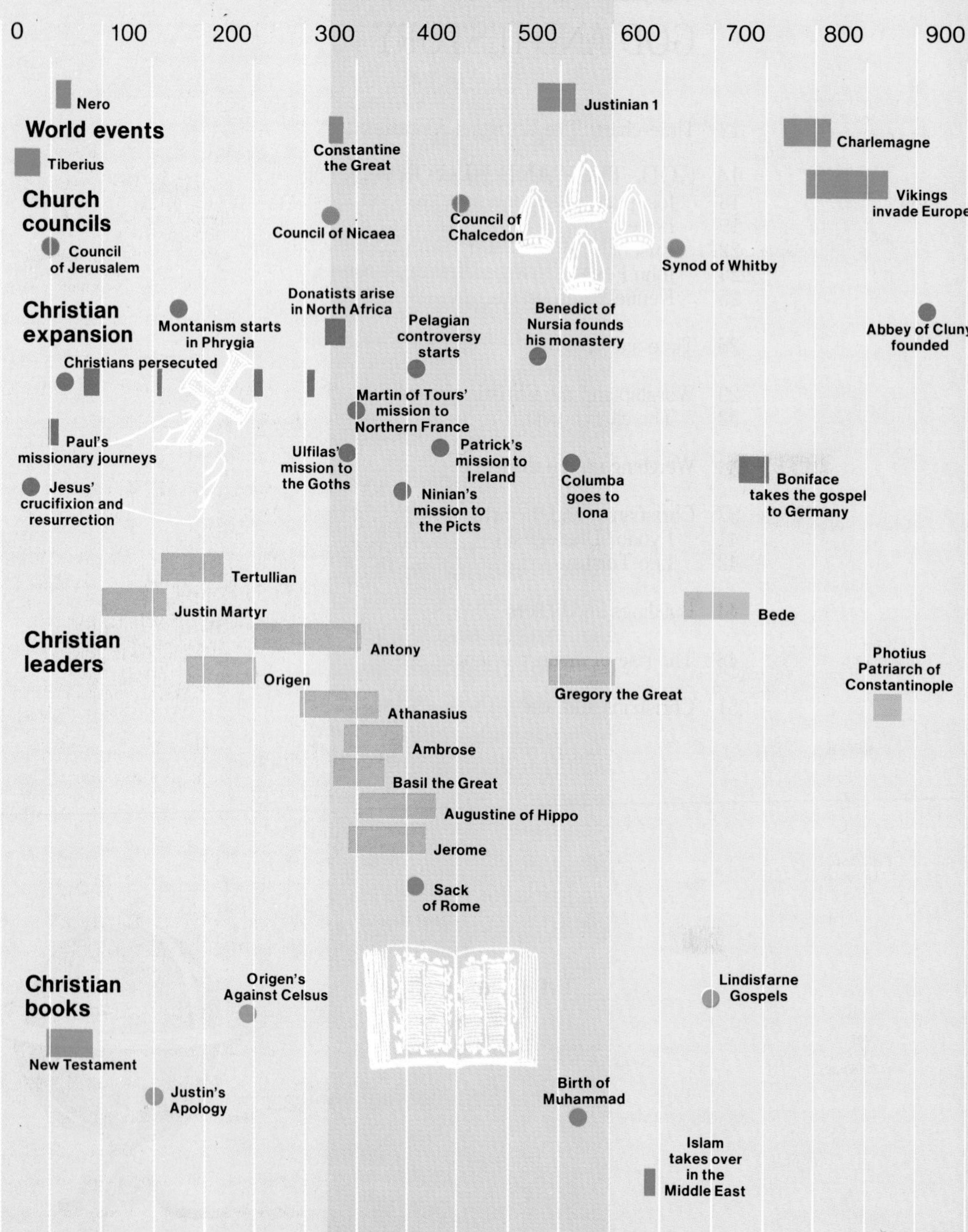
0
100
200
300
400
500
600
700
800
900
World events
Nero
Tiberius
Constantine the Great
Justinian 1
Charlemagne
Vikings invade Europe
Church councils
Council of Jerusalem
Council of Nicaea
Council of Chalcedon
Synod of Whitby
Christian expansion
Christians persecuted
Montanism starts in Phrygia
Donatists arise in North Africa
Pelagian controversy starts
Benedict of Nursia founds his monastery
Abbey of Cluny founded
Paul's missionary journeys
Jesus' crucifixion and resurrection
Martin of Tours' mission to Northern France
Ulfilas' mission to the Goths
Patrick's mission to Ireland
Ninian's mission to the Picts
Columba goes to Iona
Boniface takes the gospel to Germany
Christian leaders
Tertullian
Justin Martyr
Antony
Origen
Athanasius
Ambrose
Basil the Great
Augustine of Hippo
Jerome
Sack of Rome
Bede
Gregory the Great
Photius Patriarch of Constantinople
Christian books
New Testament
Justin's Apology
Origen's Against Celsus
Birth of Muhammad
Islam takes over in the Middle East
Lindisfarne Gospels

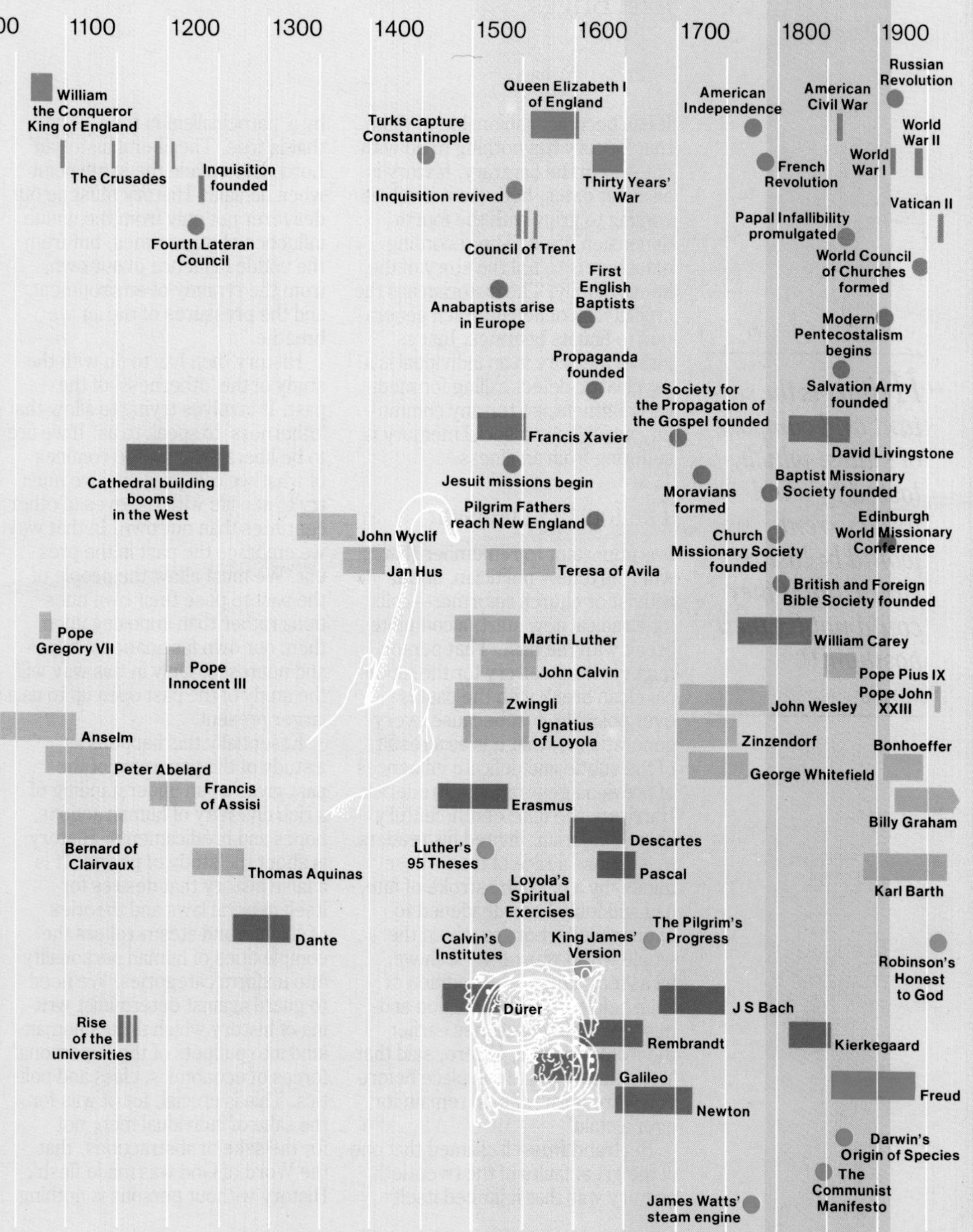
1000
1100
1200
1300
1400
1500
1600
1700
1800
1900
William the Conqueror King of England
The Crusades
Inquisition founded
Fourth Lateran Council
Cathedral building booms in the West
Pope Gregory VII
Pope Innocent III
Anselm
Peter Abelard
Francis of Assisi
Bernard of Clairvaux
Thomas Aquinas
Dante
Rise of the universities
Turks capture Constantinople
Inquisition revived
Council of Trent
Anabaptists arise in Europe
Queen Elizabeth I of England
Thirty Years' War
First English Baptists
Propaganda founded
Francis Xavier
Jesuit missions begin
Pilgrim Fathers reach New England
John Wyclif
Jan Hus
Teresa of Avila
Martin Luther
John Calvin
Zwingli
Ignatius of Loyola
Erasmus
Descartes
Pascal
Luther's 95 Theses
Loyola's Spiritual Exercises
Calvin's Institutes
King James' Version
The Pilgrim's Progress
Dürer
J S Bach
Rembrandt
Galileo
Newton
American Independence
French Revolution
Society for the Propagation of the Gospel founded
Moravians formed
Church Missionary Society founded
John Wesley
Zinzendorf
George Whitefield
James Watts' steam engine
American Civil War
Russian Revolution
World War II
World War I
Vatican II
Papal Infallibility promulgated
World Council of Churches formed
Modern Pentecostalism begins
Salvation Army founded
David Livingstone
Baptist Missionary Society founded
Edinburgh World Missionary Conference
British and Foreign Bible Society founded
William Carey
Pope Pius IX
Pope John XXIII
Bonhoeffer
Billy Graham
Karl Barth
Robinson's Honest to God
Kierkegaard
Freud
Darwin's Origin of Species
The Communist Manifesto

GOD, TIME AND HISTORY

John Briggs

It has become fashionable to claim that 'history has nothing to do with dates'. On the contrary, history is all about dates, because it involves coming to grips with the fourth dimension, time. The recording of history is to tell the story of the human family. The historian has the crucial task of helping each generation to find its bearings. Just as loss of memory in an individual is a psychiatric defect calling for medical treatment, so too any community which has no social memory is suffering from an illness.

> *"History is the sextant and compass of states, which, tossed by wind and current, would be lost in confusion if they could not fix their position."*
>
> *NEVINS*

The fourth dimension

It is important to remember this when anyone—politician, social activist or church reformer—calls for a radical new start, a complete break with the past. That person might just as well cry for the moon. No clean break with the past is ever possible, just because every generation is what it is as a result of the subtle and delicate influences of previous generations. Frederick Harrison, the nineteenth-century liberal historian, invited his readers to 'suppose a race of men whose minds, by a paralytic stroke of fate, had suddenly been deadened to every recollection, to whom the whole world was new.' 'Can we,' he asked, 'imagine a condition of such helplessness, confusion and misery?' Many centuries earlier the Roman writer, Cicero, said that 'not to know what took place before you were born' was 'to remain for ever a child'.

Bertrand Russell claimed that one of the great faults of the twentieth century was that it limited itself by a 'parochialism in time'. And that is true. The liberal historian Lord Acton made the same point when he said: 'History must be our deliverer not only from the undue influence of other times, but from the undue influence of our own, from the tyranny of environment and the pressures of the air we breathe.'

History then has to do with the study of the 'otherness' of the past. It involves trying to allow that 'otherness' to speak to us. If we are to be liberated from the confines of what we call 'present', we must try to see life with the eyes of other centuries than our own. In that way we embrace the past in the present. We must allow the people of the past to pose their own questions rather than imposing upon them our own fascinations, hopes and neuroses. Only in this way will the study of the past open up to us a larger present.

Essentially this happens as a study of the panorama of the past gives us an understanding of a rich diversity of human actions, hopes and predicaments. History is about the study of people. It is a false history that desires for itself general laws and theories of science and steam-rollers the complexities of human personality into uniform categories. We need to guard against determinist writing of history which makes humankind into puppets of the impersonal forces of economics, class and politics. This is crucial, for 'it was for the sake of individual men, not for the sake of abstractions, that the Word of God was made flesh'. History without persons is nothing.

Belief grounded in history

Christianity is essentially a historical religion. God reveals himself to his people, not in doctrinal statements nor in theoretical studies, but in action, in the outworking of a story of relationships. Moses instructed the fathers of Israel to have a story ready as an answer to their children's enquiries: 'When your son asks you in time to come, "What is the meaning of the precepts, statutes and laws which the Lord our God gave you", you shall say . . .' and then once more the story of the exodus had to be recounted. In this way the great Old Testament story was told: God's graciousness to his people in Egypt and in the wilderness, under David's kingship, in Solomon's cultured civilization, in exile in Babylon or fighting under Maccabean leadership. It is all part of the same story that continued with the story of the persecuted Christians of Rome, with the growth and expansion of the church, and yet with its constant need to be reformed and to regain the vision of the apostles.

The mysteries of the gospel cannot be confined within neat statements. We must be careful not to mistake the geometry of orthodoxy—important as it is—for the poetry of the gospel. This is a poetry that has beat, the heartbeat of the Spirit's pulse, as he energizes the people of God in their dynamic journey through history.

But this one story that covers both the Bible and church history has a focus. The theologian Oscar Cullmann puts it well: 'If we consider the Christian faith from the point of view of time we should say that the scandal of the Christian faith is to believe that these few years, which, for secular history, have no more, and no less, significance than other periods, are the centre and norm of the "totality of time". But the New Testament claims no less than this: "When all things began, the Word already was, but the Word became flesh, he came to dwell among us and we saw his glory, such glory as befits the Father's only Son, full of grace and truth." '

The birth of Jesus, the Christian church says, is reality breaking in on time, the real and the true breaking in upon our shadowy world of uncertain vision. In Jesus' life on earth, the scales are removed from our eyes and we glimpse ultimate truth. This so affects us that all other experience must be judged in relationship to this and to this alone. This is the point of reference which makes sense of the whole riddle of human experience.

So the climax of this most important story comes, not at the end, but in the middle—in the life, death and resurrection of Jesus of Nazareth. Here belief is grounded in history, for these are not legends but historical events. That is why Pontius Pilate is mentioned in the early creeds of the church. Here the world of faith and the world of history meet: Pontius Pilate, right outside the world of faith, becomes the check-point for the authenticity of Christian claims. The Messiah is not some legendary figure of conjecture or speculation, but became a human being in time and place in Jesus of Nazareth.

> *"Consciousness of the past alone can make us understand the present."*
>
> *HERBERT LUETHY*

What does the story mean?

If Christianity is an historical religion, it follows that all history is God's history. The succession of the years is not merely an unravellable tangle of events without general meaning. History witnesses to a divine purpose and is moving towards a divine goal, what Charles Kingsley called 'the strategy of God'. Indeed it was the Jews and the Christians who introduced the idea of time moving towards a goal (linear time) as against older arbitrary or cyclic views. The Christian has a scheme of reference by which to judge the particulars of history.

Events, taken in isolation, lack a flavour which can only be appreciated when they are seen in relationship with other events. The historian's far-reaching vision can be compared with the lean and thin perception of the journalist, little more than twenty-four hours deep. But history set in the context of a theology of 'beginnings' and 'ends' enables the Christian to see something of the true 'thickness' of events. He or she can see them not only in their contemporary setting, not only in their setting in human history, but in relation to 'In the beginning God', and 'I will come again'.

Many of the great cathedrals have maintained high standards of music to express their praise to God. Here the choir enters Wells Cathedral, in England.

In tracing God's continued activity in history, however, care must be taken to avoid naive arguments about power—as if the great or successful battalions in church history somehow 'prove' the truth of Christianity. One church historian has written: 'The glibness with which people still trace what they are pleased to call the hand of God in history is enough to make unregenerate historians sneer, and to shock those of us whose religion teaches them that the ways of God are past finding out, and that you cannot draw morals from the fall of towers in Siloam or from the success or failure of pious rebels in Galilee.'

God's work is a secret work. Honesty demands that when we look at a history text-book, we say that it is often difficult to discern there the finger of God. Sometimes we may think we see him at work, but for the most part the story reads in such soiled and earthy terms that we too easily exclude God from the story. It may be easier to recognize God at work in the life of Augustine of Hippo or Francis of Assisi, in the Evangelical Revival or in the heroic devotion of a Mother Teresa; much more difficult to see it in the Black Death or the dropping of the A-Bomb on Hiroshima. But it is wrong to confine God to the pleasant and the congenial. The chorus in T. S. Eliot's play *Murder in the Cathedral* takes this wider view of God's activity in history. Contemplating all the pain and suffering of human existence, they conclude:

'. . . only in retrospection, selection
We say, That was the day.
The critical moment
That is always now and here.
Even now in sordid particulars
The eternal design may
appear.'

The shadows as much as the sunlight, the agony as much as the ecstasy, are part of the divine purpose. In the tapestry of time, the hand of God weaves as many sombre skeins as bright-hued silks. In our perceptions of history, we see only the reverse side of things: with all the muddle of loose strands, back-stitching and overworked patterns. We see something of the design as it appears on the right side, but we never see it as it actually is: the clarity and beauty of the design as it appears face up are as yet denied to us.

So Christians both know and yet do not know the meaning of history. On the one hand, they have particular insight into the nature of history because they know the end of the story—and therefore can gauge the true depth or 'thickness' of events. But at the same time they do not, and cannot, know the full *meaning* of the story.

Many secular historians find it hard to live with this continuing necessity for ignorance, for it seems to suggest professional incompetence. As a result, some strive overmuch to account for everything, so that they become like gods, manipulating the past by their rival theories and hypotheses. Christian historians see such total explanation as impertinent, for this is the time of God's secret work. Thus, although Christians believe that God is the Lord of history in all its totality, they do not now pretend to know the plan of God, and cannot, therefore, construct a pattern of history upon that basis. Only at the end of time, when we are allowed to view history from God's viewpoint, will we fully see how exactly the hand of God has been at work in the process.

Does church history matter?

The Christian not only claims that all history is God's history, but that within history the Holy Spirit has not left himself without witness in any generation. This is what is meant by the word 'catholic', used in its primary sense: the presence of the living Christ, recognized, adored and obeyed, securing the catholicity of the church in every age, granting it its proper wholeness. At the beginning of the Christian era the Holy Spirit worked through the apostolic community. As that community responded to the passing of the years, to the pressures of the society in which it was set, and to the emergence of dangerous trends amongst its own members, so it both produced written records and defined its doctrine.

To make the Bible stand over against tradition at this period would be entirely false. The two are one. Scripture is the tradition of the apostles as committed to writing by them, or by those closely associated with them. Equally, of course, our knowledge of the apostolic church depends almost entirely upon the record we have in the New Testament.

But from the middle of the second century AD the word 'tradition' comes to have a secondary meaning: the teaching of the early Fathers of the church. At that period tradition was still regarded principally as an interpretation and unravelling of Scripture, but later it gradually came to stand over against Scripture. At the Council of Trent (1545–63), Scripture and tradition were defined as two distinct authorities. But Protestants still claimed that the Bible 'contained all things necessary to salvation'.

But what of the relationship between Scripture and tradition today? Cullman restates the question: 'The problem of Scripture and tradition concerns the place we give to the period of the church with reference to the period of the incarnation.' The period of the church is crucial to Christian understanding, but equally clearly it is not 'the period of the incarnate Christ and of his apostolic eyewitnesses'. It is because Paul was an *eye-witness* of the risen Lord that his writings stand in a quite different category from, for example, those of Augustine, however important Augustine may be as a theologian.

JOSEPHUS

Michael A. Smith

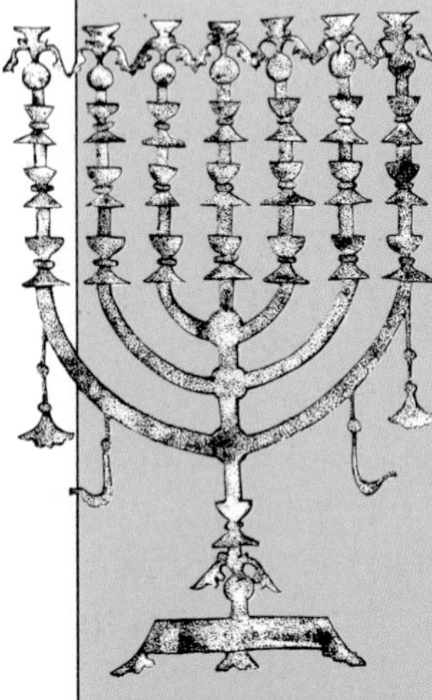

A seven-branched candlestick similar to this stood in the Temple at Jerusalem. It was part of the plunder seized by the Romans in the Jewish revolt of AD 66–70.

Josephus, the Jewish historian, was born in AD 37 of a priestly Jewish family. He was well educated, and followed the Pharisaic form of Judaism. In 64 he visited Rome as a member of a Jewish embassy. Although Josephus claimed to have advised against armed revolt against the Romans during the Jewish revolt (AD 66–70) he commanded a Jewish force in Galilee with some success. Besieged at Jotapata, he was captured by the Romans. He changed sides and began helping the Romans and trying to persuade the remaining Jews to come to terms. After the end of the Jewish revolt, he went to Rome with Titus, and lived there until his death about AD 100. Josephus became a close friend of the Emperors Vespasian and Titus, and took their family name, Flavius.

Josephus did all his writing at Rome. His works included *The Jewish Wars* and *The Antiquities of the Jews* (which tells the story of the Jews from creation to the fall of Masada), *Against Apion,* which defended Jews against pagan slanders, and a short autobiography.

Josephus wrote both to justify his own conduct and to commend what was most attractive in Judaism to the Romans. He condemned the Zealots vitriolically and praised his patrons Vespasian and Titus in glowing terms. Apart from this, Josephus gives much extremely valuable information about the period from the Maccabean revolt onwards. We depend on Josephus for most of our knowledge of the New Testament background. He has short, specific references to Jesus, John the Baptist and James, the brother of Jesus. Josephus is a rather wordy writer, but generally reliable.

Cullmann also wrote: 'The fixing of the Christian canon of Scripture means that *the church itself,* at a given time, traced a clear and definite line of demarcation between the period of the apostles and that of the church, between the time of foundation and that of construction . . . between apostolic tradition and ecclesiastical tradition . . . By establishing the principle of a canon the church recognized that from that time the tradition was no longer a criterion of truth. . . It declared implicitly that *from that time* every subsequent tradition must be submitted to the control of the apostolic tradition.'

Where is the church in history?

If it has been the error of the Roman church since the Council of Trent to magnify the authority of tradition, independent of the authority of the Bible, modern Protestants have sometimes been guilty of the opposite error—of neglecting tradition altogether. It is dangerous to suggest that the Holy Spirit was inactive in a particular period. Some of the Protestant historians of the nineteenth century preferred not to admit that the Spirit was at work in the mainstream of Catholic faith and devotion. They attempted to trace the work of the Holy Spirit from the time of Constantine to the Reformation in an 'apostolic succession' of heresies; some of them we would regard as reform movements, but others were heretical by any standard. Similarly, the claims of a number of modern deviations from Christianity (for example, the Mormons and the Jehovah's Witnesses) that they, in the latter years, have received a special revelation that promotes their supporters to the numbers of the elect, but excludes all others, must be rejected. Quite apart from other factors, they err in denying the Spirit's activity throughout history.

The same objection must also be made with regard to all attempts to restore 'the primitive church'. For there is an apostolic succession of faith, devotion and spiritual response, if not of bishops. Too many Protestants have adopted an unnecessarily negative attitude to tradition, and have therefore failed to inform their faith by the study of the story of the church. It is said that the Acts of the Apostles are more correctly described as the 'Acts of the Holy Spirit'. But it is all church history which should be written under that title and be appreciated as such. Any Christian movement which neglects this story loses the dimension of solidarity with Christ's church in all ages. The slogan 'Back to the New Testament!' represents only part of the truth. 'Onwards with the Spirit!' is the other half of this truth; together they make up the authority of the Reformers—which was always that of 'Word and Spirit'. It is the same Spirit who inspired the Bible who is alive in the church, creating the tradition and bringing afresh to every age the authority of the once-given Word.

Spirit and structure

Pentecost is the story of the outpouring of the Spirit upon waiting disciples. Such was the force of that experience that the structure of synagogue and temple were made obsolete. But, equally, the coming of the Spirit not only renewed the personal

BEDE

Harry Rosenberg

Bede (673–735), the most talented historian of the early Middle Ages, spent almost his entire life in the monasteries of Wearmouth and Jarrow in the north of England, where, by the eighth century, a vigorous Anglo-Saxon culture was flowering.

The development of Christianity in Britain found its perfect historian in Bede who was known by the title 'Venerable' from the ninth century, for the holiness of his life. His *Ecclesiastical History of the English People* is marked by careful attention to his sources of information, which are clearly identified, as well as by concern for facts as opposed to legend. His *History* is a major source of information about early England.

Bede wrote numerous other works which reflect his interest in biblical studies, including translation of the Bible into his own language. He also wrote on chronology (Bede popularized the calendar which uses the birth of Christ as the baseline for events), grammar, science, and the lives of English churchmen. In all these, as well as in his other historical and biblical works, Bede's thoughtful caution contrasts with an age when people believed the supposedly miraculous on little real evidence.

> *"If history records good things of good men, the thoughtful hearer is encouraged to imitate what is good: or if it records evil of wicked men, the good, religious listener or reader is encouraged to avoid all that is sinful and perverse, and to follow what he knows to be good and pleasing to God."*
>
> BEDE

A Celtic cross. In Bede's time the Christian leaders would teach or preach at the foot of these crosses, and often Bible stories were depicted on the cross itself.

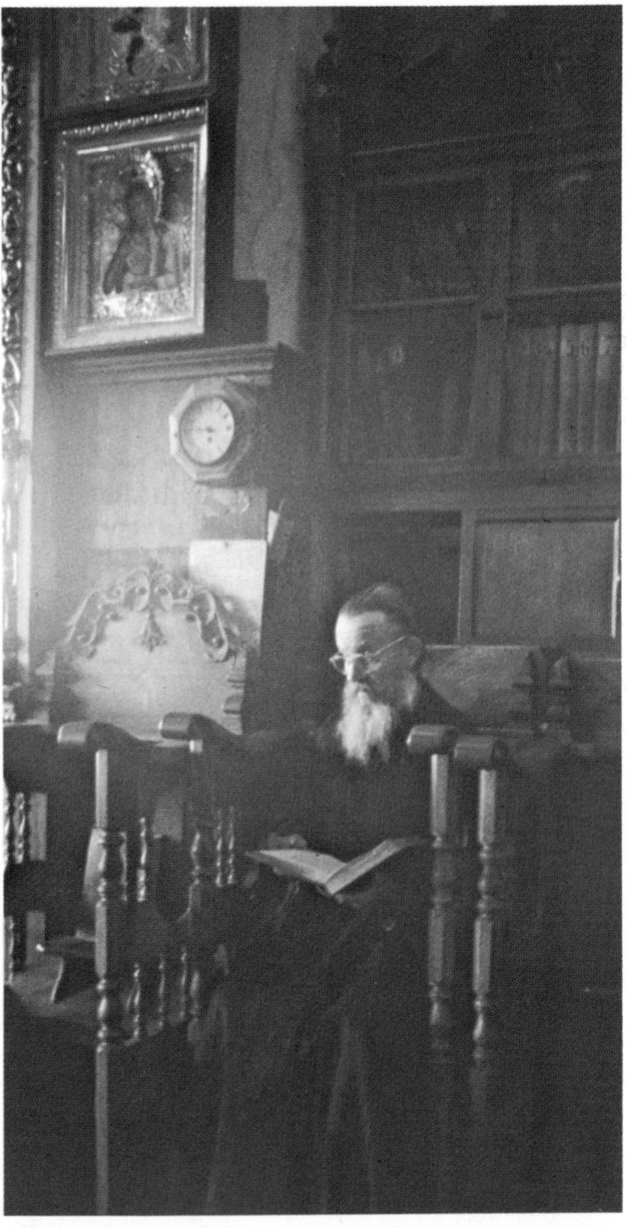

The Greek church has a great respect for tradition and continuity. The picture shows an Orthodox monk from Mount Athos, Greece, a centre of monasticism in the Orthodox church.

lives of individuals, it created a new community of shared life and work, new fellowship in the mission of a gospel to be proclaimed. And this new community was to be of strategic importance. For, called into being by the Spirit, it was also to be his witness and his agent in the world. Life in the apostolic church consisted of an interplay of Spirit, community and witness.

In one sense church history is the story of the struggle to keep those three elements in proper relationship. It is the story of the tension between the church as God's people, born of the Spirit and its visible, human organization. To describe this relationship people have often spoken of the 'church visible' and the 'church invisible'. The 'visible church' is always related to a given culture. As part of history and society it inevitably has shortcomings. Yet, at the same time, however poor its life and its witness, it points to the greater reality of the 'invisible church', 'the church as it really is before God' (Calvin).

It is tempting to be impatient with the 'visible church', to reject its services, and call for direct dependence upon the promptings of the Spirit. The record of church history is full of critics of church structures and organization. But church history also indicates that structures can never be wholly avoided.

Try as they might to escape from the notion of the 'visible church', reformers have always failed in their attempt. Luther's own biography is a classic example of this. His book *The Babylonian Captivity of the Church* (1520) has been called 'the great renunciation' of the institutions of medieval Christianity. But once he had made his protest, Luther had the painful experience of re-creating church structures to meet the continuing religious needs of Protestants in Germany.

But there are structures that allow the Spirit freedom through which, and not against which, he may work. We cannot do without organization—though equally it must not take command. All too easily the historian can confuse the two, or concentrate on structures to the exclusion of all else, because this is easier to explain and describe.

Even good structures can, however, outlive their usefulness and must constantly stand under judgement. The people of God must never forget that they are a pilgrim people who have 'no abiding city' in time. Throughout the history of the church a variety of movements has protested against static religion. So, over against the history of 'churches' in the modern period, for example, the church historian will have to look at the evangelical movement, the missionary movement, the Oxford movement, the liturgical movement, the charismatic movement, the ecumenical movement and the liberation movement. In so far as such movements are of the Spirit, the institutional churches withstand them at their peril.

History's two harvests

Jesus told two parables about the harvest of time: the parable of the sower and the parable of the wheat and the tares. The second is perhaps the more appropriate for our understanding of history. An older generation saw things differently. They took the parable of the sower as their model. They saw the seed ripening, cultivated by the church and Christian missions, to bear varying quantities of fruit. Liberals hoped that, when all defects of environment had been removed, society would improve; when education and equal opportunities had been made available to all, then misery and crime could be banished. It was left to the Marxists to re-introduce the element of conflict and tragedy into the story: they reminded Christians that evil, too, is a seed capable of bearing fruit, thirty-, sixty- and a hundred-fold.

And so we come to the parable of

"On Aidan's arrival, the king (Oswald of Northumbria) appointed the island of Lindisfarne to be his see at his own request. As the tide ebbs and flows, this place is surrounded by sea twice a day like an island, and twice a day the sand dries and joins it to the mainland. The king always listened humbly and readily to Aidan's advice and diligently set himself to establish and extend the Church of Christ throughout his kingdom. And while the bishop, who was not fluent in the English language, preached the Gospel, it was most delightful to see the king himself interpreting the word of God to his ealdormen and thanes.

He never sought or cared for any worldly possessions, and loved to give away to the poor who chanced to meet him whatever he received from kings or wealthy folk. Whether in town or country, he always travelled on foot unless compelled by necessity to ride; and whatever people he met on his walks, whether high or low, he stopped and spoke to them. If they were heathen, he urged them to be baptized; and if they were Christians, he strengthened their faith, and inspired them by word and deed to live a good life and to be generous to others.

His life is in marked contrast to the apathy of our own times . . ."

Bede looks back to the days of Bishop Aidan (died 651), History of the English Church and People

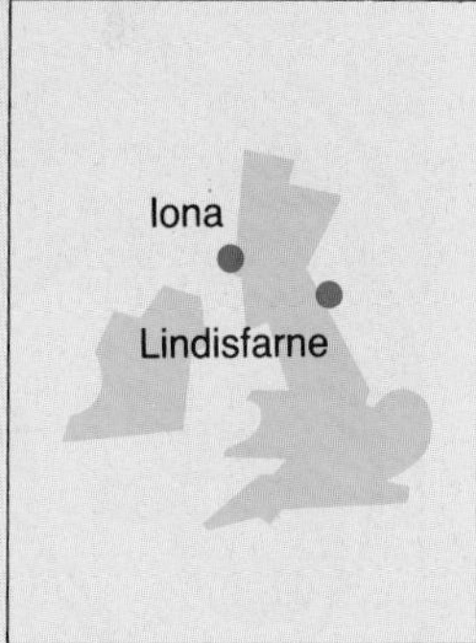

EUSEBIUS

Michael A. Smith

Eusebius (about 263-about 339) was the first to attempt a history of the church on a grand scale. Born in Palestine, he was on the run during the Great Persecution. He saw many martyrdoms in Egypt and was himself imprisoned for his faith. In 313–14 Eusebius was made bishop of Caesarea in Palestine, and later became a close friend of the Emperor Constantine, for whom he composed many flattering speeches. His political ideas helped to create the Christian Empire of Byzantium. In the Arian dispute Eusebius' own theology was suspect. He supported the banishment of Athanasius at the Council of Tyre (335). Eusebius was a typical court-bishop of the fourth century. A voluminous writer, his works include *Chronicles*, works to justify Christianity directed against pagans, biblical and theological works and letters, and above all his *Church History*. He was a keen follower of Origen.

The *Church History* was completed initially in either 303 or 311, but several supplements were added by Eusebius to bring the story up to 324 and the final triumph of his admired friend Constantine.

Eusebius dealt mainly with the succession of Christian bishops and teachers from apostolic times, heresies, the sufferings of the Jews, and the persecution and martyrdom of Christians. He also recounted traditions about the New Testament writers and details about the canon of Scripture. Eusebius wrote in a heavy, verbose and difficult style. However, his book is priceless since it preserves extracts from otherwise lost works. Much of his history is told by means of long quotations from previous writers. As a writer Eusebius was neither utterly credulous nor very critical. He does not stuff his work with improbable miracles, but accepts most of his sources at face value.

Although he was not the first church historian (Hegesippus and Julius Africanus were before him, but only fragments survive of their works), Eusebius was the first to attempt a history on a grand, comprehensive scale. He both set the pattern for future church historians, and was used extensively by later writers, for example, Jerome and Bede.

The '*Chi-Rho*' symbol, which uses the first two letters of the word Christ in Greek, was commonly used by the early Christians. This one forms part of the Roman mosaic pavement in a villa in Dorset, southern England.

the wheat and tares—which speaks of two harvests—a harvest of good and bad. It perhaps helps us to deal with a series of questions that Paul Tillich poses about the history of the church: 'What can we answer when our children ask about the child in the manger while in some parts of the world all children "from two years old and under" have died and are dying, not by order of Herod, but by the ever-increasing cruelty of war and its results in the Christian era, and by the decrease in the power of imagination of Christian people? Or what can we answer the Jews when the remnants of the Jewish people, returning from death camps, worse than anything in Babylon, cannot find a resting place anywhere on the surface of the earth, and certainly not among the great Christian nations? Or what can we answer Christian and non-Christian who have realised that the fruit of centuries of Christian technical and social civilization is the imminent threat of a complete and universal self-destruction of humanity? And what answer can we give to ourselves when we look at the unhealed and unsaved state of our own lives after the message of healing and salvation has been heard at every Christmas for almost two thousand years?' There is a harvest of tares as well as of wheat, a harvest that sometimes seems to threaten the very survival of the wheat.

But even this authenticates the Christian diagnosis of our ambiguous nature, with its impulses for both grief and glory. Sir Herbert Butterfield finds in history evidence of that 'serious gravitational pull' which the Bible calls sin: 'One of the reasons why it is so difficult to secure Utopia in our time or even anything very satisfactory in terms of a [United Nations] is the fact that no man has yet invented a form

This is the house of Martin Luther, the great Reformer, in Wittenberg, Germany.

JOHN FOXE

Alan Kreider

> *"The Lord began to work for his Church not with sword and target . . . but with printing, writing and reading . . . How many printing presses there be in the world, so many blockhouses there be against the high castle of St Angelo, so that either the pope must abolish knowledge and printing, or printing at length will root him out."*
>
> *JOHN FOXE*

John Foxe (1516–87) was an Elizabethan historian who is best known for his *Acts and Monuments*, popularly known as his 'Book of Martyrs'. Because he was a tireless compiler of accounts *(Acts)* and documents *(Monuments)* illustrating Christian heroism under persecution, his work is still an important source for historians.

But Foxe was not an impartial collector of historical data. He included these harrowing tales in his compendious work to prove a point. Throughout history, Foxe argued, a spiritual war has been raging between Christ (associated with the Protestants and the Word) and Antichrist (associated with the Catholics and the mass).

In this warfare, the English people have a unique mission. Their church has an independent history extending back to Joseph of Arimathea, who (according to Foxe) first brought the gospel to England. Since then, foreigners had repeatedly attempted to undermine the independence of the English church. They had established the pope's alien jurisdiction; they had imported superstition; they had persecuted. The recent reign of Mary Tudor had demonstrated the agony and humiliation which resulted when English people gave in to foreigners and Catholics.

But when the rulers and people of England had resisted these alien incursions, God had repeatedly blessed them. Let the English people (and, by implication, Queen Elizabeth I herself) therefore defend their national independence. Let them, as God's special people, lead history to its culmination, by reforming the Church of England according to the word of God. This view of England's history and destiny dominated the thinking of countless Englishmen for centuries. John Foxe was much more than a compiler; he was one of history's most influential mythmakers.

John Foxe, the Protestant writer, whose popular *Book of Martyrs* recounted the heroism and suffering of many early Protestants.

KENNETH LATOURETTE

Sherman Barnes

Kenneth Latourette (1884–1968) was an American pioneer in both Asian history and the global history of the church. His monumental *History of the Expansion of Christianity* (1937–45) covered all aspects of the life of the church over six continents and twenty centuries. He showed the two-way interaction between Christianity and the various environments in which it spread. Latourette believed that the record of Christianity was 'one of irregular advances and recessions'. Each fresh advance of Christianity has brought unforeseen results. For example, Christianity contributed to the rise of secularization, communism, technology and the population explosion, all of which can represent 'evils of colossal dimension'.

Latourette wrote that since 1800 Christianity has affected the world more extensively and deeply than ever before. This optimistic interpretation is presented in his five-volume *Christianity in a Revolutionary Age; A History of Christianity in the Nineteenth and Twentieth Centuries* (1958–62). In 1966 he repeated that '. . . the influence of Christianity has mounted and has never been greater than it is today'.

Latourette, a Baptist minister who never married, was a professor at Yale University. He was a close friend of students and non-academic church workers. He left an autobiography: *Beyond the Ranges* (1967).

"The influence of Christianity has mounted and has never been greater than it is today."

KENNETH LATOURETTE

of political machinery which the ingenuity of the devil would not find a way of exploiting for evil ends.'

So alongside the 'harvest' of creativity and self-sacrifice, of scientific investigation and social conscience, of mission and spirituality, there is this second harvest. But this is what the Christian faith, centred on the cross, is all about: on the cross, triumph and victory are shot through with rejection, disaster and dereliction. There the true nature of human history stands displayed.

The Christian faith does not have to contort itself to embrace the hard facts of history. It admits that the tragedy of history cannot be avoided, but claims that there is a power that redeems tragedy. Butterfield finds this one of the rewards of his own study of history: 'There is something very moving at times in Negro Spirituals—something which makes me feel that human nature under pressure can reach a creative moment, and find a higher end of life than the mere continuance of material comfort had seemed to offer them . . . It would seem that one of the clearest and most concrete of the facts of history is the fact that men of spiritual resources may not only redeem catastrophe but turn it into a great creative moment.'

So the two harvests belong together—the harvest of the wheat is not despite the tares, but because of them. As it becomes clear that all the pain, rejection and suffering is worthwhile, so history finds its meaning.

Time and progress

Sherman Barnes

Even before the invention of writing, people in Mesopotamia, Egypt, India and China felt the terror of time. Later they began to measure it with stone circles and calendars. And they looked to religion to overcome the insecurity they felt in relation to 'time, that makes the worlds to perish, when ripe . . .' (*Bhagavad-Gita*).

The early Chinese system of thought known as the *Tao* had a circular, or cyclical, view of time. The cycles derived from the source of being, Tao, which was able to transcend the distinction of past and present.

In ancient China, Confucianists believed that there had been a golden age in the past. They used past human events to teach people how to behave in the present. The practice of ancestor worship also developed in the Chinese a stronger sense of living in time.

An hour-glass. When all the sand has fallen into the lower globe, a measured interval of time has passed. Before clocks were common, sermons were sometimes timed with hour-glasses of this kind.

Greek philosophers such as Parmenides and Plato saw reality in the timeless ideals of beauty, goodness and truth. Aristotle regarded the passing of time as destructive. Truth lay in unchanging universal ideas—not in unique and particular events in history. The Roman thinker, Marcus Aurelius, wrote: 'A man of forty years . . . may be said to have seen all that is past and all that is to come; so uniform is the world.'

In the Greek and Roman worlds the goddess Clio was seen as looking after the writing of history. But there was no belief that history was moving towards a transcendent goal.

History was written by both the Greeks and the Romans. For example, Herodotus wrote his *History* to preserve the great and glorious deeds of both the Greeks and barbarians. Fair-minded to the Persians and curious about the other races, Herodotus, 'Father of History', always contrasted the Persians' slavery to a despot with the Greeks, 'free men owning no master but the law'.

The ancient Greek and Roman historians had a strong note of tragedy in their writing. Thucydides believed that human behaviour was overruled by general laws. Herodotus wrote, pessimistically: 'The states which were formerly great have most of them become insignificant, and such as are at present powerful, were weak in old times . . . human happiness never continues long in one stay.' Josephus (AD 37–100) wrote the history of the Jews in works intended to supplement the Old Testament and emphasize political history. He criticized the Greeks for their lack of historical perspective.

It was the ancient Hebrews who produced the first comprehensive

Measuring time by the sun. This sundial is set above a church porch.

and accurate historical narrative. 'The modern conception of history has its roots in the biblical story of *Jahweh* (God) and of the world which he creates as a scene for the unfolding of a divine plan.' The Bible gave history a religious significance; for it was in history that God entered into covenant with Israel, and it was in history, rather than in natural phenomena, that clues to God's nature were found. Events such as Israel's exodus from Egypt, the Assyrian destruction of Israel and the Babylonian captivity of the Jews were presented as unique events which revealed something of the divine plan. They were not mere cyclical recurrences.

The Bible gave more than a national history of Israel. God was shown as the Lord of all peoples. The Bible also encouraged the growth of the idea that time and history are important: it is in time and history that God works out his plan of salvation in dramatic confrontations.

The Bible emphasized that God's work in history and creation occurred in time. This undermined contemporary Near Eastern history which, with its dying-and-reviving nature gods such as Osiris, Tammuz and Dionysus, provided magical and mythical ways of escape from time. The Bible focussed its hope on a central historical event—the coming of the Messiah. After the incarnation, history was cut into two—BC and AD.

Christianity gave rise to new approaches to history. Augustine's *City of God* (426) attacked both Christians who expected the world to get better and pagans with a cyclical view of history. Augustine did not believe that the spread of Christianity would ensure political and economic improvement. The 'earthly city' of self-will would continue to exist amidst the rise and fall of states and empires.

In contrast to Augustine—and many centuries later—Joachim of Fiore (1135–1202) applied Christian doctrines about the future to secular affairs. He had a millenarian vision of a future age of the Holy Spirit, when love and justice would prevail on earth. Most of the secular ideas about the future in modern times are derived from Joachim's interpretation of history.

Between 1300 and 1700 many movements arose which claimed that human reason and creative power promised progress to a better world. Renaissance humanists shifted the focus from God to humanity, and substituted history for the un-historical theology of the medieval scholastics. The scientific movement from Copernicus, Galileo and Newton weakened the medieval and Reformation stress on providence and gave rise to the modern theory of progress. In spite of rearguard defences of providence by Calvin, Pascal and Bossuet, the theory of progress

"History is little more than the crimes, follies and misfortunes of mankind."

EDWARD GIBBON

"History is but a pack of tricks we play on the dead."

VOLTAIRE

> "*Every age of the world has increased, and still increases, the real wealth, the happiness, the knowledge, and perhaps the virtue, of the human race.*"
>
> EDWARD GIBBON

steadily gained ground. A number of related questions were raised at this time. Is there progress in knowledge but not in morality? In political life? In wealth? Is there progress in human nature? Can modern people surpass the ancient world in art and literature?

Theories of general progress multiplied between 1700 and 1914, and especially after 1800. The French thinker, Voltaire, and the English historian, Edward Gibbon, saw history as 'crimes and follies'; whereas the Frenchman, Condorcet, believed in human perfectibility and growing equality within and between nations. Darwin's theories assumed that nature itself determined the development and progress of all living things. This implied that any human-centred or God-centred view of the world was mere wishful thinking. By 1914 a growing number of intellectuals, such as Friedrich Nietzsche, Paul Valéry, James Joyce and Oswald Spengler, had come to disbelieve in the 'religion of progress'. Arnold Toynbee (1889–1975) is noted for his comprehensive book, *A Study of History* (1935–61), in which he described the genesis and breakdown of twenty-one civilizations. 'It looks as if the movement of civilization may be cyclic and recurrent, while the movement of religion may be on a single continuous upward line.'

Both Christians and non-Christians have criticized the idea of history as development and progress. In accounts of human history they see finiteness, conflict and frustration, irrationality and relativism. History itself is a problem, not a redemptive process bringing perfection on earth. Historical studies intensify the problem of meaning and pattern in general history. Mountains of specialist work do not add up to meaningful, coherent universal history. 'The brilliant conquest of the most distant frontiers of historical knowledge also coincides with an increasing awareness of the meaninglessness of history.'

There are signs of a desire to be free from history. Even the treatment of time in science fiction, by authors such as Isaac Asimov, Kurt Vonnegut and Arthur C. Clarke, suggests the feeling that time is never on humanity's side.

Christians believe that time will be brought to a summation by the God of history. Death is not the end of the human story.

Worship and the Christian year

Michael A. Smith

Sunday, the Christian day of worship, was observed from the very beginning of the Christian church. It was a radical departure from Judaism, which observed the sabbath (or seventh day of the week). The move to the first day of the week was to make a weekly reminder of the day when Jesus rose from the dead. Sunday was not observed as a public holiday until the time of Constantine (in the early fourth century); until then Christian meetings for worship were either early or late in the day. The main service was probably held early in the morning, although meetings for worship were also held in the evening. Because in Roman times the main meal was taken in the evening, there may well have been meetings for worship both morning and evening on Sunday. However, the early morning meeting soon became the most important.

The central service of worship on Sunday in the early church was the **'breaking of bread'** or 'communion'. This was a fellowship meal, with preaching, Bible reading and prayer, which culminated in the formal acts taken over from the Last Supper. The aim was to remember Jesus' death, and to celebrate his resurrection. Praise and thanksgiving were uppermost, and for this reason the name 'eucharist' (Greek for thanksgiving) was often given to the occasion. Gradually the eucharist became more formal, and the meal aspect secondary.

From the third century, Old Testament ideas of priesthood were used by some to interpret the eucharist as the 'Christian sacrifice'. At first the sacrifice was thought to consist of praises, but gradually it came to be held that an offering was made to God to gain forgiveness of sins. By the Middle Ages this had been developed to make the eucharist a re-offering of Christ's sacrifice on the cross. There also arose magical ideas concerning the bread and wine. By the fourth century it was held that either when the words of the Last Supper were repeated (in the Western church), or when the Holy Spirit was invoked on the bread and wine (at the prayer called the *epiclesis* in the Eastern church) a change took place. It was felt right to venerate the bread and wine as representing Jesus visibly.

The *agape* was at first the name given to the communion. Later it was often used of Christian fellowship meals apart from the communion. The separation of the two may well have been due to the growing custom of holding the main communion service early on Sunday morning, with a fellowship meal on Sunday evening. Originally the communion had been a proper meal, but as it became more of a ceremonial meal, the real fellowship meal took over the title of *agape* (meaning 'love' in Greek). The *agape* fell out of use during the third and fourth centuries.

A family celebrates the christening of a new baby in a modern Roman Catholic church.

Baptism was originally an occasion for witnessing to faith in Christ on conversion, and was the entrance ceremony to the church, identifying the person with the death and resurrection of Jesus. Only those who had been baptized took part in the communion service. Then, from an early period, considerable preparation was considered necessary before baptism took place. Candidates often had a period of three years' probation, to see if they were of good character. Then came a period of intensive instruction in Christian doctrine, often involving memorizing a short statement of Christian belief (the 'creed'). It was very likely that the creed began in the form of questions put to the candidate when he was baptized, and later became a statement of belief memorized and then recited at baptism.

Baptism was normally by immersion either in the river or in the bath-house of a large house. The person was normally immersed three times, in response to the three questions about belief in the three persons of the Trinity. From the early second century, baptism by pouring of water was allowed in cases of emergency or sickness. From the third century, the baptismal service also included the laying-on-of-hands by the chief minister of the church (the bishop), with a prayer that the candidate would receive the Holy Spirit.

Baptism seems normally to have taken place on Sundays. At first, baptism was probably only administered to adults. The first definite mention of child-baptism comes early in the third century, and infant baptism was beginning to be widespread by the mid-third century. Both adult *and* infant baptism were practised until the sixth century, after which, normally, only infant baptism was practised.

As early as the end of the second century some people had come to believe that baptism had a magical effect. Tertullian mentions prayer to 'sanctify' the water, and from then on it was widely believed that baptism automatically washed away sins. From this period, too, there arose the practice of exorcizing the candidate before baptism, often accompanied with ceremonial anointing with oil.

Daily prayer was observed in many ways by the first Christians. Some prayed three times a day, and others got up at midnight to pray. Later, daily services of prayer were held at pilgrimage centres and in monastic communities. Many written private prayers have survived from the third century onwards.

Easter was the main annual feast of the Christian church in early times. It was often called

A Christmas 'candlelight service'. In many parts of the world carols by candlelight have become a traditional way of celebrating the birth of Christ.

Part of a colourful Easter procession in modern Guatemala. The tableau represents an angel with Jesus during his agonizing prayer in the garden of Gethsemane before his arrest.

the Christian Passover, and was celebrated as the anniversary of Jesus' resurrection. During the second century considerable dispute arose about the correct date for its celebration, and at Rome various congregations observed different days. Some churches, notably in Asia Minor, kept to the Jewish calendar, even when Easter fell on a weekday. But this practice died out in the third century. Most other churches held Easter on the Sunday closest to the fourteenth day of the Jewish month Nisan. Because of problems with the calendar, there could be dispute as to which of two Sundays was correct. Several new methods of computing Easter were introduced, but agreement was not finally reached in the West until the Synod of Whitby (664).

As the great feast of the early church, Easter became a popular time for baptisms. The period of instruction before baptism became the period of preparation for Easter which we call **Lent**. This lasted forty days, to correspond with Jesus' forty days in the wilderness.

The Easter celebrations continued for seven weeks, culminating in **Pentecost** (Whitsun). This celebrated the anniversary of the giving of the Holy Spirit to the apostles, and also served as the triumphant end to the Easter period.

Good Friday and Easter Week (from Palm Sunday to Easter Day) seem to have become popular first of all in the Holy Land, where pilgrims retraced the movements of Jesus during the last week in Jerusalem. Originally both the death and resurrection of Jesus had been celebrated on the one Easter day. But during the fourth century the two events were separated, and a complex Easter cycle of services was well developed by the early fifth century.

Christmas seems to have started to be celebrated widely in the fourth century, to commemorate the birth of Jesus. There was considerable uncertainty about the correct date. Most of the Eastern churches settled for 6 January, but the West chose 25 December. It is not known for certain why these dates were picked, but it is possible that Christian churches chose days which were already public holidays for pagan celebrations. By the beginning of the fifth century, East and West had co-ordinated their practice, holding 25 December as the anniversary of Jesus' birth, while celebrating 6 January as the anniversary of the visit of the wise men. The present difference between Western and Eastern orthodox churches over the date of Christmas only arose in the eighteenth century. The West adopted the Gregorian calendar with an adjustment of twelve days, but the East retained the old calendar.

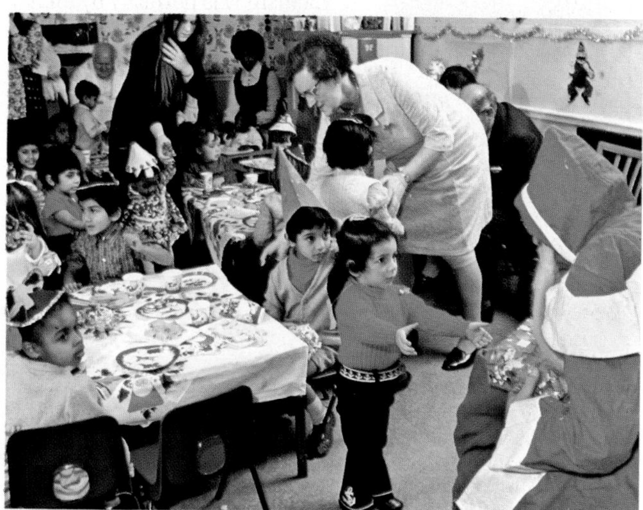

Young children receive presents from 'Santa Claus'. In many parts of the world the legend of St Nicholas (or Santa Claus) bringing gifts to children has become closely linked with the celebration of the birth of Christ.

As Christmas began to rival Easter in importance, it also acquired a preparatory period like Lent, which was called **Advent**. Because advent came at the point where the liturgical year ended, it was viewed both as preparation for

THE CHURCH YEAR

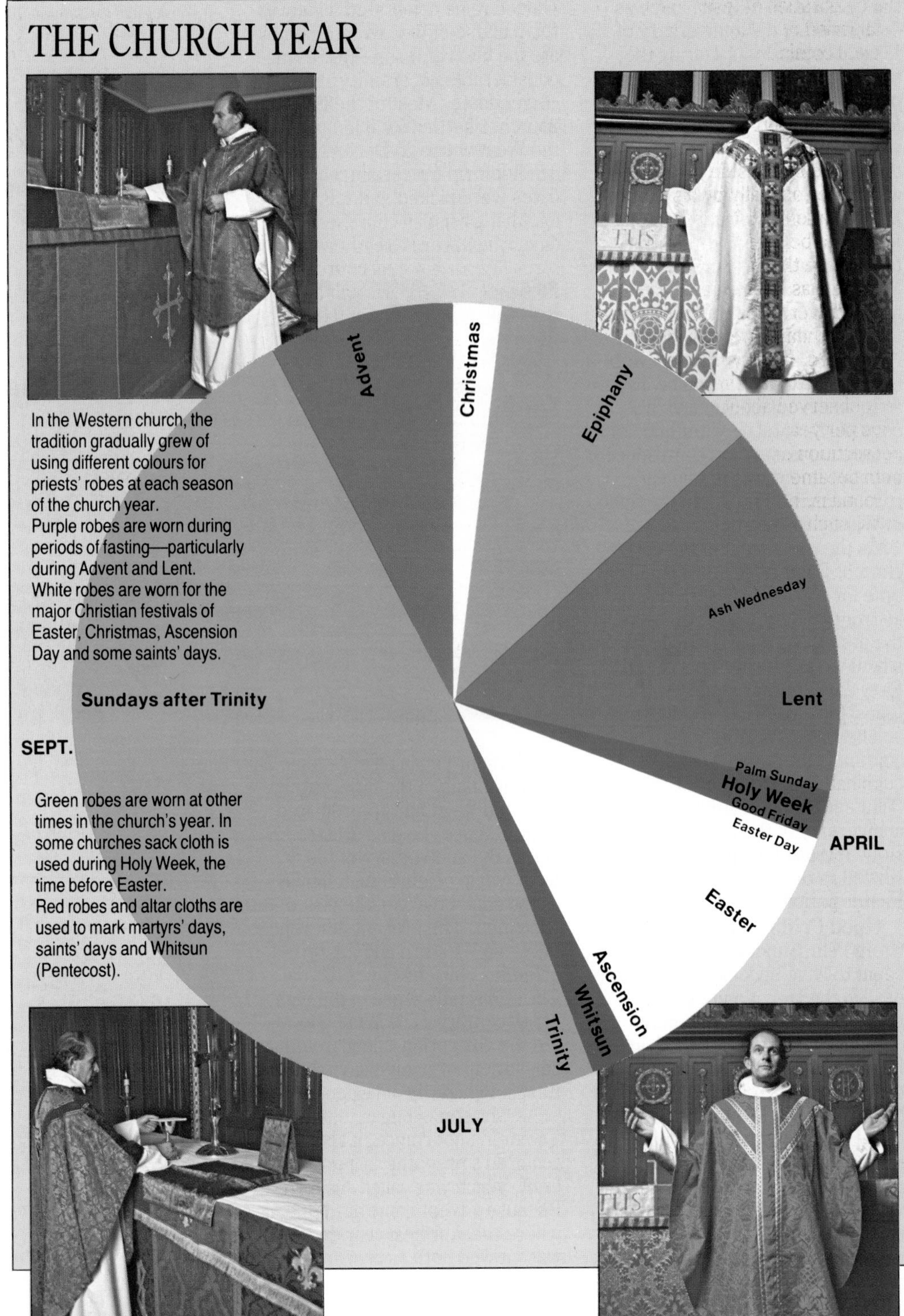

In the Western church, the tradition gradually grew of using different colours for priests' robes at each season of the church year.
Purple robes are worn during periods of fasting—particularly during Advent and Lent.
White robes are worn for the major Christian festivals of Easter, Christmas, Ascension Day and some saints' days.

Green robes are worn at other times in the church's year. In some churches sack cloth is used during Holy Week, the time before Easter.
Red robes and altar cloths are used to mark martyrs' days, saints' days and Whitsun (Pentecost).

the celebration of Jesus' birth, and as a period of looking forward to his second coming.

During the period of persecution under the Roman Empire, martyrs were regarded with the highest esteem. The date of a martyr's death, the **saint's day**, was often celebrated annually by his local congregation. Such celebrations tended to be local festivals only, although in the case of some apostles, such as Peter, Paul and John, such anniversaries (often referred to as 'birthdays') were widely celebrated. However, even by the fourth century an average church only observed about six such days per year. When, after the persecution of Diocletian, martyrdom became almost unknown for Christians, other notable Christians, such as hermits, ascetics or great missionaries, became venerated. Possibly the first of these was Martin of Tours. A special service of communion was held to celebrate the martyr's anniversary, sometimes at the tomb.

Those imprisoned for the faith had been allowed the privilege of forgiving penitent sinners. From this arose the belief that a martyr might still be able to obtain blessings for his local church. Some churches were built around the tomb of a martyr, and on the anniversary of the martyrdom it became customary to call on the martyr's prayers. A similar practice extended to include the saints and the Virgin Mary, and was often connected with the idea that the communion was an offering on behalf of the living and the dead.

The earliest-known printed Christmas card was made for an Englishman, Sir Henry Cole, in 1843. Since then Christmas cards have become part of the annual Christmas festivities in many countries.

Weighing up the evidence

John Briggs

> *"Whatever the twentieth century thinks about the irrelevance of the Christian religion, the men of the sixteenth century could not be made intelligible without it."*
>
> GORDON RUPP

> *"The historian must choose between generalizations which are never quite true in any specific instance and an incomprehensible anarchy of individual cases."*
>
> PROFESSOR NORMAN HAMPSON

The historian must always start with the evidence. Accordingly, he needs to collect as rich a diversity of materials as evidence as he can. Sometimes his difficulty will be that very little remains; at other times so much is available that only a sampling can be undertaken. The historian must always be ready to admit that the evidence is too incomplete to permit any confident conclusions. But since history is more an art than a science it often proceeds by way of reasonable conjecture, rather than by way of unshakable deduction. The historian will be happiest if his evidence shows a pattern which converges, and will be suspicious of any theory that arises out of the study of only one particular type of evidence.

Having examined all the evidence, the historian sets about writing his account. He has to be selective, not in the sense of rejecting what will not fit his theory, but in excluding the irrelevant and extraneous. At the same time he needs to have an eye for negative evidence: What could reasonably have been expected and has not materialized? Evidence of this kind may well add a crucial dimension to the picture.

Evaluation

The collecting together of source material must be followed by the all-important task of evaluation. Who is the writer? What do we know about his attitude to life? What qualifies him to speak authoritatively about the subject on which he has written? Is this document backed up by other evidence on the subject? And a host of similar questions. In particular, the historian will examine whether the document is consistent with itself. If it is not, then it must be suspect.

One judgement is crucial to the historian. Is the material he is studying significant simply for the particular situation he is studying, or does it, with other examples, suggest a more general pattern? To mistake the eccentric for the typical is a common fault.

Consider, for example, one historian's judgement on the English Victorian home. 'The real strength of Evangelicalism lay not in the pulpit or on the platform, but in the home. To those who believe that the typical Evangelical sermon was about hell-fire, that the typical Evangelical layman is fairly represented by the father of Sir Edmund Gosse and that the typical Victorian parent was Mr Barrett of Wimpole Street, this may sound surprising. But to judge from memoirs and biographies, the Evangelical families of England were conspicuously happy families, and it was in hearts of the Victorian mothers that the evangelical piety won the most signal and the most gracious of its triumphs' (Canon Charles Smyth).

As he evaluates the evidence the historian is bound to find disharmonies. But this does not necessarily mean that the evidence is rendered useless. If it reflects different view-points about an event it may in fact help to establish that the event really took place. For example, Hitler's guard and chauffeur gave evidence which differed over details concerning the burning of the bodies of Hitler and Eva Braun. But their evidence was bound to be different because of their different viewpoints. The historian Hugh Trevor-Roper shrewdly comments: 'The truth of the incident is attested by *the rational discrepancy of the evidence.*' This is equally relevant to the study of the New Testament evidence.

Interpreting the facts

Although the evidence is crucial to the writing of history, evidence, without comment, does not constitute history. Nor is history a bare narrative presented like an account sheet. The historian will hardly ever be content with a mere description of past actions. Rather he will want to reflect what actually happened in terms of an explanation. He will also want to give some assessment as to what are the most significant elements of his story. If history were to be confined to what could be stated with historical precision, then the subject would lose all interest and ability to instruct. What would be left to the historian if, for example, he had to limit his account to simply recording that, on 14 April, 1865, Abraham Lincoln was shot by J. W. Booth—with no opportunity to discuss the significance of the event?

The historian may work out an explanation in terms of a number of different patterns of connections. His account may be written, for example, in terms of causes and consequences, of development and decline, or of comparisons and contrasts.

Only at this last stage does a description emerge which bears relationship to what actually happened in the past. The past itself is more than a collection of documents or articles; for this reason interpretation is crucial to the description of the fact. It is not a mere layer of theorizing to decorate the superstructure, which can be dispensed with at will. That is, history moves not from the facts to a theory or a law, but from the sources to the facts. Those facts must include all the complexity of human psychology.

For the historian, an event can never be confined merely to action. It must always be concerned with action and agent, with all the discussion of motives that this involves. For an account of an action without the agent, and a description of the agent without the complexities of mind and emotion, would not reflect any past reality. It would only exist as an analytical abstraction of the present. History without people is nothing.

So, as he reconstructs the past, the historian brings together a variety of elements: a diversity of evidence of different kinds, weighed critically by the researcher, who selects from it the materials which will enable him to construct a pattern of relationships. He explains this pattern in terms of an interpretation which arises out of the evidence, on the one hand, and out of his experience and imagination on the other.

Can history be objective?

Historians have in recent years debated the extent to which the study of history can hope to be objective. This is a goal which many recognize as unachievable. But many also understand that over against criticism, detachment and analysis as ways of knowing, the historian must also use commitment, sympathy and imagination. One historian advised his students to read in a historical period until they heard its people speak.

An attractive way of thinking of historical study is as an encounter, a meeting-place, a conversation with the men of the past—not a kind of eternal mortuary, in which king and peasant alike are trapped, each neatly labelled with a confident analysis of his achievements and faults. Just because the historian is concerned with encountering the men of the past and gaining from them what they most can give, certainty will elude him. But this is gain and not loss; it is a sign that the counter is with real people and not mere historical stereotypes—or, more dangerously still, reflections of his own confidences and neuroses. Only if approached in this way does history increase human understanding.

The supposed detachment of the historian is rarely what it claims for itself. The historian who claims to be making an objective judgement may simply be imposing his own secular prejudices on his subject. 'We cannot see our own ideological spectacles, and because our eyes are protected by them, we do not notice that as we throw our sand against the wind, the wind blows it back again.'

It is not that a high standard of diligence in pursuing sources, or complete intellectual rigour in scrutinising them are not important. They are essential. But in themselves they are not enough. Only when the historian's imagination is brought to bear does the past come alive. Who is the historian? 'Having entered imaginatively into the experiences of the nomad, the agriculturalist and the city-dweller, having been marked by the sorrows of the persecuted and uplifted by the steadfastness of just men, having striven with Lenin and known the serenity of St Benedict, the historian is constantly recapitulating in his own person the history of man.'

In all this there is a razor-edge division between integrity and prejudice, between doing justice to the sources and justice to one's personality. There can never be any excuse for handling documents casually or sloppily. But in the end the historian has to combine the precision of the scientist with the creativity and humanity of the artist. The historian needs not only all the critical talents that he can muster but also those less tangible gifts of personality and experience if he is to use all the resources at his disposal for a complete and realistic understanding of the past, a real past inhabited by real men, flesh of our flesh, mind of our mind, with emotions that the historian also possesses. History, in fact, has to be written from person to person.

Christianity and the arts

Thomas Howard

Ever since the fourth century, the shape of civilization in the West has been heavily influenced by Christianity. Art is no exception. No account of history in the last sixteen centuries is possible without an understanding of the Christian contribution. It is ordinarily a shaky business to insist that a factor such as religion has a direct effect on particular political, economic or social events in history. But Christianity and art were causally linked between the fourth and the twentieth centuries. Even the 'post-Christian' art and literature of the last two hundred years in the West emerges from Christian roots—and often involves a more or less conscious repudiation of Christian categories, and an attempt to forge new forms, free of Christian influence.

It is very natural that Christianity should have deeply affected art. Christianity is rooted in present and real (as opposed to remote and fanciful) history. Its central events occurred in the times of public figures such as Caesar Augustus and Pontius Pilate. Christianity proclaimed not a retreat from real, historic, human existence and experience, but rather the redemption and glorification of that existence and experience. The very foundations of Christianity are the doctrines of creation and incarnation. It is inevitable that Christianity should robustly celebrate human flesh, created in the image of God, made the habitation of the incarnate God, and redeemed for the vision of God at last.

The human imagination, reflecting on this picture of things, was roused to shape and express its vision in visual, musical, narrative and dramatic forms.

There is no single common thread in all of the art of the Christian West over sixteen hundred years. What, for example, does Chartres Cathedral have in common with Sir Christopher Wren's London churches? Or the icon of the Virgin of Vladimir in Russia with a painting by Rembrandt of the holy family? Or medieval plainsong with the twentieth-century French composer Messiaen?

There is an enormously wide range of expression in Christian art. This results from the central paradoxes of the Christian faith. They include the paradoxes that arise when human imagination tries to function on the frontier that runs between time and eternity, between the transcendent and the immanent, or between the spiritual and the material. Theological language staggers on this borderline; the arts have similar difficulties.

For example, Christians have always differed about the arts. Although official church councils in

> *"Man now realises that he is an accident, that he is a completely futile being, that he has to play out the game without reason. I think that even when Velasquez was painting, even when Rembrandt was painting, they were still, whatever their attitude to life, slightly conditioned by certain types of religious possibilities, which man now, you could say, has had cancelled out for him. Man now can only attempt to beguile himself for a time, by prolonging his life—by buying a kind of immortality through the doctors. You see, painting has become—all art has become—a game by which man distracts himself."*
>
> *FRANCIS BACON, the English painter*

Christ healing the blind, from a seventeenth-century Ethiopic Gospel.

'The Holy Family', painted by Titian (1477–1576). Renowned for his versatility, Titian painted many biblical subjects on altar-pieces and church decorations.

'The Annunciation', a painting by the medieval artist Duccio.

The Pieta from the Duomo, Florence, by Michelangelo (1475–1564).

This Bach manuscript is a reminder that great musicians, as well as artists, authors and sculptors, have drawn inspiration from the biblical salvation story.

both East and West before the year 1000 had proclaimed that Christian image-making was permissible, many Christians have a lingering distrust of these images. They fear that by having an image of the thing before them, vision and devotion might attach themselves to the image, and fail to press on to the thing for which the image stands. This viewpoint was maintained by the image-rejecting 'iconoclasts' in the Orthodox church for hundreds of years, with fluctuating success. It has always been alive in some part of the church. Some Protestant traditions show a similar trend, playing down the visual. This is just one aspect of the problem that Christians face in finding ways, both visual and verbal, to express God's mysteries adequately.

Christians vary widely on the question of what sort of imagery is appropriate. For example, in depicting the annunciation, one artist would try to catch the whole idea of our mortal flesh being hailed by God's splendour. He would depict the Virgin (our flesh) crowned with gold (raised to glory by the promise of redemption), sitting under gilded arches, being approached by a shining winged creature. This is the visual expression of a theological concept—and was widespread in the Middle Ages. Another artist would want to suggest the apparently unfavourable way in which the drama of the gospel was played out on the stage of history. In this case, she would show the Virgin as a very ordinary young woman, in ordinary surroundings. The difference between the two paintings arises not so much from a difference in the two artists' doctrines, as from their contrasting ways of coming at the subject.

Christian artists have also had to ask whether they should paint 'religious' subjects (annunciations, nativities, crucifixions and saints' lives), or celebrate ordinary human life, without tackling these religious topics. Christian art from the early centuries up to the Renaissance tended to choose the first option. However, medieval artists, far from ignoring ordinary life, brought the whole of everyday life into service. We find tiny farming scenes decorating the borders of devotional books and, in cathedrals and churches, wooden carvings of craftsmen at work. On the

An illustrated page from the *Stavelot Bible*. In the corners are symbols to represent each of the Gospel writers.

Death, be not proud, though some have called thee
Mighty and dreadful, for thou art not so;
For those whom thou think'st thou dost overthrow
Die not, poor Death, nor yet canst thou kill me.
From rest and sleep, which but thy pictures be,
Much pleasure—then, from thee much more must flow;
And soonest our best men with thee do go,
Rest of their bones and soul's delivery.
Thou'rt slave to fate, chance, kings and desperate men,
And dost with poison, war, and sickness dwell;
And poppy or charms can make us sleep as well,
And better than thy stroke. Why swell'st thou then?
One short sleep past, we wake eternally,
And death shall be no more. Death, thou shalt die.

JOHN DONNE

When I consider how my light is spent,
Ere half my days, in this dark world and wide,
And that one talent which is death to hide
Lodged with me useless, though my soul more bent
To serve therewith my Maker, and present
My true account, lest he returning chide,
'Doth God exact day-labour, light denied?'
I fondly ask. But Patience, to prevent
That murmur, soon replies: 'God doth not need
Either man's work or his own gifts; who best
Bear his mild yoke, they serve him best. His state
Is kingly: thousands at his bidding speed,
And post o'er land and ocean without rest;
They also serve who only stand and wait.'

JOHN MILTON, 'On his blindness'

Adam lay y-bounden
Bounden in a bond;
Four thousand winter
Thought he not too long;
And all was for an apple
An apple that he took,
As clerkes finden written
In theire book.

Ne had the apple taken been,
The apple taken been,
Ne hadde never our Lady
A been heaven's queen.
Blessed be the time
That apple taken was!
Therefore we may singen
'Deo Gratias!'

A fifteenth-century English carol

John Milton (1608–74), the English poet, probably best known for his epic *Paradise Lost*. In his later years he was blind.

other hand, with the cultural and theological shift of emphasis in the fifteenth and sixteenth centuries, we find the artists busy celebrating plain domestic, community and professional life. Northern artists such as Rembrandt, Vermeer, van Ruysdael and Cuyp are prime examples.

When we consider the relationship of Christianity with literature—poetry, fiction, essays and drama—some of the same questions come up. For the first few centuries of Christianity most Christian writing was in the form of grammar or theology. Here and there we find imaginative discussions on the Bible, for example in the Old English *Genesis, Exodus* and *Christ*. The writing of sermons from the early centuries right on through to the Renaissance by such men as Isidore of Seville, Bede, Alcuin and Rabanus Maurus, owes much to Augustine of Hippo. He rigorously subordinated considerations of style to the service of truth and moral instruction.

Poetry may be used to help us towards God. Western writers were hampered by an austere sense of the moral uses of poetry, and an almost paralysing worry about the laws of rhetoric. Despite this, Western writing did flourish, in both prose and poetry, history (Bede, Gildas, Geoffrey of Monmouth), sermons (Gregory, Ethelred of Rievaulx, John of Salisbury) and lyric (Caedmon and Cynewulf), up to the thirteenth century peak in Dante, and, in England, to *Piers Plowman, Pearl, Patience*, and the writing of the mystics, including Richard Rolle, Lady Julian of Norwich and the author of *The Cloud of Unknowing* in the fourteenth century. All writers, whatever their talent, were officially Christian during these centuries. Their works (Chaucer's poetry, for example) are wrought with Christian assumptions, implicit or explicit.

Although the fifteenth and sixteenth centuries are often thought of as the period when the Western imagination broke free of Christian dogma and began to assert its autonomy, consciously non-Christian literature does not appear widely until well into the eighteenth century. This is not to say that all of literature before that was religious in its concerns: Shakespeare, Rabelais, Cervantes and a hundred others were not writing Christian drama and fiction. But the Christian view of the universe was still generally accepted and provided the moral backdrop against which these authors wrote. (In fact the Christian and the classical Greek moral imagination have more in common with each other than either has with the modern. Since the Enlightenment people have attempted to begin afresh, and shape human communication and culture on the assumption that humankind is autonomous.)

"The one thing that matters is that we always say Yes to God whenever we experience him."

JULIAN of Norwich,
Revelations of the Divine Love

FYODOR DOSTOEVSKY

Paul Bechtel

Fyodor Dostoevsky (1821–81), the Russian novelist, brought new qualities of insight to his work. Born in Moscow, the son of a doctor, he was trained as an engineer but soon took up writing. *Poor Fok* (1846) was acclaimed for its penetrating psychological study of the poor. Shortly afterwards Dostoevsky became involved in an underground movement, was arrested and sentenced to death. A last-moment reprieve commuted his sentence to ten years in Siberia.

Dostoevsky returned eventually to St Petersburg and in 1861 published *The House of the Dead,* a realistic account of his prison experiences. *Notes From Underground* (1864) is an extraordinary picture of a mentally disturbed and alienated man. In 1866 Dostoevsky was widely praised for *Crime and Punishment,* a novel with deep spiritual insights. For a time Dostoevsky was almost overwhelmed by gambling debts, emotional tensions, and epileptic seizures. He wandered about the continent of Europe—Germany, Switzerland and Italy—often in abject poverty as a result of compulsive gambling. *The Idiot* (1868) and *The Possessed* (1871) added to his reputation as one of the greatest novelists. Dostoevsky's masterpiece is *The Brothers Karamazov* (1880), completed the year before his death.

Dostoevsky's profound psychological insights have, in the twentieth century, made him one of the most influential and widely-read novelists. His works are novels of ideas. They are remarkable for their brilliant characterization, tense and dramatic situations, and a struggle between good and evil. Dostoevsky's Russian Orthodox faith is particularly evident in *Crime and Punishment* and *The Brothers Karamazov,* in characters who search for redemption through suffering and love. Dostoevsky seems to be saying that Russia had to come through the same routes of suffering and love to recover from the corruption of the Czarist régime.

At the end of the ancient world, drama had reached such a low point that it could only be viewed with alarm and disgust by the church. Christianity was assumed to be, and was, anti-theatre, for some hundreds of years. Before the year 1000, however, short dramatic elements were introduced into the church's liturgy. They were called *tropes*, one of the earliest and most familiar being the *quem quaeritis* ('Whom seek ye?') from the Easter service, in which monks took the parts of the women and the angel at the tomb. As time went on, more and more of the gospel story was dramatized. By the fourteenth

LEO TOLSTOY

Paul Bechtel

Leo Tolstoy (1828–1910), the great Russian novelist, expressed deeply-felt Christian principles in his work. He was born into the ruling class, and knew comfort and social prestige on the family estate in Tula. After serving in the Crimean War, he returned home to study and write. Tolstoy grew up during the era when Russians were pressing for social reform, and in 1861 he freed his serfs.

At the height of his fame as a writer, Tolstoy had a mystical experience. He threw in his lot with the peasants, adopted their dress and worked at their trades. He rejected the Russian Orthodox church and evolved his own form of faith. Central to his creed was non-resistance to evil, which he believed Christ taught. He disclaimed his title, his wealth, and the copyrights to all his books, and distributed his land amongst his wife and nine children. Tolstoy then preached a benign humanism which included some Christian elements, urging love and charity towards all people.

Tolstoy's ideas often brought him into conflict with the government and the Orthodox church, which excommunicated him in 1901, and refused him a Christian burial.

Tolstoy's best novels are *War and Peace* (1860), focussing on an epic scale on the Napoleonic invasion of Russia, and *Anna Karenina* (1877), a moving study of an unhappy woman. *The Kreutzer Sonata* (1891) and *Resurrection* (1899) reflect the social and religious beliefs which Tolstoy took up later, and lack the power of his earlier novels. *What is Art?* (1899) argues that good art is moral art. Tolstoy stresses the conflict between reason and the natural desire to live uninhibited by the conventions of society. In his fiction he writes with a unique breadth of vision. Tolstoy is a master of analysis, characterization, and moral insights.

century we find long, elaborate play-cycles of biblical history being staged by the craftsmen of such cities as York and Chester.

The most productive period in English drama follows this, in the sixteenth century, with Shakespeare at its peak. By this time again little explicitly Christian expression was coming from the theatres. Since that time there has been a widespread feeling in the church that, although drama ought to be a useful method for portraying Christian interpretations of existence, it is not easy to arrive at an understanding between church and theatre. T. S. Eliot, in *Murder in the Cathedral, The Family Reunion,* and other plays, has come as close as any poet or playwright to writing drama that is at one and the same time good and specifically Christian. But his attempt was not an unqualified success. The problem, as always, is the difficulty of depicting the mysteries of grace, which are central to any Christian handling of human experience, in artistic forms.

Of all the arts, the one most unambiguously celebrated and nourished in the Christian West has always been music. No one knows, of course, just what Western music would have sounded like without Christian influence; but from the hymns of the early church, through plainsong, motet, oratorio, and modern hymnody, we find the Christian imagination expressing its response to existence.

"I am gracious and great,
God without beginning;
I am maker unmade, all might is in me;
I am life and way unto wealth-winning;
I am foremost and first, as I bid shall it be."

God speaks in *The Creation*, the pageant performed by the tanners of York as part of the fourteenth-century York cycle of mystery plays financed by the town trade guilds for Corpus Christi Day. The drawing shows the stage for a mystery play.

"There is no age as mystical as ours. Yet it is mysticism with a difference: it is a nihilistic mysticism, for God is dead. Very old ideas are being revived: gnosticism, neo-platonic ideas of reality emanating from and returning to God, and Eastern religion, a religion with a god that is not a god but impersonal and universalist, a god which (not who!) is everything and therefore nothing, with a salvation that is in the end self-annihilation."

PROFESSOR H.R. ROOKMAAKER, Modern Art and the Death of a Culture

Buildings and beliefs

Henry Sefton

How do you know a church building when you see one? Is there a distinctively Christian architecture? Many would say that pointed windows and arches are signs of a church—and it is true that most existing churches, whether in York or New York, Lisbon or Lagos, have these features. But a building with pointed windows and arches may well be a museum or guildhall. On the other hand many older churches have round arches and round windows, and many modern churches have flat roofs and square or oblong windows. The more churches you visit the more you become aware of the diversity of styles and shapes, methods and materials used in their construction.

It would be wrong to deduce from this that there are no guiding principles in church architecture. In spite of their diverse outward appearance, churches have the same basic purpose—to provide accommodation for Christian meeting and worship. The variety of forms of building has arisen from the variety of emphases and beliefs among Christians, and the different periods in which the buildings were constructed.

Some people have, in fact, argued that the church does not really need buildings. Christians can baptize in a river, preach in the open air and celebrate the Lord's Supper on any table. The first Christians gathered in existing buildings, usually the homes of individual believers. The earliest church of which traces remain is a normal Syrian courtyard house which has been adapted for the purpose. Two rooms were put together for the celebration of the Lord's Supper, another room served as the place for baptisms and another may have been used for the instruction of applicants for church membership.

Wealthy Christians in Rome likewise adapted parts of their houses for worship. The catacombs or underground burial chambers were not used for regular meetings, but for the annual celebration of the deaths of the martyrs. This began the link with the remains of the faithful departed which has been a feature of much Christian worship and which has influenced the design and arrangement of churches. Most obviously, this has meant the use of the church as a burial-place, and its setting within a cemetery or churchyard.

The 'Edict' of Milan, AD 313, brought a great change in the circumstances of the church which is reflected in the buildings for Christian worship. Gone was the need for secrecy and the need to adapt existing buildings. Soon recognized as the official religion

Opposite:
The interior of one of the churches on Mount Athos, Greece. There are over 900 places of worship on this 'holy mountain', which is an important centre of Orthodox Christianity.

The unique chapel at Ronchamp, eastern France, designed by the revolutionary architect Le Corbusier.

of the Roman Empire, Christianity found an appropriate pattern for its impressive new buildings in the Roman basilica which was used both as a court-house and stock-exchange. The main architectural features of the basilica were a rectangular hall divided into three sections by two rows of columns parallel with the longer sides, and an 'apse' or semi-circular niche opening off one of the shorter sides. The roof covering the middle section was higher than that covering the side sections, in order to provide window-space to light the building. Here was a direct ancestor of the familiar nave and side aisles of a church.

The basilica affected the actual character of Christian worship, making it more stately and elaborate. A throne for the bishop was set up on the apse and ranged on either side of the throne were benches for the presbyters. The table for the Lord's Supper became a permanent altar on the edge of the apse and under it were often placed the remains of a saint or martyr. The rest of the worshippers assembled in the main part of the building on the opposite side of the altar. In this way the church was first divided into a part for the clergy and a part for ordinary Christians.

Besides the basilica, two other types of Christian building developed. These were the baptistery, where baptisms took place, and the *martyrion*, which was a chapel built over the tomb or relics of a martyr or saint. Both of these were constructed with a central focal point, and a dome was a frequent feature. These buildings particularly affected the development of churches in the East. The characteristic domed structure of a Byzantine church owes much to these earlier buildings.

Buildings of a similar style do occur in the West but the basilica-

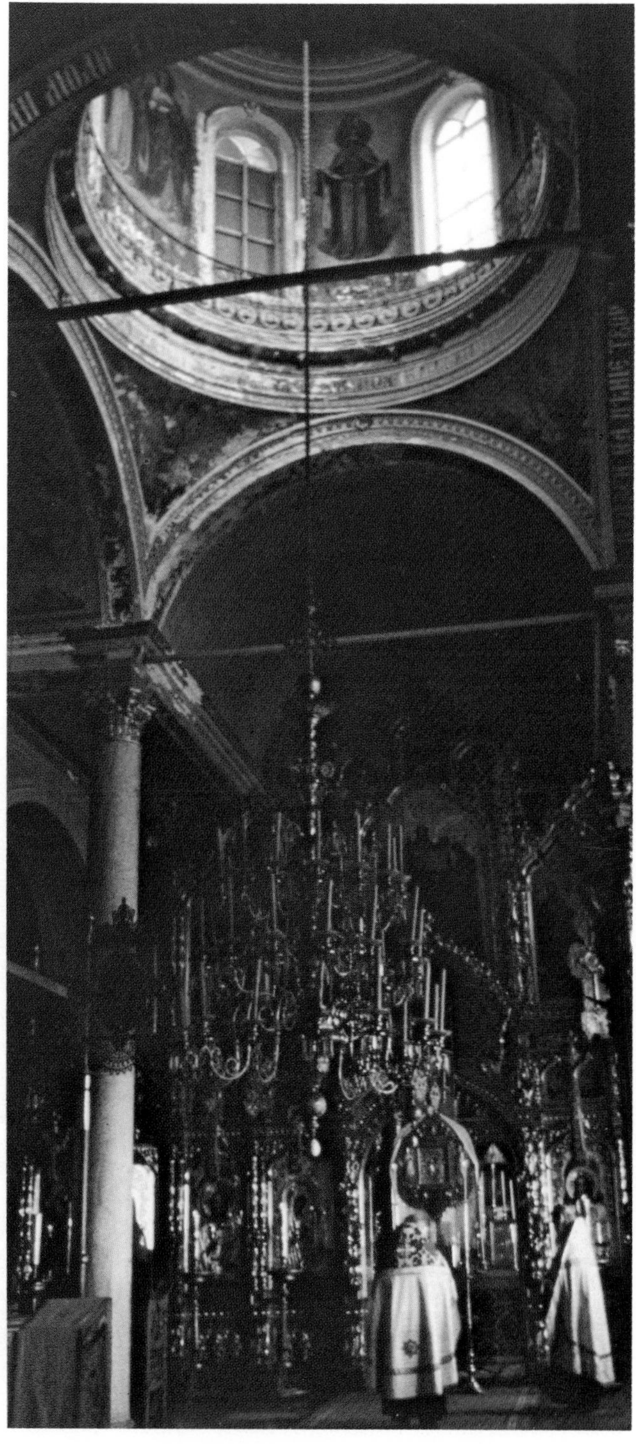

plan was the basis of most church architecture. The rounded Romanesque arches were replaced by pointed Gothic ones, and the ground-plan was often elaborated into the form of a cross. With the development of trade and the expansion of towns, churches became more and more magnificent as an expression of civic pride.

Despite their apparent differences, Eastern and Western churches have one important development in common: both separate the altar from the ordinary worshipper. This is partly the result, partly the cause, of an emphasis on the 'mystery' of the 'liturgy' in the East and of the 'mass' in the West—which became the usual ways of describing the Lord's Supper. In the East the separation is done by the *iconostasis,* a massive solid screen, adorned with icons, or pictorial representations of the saints. When the doors on this screen are closed, the altar is invisible to the ordinary worshippers who are in this way sharply distinguished from the priests who pass inside the *iconostasis.*

In the West the means of separation is different but the effect is similar. Churches in the West are divided into a chancel (or room for the clergy) and a nave (or room for the laity). The two are usually divided by an open-work screen with a large crucifix on top, known as a rood-screen, or, less commonly, by a solid screen known as *pulpitum.* The chancel contains the high altar and seats for the clergy—often intricately-carved stalls—while the nave contains the pulpit for the preaching of sermons and often a second altar. For worship the people would either stand or bring their own seats. The baptismal font is usually at the back of the nave near the entrance to the

This magnificent example of stained glass from the twelfth century is part of a window at Chartres Cathedral, France, which tells the life of the Virgin Mary in pictures. Here we see the annunciation. The great medieval cathedrals of western Europe were celebrations in light and space.

church. These arrangements prevailed throughout the Middle Ages, but were complicated by the erection of numerous side altars in the aisles of the nave, and the addition of chapels, each with its own altar. These often contained relics and were primarily for the saying of masses for the souls of the founders and their friends.

But as well as this two-chamber, or indeed multi-chamber, pattern of church building, there evolved a single-room arrangement. This reflected the very different attitude to the clergy and to worship which emerged at the time of the Reformation. Instead of emphasizing the distinctive powers of the priest in relation to the sacraments, the Reformers preached the priesthood of all believers. This view is reflected in the way that they adapted the medieval buildings which they inherited, and in the plans used in new churches.

The side altars were swept away and were replaced by a single table which might not even be a permanent fixture. The screen was either removed, so that the church became a single room again, or else it was made into a solid wall, and either the chancel or the nave used for worship. Sometimes the unused area was left to decay, but sometimes, as the population increased, each part was used by a different congregation.

Great importance was given to the positioning of the pulpit so that all might see and hear the preaching of the word of God. The close relation of word and sacrament was expressed in the closeness of the Lord's table and the baptismal basin to the pulpit. These arrangements were followed in the new churches which were built on a square or circular plan. These features can be seen in the churches built in London after the Great Fire (1666), but even more clearly in the church 'meeting-house' of the seventeenth and eighteenth centuries.

In Britain the romantic revival of the nineteenth century brought a reaction against the simplicity of these single-chamber churches. This is most obvious in the adoption of Gothic as the 'proper' style for church architecture. The altar was removed to the end of a long chancel, often for aesthetic rather than theological reasons. The architect worked for effect rather than function and many over-large and difficult-to-heat churches date from this period.

The impressive buildings of the nineteenth century reflect the prestige of Christianity in that period. The greatly altered position of the church in the twentieth century is in turn reflected in simpler and cheaper buildings. Contemporary styles show concern to make buildings relevant to the needs of Christians in the modern world.

St Paul's Cathedral, London. This world-famous church was designed by Sir Christopher Wren to replace the cathedral destroyed in the Great Fire of London in 1666.

The rise of modern science

James R. Moore

The years from 1500 to 1700 saw not one but two profound upheavals in Western thought. In religion Luther, Calvin, Zwingli and Knox were replacing a human-centred view of the world with a God-centred one. In science Copernicus, Galileo, Brahe, Kepler and Newton were replacing a universe centred on the earth with one centred on the sun. A religious reformation and a scientific revolution went hand in hand.

The search for causal connections between the Protestant Reformation and the rise of modern science has involved historians in a very complex debate. Basically, the debate has taken place between two points of view: first, that religion gave decisive encouragement to science; and second, that both religion and science were spurred by another factor, such as social and economic developments. There is distinct and plausible evidence that Protestantism gave rise to modern science.

To begin with, there is evidence of specific Protestant contributions to the 'scientific revolution'. A Lutheran prince, Duke Albrecht of Prussia, subsidized the publication of the astronomer Copernicus' *De revolutionibus* (1543); Andreas Osiander, a Lutheran theologian, arranged for the printing and wrote its preface; Joachim Rhaeticus, a Lutheran mathematician and professor at the Reformer Melanchthon's Wittenberg University, supervised the printing; and Erasmus Reinhold, another Wittenberg professor, supported Copernicus' teaching in his astronomic tables.

Tycho Brahe and Johann Kepler,

The Renaissance was a time of major breakthrough in learning. Here a medieval man pokes his head out of the world of the Middle Ages to expand his view of the universe.

the great astronomers, were both devout followers of Luther. Michael Maestlin, a Lutheran pastor, edited Kepler's *Prodromus* (1596). David Chytraeus, a Lutheran theologian, dealt with the new star of 1572 in his commentary on Deuteronomy, published a book on the comet of 1577, and discussed these phenomena in letters to Brahe. Johann Fabricius, a Lutheran layman, first observed sunspots and the rotation of the sun, and Samuel Dörffel, a Lutheran pastor, first demonstrated that comets may move in a parabola.

During the seventeenth century the followers of Calvin took the lead in advancing the cause of science. Philip van Lansberghe, a Reformed minister and renowned astronomer, became the keenest supporter of Copernicus in the Netherlands. His fellow-countryman Isaac Beeckman, a scientist and strict Calvinist, was an early defender of the atomistic philosophy.

The Royal Society

Meanwhile, in England, the Puritan movement produced men such as Henry Briggs, Henry Gellibrand, and John Wilkins, who devoted themselves to discovery and learning. Briggs and Gellibrand were professors at Gresham College, London, which was strongly Puritan. There, in 1645, Theodore Haak, inspired by the Moravian educator J.A. Comenius, commenced informal gatherings which in 1661 became the Royal Society of London. Seven of the ten scientists who formed the nucleus of those meetings were Puritans. In 1663 sixty-two per cent of the members of the Royal Society were clearly Puritan by origin—at a time when Puritans were only a small minority in England. After the Restoration (1660) the Puritan interest in science was encouraged in the dissenting academies, educational institutions for Nonconformists which emphasized scientific disciplines and experiment.

Other evidence that Protestantism encouraged the rise of modern science comes from statistics concerning the religious preferences of scientists. Protestants seem to have been relatively more numerous among scientists than in the population at large. For example, ninety per cent of the foreign members of the *Académie des Sciences* in Paris between 1666 and 1883 were Protestants. Yet in the same period Protestants made up only forty per cent of the population of western Europe outside France. Similar statistics elsewhere point in the same direction.

Historians have tried to interpret this evidence by pointing out

Nicolas Copernicus (1473–1543) the Polish astronomer revolutionized the medieval world-view with his suggestion that the universe was centred on the sun—and not the earth. 'In the middle of all sits the sun on his throne, as upon a royal dais ruling his children the planets which circle about him.'

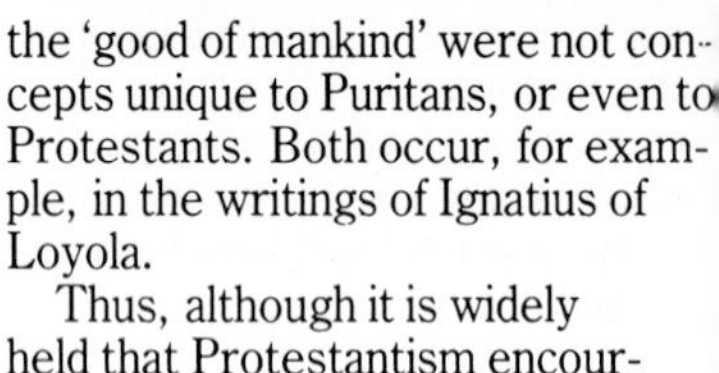

William Harvey, a seventeenth-century Englishman, discovered the circulation of the blood. He was a member of the Royal Society.

aspects of Protestantism which may have encouraged science. Lutherans taught that Christ was 'really present', in nature as well as in the eucharist. Calvinists stressed that believers would do good works to confirm that they are among the 'elect'. Protestants in general supported free enquiry and freedom of the individual. The best-known interpretation of the rise of modern science in the seventeenth century stresses the role of the so-called Puritan ethic: the demand that nature should be studied systematically, rationally and experimentally for the glory of God and the good of mankind.

Such theories face numerous problems. For example, the terms 'Protestant', 'Puritan', and 'Calvinist' do not mean exactly the same and their meanings changed over time. Doing good works could easily have been a motive for scientific activity among Protestant groups whose doctrines were not Calvinistic. The 'glory of God' and the 'good of mankind' were not concepts unique to Puritans, or even to Protestants. Both occur, for example, in the writings of Ignatius of Loyola.

Thus, although it is widely held that Protestantism encouraged the birth of modern science, there is little agreement as to how it was involved. Some historians believe that the Protestant emphasis on the priesthood of all believers significantly nurtured the growth of the scientific spirit. However, modern science cannot be traced simply to Protestant origins: Roman Catholic scientists did important work throughout the sixteenth and seventeenth centuries. Thomas Sprat gave no specifically Puritan or Protestant basis for science in his important *History of the Royal Society* (1667). The Royal Society, which had many Puritans as early members, was in fact open to men of every denomination. So also, it seems, was the scientific revolution.

John Kepler, one of the founders of modern astronomy accepted the Bible, believing that the universe itself was an expression of the being of God.

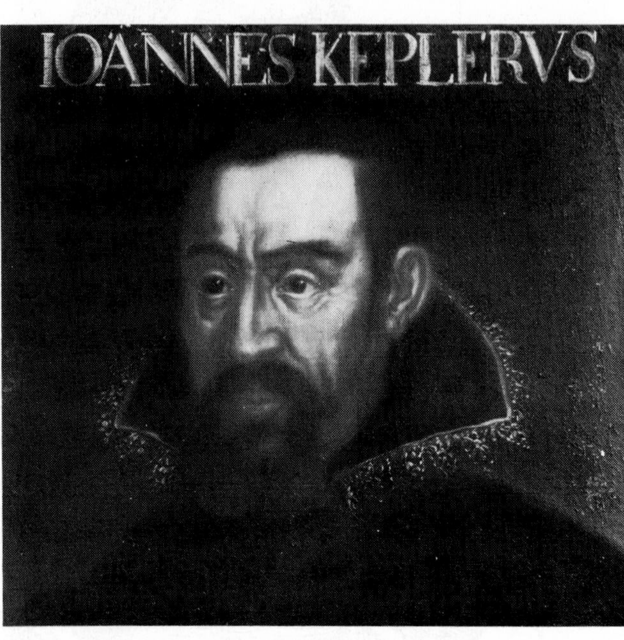

Christians and war

Alan Kreider
and John H. Yoder

Throughout Christian history, most believers have assumed that warfare is the business of sovereigns. For the ordinary subject, citizen or soldier that left only one choice—obedience. Accountability to God has been by the 'powers that be'.

There have been other Christians, however, who have gone beyond automatic obedience to think seriously about the relationship between war and the gospel. They have produced three distinct types of approach.

The most recent of these to develop—the Crusade—is almost a thousand years old. In 1095 Pope Urban II proclaimed a holy war to rout the infidel Muslims and to reclaim the Holy Land for the Christian faith. Underlying the ensuing Crusades (and underlying countless similar conflicts during the following centuries) were characteristic assumptions. Crusaders go into battle for a religious or supposedly-religious cause. Since their enemies stand for the forces of evil, they must be defeated totally; there can be no compromise between righteousness and wickedness. Ideally the enemy is vanquished by honourable means. But if you hate an enemy who embodies error, and smite him indiscriminately, that is quite excusable in the circumstances.

Over the centuries the crusader's enemy has altered from the Muslims, to the Catholics or Protestants, to the French revolutionaries, to the Germans or Allies, to the communists. But the crusading mentality has remained constant. Oliver Cromwell, in 1649, after razing Drogheda and massacring its people, rejoiced in the 'righteous judgement of God upon these barbarous [Irish] wretches'. The bishop of London during World War I urged young English soldiers: 'To kill Germans—to kill them, not for the sake of killing, but to save the world, to kill the good as well as the bad, to kill the young men as well as the old . . . I look upon it as a war for purity. I look upon everyone who dies in it as a martyr.'

Older than the crusade, though by no means so popular, is the second approach—the 'just war'. Although the idea was rooted in Roman Stoic philosophy, Ambrose and Augustine formed the just war into a Christian approach to the problem of warfare in the late fourth century. Thomas Aquinas, the Spanish Dominican Francisco de Victoria and the Dutch Protestant Hugo Grotius developed it further.

The just war theory has come to provide a series of criteria by which the permissibility of war in a particular situation can be weighed. Some of these criteria have to do with the origins of war: Is there a just cause (for example, a clear injury which needs to be redressed)? Has every reasonable attempt been made to get redress without bloodshed? Will war be declared by a legitimate authority? Other criteria concern the way in which the war is fought. Is it to be waged solely by legitimate and moral means? Is the damage which is likely to be incurred by the war less grievous than the prior injury? Is success likely?

If the answers to these questions are 'Yes', one may justly declare war. Unfortunately this will entail killing. But Augustine emphasized that this does not clash with loving

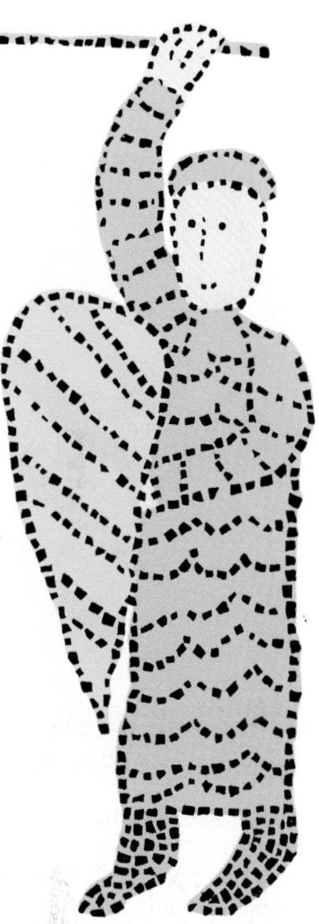

A Western soldier of the Fourth Crusade. An illustration from a thirteenth century mosaic in Ravenna.

the enemy. What really matters are the intentions of the combatants' hearts.

Although these criteria for the just war may seem to be clear, in practice they have often proved difficult to apply. Augustine's assumption that in any conflict justice will lie mainly on one side is clearly wrong. In any event, 'justice' is an elastic standard. It has rarely been clear who has the insight and objectivity necessary to decide what justice means in a given situation. In practice, decisions about the meaning and application of 'justice' have almost always been made by the interested parties in a dispute. And they in turn have used the criteria of the just war simply to justify wars in which they were already engaged. For example, in the Spanish-Dutch wars of the late sixteenth century both sides attempted to demonstrate learnedly that justice was on *their* side.

Oliver Cromwell, who was Lord Protector of England following the English Civil War. He gained notoriety for his massacre of the Roman Catholic inhabitants of Drogheda and Wexford in Ireland, when they refused to submit to his besieging army.

In the heat of battle it has also been difficult to ensure that only moral and legitimate means are used. The Christian warrior has often been overcome by exhaustion and over-excitement. Atrocities have been inevitable. One British observer commented about excesses at the Battle of the Somme: 'If you start a man killing you can't turn him off again like an engine.'

The third and oldest Christian approach to war is pacifism. The Christian church of the first three centuries was pacifist. The early Christians combined a simple obedience to the words of Jesus ('Love your enemies'; 'put up your sword into its place') with a genuine international spirit (Christians 'love all men as their brothers'; 'Christ is also among the barbarians'). They were also repelled by the idolatry which permeated Roman army life.

In practice the early Christians were not quite as strictly pacifist as the theologians' writings would seem to indicate. By the third century some Christians were in the legions. However, it is probable that the majority of these Christian soldiers confined themselves to police duties. Some Christian converts left the forces upon their conversion. Martin of Tours, following his conversion in 339, exclaimed, 'I am Christ's soldier; I am not allowed to fight.'

After the triumph of Constantine in the early fourth century, this early Christian pacifism withered rapidly. In 392 the Emperor Theodosius declared Christianity to be the sole legal religion in the Empire; and in 416 all of the non-Christian troops were purged from the Roman army. Only a few monks and mendicants remained pacifist, until the Waldensians in thirteenth-century Italy and the Czech Brethren in the fifteenth century revived pacifism.

In the Protestant Reformation the Anabaptists were the first to revive pacifism. Many of their emphases echoed the concerns of the early church theologians. But the anabaptists added two new concerns. They denied that the government may legitimately interfere with the reformation of the church, and argued that the Christian is called to share in Christ's suffering love for his enemies.

The Anabaptists called all believers to participate in a renewed society in which 'repentance was in evidence by newness of life in Christ'. Nations would go on warring, but 'the regenerated do not go to war'. Some Anabaptists attempted to participate in government; others tried to avoid all contact with the civil order. But for centuries most of them were forced into withdrawal by harsh persecution. Anabaptist ideas have continued to shape the life and thought of the Mennonites and the members of

Martin Luther King was one of the great Christian champions of non-violent protest. Here he leads 10,000 civil rights marchers heading for Montgomery, in March 1965, representing the black population of the United States.

the Church of the Brethren, and most recently have influenced the 'Young Evangelical' movement in the United States.

In England in the mid-seventeenth century pacifism appeared in yet another guise among the Friends. The 'Quakers' were aware of the battle being waged between the forces of good and evil. In this struggle, which they called the 'Lamb's War', they committed themselves to struggle in a loving and non-violent way against the 'powers of darkness'. The Friends felt sure of victory. For in their lives they had experienced the triumph of God's light and truth over their own rebelliousness. They therefore trusted that Power to enlighten every person, including their enemies. By the end of the seventeenth century, the nature of much of the Quaker witness to peace had begun to change. Humanitarian concerns became predominant—war's unreasonableness, its economic waste, its injury of the innocent. Friends could now appeal to people whose ethics were based on different grounds from their own. After some early persecution, the Quakers have continued to try to influence governments. At times, as in Pennsylvania in the colonial period, and later in many international agencies, they have also participated effectively in governments.

In the 1920s and 1930s yet another variety of Christian pacifism developed, that of the liberal Protestants. World War 1 was still a recent and vivid memory; its stupidity, bestiality and unresolved problems gave the liberals an arsenal of anti-war arguments. But the liberals were positive as well as negative. They were confident that humanity could come to rational solutions of international disputes by peaceful means, particularly through new political instruments such as the League of Nations.

Unlike the early Christians and the Anabaptists, they assumed that if war is morally wrong it must be possible to run the world without it. A common liberal slogan therefore advocated as a possible political procedure the 'renunciation of war as an instrument of national policy'. By their political activities, the liberals hoped to put an end to political boundaries and nation-states. Instead, the rise of Adolf Hitler put an end to liberal pacifism as a mass movement.

In the years since World War II, many Christian pacifists have adopted self-conscious techniques of non-violent action to obtain specific political goals. There was nothing novel about non-co-operation, the boycott, or the demonstration; these had been used for centuries as a means of protest. But Mahatma Gandhi and Martin Luther King popularized them as instruments for resolving conflict constructively. Advocates of non-violent action point out that these techniques—unlike violence—do not dehumanize or alienate the adversary. Nor do they—unlike warfare in the nuclear age—threaten to obliterate the human race. For these reasons, non-violent techniques have been carefully scrutinized by military strategists as well as by pacifist activists.

Except for the first three centuries of the church's history, pacifism has always been held by only a minority of Christians. The pacifists have therefore been tempted to retreat from involvement in the world; indeed, persecution has often forced them to withdraw. Many pacifists have tended to be self-righteously irresponsible. Yet they have also kept asking one question which might otherwise have been overlooked: 'Where is God's primary action in the world, among the powerful, or in the church?' Pacifists have also been accused, sometimes justly, of enjoying the benefits of a society without contributing to its defence. Yet the pacifist movement has, over-all, been a movement of suffering. Even in the 1970s Christian conscientious objectors suffered in Soviet and Spanish prisons. Finally, many pacifists have believed in human perfectibility. At times they have been unwilling to face the extremity of human sin, which has given their thought an odour of unreality. But when one surveys the mountain of corpses in the history of Christendom—to say nothing of the prospect of nuclear annihilation that confronts the entire human family—one wonders how genuinely real is the reality, or how genuinely just is the war, which the advocates of the just war and crusade put forward.

SECTION 2

BEGINNINGS 1–325

0
25
50
75
100
125
150
175
200
225
250
275
300
Roman Emperors
Domitian
Septimius Severus
Claudius
Hadrian
Decius
Vespasian
Antoninus Pius
Valerian
Nero
Trajan
Gallienus
Tiberius
Titus
Marcus Aurelius
Empire divide East/West
Fall of Jerusalem
Eruption of Vesuvius
Christians persecuted
Polycarp martyred
Rome
Rome and North Africa
Asia
'Great Persecution'
Rome, Gaul and Africa
Writings
Didache
Josephus' History
Justin's Apology
Origen's Against Celsus
Ignatius' Letters
Irenaeus' Against Heresies
Paul's letters
Synoptic Gospels
Tertullian's Apology
General New Testament Letters
Church leaders and writers
Marcion excommunicated
Montanism starts in Phrygia
Novatianists set up congregation in Rome
Council of Jerusalem
Irenaeus
Paul's missionary journeys
Origen
Cyprian
Justin Martyr
Antony
Tertullian
Jesus' crucifixion and resurrection
Clement of Rome

THE CHURCH EXPANDS: JERUSALEM TO ROME

W. Ward Gasque

Jesus was executed by the Roman authorities in the city of Jerusalem in the year AD 30 on a trumped-up charge of sedition. Not a very promising start for a new religion!

But within three days the rumour was spreading round the city that he was alive, that he had been raised from the dead. Some of his closest followers claimed that they had actually seen him. Seven weeks later his resurrection was being boldly proclaimed in public in the very city where he had been executed. The effects were startling: thousands of Jews and Jewish converts, who had returned from other parts of the Roman Empire to live in or visit Jerusalem, came to believe that Jesus was alive, and that his death on a cross was, in fact, part of God's plan to save humanity. During the following weeks and months many others joined them.

This marked the birth of the Christian church, as recorded in the book of Acts.

Jesus commissions his disciples

During the days immediately following his resurrection, Jesus met with some of his followers. After these encounters with the risen Jesus no one could ever convince them that they were following mere pious hopes. They were not deluded: they had really *seen* their master and he was alive for ever!

Jesus explained to them things which they had never understood before; for example, that it had been necessary for him to suffer and die before entering into his rightful glory. Now, seen in the light of his resurrection and the explanations he gave, the cross of Jesus took on an eternal dimension of splendour, in spite of the wickedness of the people responsible for his death.

But Jesus did more than simply rebuild the faith of his disciples and cast new light on the meaning of his death. He also commissioned them to take into all parts of the world the good news of what God had done by sending him to rescue the human race. But they would not be alone in this task. Jesus promised them God's Holy Spirit to empower them (Matthew 28, Luke 24 and Acts 1).

Jerusalem, at the time of Jesus, was dominated by Herod's Temple. After the Jewish revolt of AD 66, the Roman general Titus destroyed the fortifications and the Temple. The Muslim Dome of the Rock, built on the site of Herod's Temple, is prominent in this view from the Mount of Olives today.

The promised Holy Spirit

Some writers have suggested that a better name for 'Acts of

A view from the walls of Jerusalem.

When Jesus' followers visited his tomb they found the 'door' rolled away and his body gone. This rock-cut tomb from first-century Nazareth has a similar rolling-stone as a door.

the Apostles' would be 'Acts of the Holy Spirit'. The book tells of the coming of the promised Holy Spirit, and how the earliest Christians witnessed to their Lord in various parts of the Roman Empire.

The account in Acts gives only part of the picture. It tells of only a few important churches and individuals—particularly Peter (the key figure in chapters 1–12) and Paul (who comes to the fore in chapters 13–28). But Acts gives a clear insight into the patterns of growth of early Christianity and, together with the New Testament letters, provides most of what is known about the spread of the gospel in the first century.

Above all, Acts stresses that the Holy Spirit's power enabled the disciples to witness effectively in their world. A tiny band of discouraged and disillusioned men and women was suddenly transformed into a bold company of enthusiastic evangelists. Their work began in Jerusalem, but quickly spread to other centres. Thirty years later the new faith had reached most parts of the eastern section of the Roman Empire, and probably even beyond, as well as westwards to Rome itself.

The Christians in Jerusalem

In spite of Jesus' commission to preach the good news in all the world, most of his followers in Jerusalem at first restricted themselves to evangelizing the Jews. This was not quite so limited as might appear, since thousands of Jews regularly flocked to Jerusalem for their most important religious festivals, and many actually settled permanently in Jerusalem—though doubtless maintaining links with their home countries. (Paul's companion, Barnabas, provides one example.) It was probably largely through the witness of these unknown Jewish converts from the earliest days that the Christian faith spread throughout the Empire and beyond in the first few decades, though Acts reveals little about this.

But among the Jerusalem Christians there were a few who were more forward looking. They grasped the full meaning of Jesus' final command to his disciples and tried to reach beyond the orthodox Jews. One disciple, named Stephen, saw more clearly than others that the faith was for all people, and that a break with Judaism was inevitable. He belonged to a group of Jews called 'Hellenists' who spoke Greek and adopted a freer life-style than the more conservative Jews. Stephen came into conflict with some of the Jewish leaders as a result of his bold preaching. This led to his quick trial and summary execution, and a general outburst of persecution against the Jerusalem Christians and particularly the Hellenists.

The good news reaches Samaria and Antioch

Many Christians were forced to flee from Jerusalem because of this persecution, but they spread the good news about Jesus wherever they went—throughout the province of Judea and into Samaria. Philip, another Hellenist, led the way by evangelizing extensively among the despised Samaritans, who were half-caste and unorthodox Jews. This resulted in mass conversions.

Other Christians travelled to the coast, the island of Cyprus and to Antioch in Syria, the third city of the Empire, preaching the message of Jesus with great success. It was in the metropolis of Antioch that the revolutionary step of evangelizing non-Jews was first taken by some of these nameless refugees from Jerusalem. This move was only reluctantly accepted by the Christians back in Jerusalem. It was in Antioch too that the followers of Jesus were first called 'Christians'.

During these early years, Peter evangelized among his fellow-Jews, but only within his own country. On one occasion he was rather reluctantly forced to preach the good news directly to Gentiles; but it took him at least ten years to decide that the gospel was for all people. It was left to a one-time opponent of Christianity to become the champion of Gentile evangelism and to pave the way for the integration of Jews and Gentiles into a common community.

Paul: the model missionary

Saul of Tarsus is better known to

In the first century AD Antioch, on the River Orontes, was an important commercial centre, and capital of the Roman province of Syria. Part of the modern town of Antakya, Turkey, can be seen in this view from the site of the earliest known church in Antioch.

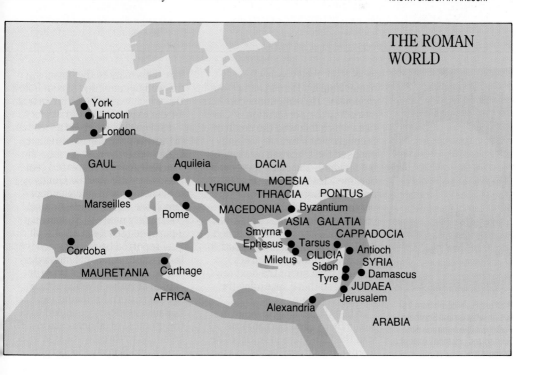

THE ROMAN WORLD

York
Lincoln
London
GAUL
Aquileia
DACIA
MOESIA
ILLYRICUM
THRACIA
PONTUS
Marseilles
Rome
MACEDONIA
Byzantium
ASIA
GALATIA
Smyrna
CAPPADOCIA
Ephesus
Tarsus
Cordoba
Miletus
CILICIA
Antioch
SYRIA
MAURETANIA
Carthage
Sidon
Damascus
Tyre
JUDAEA
AFRICA
Jerusalem
Alexandria
ARABIA

PETER

Michael A. Smith

Peter came from Bethsaida, on Lake Galilee, and his fisherman father John originally named him Simon. He was living in Capernaum with his wife, brother and mother-in-law when first introduced to Jesus by his brother Andrew. He quickly became the leader of Jesus' twelve close followers and was often their spokesman. He was the first to declare publicly that Jesus was the Messiah, at Caesarea Philippi.

Jesus gave him the nickname 'Peter' (*Cephas* in Aramaic) meaning 'rock'. Rash and hot-blooded, Peter said he was ready to die with Jesus, then three times denied knowing him on the night of Jesus' arrest. But Peter was one of the first to meet the risen Jesus, who specifically restored him to his position as leader.

After Jesus ascended, Peter took the initiative in the appointment of a successor to Judas among the Twelve and was the chief preacher when the Holy Spirit came on the Day of Pentecost. Peter and John took the lead in the early days of the church, disciplining Ananias and Sapphira after they deceived the believers, healing and preaching, and taking a special interest in the mission to Samaria.

Later, Peter had a vision which launched the mission to take the gospel to the Gentiles. Although he was wary of this new venture, and later wavered under the criticism of strict Jewish Christians at Antioch, Peter welcomed Paul's work among the Gentiles, and gave it his full support at the Council of Jerusalem (which welcomed Gentile converts without imposing on them all the rigours of the Jewish law). Peter was imprisoned by King Herod Agrippa I (AD 41–44) but miraculously escaped the night before he was due to be executed.

Paul originally came from Tarsus (in what is now Southern Turkey). Little remains of the Romanized city today except for this arch.

us as Paul. Saul was his Jewish name; Paul his Roman name—or *cognomen*. He is mentioned in Acts as leading the persecution of Christians which followed the death of Stephen. For a time he violently opposed the Christian movement; but suddenly the chief persecutor became a leading witness to the risen Christ, as a result of his personal encounter with Jesus on the road to Damascus. After a period in Arabia, Paul returned home to Tarsus (near the south-east coast of modern Turkey). He may have spent the next ten years or so there spreading the gospel.

When the Jerusalem believers sent a man called Barnabas to visit the Christians in Antioch, he fetched Paul from Tarsus to assist him. This marked the beginning of the well-documented part of Paul's life, which was to be so important for the expansion of Christianity.

Paul quickly emerged as leader of the strong group of Christians in Antioch, who now became the beach-head for a concerted campaign to evangelize the Gentiles. Jerusalem was to remain important in the world-wide Christian community until the Roman army destroyed the city in AD 70—and Paul reported back to the believers there after each of his missionary journeys abroad. But it was the church at Antioch which actually set the pattern for the future.

Paul was ideally equipped to be the greatest of all missionaries. He belonged to three worlds: Jewish, Greek and Roman. His parents

Peter's later career is obscure. He may have worked in Asia Minor, perhaps visited Corinth, but ultimately settled in Rome. Here he described himself as a 'fellow elder', which may mean he was one of the church leaders, but not the sole leader. Two New Testament letters bear his name, and he was probably the main source of information for Mark's Gospel. Peter is believed to have been martyred at Rome during Nero's persecution of Christians, around AD 64.

Although he did not found the church at Rome, Peter's martyrdom in Rome gave it great prestige. Paul's association with the church added to this, and the church of Rome later claimed to be the chief church in the West of the Empire, and the only one with assured apostolic roots.

A considerable cult began to surround Peter and Paul from about AD 200. By the time of the Emperor Constantine the site of Peter's martyrdom was held to be that now occupied by the Vatican basilica of St Peter's. Recent excavations have revealed a shrine in honour of Peter dating from the late second century. In the time of Pope Leo the Great, who died in 461, Peter was given more prominence. The popes of Rome now claimed direct spiritual descent from Peter, the leader of the Twelve.

Several apocryphal works are attributed to Peter. The *Gospel of Peter* was banned at Rhossus (near Antioch) in AD 190 because of its heretical tendencies. The *Apocalypse of Peter*, which includes a graphic description of hell, and the *Acts of Peter*, which claims to describe his martyrdom, also date from the later part of the second century.

Peter originally worked as a fisherman on Lake Galilee. The name of his home city, Bethsaida, means 'place of nets' or 'fishery'.

were strictly orthodox Jews who used the Hebrew language and observed Jewish customs at home. They were sufficiently concerned about a correct religious upbringing to send Paul to Jerusalem at an early age—possibly to live with an older, married sister. In Jerusalem Paul learned the traditions of his people and was ultimately taught by Gamaliel the elder, one of the most famous rabbis of the day.

But Paul also inherited Greek culture, which had permeated the eastern Mediterranean following the conquests of Alexander the Great (335–323 BC). Paul later showed his mastery of Greek in his Pastoral letters (1 and 2 Timothy, and Titus), which can be counted among the classics of Greek literature.

In addition, Paul was a Roman citizen, which gave him special freedom of movement, protection in his travels and access to the higher strata of society. Ultimately it meant that he probably died by the sword, a Roman privilege, rather than on a cross.

What Paul achieved

Paul's missionary achievements were immense. The years AD 35–45 remain obscure, but during the next ten or twelve years his activity was astounding. Between AD 47/48 (when he set sail with Barnabas on his first missionary journey) and AD 57 (when he returned to Jerusalem for the last time) he established flourishing churches in major cities in the

PAUL

Michael A. Smith

"A man small in size, with meeting eyebrows and a rather large nose, bald-headed, bow-legged, strongly built, full of grace; for at times he looked like a man, and at times he had the face of an angel."

A second-century description of Paul

Paul was born into a Jewish family in Tarsus, where his parents were Roman citizens. He was a strict Pharisee, and even as a young man was outstanding in his orthodox beliefs and in his hatred of Christians. He was present at the stoning of Stephen, and was commissioned by the High Priest to arrest Christians at Damascus.

Paul was converted through a vision of the risen Christ on his way to Damascus. Temporarily blinded, he was befriended by a Christian called Ananias, and when cured he began to preach Christ in Damascus. However, attempts were made against his life, and he had to escape by being lowered down the city wall in a basket.

After a spell in Arabia, Paul may have returned to Damascus, but later came to Jerusalem, where he was befriended by Barnabas and introduced to Peter. Further Jewish threats against his life forced him to flee again, and he returned to Tarsus. There followed a period of roughly ten years about which little is known; but Paul must have been active in Christian work, for when the Gentile mission began to flourish at Antioch, Barnabas summoned him from Tarsus to join in the work.

It was through country such as this (in modern Turkey) that Paul and his companions travelled on their arduous mission.

Paul visited Jerusalem again, taking famine-relief funds, and discussed the Gentile mission with Peter. Then Paul began the evangelistic work which made him the most outstanding Christian missionary of the first century. He went with Barnabas and John Mark to Cyprus and central Asia Minor, founding a number of churches. On his return he had a violent disagreement with Peter at Antioch about how far Gentiles had to accept Jewish customs when they became Christians. However, this question was settled soon after at the Council of Jerusalem (Acts 15).

Paul now set out again, this time with Silas, and they travelled through Asia Minor and crossed into Macedonia. Further successful missionary work followed, especially in Macedonia, Corinth and Ephesus. After another visit to Jerusalem, Paul left with Timothy for further evangelistic work, finally returning to Jerusalem with money collected for the poor Christians there.

On his arrival, Paul was seized by a Jewish mob and would have been lynched, but for the prompt intervention of the Roman garrison. He was kept in protective custody at Caesarea for two years by the Roman governor Felix, whose successor, Festus, suggested that Paul be tried at Jerusalem. But Paul refused to face such a biassed court and appealed to the Roman Emperor for justice.

Paul was taken under escort to Rome, surviving a shipwreck at Malta on the way. After two years in Rome (at which point the account in Acts ends) Paul was probably released and spent further time in missionary work before being martyred on a second visit to Rome during Nero's persecution of AD 64.

Paul's surviving letters are found in the New Testament. Galatians was probably written before the Council of Jerusalem. 1 and 2 Thessalonians date from Paul's first journey into Greece; Romans and 1 and 2 Corinthians come from his last spell in Greece before his arrest at Jerusalem. Philippians, Colossians, Ephesians and Philemon were probably written from Rome during Paul's first imprisonment (although some scholars date them from an earlier imprisonment in Ephesus). 1 and 2 Timothy and Titus were probably written after Paul's first stay in Rome.

Paul's letters were highly valued during his lifetime, and were probably collected together soon after his death. In *1 Clement* (written about AD 95) they are already accepted on an equal basis with other Scripture. They were certainly in their present collected form by the time of Marcion (about AD 140).

Paul's theology was not well understood in the period immediately after his death. This was partly because the heretic Marcion rejected the Old Testament and much that was Jewish in the New Testament, and made great use of Paul's writings to support his own ideas. As long as Marcion's heresy was a threat, mainstream Christian teachers did not stress many of Paul's distinctive doctrines, such as law and grace. Augustine was the first to give full weight to Paul's theology.

Roman provinces of Galatia, Asia, Macedonia and Achaia. When he wrote to the church in Rome, towards the end of this period, he spoke of his work in the eastern provinces as being essentially finished, and indicated that he was now thinking about visiting Spain.

How was it that Paul played such a decisive role in the early Christian mission? First, it was he who championed the mission to the Gentiles and won its acceptance by the rest of the church. Second, it was Paul who developed the theological defence of the Gentile mission which is clearly set out in Romans 1–11. He worked very hard to keep Jewish and Gentile Christians united. With this purpose in view he kept in constant touch with the mother church in Jerusalem, collected a considerable sum of money among Gentile converts for the needs of the Christians in Judea, and regularly underlined the importance of Christian unity in his letters.

Finally Paul's principle of being 'all things to all people' helped him to move with relative ease between the synagogues, his base of operations, and Greco-Roman society, where ultimately the gospel received its greatest response. Paul's personal example as a self-supporting travelling missionary, and his concentration on important cities rather than rural areas, provided a pattern for others to follow.

Christians travel the Empire

Paul was not the only pioneer missionary among the early generation of Christians. In spite of the earlier hesitancy of Peter and the other apostles, they too probably travelled far and wide in the cause of Christ. Almost certainly Peter preached the gospel in Rome and the apostle John evangelized

CHRISTIANITY EXPANDS

Jerusalem

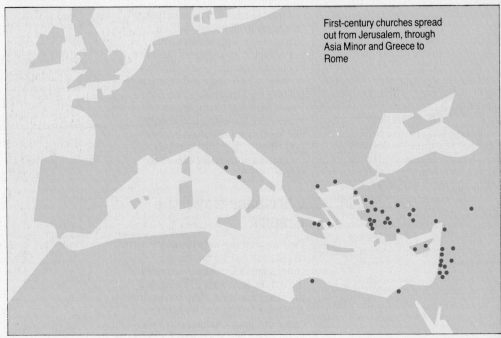

First-century churches spread out from Jerusalem, through Asia Minor and Greece to Rome

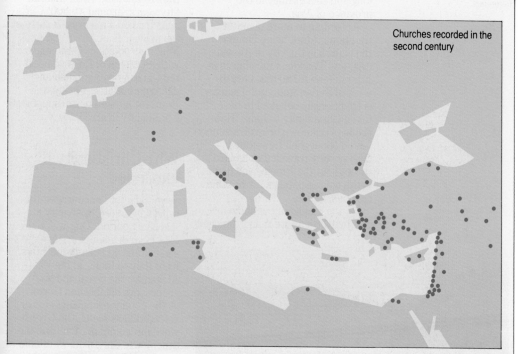

Churches recorded in the second century

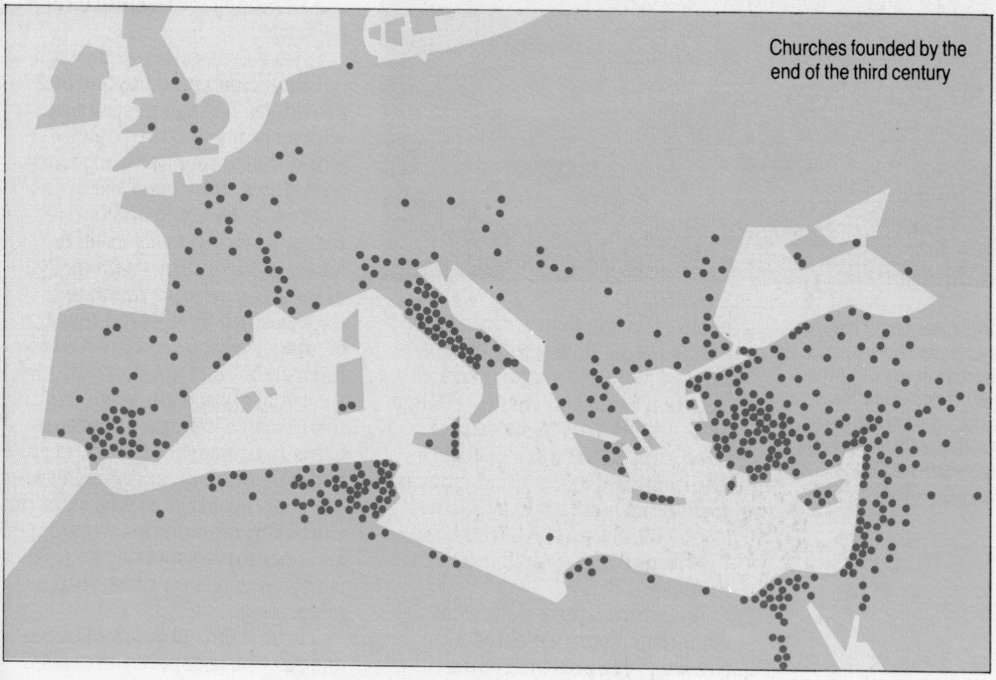

Churches founded by the end of the third century

long and successfully in the province of Asia.

According to more disputed traditions, Mark helped found the church in the city of Alexandria, and Thaddeus the church in Edessa (about 180 miles north-west of Syrian Antioch). Thomas is traditionally believed to have taken Christianity to India. Hundreds of unknown believers simply talked about their new-found faith as they travelled to and fro throughout the Empire and beyond in the course of business or other responsibilities.

By the middle of the second century, little more than a hundred years after the death and resurrection of Jesus, flourishing churches existed in nearly all the provinces between Syria and Rome. Though their origins are shrouded in obscurity, there were probably also churches in the great cities of Alexandria and Carthage, as well as beyond the eastern fringes of the Empire and in Gaul (modern France).

Athens was one of the strategic targets in Paul's mission. The market-place in Athens was overlooked by the Acropolis (background left) and Areopagus (background right), from which the Court where Paul argued took its name.

A century later a significant Christian minority existed in almost every province of the Empire and also in several countries to the east. After another fifty years, around AD 300, Christians formed a majority in parts of the provinces of Africa and Asia Minor. In addition, Osrhoene, with its capital of Edessa, adopted Christianity nationally, as did Armenia later. Finally, the Emperor himself began supporting Christianity in AD 312.

Why Christianity expanded

Several factors encouraged the rapid spread of Christianity in this short period. One was the existence of a unifying language and culture, at least in the cities, from Italy to India. In the East Alexander the Great and his successors established Greek as the common language—often referred to as *koinē,* the Greek word for 'common'. Paul and the other early Christians were able to use this language to spread their message.

Jews were scattered throughout the Empire and beyond and provided Christian missionaries with an entry into the pagan world. Since the first Christians were Jews, they used the synagogues, both inside and outside Judea, as ready-made centres for evangelism. Although most of their fellow-Jews remained unconverted, many God-fearing Gentiles, who were attracted to Judaism but had not gone through the ritual of total integration into the Jewish community, became Christian converts. In fact, in spite of the growing divergence between the church and the synagogue, the Christian communities worshipped and operated essentially as Jewish synagogues for more than a generation.

Three hundred years of peace and general prosperity prevailed throughout the Roman Empire

THOSE CHRISTIANS

"For Christians are not differentiated from other people by country, language or customs; you see, they do not live in cities of their own, or speak some strange dialect, or have some peculiar lifestyle.

This teaching of theirs has not been contrived by the invention and speculation of inquisitive men; nor are they propagating mere human teaching as some people do. They live in both Greek and foreign cities, wherever chance has put them. They follow local customs in clothing, food and the other aspects of life. But at the same time, they demonstrate to us the wonderful and certainly unusual form of their own citizenship.

They live in their own native lands, but as aliens; as citizens, they share all things with others; but like aliens, suffer all things. Every foreign country is to them as their native country, and every native land as a foreign country.

They marry and have children just like every one else; but they do not kill unwanted babies. They offer a shared table, but not a shared bed. They are at present 'in the flesh' but they do not live 'according to the flesh'. They are passing their days on earth, but are citizens of heaven. They obey the appointed laws, and go beyond the laws in their own lives.

They love every one, but are persecuted by all. They are unknown and condemned; they are put to death and gain life. They are poor and yet make many rich. They are short of everything and yet have plenty of all things. They are dishonoured and yet gain glory through dishonour.

Their names are blackened and yet they are cleared. They are mocked and bless in return. They are treated outrageously and behave respectfully to others. When they do good, they are punished as evildoers; when punished, they rejoice as if being given new life. They are attacked by Jews as aliens, and are persecuted by Greeks; yet those who hate them cannot give any reason for their hostility.

To put it simply—the soul is to the body as Christians are to the world. The soul is spread through all parts of the body and Christians through all the cities of the world. The soul is in the body but is not of the body; Christians are in the world but not of the world."

From an anonymous Letter to Diognetus, possibly dating from the second century

from the time of Augustus, with a few notable exceptions. This has become known as the *pax Romana* (Roman peace). It allowed great freedom of travel throughout the Mediterranean world. For example, Paul could travel along superbly engineered roads, and also expect the protection of the Roman government until the final years of his life.

The pagan world was experiencing a certain insecurity. Local political independence had disappeared, old loyalties and traditions were losing their hold, and sensitive people felt their age was morally and religiously bankrupt. Many sought security in the intimate fellowship provided by the newly-popular Eastern religious cults, while others found escape in the excitement of the ever more brutal public games and

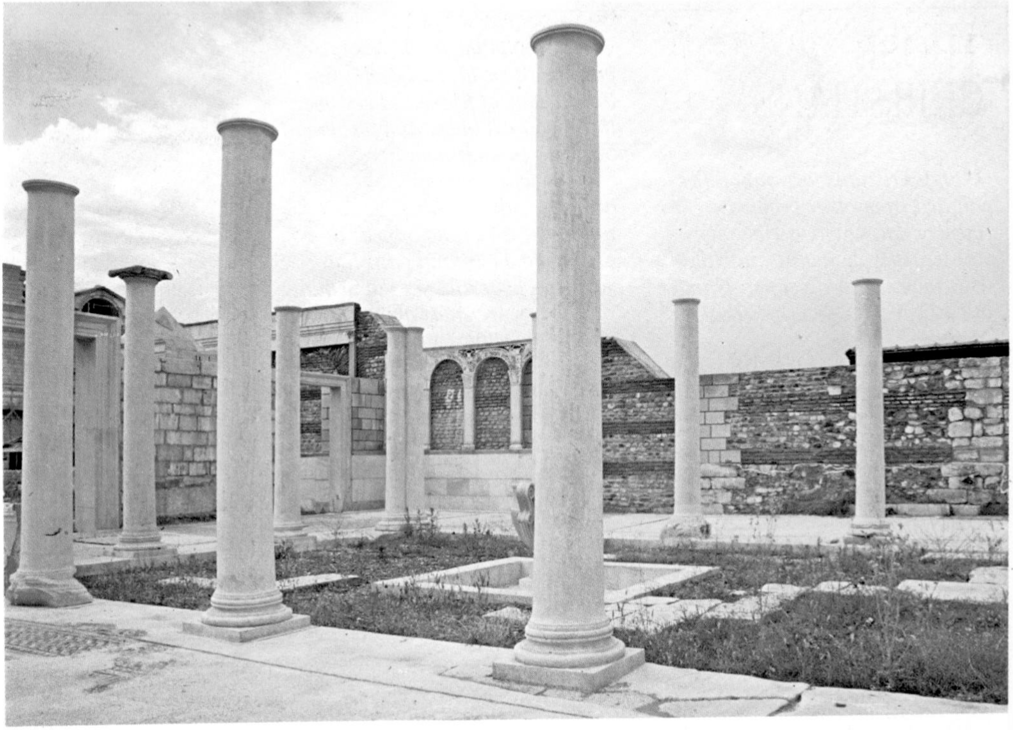

Paul regularly used the local synagogue as his starting-point when bringing the gospel to a new place. Later, the bridges between Jews and Christians were broken. This reconstructed second-century synagogue is at Sardis (in modern Turkey).

The Christian gospel took root in the Roman world. This aqueduct once carried water to Pisidian Antioch, where Paul preached. By their use of concrete, Roman engineers greatly extended the use of arches and vaults. They constructed bridges longer and higher than any previously built.

entertainments. Such an atmosphere of dissatisfaction and unease prepared people to listen to the Christian gospel.

Early Christianity in no way depended solely upon professional leaders for its practice and growth. Each Christian was both 'priest' and 'missionary'. The churches have been described as the most inclusive and the strongest of all the various associations in the Roman world. The distinctions between Jew and Gentile, slave and freeman, male and female were in theory, and usually also in practice, abolished in the Christian community. All were active in sharing the message of Christ with others.

Archaeological light on earliest Christianity

Colin J. Hemer

Archaeology is properly the study of ancient times. In a narrow sense, the term is restricted to the techniques of excavating ancient sites and interpreting the objects found there. But it may also be used in a much wider sense to mean the study of many areas of ancient evidence which go beyond the province of the traditional historian using literary sources. There is no rigid boundary between history and archaeology in this sense. Where the early church is concerned, the archaeologist's interests may lie, for instance, in the study of papyri, of stone inscriptions (epigraphy) or of the development of church architecture.

The special value of archaeology is not usually to prove anything. It helps build up a complete picture. Its data must be assessed and compared with literary sources. Archaeology cannot prove the Bible true. If a historical text is accurate in the kinds of detail which archaeology can confirm, there will be links between the two. Such details are valuable illustrations and may help to rule out mistaken theories. But they must not be given more weight as 'proof' than they deserve.

The book of Acts is a case in point. Many details of the names of people and officials, places and customs can be exactly illustrated from inscriptions. This does not prove the account to be historically true—but it rules out any view which holds that the writer was careless about such details. It also makes it harder to believe that the book was written long after the events.

All this may be an encouragement to faith. People can see here a world, not remote and shadowy, but as real and actual as our own, however different in its culture.

Archaeology has caught the popular imagination through spectacular discoveries, such as the Dead Sea Scrolls and the dramatic story of Masada. These great finds shed important light on the contemporary Jewish world and this in turn helps us to understand the background to Christian beginnings. But these matters need cautious and rigorous assessment. The instant sensations often turn out to have been ill-founded.

'Since the Jews constantly made disturbances at the instigation of Chrestus, Claudius expelled them from Rome,' wrote Suetonius (who may have thought 'Chrestus'—an alternative for 'Christ'—was in Rome). The coin shows the head of Emperor Claudius.

Traditional sites

The Romans destroyed Jerusalem so thoroughly in AD 70 that today little remains visible of the city Jesus knew. The many traditional sites are covered by churches, and the evidence for the original state

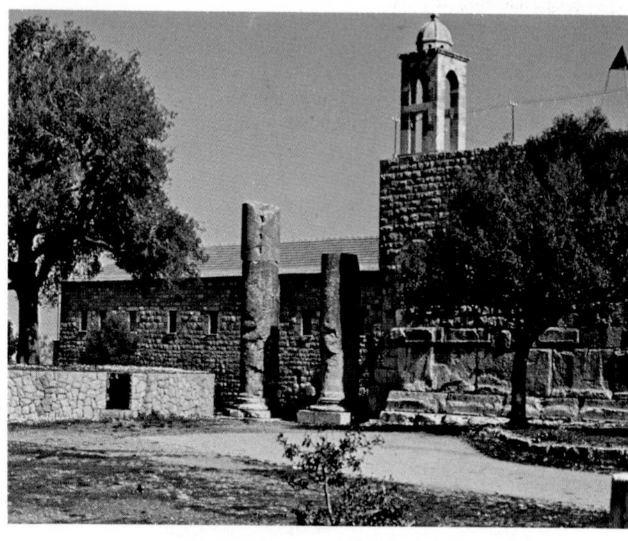

At Beit Mery (Lebanon) a Christian church was constructed incorporating the base and columns of a previous Roman temple.

of the localities has been destroyed or made inaccessible. We cannot picture the tomb of Jesus by standing in the Church of the Holy Sepulchre—which probably stands at or near its actual site. But we can illustrate what it was probably like from other tombs, like the so-called 'Tombs of the Kings', where a disc-shaped rolling stone fits into a slot in the rock.

The first missions to the Gentiles, as presented in Acts, offer a most fruitful field for archaeological study. Different kinds of detail interlock. For example, Paul met a Jewish couple in Corinth, after the Emperor Claudius had expelled the Jews from Rome (Acts 18: 2). This expulsion is mentioned in pagan literature and dated to AD 49 by a later writer. During Paul's long stay in Corinth, Gallio became governor (Acts 18:12). Gallio is known elsewhere from the writings of his famous brother Seneca, and his governorship can be dated to AD 51–2 by an inscription found in Delphi. This evidence helps build a consistent and fairly precise outline for this part of Paul's life, and helps relate Acts and Paul's letters.

A test case is Paul's letter to the Galatians. The famous investigator Sir William Ramsay used the evidence of inscriptions to establish clearly the extent of Galatia, and then argued that the letter was sent to the southern cities such as Pisidian Antioch, in Phrygia, which Paul had visited on his first journey (Acts 13–14). This in turn suits a very early date for the letter. Thus the details of Paul's life contained in the letter may be straightforwardly related to those in Acts.

City life

The city was a vital force in the ancient world. It is crucial to see Christianity in its city setting. The faith first spread in those areas of the eastern Roman Empire where the cultures had become very mixed. Roman rule and institutions were imposed on Greek-speaking peoples, who were often deeply influenced by Eastern religions. There were also many Jews. It must all have been very different from the picture given in literature; Roman literature was only for the educated few, who despised such popular movements as Christianity.

The everyday life of a Roman city has been remarkably preserved at Pompeii and Herculaneum in Italy, which were overwhelmed by the eruption of Mount Vesuvius in AD 79. Paul had found Christians at nearby Puteoli twenty years earlier, and there were probably Christians here, too, though the traces are tantalizingly uncertain. In Herculaneum a tiny room, perhaps belonging to a family slave, had had a wooden cross nailed to the wall and later wrenched off. In Pompeii two examples of the *ROTAS-SATOR* word-square, which may have been of Christian origin, were found scratched on walls.

The book of Revelation was probably written about AD 95, at a time of conflict and persecution. Study of the cities of Asia, to which the book was addressed,

Life stopped suddenly at Pompeii in AD 79, when Mount Vesuvius erupted. This young girl died of suffocation in the fumes from the falling ash and cinders. All over Pompeii archaeologists have discovered bodies of the dead; or, more accurately, holes which can be filled with plaster to show what the bodies once looked like.

ROMAN RELIGION

The ancient city of Pergamum, site of one of the seven churches of Asia, was dominated by the great altar of Zeus (Jupiter), god of the sky. Paul and Barnabas were taken to be Jupiter and Mercury by the people of Lystra.

Hermes (Mercury) was regarded as guide of the living and dead, and patron of commerce, literature and youth.

The Romans took the abstract qualities they admired and represented them with gods and goddesses. Most towns had temples dedicated to several gods. This winged 'Victory' (from Ephesus) stood for military success.

> *"Fill me with the Fish, I pray thee, Lord Saviour.*
>
> *May my mother sleep well, I pray thee, Light of the dead.*
>
> *Aschandius my father, dearly beloved of my heart, with my sweet mother and my brethren, remember thy Pectorius in the peace of the Fish."*
>
> *Part of a third-century epitaph from Autun, Gaul*

reveals more of that period. The imagery used in the book was often much to the point. The people of Laodicea had built an aqueduct to supply their city, but the water was lukewarm and impure. The remains can still be seen, and thick deposits of calcium carbonate inside the pipes witness plainly to the warmth of the water which once flowed through them. The words of Revelation 3:14–15 must have hit home powerfully in Laodicea: the writer said that the church was as useless and distasteful as that bad water.

The written word

The written word is the most important source of evidence. Books in the ancient world had usually been written on rolls made of papyrus or parchment. But this form of book was awkward to use, and the first Christians wanted to make their good news available as widely as possible. They may have been the first people to make wide use of the *'codex'*, the bound book with pages, such as we have today.

Tens of thousands of papyri have been preserved in the dry climate of Egypt. Those discovered include the oldest known fragment of the New Testament, a scrap of a papyrus *'codex'* of John's Gospel, copied about AD 130, and now in Manchester.

These papyri are important in other ways. They include hundreds of letters, accounts, certificates, receipts and other private documents. These give a vivid picture of everyday life and society, and of the kind of Greek which was spoken and written by ordinary people. This is important because the New Testament was not written in very literary or religious language. It is often illustrated and clarified by these examples of more popular language.

Graves and epitaphs

Epitaphs differ from most of the papyri in being phrased with a view to public display and posterity. The tombs of Christians are not at first easily recognized, for they use almost the same names and styles as their pagan neighbours. A famous and distinctive Christian

ΡΟΥΦΙΝΑ
ЄΙΡΗΝΗ
+

The cross on their epitaph witnesses to the faith of Rufina and Irene, buried in the catacombs in Rome early in the third century.

The first Christians were forbidden to cremate their dead, and therefore needed burial space. In Rome they adopted a form of cemetery sometimes used by pagans: a network of underground tunnels known as 'catacombs'.

epitaph is that of Abercius of Hierpalis, in Phrygia, dating from the late second century. Here poetic language about symbols, such as the shepherd and the fish, carried a hidden meaning for the Christian reader. Open confessions of faith are rare on tombstones. But there are some remarkable third-century examples from Phrygia which read 'Christian to Christian'. These appear to belong to the Montanists, who insisted that Christians publicly proclaim their faith in the face of persecution.

The most important evidence comes from the catacombs in Rome. These were huge complexes of underground burial-galleries, excavated by the Christians in the soft tufa-stone near the roads outside the city. The total length of their corridors is said to be over 500 miles. Some thirty-five catacombs are known, the oldest of which, bearing the names of Lucina, Callistus, Domitilla and Priscilla, date from later in the second century.

Inscriptions and paintings from the catacombs help clarify the development of Christian art and symbolism, and thereby of Christian beliefs and devotion. The cross and the fish are common Christian emblems, but the history of their use remains a puzzle. The fish probably came from an acrostic. The first letters of the Greek words *Iesous CHristos THeou Uios Soter* (Jesus Christ,

A PUZZLE

A mysterious square made up of Latin words has been found scratched on walls in places as far apart as Cirencester in England, Pompeii, and Dura-Europos in Mesopotamia. The letters are so arranged that the words read backwards and forwards as well as up and down. Many people think it has a Christian significance, but its exact meaning remains a puzzle. The straight translation does not seem to make much sense; various attempts have been made to find a hidden meaning.

R	O	T	A	S	*the wheels*
O	P	E	R	A	*with care*
T	E	N	E	T	*holds*
A	R	E	P	O	*Arepo*
S	A	T	O	R	*the sower*

It contains, jumbled-up, the words PATER NOSTER ('Our Father', the first two words of the Lord's prayer in Latin), together with A and O (the Greek letters 'alpha' and 'omega', used of God, for example in Revelation). So the square could be re-arranged like this:

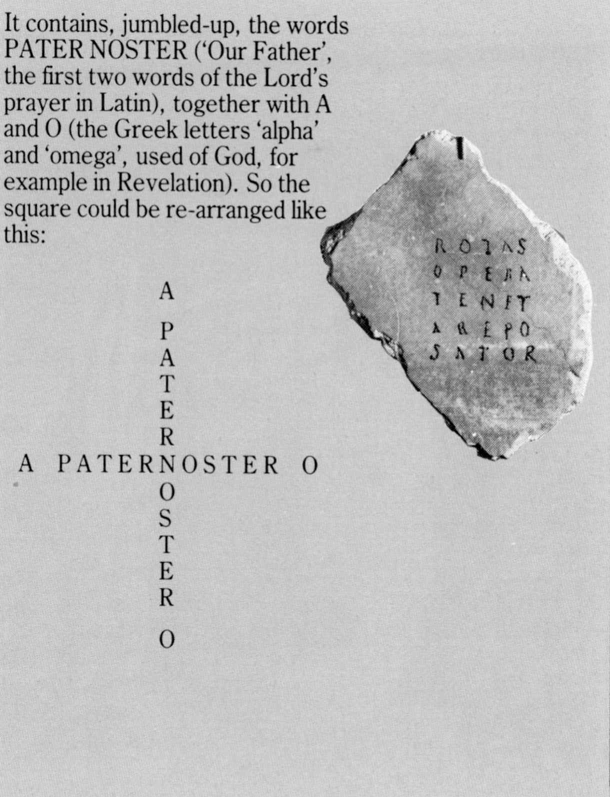

THE RELIGION OF THE ROMANS

Edwin Yamauchi

The Romans originally practised an agricultural religion in which they worshipped a mysterious, impersonal force which pervaded nature. The Romans placed strong emphasis upon correct ritual. For them religion was a contract, summarized in the Latin saying, 'I give that you may give.'

The Romans believed that they had to work to preserve 'the peace of the gods' by such means as sacrifices and by a special banquet where the images of the gods were featured. Every Roman made offerings at each meal to the spirits of the farm, and spirits of the larder.

This grotesque theatre-mask from Pompeii, was probably used in performing tragedy. The wreath of ivy leaves and berries suggests that it is linked with the frenzied Roman cult of Dionysus.

The Roman gods

In the period of the Roman Republic (509–27 BC) the Romans adopted Greek myths and identified the Greek gods with their own native gods.

Jupiter (the Greek god Zeus) was 'the best and the greatest'. His temple, built on the Capitoline Hill in Rome, was the most important of all. He made known his will by lightning and thunder. It was to Jupiter's temple that a victorious general or emperor made his way in the 'triumph', a ceremonial procession in which prisoners and plunder were paraded.

Juno (Greek, Hera) was responsible for women and marriage. Her month of June, or more precisely the second half, was considered particularly favourable for marriages. Mars (Greek, Ares), the god of war, was second in importance only to Jupiter.

Neptune (Greek, Poseidon) was the god not only of the sea but of rivers. His priests were known as 'bridge builders' (in Latin, *pontifex*). The *pontifex maximus* (high priest) was an elected official, who supervised the religious calender and sacrifices. The title has survived, and is today applied to the pope.

Mercury (Greek, Hermes) was the god of both merchants and thieves—an intriguing combination. Venus (Greek, Aphrodite) was the goddess of love and beauty. In Corinth, a thousand sacred prostitutes plied their trade as part of her cult.

The model shows part of the ancient city of Rome. To the left may be seen the Circus Maximus, where games and races took place.

Many of the months of our year are named after terms in Roman religion. For example, January is named after the two-faced god Janus, whose gate was kept open during times of war and shut in times of peace. It was usually open.

Reading the signs

The prediction of future events and the interpretation of past occurrences played a mayor role in Roman religion, politics and warfare.

The Romans regarded unusual occurrences as signs that the 'peace of the gods' had been broken. Signs or 'prodigies' included such freaks as a foal with five feet, hot stones falling from heaven, or shields sweating blood.

The Romans were especially concerned to discover the will of the gods from observing the signs given by birds. From the temple precinct they would observe the flights of birds, their numbers and their calls. The Romans also carefully observed the feeding of chickens on their military campaigns. When some of his sacred chickens did not eat, one impatient naval commander threw them into the sea with the remark, 'Let them drink since they will not eat!' But this impious act was said to have cost him the battle.

No military campaign or official act was supposed to be conducted without discovering the will of the gods by some act of divination. To disregard the signs was an act of ill omen, and to ignore the stars promised 'disaster'. Caesar was forewarned of his assassination by dreams and other omens which he ignored.

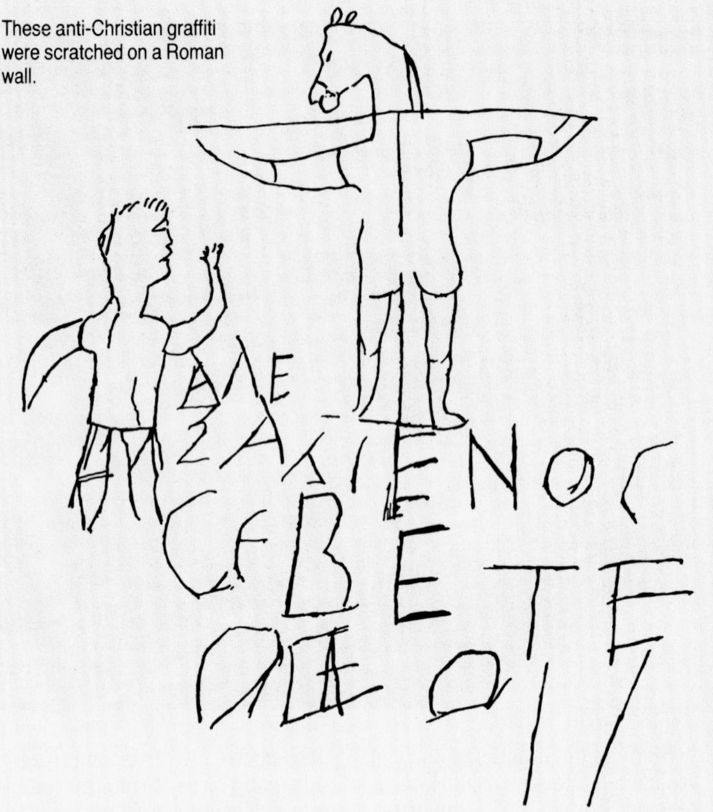

These anti-Christian graffiti were scratched on a Roman wall.

The Good Shepherd, the anchor (standing for the cross), and the dove holding an olive-branch (meaning peace) are three recurring early Christian symbols.

God's Son, Saviour) make up the word *ICHTHUS* (Greek for fish). Here was a secret sign which also summed up the heart of Christian belief and served as a simple aid to help explain it.

There are great gaps in the records. Archaeology reveals little about many important subjects. Most of the information concerning the growth of the church comes from literature, and particularly from the historian Eusebius. Christianity had become a powerful force when in the third century Rome tried to suppress it. There are traces in the inscriptions of the renewed strength of pagan cults.

Yet material remains of the life and witness of the Christians are rarely found. Eusebius tells of a whole Christian town exterminated in the persecution of Diocletian: this may have been Eumenea in Phrygia, where there are many Christian epitaphs.

There is the occasional glimpse of personal faithfulness to Christ. A crude third-century drawing in Rome depicts a boy with one hand raised in an attitude of worship before a crucified figure with an ass's head. Beneath are scribbled the mocking words, 'Alexamenos worships his god.'

The first church buildings

The earliest Christians had no special buildings, but met in private houses, as mentioned in several places in the New Testament. The earliest known church building

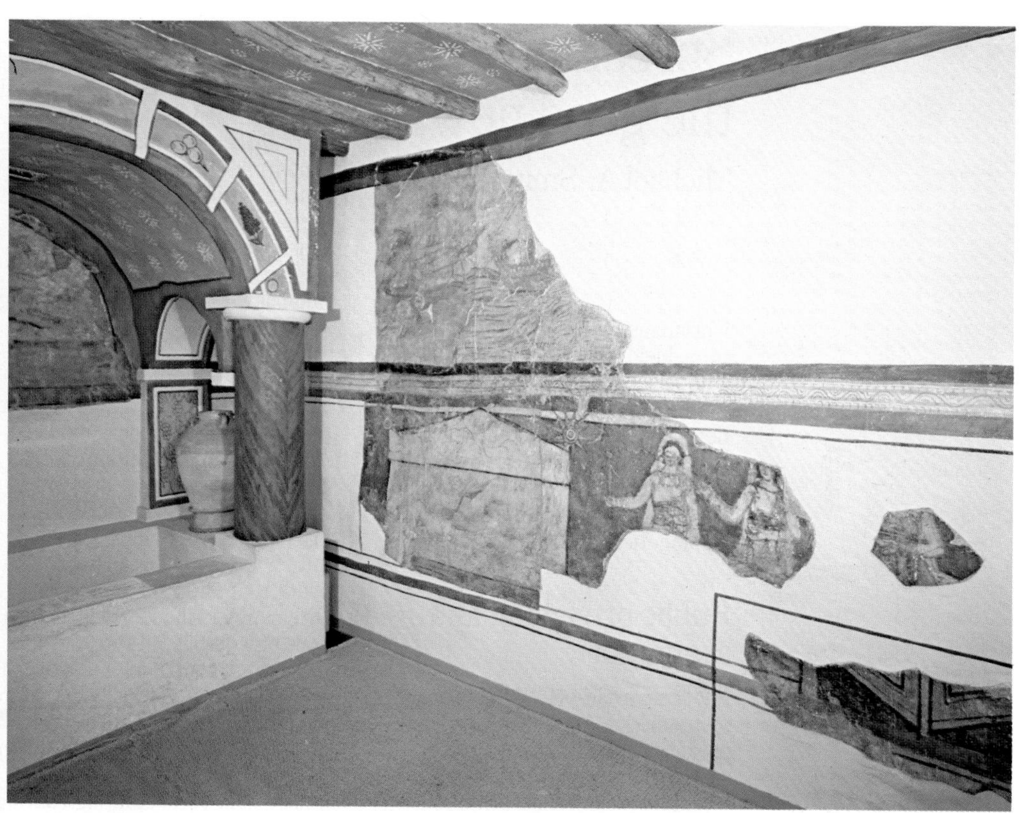

is usually thought to be at Dura-Europos on the River Euphrates, where a house dating from AD 232–3 was adapted soon after its construction to make a larger hall suitable for about a hundred people to assemble for worship. The walls have painted scenes from both the Old Testament and the Gospels.

Recent discoveries at Capernaum in Galilee have led some to believe that a very early house-church met there in what may once have been the house of the apostle Peter. But so far most scholars remain unconvinced.

In Rome about eighteen churches still bear the name of an early owner or patron, and their origins as house-churches go back before Constantine. They are now almost wholly replaced by, or incorporated in, later buildings. After Constantine the picture changed completely; Christianity was officially recognized, and large, impressive churches were built in many places.

Recent archaelogical work at Rome and elsewhere has shown that the early Christians' regard for their dead, especially martyrs, was important in developing structures and buildings for meetings.

In AD 231 this house at Dura-Europos (modern Salhiyeh) was adapted for the use of a Christian congregation. One room was enlarged to hold about a hundred people, with a small platform for the bishop, and in the corner a baptistery—a bath covered by a canopy decorated with wall-paintings. Illustrations included Adam and Eve, the Good Shepherd, Christ walking on the waters, David and Goliath and a procession of women carrying candles.

Spreading the good news

Michael A. Smith

Christians took two main approaches to spreading their faith. They used a variety of direct methods to communicate the good news, but in addition they took care to explain the faith intelligently and counter the attacks of critics. This second activity is often known as 'apologetics'.

Public preaching and argument

Public open-air preaching is often mentioned in Acts. The Christian preacher would choose a place where a crowd gathered, and attempt to catch their attention and proclaim the Christian message. This method must have become very hazardous after Nero's persecution, and it is rarely mentioned during the second and third centuries. It was possibly still practised in some places, because apocryphal stories about apostles, dating from the second and third centuries, still mention it.

Preaching in the Jewish synagogues was a very common tactic in the age of the apostles. Paul almost always started by preaching at the synagogue when he first arrived at a town. However, after the destruction of Jerusalem in AD 70, Jews took strong action against Christians in their midst, and certain anti-Christian additions were made to the synagogue prayers. Although there were Jewish Christians throughout the second century, the synagogues were now closed to Christian evangelism.

Preaching in the Christians' own places of worship offered another method of evangelism. The normal Sunday 'service' gradually began to split into two parts. The first part was open to all; but the communion which followed was restricted to baptized believers. Although during the second century most church attenders were people already sympathetic to Christianity, later

At Athens Paul took the opportunity to explain the gospel to the 'Court of the Areopagus', which met in one of the colonnaded buildings surrounding the market-place (*agora*). This part has been reconstructed.

the audience widened. During the long periods in the third century when Christians were not actively persecuted, many interested outsiders attended the first part of Sunday worship. From them came a considerable number of candidates for baptism.

Philosophic argument in public can be traced at least as far back as the time of Socrates and the sophists of the fifth century BC. Christians entered such debates very early. For a period Paul argued daily with the philosophers in the market-place at Athens. The method was continued, and often these public arguments were recorded. For example Justin Martyr's famous dialogue with the rabbi Trypho at Ephesus, and the discussion recorded by Minucius Felix, are now in written form.

When public preaching became dangerous, semi-private instruction took over. It had already been used to supplement public preaching. Paul hired the lecture-hall of Tyrannus at Ephesus for Christian teaching. In mid-second century Rome, Justin Martyr held classes for enquirers in a room over public baths. In early third-century Alexandria, Pantaenus, Clement of Alexandria and Origen in turn headed a well-known 'school of instruction' for those wishing to become Christians. Later such teaching became formalized into new converts' instruction-classes for baptism held each year in the period before Easter, which developed into Lent. This instruction was also the method most frequently used by splinter-groups for propagating their different doctrines.

Personal witness

This was by far the most common method of evangelism used by Christians, because it was the easiest to organize. Personal friendship formed the basis for bringing many people to Christ. But more casual encounters were used as well. Justin Martyr became a Christian after talking with an old man at Ephesus. Cyprian was converted through talking to a church elder. Later family influence became strong: Origen came from a Christian family and owed much to his parents for his Christian faith.

Some idea of the effectiveness of Christian witness is given by Celsus, a great opponent of the faith. He mentions how even Christians with little or no education seized every opportunity to witness to people, and when confronted by educated pagans they still would not stop pushing their opinions.

Personal evangelism was often backed up by outstanding acts of kindness. Another opponent of Christianity, Lucian of Samosata, told how a charlatan, Proteus

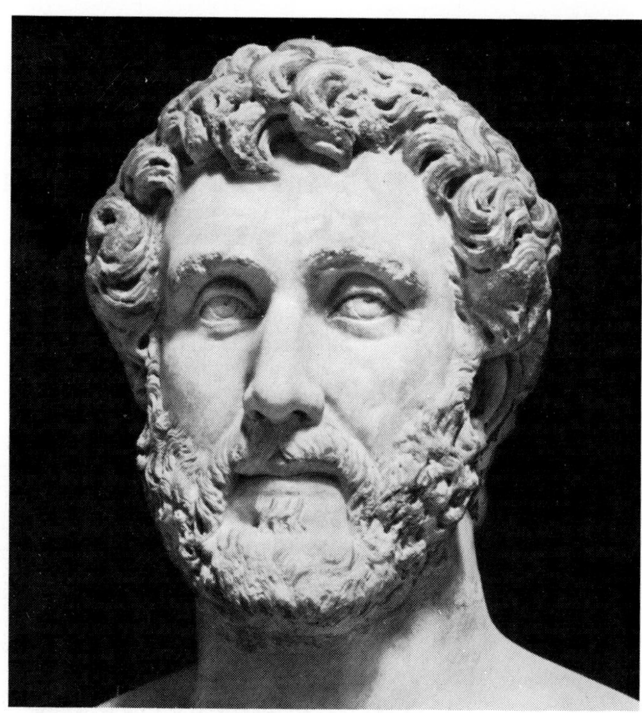

Justin's *First Apology*, addressed to the Emperor Antoninus Pius (138–61) (*above*), attempted to explain the true nature of Christianity.

Peregrinus, was befriended by Christians. During outbreaks of plague at Alexandria, Christians tended the sick and buried the dead when nearly everyone else had fled. In fact, the Christian life-style itself was a very powerful influence in evangelism. In a society where kindness, honesty and personal purity were rare, Christians who lived out these virtues were sure to attract comment and often serious enquiry.

The personal witness of Christian martyrs also had some effect. Even hostile observers, like the Emperor Marcus Aurelius, had to admit that Christian bravery in the face of death was praiseworthy. As a result of the martyrdom of Perpetua and Felicitas at Carthage, it was reported that the prison governor was converted. The sufferings of the martyrs at Lyons and Vienne in AD 177 encouraged several bystanders to declare themselves Christians, even though it meant almost certain death for them too.

In Alexandria, in Egypt, with its great libraries and tradition of learning, Christians first began to examine their faith as 'the true philosophy'. This figure of a Christian philosopher is from a third-century sarcophagus.

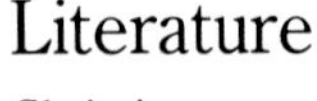

Literature

Christians were writing throughout this period to explain the faith and refute unfounded attacks. Luke and Acts may be the first examples; they were certainly written to instruct. By the second century such writing was well under way, aiming to commend the faith to pagans and Jews, and to counter slanders against Christians. Quadratus, Aristides, Justin Martyr, Athenagoras and Theophilus of Antioch all wrote such works in the second century. From the third century comes the great work of Origen, refuting the extended attack made on Christianity by the pagan philosopher Celsus.

As Christians became more competent, their writings tended to specialize. Some writers concentrated on a particular audience (for example, the Jews), while others took a particular theme (for example, Lactantius's *The Deaths of the Persecutors,* which claimed that all emperors who persecuted Christians came to a bad end).

Orthodox Christians also spent much time combating unorthodox groups. An example is Tertullian's monumental work *Against Marcion.*

Translation of the Scriptures from Greek into other languages also helped evangelism. By AD

300 there were versions of the New Testament in Latin, Syriac and Sahidic (a Coptic dialect), as well as collections of biblical texts.

Finally, some apocryphal fiction of this period may have had an evangelistic aim. It is possible that stories like the *Acts of Paul and Thecla* were produced to compete in the market of light, romantic fiction, and to commend Christian life-styles.

Christians were sometimes expatriates who could interest people from similar backgrounds. For example, the Christians of Vienne and Lyons in Gaul came from Asia Minor. At this time Christianity was largely an urban movement; Paul tended to preach in big cities, and small Christian groups could more easily spring up in the anonymity of large towns. Deep penetration of the countryside only began in the third century, though the methods used are unclear.

Nearly every known Christian congregation started by meeting in someone's house. One example is Philemon's house-church, perhaps at Laodicea. The home formed an important starting-point, although by the mid-third century congregations were beginning to have their own special buildings, because congregations were too large to meet even in the courtyard of a large Roman house.

Although the apostles performed many miracles during the course of evangelism, miracles did not form a large part of evangelism during the following years. Eusebius mentions only a very few miracles in his history of the church during this period—and only in one incident (the exorcizing of the Paneas spring) was any evangelistic use made of them. In fact, most Christian writers were surprisingly rationalistic, and tried to discredit contemporary pagan superstition, focussing on good living rather than supernatural 'signs'.

In the late third century came the first deliberate attempts by Christian missionaries to 'baptize' features of pagan religions, and thus overcome them by absorbing them into Christianity. Churches took over from temples, martyrs replaced the old gods in popular devotion, and the festivals of the Christian year took the place of the high-days and holy days of paganism. Reports of the work of people like Gregory the Wonderworker in Pontus, northern Asia Minor, and Gregory the Illuminator in Armenia also tend to exaggerate the success brought about by miracles. In Armenia the conversion of the royal family was followed by a national acceptance of Christianity. Such superficial methods of 'Christianization' became common in later centuries throughout Europe.

THE CHALLENGE TO FAITH

W. Ward Gasque

Roman emperors came to be regarded as divine. This inscription from the Forum in Ephesus speaks of the 'divine Augustus' (30 BC–AD 14).

The early followers of Jesus were marked out by their clear convictions about doctrine and ethics. They recognized only one message of salvation, only one God, only one Saviour. Once a person became a follower of 'the Way', a new life-style was demanded of him. This exclusiveness of early Christian belief and behaviour attracted many people. But it was also a cause of offence; enemies accused Christians of aloofness and of hating the present world.

But strong forces were acting against the spread of Christianity. Paganism still maintained a strong grip on people. The world was as morally corrupt as it has ever been, and the young church soon attracted the unyielding opposition of the ruling authorities. Jesus, Paul and Peter had all been executed by the government, and other leaders were similarly dealt with.

"If the River Tiber reaches the walls, if the River Nile does not rise to the fields, if the sky does not move or the earth does, if there is famine, if there is plague, the cry is at once: 'The Christians to the lion!' What, all of them to one lion?"

TERTULLIAN, Apology

Caesar versus Christ

As long as the church was regarded simply as a Jewish sect, it was tolerated by the Roman authorities. For its first thirty years Christianity, like Judaism, enjoyed protection by Roman law. Partly for this reason Paul emphasized the benefits of good government. But once Judaism and Christianity began to diverge Christians lost the special privileges given to Jews.

Jews were specially exempted from taking part in the cult of emperor-worship. Christians also sought this exemption, since they recognized only one God and served one Lord, Jesus Christ. But when the church became largely composed of Gentiles, it was no longer possible to shelter under the wing of Judaism. Christians refused to offer a pinch of incense on an altar to the divine Emperor—an act which most intelligent people considered to be merely symbolic—and this was interpreted as unpatriotic. In this way the official Roman attitude towards Christianity became less and less favourable.

Adherents of the new religion were subjected to a series of persecutions. These began with brief and apparently localized persecution in Rome under Nero in July 64. According to Tacitus, a Roman historian writing fifty years later, Nero tried to shift the blame on to the Christians after a rumour arose that he had started a fire which destroyed much of the city of Rome.

The scale and length of these persecutions seem to have become exaggerated. But Revelation, the final book of the Bible, gives evidence of the persecution of Christians in the province of Asia under the Emperor Domitian (AD 81–96).

Letters have survived between the Emperor Trajan and Pliny the

Younger (governor of Bithynia, AD 111–113) which make it clear that by their time profession of Christianity could be a capital offence. The policy which Pliny followed, which was commended by the Emperor, did not involve seeking out Christians for special punishment. But if a person was discovered to be a Christian, he or she was given an opportunity to renounce the faith. Refusal to do so meant that he or she was executed. This was probably normal policy at this period.

Seven letters of Ignatius, bishop of Antioch, written when on his way to Rome to be executed for being a Christian, survive from the beginning of the second century. In the letters he mentions others who 'preceded me from Syria to Rome for the glory of God'. One of his letters is addressed to Polycarp, bishop of Smyrna (Izmir in modern Turkey), who in turn became a martyr at the age of around eighty-six, about AD 156–160.

Around the middle of the second century Bishop Telesphorus of Rome was executed. During the reign of the Emperor Marcus Aurelius (161–180), who thoroughly disliked Christians, believers were executed in Rome itself, and the provinces of Gaul and Africa.

The legal grounds for the persecution of Christians are often obscure. Popular rumour suggested that Christians were cannibals (based perhaps on a misunderstanding of the Lord's Supper), atheists (like the Jews, Christians had no images in their shrines) and incestuous (their 'love' for one another was well known). These accusations were easily answered by Christian writers, but little notice seems to have been taken of their arguments. Apparently, simply to bear

Domitian took the title 'Master and god', and insisted that people took the official oath 'By the genius of the Emperor'. Such claims could not be accepted by Jews or Christians.

IGNATIUS OF ANTIOCH

Michael A. Smith

Ignatius was the bishop of the church at Antioch early in the second century. What little is known of him comes almost entirely from seven letters written during his journey to Rome to be executed, about AD 110–115.

Ignatius believed that he possessed the Holy Spirit's gift of 'prophecy', though he considered himself inferior to the apostles. He was a rather neurotic man, given to strong ideas and forceful language.

His seven letters (others attributed to him were added in the fourth century) were addressed to the churches at Ephesus, Magnesia, Tralles, Rome, Philadelphia and Smyrna, and to Polycarp, bishop of Smyrna. He argued strongly that there should be one 'bishop' in charge of each congregation, in order to prevent splits in the church and to ensure that correct beliefs were preserved.

He strongly condemned Docetist ideas current in churches in Asia Minor, where it was held that Jesus only seemed to be a man, and was in fact a pure spirit-being, uncontaminated by this material world. Ignatius put high value on the eucharist, or communion, as a means of ensuring unity, and of stressing the reality of Jesus' becoming man.

Ignatius was so enthusiastic to become a martyr that he begged the Christians in Rome not to prevent his expected execution.

the name 'Christian' was a crime, probably because rejection of the gods of the Romans was felt to threaten the peace and prosperity that the gods were believed to bring. Refusal to worship the Emperor could also be taken as a sign of treason.

Despite periods of persecution, the church continued to grow. The storms of opposition made the flame of the gospel burn all the brighter. Tertullian wrote: 'The blood of the martyrs is seed.' Even the later full-scale, systematic persecutions under the Emperors Decius (249–251) and Diocletian (284–305), the fiercest of all the early opponents of the Christian faith, helped to purge the church of some of its more lukewarm members.

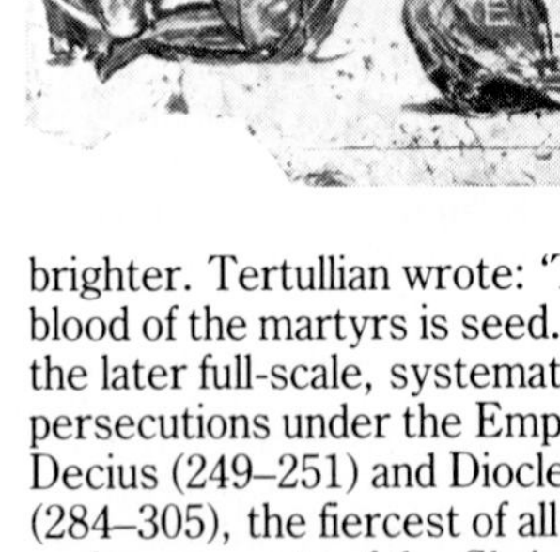

Three unnamed martyrs kneel blindfold, awaiting the executioner's sword. This wall-painting was found in a room used to house the relics of a martyr in Rome; it was later incorporated into the fifth-century church of St John and St Paul.

Very little is known about the details of church expansion during the second and third centuries. There are glimpses of a lively church, steadily expanding in size and in its influence on society. The faith of a persecuted minority was quietly and gradually becoming a major force in the Empire.

Christians meet challenges from within

When we read Paul's first letter to the church at Corinth, it becomes clear that many problems faced the church within its own membership. There was a tendency to divide into parties centred on the personalities of human leaders, and possibly also differences in emphasis over doctrines. A prominent member of the church was living in immorality, individual Christians were taking each other to the lawcourts over minor disputes, there were misunderstandings about the meaning of Christian liberty, disorders during the weekly worship service and even false teaching about the resurrection.

Paul's other letters also reveal controversies and power-struggles in the midst of encouragement and growth. Some people opposed the mission to the Gentiles and others questioned Paul's role in the church. Some people tried to mix Christian and non-Christian religious beliefs. The first letter of John speaks of those who once belonged to the Christian community but had now departed. They denied the true humanity of Jesus Christ.

Early in the second century Gnostic ideas began to be strongly promoted within the churches. Church leaders recognized that such views would lead to the total destruction of the Christian faith and had to be vigorously opposed.

The gospel came early to the notorious Seaport of Corinth. Here the Temple of Apollo dominates the ruins of ancient Corinth; in the background the rock of Acrocorinth, a stronghold for the city.

Another challenge came from

Marcion, a wealthy ship-owner, who came to Rome shortly before AD 140 and began teaching his own brand of anti-Jewish Christianity. Marcion organized his followers into a movement rivalling mainstream Christianity, which established its own communities throughout the Empire, and presented a real threat to the true faith.

A few decades later a movement arose in Phrygia, central Asia Minor, strongly emphasizing the imminent return of Christ and the end of the age. It became known as Montanism, and combined prophetic enthusiasm with strict asceticism, leading to a split in the church which lasted for over a century. Later, theological controversies concerning the nature of Christ occupied much attention, disrupting Christian unity and weakening the church's witness.

So the church brought together ideas and people from many backgrounds. It had to cope with people who had become Christians in such disreputable seaports as Corinth, notorious for its immorality. It had to resolve the pressures to revert to pagan practices and to Judaism, to sort out its attitudes towards contemporary customs and cultures, and thrash out beliefs and opinions about issues on which there were no precedents to guide its thinking.

Christianity attracts leading thinkers

By the end of the second century the new faith was on the way to becoming the most forceful and compelling movement within the Empire. Many of the keenest minds of the day were becoming followers of 'the Way'.

A series of writers defended the Christian faith against both popular accusations and more

NERO'S SPECTACULAR MASSACRE

"To kill the rumours, Nero charged and tortured some people hated for their evil practices—the group popularly known as 'Christians'. The founder of this sect, Christ, had been put to death by the governor of Judea, Pontius Pilate, when Tiberius was Emperor. Their deadly superstition had been suppressed temporarily, but was beginning to spring up again—not now just in Judea but even in Rome itself where all kinds of sordid and shameful activities are attracted and catch on.

First those who confessed to being Christians were arrested. Then, on information obtained from them, hundreds were convicted, more for their anti-social beliefs than for fire-raising. In their deaths they were made a mockery. They were covered in the skins of wild animals, torn to death by dogs, crucified or set on fire—so that when darkness fell they burned like torches in the night. Nero opened up his own gardens for this spectacle and gave a show in the arena, where he mixed with the crowd, or stood dressed as a charioteer on a chariot. As a result, although they were guilty of being Christians and deserved death, people began to feel sorry for them. For they realized that they were being massacred not for the public good but to satisfy one man's mania."

TACITUS, Annals 15.44

Nero (54–68) behaved monstrously towards his own family—but the Greeks flattered him over his literary efforts. After his early death rumours arose that he would be reincarnated.

The most famous amphitheatre in the Roman world was the Colosseum in Rome itself. Dedicated in AD 80, it could hold around 45,000 spectators, and be used for gladiators' fights, or flooded for mock-naval battles. Prisoners, in some instances Christians, were thrown to lions and bears in the arena.

sophisticated attacks. Although most of the writings of these 'apologists' were dedicated to the emperors, their real audience was the educated public of the day. If they could answer the accusations of the enemies of Christianity and point out the inherent weakness of paganism, they hoped this would help to change public opinion concerning the good news and lead to conversions. Men such as Aristides, Justin Martyr, his disciple Tatian, Athenagoras, Theophilus of Antioch, the unknown author of the *Letter to Diognetus* and Melito, bishop of Sardis, all directed their intellectual and spiritual gifts to this cause.

Towards the end of the second century Irenaeus, bishop of Lyons in Gaul, wrote five monumental books against the Gnostic heresies of his area, together with a book entitled *Proof of the Apostolic Preaching.* Several of his other books have been lost. His theology was grounded in the Bible and the church's doctrines and helped provide a steadying, positive influence in the church. He wrote of the cosmic implications of the work of Christ and God's plan in history, and paved the way for the later Christian interpretations of history by writers such as Augustine.

But the real intellectual giants were still to come.

Tertullian, the 'father of Latin

THE MONTANISTS

David F. Wright

An enthusiastic young Christian named Montanus began to attract attention as a prophet around AD 172 in Phrygia, a region of western Asia Minor. Two prophetesses, Prisca and Maximilla, soon joined him. They claimed to be mouthpieces of the Paraclete, the Greek title used in John's Gospel for the Holy Spirit. At times God spoke through them in the first person, as with the Old Testament prophets: 'Man is a lyre, and I move over him like a plectrum.' They were the 'New Prophecy'.

Their main message was the nearness of the end and the return of Christ. For this, Christians needed to be fully prepared.

Montanists called all Christians to a demanding asceticism. Marital relations were to be abandoned in favour of chastity, fasts multiplied, and food eaten dry. The Montanists' holy, Spirit-led communities at Pepuza and Tymion in Phrygia were named 'Jerusalem'. Maximilla predicted: 'After me there will be no prophecy, but the End.'

Through their oracles they urged Christians to relish persecution: 'Do not hope to die in bed . . . but as martyrs.' Montanists were 'gloriously martyred' in Gaul and Africa.

The most distinguished Montanist was Tertullian of Carthage in his later life. He too believed that the prophecies given by the Paraclete perfected the church's discipline—by refusing forgiveness for serious sins after baptism, and banning remarriage and flight from persecution.

The Montanists soon ran into trouble. In Asia they were excommunicated by the first synods of bishops known of in the history of the church. Why they were condemned is uncertain. They were fanatics but not heretics. (One bishop of Rome apparently recognized their gifts as of the Spirit, but later changed his mind.) Their visions, speaking in tongues and intense religious excitement attracted suspicion. The claims made for their prophecies seemed to question the emerging canon of New Testament Scriptures. Maximilla's predictions were not fulfilled. The Montanists scolded the 'unspiritual' church for rejecting their Paraclete. In short, allegiance to the New Prophecy created discord at a time when the bishops were working towards a united, stable church which conformed with the tradition of the apostles.

Montanist groups survived into the fifth century in Africa and longer still in Phrygia. The church lost something by excluding them. Despite their excesses, the Montanists stood for the conviction that the Spirit was as active in the contemporary church as at the beginning; greater manifestations, not lesser, were promised for 'the last days'. Their similarity to today's Pentecostal and charismatic movements has often been exaggerated.

theology', was born in Carthage, in the province of Africa, around AD 150. He was converted to Christianity as a man of about forty, and soon began writing books to promote the Christian faith. The large number he wrote in Greek are now lost, but thirty-one in Latin survive.

Tertullian's *Apology* underlined the legal and moral absurdity of the persecution directed against Christians, while other books offered encouragement to those facing martyrdom. He attacked the heretics, explained the Lord's Prayer and the meaning of baptism, and helped develop the orthodox understanding of the Trinity. He was the first person to use the Latin word *trinitas* (trinity). Tertullian later joined the Montanist movement. His intellectual brilliance and literary versatility made him one of the most powerful writers of the time, and almost as influential as Augustine in the development of theology in the West.

While Tertullian was at work in Carthage, Alexandria, to the east, was becoming another key intellectual centre for the Christian faith. Alexandria had been an important cultural capital since its foundation by Alexander the Great in the fourth century BC, and it possessed one of the great libraries of the ancient world. It was probably in Alexandria that the Old Testament was first translated from Hebrew into Greek. The famous Jewish philosopher, Philo, lived in Alexandria at about the time of Jesus: he tried to re-interpret Judaism in terms of Greek philosophy.

By about AD 185 a converted Stoic philosopher named Pantaenus was teaching Christians in Alexandria. He probably also travelled to India, and was a very able thinker. He was succeeded as leader of the school for those preparing for Christian baptism (catechumens) first by Clement, then by Origen. In spite of periods of intense persecution, the school at Alexandria gained great importance, strengthening the faith of Christians and attracting new converts to the faith.

The crucial achievement of Clement and Origen was to put over the gospel in terms which could be understood by people familiar with the highest forms of Greek culture. They established once for all the intellectual respectability of the new faith.

In addition to being a creative theologian, Origen also made an immense contribution to biblical scholarship. He was one of the few Christian scholars before the Reformation who took the trouble to learn Hebrew so that he could read the Old Testament in its original language. He was later forced to leave Alexandria for Caesarea, where he continued writing and teaching.

In the third century the church extended its frontiers, both geographically and socially, at an unparalleled rate. It was beginning to assume the proportions of an empire within the Empire. The constant travel between different churches, the synods of bishops, the letters carried by messengers back and forth across the Empire and the loyalty which the Christians showed to their leaders and to one another impressed even the emperors. Yet such things could be easily interpreted as a threat to the government.

Violent persecution

In AD 250 the most violent persecution the church had yet faced was instigated by the Emperor Decius (249–251). Imperial edicts commanded all citizens of the Empire to sacrifice to the traditional Roman gods. Those who did so were given certificates (*libelli*, in Latin) as evidence that they had obeyed the order. Those who refused to obey and were unable (or unwilling) to obtain false *libelli* from sympathetic or corrupt officials were executed.

Many Christians actually complied to save their lives. Others were able to obtain certificates without having actually sacrificed. But an unknown number of Christians were imprisoned or executed—among them the bishops of Rome, Antioch and Jerusalem.

Fortunately for the church, this testing did not last very long.

NOVATIANISTS

Michael A. Smith

The Novatianists were a small puritanical group which split off from the church at Rome. Their founder, Novatian, was defeated in the election for bishop in AD 251, and set up a rival congregation. The main point at issue between the factions in the election was how to treat those who had renounced Christ during the persecutions. Novatianists took a very rigid line, and refused to receive back anyone who had given way under persecution.

Novatian was a gifted theologian and one of the earliest Latin authors among the Christians. Several of his works survive, the most important dealing with the doctrine of the Trinity. He is believed to have been martyred during the persecution of the Emperor Valerian about AD 258.

Novatianists were theologically orthodox and in the 250s spread quickly. They set up a rival bishop at Carthage, gained the support of Marcian, bishop of Arles, and also made headway in the East. They soon built up a network of small congregations, calling themselves 'Cathari' (pure ones) to distinguish themselves from all other churches, which they considered to be polluted as a result of their lenient attitude towards sinners.

Those who joined the Novatianists had to be baptized afresh, as if they were joining the only true church. Novatianists later took their rigid stand further, refused to have communion with people who had been married more than once, and rejected the possibility of penance for any major sin after baptism.

Novatianists were treated as heretics until the time of Constantine, when an edict in 326 granted them toleration and the right to own church buildings and burial-places. A Novatianist bishop, Acesius, was present at the Council of Nicaea in 325. In the fourth century, Novatianists spread into Spain and Egypt.

Despite official toleration, Novatianists continued to be harassed by official churchmen. Nestorius attacked them in 428 at Constantinople, but was restrained by the Emperor. In 429 Celestine, bishop of Rome, deprived them of their buildings. The Novatianists were especially strong in Constantinople, and the church historian Socrates (about 380–440) probably belonged to them. They were still important enough to be attacked in the writings of Eulogius, patriarch of Alexandria (580–607), but were probably reabsorbed into the mainstream churches with the passage of time. As early as Nicaea, Novatianist clergy were allowed to retain their rank if they returned to the 'catholic church'.

During the persecution under the Emperor Decius (249–51) both Pope Cornelius, and his rival, Bishop Hippolytus, died in the mines in Sardinia.

Within two years Decius died in battle against the Gothic invaders from the north. Although his successor, the Emperor Gallus (251–253), kept the anti-Christian measures alive, persecution was not so widespread as under Decius.

A few years later, persecution was renewed with a fresh ferocity, towards the end of the reign of the Emperor Valerian (253–260). On this occasion church leaders were singled out and ordered to worship the old gods, under the threat of exile and imprisonment. Christians were forbidden to hold church meetings or to visit Christian cemeteries, on pain of death. Finally, a particularly severe edict prescribed death for church leaders and the confiscation of property, slavery and even death for other Christians who would not desert the faith. Again only a war with foreign invaders, this time the Persians, put an end to the ordeal.

A few decades of relative peace and prosperity followed, only to be interrupted in 303 by the most severe persecution the church had yet faced.

By this time Christianity had reached as far as the immediate family of the Emperor Diocletian (284–305). Many of his slaves and servants, as well as his wife and daughter, were believers, together with many others in high places—either Christian or favourably disposed to Christianity. Diocletian issued four edicts against Christianity which were enforced with varying degrees of severity. His action may have been intended to gain more enthusiastic support from the army, which tended to be strongly anti-Christian.

The decrees of 303 ordered the destruction of all church buildings, the confiscation of Christian books, the dismissal of Christians from the government and army, and the imprisonment of the clergy. A further edict, in 304, ordered all Christians to offer sacrifices to the pagan gods.

In Asia Minor an entire town and its inhabitants, who were predominantly Christian, were destroyed by soldiers. In Rome church property was confiscated and many Christians were martyred. Christians in Palestine, Syria and Egypt seem to have suffered particular violence.

What should be done with lapsed Christians?

Many Christians were willing to suffer as martyrs rather than betray their Lord by acknowledging false gods. Some, however, renounced their faith under pressure of torture and imprisonment. Others got pagan neighbours to sacrifice on their behalf, or obtained false certificates from sympathetic officials. At the opposite extreme, some Christians eagerly sought out martyrdom, even when it was not forced upon them, though this was strongly discouraged by Christian leaders.

Following each wave of persecution, the church was faced with the problem of what to do with those who repented after lapsing under the pressure of persecution.

Baptism was generally held to cover only sins already committed. Serious post-baptismal lapses required special treatment. Some Christian leaders claimed that offences such as idolatry after baptism were unpardonable on earth; but others allowed one such occasion of forgiveness subsequent to baptism. The lapsed Christian who showed genuine penitence could be received back into church communion.

Callistus, bishop of Rome (217–22), was among the more moderate and appealed to Paul's letters and the parables of the lost

PERPETUA

"While we were still under arrest my father out of love for me was trying to persuade me and shake my resolution. 'Father,' said I, 'do you see this vase here, for example, or waterpot or whatever?'

'Yes, I do', said he.

And I told him: 'Could it be called by any other name than what it is?' And he said: 'No.'

'Well, so too I cannot be called anything other than what I am, a Christian.'

At this my father was so angered by the word 'Christian' that he moved towards me as though he would pluck my eyes out. But he left it at that and departed, vanquished along with his diabolical arguments.

During these few days I was baptized, and I was inspired by the Spirit not to ask for any other favour after the water but simply the perseverance of the flesh. A few days later we were lodged in the prison; and I was terrified, as I had never before been in such a dark hole. What a difficult time it was! With the crowd the heat was stifling; then there was the extortion of the soldiers; and to crown all, I was tortured with worry for my baby there.

These were the trials I had to endure for many days. Then I got permission for my baby to stay with me in prison. At once I recovered my health, relieved as I was of my worry and anxiety over the child. My prison had suddenly become a palace, so that I wanted to be there rather than anywhere else.

One day while we were eating breakfast we were suddenly hurried off for a hearing. We arrived at the forum, and straight away the story went about the neighbourhood near the forum and a huge crowd gathered. We walked up the prisoner's dock. All the others when questioned admitted their guilt. Then, when it came my turn, my father appeared with my son, dragged me from the step, and said: 'Perform the sacrifice – have pity on your baby!'

Hilarianus the governor, who had received his judicial powers as the successor of the late proconsul Minucius Timinianus, said to me: 'Have pity on your father's grey head; have pity on your infant son. Offer the sacrifice for the welfare of the emperors.'

'I will not,' I retorted.

'Are you a Christian?' said Hilarianus.

And I said: 'Yes, I am.'

Then Hilarianus passed sentence on all of us: we were condemned to the beasts, and we returned to prison in high spirits.

But my baby had got used to being nursed at the breast and to staying with me in prison. So I sent the deacon Pomonius straight away to my father to ask for the baby. But father refused to give him over. But as God willed, the baby had no further desire for the breast, nor did I suffer any inflammation; and so I was relieved of any anxiety for my child and of any discomfort in my breasts."

Extract from Perpetua's diary of her imprisonment.

sheep and prodigal son for proof that no sin is unforgivable if the sinner truly turns from his sins. His views enjoyed wide acceptance in the church, but were strongly opposed by Novatian, a presbyter in the church of Rome, during the persecution under Decius.

Cornelius, a more liberal man, was elected bishop of Rome: but a minority voted for Novatian and demanded that those who had given up faith under pressure should not be welcomed back into fellowship. Novatian split the church over this issue and other separatist bishops were appointed for churches in Africa, Asia Minor and elsewhere. This division persisted until the seventh century, though the Novatianist churches gradually waned in influence.

A similar division took place in North Africa following the persecution under Diocletian. Here the arguments were clouded by personalities and questionable motives. A bishop of the church in Carthage was consecrated by a bishop who was believed to have surrendered the Scriptures to the police. He was therefore regarded as fatally tainted by the stricter members of the church. A rival bishop was elected by the stricter group and he was in turn succeeded by Donatus, from whom the Donatist movement derives its name.

This controversy ultimately led to the principle that the reality of baptism and of ordination does not depend on the moral character of the person who performs it but on Christ and the Spirit. It now became general practice to accept people back into the church following a temporary lapse from the faith, provided they gave evidence of repentance. But the Donatists rejected this position—and even rebaptized orthodox Christians who joined their ranks.

Diocletian rose from the army to become Emperor (287–305) and managed to restore order by imposing totalitarian rule. He tried to complete his task by liquidating the church.

Miracles and martyrs

From the beginning, those Christians who gave their lives rather than betray their Lord were held in high honour by the church. The book of Acts gives considerable space to the martyrdom of Stephen. Revelation honours an otherwise unknown disciple named Antipas, acknowledged by Jesus as 'My witness, my faithful one, who was killed among you,' and elsewhere promises a special reward for those who have sealed their witness for Christ with their blood.

During the later persecutions, the martyrdoms of Peter and Paul were given special significance. Ignatius thought of his own journey to Rome for execution as a conscious imitation of the Lord's last journey to Jerusalem and the cross. Martyrdom became regarded by many as the ultimate sign of Christian discipleship. Even Origen as a boy in Alexandria had to be restrained forcibly by his mother from leaving home to join the martyrs voluntarily in their sufferings. (Origen lived a strictly ascetic life; he may have taken the instruction of Matthew 19:12 literally and had himself castrated.)

The martyrdom of Polycarp, whose execution was recorded so lovingly by a disciple, was celebrated annually by his church at Smyrna. This celebration became the pattern for the practice of venerating the martyrs' remains and commemorating their death. Later the belief developed that prayers addressed to God through the martyrs were especially effective.

In the late third and early fourth centuries the practice of the veneration of the martyrs grew rapidly. The events of the last and violent persecutions led to an exaggeration of the scale and extent of earlier persecutions.

CYPRIAN AND NORTH AFRICA

David F. Wright

Cyprian became a Christian about AD 246, when he was already a rich and cultured man of Carthage, the chief city of Roman Africa, and probably destined for high government office. He himself wrote that: 'A second birth created me a new man by means of the Spirit breathed from heaven.' He now dedicated himself to celibacy, poverty and the Bible with such distinction that within two years he was made bishop of Carthage.

When the persecution of the Emperor Decius began in AD 250, Cyprian left the city. Many church leaders scorned flight from persecution, and Cyprian lost face. From his hiding-place he had difficulty restraining the 'confessors', Christians whose sufferings earned them great spiritual prestige. They were urging lenient treatment for 'lapsed' Christians who denied the faith under pressure. After Cyprian returned in AD 251 a council of bishops fixed stricter terms for readmitting them to the church, whereupon the dissidents split off. To oppose their action, Cyprian wrote his most important work, *The unity of the Catholic Church*.

From AD 255 Cyprian defiantly opposed Stephen, bishop of Rome, over the question whether Christian baptism could be received outside the catholic (mainstream) church. Cyprian believed that the Spirit's gifts of life and salvation were restricted to the catholic church. Unlike Stephen, he demanded that people baptized in separatist groups who entered the church should be rebaptized. The dispute faded after Stephen's death and Cyprian's exile and courageous martyrdom in AD 258.

Cyprian was above all a churchman—a clear-headed administrator but simple theologian. His writings deal with practical church matters. By calling regular councils of bishops he put into practice his conviction that the church depended for its unity on their harmony and equality.

Cyprian believed that all bishops were in theory equal—just as the apostles had been. He regarded ministers as priests, and the Lord's Supper as the sacrifice of the cross. He tried to integrate the Spirit-dominated puritanism of Tertullian with the church of the bishops. His pastoral zeal was best shown when he helped people during a terrible plague in AD 252–4. His influence on the later Western church was immense and largely harmful.

The numbers of martyrs and their sufferings were greatly magnified; the stories of their deaths were embroidered with all sorts of fantastic miraculous happenings and superstitions.

Some converts from paganism brought with them pre-Christian ideas so that in the church the martyrs began to take on the role that the gods had earlier played in the old religions. Relics of the martyrs were superstitiously cherished, their graves became sites of pilgrimages and prayer, and they were believed to work miracles and guarantee special blessings to believers. Although not all church leaders approved of such things, the veneration of martyrs and

JUSTIN MARTYR

Colin J. Hemer

Justin welcomed classical philosophy. He believed that Plato's teaching on eternal forms referred to the God of the Bible; that Socrates, like Abraham, was 'a Christian before Christ', and his death an example for Christian martyrs. This Roman statuette of Socrates is copied from a Greek original.

Justin was a convert from paganism, but became the most notable of the second century 'apologists' (writers defending the Christian faith). Details of his life come chiefly from his own writings.

Justin was born at Flavia Neapolis (now Nablus) in Palestine. As a young man he searched energetically for truth in a variety of philosophical schools. One day, while meditating alone by the seashore, perhaps at Ephesus, he met an old man who exposed the weaknesses of his confident thinking. The stranger then pointed him to the Jewish prophets who bore witness to Christ. Justin had already been impressed by the remarkable moral constancy of Christians in the face of death. These themes were to recur later in his writings.

Justin responded wholeheartedly by becoming a Christian. He took his new faith into the philosophical schools. He believed he now possessed in Christ a more perfect philosophy, revealed fully by the God who had been known only in part through the wisdom of the ancient world. He taught in Ephesus and Rome, where Tatian was one of his pupils.

Justin had close links with Ephesus, capital of the Roman province of Asia. The city has been extensively excavated. A wide road led from the harbour (now silted over, to become a fertile plain) to the city (the amphitheatre is in the foreground).

Justin's writings give an attractive impression of him. They are vigorous and earnest, but discursive—urgent appeals to reason, thrashed out under the threat of persecution.

Justin's *First Apology* was addressed to the Emperor Antoninus Pius (AD 138–161) and aimed to clear away prejudice and misunderstanding about Christianity. He claimed that popular charges that Christians were atheists and immoral were unfounded. He argued that Christian beliefs and practices actually reflect a higher reason and morality. His *Second Apology* is brief and passionate, protesting against injustice. It was provoked by the summary execution of people innocent of any crime, except confessing the name of Christ.

The longest of Justin's three surviving works is the *Dialogue with Trypho.* It apparently recounts an actual encounter at Ephesus years earlier. Trypho was a cultured Jew who objected that Christians broke the Jewish law, and worshipped a human being. The debate was conducted with respect and courtesy on both sides, despite deep disagreement. Justin argued from the Scriptures they shared. The Scriptures spoke of Christ, in whom the law is set aside. Justin's words are valuable examples of the way early Christians interpreted the Bible.

Justin was martyred in Rome about AD 165. It seems likely that his bold ministry was cut short in its full vigour. He had presented his faith as both scriptural and reasonable in the face of objections by both Jews and pagans.

other saints took a greater and greater place in popular religion.

The North African Christians

North African Christianity tended to be extremely rigorous. Martyrs were seen as ideal Christians. Churchmen in North Africa thus tended towards a view of the church which regarded it as so pure as to forget that it consisted of a community of redeemed sinners. This led to repeated controversies and divisions, fragmenting the united witness to Christ.

Bishop Cyprian of Carthage (about 248–258) provides a good example of the rigorous North African faith, though he advised moderation towards the backsliders during the persecution under Decius, and in certain circles gained a reputation for compromise. He was under vows to remain single, and lived a life of poverty, though he was born into wealth. Cyprian rejected the reading of all literature other than the Bible and distinctively Christian books, in spite of being educated in the best schools of the day.

It was in Syria and Egypt that the earliest Christian monks appeared, in the late third century. Christian hermits or anchorites (from a Greek word meaning 'one who withdraws') forsook ordinary society for a life of prayer and solitude in the desert. One of the most famous of these early hermits was Antony of Egypt (about 251–356), who gave away all his earthly possessions at the age of twenty, in order to serve Christ free from distraction. In spite of his desire to be alone, he was constantly beset by visitors and finally organized a cluster of hermit cells around him. Although physically withdrawn from the world, Antony strongly influenced Christians of his day and inspired many conversions to Christ.

Constantine becomes Emperor

At the height of the most severe of the persecutions directed against the Christians, the Emperor Diocletian voluntarily retired to live as a gentleman-farmer on his estate on the coast of Dalmatia (modern Yugoslavia). He aimed to stabilize the government and to avert civil war, by setting a precedent for orderly and peaceful succession to the office of Emperor. He had earlier divided the Empire into two parts, the East and the West, each with its own capital and senior and junior emperors.

Diocletian succeeded in setting the administrative pattern for a divided Empire (and, later, a divided church) for centuries to come. But he did not avert civil war.

Upon the death of Constantius, the chief ruler of the Western Empire, his son Constantine took command of the army in Britain and Gaul and demanded recognition as his successor. Galerius, the preeminent Emperor in the East, granted him only junior status. Soon Maxentius, son of Constantius's predecessor in the West, murdered the senior western Emperor and usurped his position.

Constantine returned to Italy and marched upon Rome. His rival, Maxentius, foolishly sallied forth to meet him and was defeated at the famous battle at the Milvian Bridge in 312. In this way Constantine, later called the Great, became the sole master of the West. After a further struggle with Licinius, successor to Galerius in the East, Constantine emerged as supreme victor in the Empire.

Constantine was proclaimed Emperor by soldiers at York in AD 305. This copper coin was minted in London in AD 310.

The Gnostics

Edwin M. Yamauchi

The Gnostics were followers of a variety of religious movements in the early Christian centuries which stressed that people could be saved through a secret knowledge (*gnōsis* in Greek). The clearest evidence for these movements, collectively known as Gnosticism, comes in Christian writings of the second century. These viewed the various Gnostic groups as heretical perversions of Christianity.

Gnosticism may also have been more independent of Christianity. For instance, some scholars find Gnostic traces wherever there is an emphasis on 'knowledge' for salvation, as for example in the Dead Sea Scrolls. Others emphasize the stress on an opposition between the spiritual world and the evil, material world.

The teachings of the Gnostics

In Gnostic beliefs there is a sharp dualism—they set a transcendent God over against an ignorant creator (who is often a caricature of the God of the Old Testament). Some taught that the creation of the world resulted from the fall of *Sophia,* 'wisdom'. All Gnostics viewed the material creation as evil. Sparks of divinity, however, have been encapsuled in the bodies of certain 'spiritual' individuals destined for salvation.

These 'spirituals' are ignorant of their heavenly origins. God sends down to them a redeemer who brings them salvation in the form of secret knowledge *(gnōsis)* of themselves, their origin and their destiny. Thus awakened, the 'spirituals' escape from the prison of their bodies at death and pass safely through the planetary regions controlled by hostile demons, to be reunited with God.

Since they believed that salvation depended solely upon the knowledge of one's 'spiritual' nature, some Gnostics indulged in extremely licentious behaviour. They claimed that they were 'pearls' who could not be stained by any external mud. Carpocrates, for example, urged his followers to sin; and his son Epiphanes taught that promiscuity was God's law. The Cainites perversely honoured Cain and other villains of the Old Testament and the Ophites venerated the serpent for bringing 'knowledge' to Adam and Eve.

Most Gnostics, however, had a radically ascetic attitude towards sex and marriage. Humans were

The Gospel of Thomas was found with other Gnostic texts at Nag Hammadi, Egypt. The opening words are: 'These are the secret words which the living Jesus spoke, and Didymus Judas Thomas wrote them down. . .'

originally unisex. The creation of woman was the source of evil; the procreation of children simply multiplied the souls in bondage to the powers of darkness.

Gnosticism clearly enjoyed great success in the ancient world, especially on the fringes of Christianity. It offered explanations of the evil and confusion of the world and the human race, and a way of escape which led back to humanity's spiritual home.

Until the nineteenth century, our knowledge of the Gnostics rested entirely on the writings of Christians such as Irenaeus, Hippolytus, Origen, Tertullian, and Epiphanius. Some of them preserved extracts from original Gnostic documents, but for the most part their accounts are in the form of counter-arguments. Scholars were not sure how accurate these accounts were; recent discoveries, such as the Nag Hammadi texts, have confirmed some of them.

New evidence about the Gnostics

In the nineteenth century two original Gnostic manuscripts were published: the *Codex Askewianus* containing the Pistis Sophia, and the *Codex Brucianus* containing the Books of Jeu. All of these are relatively late Gnostic documents. A third manuscript, the *Codex Berolinensis,* though acquired in the nineteenth century, was not fully published until 1955. It contains a Gospel of Mary (Magdalene), a Wisdom of Jesus, Acts of Peter, and an Apocryphon of John (a work mentioned by Irenaeus in AD 180). These three manuscripts are in Coptic, a late version of the Egyptian language.

In 1946 a priceless cache of twelve Coptic codices and fragments was discovered near Nag Hammadi in Upper Egypt by a peasant searching for fertilizer. The collection, which was deposited about AD 400, contains about fifty works. These texts have already thrown much new light on Gnostic beliefs and practices. Among those which have been published are: *The Gospel of Truth,* which some have ascribed to the famous Gnostic leader Valentinus, and which deals with ignorance as the cause of humanity's lost state.

The letter of Rheginos, possibly by Valentinus, claims that the resurrection was not a physical event.

The Gospel according to Thomas, an important collection of 114 *logia* or sayings attributed to Jesus. (This is distinct from another apocryphal *Gospel of Thomas,* which describes the miracles supposed to have been done by the child Jesus.)

The Gospel according to Philip, by Valentinus, which discusses several sacraments, including baptism, anointing with oil and the 'wedding chamber'.

The Apocryphon of John, giving a detailed account of the origins of the universe, similar to that of the Sethians and Ophites, Gnostic groups mentioned by early Christian writers.

The Revelation of Adam, in which Adam reveals to Seth how Noah was saved from the flood and Seth's seed is saved from destruction by fire. Although some allusions—for example to a virgin birth and physical suffering—may be explained as references to Christ, Christianity is not explicitly mentioned in the text. Some have therefore argued that this document represents pre-Christian Gnosticism.

The Mandaean communities living today in Iraq and Iran are the sole surviving remnants of ancient Gnosticism. Three major texts from the Mandaeans were translated early in this century: The

The Dead Sea Scrolls, some of which show traces of Gnostic teaching, were discovered in 1947 in caves in these hills. The Qumran community lived nearby until the war with Rome of AD 66–73.

Many Gnostic manuscripts circulated in the first centuries of the church. The *Pistis Sophia,* here in a late fourth-century Coptic version, set out the influential teachings of Valentinus.

MANICHAEANS

Edwin Yamauchi

Mani (AD 216–76), a Persian born in Mesopotamia, established a religion which claimed to be the final, universal revelation. It was a dualistic religion which maintained the sharp opposition between the principles of light and of darkness, like other Gnostic movements. Mani's followers, the Manichaeans, were zealous missionaries who carried their gospel to Africa, to Europe and even to China. The Manichaeans posed a threat to the church in the fourth century, and numbered Augustine among their adherents before his conversion. The Manichaeans probably bequeathed some of their beliefs to heretical groups which flourished in Asia Minor and Europe in the Middle Ages.

Mani was brought up among a sect of Jewish Christians, but left them when he received 'revelations'. He called himself 'the apostle of Jesus Christ'. Mani converted members of his family and began his far-flung ministry of over thirty years. An early source describes Mani's appearance with a book in one hand and a staff in the other—he may have been lame. He wore flamboyant clothing, a blue cloak, and red and green trousers.

He preached in Mesopotamia and throughout Persia, and even reached India. He allegedly delivered many from demons and diseases.

Mani died in prison in AD 276. He was decapitated, and his corpse was buried by his followers at Gundishapur in south-western Persia. Mani, who was a gifted painter, composed the *Ardahang,* a picture book, to propagate his faith among the illiterate. He also wrote seven works.

Mani taught that there were two independent eternal principles, light and darkness, God and matter. In the first epoch, light and darkness were separate; in the second epoch they were intermingled; and in the final epoch they were to be separated once more. Jesus and other religious leaders came in order to release souls of light from the prison of their bodies.

Ginza, a detailed account of the beginnings of the universe.

The Johannesbuch, containing some late traditions about John the Baptist.

The *Qolasta,* a collection of prayers and liturgies.

The manuscripts of these texts date from the sixteenth to the nineteenth centuries; there are earlier magic bowl texts (AD 600) and some magical lead amulets which may possibly date from as early as the third century AD. Though a number of scholars have assumed a pre-Christian date for the origin of the Mandaeans, the firm evidence suggests a date no earlier than the second century AD. Hence it is anachronistic to interpret the New Testament on the basis of Mandaean texts.

Gnostic leaders

Although the New Testament itself (Acts 8) does not describe Simon Magus as a Gnostic (he is called a *magos,* 'magician'), early Christians writers unanimously regarded Simon as the fount of all heresies. Unlike the later Gnostics, Simon appears to have claimed to be divine, and taught that salvation

The Manichaean community

The Manichaeans were sharply divided between an elite circle known as the elect, and the mass of lay people known as hearers. The hearers lived the lives of ordinary citizens. They offered daily gifts of fruit, cucumbers and melons—which were believed to possess a great deal of light—to the elect, who were ascetics and vegetarians. At death the souls of the hearers were reborn as other people. Only the elect, who were distinguished by white robes, were eligible for offices and for the most sacred rites.

The spread of Manichaeism in the West

Manichaeism spread at an early date to Syria and Palestine. An army veteran brought the new religion from Mesopotamia in AD274. Their invasion of North Africa elicited Diocletian's harsh edict of AD297 which condemned the Manichaeans as hostile Persian agents who were to be executed.

After the spread of Manichaeism in many areas in the fourth century, the forceful refutations of Augustine, his disciple Evodius, and other church leaders stemmed the tide. By the sixth century Manichaeism was in decline in the West.

The Paulician movement which spread in Armenia from the seventh to the twelfth century, though it repudiated Manichaeism, resembled it in its dualist views. The Paulicians came to Bulgaria in the tenth century and helped to develop the Bogomils who flourished in the Balkans in the eleventh and twelfth centuries. The latter movement in turn stimulated the important Manichaean-like heresy of the Cathars or Albigensians, who were dominant in southern France and northern Italy in the twelfth and thirteenth centuries. A crusade was proclaimed against them by Pope Innocent III in 1208. By the fourteenth century the last heirs of Manichaeism had been finally suppressed by the Inquisition.

involved knowledge of himself rather than any knowledge of one's self.

Simon was followed by a fellow Samaritan, Menander, who taught at Antioch in Syria towards the end of the first century. He told his followers that those who believed in him would not die. Needless to say, his own death demonstrated that he was a false prophet. Also teaching in Antioch, at the beginning of the second century, was Saturninus, who believed that Christ was the redeemer. But like other Gnostics he maintained that Christ was not a material being and only appeared to be a human (the Docetic view).

Cerinthus taught in Asia Minor. (Irenaeus tells the story that the apostle John fled from a bath-house at Ephesus when he learned that Cerinthus was there!) He taught that Jesus was merely a man upon whom 'the Christ' descended as a dove. As Christ could not suffer, he departed from Jesus before the crucifixion. (This tradition is also found in the Qur'an. 'They slew him not nor crucified, but it appeared so unto them.')

Marcion of Pontus was an important, though not typical, Gnostic.

IRENAEUS

Everett Ferguson

Irenaeus was born in Asia Minor and studied under Polycarp, bishop of Smyrna. He then went to Gaul where he became bishop of Lyons in AD 177. His books aimed to counteract the Gnostic ideas common in this region.

Two major writings by Irenaeus survive: *Against Heresies* ('Five Books Exposing and Overthrowing the So-Called "Knowledge"') and *Proof of the Apostolic Preaching,* an instructional book, demonstrating that the basic Christian faith fulfils the Old Testament.

Irenaeus stressed the fundamental Christian doctrines that were being challenged by Gnosticism: that the world was created by one God; that Jesus Christ, son of the Creator, died to save humanity; that there will be a resurrection of the body. He appealed to the historical roots of the Christian faith, and argued that Scripture contained a succession of covenants through which 'one and the same God' progressively revealed his will to men and women, as they were ready to receive it.

Irenaeus developed the idea that Christ, fully man as well as fully God, retraced the steps of Adam, with a different result. Because Christ passed through every age of life, all humanity share in his sanctifying work.

The Gnostics claimed to possess secret traditions passed down from the apostles. To counter this Irenaeus developed an argument involving another kind of apostolic succession. He claimed that the churches preserved public, standard beliefs handed down from apostolic times by the teachers in the churches.

Irenaeus thus developed Christian theology in several ways; for example, the 'canon (or rule) of truth' preserved in the church as the key to interpreting Scripture; his view that the eucharist contains 'an earthly and a divine reality'; and the place of the virgin Mary (the new Eve) in his theology. At the same time he tried to base his teachings and arguments on Scripture.

He insisted upon faith in Christ, but rejected the humanity of Jesus and the resurrection of the body.

Other Gnostic teachers included Basilides and his son Isidore, and Carpocrates and his son Epiphanes—all of whom taught at Alexandria, in Egypt. The most famous Gnostic teacher was Valentinus, who taught at Alexandria and who came to Rome in AD 140. He had a number of able followers, among them Theodotus in the East, and Ptolemy and Heracleon in the West. Heracleon's commentary on the Gospel of John is the earliest known commentary on a New Testament book.

WHAT THE FIRST CHRISTIANS BELIEVED

David F. Wright

As the 'Jesus movement' grew and spread throughout the Mediterranean world, pressures from inside and outside presented it with a series of important challenges. Internally, it had to spell out its foundation charter and terms of membership, and develop its structure and leadership. Externally, it had to work out its relations with Judaism, with other religions and philosophies, and with the Roman Empire itself.

As it came to terms with these challenges during the first three centuries, Christianity began to acquire a recognizable shape and a sense of identity through various features: the New Testament Scriptures, the concepts of orthodoxy and heresy, the 'Rule of Faith' and the earliest creeds, the offices of bishop, presbyter and deacon, the rise of Rome as a centre of reference and arbitration, patterns of argument against Jewish and pagan critics, schemes for the instruction of new converts (catechumens) before baptism, elaborate orders of worship, and the basic outline of the Christian year.

Christianity attempted to take over from both the cults and the philosophies of the Roman world, and to satisfy both religious and intellectual needs. Its success was due partly to the rich variety of thought and life that developed within the one 'Jesus movement'.

Christianity and the Jews

The first Christians were all Jews. They had come to believe the apostles' message that Jesus was the promised Saviour of God's people. 'Jesus is the Messiah (Christ)' summed up all that the Jews were called upon to accept. The resurrection of Jesus was

The Good Shepherd is one of the most common themes in early Christian art. This painting on the plaster walls of the catacomb of Domitilla in Rome shows the shepherd surrounded by his flock, holding pan-pipes reminiscent of Orpheus. The Christians often adapted classical subjects in this way.

emphasized more than his death in the earliest preaching to Jews, because it demonstrated that the person executed as a criminal was nevertheless God's Messiah.

Following guidelines laid down by Jesus himself, the apostles pointed to Old Testament passages which had been fulfilled in his career and in the beginnings of the church. 'This is what was prophesied' was a phrase frequently on their lips. They used Old Testament images to describe Jesus. He was the Passover lamb, the second Adam, the kinsman-redeemer. He was the stone rejected by the builders, but chosen by God to be the 'cornerstone' in the construction of his church.

Until its destruction in AD 70, worship and sacrifices continued daily in Herod's Temple in Jerusalem (reconstructed in this model).

This central concern of the earliest Christian preaching and teaching is especially emphasized in Matthew's Gospel and, from a different angle, in the letter to the Hebrews. But all early Christian theology was Jewish, since the language and concepts it used were quarried chiefly from the Old Testament.

Some Jewish Christians were so conservative that they demanded, in effect, that Gentiles had to become Jews in order to be true Christians. They insisted on circumcision and other Jewish legal requirements, and frowned on social contact with 'unclean' Gentiles. These 'Judaizers' appealed to the Jerusalem church where James, the brother of Jesus, led a community of thousands of 'staunch upholders of the Law'. But Paul refused to tolerate any demands imposed on Gentile converts which threatened the good news of 'grace alone through faith alone'.

In Jerusalem the harmony maintained between James and the Jewish authorities failed to survive his martyrdom in AD 62 and the Jewish war with Rome which began four years later. Jewish-Christian relations continued to deteriorate later in the first century. Judaism entrenched itself within the tight limits set by the rabbinic Pharisees. It excluded non-conformist Jews like the followers of Jesus.

Conservative Jewish-Christianity disappeared into obscurity. Its strength filtered off into side-channels, such as the heretical Ebionite groups. It may also have merged with currents from other brands of Judaism, which also lost out after the disastrous war with Rome. The Qumran community whose library, known as the 'Dead Sea Scrolls', was discovered in 1947, helped to produce strongly ascetic forms of Christianity east of the River Jordan and in Syria to the north. Fringe Judaism of one kind or another fertilized the emerging Gnostic sects which loomed so large in the second century.

The martyr Stephen's boldness in declaring the old covenant obsolete reflects the ideas of more liberal Greek-speaking Jewish Christians scattered throughout the Empire. They had been won to the new faith from the Jewish communities of the Dispersion found throughout the Mediterranean world. They preached the new faith in Alexandria: there too the thoroughly Hellenized Judaism of Philo contributed to distinctive Alexandrian varieties of Christianity.

Towards the middle of the second century Justin Martyr was asked by a Jewish teacher whether Jewish converts to Christianity would be saved if they continued to keep the law of Moses. Justin replied that they would, provided they did not insist on other Christians doing likewise. But he also warned that not all Christians shared his tolerant attitude. The incident reveals that the church was by this time a predominantly Gentile body.

According to Christian writers in the second and third centuries, relations between Christians and Jews apparently became increasingly hostile. These writers tried to support believers faltering under the force of the Jewish objection, 'How can Jesus be the Messiah if so few Jews have accepted him?' They responded by portraying Israel as an unbelieving and apostate people from first to last.

But Jews and Christians were often on friendlier terms as neighbours in the local community than official hostility and irregular persecution would indicate. Church leaders repeatedly denounced Christians who joined in Jewish practices. Sometimes this followed the 're-discovery' of Old Testament commands. Even without this, Jewish festivals could be enjoyable occasions, as Christmas is for post-Christian pagans in the West today.

The second-century churches of Asia held the Christian *Pascha* to celebrate the passion, resurrection and exaltation of Christ, on the same day as the Jewish Passover. (This was probably the general custom of the earliest Christians). Some of their opponents believed that Sunday was the only appropriate day to end the fast that preceded the *Pascha*, and accused them of Judaizing, labelling them '*Quartodecimans*'—'fourteenthers'. (Passover fell on the fourteenth day of the month *Nisan.*) In time, the Sunday *Pascha* became the standard practice, and formed the basis of Easter today.

How the Christians used the Old Testament

Jews keenly resented the Christians' claim that the Old Testament belonged to them exclusively since they alone understood it aright. Christians followed the example of Jesus and the apostles, and accepted the Old Testament as inspired and authoritative Scripture. They normally used the Greek *Septuagint* version of the Old Testament. Latin translations of the *Septuagint* first became available in the West late in the second century.

At some periods sections of the early church also used a number of other Jewish writings. Most of these, such as the Wisdom of Solomon and Ecclesiasticus, were first written in Greek and were included in the *Septuagint.* They are now known as the Apocrypha. There is much argument about how far they were given a status equal to the books of the Hebrew Bible. In the West, largely through Augustine's influence (but against Jerome's arguments), they later became widely accepted as part

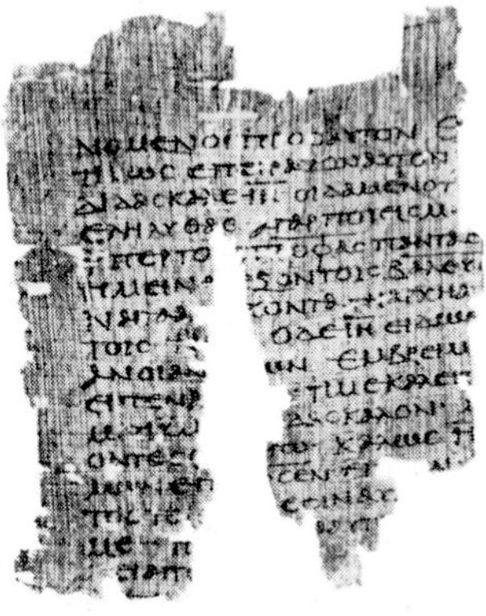

of the 'canon' of Scripture. Eastern churches usually recognized only the Hebrew books. Melito of Sardis travelled to Palestine in about AD 170 to investigate the contents of the Hebrew Scriptures.

Early Christians went to exaggerated lengths to make the Old Testament into a Christian book speaking everywhere about Christ and his church. Their interpretations of Scripture often kept to the historical pattern of promise and fulfilment, shadow and substance, which the New Testament writers largely used. But they soon became much freer and looser.

Most of the Gnostics rejected the entire Old Testament, at least in any straightforward meaning. They blamed the inferior God of the Old Testament for creating the evil material world. Marcion himself posed sharper problems by listing the contradictions between Old and New. He claimed that the Old Testament God who ordered battles and slaughter, and was driven by anger rather than love, was incompatible with the merciful Father of Jesus Christ.

Other critics pointed the finger at the polygamy and other misbehaviour of the Jewish patriarchs, the psalms which lusted for

MARCION

H. Dermot McDonald

Marcion was born in Sinope, Pontus, on the Black Sea, the son of the bishop. He arrived in Rome about AD 140 and immediately fell under the spell of the Gnostic teacher Cerdo, who believed that the God of the Old Testament was different from the God and Father of the Lord Jesus Christ. The God of the Old Testament was unknowable; the latter had been revealed. The former was sheer justice; whereas the God of the New Testament is loving and gracious.

Marcion became the chief spokesman of this message and introduced his own distinctive ideas. Was Marcion a Gnostic? He was certainly gnostic in his belief that the physical body was inherently evil. And so he argued for asceticism and a docetic understanding of Christ. But he never supported the fanciful and mythological views of redemption held by other Gnostics. His garbled Christian views were firmly repudiated by the church in Rome and Marcion was excommunicated in AD 144.

Justin Martyr asserted that Marcion was aided by the devil to blaspheme and deny that God was the creator of the universe. Tertullian wrote *Against Marcion* about AD 207, and regarded Marcion as a formidable foe of true Christian doctrine.

Marcion's ideas about God

Marcion developed Cerdo's division between the God of the Old Testament and the New. He held that the Old Testament God was basically vengeful and the author of evil. God was solely concerned for the Jewish people, for whom he was prepared to destroy all others. In contrast, the New Testament God is a God of grace and love for all, who disclosed himself in Jesus Christ, his Son.

Marcion stated that Jesus Christ was not born of a woman; he suddenly appeared in the synagogue at Capernaum in AD 29 as a grown man. For he was not like any other man except in his the destruction of enemies, and the crude descriptions of God's 'back parts' and the like. The Old Testament also seemed to concentrate on earthly prosperity as the reward of piety; this was embarrassing in an age of martyrs and widespread asceticism.

Christianity inherited many of the objections Greek and Roman intellectuals levelled against the Jewish Bible. Therefore it could take over traditional Jewish arguments to refute them. But Marcion's charge that the Old Testament was sub-Christian was not so easily answered. Tertullian's defiant response was to 'mingle the law and the prophets with the Gospels and apostolic writings'. As a result, his own Christianity has been called 'baptized Judaism'; and his follower Cyprian 'mingled' Christian ministers with Old Testament priests, and Christian ordinances with Old Testament sacrifices.

Most churchmen found peace on this front only by allegorizing or spiritualizing the Old Testament. They followed the example set by Philo and some of the Gnostics, as well as Platonic interpreters of Homer and Hesiod (the sacred poets of Greece). The *Letter of Barnabas* from Alexandria claimed

Many gospels and letters which find no place in the New Testament were in circulation. These papyrus fragments form part of an unknown gospel in Greek, found in Egypt and dated to the early second century.

appearance: he was a new being on the earth. Marcion's view of Christ was similar to that of the Docetists. Although he stated that Christ's life and crucifixion were necessary for salvation, he also believed that Christ's human experiences and sufferings were merely apparent, not real. Since creation was not an act of the good God of the New Testament, the Christian must reject the world. The body must be denied and discarded, since the soul and spirit alone are redeemed. As a result Marcion rejected the idea of the resurrection of the body.

Because he believed that the God of the Old Testament favoured the Jews exclusively, Marcion rejected the entire Old Testament and also those New Testament writings which he considered favoured Jewish readers—for example Matthew, Mark Acts and Hebrews. He cut out from the rest of the New Testament what appeared to him to compromise his own views, including the Pastoral letters (1 and 2 Timothy and Titus). So he was left with only a mutilated version of Luke's Gospel (omitting the nativity stories) and ten letters of Paul. He believed that Paul was the only apostle who did not corrupt the gospel of Jesus.

The Marcionites set up their own churches, modelled on othodox congregations. They did not use wine at communion, as a result of the ascetic emphasis of their teaching. Some of the Marcionite ideas spilled over into the various Gnostic sects, and Marcionites were themselves affected by Gnostic views. Their ideas spread throughout Italy, and as far afield as Arabia, Armenia and Egypt. In the East they exercised a considerable influence for many decades. A number of Marcionite villages are known to have existed near Damascus and late as the fourth century. In the West their influence declined mainly as a result of their becoming linked with the Manichaeans.

A Roman feasting-hall has been excavated in Alexandria. This Egyptian port was a great metropolis of the Roman Empire; and from the second century was the centre of Greek-speaking Christianity.

that the law of Moses had never been meant to be taken literally; even the number of Abraham's 318 servants pointed to the cross of Jesus!

Origen was the most influential allegorizer of Scripture. He developed a sophisticated theory of the different levels of Scripture:

'The Scriptures were composed through the Spirit of God, and have both a meaning which is obvious, and another which is hidden from most readers. For the contents of Scripture are the outward forms of certain mysteries, and the reflection of divine things . . . The whole law is spiritual, but the inspired meaning is not recognized by all—only by those who are gifted with the grace of the Holy Spirit in the word of wisdom and knowledge.'

The use of allegorical interpretations infuriated pagan objectors, whose criticisms depended on taking the Old Testament at face value. It also enabled Origen to discover secret teaching concealed beneath the surface of the Scriptures, like a Christian Platonist or true Gnostic. After Origen, Christians found it easier to live with their conviction that the Bible was inspired and therefore both consistent and significant in every detail, when spiritually understood.

Christians recognize the New Testament

The earliest Christian congregations quickly appreciated the value of letters written by apostles such as Paul. Some of them were obviously intended for public reading, perhaps in place of, or alongside, a sermon on the Old Testament, and for circulating among the churches. Christians also treasured what they learned about the life and teaching of Jesus. The first Gospels were not produced until the 60s, but their contents were partly available in written form before this time.

It is uncertain how long reliable spoken traditions about Jesus lived on. Papias, a Phrygian bishop early in the second century, confidently believed that he discovered fresh information from the 'living and abiding voice' of the elders or followers of the apostles. The little that remains of his writings suggests he was mistaken!

The example of the Old Testament 'canon' encouraged the gradual collection of a list of Christian writings which should constitute the standard or rule of the churches. (The Greek word *kanōn* meant 'measuring rod'.) These were the books read publicly in the congregations and regarded as having special authority.

Paul's letters were brought together first of all, probably around the end of the first century. The synoptic Gospels (Matthew, Mark and Luke) were formed into a group by the middle of the second century. John's Gospel, which appealed particularly to the Gnostics and later the Montanists, was treated with some reserve and took longer to be generally accepted.

Marcion is generally believed to have published the first formal canon-list about AD 140. It consisted of the expurgated Gospel of Luke and ten of Paul's letters (but not the Pastoral letters). This restricted collection, together with the Gnostics' use of their own gospels and apocalypses bearing apostolic names, challenged the church. It was also feared that the Montanists would claim the status of scripture for the utterances of their New Prophecy. Possibly the earliest appearance of 'New Covenant (Testament) of the Gospel' to mean a body of writings is found in an anti-Montanist writer late in the second century.

The late second century also

ORIGEN

Everett Ferguson

Origen was the greatest scholar and most prolific author of the early church. He was not only a profound thinker but also deeply spiritual and a loyal churchman.

Origen was born into a Christian family in Alexandria about AD 185. He became a teacher, first of new converts, and later of more advanced students. Origen, who led a very ascetic life, was forced to move to Caesarea, in Palestine, because of the antagonism of Bishop Demetrius of Alexandria. Origen travelled widely in response to invitations to mediate in church disputes, or to speak in front of prominent people. His death in AD 254 was the result of injuries inflicted during the persecution under the Emperor Decius.

Origen produced the *Hexapla*, the greatest piece of biblical scholarship in the early church. It put in parallel columns the Hebrew text of the Old Testament, a Greek transliteration, the Greek translations by Aquila, Symmachus and Theodotion, and the *Septuagint*. Origen made the *Hexapla* the basis for his interpretations of the Old Testament. His church sermons and massive biblical commentaries illustrated his theory that there are three levels of meaning in any biblical text: the literal sense, the moral application to the soul, and the allegorical or spiritual sense, referring to the mysteries of the Christian faith.

Origen's major work on theology, *First Principles*, attempted to present the fundamental Christian doctrines systematically: God, Christ, the Holy Spirit, creation, the soul, free will, salvation and the Scriptures. Origen tried first to set out clearly the faith expressed in the church, and then to clarify and draw out what was only implicit in the faith.

Exhortation to Martyrdom and *Prayer* are examples of Origen's writing on the Christian life. *Against Celsus* was his one major writing against pagan criticisms of Christianity.

Alexandria, the city in Egypt where Origen was born, rivalled Rome itself. It had a huge population, commercial strength, and was the greatest existing centre of Greek culture.

Origen tried to express the Christian faith in terms of the prevailing Platonic philosophical ideas of his time. Some of his speculations, for example about the pre-existence of souls and universal salvation, were repudiated by the church, and helped bring about his later condemnation. But Greek Christian theology continued to be concerned with the problem which Origen tackled —the relationship of philosophy and the Christian tradition.

saw the production of several 'acts' of apostles whose missionary labours are not recorded in Luke's Acts. In addition there appeared the first of a number of gospels written to satisfy curiosity about, for example, the childhood of Jesus and the life of Pilate. These mainly imaginative books served as the novels and romances of popular Christianity. Most of them popularized the ideas of fringe Christian groups, particularly Docetism and the rejection of sex and marriage.

Canon lists

By the late second century Christian writers felt it vital to spell out which books were accepted by the church. Irenaeus had no doubt that there could be only four gospels, neither more nor less. A list known as the *Muratorian Canon* lists the four Gospels, thirteen letters of Paul, Acts, two letters of John, Jude and the Revelation of John, together with the Wisdom of Solomon and, with reservations, the Revelation of Peter. Hebrews is, surprisingly, missing; it had been much used by Clement of Rome a century earlier. This list has traditionally been dated around 200, but several scholars now place it much later.

The Romans took over many cultural and religious traditions from the Greeks. This bronze head of *Hypnos* ('Sleep') was copied by a Roman craftsman from a Greek original.

By the early third century, a consensus had been reached throughout the church concerning the main contents of the canon. Only a handful of books continued to be debated. Hebrews was not accepted in the West, possibly because doubts about who wrote it were stiffened by the Montanist use of chapter six. Revelation was unpopular in the East because it supported millenarian ideas.

Eusebius summed up the situation at the outset of the fourth century. The only books still disputed at that stage were James, 2 Peter, 2 and 3 John and Jude. These were 'spoken against' by some but 'recognized by most churchmen'. Eusebius was clearly bewildered by the Revelation of John. He placed it with the undisputed books, but knew its authorship was uncertain and its contents unwelcome to some. Dionysius of Alexandria had earlier worked out, with remarkable skill, that Revelation was not by the author of the Fourth Gospel: but he did not for that reason deny its authority.

The Eastern church finally arrived at a consensus by 367. In that year Athanasius' Easter Letter from Alexandria listed solely the twenty-seven books of the New Testament. It also allowed new converts to read the *Didache* and the *Shepherd* of Hermas. Other orthodox books which had until then been accepted for a time in some churches were *1 Clement* and the *Letter of Barnabas*. The Syriac church used for centuries Tatian's *Diatessaron*, a harmony of the Gospels, instead of the four separate ones. Later it also rejected Revelation and demoted the general letters. They were all restored by the mid-sixth century.

In the West complete canon lists were approved by the African

Councils of Hippo, 393, and Carthage, 397. In time the Western church followed the East in accepting Hebrews within the canon. Its contents proved so attractive that they overcame doubts about its writer. Christians at Alexandria claimed at an early stage it was by Paul; this view was eventually accepted everywhere.

Although church leaders in a literal sense created the canon, they were only recognizing the books that had stamped their own authority on the churches. The criteria for accepting a book as canonical were sometimes complex. Above all, it had to be written or sponsored by an apostle, and also be recognizably orthodox in content, and publicly used by a prominent church or majority of churches. Known forgeries, such as the *Acts of Paul,* were rejected; as were other books which contained heretical teaching.

Some books suffered because of the unacceptable use other Christians made of them. The Montanists' love of Revelation was made the excuse for discrediting the book for a time. Some people were embarrassed about the differences between John and the other Gospels; and also at the variations and massive overlap between the synoptic Gospels.

But the eventual shape of the New Testament shows that the early church wanted to submit fully to the teachings of the apostles. It had been created by their preaching and now grounded itself upon their writings.

The meaning of the faith

The ancient world had a great respect for tradition and precedent, especially in religion. Christianity seemed to be quite new; this set a serious stumbling-block. Christian writers tried to overcome this problem by demonstrating that the faith had centuries-old roots in Israel and in the wisdom of the Greek philosophers. Justin Martyr wrote: 'Christ is the Logos in whom every race of men shared. Those who lived in accordance with *Logos,* true reason, are Christians, even though they were regarded as atheists; for example, Socrates and Heraclitus among the Greeks.'

Tertullian and most early Christian writers believed truth was older than error. Heresy came later than orthodoxy, like some corrupting parasite. Origen wrote: 'All heretics are at first believers; then later they deviate from the rule of faith.' The early Christian writers believed that the orthodox faith was transmitted full-grown to the churches by the apostles. A delightful legend described how the Twelve composed the Apostles' Creed jointly, with each contributing a clause.

But the preaching and teaching of the apostles was not the same as the orthodoxy about which the theologians wrote. Historical development had been at work in the interim. Nevertheless, from a very early stage sharp lines were drawn between true

The Romans made an enormous contribution to law; their system was, above all, based on common-sense principles. The Forum in Rome was the centre of the Empire's administration.

and false versions of the Christian message. Rival gospels were condemned outright. In Galatians Paul curses those who add Jewish legal requirements to the gospel. 1 John established that Christians must believe that Christ came 'in the flesh'. 1 Corinthians fixed belief in the historical resurrection of Jesus as another indispensable basis of salvation.

False accounts of Christ and his achievement were in circulation from the very beginning. Many scholars believe that in some regions views later condemned as heresy predominated at first. It appears that in Alexandria Christian teaching was quickly combined with Jewish and Greek beliefs. Then prominent Christian Gnostic groups arose there, before orthodox Christianity became dominant towards the end of the second century. It was not until this period that orthodox teaching prevailed in Syriac-speaking Christianity. Here however the extreme asceticism, known as 'encratism', deriving from unorthodox Jewish Christianity, continued to dominate.

The churches were hardly ever free from disputes over vital aspects of the faith. In the early centuries Christian leaders did not distinguish clearly between heretical movements and schisms which split the mainstream church. It was difficult to believe that separatists could be really orthodox; while heretics who denied the faith of the church logically belonged outside the church. But paradoxically, heretics contributed to the way in which Christianity developed. The pioneering challenge of heresy did much to shape Christian orthodoxy—a rounded, systematic exposition of the implications of basic Christian convictions.

The core of earliest Christianity centered on the Scriptures, the Lord's Supper and fellowship (*koinōnia*) in the Spirit, as well as faith in Christ and the Father. Out of this core, provoked by the challenge of heretics, patterns of orthodoxy were developed. They were not identical in every region, but they were sufficiently similar for each region's church to be in communion with the others. Prior to the Council of Nicaea, 325, no universal touchstone of orthodox faith existed—except perhaps in the New Testament.

The differences between the orthodoxy of, for instance Alexandria and Carthage, arose out of the different ways of thinking of their theologians. Each reflected his own culture. Tertullian used the language and thought-forms of law, rhetoric and Stoicism—and Montanism; Clement and Origen used the concepts of Platonism and Pythagoreanism—and Christian Gnosticism. Origen, and even Tertullian, may at times have been so heavily influenced by them as to cross the narrow frontier that separates orthodoxy from heresy.

How could the Creator God share our human life?

Christians inherited from the Jews the belief that the world was created by God. But the Creator also entered fully into human life in the incarnation. The Word who 'became flesh' was the same Word through whom 'all things came to be'.

The philosophers rejected these Christian fundamentals. They held that a transcendent god could not be directly involved in the physical world; nor change, as the doctrines of creation and incarnation implied. Gnostics denied them too since they believed that spirit alone belonged to God; the material world was corrupt and corrupting. Many Gnostics held that Christ only *appeared* to be human, like a phantom.

Others who took this view of Christ were known as 'Docetist', from the Greek verb 'to seem or appear'. Their views were attacked in 1 and 2 John. Jews too objected to the idea of divine incarnation, and Jewish Christians sometimes described Christ's coming as a 'theophany', a temporary visitation by God, more angelic than human.

For all these reasons, second-century writers stressed that God's world was good; that the body as well as the soul was destined for salvation; and, consistent with both these doctrines, that Jesus was a man of flesh and blood. Ignatius wrote: 'Jesus Christ was of the race of David, the child of Mary, who was truly born and ate and drank, was truly persecuted under Pontius Pilate, was truly crucified and died.'

The most important anti-Gnostic author was Irenaeus of Lyons. He taught that if the body could not be saved, 'the Lord did not redeem us with his blood, nor is the cup of the eucharist the communion of his blood, nor is the bread which we break the communion of his body.' Theology, worship and salvation were all connected. Ignatius believed that martyrdom was meaningless if Christ had not truly shed his blood.

Christians writers developed a theology of the *Logos* in order to justify their belief in divine creation and incarnation. *Logos,* translated 'Word' in John 1, also meant 'reason, purpose, wisdom'. The term was used in Stoicism, Middle Platonism and the writings of Philo to mean a cosmic principle of order and harmony, or the pattern or power by which God impinged upon the world.

Justin Martyr and others developed these two meanings, and taught that the *Logos* was eternally with God, as his mind or wisdom. But in creation, revelation and finally incarnation the *Logos* went forth, acting upon and within the world. God the Father was therefore not directly in contact with the physical world, nor subject to change; for the *Logos* never ceased to be his eternal wisdom. Some Christian writers were too strongly influenced by philosophical ideas of divine unchangeability, quite different from the consistent steadfastness of the living God of the Bible.

The *Logos* who issued from God was certainly seen as divine. But the *Logos* easily appeared to be some impersonal power of God. It was often argued that the *Logos* was generated as Son (so that God became Father of the Son) only prior to creation (Tertullian), or even the incarnation (Hippolytus).

Some of the difficulties arose from language. If God was Father, this seemed to imply that he once existed without his Son. Origen established that such language referred to an eternal relationship between the Father and the Son. His doctrine that the Son was eternally being generated was an important step forward.

The theologians of Alexandria did not assert divine creation and incarnation as unambiguously as, say, Irenaeus. Origen lived in an age of persecution and was a Christian Platonist; therefore he instinctively looked through and beyond the visible, historical world to the transcendent and spiritual. For him, the material world was only a passing phase, where spirits who had fallen in an earlier existence were purified as punishment.

Was Christ really God?

The Christians took over the Jews' uncompromising belief that: 'The Lord our God is one God.' But they also soon came to the belief

TERTULLIAN

Everett Ferguson

"God made this universe by his word, reason and power. Your philosophers also agree that the maker of the universe seems to be Logos—that is, word and reason . . . (for example, Zeno and Cleanthes) . . . We also claim that the word, reason and virtue, by which we have said that God made all things, have spirit as their substance . . . This Word, we have learnt, was produced from God, and was generated by being produced, and therefore is called the Son of God, and God, from unity of substance with God. For God too is spirit.

When a ray is projected from the sun it is a portion of the whole sun; but the sun will be in the ray because it is a ray of the sun; the substance is not separated but extended. So from spirit comes spirit, and God from God, as light is kindled from light . . . This ray of God . . . glided down into a virgin, in her womb was fashioned as flesh, is born as man mixed with God. The flesh was built up by the spirit, was nourished, grew up, spoke, taught, worked, and was Christ."

TERTULLIAN, Apology XXI

Tertullian was the first major Christian author to write in Latin. He was therefore the first to use many of the technical words common in later Christian theological debates.

Tertullian lived most of, if not all, his life in Carthage, capital of the Roman province of Africa. He received the typical education of the late second century, and his surviving works date from between 196 and 212.

Tertullian's books reflect three main concerns: Christianity's attitude to the Roman state and society; the defence of orthodox beliefs against heresy; and the moral behaviour of Christians. His own strict moral views led him to join the Montanists around AD 207.

Tertullian wrote in a witty and vigorous style, marked by startling turns of phrase. It was he who claimed that 'the blood of the martyrs is seed'. But his well-known question, 'What has Athens to do with Jerusalem?' expressed a rejection of philosophy that was not true of his own work, since he demonstrated how pagan intellectual achievements could be made to serve Christianity.

Tertullian's masterpiece was the *Apology*, which argued effectively that Christianity should be tolerated. His longest work, the five books *Against Marcion,* defended the use of the Old Testament by the Christian church, and the oneness of God, both Creator and Saviour. In *Against Praxeas,* Tertullian developed the doctrine of the Trinity. Tertullian had two things against Praxeas: his opposition to the Montanist 'New Prophecy', and his view of God. Tertullian said that Praxeas 'did two works for the Devil in Rome: he put to flight the Paraclete and crucified the Father.'

Tertullian covered a number of other subjects. In the *Exclusion of Heretics* Tertullian used an argument from Roman law to claim the Scriptures as the exclusive property of the church, against Gnostic heretics. Tertullian's *On the Soul* is the first Christian writing on psychology. *On Baptism* in the earliest surviving work about baptism; in it Tertullian criticized the baptism of children. In other books Tertullian argued for a strictness in church discipline, remarriage and fasting, which goes beyond biblical requirements; and opposed flight to avoid persecution.

:hat 'Jesus is Lord.' They applied .o Christ Old Testament passages 'eferring to *Yahweh,* the Lord; hey worshipped Christ as God.

In worship and other activities he Christians did not necessarily eel any tension between these wo basic beliefs. But both Jews ınd pagans such as Celsus accused Christians of having two gods. Some Christians were also making ınacceptable statements about Christ. The issue of the Trinity (a ater term) became an unavoidable problem. It was particularly diffi-cult to resolve because of the influ-ence of the Greek concept of unity, ıs perfect oneness, excluding any nternal distinctions.

Docetists and Jewish Christians, such as the Ebionites, saw no problem. The Docetists regarded Christ as merely a temporary ppearance of God disguised as a ıuman. The Ebionites saw Jesus s an ordinary person indwelt y God's power at his baptism. Neither believed that Jesus Christ was truly God.

Some writers tried to safeguard oth monotheism and the deity f Christ with the *Logos* theol-gy—which tended to be rather cademic. It failed to give an dequate picture of the personal ivinity of the *Logos,* especially rior to creation. Writers like renaeus and Tertullian developed into an 'economic' doctrine of he Trinity—so called because it poke of the relations between Father, Son and Spirit chiefly in erms of the divine 'economy' or lan for the world, rather than in erms of the internal life of God in ternity. It emphasized the succes-ive activities of Father, Son and pirit as God dealt with creation. t stressed that the one God was esponsible for both creation and edemption, and thus countered Gnostic views.

In the late second and early hird centuries a backward-looking theology known as Monarchianism emerged in Asia Minor and flour-ished in the West. It was anxious to emphasize the divine unity or 'monarchy' (Greek, 'single prin-ciple'). (The Monarchians are also known as Sabellians after one of their leaders, Sabellius.) They claimed that God existed in different 'modes' (so were some-times called Modalists), but only in one mode at any one time. God's different names—Father, Son and Spirit—described the different roles he played at different times.

The Monarchians were also called Patripassians by their opponents, because they taught in effect that the Father (Latin, *pater*) suffered (Latin, *passus*) as the Son. They felt they could not believe that God was one, and that Christ was fully God, without rejecting the belief that God was always three.

The Monarchians were assailed on all sides—in Rome by Hippolytus and Novatian, in Africa by Tertullian and in Alexandria by Origen. In writing a book to refute Praxeas, perhaps a nickname for a Roman bishop, Tertullian gave the Latin West a theological vocabu-lary that has hardly yet been bettered. He drew upon Stoicism and Roman law for his language, and taught that God was one being (*substantia*) but three concrete individuals (*personae*). The Son and the Spirit did not issue from the Father by a division of his being, but as extensions from his being, like rays from the sun. Tertullian's theology was backed up by the Roman theologians and ensured that the Western church was scarcely disturbed by the problems raised by Arius in the fourth century.

Origen's teaching dominated the East in the third and fourth cent-uries. Against the Monarchians he insisted that Father, Son and Spirit were three eternally distinct per-sons (Greek *hypostaseis*—roughly the same as *personae*). The Son owed his being eternally to the Father (the eternal generation of the Son), and was inferior to him. As genuine Son of the Father he was truly divine, but subordinate; the Spirit was even lower. Origen's ideas were deeply coloured by Middle Platonism, which graded existence into different levels. They pointed in various directions, and for this reason could be appealed to later by most parties in the Arian controversy.

Before the Council of Nicaea (AD 325) all theologians viewed the Son as in one way or another subordinate to the Father. Around AD 250 a dispute between Dionysius of Rome and Dionysius of Alexandria illustrated the different approaches of the churches in the West and East. The West was stronger on the unity of God and weaker on the permanent distinctness of the three; in the East the position was reversed.

A Christian baptism pictured on a third-century sarcophagus in Rome; the Holy Spirit is represented by a dove.

Christians summarize their beliefs

The early Christians often summarized what they believed. These summaries varied according to the contexts in which they were used, the writers or churches which produced them, and the errors or attacks they had to resist.

In addition to statements made at baptism (for example, Acts 8:37) and solemn commands (for example, Acts 3:6 and 2 Timothy 4:1), scholars have discovered summaries of the teaching of the apostles (for example, 1 Corinthians 15:3 and 4), as well as statements of belief in hymn form:

(Christ) appeared in human form,
Was shown to be right by the Spirit,
And was seen by angels.
He was preached among the nations,
Was believed in the world,
And was taken up to heaven.'
(1 Timothy 3:16)

Some formulas mention Christ alone, for example: 'Jesus is the Christ' (for a Jewish setting) or, more widely: 'Jesus is Lord' (1 Corinthians 12:3). Persecutors often demanded that Christians should curse Christ and say: 'Caesar is Lord.' Other formulas include God the Father too (1 Corinthians 8:6; 1 Timothy 2:5), while forms naming Father, Son and Spirit appear in baptism (Matthew 28:19), worship (2 Corinthians 13:14) and summaries of doctrine (Ephesians 4:4–6).

Later writers recorded more elaborate declarations of faith. Ignatius's declaration against Docetism was quoted earlier.

Hostile or inquisitive outsiders called for statements of what Christians believed. Here is the account of Aristides, one of the earliest writers to defend Christianity:

'As for the Christians, they trace their origins to the Lord Jesus Christ. He is confessed to be the Son of the most high God, who came down from heaven by the Holy Spirit and was born of a virgin and took flesh, and in a daughter of man there lived the Son of God . . . This Jesus . . . was pierced by the Jews, and he died and was buried; and they say that after three days he rose and ascended into heaven. . . They believe God to be the Creator and Maker of all things, in whom are all things and from whom are all things.'

Similar summaries were made by Justin Martyr.

One important outline of basic Christian beliefs in the late second and early third centuries was the 'Rule of Faith'. Origen described it as: 'the teaching of the church preserved unaltered and handed down in unbroken succession from the apostles'. In reality it indicated what particular writers or churches taught, especially against heretics, but also to new converts, as the central message of the Bible. The Rule was also known by several other names: 'the faith', 'the tradition', 'the preaching' and the 'Rule of Truth'. It claimed to represent an apostolic tradition of teaching, and was even appealed to in the dispute over the Christian *Pascha*.

Irenaeus is the first writer to record a clearly identifiable Rule. Its main content was as follows: '. . . this faith: in one God, the Father Almighty, who made the heaven and the earth and the seas and all things that are in them; and in one Christ Jesus, the Son of God, who was made flesh for our salvation; and in the Holy Spirit, who made known through the prophets the plan of salvation, and the coming, and the birth from a virgin, and the passion and the resurrection from the dead, and the bodily ascension into heaven of the beloved Christ Jesus, our

"Jesus is Lord. Jesus is the Christ."

Lord, and his future appearing from heaven in the glory of the Father to sum up all things and to raise up anew all flesh of the whole human race . . .'

It is clearly anti-Gnostic. It emphasizes the 'bodily ascension' and alludes to Irenaeus's distinctive idea of the 'summing up' in Christ of all God's dealings with humanity.

Other versions of the Rule reflect not only the battle with Gnostics and heretics, but also the writers' personal concerns. The Montanist Tertullian described lengthily 'the Holy Spirit, the Paraclete, the sanctifier of the faith of those who believe in the Father, the Son and the Holy Spirit'.

"Do you believe in Christ Jesus, the Son of God, who was born by the Holy Spirit of the Virgin Mary, and was crucified under Pontius Pilate, and was dead and buried, and rose again the third day, alive from the dead, and ascended into heaven, and sat at the right hand of the Father, and will come to judge the living and the dead?"

HIPPOLYTUS, Apostolic Tradition

This wall-painting from late third-century Rome pictures the baptism of Christ, with the Holy Spirit in the form of a dove.

The speculative Origen not only includes paragraphs on the soul, free will, devils and angels, but also claims that the apostles left much else 'to be investigated by those who were fit for the higher gifts of the Spirit'.

Creeds at baptism

But the Rule of Faith was not a creed with fixed wording. Fixed creeds of this kind developed chiefly in the context of baptism, and originally consisted of question-and-answer. Although a first people were often baptized i the name of Christ alone, it soon became standard to be baptized i the name of the Trinity. By Justir time at Rome those being baptize answered questions about their belief in 'God, the Father and Lo of the universe', 'Jesus Christ, w was crucified under Pontius Pilat and 'the Holy Spirit who through the prophets foretold all things about Jesus'.

Hippolytus's account of baptis at Rome at the outset of the third century is very important: 'When the person being baptized goes down into the water, he who bap tizes him, putting his hand on hin shall say: "Do you believe in God the Father Almighty?"
And the person being baptized shall say: "I believe."
Then holding his hand on his hea he shall baptize him once. And th he shall say:
"Do you believe in Christ Jesus, the Son of God, who was born by the Holy Spirit of the Virgin Mar and was crucified under Pontius Pilate, and was dead and buried, and rose again the third day, aliv from the dead, and ascended int heaven, and sat at the right hand the Father, and will come to judg the living and the dead?"
And when he says:
"I believe," he is baptized again.
And again he shall say:

"Do you believe in the Holy Spirit, in the holy church, and the resurrection of the body?"
The person being baptized shall say:
"I believe," and then he is baptized a third time.'

By now other items of belief had been attached to the third question, which sometimes mentions 'the forgiveness of sins'. In addition the question about Christ had been considerably expanded, probably influenced by the Rule of Faith, to uncover and exclude Gnostics and heretics. Although it is in question-and-answer form, Hippolytus's 'Old Roman' creed is the earliest close parallel to the *Apostles' Creed*—which has no direct link with the apostles, and of which the earliest exact text dates from about AD 400.

Creeds in statement form (I believe . . .) developed from the mid-third century by adaptation of the questions-and-answers. They were originally used in the closing stages of the instruction of converts prior to baptism. The earliest clear example is the creed of the church of Caesarea in Palestine.

The creed of Nicaea inaugurated a new era. The old creeds were creeds for converts, the new creed was a creed for bishops. The old creeds had been local, the new one was to be universally binding. It took over from the old Rule of Faith as a test of orthodoxy.

Instruction before baptism

At the birth of the church, converts were baptized with little or no delay. But a course of instruction prior to baptism soon became customary, especially for non-Jewish converts. Justin explained that before baptism: 'All those who are convinced and believe the things which are taught by us and said to be true, and promise to live accordingly, are instructed to pray and to call on God with fasting.'

Hippolytus of Rome again provides valuable evidence. A convert's occupation and personal relations were scrutinized, and then came pre-baptismal instruction which took three years (even longer in Syria!). Good progress, or the imminence of persecution, could shorten the period. A convert who was martyred before baptism was regarded as experiencing a better 'baptism in blood'. More intensive preparations, including fasting, exorcism and blessing, immediately preceded baptism. The converts were often taught by laymen, such as Justin in Rome or Origen in Alexandria, in independent Christian 'schools'

Because the person being baptized was called '*infans*' (Latin, infant), he is pictured as a child. This baptism is part of a wall-painting in the catacomb of Calixtus, from third-century Rome.

open to enquiring pagans too.

By the fourth century, the clergy had taken over the instruction of converts ('catechumens'), and the bishop had become personally responsible for the concentrated teaching and discipline immediately before baptism. (Here lay the origins of Lent; from the second century baptisms normally took place at Easter.)

By now this period included the ceremonial 'handing over' of the creed, which the candidates would affirm in the baptismal questions-and-answers. After the bishop had explained it and they had memorized it, they would 'give it back' in a later ceremony. The same was often done with the Lord's Prayer. These formulas were not presented in written form; they were treasured secrets to be concealed from the uninitiated, in the same way as what happened at the Lord's Supper. From this era survive several notable series of addresses delivered before and immediately after baptism.

'I am the Good Shepherd,' Jesus said. This carving of the Good Shepherd is on the side of a sarcophagus in Rome, about AD 270.

Careful preparation for baptism was seen as essential, because baptism was commonly thought of as dealing with a person's past corruption but not his future faults. This explains the practice of delaying baptism, the development of a system of penitence to cover sins after baptism, and even Tertullian's insistence on purity before baptism so that baptism became almost a prize.

The systematic teaching of new converts along these lines flourished particularly in the great era of Christian expansion in the third and fourth centuries. As infant baptism became increasingly common the practice faded. Little is known about the instruction of children within the early Christian community.

Who led the churches?

The first leaders of the church were the apostles, assisted in Jerusalem by 'the elders' and the practical help of the Seven (Acts 6). Other gifted and Spirit-filled individuals were prominent in the early decades: missionary preachers, evangelists (including some of the Seven), teachers and prophets. They were not normally officially appointed, but undertook a widely-recognized travelling ministry.

This Spirit-gifted leadership had largely disappeared by the early second century. The *Didache* shows that, in one region, some prophetic teachers were settling down, others had become self-seeking, and 'bishops and deacons' were gaining new prominence. Nevertheless, the prophetic tradition continued with people such as Ignatius, Hermas, Melito and the Montanists; and free-lance teachers or philosophers still existed—such as Justin, Clement of Alexandria, Origen and even Tertullian.

Local leaders emerged at an early stage. Congregational life was directed by a team or group, commonly known as 'presbyters'—that is, elders or fathers in the faith (possibly based on Jewish or Old Testament models)—or 'bishops' (that is, guardians or overseers, probably derived from Hellenistic patterns, although there were interesting parallels at Qumran). Other titles were used—pastor or shepherd, teacher, deacon or servant, ruler and president. The status and function of the different posts were still flexible. There was no counterpart to 'the minister' of today in earliest Christianity. Churches met in small, house-based gatherings until at least the third century.

By Ignatius's time churches in Asia Minor were ruled by the 'three-fold ministry'. This consisted of a single-bishop (Ignatius links his authority to that of the single God), a body of presbyters (patterned on the band of apostles) and several deacons (who 'served' as Christ did). This pattern became universal before the third century, though the churches of Rome and Greece had no single bishop in Ignatius's day, nor did Alexandria until about AD 180.

The number of bishoprics varied considerably from region to region. Numerous small communities in Asia Minor and Africa acquired their own bishops; elsewhere, for example in Gaul, the bishop of a large town would supervise the surrounding congregations. About AD 250 the church at Rome still had only one bishop, together with forty-six presbyters, seven deacons and seven sub-deacons, as well as forty-two 'acolytes' or attendants and fifty-two exorcists, readers and door-keepers.

The bishop gradually emerged as undisputed leader of the Christian community; this was brought about by a number of factors. Congregations often needed one from the group of presbyters or bishops to take the initiative, or represent them—for example, by presiding at the Lord's Supper, contacting other churches, teaching, or guarding church property and offerings. One-person leadership was suggested by the roles played by the founding apostle or missionary, especially if he had settled in one place for an extended period; by agents of the apostles, such as Timothy and Titus; and by James who was apostle-cum-bishop-cum-high-priest of the Jerusalem church. Some of their functions had to continue in the churches.

Heirs to the apostles?

Clement of Rome urged the Christians at Corinth to preserve the arrangements made by the apostles for controlling the congregation's affairs. But this was simply the kind of provision any pioneer missionary organizes for the leadership of a new church.

The Gnostics soon began to appeal to a succession of teachers traced back to the apostles (normally Philip, Thomas and Matthias) to whom, they claimed, Jesus entrusted secret wisdom before he ascended. Their views were countered by stressing the continuity of the open teaching (for instance, the Rule of Faith) and teachers (bishops or presbyters) from the time when the apostles founded the churches.

The argument was first outlined by Hegesippus. He travelled from Palestine to Rome in the mid-second century, associated with numerous bishops, and heard (so he says) the same teaching from all. 'In every succession and city, what the law and the prophets and the Lord preached is faithfully followed.' He drew up succession-lists of bishops, at least for Corinth and Rome. He may have taken note of the Jerusalem church's attempt to maintain a hereditary leadership from among the 'relatives of the Lord', similar to the succession of Jewish high priests.

Irenaeus, Tertullian and others in the West followed in the anti-Gnostic path mapped out by Hegesippus. They held that the succession of bishops stemming from the apostles guaranteed the unbroken handing-on of the apostles' doctrine. Irenaeus still felt close to living tradition; only the generations of Polycarp and John separated him from Jesus. But in fact the apostles had not appointed bishops in every church, and succession-lists of bishops were seriously unreliable.

Later the threat from the Gnostics receded, and lapse of time eroded the appeal to tradition. But apostolic succession was given a new lease of life, chiefly by Cyprian. Now the bishop became the basis and criterion of the church's life. Being in the church was made dependent on communion with the bishop. Now the apostles were seen as the first bishops, and bishops were called apostles. Succession assumed a more mechanical character.

Cyprian's theory prevailed in the medieval West; but the East was never sold on the idea. For Cyprian, the 'one and undivided episcopate' was embodied in the provincial or pan-African councils he frequently called and presided over. In Africa and elsewhere the provinces of the Roman Empire supplied the basis for the regions of the church. The provincial capital normally became the ecclesiastical centre and its bishop enjoyed special status as metropolitan bishop.

The church at Rome develops a special role

When Irenaeus presented his succession-list for the church of Rome, he described it as: 'the very great, very ancient and universally known church, founded and organized at Rome by the two most glorious apostles, Peter and Paul.' Because Christians from all parts were found there, it was a microcosm of the whole Christian world.

His statement hints at some of the reasons why Rome acquired a leading position among the churches. All roads led to Rome, the capital of the Empire, not least the roads on which Christians travelled. A remarkable number of prominent Christians made their way to Rome: Ignatius, Polycarp, Marcion, Valentinus, Tatian, Justin, Hegesippus, Irenaeus, Tertullian, Praxeas and other Monarchians and Origen—as well as Peter and Paul in the sixties.

Rome was the only Western church which received a letter from an apostle (and what a letter!). Luke's long, miraculous account of Paul's journey to Rome reflects the importance attached to his reaching the capital. Nothing boosted the prestige of Christian Rome so much as the fact that the two chief apostles were martyred there under Nero. By the mid-second century memorial shrines to Paul and Peter had been erected in Rome, on the Appian Way and the Vatican Hill respectively. Remains of the latter have been uncovered in modern excavations.

The Fall of Jerusalem in AD 70 enhanced the standing of the Roman church in the long term. It now became almost impossible to evangelize the Jewish settlements

The Appian Way, chief road from Rome to the south – the road travelled by Paul – is still lined with ancient Roman monuments.

in the province of Parthia to the east, and Christianity's centre of gravity shifted west—where Rome was well suited to play a central role. However, the letter to the Corinthian church known as *1 Clement* did not imply any Roman claim to superior authority.

Second-century Christianity in Rome appears very varied. It included independent schools like Justin's, and immigrant groups such as the Asians who followed their traditional observance of the *Pascha.* Not until the 190s did a strong bishop emerge—Victor, an African and the first Latin speaker. He threatened to excommunicate the Asian churches over the *Quartodeciman* dispute. Meanwhile the new succession-lists and the shrines of Peter and Paul bolstered a growing self-confidence, and the Roman bishop's attitude to Montanism was widely noted.

The first bishop to claim a special authority derived from Peter by appealing to Matthew 16:18–19, was Stephen in his dispute with Cyprian. Paul's position alongside Peter in the earliest Roman church now began to be lost sight of. Cyprian regarded every bishop's seat as 'the see of Peter', although he admitted that the Roman church had a special importance because it had been founded so early.

The Roman church soon possessed considerable wealth, including the first of its underground burial-chambers (catacombs) outside the city, and several large houses whose upper floors were adapted for use as churches *(tituli).* Constantine's family enriched it by giving the Lateran palace and by erecting basilicas, including two as memorials to Peter and Paul. In the 270s, when the Emperor Aurelian was petitioned to settle a dispute about church property in Antioch, he allocated it 'to those with whom the bishops of the doctrine in Italy and Rome should communicate in writing'.

During the fourth century the church of Rome and its bishop considerably enlarged their claims to first place in honour and jurisdiction. They benefited from reaction against excessive interference by the Emperor in Eastern church affairs, and because Rome was consistently orthodox throughout the upheavals over doctrine in the East.

Christians and the Roman state

Different attitudes towards the Roman Empire are evident in the earliest Christian writings. This variety of views persisted into the second and third centuries. Following Romans 13 and Acts, apologists writing in defence of their faith stressed that the Christians were law-abiding citizens, who paid their taxes and prayed for the emperors. They did not serve in the armies, but engaged in a more effective spiritual warfare, and by prayer contributed to Rome's victory in just wars.

These writers attempted to demonstrate that those who did not worship the Roman gods could

The Persian god Mithras can be seen killing the bull as a sacrifice on the altar of his temple from third-century Rome. Mithraism, a tough mystery religion, was particularly popular with soldiers, since it could involve various endurance tests.

nevertheless be good Romans. They argued that the special connection between Roman religion and the Roman state should be broken, and that emperors should allow the practice of other religions, such as Christianity.

Some Christian writers falsely claimed that only corrupt emperors had persecuted the church. Some suggested that the church and Empire might have a common destiny; they began together (Jesus was born in the reign of the first Emperor, Augustus) and prospered together. They claimed that the peace won by the Emperor—the *Pax Romana*—was God-given to facilitate the spread of Christianity, 'the philosophy which goes with the Empire' (Melito).

Tertullian was less optimistic, and followed the apocalyptic tradition of the Revelation of John. He believed that the whole fabric of social and public life was fouled by idolatry. It was unthinkable that a Christian should enter the imperial service, let alone be an emperor. North African Christians generally displayed a more scornful and defiant attitude to Roman power. In AD 180 one of the martyrs from Scillium declared, 'I do not recognize the empire of this world.'

During the first half of the third century it became fashionable to combine the worship of different gods in one religion. Some of the emperors showed a particular interest in Christianity. The Emperor Alexander Severus reputedly included a representation of Jesus among the statues in his chapel. His mother had contact with Hippolytus and Origen, who also corresponded with the Emperor Philip the Arabian and his wife.

But Christianity first became the religion of kings and princes outside the Roman Empire. Royal families adopted it in Edessa, one of the chief centres of Syriac-speaking Christianity, in the early third century, and in Armenia and Georgia a century later.

How the first Christians worshipped

Ralph P. Martin

ince the first Christians came o faith in Jesus as Messiah nd Lord out of a Jewish back- round, it is not surprising that ewish influences are seen in he patterns of early Christian vorship.

The two great centres of ewish worship, the Jerusalem Temple and the network of local ynagogues throughout Palestine nd the ancient world wherever ews had scattered, handed on a ecognizable legacy to the Chris- ian church. The synagogue played he more dominant role in both udaism and early Christianity. ts pattern of Scripture readings nd sermon within a framework of raise and congregational prayers vas taken over by the Jewish Christians. Luke 4:16–30 gives valuable description of Jewish vorship. Later the apostles used he synagogue as a springboard or their evangelism and teaching. Scripture reading is referred to ccasionally in the New Testa- nent, and the sermons reported n the book of Acts give models of arly Christian preaching, some- imes in synagogues.

aul's contribution

n 1 Corinthians, which gives robably the earliest description f worship in the Christian church, Paul constantly draws on the Old Testament. This letter, written bout AD 55, pictures the church as the new Israel, living a pattern of the Christian life that is based on the new exodus. Paul uses ideas drawn from the Jewish Passover, which celebrated God's saving favour and strength in calling Israel to be his people, and rescuing them from tyranny in Egypt.

According to Paul, the church succeeded the old Jewish community, and combined both Jews and Greeks within God's one family of converted men and women. This fellowship of believers in Jesus stood at the dawn of a new age in God's dealings with the old Israel. They were the first generation of a new people in world history. They were marked out by their joyful awareness of living in a new relationship to God, and sharing in a new age of grace and power. All this was possible through the gift of the Holy Spirit, which followed the resurrection and ascension of Jesus. This one fact of experience stamps New Testament worship as unique, however much the church owed to its Jewish inheritance.

That inheritance was, of course, considerable. Paul used the framework of the Passover meal to interpret the Lord's Supper. But other elements were intertwined, such as the fellowship meal, called the *agape*, or 'love feast', which had its counterpart in Jewish table-customs. At public prayer, the response of *amen* (a Hebrew word meaning a confirming of what was being expressed in prayer) was the natural way to show agreement.

The setting of worship was 'the first day of the week'. This referred to the day of Christ's resurrection, as in the Gospels, and is distinct from the Jewish sabbath. The Christian Sunday was not made a 'day of rest' until Constantine decreed it in AD 321. Paul also speaks about baptism, a rite of initiation with roots in Jewish washings for ceremonial purposes, and especially in the

---

"You were washed, you were sanctified, you were justified in the name of the Lord Jesus Christ and in the Spirit of our God."

1 Corinthians 6:11

THE PASSOVER

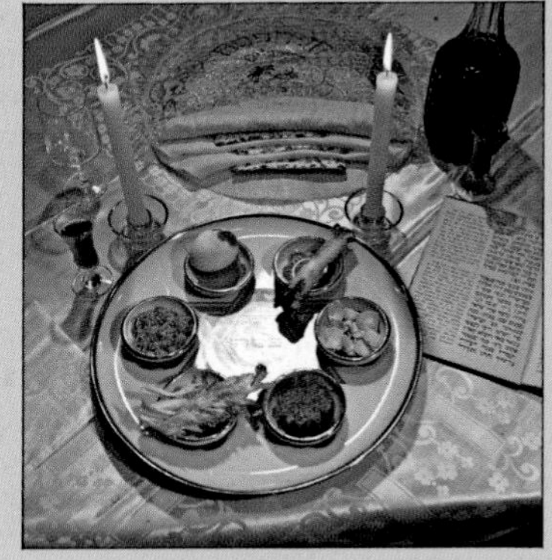

In New Testament times the Passover lamb was slaughtered in the Temple, but the meal could be eaten in any house inside Jerusalem. A group such as that of Jesus and his disciples would celebrate like a family. Christians realized early in the second century that the Lord's Supper completely replaces the Passover.

Passover followed a fairly standard pattern. First an opening prayer, the blessing of the cup. Then each person took herbs and dipped them in salt-water. The head of the family took one of three flat cakes of unleavened bread, broke it, and put some aside. The story of the first Passover was recounted, and the second cup filled and passed round.

Before the meal itself, all washed their hands, grace was said, and the bread broken. Bitter herbs dipped in sauce were distributed. The climax was the festive meal of roast lamb, which was followed by the third cup of wine, a final psalm and the fourth cup of wine.

service of *tebilah,* the 'bath' necessary for all converts to Judaism from paganism.

Several of these practices were being misused at Corinth, and Paul objected to their abuse and misunderstanding. Baptism should be in the name of Jesus, not in the name of Christian leaders, as if these apostolic figures were leaders of some cult. 'In the name of Jesus' meant that the new converts passed under his authority, and confessed him as Lord.

Two special meals

The love feast or *agape* meal had become an occasion for selfishness and drunkenness, and Paul pointed out the breakdown of fellowship —which it was the purpose of both the *agape* and the Lord's Supper to promote. Paul believed the Lord's Supper served both to unite Christians with the Lord in his death and risen life, and to join believers in a bond of union as 'one body' in Christ. The excesses at Corinth destroyed both aims. By heir greed and drunkenness they vere turning the meal into an orgy; y their superstitious attitude to he bread and the wine they were ndermining Paul's teaching on the eed for a personal receiving of Christ by faith and in love.

The enthusiasm of the Corinthian Christians led them to nisuse 'ecstatic tongues' and other gifts of the Spirit. Paul tried to curb his by insisting that worship must promote the healthy growth of the ntire community of Christians. Personal whims and the private njoyment of the gifts of the Spirit vere to be brought firmly under ontrol.

Not all the features of early Christian worship at Corinth are lear. It is not known what 'bap-ism for the dead' implied. Paul id not attach great importance to , but used it simply to illustrate nother matter. He also men-ioned the 'kiss of peace' without xplanation.

Singing and prayers

Singing' with the mind and with he spirit indicates a musical side o the meeting, but references o musical instruments do not nake it clear whether they were sed in worship. Exactly what hese hymns were, and whether natches of them have survived, s unclear. Passages such as Philippians 2:6–11, Colossians :15–20 and 1 Timothy 3:16 con-ain what may be early hymns, offered, as later among Christians n Bithynia about AD 112, to Christ s to God. Ephesians 5:14 is the nost likely example of a hymn rom the churches instructed by Paul. The setting of that three-line nvocation is clearly a service of baptism.

Prayers, whether very short like *Maranatha,* meaning 'Our Lord, come', or longer, played an impor-ant part in worship at Corinth.

In the early days, Christians stood with their arms raised when praying—like this woman carved on the side of a sarcophagus in third-century Rome.

Problems arose concerning women who attempted to pray with uncovered heads. Paul resisted this practice, though he freely granted the right of women believers to act as prophets and leaders of prayer in the assembled church.

Both prophesying and praying are gifts of the Spirit. The freedom that the Corinthians were exercising to the full was to be held in check. Paul crisply summed up: 'Let all things be done decently and in order.'

Evidence about Christian worship from writers who lived between the time of Paul and the middle of the second century is scarce and difficult to piece together.

Worship gradually became more formal and stereotyped in the period following Paul's death. Bishops and deacons possibly helped in this trend. New converts (catechumens) were given instruction in preparation for baptism. Worship forms connected with this have been seen in such writings as 1 Peter and 1 John.

Short snatches of an elementary creed are found in such verses as

"For I received from the Lord the teaching that I passed on to you: that the Lord Jesus, on the night he was betrayed, took a piece of bread, gave thanks to God, broke it, and said, 'This is my body, which is for you. Do this in memory of me.' In the same way, after the supper, he took the cup and said, 'This cup is God's new covenant, sealed with my blood. Whenever you drink it, do so in memory of me."

1 Corinthians 11:23–25

'Any one who denies being a Christian and actively proves it by adoring our gods must be forgiven on the basis of his repentance, no matter how suspect his past.'

Emperor Trajan (AD 98–117).

Romans 10:9 ('Jesus is Lord'); later examples are lengthened and developed, as in 1 Timothy 3:16 and 1 Peter 3:18–22.

Statements of faith

The rise of false teaching, against which the letters of John were written, required Christians to state their faith in Jesus Christ as true man and true God. This was to counteract the Docetists, who denied Christ's humanity, and the Ebionites, who threw doubt on Jesus' unique status as Son of God.

At first when a person was baptized he or she affirmed a creed which was concerned mainly with statements about Christ's person, as in the addition to the text at Acts 8:37. Examples of more formal creeds, stating belief in the three persons of the Godhead, which goes back to the baptismal commission recorded in Matthew 28:19, occur in descriptions of baptismal services reported by Irenaeus and Hippolytus of Rome. The Apostles' Creed derives from the late second-century baptismal creed used in Rome.

The puzzling document known as the *Didache* probably originated in the Syrian churches. It consists of a moral tract concerning the 'Two Ways' of life and of death,

CLEMENT OF ROME

Michael A. Smith

Little is known of the life of Clement, who was one of the early bishops or presbyters of Rome, and died about AD 100. His name was linked to a general letter usually known as *1 Clement.*

1 Clement is an open letter from the church at Rome to the church at Corinth, probably written at the end of the first century, shortly after the persecution by the Emperor Domitian. It is probably the earliest surviving Christian writing apart from the New Testament. It was written to counter the disruption and disturbance in the church at Corinth, where some of the older leaders had been deposed by a younger clique.

The letter sheds interesting light on church life soon after the age of the apostles. There is no trace of a single ruling bishop; instead the leaders of the church are called either bishops and deacons or elders (presbyters). The martyrdoms of Peter and Paul are referred to—but only in very vague terms. The letter appeals to a simple form of apostolic succession.

1 Clement puts great stress on good order, and on Christian faith being accompanied by good works, claiming that Abraham was saved 'by faith and hospitality'. The book quotes extensively from the Old Testament, Jewish books outside the canon, and writings of the apostles. It became widely known and popular because it was believed that its author knew Peter and Paul, and because it contained earnest exhortations to Christian humility and love. It was known to Hermas and Dionysius of Corinth in the later second century and was occasionally even read in church.

2 Clement, another early work, was claimed to be by Clement of Rome, but is an anonymous sermon perhaps dating from AD 150. Several additional writings of the fourth century were falsely claimed to be by Clement.

ollowed by sections about early rocedures for baptism, the *agape* nd the Lord's Supper. It is clear hat the *agape* and Lord's Supper ncluded set prayers during a public athering on the Lord's day, when hristians assembled 'to break read and give thanks'. This was receded by the confession of sins nd offering of gifts.

Clement of Rome also gives vidence that Sunday worship was ecoming formalized. Clement ncluded a great prayer of intercession, drawn from the church's turgy (a word used for the form f service, normally the Lord's upper), in his letter, *1 Clement.* le also insisted that worthy elebration of the Lord's Supper is ossible only when conducted by hurch leaders, called bishops or resbyters.

Ignatius also emphasized that he eucharist is the focal point of he church's unity, and so must be elebrated only under the authored church leader, the bishop r his delegate. Ignatius' letters hed much light on early Christian orship, and include an early hymn Christ and an explanation of the eaning of the Lord's day.

The correspondence between he Emperor Trajan and Pliny, the overnor of Bithynia, reveals that hristians used to meet for public orship on a 'fixed day' (Sunday) efore sunrise. They would join a hymn sung responsively, fered to Christ 'as God', and ow to renounce all practices consistent with their Christian ith. They shared 'holy meals', d it seems that by now the *gape* had been separated from the ord's Supper. In fact, continuing ouse of the love feast led to its adual disappearance in its original rm. The solemn meal of 'holy ommunion' was given more and ore significance as a sacrament. natius described it as 'a medicine immortality, the antidote that we should not die, but live for ever in Jesus Christ'.

Later patterns of worship

The Christians gradually standardized their worship and gave prominence to the Lord's Supper as the focal point of the liturgy. From the time of Justin Martyr to Athanasius three major descriptions offer new evidence.

Justin's *First Apology,* written about AD 150, contains what has been called 'the oldest systematic description of Sunday worship', based on practices in the church in Rome at that time. In Justin's day, Christian worship was becoming distinctively ecclesiastical by shedding its Jewish elements, though the framework was still modelled on that of the synagogue. The domestic atmosphere of the Passover meal was giving way to formality, and a new vocabulary introduced to give a more otherworldly, even transcendental, character to worship.

For Justin the act of communion was a 'memorial of the passion' of Christ. The elements of bread and wine over which thanks had been given nourished the lives of Christians by assimilation—a thought derived from John 6. This idea played an increasing role in explanations of the eucharist as a sacramental sharing in the divine life. Justin and Irenaeus may possibly allude to a special prayer, later known as the *epiclesis,* which 'called upon' the divine Word to come upon the bread and wine. It is not surprising that, especially among Gnostics, magical ideas about the nature of the consecrated elements began to emerge. Irenaeus also wrote of the 'altar in heaven' to which prayer and offerings were directed.

Justin's evidence is important for other reasons. He described the framework of Scripture readings

An observer's view of Christian worship

"They were in the habit of meeting on a certain fixed day before it was light, when they sang an anthem to Christ as God, and bound themselves by a solemn oath (sacramentum) not to commit any wicked deed, but to abstain from all fraud, theft and adultery, never to break their word, or deny a trust when called upon to honour it; after which it was their custom to separate, and then meet again to partake of food, but food of an ordinary and innocent kind."

PLINY, Letters x.96; AD 112

A SERVICE IN SECOND-CENTURY ROME

"*At the end of the prayers, we greet one another with a kiss. Then the president of the brethren is brought bread and a cup of wine mixed with water; and he takes them, and offers up praise and glory to the Father of the universe, through the name of the Son and of the Holy Ghost, and gives thanks at considerable length for our being counted worthy to receive these things at his hands. When he has concluded the prayers and thanksgivings, all the people present express their joyful assent by saying Amen. ('Amen' means 'so be it' in Hebrew) . . . Then those whom we call deacons give to each of those present the bread and wine mixed with water over which the thanksgiving was pronounced, and carry away a portion to those who are absent.*

We call this food 'Eucharist', which no one is allowed to share unless he or she believes that the things which we teach are true, and has been washed with the washing that is for remission of sins and unto a second birth, and is living as Christ has commanded. For we do not receive them as common bread and common drink; but as Jesus Christ our Saviour, having been made flesh by the word of God, had both flesh and blood for our salvation; similarly we have been taught that the food which is blessed by the word of prayer transmitted from him, and by which our blood and flesh are changed and nourished, is the flesh and blood of that Jesus who was made flesh. For the apostles, in the memoirs called Gospels composed by them, have thus delivered unto us what was enjoined upon them; that Jesus took bread, and when he had given thanks, said, This do in remembrance of me, this is my body; *and that, in a similar way, having taken the cup and given thanks, he said,* This is my blood; *and gave it to them alone.*"

JUSTIN, Apology I 65–66: AD 150

Justin describes the breaking of bread at a eucharistic meal. Here seven people share bread and fish, 'the food of life', in a wall-painting in the catacomb of Priscilla, dating from early third-century Rome.

INSTRUCTIONS FOR WORSHIP AND LEADERSHIP

"On Sunday, the Lord's own day, come together, break bread and carry out the eucharist, first confessing your sins so that your offering may be pure. Let no one who has a quarrel with his friend join the meeting until they have been reconciled, so that your offering is not polluted. For this is the offering spoken of by the Lord: 'Everywhere and at all times offer me a pure sacrifice. For my kingdom is great, says the Lord, and my name is wonderful among the nations.'

Appoint for yourselves therefore bishops and deacons worthy of the Lord; men who are meek and not money-lovers, true and approved, for they also perform for you the ministry of prophets and teachers. So do not despise them; they are the honourable men among you, together with the prophets and teachers."

Didache 14:1–15:1

as including 'the memoirs of the apostles' (that is, the Gospels of the New Testament), the exposition delivered by the presiding leader, prayers for all people, offered standing, and the kiss of peace. This 'service of the word' (as it was later called) led into the eucharist itself, when bread and wine were presented to the leader who offered a thanksgiving prayer extempore, to which the congregation assented with 'Amen'. The deacons handed the bread and wine to all present, and arranged to have them distributed to those believers who were absent. A collection was taken, looked after by the leader and then distributed to those in need.

Clearly what has come to be regarded as a service of worship was already more or less fixed in Justin's time. It soon became clear, as Origen implies, that the first part of the service was open to converts under instruction and probably enquirers, but the second part restricted to baptized communicants. This distinction became standard, with a clear dividing-line between the two parts—particularly in the Syrian *Apostolic Constitutions* and later in Chrysostom's writings.

The *Apostolic Tradition* of Hippolytus, usually dated about AD 215, contains a very full account of the ordaining and ordering of ministers. It also includes much interesting information about baptism. But its chief value lies in its teaching about the Eucharist. The Holy Spirit was invoked on 'the offering of the church', but this was more a prayer for the Christians in their act of offering than for the elements themselves. The bishop who laid his hand on the offering was to do so 'with all the presbyters' sharing with him. The act clearly involved both the bishop and the presbyters.

The Sacramentary of Serapion (who was an Egyptian bishop at the time of Athanasius) was written primarily for bishops, but gives interesting general descriptions of worship and particularly prayer. The Word (*Logos*) is asked to come upon the offerings to make them 'the body of the Word', 'the blood of the Truth'. The bread on the church's altar is believed to *become* 'the likeness of the holy body' of the Lord.

How the New Testament has come down to us

Larry W. Hurtado

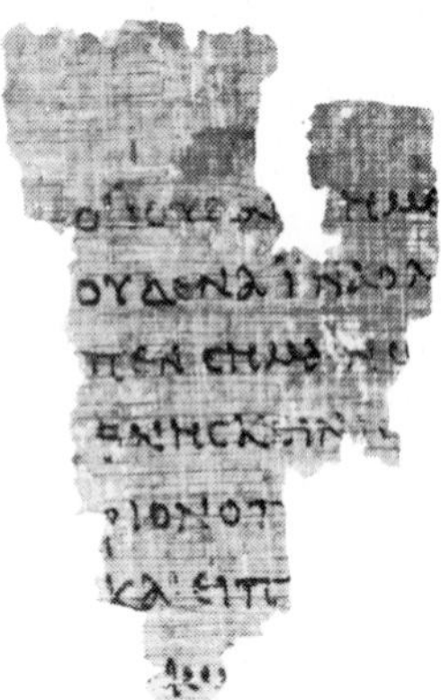

The earliest surviving fragment of the New Testament is this papyrus containing part of the Greek text of John 18:31–33 and 37. It dates from about AD 130.

An overwhelming number of handwritten texts are available for studying the New Testament in the original Greek. A recent count lists nearly ninety papyri (manuscripts made of papyrus, and generally the earliest), over 260 uncial manuscripts (written in Greek capital letters, generally on leather), and over 2,700 minuscule manuscripts (written in flowing Greek script, usually later in date than uncials). In addition, there are more than 2,200 lectionary manuscripts—church reading books which contain the parts of the Gospels and letters to be read on fixed days of the church year. But most of these manuscripts date from the eighth century or later, and few have been studied in detail.

The earliest complete New Testament manuscript still available is the *Codex Sinaiticus* which dates from the fourth century. '*Codex*' is the name for an early form of book, made by sewing leaves of writing material together. *Codex Vaticanus,* from which a few leaves are missing at the end of the New Testament, dates from the same period.

Less complete New Testament manuscripts date back as early as the late second or early third century, and one fragment of the Gospel of John (now at the John Rylands University Library, Manchester) dates from approximately AD 130. The Chester Beatty papyri contain parts of the Gospels, Acts, Paul's letters, Hebrews and Revelation, and date from the first half of the third century. Bodmer Papyrus II, dating from about AD 200, has

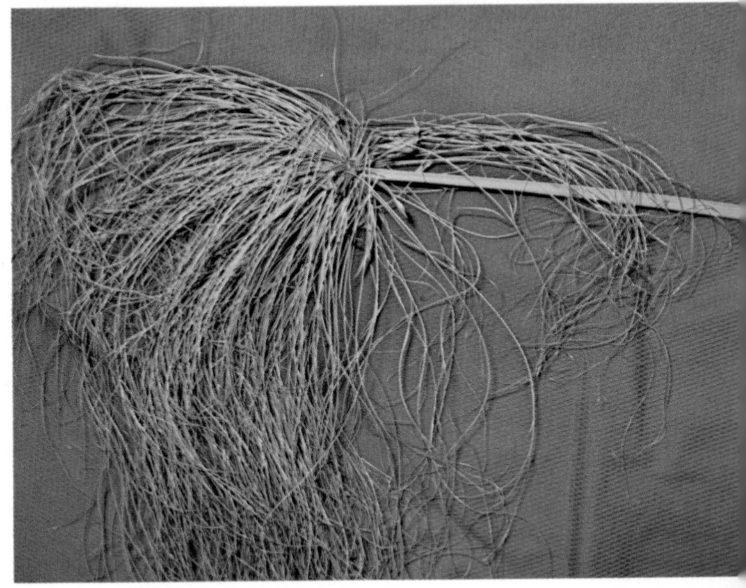

Papyrus 'paper' was made from the stems of the papyrus plant, found in ancient Egypt. Strips about sixteen inches long were laid side by side, and covered by another layer of strips across them. The layers were welded by beating, trimmed and smoothed to give a whitish paper. Sheets could be pasted together end-to-end to form a papyrus roll. Scrolls preceded the book form by many centuries.

RESCUING A MANUSCRIPT

The manuscript is a *codex*—that is, it is paged and bound in a similar way to books as we know them.

Codex Sinaiticus is written on parchment—the skin of sheep or goats, dried and polished with pumice. Careful techniques are used to preserve such valuable manuscripts.

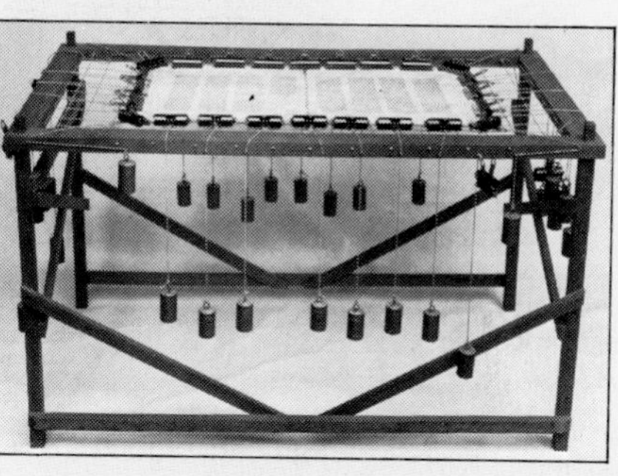

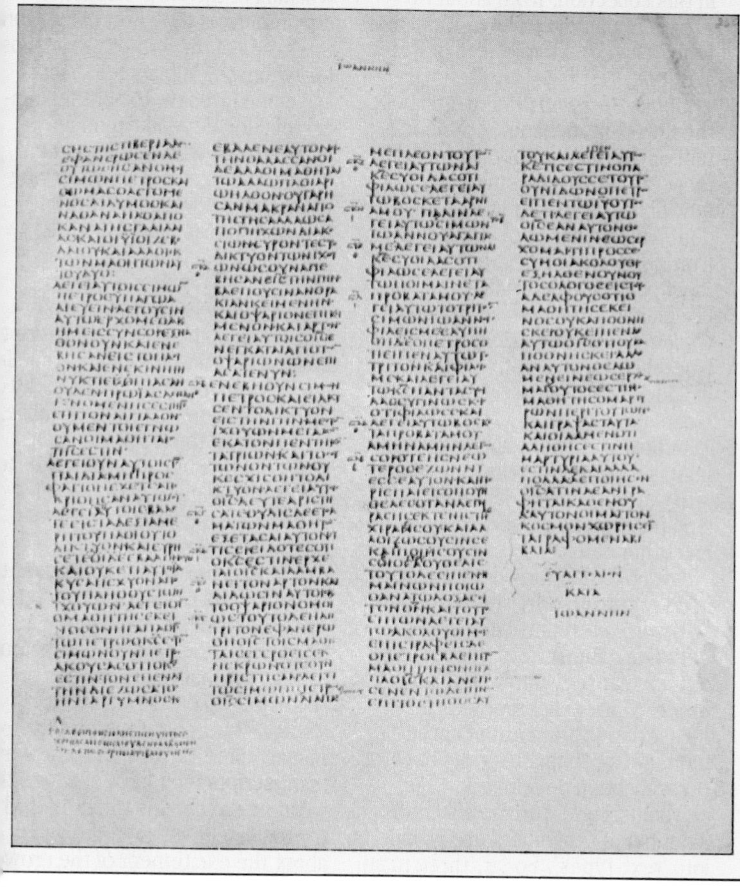

Codex Sinaiticus, one of the most important Greek manuscripts of the New Testament, was discovered at St Catherine's monastery, at the foot of Mount Sinai, in the nineteenth century. It was later bought by the British Government from USSR for £100,000 on Christmas Day, 1933.

This page from *Codex Sinaiticus* contains the last chapter of John's Gospel.

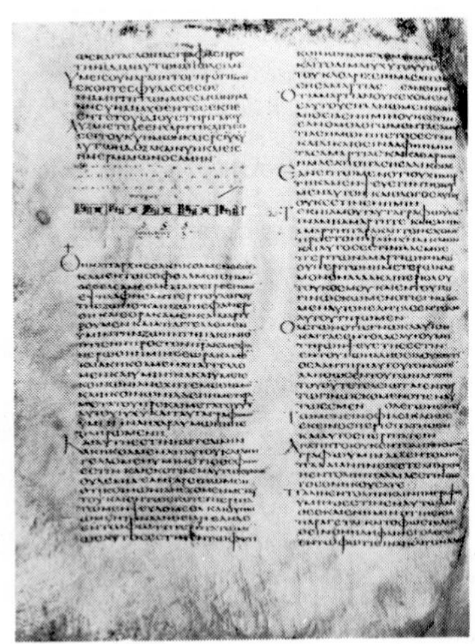

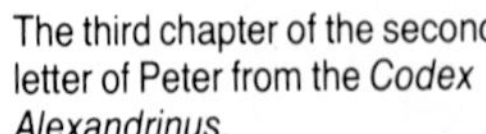

The third chapter of the second letter of Peter from the *Codex Alexandrinus.*

fragments of John's Gospel; others in this collection, from about AD 175–225, contain parts of Luke and John, as well as the letters of Peter and Jude.

Codex Alexandrinus, from about the fifth century, another important early manuscript containing most of the New Testament, is now in the British Library, London. At Cambridge *Codex Bezae,* from the fifth century, contains most of the Gospels and Acts, in Greek and Latin on facing pages; *Codex Washingtonianus,* dating from the fourth or fifth century, includes nearly all of the four Gospels.

Scholars examine these Greek manuscripts in the following ways:

By attempting to date and place a manuscript by its style of writing and other clues.

By looking for any divergences in its text from other manuscripts.

By discovering relationships between manuscripts, they work out how far they agree with each other. More exact methods for measuring the amount of agreement between manuscripts have recently been developed.

Manuscripts with significant amounts of agreement are grouped into 'text-types'. So far, three main 'text-types' have been found: the Neutral or Alexandrian text-type; the Western text-type—much less clearly defined; and the Byzantine text-type (also called the Syrian or Ecclesiastical text-type) which seems to have given rise to the relatively standard New Testament text which most later manuscripts use. Some scholars suggest there is a fourth group, which they call the 'Caesarean' text.

Getting back to the original New Testament

The main aim of all this detailed work is to establish a Greek text which is as close as possible to the wording of the New Testament documents as they first came from the hands of the authors. For those for whom the Bible's teaching is the starting-point, exact theological thinking depends upon an accurate Greek New Testament.

In addition, scholars are trying to discover how the history of the church may have affected the copying of the New Testament text.

The overwhelming mass of variations in the many manuscripts studied consist of accidental spelling differences or omissions. But some variations are clearly deliberate. Most of these appear to be attempts to 'improve' the style, to remove ambiguity or sometimes to harmonize parallel accounts in different books.

A few of the variations appear to be caused by a copyist's concern about doctrine. For example, in Mark 3:21, the original text seems to suggest that Jesus' friends or relatives were worried about his sanity. This apparently embarrassed some scribes; in some ear manuscripts they have changed th wording so that it is the crowd wh try to seize Jesus, and the worry about the excitement of the crow

CAN THE TEXT BE TRUSTED?

'Perhaps we can appreciate how wealthy the New Testament is in manuscript attestation if we compare the textual material for other ancient historical works. For Caesar's *Gallic War* (composed between 58 and 50 BC) there are several extant manuscripts, but only nine or ten are good, and the oldest is some 900 years later than Caesar's day. Of the 142 books of the *Roman History* of Livy (59 BC–AD 17) only thirty-five survive; these are known to us from not more than twenty manuscripts of any consequence, only one of which, and that containing fragments of Books iii–vi, is as old as the fourth century. Of the fourteen books of the *Histories* of Tacitus (about AD 100) only four and a half survive; of the sixteen books of his *Annals*, ten survive in full and two in part. The text of these extant portions of his two great historical works depends entirely on two manuscripts, one of the ninth century and one of the eleventh. The extant manuscripts of his minor works (*Dialogus de Oratoribus, Agricola, Germania*) all descend from a codex of the tenth century. The *History* of Thucydides (about 460–400 BC) is known to us from eight manuscripts, the earliest belonging to around AD 900, and a few papyrus scraps, belonging to about the beginning of the Christian era. The same is true of the *History* of Herodotus (about 488–428 BC). Yet no classical scholar would listen to an argument that the authenticity of Herodotus or Thucydides is in doubt because the earliest manuscripts of their works which are of any use to us are over 1,300 years later than the originals.

'But how different is the situation of the New Testament in this respect! In addition to the two excellent manuscripts of the fourth century . . . which are the earliest of some thousands known to us, considerable fragments remain of papyrus copies of books of the New Testament dated from 100 or 200 years earlier still. The Chester Beatty Biblical Papyri, the existence of which was made public in 1931, consist of portions of eleven papyrus codices, three of which contained most of the New Testament writings. One of these, containing the four Gospels with Acts, belongs to the first half of the third century; another, containing Paul's letters to churches and the Epistle to the Hebrews, was copied at the beginning of the third century; the third, containing Revelation, belongs to the second half of the same century.

'Earlier still is a fragment of a papyrus codex containing John xviii. 31–33, 37 ff., now in the John Rylands University Library, Manchester dated on palaeographical grounds around AD 130.'

F.F. Bruce, *The New Testament Documents*

"The variant readings about which any doubt remains among textual critics of the New Testament affect no material question of historic fact or of Christian faith and practice."

THE EARLY CHURCH RECOGNIZES THE NEW TESTAMENT

AD 100

All dates approximate

Different parts of our New Testament were written by this time, but not yet collected and defined as 'Scripture'. Early Christian writers (for example Polycarp and Ignatius) quote from the Gospels and Paul's letters, as well as from other Christian writings and oral sources. Paul's letters were collected late in the first century. Matthew, Mark and Luke were brought together by AD 150.

AD 200

New Testament used in the church at Rome
(the 'Muratorian Canon')

Four Gospels
Acts
Paul's letters:
- Romans
- 1 & 2 Corinthians
- Galatians
- Ephesians
- Philippians
- Colossians
- 1 & 2 Thessalonians
- 1 & 2 Timothy
- Titus
- Philemon

James

1 & 2 John
Jude
Revelation of John
Revelation of Peter
Wisdom of Solomon

To be used in private, but not public, worship
The Shepherd of Hermas

AD 250

New Testament used by Origen

Four Gospels
Acts
Paul's letters:
- Romans
- 1 & 2 Corinthians
- Galatians
- Ephesians
- Philippians
- Colossians
- 1 & 2 Thessalonians
- 1 & 2 Timothy
- Titus
- Philemon

1 Peter
1 John

Revelation of John

Disputed
Hebrews
James
2 Peter
2 & 3 John
Jude
The Shepherd of Hermas
Letter of Barnabas
Teaching of Twelve Apostles
Gospel of the Hebrews

AD 300

New Testament used by Eusebius

Four Gospels
Acts
Paul's letters:
Romans
1 & 2 Corinthians
Galatians
Ephesians
Philippians
Colossians
1 & 2 Thessalonians
1 & 2 Timothy
Titus
Philemon

1 Peter
1 John

Revelation of John (authorship in doubt)

Disputed but well known
James
2 Peter
2 & 3 John
Jude

To be excluded
The Shepherd of Hermas
Letter of Barnabas
Gospel of the Hebrews
Revelation of Peter
Acts of Peter
Didache

AD 400

New Testament fixed for the West by the Council of Carthage

Four Gospels
Acts
Paul's letters:
Romans
1 & 2 Corinthians
Galatians
Ephesians
Philippians
Colossians
1 & 2 Thessalonians
1 & 2 Timothy
Titus
Philemon
Hebrews
James
1 & 2 Peter
1, 2 & 3 John
Jude
Revelation

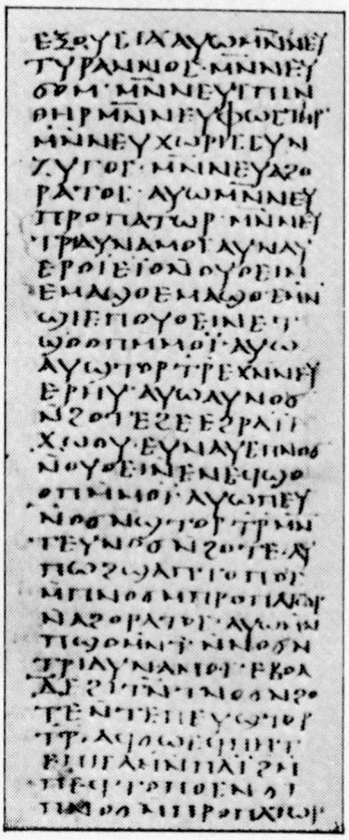

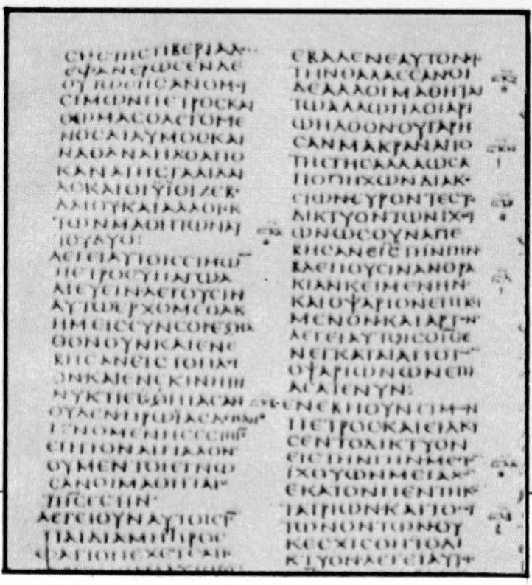

Part of the last chapter of John's Gospel in Greek, from the fourth-century *Codex Sinaiticus*

Part of the *Pistis Sophia*, a Gnostic work which circulated in the first centuries of the church.

Second-century African missionaries may have made this first Latin version of the Greek Old Testament (*Septuagint*) around AD 150. This 'Old Latin' version was widely used until gradually replaced by Jerome's *Vulgate*. This papyrus fragment includes parts of Genesis 5 and 6.

rather than Jesus' sanity. Because of its rather non-literary Greek, Mark's Gospel appears to have suffered most often from these kinds of deliberate alterations during copying.

Copying the New Testament

Clearly the New Testament writings were considered important in the early church, since many copies were made—for private reading as well as church use. However, though the writings were considered important, this did not always guarantee scrupulous, exact copying of them. While no manuscript is free of either accidental or deliberate variations, some manuscripts seem to reflect a more careful tradition of copying, while others reveal a much freer attitude towards the actual words of the New Testament.

Several translations of the New Testament were made at an early date. The most important are the Syriac, Latin and Coptic. There was an intense interest in making the New Testament available to different language-groups in the Roman world. These versions can often show how the New Testament was interpreted during the second and third centuries and later, when they were first produced. But these translations were not always prepared by people with a good command of Greek, and are often very imperfect.

Quotations from the New Testament in the works of some of the early Christian writers can also help in studying the New Testament text. But these early writers were often very free in their use of the New Testament, and quoted from memory or merely paraphrased the passage. This makes it difficult to decide what type of New Testament text they used. The early Christians revered and used the New Testament greatly, but did not treat the exact wording with care.

From the time they were first produced, the New Testament writings were always closely linked with the church and its worship, evangelism, beliefs and institutions. The information available concerning the New Testament in the early period shows how New Testament Scripture and the church interacted and affected each other at that time. The church was concerned to make Scripture widely available; some of the variations in early New Testament manuscripts reveal a concern over misunderstanding of Scripture, or perhaps misuse by heretics.

SECTION 3

ACCEPTANCE AND CONQUEST 325–600

ACCEPTANCE AND CONQUEST

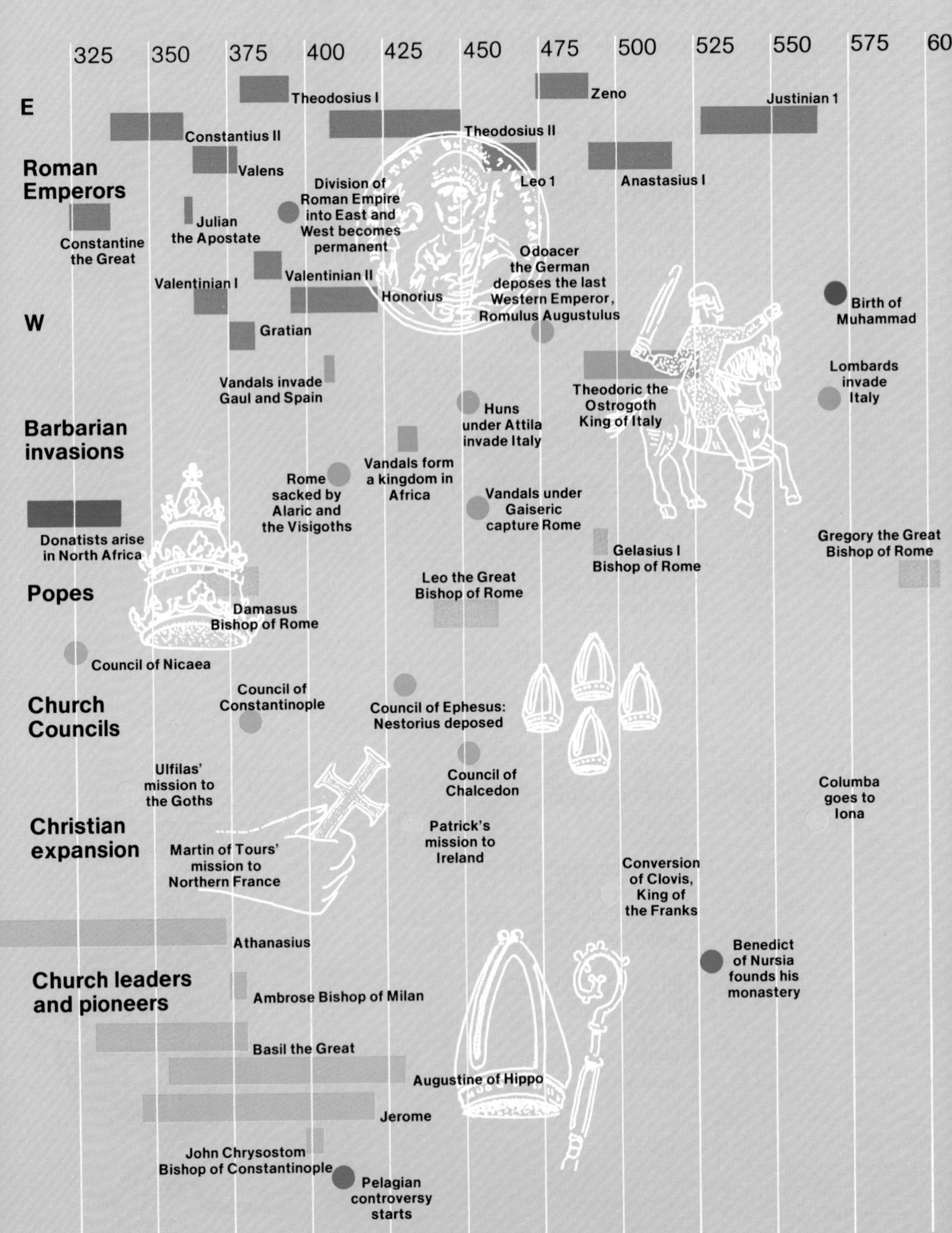
325
350
375
400
425
450
475
500
525
550
575
600
E
W
Roman Emperors
Theodosius I
Zeno
Justinian 1
Constantius II
Theodosius II
Valens
Leo 1
Anastasius I
Division of Roman Empire into East and West becomes permanent
Julian the Apostate
Constantine the Great
Valentinian I
Valentinian II
Honorius
Gratian
Odoacer the German deposes the last Western Emperor, Romulus Augustulus
Birth of Muhammad
Barbarian invasions
Vandals invade Gaul and Spain
Huns under Attila invade Italy
Theodoric the Ostrogoth King of Italy
Lombards invade Italy
Rome sacked by Alaric and the Visigoths
Vandals form a kingdom in Africa
Vandals under Gaiseric capture Rome
Donatists arise in North Africa
Popes
Damasus Bishop of Rome
Leo the Great Bishop of Rome
Gelasius I Bishop of Rome
Gregory the Great Bishop of Rome
Church Councils
Council of Nicaea
Council of Constantinople
Council of Ephesus: Nestorius deposed
Council of Chalcedon
Christian expansion
Ulfilas' mission to the Goths
Martin of Tours' mission to Northern France
Patrick's mission to Ireland
Conversion of Clovis, King of the Franks
Columba goes to Iona
Church leaders and pioneers
Athanasius
Ambrose Bishop of Milan
Basil the Great
Augustine of Hippo
Jerome
John Chrysostom Bishop of Constantinople
Pelagian controversy starts
Benedict of Nursia founds his monastery

CONSTANTINE AND THE CHRISTIAN EMPIRE

Richard A. Todd

Momentous changes occurred both in the church and in the political structure of the West during the fourth, fifth and sixth centuries. The Western Roman Empire disappeared under the repeated assaults of the German barbarian tribes on its northern frontier. Christianity, a persecuted minority faith at Constantine's conversion in AD 312, had become the religion of the Empire by the end of the century. The bishop of Rome, whose leadership in the church had been largely a primacy of honour, now claimed supreme and universal authority in Christian lands, and began to make good this claim in the West, at least over the church. By the time of Pope Gregory I (590–604) the collapse of the Western Empire left the Roman bishop the real ruler of much of central Italy.

The conversion of Constantine

Throughout the fourth century relations between the church, the emperor and pagan religion were continually changing. Constantine's defeat of Maxentius at the battle of the Milvian Bridge in the autumn of 312, and his interpretation of that victory as the response of the Christian God to his prayer for help, propelled church and state into a new age for which neither was prepared. Out of this new relationship between Christian church and Christian emperor stemmed the history of church/state relations in the later Roman Empire and throughout the Middle Ages.

Constantine's account of his conversion, told by the Emperor himself to the church historian Eusebius of Caesarea, towards the end of his life, is well known. Constantine, alarmed by reports of Maxentius' mastery of magical arts, prayed to the 'Supreme God' for help. The response was a sign, a cross in the noonday sky 'above the sun', and with it the words, 'Conquer by this.' That night Christ appeared to him in a dream and commanded him to use the sign—apparently Chi-Rho , the initial letters of the name of Christ—'as a safeguard in all engagements with his enemies'. According to the historian Lactantius, Constantine placed the sign on the shields of his soldiers. He then marched on Rome, confronted Maxentius, who was miraculously induced to fight outside the city fortifications, and conquered.

The story has been doubted. But Constantine's attitude towards the Christian church after he

Constantine's momentous victory at the Milvian Bridge was commemorated by the construction of a triumphal arch in Rome.

Sun-worship lingered on in Roman Christianity. Christ is shown as the sun-god mounting the heavens in his chariot in this third-century Roman mosaic ceiling.

became emperor, and his new laws, show that his allegiance to Christianity was genuine, though his understanding of the Christian faith was at first no doubt imperfect. Constantine did, indeed, retain the pagan high priest's title of *Pontifex Maximus*, and for a decade his coins continued to feature some of the pagan gods, notably his own favourite deity, the Unconquered Sun. He also delay Christian baptism until the end of his life. But delayed baptism was the custom of the age, a device f avoiding mortal sin, and retaining the pagan symbols was a necessary compromise with his pagan subjects, still very much in the majority.

Constantine treated Christiani as the favoured, though not yet t official, religion of the Empire. H granted immunities to the clergy and lavished gifts on the church; his letters and edicts he spoke as the Christian God were his own.

It is important to understand Constantine's previous religion, the worship of the Unconquered Sun. If the story of the cross in the sky is true, he may have inte preted the sign as his own specia deity recommending the worship of the Christian God. Perhaps Constantine continued to identify the sun with the Christian God in some way—a belief made easier the tendency of Christian writers and artists to use sun imagery in portraying Christ. For them Chri is the source of light and salvatio and a mosaic from a third-century tomb found under St Peter's, Rome, even shows him as the su god in his chariot. When in 321 Constantine made the first day of the week a holiday, he called it 'the venerable day of the Sun' (Sunday).

Another result of Constantine' conversion was renewed interest in the Holy Land by people in the West. Since the failure of the sec ond Jewish revolt of Bar Kokhba (132–35), Jerusalem had been a pagan city. Constantine, and his mother Helena, made it into a Christian city. The traditional pla of Jesus' burial was found under the Emperor Hadrian's Temple of Venus, and Helena discovered what was believed to be the 'Tru Cross' on which Jesus had been crucified. Here, and elsewhere,

Constantine and Helena built churches, and pilgrims came in increasing numbers to the holy places.

Isis with her son Horus. They were sometimes connected with the Virgin Mary and child Jesus. The popular religion of Isis was a rival to Christianity.

Christianity and pagan customs

The Christian church took over many pagan ideas and images. From sun-worship, for example, came the celebration of Christ's birth on the twenty-fifth of December, the birthday of the Sun. *Saturnalia,* the Roman winter festival of 17–21 of December, provided the merriment, gift-giving and candles typical of later Christmas holidays. Sun-worship hung on in Roman Christianity and Pope Leo I, in the middle of the fifth century, rebuked worshippers who turned round to bow to the sun before entering St Peter's basilica. Some pagan customs which were later Christianized, for example the use of candles, incense and garlands, were at first avoided by the church because they symbolized paganism.

The veneration of the Virgin Mary was probably stimulated by parallels in pagan religion. Some scholars believe that the worship of Artemis (Diana) was transferred to Mary. Ephesus, a city which belonged to Artemis until the end of the pagan era, was also associated with Mary from an early date.

Many people connected Mary with Isis, the Egyptian goddess whose worship had spread throughout the Empire in the Christian era. Isis in her travels became identified with many other goddesses, including Artemis, and was the 'universal mother' of later pagan religion. The devotees of Isis, herself called 'the Great Virgin' and 'Mother of the God', naturally tended to look to Mary for comfort when paganism was outlawed and their temples destroyed at the end of the fourth century. Some surviving images of Isis holding the child Horus are in a pose remarkably similar to that of some early Christian madonnas. However, the original aim of titles such as 'bearer of God' for Mary was to honour the divine Son.

The cult of saints and martyrs grew rapidly in the fourth century, another example of the blending of the old paganism with Christianity. Chapels and even churches began to be built over the tombs of martyrs, a practice which influenced church architecture. Competition for saintly corpses soon degenerated into a superstitious search for relics. In parts of the East it sometimes became a fight for the bodies of saintly hermits, still alive but expected to expire shortly. The cult arose among the people, but was approved and encouraged by the great Christian leaders of the age—Jerome, Ambrose and Augustine. Ambrose, for instance, discovered the bodies of several forgotten saints.

The Christian historian Theodoret boasts that in many places saints and martyrs took the place of pagan gods, and their shrines the place of pagan temples. Some saints were claimed to cure barrenness, others

The great temple of Artemis (Diana) at Ephesus on a coin of the Emperor Maximin (AD 235–38). Some believe the worship of this goddess was transfered to Mary.

Constantine described himself as 'defender of the church'.

protected travellers, detected perjury, foretold the future, and many healed the sick. The shrine of saints Cyrus and John, physicians who in their earthly practice charged no fees, near Alexandria, was particularly popular. To the shrine of St Felix of Nola, who detected perjury, Augustine sent two clergymen who had accused each other, to discover which was lying.

The church never went as far as to teach that saints were to be worshipped. It was only suggested that they were in a special position to hear petitions and present them directly to God. The saint's position in heaven was compared to that of the great man at court, who might be expected to get results for a lowly petitioner by presenting his request directly to the Emperor.

Augustine and others protested against abuses of the traffic in relics. An African church council in 401 insisted that a saint or martyr must be proved genuine before a chapel was consecrated. Only one suggestion remains by an orthodox Christian that attachment to particular shrines or relics marked a return to pagan superstition. Vigilantius, an obscure priest from Aquitaine, wrote, 'We almost see the rites of the pagans introduced into the churches under the pretext of religion; ranks of candles are lit in full daylight; and everywhere people kiss and adore some bit of dust in a little pot, wrapped a precious fabric.' Vigilantius' protest survived only because some outraged priests sent a copy to Jerome who refuted it in a scathing reply.

Tradition holds that the body of John the Baptist is buried at the cathedral church of St John the Baptist at Sebaste (Samaria), now part of the West Bank.

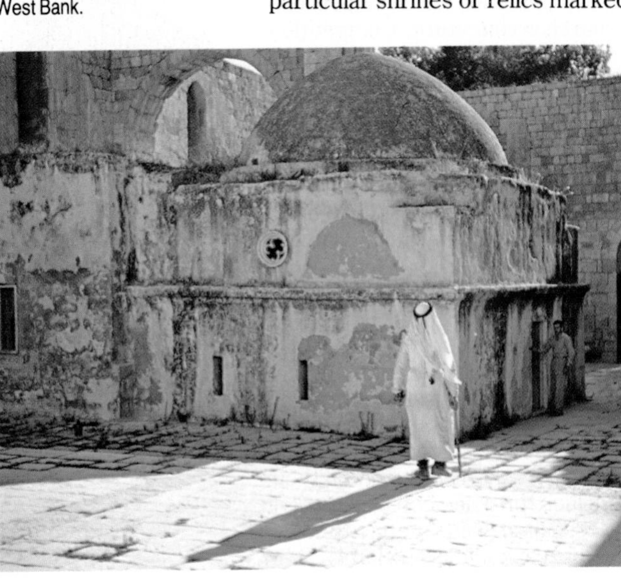

Constantine and the church

'What has the Emperor to do with the church?' retorted Bishop Donatus when presented with an unfavourable decree from the Emperor Constans. Most of the conflict between church and state during the fourth century relates to this question. From the very beginning of Constantine's reign, most Christians agreed with the Emperor that he had a great deal to do with the church.

Although they later complained about the Emperor's interference, it was the Donatists who first asked Constantine to intervene, less than six months after his victory over Maxentius. The Donatists were a strict party in North Africa who refused to recognize Caecilian as bishop of Carthage because, they alleged, he had been ordained by a *traditor*, one who had 'handed over' or 'betrayed' Scriptures to the authorities in the recent persecution.

Constantine did not hesitate to accept jurisdiction, though he referred the matter to a council of bishops. When the Donatists refused to accept the authority of this and a subsequent council, the Emperor lost patience and threatened to go to Africa to set things right himself:

'I am going to make plain to

them what kind of worship is to be offered to God . . . What higher duty have I as emperor than to destroy error and repress rash indiscretions, and so cause all to offer to Almighty God true religion, honest concord and due worship?'

The visit to Africa did not materialize, but Constantine ordered the Donatist churches to be confiscated and their leaders banished. The Donatists resisted tenaciously; over the years they produced a host of martyrs. Constantine soon saw that his policy of repression was futile and revoked it. The Donatists survived for three centuries, despite intermittent attempts to root them out; they only disappeared with the obliteration of Christianity in North Africa after the Muslim conquest.

The Roman Emperor, as head of the state religion, had always been responsible for maintaining good relations between the people and their gods. Constantine naturally saw himself in a similar role as Christian Emperor. Strife in the church, such as the Donatist and Arian controversies, was likely to bring down the wrath of the Christian God on him and the people entrusted to his care.

The willingness of the church to accept, indeed to ask for, the intervention of the Emperor in matters so clearly outside his expert knowledge is surprising. The explanation is in part simply the selfish desire of one faction or another to gain advantage in the desperate struggles of the fourth century. Another problem for the church was that the only Christian precedent for the role of a Christian emperor was that of the Old Testament kings of Israel, who had a great deal to do with maintaining peace and purity of religion in their kingdoms. In the Byzantine East, once the doctrine that the Emperor was above the church had been established, it was never effectively challenged.

Constantine's handling of the Arian controversy was more astute and at first more successful than his approach to the Donatist split. The council of Nicaea, where the controversy should have ended, was his great triumph.

When Constantine became master of the East in 324 he found a dispute already raging between Alexander, bishop of Alexandria, and his presbyter, Arius. Arius was attempting to solve the difficult problem of the relation of the Son to God the Father. He suggested that the Son, though Creator, was himself created and therefore could not be truly divine like the Father. Alexander and his bishops judged this heretical and excommunicated Arius, who found support elsewhere in the East.

Constantine hoped to settle the matter 'out of court' and sent a letter to the contending parties describing the dispute as 'very trifling and indeed unworthy to be the cause of such a conflict'. When he saw that the dispute was not to be settled so easily Constantine called a Council of the whole church, the first 'ecumenical' (general) council, at Nicaea in 325.

The Emperor himself presided over the critical session, and it was he who proposed the reconciling word, *homoousios* (Greek for 'of one essence'), to describe Christ's relationship to the Father (though it was probably one of his ecclesiastical advisers, Ossius of Cordova, who suggested it to him). Nicaea was a triumph both for orthodoxy, since Arius could not accept the word, and apparently for Constantine's goal of church unity, since only two bishops finally stood with Arius.

The orthodox statement of doctrine produced at Nicaea, with some later modifications, became one of the great creeds of Western

The huge head from a statue of Constantine, which once stood in the basilica of Constantine in Rome. The head alone is over 8 feet/2.46 metres high and weighs about nine tons.

Christianity. But Constantine's achievement of unity proved a hollow victory. Conflict flared up again when the anti-Arian party, led by Athanasius who succeeded Alexander as bishop of Alexandria, refused to receive back repentant Arians into the church. Constantine's continued attempts to attain unity were frustrated, as he saw it, by the obstinate refusal of first one faction and then the other to make any compromise.

Constantine died in 337, tolerant towards Arian sympathizers, with Athanasius defiant in exile. Constantine thus failed to achieve his goal of unity in the church. Against this must be balanced his successes. He had begun to Christianize the Empire. He founded Constantinople (in 330) and thus shifted the focus of the Empire eastward, contributing both to the decline of the West and the independence of the Western church. The effect of Nicaea and its Creed far outlived his own failure to solve the Arian controversy. Finally, he established, permanently in the East and for a time in the West, his own answer to the question, 'What has the Emperor to do with the church?'

The Emperor Constantius repeatedly banished Athanasius.

Church, state and paganism

The division of the Empire between Constantine's three sons, after his death in 337, soon resulted in a civil war with theological overtones. From this struggle Constantius, who was inclined towards Arianism, emerged victorious in 353.

Constantius' efforts to unite the church under an anti-Nicene banner are seen in the series of councils held in various parts of the Empire from 354 to 360. Through these he finally succeeded in forcing an anti-Nicene creed on reluctant bishops, and secured the condemnation of Athanasius, leader of the Nicene party. The climax of imperial intervention came at Milan in 355, if Athanasius account is accepted. Certain bishops were summoned before Constantius at his palace and ordered to condemn Athanasius. When they dared to appeal to the canons of the church, the Emperor replied, 'Whatever I will, shall be regarded as a canon . . . Either obey or go into exile.'

In spite of all this, neither Athanasius nor the other Nicene bishops at first questioned the Emperor's authority to intervene in church disputes. They held that he was simply wrong, deceived by his advisers. By 358, however, Athanasius' views had changed: 'When did a judgement of the church receive its validity from the Emperor? . . . There have been many councils held until the present and many judgements passed by the church; but the church leaders never sought the consent of the Emperor for them nor did the Emperor busy himself with the affairs of the church . . .' This was not quite true—but Athanasius might well forget the events of Constantine's reign when confronted with the audacity of Constantius.

Even the old Ossius of Cordova, who had helped shape Constantine's policy towards the church, now quoted Jesus against imperial interference: 'Do not intrude yourself into church matters, nor give commands to us concerning them . . . God has put into your hands the kingdom; to us he has entrusted the affairs of his church . . . It is written, "Render unto Caesar the things that are Caesar's and unto God the things that are God's."'

The sons of Constantine were bolder than their father in the attack on paganism. Constantine had to proceed slowly since

ATHANASIUS

Everett Ferguson

Athanasius (about 300–73) is one of the giants of Christian history because of his part in defining the doctrine of the Trinity in the Arian struggles.

As a deacon of the church at Alexandria, Athanasius accompanied his bishop, Alexander, to the Council of Nicaea in 325. He succeeded Alexander as bishop in 328. Changing political fortunes due to the involvement of the Emperor in the affairs of the church resulted in Athanasius being exiled five times (335–37, to Trier in Gaul; 339–46, when he went to Rome; 356–61, when he lived among the monks in the Egyptian desert; 362–63 and 365–66 in concealment in Egypt). Athanasius' flock stayed loyal to him and each time he was welcomed back from exile.

On the Incarnation, (335–37, but dated by some as early as 318) sets out Athanasius' basic theological viewpoint. Christ 'was made human that we might be made divine'. This concern with salvation motivated Athanasius as he argued against Arius and his followers. The Arians said that Christ was a created being, made by God before time. Athanasius argued that if Christ was less than God then he could not be our saviour. Only God could restore the human race to communion with himself. For this reason he defended Nicaea's definition of Christ as of the same substance with God, and Nicaea's rejection of Arianism.

Most of Athanasius' writings are aimed at opposing Arianism, dealing with it historically, doctrinally, or from Scripture. Athanasius stood like a rock in defence of the creed adopted at Nicaea. His personality, preaching and writings did more than anything else to achieve victory for the Nicene position. His zeal made him uncompromising—even harsh—in dealing with opponents, and slow to recognize good in those he disagreed with. Athanasius' *Life of Antony* did much to promote monasticism by praising the life of the desert ascetics. Athanasius found echoes of his own experiences and emotions in the psalms *(Letter to Marcellinus)* and helped to introduce the personal devotional use of the psalms which Christians have ever since adopted. His Easter Letter 39 (367) is the earliest witness to the twenty-seven-book New Testament canon.

One of the oldest known representations of the crucifixion. This wooden carving forms part of the doors of the church of Santa Sabina, built in Rome 422–32. It is interesting that Christ is shown as bearded (earlier he was always shown as a clean-shaven youth) and that the cross itself is not represented.

most of his subjects were still pagan—particularly the army, and the nobility from whom he drew his officials. His 'Edict' of Milan (313) proclaimed toleration for both pagan and Christian subjects. He did close a few temples particularly offensive to Christians for such things as ritual prostitution, and stripped many others of their treasures to deck his new capital city. He also banned private sacrifices and divining. He probably prohibited public sacrifice too, near the end of his reign.

The sons of Constantine proceeded more vigorously. A law of 341 apparently suppressed pagan cults. A stronger decree of Constantius, in 356, closed the temples and prohibited sacrifice on pain of death. Some temples were closed but the law seems not to have been rigidly enforced, for the priesthoods and rituals continued at Rome and probably elsewhere. In 357, Constantius, on a visit to Rome, removed from the Senate House the altar of Victory on which incense had been offered by the senators since the age of the Emperor Augustus.

Athanasius came to regard Constantius as worse than Saul, Ahab or Pilate and herald of the Antichrist. This view is too harsh. Constantius was, after all, acting in the spirit of Constantine to bring about unity in the Empire. Furthermore, he thought the church was on his side since he had the support of a large part of the Eastern church—and Christianity was stronger in the East. But Constantius' reign does show how truth and liberty may suffer when unity is made the ultimate goal.

Julian the Apostate died fighting the Persians in 363. He was ridiculed for his beard by the people of Antioch.

Julian the 'Apostate'

Some of the Nicene leaders thought better of Constantius when confronted with Julian, who became emperor in 361. Julian was a nephew of Constantine who barely escaped the general massacre that had followed his death in 337. As emperor he could at last reveal that he had been for some years a secret pagan. His conversion was due to many factors. There was the massacre of his family and his long, lonely childhood filled with fears, imagined and real, of enemies at the Christian court of Constantius. In his education he had felt closest to Plato and other great writers of ancient Greece, whom he studied under sympathetic tutors. Finally, he was influenced by the skill of the Neoplatonic magician and medium, Maximus.

Julian now attempted to convert the Empire to a religion which he called 'Hellenism'. This was more than a mere revival of the old, unco-ordinated paganism. Julian made a unique attempt to combine many old elements in an organized pagan 'church'. The principal deity was Plato's 'Supreme Being', whose chief visible representative was the life-giving Sun, identified with Helios and Mithras in the mythologies of the day. Syncretism prevailed, and it was possible to regard all the old and new gods with their cults and rituals as originating from the Sun. Thus the world of Greek culture, mythology and ritual could be retained without sacrificing the lofty monotheism of the Sun.

Julian paid tribute to the Christian church by attempting to incorporate in his 'Hellenism' some of the more successful features of Christianity. He tried to set up a hierarchy, like that of the church, with metropolitans of provinces set over the local priesthoods and answerable to the Emperor as *Pontifex Maximus*. Julian was much concerned that the 'Hellenists' should not be outdone in holiness and charity by the 'Galileans', as he called the Christians, and that the lives of his priests should be worthy of their high calling. A letter to Arsacius, High Priest of Galatia, is in this spirit:

'Why do we not notice that it is their kindness to strangers, their care for the graves of the dead and the pretended holiness of their lives that have done most to increase atheism [i.e. Christianity]? I believe that we ought really and truly to practise every one of these virtues. And it is not enough for you alone to practise them, but so must all the priests in Galatia, without exception . . . In the second place admonish them that no priest may enter a theatre or drink in a tavern or control any craft or trade that is base and not respectable . . .'

Arsacius was to set up hostels on the Christian model:

'In every city establish frequent hostels in order that strangers may profit by our generosity; I do not mean for our own people only, but for others also who are in need of money . . . For it is disgraceful that, when no Jew ever has to beg and the impious Galileans [Christians] support both their own poor and ours as well, all men see that our people lack aid from us . . .'

Although Julian restored pagan worship all over the Empire, and the special privileges enjoyed by Christian clergy were taken away, there was no open persecution of Christians. In fact, toleration was decreed for all religions. Pagans were, of course, particularly favoured in the civil service, and imperial justice was not always even-handed when settling the violent disputes that arose in some cities over the religious changes.

But Julian raised the strongest protest by prohibiting Christians from teaching literature in the schools. He knew that upper-class Christians would continue to send their children to the ordinary schools, which prepared them for public life, even if their teachers were pagan; they would thus be exposed to pagan propaganda. A curious solution to the dilemma was found by two Christian professors. They attempted to make the Scriptures a suitable vehicle for the preferred classical education by translating the Old Testament into epic and tragedy and the New Testament into Platonic dialogue; but Julian died in 363 before it could be tried.

'Be of good courage; it is but a cloud which will quickly pass away', Athanasius told his weeping congregation on hearing that Julian had ordered him into exile. Athanasius was right, for the zeal had gone out of paganism—at least Julian's kind of paganism. Its failure was apparent even before Julian's death.

Christian emperors

Jovian, the emperor who followed Julian in 363, was a Christian. He proclaimed toleration, as did Valentinian 1 (364–75), who soon succeeded him. Ammianus, a pagan historian, praised Valentinian because: 'he kept a middle course between the different sects of religion; and never troubled anyone, nor issued any orders in favour of one kind of worship or another . . .' Valentinian extended toleration to Arians and most other heretics, though he himself was of the Nicene faith.

Valens (364–78), the younger brother of Valentinian, chosen by him to rule the East, was less tolerant. He did not attack paganism, but felt obliged to proceed against the Nicene party, and exiled some bishops. Valens, however, was killed at the battle of Adrianople in 378 and subsequent emperors, in the East as in the West, were orthodox.

A dispute over the election of the bishop of Rome in the

Magnus Maximus (383–88), the emperor who executed Priscillian for heresy.

reign of Valentinian scandalized the pagan Ammianus. A bloody battle between the followers of Damasus and Ursinus left, at the end of a day's strife, one hundred and thirty-seven dead in the basilica of Sicininus which, Ammianus noted, 'is a Christian church'. The historian concluded that the Roman bishopric had become a prize worth fighting for, and described the luxury of the Roman clergy: 'enriched by offerings from women, riding in carriages, dressing splendidly, and feasting luxuriously, so that their entertainments surpass even royal banquets'. Not all lived luxuriously however. Many lived frugal, even austere lives, as did bishops Ambrose and Augustine, and recommended the same simple life to their congregations.

Gratian (375–83) succeeded his father, Valentinian, in the West, and became ruler of the East as well on the death of Valens. Wisely recognizing that he could not govern the whole Empire alone, he chose an experienced soldier, Theodosius, to rule the East. Gratian was a talented, pious and cultured young man who received a classical, but Christian, education from the poet Ausonius. He was also an accomplished sportsman, who could have 'excelled in every sphere if he had put his mind to the art of government, for which he was unsuited by temperament and training'. Gratian's inability to win the loyalty of the armies led to his death during the rebellion of a Spanish officer, Magnus Maximus (383).

The end of pagan religion

The reigns of Gratian and of Theodosius I (379–95) finally decided the fate of paganism. Both Gratian and Theodosius strongly supported the orthodox faith. But the imperial policy of outlawing heresy and pagan religion during these years was partly the work of the great bishop Ambrose who was elected to the see of Milan in 374.

When Auxentius, the Arian bishop of Milan, died in 373, the new governor, Ambrose, was afraid that the Catholic–Arian controversy would break into violence. When the people of Milan poured into the cathedral to elect their bishop, Ambrose spoke a few words to calm the crowd. Suddenly a voice was heard (a child's voice, it is said), 'Ambrose, bishop!' The congregation took up the cry and Ambrose found himself elected bishop, much to his surprise and against his will, for he was unbaptized and had had no church training. He tried to flee and hide,

A HYMN OF AMBROSE

Maker of all things, God most high,
Great ruler of the starry sky,
Who, robing day with beauteous light,
Hast clothed in soft repose the night,

That sleep may wearied limbs restore,
And fit for toil and use once more,
May gently soothe the careworn breast,
And lull our anxious griefs to rest.

We thank thee for the day that's gone;
We pray thee for the night come on;
O help us sinners as we raise
To thee our votive hymn of praise.

From every carnal passion free
O may our hearts repose in thee!
Nor envious fiend, with harmful snare,
Our rest with sinful terrors share.

Christ with the Father ever one,
Spirit! the Father and the Son,
God over all, the mighty sway,
Shield us, great Trinity, we pray.

Translated by John D. Chambers, 1864

but eventually was persuaded that this was the will of God.

Ambrose became bishop at the age of thirty-four and held the position for twenty-three years. He was particularly influential because Milan, rather than Rome, was at the time the Emperor's residence in the West. The Western Emperors Gratian and Valentinian II (383–92), came under his direct influence, as did Theodosius when in the West during some of the most critical years of his reign.

Gratian at first tolerated other religions as well as orthodox Christianity. He soon changed his mind under Ambrose's influence and began to suppress pagans and heretics. He once again removed the altar of Victory from the Senate House in Rome (Julian had restored it), confiscated the revenues of the Vestal Virgins and other Roman priesthoods, and refused the title of *Pontifex Maximus* (High Priest), which previous Christian emperors had taken.

Theodosius, in 381 and 385, prohibited sacrifices for divination, which seems to have stopped all sacrifice. Petitions to destroy individual temples, or convert them into Christian churches, were received and many were destroyed. Theodosius ordered all the temples in Alexandria to be demolished following pagan-

AMBROSE OF MILAN

Michael A. Smith

In 374, after the death of the Arian bishop of Milan, Ambrose was elected bishop by popular acclaim even though at that time he was not even baptized. Ambrose (339–97) came from a noble Roman family and received a classical education. He became a provincial governor in northern Italy residing at Milan.

He read widely, especially the Greek theologians, and became famous both as a preacher and as a church administrator and politician. He was the leading spokesman against the petition of the pagan Symmachus in 384 to have the altar of the goddess Victory restored to the Senate House in Rome; his influence ensured that the altar was not restored.

Ambrose took a strong stand against Arianism, and completed its overthrow in the West. He clashed with the Empress-mother Justina, mother of Emperor Valentinian II, and in 385 organized a sit-in when she tried to take over one of the churches of Milan for Arian worship. This made her give up the idea.

Later Ambrose became a close adviser of the Emperor Theodosius, when he had his court at Milan. He used his position to prevent the Emperor from punishing rioting monks who had burned down a synagogue at Callinicum, but he also forced the Emperor to make a form of public confession after he had sanctioned a massacre of civilians at Thessalonica. Ambrose was the first church leader to use his office successfully to coerce civil rulers.

Ambrose did much to encourage early monasticism in the West; he had considerable influence on Augustine, and baptized him at Milan in 387. He was the first to introduce community hymn-singing in the church, during the sit-in against Justina, and at least four Latin hymns are correctly credited to him. His writings mainly concern matters of Christian practice.

> *"Nothing can be found in this world more exalted than priests or more sublime than bishops."*
>
> AMBROSE

Christian unrest. It is reported that when the first blow at the great bronze statue of the god Serapis in the famous Serapeum produced only a swarm of rats, and divine retribution failed to follow the destruction of the temple, many pagans became believers.

Finally, in 391, Theodosius prohibited all sacrifices and closed all temples. The next year private pagan worship was forbidden too. Paganism had one last chance in the West during the brief reign of the usurper Eugenius. His chief supporters were zealous pagans who restored the ancient worship in Rome, but the final triumph of Theodosius in 394 put an end to that.

Theodosius was the last great absolute ruler of both parts of the Empire. He is pictured enthroned in power, on an ornamental silver shield. It is interesting that his pose is similar to that of the 'enthroned Christ' of later Orthodox art.

Nevertheless, the laws against paganism were not rigidly enforced, and pagan worship continued openly in some places for several generations—and secretly for much longer. In much of the Empire the countryside remained pagan for several centuries. Pagan *belief* was not prohibited, and pagans still managed for some time to attain high positions in the Empire.

Theodosius began to act against heretics early in his reign. In 380 he ordered all his subjects to subscribe to the faith brought by Peter to Rome and now held by Pope Damasus and by Peter, bishop of Alexandria. The next year he summoned the Council of Constantinople which drew up a definition of faith on the Nicene model. But Arianism had by now lost its vitality, except among the Gothic tribes, still mostly outside the Empire, and he met little opposition.

Priscillian executed for heresy

In Gratian's reign began the strange and sad case of Priscillian. The usurper, Magnus Maximus, became the first Christian emperor to inflict the death penalty on a heretic. These events foreshadow the later medieval practice of handing over heretics condemned by the church for execution by the state.

Priscillian was the Spanish leader of a strict Christian ascetic movement, and was suspected of heretical beliefs, and immoral practices. He was first accused by prominent Spanish church leaders but escaped outright condemnation. Later his case was referred to Maximus, who was biassed against Priscillian and his followers. Finally, Priscillian and six of his associates were condemned and executed at Trier, in spite of the personal appeal of the saintly bishop, Martin of Tours. Martin also objected to the case being tried before secular rulers. Although Priscillian and his followers were ultimately condemned for the civil crime of sorcery, no one doubted that their real offence was Priscillian's unusual beliefs and religious practices. He was perhaps more an eccentric than a heretic—although he was involved in magic and the occult.

To the credit of the church, the executions brought a strong reaction. Martin reappeared at Trier to denounce the Emperor Maximus; Ambrose and Pope Siricius refused to have fellowship with Priscillian's accusers. Finally in 388 the anti-Priscillian bishops were deposed and their party destroyed. Though a few fanatical church leaders were willing to execute people for heresy and use the state as the church's executioner most drew back from that severe view.

What has the Emperor to do with the church?

Two encounters between Ambrose and the Emperor Theodosius show a dramatic increase in the power of the church since the time of Constantius. The first occurred in 388 after rioting in the town of Callinicum on the River Euphrates. The Christians had been led on by the bishop to rob and burn a Jewish synagogue. Theodosius ordered the stolen property to be restored and the synagogue rebuilt at the bishop's own expense; just compensation, it appears. But Ambrose sent Theodosius a letter insisting that to make a Christian bishop rebuild a place of worship for the Jews, the enemies of Christ, amounted to apostasy. 'The maintenance of civil law is secondary to religious interests,' wrote Ambrose. When Theodosius ignored Ambrose's letter, the bishop felt obliged to preach on the subject in the presence of the Emperor. Theodosius, partly because he was weak in the West, finally had to give in and withdraw his order.

The second encounter, in the summer of 390, shows Ambrose in a better light. The people of Thessalonica had murdered the military commander of the city because he had refused to release a favourite charioteer. Theodosius avenged his death by a massacre of the inhabitants, despite Ambrose's protest. The Emperor repented, but too late; 7,000 or more citizens, both guilty and innocent, were slaughtered in the theatre. Ambrose sent a secret letter excommunicating the Emperor until he did public penance. Theodosius was again obliged to give way, and publicly in the church asked forgiveness for his sin.

Ambrose's answer to the question. 'What has the Emperor to do with the church?' was that the Emperor was within the church, not above it. But this did not mark the end of imperial interference in the church's affairs. The Emperor in Constantinople kept control of the Eastern church and occasionally interfered in the West, particularly in the sixth century after Justinian reconquered Italy.

By the late fifth century the bishop of Rome, Gelasius I, had developed the view that the Emperor was directly subject to the head of the church, the bishop of Rome (or pope), and should rule the Empire for the good of God's people. This exalted idea could not be applied in the late Empire because of its political weakness, but was picked up in the Middle Ages. Ambrose showed how it might work in practice.

Modern Thessaloniki is the second largest city of Greece. The great Roman West-East highway, the Egnatian Way, passed under the Arch of Galerius, pictured here.

Worship and the Christian year

Michael A. Smith

When Christianity became a tolerated religion in the time of Constantine, worship and festivals had not yet been rigidly formalized. The main festivals of the Christian year were Easter (the *Pascha*) and Pentecost. Easter was still at this time only a one-day festival, celebrating together the death, resurrection and exaltation of Christ on the Sunday following 14 Nisan in the Jewish calendar. It ushered in a period of rejoicing over the resurrection of Christ which lasted for the seven weeks until Pentecost. (The whole period was often known as Pentecost.) The weeks immediately before Easter Sunday were used for preparing candidates for baptism. In addition, a number of days were probably kept as the anniversaries of local martyrdoms.

Christian worship in this period was almost entirely in Greek, although in a few places local languages such as Syriac, Coptic, or Latin were probably beginning to be used. In general, services in this period were extempore, the local bishop being free to pray or preach as the Spirit led, within certain fairly broad guidelines. There were a few fixed formulas in use, including the dialogue beginning 'Lift up your hearts' (*Sursum corda*), the hymn beginning 'Holy, holy, holy' (*Sanctus*) based on Isaiah 6, and the 'Words of Institution', commemorating the Last Supper, at the communion service. The doxologies at the end of prayers, the creed and the form of words at baptism were also of a set pattern, although the words of the creed could vary slightly from one church to another.

Sunday a holiday

The toleration of Christianity under Constantine produced a few immediate changes. Constantine ordered that Sunday was to be a public holiday similar to other Roman holidays. This made possible wider development in worship, and larger congregations in the churches. Sunday services became bigger occasions and worship imported some practices from court ceremonial, such as the use of incense, the carrying of candles as a mark of honour, and curtaining around the altar used at the eucharist. But Constantine's act of toleration also started several trends which only became really noticeable later. The growth of formality, of ceremonial and of superstition took place only gradually. New festivals were introduced slowly. Churches still had to draw people in. In the fourth century this was often done by the great pulpit-orators, who were cheered (or occasionally booed) by intensely-involved congregations.

Greater leisure meant that Christian festivals tended to multiply. Constantine's mother Helena made a pilgrimage to the Holy Land (326–27) which made a great impression. Pilgrimages to Bible lands now became quite common. A short pamphlet appeared in 333 giving a route from Bordeaux to Jerusalem. Great efforts were devoted to finding the various biblical sites, erecting churches on them (such as the Church of the Holy Sepulchre) and celebrating there the events connected with them. The church at Jerusalem took the lead in this, and was

---

Sunday observance

"*All judges, city-people and craftsmen shall rest on the venerable day of the Sun. But countrymen may without hindrance attend to agriculture, since it often happens that this is the most suitable day for sowing grain or planting vines, so that the opportunity afforded by divine providence may not be lost, for the right season is short. 7 March 321.*"

CONSTANTINE'S Edict (Cod. Justinianus III xii 3)

THE APOSTLES' CREED

I believe in God almighty [the Father almighty]
And in Christ Jesus, his only Son, our Lord
Who was born of the Holy Spirit and the Virgin Mary
Who was crucified under Pontius Pilate and was buried
And the third day rose from the dead
Who ascended into heaven
And sits on the right hand of the Father
Whence he comes to judge the living and the dead.
And in the Holy Ghost
The holy church
The remission of sins
The resurrection of the flesh
The life everlasting.

'The Old Roman Creed'

Constantine gave permission for archaeological excavations in Jerusalem in an attempt to discover the tomb of the Christ. The church of the Holy Sepulchre was built in the fourth century as a witness to the resurrection, on the site they uncovered.

rapidly followed by others. In this way the idea of the Christian year as a re-enactment of the life of Jesus became more and more central.

Easter

It was probably early in the fourth century that Easter became expanded into a week-long festival The marking of Christ's death was separated from the Easter Sunday

EGERIA'S PILGRIMAGE TO THE HOLY PLACES

"Next we came, in the name of Christ our God, to Edessa. When we arrived there we immediately went to the church and memorial chapel of the holy Thomas. And when we had offered up our prayers there in the customary way, and had done all the usual things at the holy places, we read something there about the saintly Thomas. Now the church there is very large, very beautiful, and built in a new style; it is a worthy home of God.

And since there were many things I wished to see, I had to stay there for three days. I saw in the city several commemorative chapels and also holy monks, some of whom live near the chapels and others in hermitages further from the city, in more isolated places. The bishop of the city, a truly pious man, a monk and confessor, received me warmly and said: 'Since I see, my daughter, that from a spirit of religion you have gone to such great efforts to journey here from distant places, we shall, if you desire it, show you all the places here which Christians like to see.' Then I thanked God first of all and afterwards him, and eagerly urged him to carry out his promise. He brought me first to the palace of King Agbar . . ."

Travels of Egeria 19

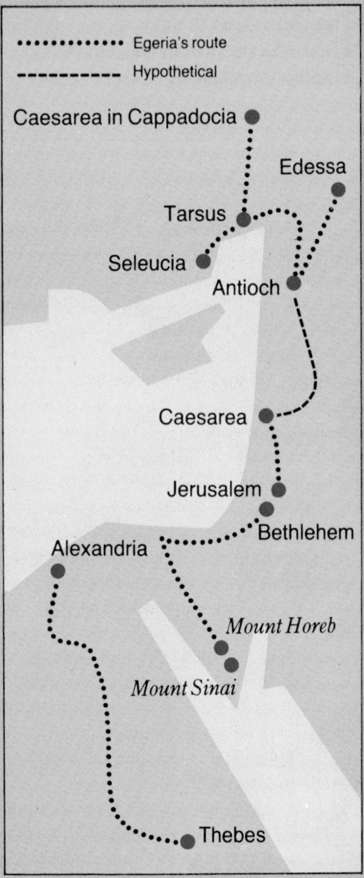

A Palm Sunday procession in modern Jerusalem.

resurrection festivities. Good Friday, Maundy Thursday and Palm Sunday were all celebrated by the early part of the fourth century. Easter had often been spent by baptismal candidates fasting on a vigil and this was now adopted generally by the church. At the same time, the week after Easter was made the special period when newly-baptized Christians received teaching about baptism and the eucharist.

The period for preparing candidates for baptism before Easter became formalized into the forty days of Lent. Several sets of baptismal instruction addresses survive, usually consisting of an extended explanation of the creed which the candidates had to memorize. At the beginning of Lent people who wanted to be baptized gave in their names at church and their moral fitness for baptism was examined. Lent as a period of austerity and fasting only developed in the Middle Ages.

The first mention of Christmas as a festival of the church on 25 December, refers to AD 336. It comes in the *Philocalian Catalogue* (354), a civil and religious calendar compiled at Rome. In the East, 6 January, known as Epiphany, was favoured as the anniversary of Christ's birth and baptism. The Western date was introduced into the East by John Chrysostom near the end of the fourth century. Subsequently the birth of Christ was celebrated by both East and West on 25 December. Meanwhile Epiphany had come from the East to the West, where it commemorated the revealing of Jesus to the Gentiles—originally to the Wise Men.

Although there was no great increase in the number of festivals of martyrs in the fourth century, they did receive greater attention. Private ceremonies were held in the cemeteries, although they were often condemned because of disreputable behaviour. Meanwhile many of the martyrs' tombs were decorated. For instance, Bishop Damasus had many fine inscriptions set up in the catacombs in Rome. New discoveries of supposed relics of martyrs were celebrated with great joy, as at the finding of the 'relics' of Gervasius and Protasius at Milan in 386. A few churches at this time were formally dedicated, for example the great new church at Antioch in 341. The Roman festival of the throne of Peter *(Cathedra Petri)*, first mentioned in the *Philocalian Catalogue,* is probably the earliest celebration of the patron saint of a particular church.

Written liturgies

With Christian worship evolving into public ceremonial, there came a move towards fixed, written forms of service. During the fourth century this change was fairly slow. The catecheses given at Jerusalem by Bishop Cyril (348–86) and Bishop John (386–417) include fixed wording but also opportunity for extempore prayer. Ambrose of Milan quotes several long passages from the great eucharistic prayer in his work on the sacraments written 390–91.

At the same time, languages other than Greek were being used in worship. Egeria, a pilgrim to Jerusalem in the late fourth or early fifth century, mentions services there being conducted in Greek, Latin and Syriac, and preaching to baptismal candidates in all three languages. Both Coptic and Greek were used for worship in Egypt. Although there was a gradual move towards fixed forms in worship, language and regional differences ensured considerable variations from one church to another. The differences could even involve additional ceremonies. The church at Milan, for example, practised ceremonial foot-washing at baptism (based on John 13) though this was unknown at Rome. Prominent churches such as Rome used their power to try to enforce some kind of uniformity, but local variations continued for a long time.

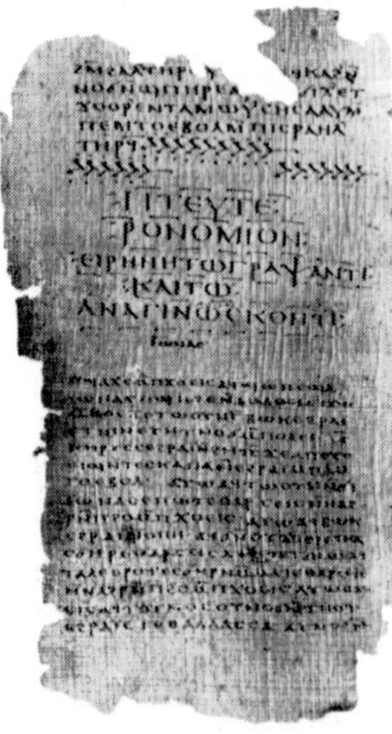

By the fourth century, local dialects and languages were increasingly used in Christian worship and instruction. This fourth-century papyrus of part of Deuteronomy 34 is in Sahidic dialect Coptic.

During the fifth and sixth centuries the trends begun in the fourth century continued. However, East and West now diverged more sharply. In the East the ritual tended to become uniform, leaving no room for variation. This was perhaps due to the greater political stability there which allowed uniformity to be more easily enforced. But fixed forms of worship were also the rule in churches disowned by the state-church, such as the Nestorians and the Monophysite Coptic church. Only in the Syrian Jacobite church did the practice of composing eucharistic prayers, tried by almost every great churchman, live on. But even here the liturgy of James was pre-eminent. At least eight local rites are known from the sixth century, but these gradually gave way to the liturgies of Chrysostom and Basil.

The Christian year

In the West the liturgy varied according to the calendar. The Roman rite soon included a fixed eucharistic prayer, probably by the mid-fifth century. Leo the Great is traditionally credited with making a minor alteration to it. A wide selection of prayers was available in the sixth-century compilation from Verona in Italy known as the *Leonine Sacramentary;* however, the central prayer is fixed in form.

A similar arrangement was to be found in other rites in the West; for example, the Mozarabic in Spain, the Gallican rites of France, the Celtic rites and some early rites in north Italy. It was possible to vary all but their basic form (for instance, in the mass only the opening preface, the *Sanctus* and the Words of Institution could not be varied), but written forms were provided for different festivals. No two mass-books were identical, but all provided fixed written prayers, although in an emergency an eloquent bishop such as Sidonius Apollinaris might still extemporize a whole service.

The Roman rite gradually spread throughout the West, and was already beginning to displace various local rites when it was made official by Charlemagne in the late eighth century.

By the year 600 many other festivals had been added to the Christian calendar, several going back to the fourth century. The Christmas period acquired a number of saints' days—St Stephen, and St James nd St John—as well as Holy Innocents' Day, to commemorate the babies massacred at Bethlehem, nd the Circumcision of Jesus. The entire week after Easter vas specially observed and the Ascension of Jesus was celebrated s well as Pentecost. In the veek before Easter, Maundy Thursday was celebrated as the ay when the Eucharist was instituted. Saints' days became more ommon, and included not only postles, but also the Virgin Mary nd various local saints such as Martin, Germanus, Cyprian and Leudegarius. Celtic churches now egan to celebrate All Saints' Day, nd to make long prayers to the aints. By 600, what became the lassical pattern of the Christian ear had been established in all but few details.

Liturgical books

1 the West, Latin had replaced Greek as the language of worship y the mid-fourth century. Greek nd Latin prayers were both used t Rome until about 350. Latin emained alive after the fall of the Western Empire because most of ne barbarian languages had not een reduced to written form.

As the Christian year evolved in e West service books were comled for use by the clergy. They cluded 'sacramentaries', which ontained all the forms of services eeded in a church during the year, nd 'lectionaries', with the set ible readings for the various days the year. There were also books sermons (homiliaries) for the se of clergy who were not well nough educated to write their wn.

New ceremonies were gradually dded to the church services from e fifth century onwards, while ome older ceremonies fell out of se. Believer's baptism declined nd the baptism of infants became normal. Because infant mortality rates were high, baptism usually took place early in life, becoming a private ceremony, often not even performed in a church building. At the same time, the examples of Jerusalem and the growing monastic communities encouraged daily services of prayers and Bible readings. Ordination, at one time a ritual merely tacked on to the communion, had grown into an important distinct ceremony. Laying-on-of-hands was accompanied by the giving of articles to symbolize the job—a Gospel-book for the deacon, a chalice for the priests. In the West, bishops were becoming landed magnates as well as the chief clerics of the church.

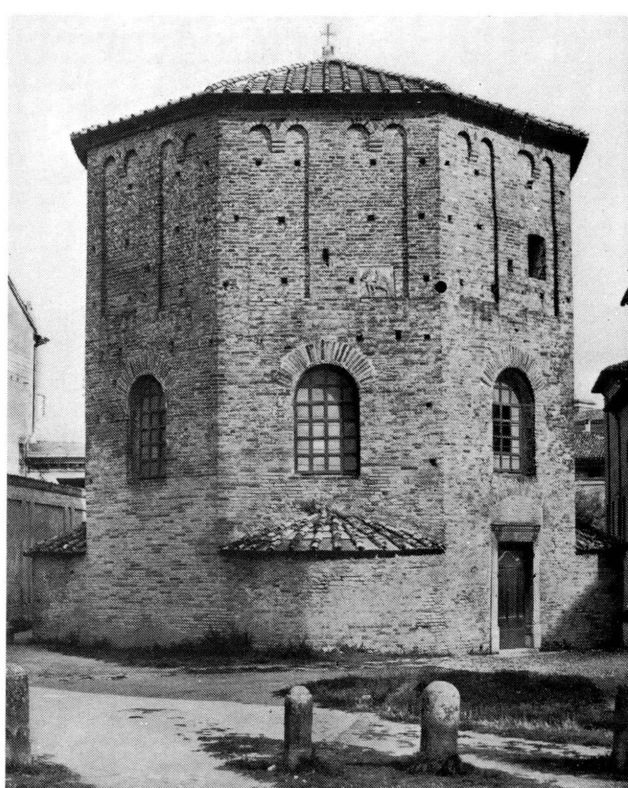

The eight-sided baptistery at Ravenna (Italy) was built about 450. It is very richly decorated inside, where baptism took place.

Building for worship

Henry R. Sefton

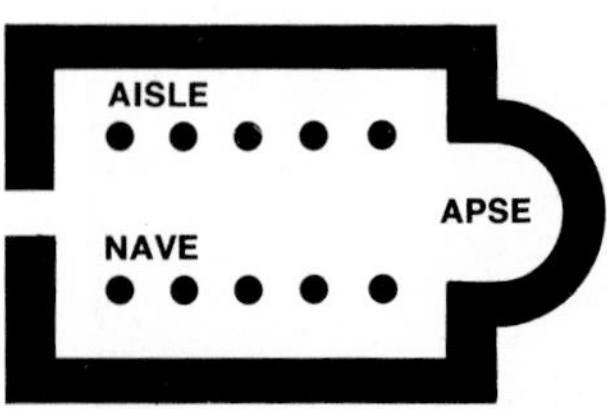

For centuries, Christians everywhere built churches to this plan, known as a basilica.

The plan of a basilica, with its semi-circular apse, can be clearly seen in this picture of the famous memorial church of Cyprian at Carthage. Augustine most probably preached here.

Constantine's pronouncement of freedom of worship for all in the 'Edict' of Milan (313) was soon reflected in the buildings used for Christian worship. The Emperor himself built a new church in Rome which symbolized the dawn of a new era. This Church of St John Lateran was a basilica, and in all the main centres of the Empire this style of church seems rapidly to have replaced the house-church.

The basilica was a rectangular hall with a semi-circular niche or 'apse' opening off one of the shorter sides. Inside, it was divided by two, and sometimes four, rows of columns into a wider central space and two or four parallel long narrow spaces. The roof covering the wider central space was higher than the roofs over the side sections. The outer walls, including that of the apse, were blank, and the only daylight came through the doorways or windows pierced in the walls of the central space above the columns. These are the ancestors of the 'clear-storey' (or clerestory), nave and side-aisles long associated with churches.

The appearance of this new and fully-developed plan for church buildings has led to the suggestion that Constantine imposed it on the church and commanded that it should be followed everywhere. It seems more likely that the plan was gradually adopted by the builders of churches simply because it was the most suitable available, and that these developments began before the time of Constantine.

The basilica plan was followed because it provided what the church needed in its altered circumstances. Most obviously it provided the space needed for

he much larger congregations vhich now gathered for worship. The house-church had usually rovided enough room for the ersecuted Christians. Now that Christianity was respectable and fficially recognized the numbers of worshippers increased rapidly nd bigger accommodation was eeded. Pagan temples were not lesigned to house a worshipping ssembly, whereas various forms f basilica were commonly built to ccommodate crowds attending a aw court, market or any kind of ssembly.

Occasionally pagan temples were taken over and adapted by the Christians for their own worship, but this was done only in smaller or less wealthy communities. Such adaptation has been described as 'turning the temple inside out'. The space between the pillars was filled up with walls, the original inner walls of the temple were pierced to give the impression of two rows of pillars, and an apse was added. In other words, the temple was made as similar to a basilica as possible.

Worship in the house-church

Pictured here is the apse of the fifth-century church of Santa Maria delle Grazie, Grado (Italy). The clergy used to sit on the circular bench; the central chair was reserved for the bishop.

had been of an intimate kind in which all present had taken an active part. But by the beginning of the fourth century the distinction between clergy and lay people was becoming more prominent. About this time the liturgy changed from being 'a corporate action of the whole church' into 'a service said by the clergy to which the laity listened'. This may have influenced the choice of the basilica plan for the new churches.

Certainly the basilica pattern made it easier for the distinction between clergy and lay people to harden. The apse was reserved for the clergy, and those not actively taking part in the service sat on a bench against the wall. A throne was set up in the centre for the bishop, and this stately chair reflected his position as a trusted imperial servant as much as a pastor of the flock. The table for the Lord's Supper became a permanent altar at the front of the apse. The central space, or nave, was occupied by the choir, who sang the service, and by the lower ranks of clergy. The ordinary worshippers tended to be confined to the side aisles—men on one side and women on the other. Those under instruction (the catechumens) or under discipline (the penitents) were restricted to the porch, at the rear of the nave.

The basilica had no direct lighting, for the windows were directly under the roof of the nave in the 'clear-storey'. This was not regarded as a disadvantage, for it enhanced the light of the candles and lamps near the altar and heightened the sense of mystery. Churches were normally orientated towards the west so that the rays of the rising sun fell on the face of the clergyman celebrating

The clear-storey windows of a basilica are plainly visible in this picture of the fourth-century cathedral of Aquileia in Veneto, Italy.

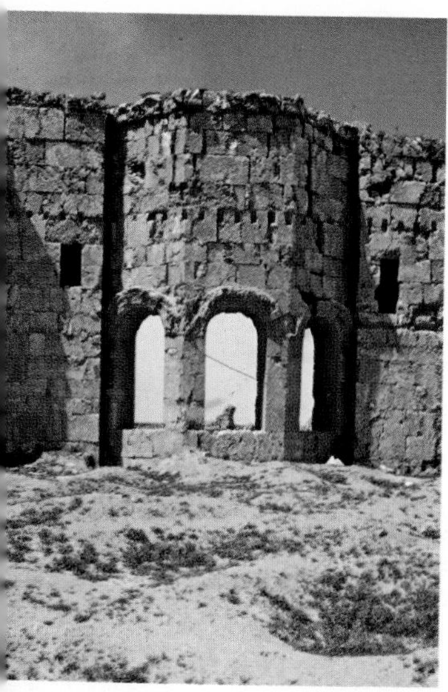

he eucharist as he stood behind he altar facing the congregation.

Constantine's Church of St John ateran in Rome was built on a site vithout any special associations, ut the churches of St Peter and of t Paul were built by Constantine n the traditional sites of the postles' martyrdom or burial. In he Holy Land, churches were built n sites associated with particular vents in the life of Christ. This ffected the plan of the church, or attention had to be drawn o the sacred spot which was ne reason for the church being uilt there. Thus in the church f the Nativity at Bethlehem the raditional birthplace is covered y an eight-sided building which is nked to a rectangular basilica. In t Peter's the place of martyrdom as marked by a structure at the ont of the apse and given further rominence by the addition of ansepts (cross-aisles) on either de of the basilica. The altar, also t the edge of the apse, often had ints' relics placed under it.

But in the East it was thought nportant to keep the altar distinct om the relicts of the saint, which ere often housed in a separate building. These chapels were constructed with their focal point in the centre, and often featured a dome. When these buildings were designed for congregational use, the altar was not placed in the centre over the tomb but in an apse added to the original plan.

The tradition of the buildings built for martyrs (*martyria*) was strong enough for their centralized plan to influence church architecture. In the Holy Land, Syria and Mesopotamia centralized churches became the rule; and since such churches required a dome, architects developed their skills until they succeeded in constructing a cupola over a square. In this way the basilica and centralized styles of construction could be combined, making possible the architectural miracle of St Sophia, Constantinople, the supreme example of the domed basilica. St Sophia was built by the command of the Emperor Justinian and completed in 537. The great central dome was damaged by an earthquake twenty-one years later but was repaired by 563, since when it has remained to deter any attempts at imitation.

The great church of St Sergius, built on the traditional site of his martyrdom at R'safah (Syria)

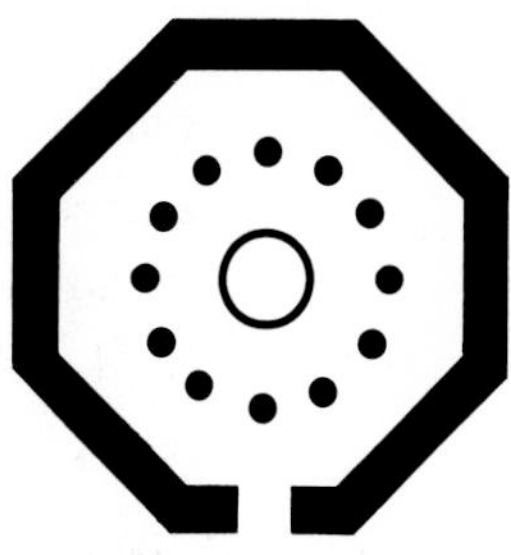

A sanctuary was often built over the tomb of a martyr. It could be square or circular, to emphasize the actual spot where the saint or martyr was buried.

Church builders eventually worked out a method of combining the basilica plan and the dome. St Sophia, in Istanbul, has never been surpassed as an example of this achievement.

ACCEPTANCE AND CONQUEST

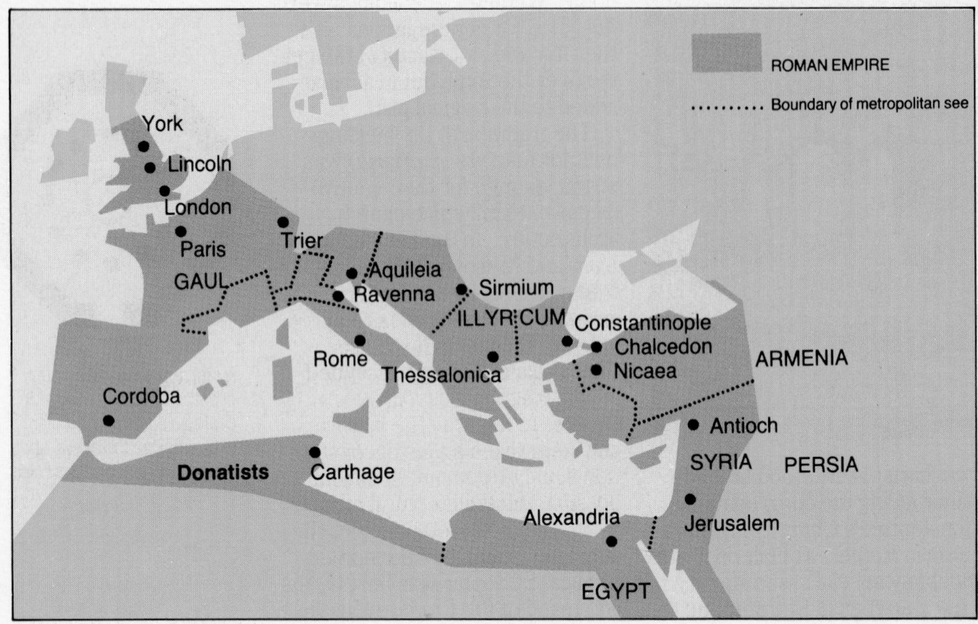

The church in the fourth century

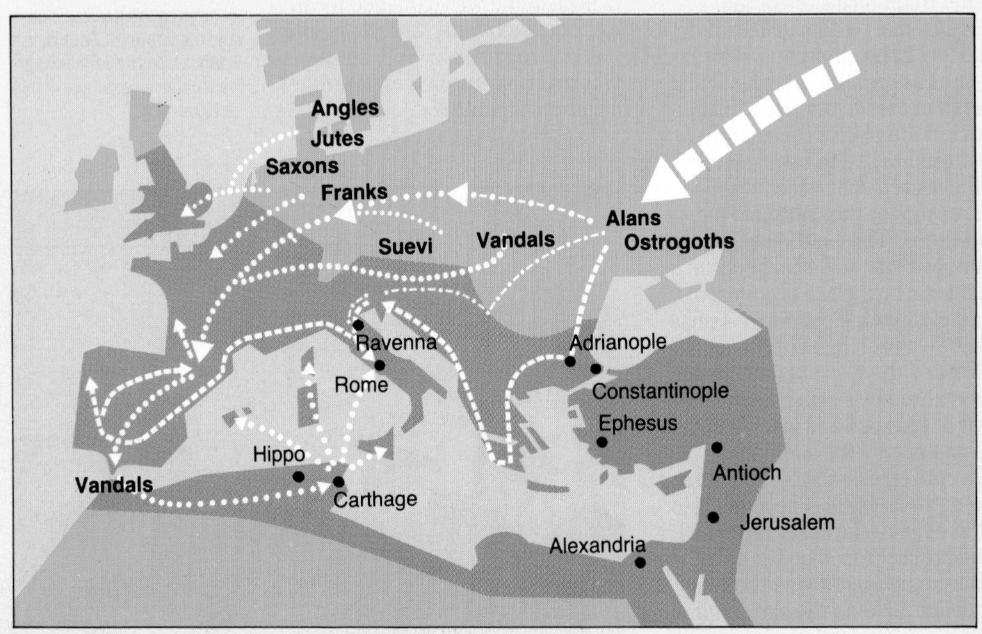

The barbarian invasions of the fourth and fifth centuries

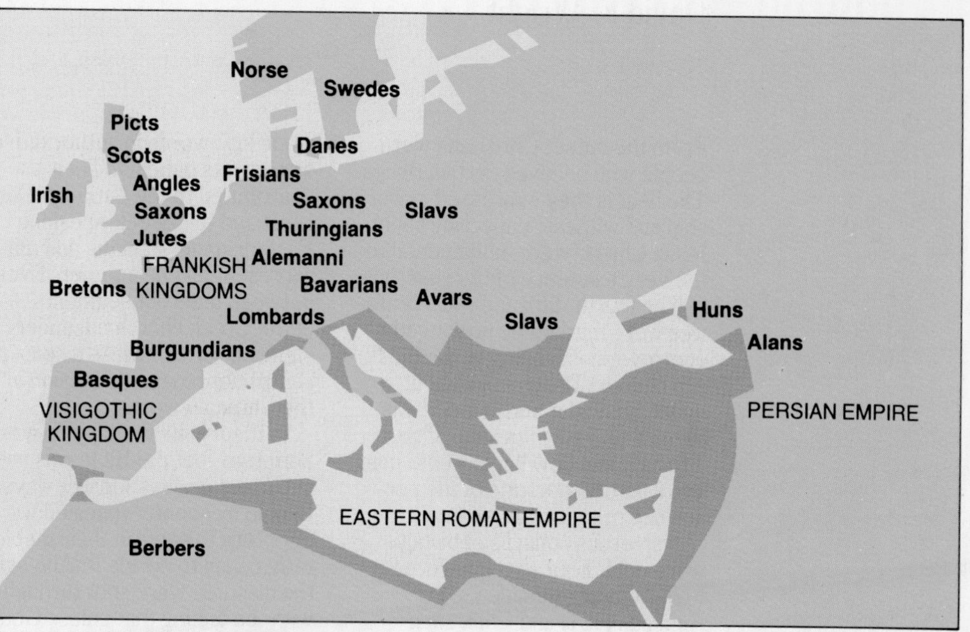

The barbarian kingdoms about 600

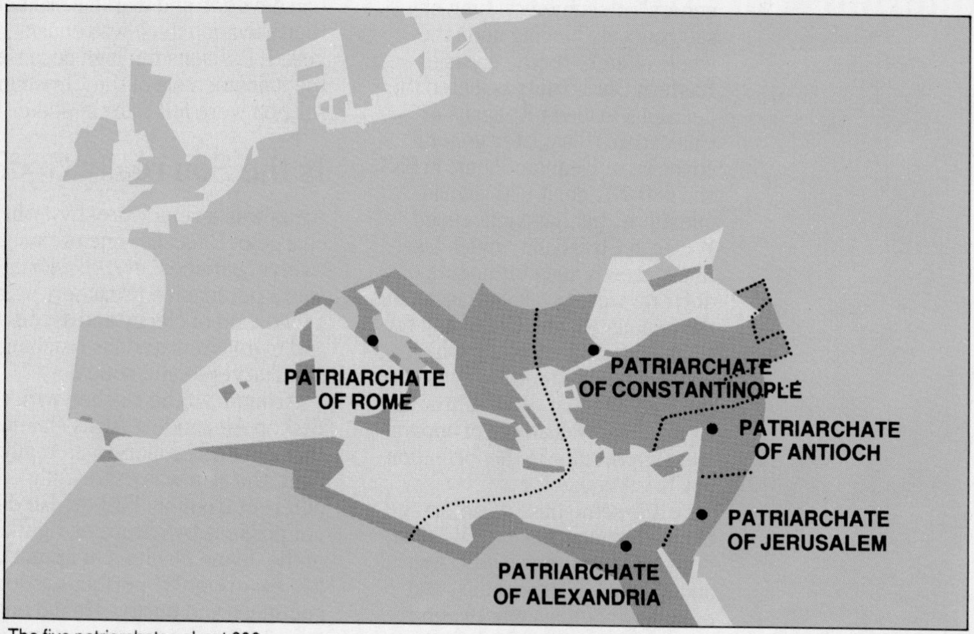

PATRIARCHATE OF ROME

PATRIARCHATE OF CONSTANTINOPLE

PATRIARCHATE OF ANTIOCH

PATRIARCHATE OF JERUSALEM

PATRIARCHATE OF ALEXANDRIA

The five patriarchates about 600

COUNCILS AND CREEDS

David F. Wright

From the outset Christians were people who believed certain things. The beliefs they expressed in worship and witness, especially about Jesus Christ, were fundamental to the very existence of the church.

The fourth, fifth and sixth centuries were marked by prolonged controversies, chiefly in the Eastern church. These were about how Christ, the Son of God, was himself God (the doctrine of the Trinity), and how he was both man and God (the doctrine of the person of Christ, or Christology).

Numerous councils of bishops were held. Four of them, Nicaea (325), Constantinople (381), Ephesus (431) and Chalcedon (451), came to be accepted as general or ecumenical (universal) councils, binding upon the whole church. (Some areas of Eastern Christianity rejected the decisions made at Ephesus or Chalcedon.) Two later general councils, at Constantinople in 553 and 680–81, dealt with similar questions, but have influenced Western Christianity much less. Many creeds and statements of doctrine were produced, including the famous Nicene Creed and the Chalcedonian Definition, which became touch-stones of orthodoxy throughout most of the Christian world. This was an era of unparalleled importance in the formation of Christian theology.

At the same time it was an age of interference and even domination by the emperors, of colourful and abrasive personalities, and of bitter antagonism between leading bishoprics. Technical terms without biblical origins were made key-words in authoritative statements of belief. Their use contributed to the Latin-speaking West and the Greek-speaking East misunderstanding and misrepresenting one another. Even between different segments of the Greek church misunderstandings arose; these disputes contributed to major division in the Christian world.

In theory the first appeal was to Scripture, but the Bible was used in curious or questionable ways. People frequently appealed to Scripture to confirm their theology rather than to decide it. Above all, the disputes were shot through with the feeling that unless God and Christ were truly what Christian devotion and worship claimed, then salvation itself was endangered. Passions ran high because the fundamentals of the Christian religion were felt to be at stake.

Is the Son really God?

Arius was a senior presbyter in charge of Baucalis, one of the twelve 'parishes' of Alexandria. He was a persuasive preacher, with a following of clergy and ascetics, and even circulated his teaching in popular verse and songs.

Around 318 he clashed with Bishop Alexander. Arius claimed that the Father alone was really God; the Son was essentially different from his Father. He did not possess by nature or right any of the divine qualities of immortality, sovereignty, perfect wisdom, goodness and purity. He did not exist before he was begotten by the Father. The Father produced him as a creature. Yet as the creator of the rest of creation, the Son existed 'apart from time before all things'. Nevertheless, he did not share in the being of God the Father and did not know him perfectly.

As if to salvage something from the wreckage, Arius allowed that the Son was called 'God' by grace and favour, and was sinless and unchangeable in practice, if not by nature. Moreover, the Son received enough wisdom and light from the Father to enable him to reveal the Father to mankind.

Nevertheless, by dividing off the Son from God the Father, Arius undermined Christ's standing as God's revelation, and the redeemer of mankind.

We are not certain of Arius' precise teaching and motives. It may be that he chiefly wanted to explain the incarnation without difficulties. He undoubtedly believed that the *Logos,* or Son, took the place of the human soul in the earthly Christ. The *Logos* was united only with a human body, not with a full human nature. It was much easier to understand how the *Logos* could be united with human flesh when he was lowered to the status of a perfect creature or honorary god.

Arius' ideas parallel and contrast with Origen's teaching; they owe much to secular Greek concepts of God. He had a sharply logical mind and appealed to biblical texts which apparently backed up his arguments—for example, John 17:3 ('the only true God'), 1 Timothy 6:16 ('alone possesses immortality'), Colossians 1:15 ('first-born of all creation') and Proverbs 8:22 (in the *Septuagint,* 'the Lord created me at the beginning of his work').

A council at Alexandria of Egyptian and Libyan bishops soon excommunicated Arius and a dozen other clergy, including two bishops, but the affair was not so easily settled. Arius sought the backing of former fellow-pupils of Lucian of Antioch, an influential teacher martyred a few years earlier. They included Eusebius, bishop of Nicomedia, the imperial headquarters on the Asian side of the Bosphorus. Eusebius skilfully used his closeness to the court to benefit 'the Eusebians', as sympathizers of Arius came to be known. He later moved across the Bosphorus to the see of Constantinople, the new capital.

Constantine calls the Council of Nicaea

Eusebius of Caesarea, the church historian, also rallied support for the Arians in his region, and soon found himself in deep water as a consequence. Constantine, now Emperor of East as well as West, was dismayed to discover in 324 that his new territories were split over a 'theological trifle'. His religious adviser, the Spanish bishop Ossius, was sent to Alexandria but failed to reconcile the parties, and Constantine summoned a general assembly of bishops to meet at Ancyra (modern Ankara) the

The Roman gateway into Nicaea (modern Iznik), venue of the great general Council of the church.

following year.

The Emperor subsequently changed the venue to Nicaea, near Nicomedia, hoping to avoid a divisive result. The Council met in the imperial palace under imperial auspices. Constantine presided at the opening session, surrounded by survivors of the Great Persecution. He, or Ossius, may also have taken the chair when the Arian question arose.

All this underlined the change in relations between church and state. Constantine's ambitions for a fully church-wide attendance were disappointed. Of some two hundred and twenty bishops present, only a handful, including Ossius, were from the West. Bishop Sylvester of Rome was represented by two presbyters. The Council's 'universal' status depended largely on its subsequent universal acceptance.

The Creed of Nicaea

Much more is known of the outcome of the Council than of its proceedings. Arius was quickly condemned by his own words. Three bishops previously banned or suspended, including Eusebius of Caesarea, were cleared.

To exclude Arian error, the Council produced its own creed, which we call the Creed of Nicaea to distinguish it from the Nicene Creed:

'We believe in one God, the Father, Almighty, maker of all things visible and invisible;

'And in one Lord Jesus Christ, the Son of God, begotten of the Father, only-begotten, that is, from the substance (*ousia*) of the Father; God from God, Light from Light, Very God from Very God, begotten not made, of one substance (*homoousios*, consubstantial) with the Father,

through whom all things were made, both in heaven and on earth; who for us men and for our salvation came down and was incarnate, was made man, suffered, and rose again on the third day, ascended into heaven, and is coming to judge the living and the dead;

'And in the Holy Spirit.

'And those who say: "There was a time when he was not", and: "Before he was begotten he was not", and: "He came into being from nothing", or those who pretend that the Son of God is "Of another substance (*hypostasis*), or essence (*ousia*)" [than the Father] or "created" or "alterable" or "mutable", the catholic and apostolic church places under a curse.'

Based on a traditional Syrian or Palestinian creed, the Creed of Nicaea became entirely distinctive because of its technical language and solemn curses (anathemas). Apparently Arius could agree to any statement using solely biblical language. Constantine supported the introduction of the word 'consubstantial'—probably suggested by a Western bishop.

'Consubstantial' (*homoousios*) had been introduced to Christian theology by Gnostics who believed that the heavenly powers shared in the divine fullness. Similarly Origen probably applied it to the Son as a true offspring of the Father, but later bishops had been unhappy about its implications. For many at Nicaea it probably implied that the Son was no less divine that the Father; that the two were equally divine, as an earthly father and son are equally human. For the Westerners and a few Easterners, Alexander and Athanasius, his personal assistant, Eustathius of Antioch and Marcellus of Ancyra, it meant that Father and Son were one in a single Godhead.

Both these senses ruled out

The carvings on a fourth century Christian sarcophagus portray biblical incidents. *Left to right*: the wise men bring gifts; the healing of a man born blind; Daniel and Habakkuk; Peter hears the cock crow; Jesus arrested in the garden.

> *"We believe in one God, the Father, Almighty, maker of all things visible and invisible; And in one Lord Jesus Christ, the Son of God . . ."*
>
> *The Creed of Nicaea*

Arian misconceptions. But some bishops hesitated at the Council, and many more reacted in alarm afterwards, from fear that the Greek word *homoousios* split the Godhead into two as if it were a material substance. The word was used, for example, to describe two coins made from the same metal. Its use in the Creed of Nicaea must have resulted largely from Constantine's intimidation or overawing persuasion.

Only two bishops refused to subscribe to the Creed. Constantine rejoiced in the God-given concord, which events showed to be so deceptive. Eusebius of Caesarea signed only by making tortuous evasions. Eusebius of Nicomedia also signed, but was later exiled for entertaining the Arians *en route* for Illyria on the Danube frontier, where Constantine had banished them. Genuine Arians were very few in number.

The church's organization

The Council of Nicaea also issued twenty 'canons' regulating various aspects of the church's life. Because of the prestige surrounding the Council, they became the core of later collections of canon law. They dealt with the admission of members of splinter groups, restrictions on the functions of deacons and on business activities by the clergy, the giving of the eucharist to those about to die out of communion, probation before ordination after baptism, and a ban on clergy transferring from one city to another.

Other canons strengthened the organization of the church into provinces and recognized that the bishops of Rome, Alexandria, Antioch, Caesarea and Jerusalem had superior authority. While Rome alone is mentioned in the West, the four in the East were soon joined by Constantinople. The pretensions of this upstart, as well as the rivalry between ancient Antioch and Alexandria, rapidly aggravated the continuing conflict over doctrine.

The Council of Nicaea set many precedents. The Emperor called it, influenced its decision-making and used his civil power to give its decrees virtually the status of imperial law. The Council introduced a new kind of orthodoxy, which for the first time gave non-biblical terms critical importance. The Creed's own form of expression was influenced by the heresy it outlawed. Only in the long term did the whole church recognize that Nicaea had decisively developed its understanding of the divinity of Christ.

The reaction against Nicaea

Nicaea was followed by more than half a century of discord and disorder in the Eastern church, which at times spilled over into the West. The 'faith of Nicaea', as the Creed was commonly called, was for most of the period out of favour with most churchmen. Numerous other statements of belief were drawn up, some quite near to it, others a great distance from it, none containing the word *homoousios*. The Eastern emperors between Constantine and Theodosius I were at best unsympathetic to Nicaea, at worst openly friendly towards Arianism.

Athanasius, backed by the solid ranks of Egyptian churchmen and monks, remained the one unyielding champion of Nicaea in the East. Five times exiled from Alexandria, he lived long enough to welcome the 'new Nicene' theology of the 360s and the Cappadocian Fathers.

Throughout this half-century

the basic dispute about doctrine was intertwined with other complications—local factions, rivalries between the leading bishoprics, the personal failings or follies of Christian leaders, the emperors' intervention, and confusion arising from differences in language, especially as rifts opened up between the Latin and Greek churches.

The Western church had able theologians such as Hilary of Poitiers and Ambrose of Milan, but they contributed little to solving the troubles of the East. The Western church consistently supported Nicaea and Alexandria (whose isolation in the fourth century arose partly because it expelled Origen in the third). This did their cause little good, and much harm, in the East.

While Constantine remained alive, no one openly dared to attack his beloved Council. The reaction against Nicaea had to proceed indirectly, seizing the opportunities offered by the Emperor's restless quest for harmony. The Eusebians and even Arius were brought back into favour, the leading enthusiasts for Nicaea were sent packing.

A Christian emperor

After he had been cleared at Nicaea, Eusebius of Caesarea went on to develop a theology of the Christian empire and emperor. He claimed that both empire and church were images of the kingdom of heaven. Through both God was saving humanity. The empire replaced anarchy by monarchy, which represents on earth the God who alone rules in heaven. The church replaced polytheism with the worship of the one God. In the Christian emperor the two images began to merge. Constantine is seen as the earthly image of the *Logos* who had fully revealed the heavenly monarchy and kingdom. He was specially inspired to rule by the *Logos*.

Eusebius drew his ideas from Hellenistic writers on divine kingship—although the Old Testament offered similar patterns. His thinking was taken up by Eastern Christians. Inevitably the emperors became supreme in church as well as state. Since Alexander the Great the East had been used to regarding rulers as divine.

Eusebius of Nicomedia was recalled from exile after a couple of years, and threw himself into organizing opposition to Nicaea. Arius was likewise recalled after confusing Constantine with a statement of faith which dodged all the crucial issues. He no longer had any influence.

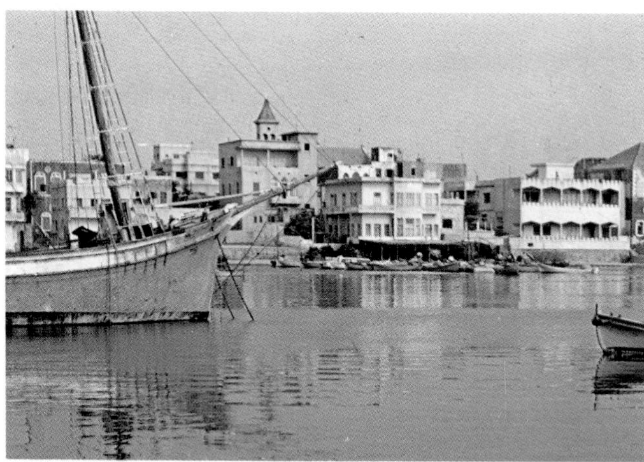

Tyre, where the Eusebians plotted to depose Athanasius, was a busy Mediterranean port.

Among the supporters of Nicaea, Eustathius of Antioch was the first to be dislodged. The reasons given ranged from insulting Constantine's mother Helena to exaggerated criticism of Origen. Marcellus of Ancyra was condemned directly for heresy. He was another critic of Origen's ideas and presented a single God who expanded into three in creation and redemption and then contracted to one again. This seemed like a form of Sabellianism, which Origen had taught Eastern churchmen to resist with unparalleled intensity. Marcellus' appeal to 1 Corinthians 15: 24–28 (the Son at the end hands the kingdom over to the Father, and is made subordinate to him, so that God is all in all) led eventually to the inclusion in the Nicene Creed of the words 'whose kingdom shall have no end'.

Athanasius annoyed Constantine by refusing to rejoice when the Arians were reconciled. The Eusebians plotted to depose him in 335 at Tyre, where the bishops assembled before celebrating the thirtieth anniversary of Constantine's reign with the dedication of his Church of the Holy Sepulchre at Jerusalem. Athanasius was charged with conduct unbecoming a bishop, including violent treatment of dissident clergy. The charges had some substance. When Athanasius fled to Constantine himself, his enemies accused him of threatening to cut off vital grain supplies for Constantinople by calling a dock strike in Alexandria. Constantine banished him to Trier in Gaul—banishment had become customary for those the church condemned.

> *"Athanasius—this troublesome bit of a man."*
>
> *JULIAN the 'Apostate'*

When Constantine died, baptized by Eusebius of Nicomedia and praised by Eusebius of Caesarea, the Creed of Nicaea remained officially in force. Until the end Constantine had worked for peace in the church. His son Constantius, Emperor of the East until 361, and of the West too after Constans' death in 350, followed the same policy. The only difference was that his quest for unity did without the settlement of Nicaea.

Confusion under Constantius

A breathing-space after Constantine's death allowed the exiles to return—Athanasius, Marcellus an Paul, the bishop of the strategic see of Constantinople, who was expelled as often as Athanasius. But the slide towards total ruptur between East and West soon resumed. Although efforts to heal the divisions had some success, when Constantius died Arianism was practically dominant in the East, while the Emperor's theology of compromise ruled the West. Yet there were hints of a brighter future for the 'faith of Nicaea'.

Constantius was not long in power before Athanasius and Marcellus were banished again. Eusebius had now moved from Nicomedia to Constantinople. The two exiles went to Rome, where in 340 a council under Bishop Juliu undid their excommunication and declared Marcellus orthodox. The Eastern church saw these acts as arrogant and simple-minded. The thought that Rome had been hood winked by Marcellus who manage to avoid being pressed on the wea points of his beliefs. Moreover, Rome did not have the power to overrule councils of Eastern bishops.

At a council at Antioch in 341 the Greek bishops were free to express their own views. They repudiated both Arius and Marcellus, their chief target, and refused to reconsider Athanasius' case. They drew up creeds, not intending to supplant Nicaea's, bu implying that it was inadequate. The second creed of Antioch was repeatedly referred to in the years following as a true mirror of Eastern theology. It was inadequate in teaching that Father, Sc and Spirit are 'three as persons' but one only 'in agreement' or harmony of will. It clearly exclude Arianism but went out of its way to condemn Marcellus and his supposedly Sabellian ideas.

Constans persuaded Constanti

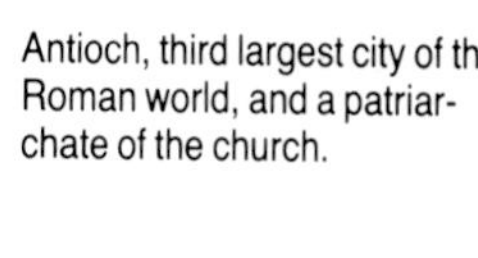

Antioch, third largest city of the Roman world, and a patriarchate of the church.

ɔ call a general council at Sardica modern Sofia, Bulgaria) in 42/3. But this council split into pposing camps which bombarded ach other with anathemas. A heological statement issued om the Western side innocently xposed the problems of mutual nderstanding. By refusing to escribe Father, Son and Spirit s 'three *hypostaseis*' (which it nderstood as implying 'three ;ods'), and by arguing for a single *ypostasis* of Father and Son it onfirmed Eastern fears that the Vest sincerely backed Marcellus' abellian viewpoint. To add offence ɔ the Eastern church the Western ouncil gave the Roman bishop the ight to hear appeals from bishops ondemned in their own provinces.

For the first time East and West ere in a state of virtual schism, om which they never fully recovred. The situation improved ɔr a time as Constans pressed, nd Constantius was distracted y the Persians. The West and thanasius quietly abandoned Marcellus, and Athanasius was even allowed to return to Alexandria, where in 346 he embarked upon his 'golden decade'.

But after taking over control of the Western Empire in 350, Constantius allowed the Arians to advance to fresh triumphs. He pursued his goal of harmony in the church at the expense of Nicene theology and theologians. At councils he forced the Western bishops to condemn Athanasius and banished those who resisted to the end, such as Ossius and Hilary. He could then confidently exile Athanasius again in 356, though his replacement was inducted only by force against massive popular opposition.

Arianism in the ascendant

The provinces of Illyria had become a stronghold of Arianism as a result of Arius' banishment to the region. (It was from here that the Visigoths adopted Arian Christianity, launching it on its second career as the new religion of the migrant peoples who overwhelmed the Western Empire.) A local anti-Nicene bishop, Valens of Mursa, influenced Constantius strongly during the 350s. A creed published at nearby Sirmium in 357, which Hilary labelled 'the Blasphemy of Sirmium', banned the use of philosophical words like *ousia,* and implied clearly Arian beliefs. It was welcomed by the Anomoians, extreme Arians who claimed that the Son was unlike *(anomoios)* the Father.

> "*The whole world groaned in astonishment at finding itself Arian.*"
>
> *JEROME*

These excesses provoked a reaction, spearheaded by Marcellus' successor, Basil. His supporters, sometimes misleadingly called semi-Arians, taught that the Son was like the Father in all respects, including his essential being *(ousia)*. They described the Son as 'of the same substance' *(homoiousios)* as the Father rather than 'of one substance' *(homoousios)*, and thus unmistakably distinguished between Father and Son. Hilary and Athanasius viewed the movement as the most promising development since Nicaea itself.

Constantius' reign ended with a moderated Arianism dominant. In the West all dissent had ceased, except for Hilary, in exile. Constantius extorted from joint councils at Rimini in Italy and Seleucia (on the coast of Asia Minor) a universal creed which feebly confessed the Son to be like *(homoios)* the Father. Jerome wrote, 'The whole world groaned in astonishment at finding itself Arian.' This shock was similar to the dismay which had followed Nicaea in the Eastern Empire. Churchmen would not acquiesce in an imperial settlement which had not won their own agreement. But Basil's constructive contribution was still to bear fruit. It focussed attention in a new way on the central theological issue.

Emperor Julian the 'Apostate' permitted all Constantius' exiles to return. Instead of the destructive inter-church warfare which he expected, there came major advances in mutual understanding. Athanasius, now a mellowed elder-statesman, called a synod in Alexandria in 362. The bishops agreed that the Creed of Nicaea should be confessed by all without any additions, and discovered that in spite of differences in technical terms, they were in agreement. 'Three *hypostaseis*' did not mean three Gods, or three beings with different natures or as separate from each other as three men. Nor did 'one *hypostasis*' involve its users in Sabellianism; it spoke of the oneness of the Godhead as a single essence.

Other problems that concerned the Council were the God-man union in the incarnate Christ, and the teaching of Egyptian supporters of Nicaea that the Holy Spirit was a superior angel, not of one substance with the Father and the Son. Athanasius had written against them, and the synod backed him up. Although Scripture was less explicit on this matter and Nicaea itself had said little, the acceptance that the Son was fully God cleared the way for the same acceptance concerning the Spirit. For Athanasius only a divine Spirit could make us 'partakers of the divine nature'. The issue arose more threateningly outside Egypt.

Elsewhere in the East many people rallied to the faith of Nicaea or the second creed of Antioch of 341. But divisions continued among the Antioch Christians and threatened further progress. Ever since Eustathius had been deposed in 330, the Nicene Christians had met in a separate congregation, now led by Paulinus. The official bishops of Antioch were Arians of one variety or another until Meletius, who was deposed when ıe showed his colours.

Meletius' supporters formed second anti-Arian congregation ı Antioch, with wide backing in he East. Athanasius, followed by ome and the West, continued in ommunion with the old Nicenes nder Paulinus. Church order and heology could not have been more ightly interwoven. Antioch was n important church. By refusing o recognize Meletius and the ew Nicenes, Alexandria and Rome ffended Eastern churchmen.

Valens, the Eastern Emperor 364–78), reminded the world that he 'Homoian' creed of Constantius vas still official orthodoxy. During is 'second Arian persecution', old nd new Nicenes suffered alike, lthough Athanasius' fifth exile did ot last long.

The Emperor devastated ongregational life, and heretical roups proliferated. The confusion vas 'like a sea-fight in the fog'. pollinarius' teaching was popu- ır, and around Constantinople ıe Pneumatomachians, 'fighters gainst the Spirit', denied that the pirit was fully God in the same ense at the Son. (They were ter improperly called 'Macedo- ians' after a former bishop of onstantinople.) They claimed ıat the Bible says nothing to deny ıat the Spirit is a lower being. Iarcellus was also still active, and thanasius had still not disowned im.

Blindness—or excessive indul- ence—to the faults of friends and ıpporters was one of Athanasius' eaknesses. It was the counter- ırt of his harshness against pponents, especially as a young ishop, largely due to his belief ıat Arianism spelt the doom of the hristian faith. Christianity was oove all else about redemption. nly a Word of God who was fully ıd uncompromisingly divine could escue mankind from the corrup- on and death issuing from the fall.

Athanasius was not a specula- tive theologian. What mattered for him was not so much the terms used in the Creed of Nicaea as its message. He used Scripture as inadequately as his contemporaries. He did not refute Arius by rejecting the relevance of Proverbs 8:22 and even quoted Psalm 110:3 (in the *Septuagint*) to prove that the Son was not a created being. His greatest contribution was in routing main- stream Arianism. He had less success in re-establishing the faith of Nicaea. As his attitude softened with the years, he happily accepted the new approaches of Basil of Ancyra, Meletius and Basil the Great, bishop of Caesarea in Cappadocia (eastern Asia Minor), 370–79.

Repairing the damage

Basil the Great was an extremely able administrator. He set about repairing 'the tattered old coat of the church' by letters and by influencing the appointment of bishops in the provinces of Asia. But in relations with the West he had little success. Basil sent four delegations to Pope Damasus which produced no tangible aid. The two sides disagreed strongly about the division in Antioch. Western churches still suspected the theology of the 'new Nicenes' such as Meletius and Basil him- self. Damasus' insensitive and ill-informed detachment further endangered the recovery of harmony between East and West.

Basil worked closely with his brother Gregory of Nyssa and their friend Gregory of Nazianzus. These three Cappadocians finally convinced the East that it was quite possible to accept both Nicaea *(homoousios)* and the distinct persons *(hypostaseis)* of Father, Son and Spirit at the same time. It was not enough to show that the Son was equal with the Father, for this might suggest there were two Gods. Father and Son must also be recognized as one God. The Cappadocians established *ousia* as the Greek equivalent to the Latin *substantia.* At the same time, further linguistic confusion reared its head. The closest Greek parallel to the Latin 'three *personae*' was 'three *prosōpa*'; but the latter term, meaning 'face, mask or role', was popular with the Sabellians. The Cappadocians insisted on the stronger 'three *hypostaseis*' (beings).

"Every divine action begins from the Father, proceeds through the Son and is completed in the Holy Spirit."

The Cappadocians' doctrine of the Trinity is complex and at points controversial. They were accused of suggesting that there are three Gods and also of the opposite error, Sabellianism. They used analogies that they knew were inexact—but one in particular, of the single humanity shared by father, mother and child, easily misled.

Basil argued that the Trinitarian baptismal formula and doxology (whether 'Glory be to the Father together with the Son, with the Holy Spirit' or 'Glory be to the Father through the Son in the Holy Spirit') demanded that Father, Son and Spirit are equal but distinct. According to the Cappadocians, the three operated inseparably, none ever acting independently of the others. 'Every divine action begins from the Father, proceeds through the Son and is completed in the Holy Spirit.' They 'coinhere'—inter-penetrate each other; 'everything that the Father is is seen in the Son, and everything that the Son is belongs to the Father'.

On the basis of John 15:26 they taught that the Spirit 'proceeds' from the Father through the Son, as the counterpart of the Son's generation. Basil remained diffident about calling the Holy Spirit 'God'.

In obedience to a dream, Constantine founded a new capital for the eastern half of the Empire. He sited it strategically on the Bosphorus, and intended it to be a 'New Rome'. Naturally it became known as Constantinople.

The Council of Constantinople

The Cappadocians' theology made little formal headway until Theodosius, a Westerner and keen supporter of Nicaea, became Eastern Emperor in 379. It was he who conclusively established Christianity as the official religion of the Empire. A famous decree of 380 required all peoples to adhere to 'the religion that is followed by Pope Damasus and Peter, bishop of Alexandria'.

In 381 Theodosius summoned the Council of Constantinople to reaffirm the faith of Nicaea. No doctrinal statement put out by the Council has survived, but at the Council of Chalcedon in 451 the Nicene Creed, regarded as the Creed of Nicaea appropriately modified after later controversy, was attributed to this council. The Nicene Creed was probably independently produced by the Council of Constantinople, republishing the teaching of Nicaea rather than repeating its wording.

The Council marked the end of Arianism within the Empire. Unlike the other three early ecumenical councils, it was not followed by decades of doctrinal strife. Theodosius had proved the man for the moment. But in matters

BASIL THE GREAT

H. Dermot McDonald

Basil displayed his immense gifts in public speaking, church statesmanship and theological insight, and was outstanding in social concern and the monastic way of life. The trio of Basil, his brother Gregory of Nyssa and friend Gregory of Nazianzus are often known as the 'Cappadocian Fathers'.

Basil was born into a distinguished and wealthy Christian family in Caesarea in Cappadocia about 330. Despite a first-class education there and at Constantinople and Athens, he turned aside from a career in rhetoric, was baptized and became an ascetic on his family estate in Pontus (357). From the outset he was completely dedicated, especially to biblical study. With Gregory of Nazianzus he compiled an anthology of Origen's works. His sure theological touch helped to strengthen Origen's place within orthodoxy.

In 364 Basil was ordained presbyter and in the spring of 370 he succeeded Eusebius as bishop of Caesarea. His new monastery was at the heart of the complex of hospitals and hostels he founded, largely out of his own pocket, out of his concern for the sick and needy. He took a firm stand against the state-supported Arian party, and wrote several works to oppose their errors. He backed Meletius (bishop of Antioch, 360–81) which damaged his attempts to win practical help from Damasus, bishop of Rome, and cooled his relationship with Athanasius. Basil refused to accept the Roman bishop as supreme judge of the universal church, although he recognized the authority in the area of doctrine.

Basil's writings on the monastic life have had enormous influence in Eastern Christianity. No one before had laid so much stress on community and love in the monastic life. In *On the Holy Spirit* Basil opposed the Pneumatomachians ('fighters against the Spirit') who denied that the Holy Spirit was truly divine. He also wrote homilies on a number of the psalms, a long commentary on Isaiah 1–6, and many sermons and letters.

By giving precise meanings to the terms used in talking about the Trinity, Basil paved the way for the work of the Council of Constantinople in 381. He was the first to fix the accepted formula for the Trinity: one *substance (ousia)* and three *persons (hypostaseis)*. Basil was suspected in turn of the opposite errors of Sabellianism and tritheism, but could not be convicted of either. He died in Caesarea on the first day of 379.

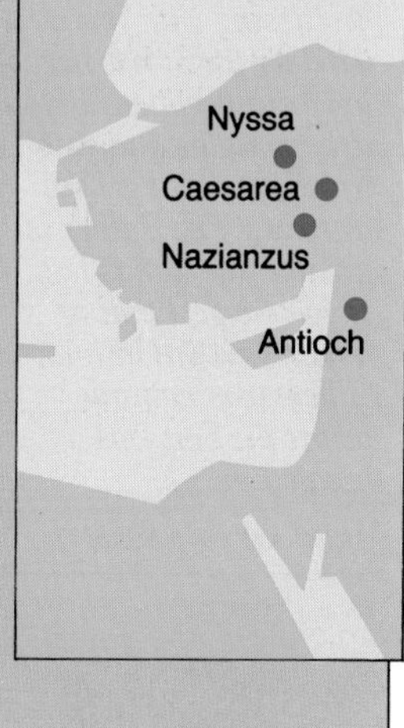

Artists often used symbols to convey Christian truth. These three figures on a fourth-century stone coffin represent the three persons of the Trinity.

of church order, peace was more elusive.

The Council confirmed Gregory of Nazianzus' appointment as bishop of Constantinople, rejecting the rival claimant backed by Alexandria. When Meletius died, Gregory succeeded to the presidency of the Council. In this exposed seat he was buffeted from all sides, and he retired sadly into private life. In his place the Council chose as bishop of Constantinople and its own president a prominent layman, who belonged to no party and was unbaptized. Anti-Western feelings were strong, and the schism at Antioch went on.

Alexandria's interference in Constantinople and Antioch was clearly in mind when the Council drew up its canons. The second of these adopted the dioceses (groupings of provinces) in the Eastern Empire as regions for church purposes, and forbade intervention in the affairs of another diocese. The third canon read: 'The bishop of Constantinople shall have the primacy of honour after the bishop of Rome because Constantinople is new Rome.' The elevation of this upstart see greatly offended the ancient church of Alexandria, for centuries the leading city in the Greek world. It provoked bitter conflict between the two. Rome, too, was dismayed because the canon assumed that political importance determined status in the church. Rome based her supremacy on religious grounds, claiming to be founded by Peter, the apostle. The new ruling would leave Rome's future position uncertain instead of unassailably supreme on the basis of history and tradition. The Roman church repudiated it—delaying Western recognition of the Council (which was attended only by Eastern bishops) as ecumenical until the sixth century. (The canon itself was accepted at the Lateran Council in 1215.)

The new settlement of orthodoxy concerning the Trinity was enforced by imperial edict in both East and West, where Ambrose spurred the emperors into clearing up the last pockets of Arianism. But in government and discipline East and West went separate ways, still divided over Antioch. Doctrinal order had been restored, but in the process the

All Constantinople talks theology

“*If you ask any one in Constantinople for change, he will start discussing with you whether the Son is begotten or unbegotten. If you ask about the quality of bread, you will get the answer: 'The Father is greater, the Son is less.' If you suggest taking a bath you will be told: 'There was nothing before the Son was created.'*”

GREGORY OF NYSSA

Peter hears the cock crow and repents. The cock came to symbolize repentance and baptism. Included on this fourth century sarcophagus is a baptistery (left) as well as two basilicas (centre and right).

seeds of irreparable disruption had been sown between East and West, and in Alexandria's isolation in the East.

The Athanasian Creed

The Cappadocians' theology of the Trinity remained fundamental to all subsequent Greek and Byzantine statements, such as John of Damascus' eighth-century *The Orthodox Faith*. He developed their doctrine of the mutual indwelling of the three persons of the Trinity.

Latin expositions reached their peak in Augustine's writings, especially his principal work on *The Trinity*, an intensive and profound discussion from the traditional Western starting-point that God is one single substance. His distinctive contribution was to elaborate analogies: of the lover, the loved, and the love which binds them, as a picture of relationships within the Trinity; and of the inner man reflecting the image of God in a trinity of mind or memory, knowledge or understanding, and will or love. Marius Victorinus, a converted Neo-platonist, had speculated along somewhat similar lines in refuting Arianism shortly before Augustine wrote.

Augustine, like Ambrose and Jerome, taught that the Spirit proceeded not from the Father alone but also from the Son. (The Greek theologians for the most part thought of the Spirit proceeding from the Father through the Son.) This so-called 'double procession' of the Spirit was incorporated into the *'Athanasian' Creed*, which in reality was written in Latin, probably in southern Gaul in the late fifth century. This creed, Augustinian in inspiration, is directed against the 'modalism' (similar to Sabellianism) which Priscillianism had revived in Gaul

THE NICENE CREED

Jesus calls Lazarus from the tomb. The sculptor has used this incident to emphasize the Christian hope of life beyond the grave.

We believe in one God,
the Father, the almighty,
maker of heaven and earth,
of all that is,
seen and unseen.

We believe in one Lord, Jesus Christ,
the only Son of God,
eternally begotten of the Father,
God from God, Light from Light,
true God from true God,
begotten, not made,
of one Being with the Father.
Through him all things were made.
For us men and for our salvation
he came down from heaven;
by the power of the Holy Spirit
he became incarnate of the
Virgin Mary, and was made man.
For our sake he was crucified under
Pontius Pilate;
he suffered death and was buried.

On the third day he rose again
in accordance with the Scriptures;
he ascended into heaven
and is seated at the right hand of the Father.
He will come again in glory
to judge the living and the dead,
and his kingdom will have no end.

We believe in the Holy Spirit,
the Lord, the giver of life,
who proceeds from the Father and the Son.
With the Father and the Son he is worshipped
and glorified.
He has spoken through the Prophets.

We believe in one holy catholic
and apostolic Church.
We acknowledge one baptism for the
forgiveness of sins.
We look for the resurrection of the dead,
and the life of the world to come. Amen

From *The Alternative Service Book*

and Spain in the fourth and following centuries, and against the Arianism of the Goths and Vandals, which made the Son and the Spirit into second- and third-rank divinities.

The 'double procession' of the Spirit found its way into the Nicene Creed by the addition of the word *Filioque* (Latin, 'and the Son'), the first evidence of which comes from the Third Council of Toledo, in Spain (589). The Roman church refused for centuries to accept this addition, but it later became a major bone of contention between the Latin and Greek churches.

Pompey's Pillar at Alexandria, where Athanasius' synod took place in 362.

Was the Lord of glory crucified?

The relationship between the divine and human natures in the incarnate Christ was inevitably interwoven with the questions about the Trinity in the Arian controversy. It remained, however, a minor theme until the divinity of the Son had been firmly established. So long as the Son was viewed as inferior to the Father in his deity, its union with humanity in Christ was not an urgent problem.

The issue was discussed at Athanasius' synod at Alexandria in 362, probably in connection with the teaching of Apollinarius, bishop of Laodicea in Syria. What was decided is not clear, except that it was agreed that the incarnation was not 'the Word indwelling a holy man, as he did the prophets', but 'the Word himself becoming man for us from Mary after the flesh'.

Athanasius' account of the agreement reflects the approach to the subject favoured in Alexandria. Apollinarius' bold exposition of this approach was universally condemned.

Origen regarded Christ's rational soul as the ideal meeting-point with the *Logos,* because they shared a perfect natural affinity. (Platonists viewed the soul as the essential person and, like Stoics, held that the *Logos* directing the universe and the *logos* in human individuals were homogeneous.) It was a short step to conceive of the *Logos* not merely swallowing up the soul but replacing it.

The Word, therefore, was the sole agent in the life of Christ. This framework of understanding was followed by both Arius and Athanasius, although they differed totally in their estimates of the Word. Whether or not Athanasius disbelieved in, or changed his mind about, the existence of a human soul in Christ (the debate still rages), he certainly attached no theological significance to it. For him, Christ is always the divine Word active in human flesh. It was the Word-as-incarnate who was tired or ignorant or suffered. From start to finish the incarnation was a divine work of salvation. The Alexandrians' use of allegory in understanding Scripture enabled them to be less bothered by the human experiences of Jesus in the gospel story.

As a consequence, this doctrine of Christ grasped strongly the unity of his person, and was at times inclined to mix divine and human. The incarnate union brought about a real interchange of attributes between the two. The Lord of glory actually suffered crucifixion.

Apollinarius was a staunch theologian in the Nicene tradition. Reacting against teaching from Antioch, he brazenly denied that Christ possessed a human soul. The soul was intrinsically corrupt and could not be responsible for motivating a Saviour of sinful people. The virgin birth marked the divide between the human race and Christ. Humanity was the sphere not the instrument of salvation. Christ was 'one nature composed f impassible divinity and passible lesh', 'one enfleshed nature of the livine Word'. In the union Christ's lesh took on a divine character. In he eucharist a communicant could e confident of receiving Christ's fe-giving flesh.

Apollinarius' teaching first ttracted notice in the 350s but vas not prominent until the 370s, vhen that supreme heresy-hunter, piphanius, bishop of Salamis in yprus, denounced it. It was ondemned in East and West nd conclusively at the Council of onstantinople in 381. If God in hrist did not lay hold of our full umanity, then it is not saved. What is not assumed (by the Vord) is not healed' (Gregory of Jazianzus). Apollinarius made he incarnation seem like a mere ppearance of God and Christ's umanity monstrous or mutilated.

After the condemnation f Apollinarius, Alexandrian heologians no longer denied hat Christ had a human soul. Yet ttle significance was attached to uman agency or experience in he incarnation. Apollinarius' writ- ngs continued to circulate, often nasquerading under orthodox ames such as Athanasius.

Two natures?

he Antioch school of theologians ormally interpreted the Scrip- ures in a straightforward historical nanner. Serious consideration was iven to the human figure of the ospels. His example and achieve- nent were regarded as possessing aving virtue. In Christ the human vill, which in other people turns eely to sin, proved obedient and ictorious.

Antiochene theologians onsequently stressed the com- lete humanity of Christ, regarding uman nature as a unity of body nd soul, following Aristotle. The nion did not in any way affect the completeness and normality of the human nature. Antiochenes feared that if the human soul were excluded, the Word would be demoted in Arian fashion in order to accommodate the evidence of the Gospels. It might be possible to ascribe Christ's physical experiences, such as growth, hunger and pain, to flesh alone; but not his mental and emotional life of sorrow, ignorance and exasperation.

After the Word became flesh, the two natures remained distinct. In Antiochene teaching they could easily seem like two beings, God and the man Jesus, Son of God and son of Mary, joined, associated, even juxtaposed rather than personally united. This seemed to open up the possibility of separating 'the man who was assumed' from 'the Word who assumed'. As a vessel indwelt by the Word he was not unlike prophets and apostles, except that he enjoyed perfect fullness of grace and power.

This dualistic approach allotted what Christ did or underwent either to his divine or to his human nature. Undeniably the New Testament spoke of the Son of God suffering or the human Jesus working miracles, but this was seen as merely a literary convention, acceptable to the ordinary believer, but not to the theologian.

These characteristic emphases were developed by Eustathius, by Diodore, bishop of Tarsus (378 to about 390), and supremely by Theodore, bishop of Mopsuestia (east of Tarsus) (392–428), in direct opposition to Apollinarius. Diodore and Theodore had been presbyters at Antioch.

Nestorius was a famous preacher at Antioch before being made bishop of Constantinople by Theodosius II in 428. It is difficult to prove that his teaching went beyond that of his master, Theodore. Like the latter he doubted whether it was right to describe Mary as *theotokos,* 'God-bearer'. The description had been used by Apollinarius, but it was also well established in Christian devotion, especially in monastic circles.

Nestorius was undoubtedly rather outspoken in expounding his Christology. The incarnate Christ he weakly described as 'one *prosōpon*', the single historical figure of the Gospels. In his own words, 'I hold the natures apart, but unite the worship.'

Nestorius was condemned more for ecclesiastical than doctrinal reasons. He was the Emperor's nominee in the hot seat of Constantinople, where he was soon widely hated for his assaults on Jews and heretics. H[e] rapidly incurred the implacable hostility of Cyril, the patriarch of Alexandria (412–44). Cyril was a distinguished expositor and theologian, but an unscrupulous and violent controversialist. Cyril was sufficiently alarmed by Nestorius' teaching and 'new Nicene' background; he was outraged when Nestorius listened t[o] the complaints of some Alexandrian clergy deposed by Cyril. Western disapproval of Nestoriu[s] was ensured when he gave refug[e] to some Pelagian exiles, who ha[d] been excommunicated in the We[st]. His action had probably nothing

NESTORIUS

H. Dermot McDonald

> *"God is not a baby two or three months old."*
>
> *NESTORIUS*

Nestorius, condemned for heresy at Ephesus, was a native of Germanicia in Euphratesian Syria. Born after 381, he was taught the theology of Antioch by Theodore of Mopsuestia whose views he faithfully echoed. He was instituted bishop of Constantinople in 428, and immediately began an offensive against Arian heretics and the Novatians. His support of his chaplain Anastasius made him declare his own views, which brought about his condemnation for heresy at the Council of Ephesus (431). (Anastasius objected to the popular designation of Mary as 'bearer of God'.)

Nestorius, in his defence of Anastasius and his repeated rejection of the word *theotokos,* made it appear that he held Christ to be constituted of two persons. He did not deny the deity of Christ; but in emphasizing the reality and integrity of his humanity he pictured the relation between the two natures in terms of a moral 'conjunction' or a merging of wills rather than that of an *essential* 'union'. Although he never divided Christ into 'two sons', Son of God, and son of Mary, he refused to attribute to the divine nature the human acts and sufferings of the man Jesus. He objected that to assert that Mary was mother of God was tantamount to declaring that the divine nature could be born of a woman, or that God could be three days old. Nestorius distinguished the two natures in Christ with admirable realism, but he was unable to reduce the two to the unique and clearly undifferentiated one Jesus Christ of the Gospels. The twelve anathemas hurled against him by his chief opponent, Cyril of Alexandria, were countered by twelve from him. After exile in 431 he wrote his apology, which survives in Syriac, under the pseudonym *The Bazaar of Heraclides.* Here Nestorius attempts to justify his position and answer Cyril's criticisms. Nestorius died in Upper Egypt after 451.

o do with the fact that some Pelagian emphases were similar o Antiochene theology. There was also confusion over language: *physis* was used by Alexandrians of the single 'person' of Christ, but by Antiochenes of his two 'natures'.

Cyril opened his attack on Nestorius late in 428. His forceful arguments for Alexandrian Christology were bedevilled by his own unwitting use of works of Apollinarius. He stirred up accusations that Nestorius was an adoptionist and slandered him to Rome where Pope Celestine was upset about his having received the Pelagians. Celestine commissioned Cyril to carry out a Roman synod's judgment against Nestorius, and Cyril demanded that Nestorius should agree to twelve 'anathemas' which condemned the Antiochene doctrine in the harshest terms.

At the Council of Ephesus in 431, called by Theodosius II who had until then supported Nestorius, Cyril got Nestorius deposed before the late arrival of his Syrian supporters. They in turn, under John of Antioch, condemned Cyril and Bishop Memnon of Ephesus. Finally the Roman legates arrived and approved Cyril's action. His synod reassembled to excommunicate the Syrian bishops and distribute favours to his allies. Cyril was able to count on the backing of metropolitan bishops such as Ephesus, who resented Constantinople's superior authority, and Jerusalem, who desired independence of Antioch. His campaign also rallied the ordinary Christians, who only too easily pictured Christ as God in human guise and worshipped his incorruptible flesh in the eucharist. The monks were front-line troops at Ephesus.

From Ephesus to Chalcedon

After further machinations,

The baptistery at the church of Our Lady, Ephesus. It was at Ephesus that the Councils of 431 and 449 were held.

Theodosius II eventually acquiesced in the decisions of Cyril's first assembly at Ephesus, which became the third ecumenical council. Nestorius was sent off to Antioch, and died around 450 in exile in Egypt. Few of his supporters accepted his excommunication.

Under pressure from the Emperor, Cyril and the Syrians began to understand each other, and in 433 they signed a Formula of Union drawn up by Theodoret, bishop of Cyrrhus (north of Antioch). Largely Antiochene, it included the description *theotokos* (bearer of God) and showed that some mutual understanding had existed at Ephesus in 431, when most of it was drafted. Both sides agreed to drop demands—the Syrians for Nestorius' reinstatement, Cyril for recognition of his twelve anathemas. Extremists on both wings were dissatisfied, but the compromise held while Cyril and John of Antioch were alive.

In the early 440s a new generation took over. John died 441/2; Leo I became bishop of Rome in 440; the ruthless Dioscorus succeeded Cyril in 444; Flavian was made patriarch of Constantinople in 446. Of the earlier protagonists only Theodoret survived.

Dispute soon raged around Eutyches, an aged monastic superior in Constantinople, who provocatively attacked the doctrine of 'two natures after the union'. In almost 'single-nature' (Monophysite) terms, he suggested that Christ's humanity was absorbed by his divinity like a drop of wine in the sea. Although attacked by Theodoret and condemned under Flavian in 448, he had influence at court and was supported by the unprincipled Dioscorus.

Amid counter-charges, intrigue and disorder, Theodosius II summoned another council for Ephesus in 449. Leo sent a statement of doctrine for the bishops to approve. This was the first major Western contribution—unoriginal but a useful mediating statement. It rejected Eutyches and supported 'two natures after the union', yet incorporated some Alexandrian positions. (Tertullian had long ago provided the structure and language—two *substantiae* in one *persona*—of a Latin Christology

CYRIL OF ALEXANDRIA

H. Dermot McDonald

Although he was an important figure who became a brilliant representative of the Alexandrian theology, the early life of Cyril is obscure. He was accepted into the ranks of the clergy by his nephew Theophilus, patriarch of Alexandria, and in 403 he accompanied Theophilus to Constantinople.

The Roman theatre at Alexandria, a city with a major tradition in theology.

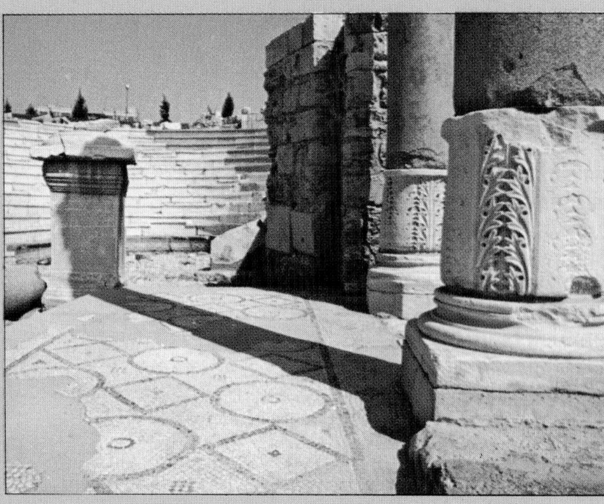

Despite opposition he was elected in 412, to succeed Theophilus as patriarch of Alexandria. His main concern was to combat Nestorianism. Acting on behalf of Celestine of Rome, Cyril convened the Council of Alexandria in 430, which demanded that Nestorius recant. Cyril's twelve anathemas against Nestorius were countered with twelve from Nestorius. Cyril headed the Council of Ephesus in 431, which deposed Nestorius.

Cyril's theological talent was devoted to preserving Christ's person as a living unity, against Nestorian dualism. While acknowledging the completeness of Christ's human nature, he held that the human nature which the Word assumed was not really 'personal'. In his resulting definition, however, the two natures were virtually resolved into one. And by using the phrase 'one nature' he was blamed for reviving Apollinarianism, and giving rise to Eutychianism with its resulting Monophysitism.

Against Nestorius, as well as heretics, Jews and pagans, Cyril showed himself a ruthless antagonist. The conflict with Nestorius was in part a clash between the rival sees of Alexandria and Constantinople. Cyril died in 444.

which to a remarkable extent anticipated the outcome of these Eastern disputes.)

Dioscorus dominated the council. Leo's *Tome* (his statement of doctrine) was refused a hearing, Flavian was deposed and Eutyches rehabilitated. The Formula of Union and its two-nature doctrine was banned, and its supporters, including Theodoret, excommunicated. Leo labelled the synod a 'robber band'. It was a shameless attack on Constantinople by Dioscorus.

No redress was possible until Theodosius II died the next year in a fall from his horse. His sister Pulcheria succeeded him, reigning jointly with her new husband Marcian. Pulcheria had been sympathetic to the cause of Leo and Flavian, and the great Council of Chalcedon (across the Bosphorus from Constantinople) was summoned for late 451.

Over four hundred Greek bishops attended, with legates (representatives) from Rome. Pulcheria's own commissioners controlled the proceedings. The acts of the 'robber synod' were undone and Dioscorus deposed. Theodoret at last disowned Nestorius. The Council put out a composite Definition which consisted of the Creeds of 325 and 381, two letters of Cyril refuting Nestorius, Leo's *Tome* and, despite some reluctance, a new confession, compiled largely from Cyril, Leo and the Formula of 433:

'We all with one voice confess our Lord Jesus Christ one and the same Son, at once complete in Godhead and complete in manhood, truly God and truly man, consisting of a reasonable soul and body; of one substance with the Father as regards his Godhead, of one substance with us as regards his manhood, like us in all things, apart from sin; begotten of the Father before the ages as regards his Godhead, the same in the last days, for us and for our salvation, born from the Virgin Mary, the God-bearer *(theotokos)*, as regards his manhood; one and the same Christ, Son, Lord, Only-begotten, to be acknowledged in two natures, without confusion, without change, without division, or without separation; the distinction of natures being in no way abolished because of the union, but rather the characteristic property of each nature being preserved, and coming together to form one person *(prosōpon)* and one entity *(hypostasis)*, not as if Christ were parted or divided into two persons . . .'

This distinguished statement undoubtedly reflects the fact that the Antiochene standpoint had the stronger influence.

Rome was disturbed by some

Rome: in the fourth century the city was building up its claim to lead the Christian world.

of the Council's canons, which included important regulations concerning monks and monasteries. Canons 9 and 17 allowed appeals from eastern provinces to be addressed to Constantinople instead of to the chief bishop (exarch) of the diocese. Canon 28 reaffirmed the third canon of 381, explicitly stating that the earlier Council gave Rome the primacy because she was the imperial city. The Roman legates appealed in vain to Nicaea's canons, before Constantinople even existed! Leo even delayed recognizing the Council's doctrinal settlement for a couple of years.

A new division

Chalcedon's decrees became imperial law, which was now normal practice. They offended Eastern churches who cherished Cyril's one-nature portrayal of the incarnate Christ; these dissidents were henceforth known as 'Monophysites'. For the most part they could no more be called heretics than Cyril himself.

Anti-Chalcedonianism soon dominated Egypt, where the Coptic language served to express dissent, especially among the monks. The Greek-speaking Chalcedonian minority was dubbed 'the Emperor's men'. In Syria, where the Syriac language played a similar role, the Monophysites had to struggle for ascendancy, but here too their leadership far excelled that of the Chalcedonians.

The division threatened the imperial throne itself during the Emperor Zeno's reign.

LEO THE GREAT

Michael A. Smith

Leo the Great was born in Tuscany (Italy) and rose through the bureaucracy of the church of Rome to become bishop of Rome in 440. He advanced the primacy of the Roman church in the West and was the first bishop of Rome to make extensive use of the text 'You are Peter' (Matthew 16:19) as speaking of the pope himself. He also got legal backing for the status of the bishop of Rome from the Emperor Valentinian III, although by this time edicts from the Western Emperor were for the most part unenforceable. Leo was one of the church's earliest great administrators. His style was strongly influenced by Roman law; he was also a notable preacher.

Leo took a leading part in the controversies about the nature of Christ of the fifth century. He fought energetically against ideas that stressed the deity of Christ at the expense of his humanity. The *Tome* of Leo, his statement about the person of Christ, was disregarded at the 'robber-synod' of Ephesus (449) but two years later at the Council of Chalcedon (451) it was one of the main sources used to draw up the Chalcedonian Definition on the person of Christ. Leo stated, in line with mainstream beliefs, that Christ has both a fully human nature and a fully divine nature, and yet was not a split personality.

Leo increased his personal prestige, as well as that of his office as Roman bishop, when he persuaded Attila the Hun to turn back from Rome (452) and later managed to minimize the damage done to the city when it was captured by the Vandal leader Gaiseric (455). The Roman bishop was beginning to act as a civil ruler.

He subsequently issued the *Henoticon*—a peace formula which condemned Nestorius and Eutyches, sanctioned Cyril's anathemas in addition to the Creeds of 325 and 381, and put a curse on any contrary doctrine 'whether taught at Chalcedon or elsewhere'.

From 484 to 518, under Zeno and Anastasius, the *Henoticon* was official orthodoxy. The pope's excommunication of Zeno and Acacius, the patriarch of Constantinople, created the 'Acacian schism' between the Greek and Latin churches, the longest formal breach thus far.

The Coptic church was developing its own distinctive traditions of art and worship. This icon from a Coptic monastery pictures Christ and St Menas. A *Chi-rho* has been drawn between their haloes.

The Empire's adoption of this compromise Monophysitism encouraged the Persian church to accept Nestorianism, in order to widen its divorce from the imperial church, and so appear less obnoxious to Persia's rulers. After Nestorius' condemnation in 431, Nestorian strength had concentrated at Edessa, east of the Euphrates. The Monophysite reaction after Chalcedon prompted the Nestorians to migrate across the frontier into Persia, and make Nisibis their centre. In 486 the Persian church became officially Nestorian. The works of Diodore and Theodore were preserved in Persian as well as Syriac.

After the *Henoticon* was abandoned, efforts to meet the Monophysites half way continued, especially under Justinian (527-65), who set his sights on the political and religious reunification of East and West. In 543/4 he condemned the *Three Chapters* which listed, first, Theodore of Mopsuestia and his works, and specified writings of, second, Theodoret and, third, Ibas, bishop of Edessa 435-57—all three alleged Nestorians left uncondemned by Chalcedon. Pope Vigilius hesitated under extended pressure, but finally consented to the anathematizing of the *Chapters* at the fifth ecumenical council at Constantinople in 553. The West was divided over the affair. The same council condemned Origen as a heretic and approved the development of Chalcedon's doctrine worked out by Leontius of Byzantium.

The emperors persecuted, as well as wooed, the Monophysites, which stimulated the formation of separate ecclesiastical organizations. Severus, patriarch of Antioch (512-38), gave Monophysite theology its definitive Cyril-derived shape, and Jacob Baradeus vigorously created Monophysite bishoprics throughout the East in the mid-sixth century. And so the Syrian Jacobites and the Copts of Egypt and Ethiopia, which was always closely dependent on Alexandria, formed themselves into autonomous Monophysite churches. Armenia too became Monophysite in the same period, largely in order to gain her independence of the Empire and of Constantinople. Georgia took up Chalcedonianism partly to gain imperial aid in resisting Armenian control.

In the seventh century Persian and, later, Arab invasions made reconciliation with the Monophysites even more imperative. But two further attempts at harmony of doctrine came to nothing. The beliefs that Christ possessed a single principle of activity or 'energy' (Monergism) and a single will (Monotheletism) were both condemned at the sixth general council at Constantinople in 680-81. The Council decreed that in Christ 'there are two natural wills and modes of operation without division, change, separation or confusion . . . His human will follows, without any resistance or reluctance but in subjection, his divine and omnipotent will.'

Once again the resolving of doctrinal conflict was a major factor in the creating of ecclesiastical divisions, which in the eastern Mediterranean area weakened the Empire's defences against the Muslim invaders. Issues of faith and order had proved to be disastrously interwoven. The creeds and confessions of the ecumenical councils were bought at considerable cost to peace.

THE FALL OF THE ROMAN EMPIRE

Richard A. Todd

rom the time of Augustine, many ıinkers have tried to explain the ıll of the Roman Empire, by which › meant the end of the Roman mpire in the West. The Eastern mpire, based on Constantinople, East Rome', survived for another ıousand years. Although the nderlying reasons for the fall of ıe Western Empire are still disuted, the immediate cause was ıe Germanic invasions of the fifth entury.

laric sacks Rome

ermanic tribes had threatned the Roman frontier for everal centuries. But the ibes who finally destroyed the Vestern Empire were new to ıe Romans—Goths, Vandals, urgundians, Lombards and othrs. Most important of these were ıe Goths, who began to attack ıe Empire about the middle of ıe third century. The Visigoths, ıe western branch of the Goths, ccupied the Roman province of acia and forced the Emperor urelian to abandon it in 271.

The Visigoths were introduced › Christianity during their occupaon of Dacia, by Roman prisoners ıken on raids into the Empire. bout the end of Constantine's ign, Ulfilas, a descendant of one the Christian Roman prisoners, as consecrated head of the Chrisan community there by an Arian shop. The Visigoths, therefore, ecame Arian Christians and ventually spread their particular nd of Christianity to most of the her German tribes on the borer of the Empire. Ulfilas' most important achievement was the translation of the Bible into the Gothic language, for which task he had to invent a Gothic alphabet.

After its recovery from the chaos of the third century, the Empire enjoyed almost a century of relative security. The first hint of ultimate disaster was the battle of Adrianople in 378. The Visigoths had obtained refuge within the Empire from the Huns, but when mistreated by the Romans, they rebelled and destroyed the Emperor Valens and his army at Adrianople. Theodosius, chosen to settle the East by the Western Emperor Gratian, managed to subdue the Visigoths; but they were allowed to remain within the Empire as Roman allies, under their own rulers, and with a regular subsidy.

"The city which has taken the whole world is itself taken!"

JEROME

In 395 the Empire was divided between Arcadius and Honorius, the two young sons of Theodosius. Alaric, the new king of the Visigoths, began to exploit the differences that now developed between East and West. Encouraged, apparently, by Constantinople, he invaded Italy in 401.

On the night of 24 August 410, Alaric stormed the walls of Rome in a surprise attack and pillaged the city for three days. The event had little permanent effect on the Empire since Alaric soon abandoned the city; but the psychological blow was enormous. For the first time in 800 years Rome had been taken by a foreign enemy. Jerome, far away in his monastery at Bethlehem, wept: 'The city which has taken the whole world is itself taken!'

A divine punishment?

Some pagans claimed that the catastrophe was due to the recent rejection by the Romans of their ancestral gods. Augustine of Hippo, the great North African bishop and theologian, countered this accusation in his book *The City of God.*

Augustine wrote that within the Roman Empire two 'cities' were intertwined: the City of God, the community of true Christians living according to God's law, and the City of Man, pagan society following its own desires and seeking material gain. Such a community could only come to a disastrous end. But to Christians, citizens of the City of God, the sack of Rome was not a catastrophe, in spite of their suffering. The loss of goods can deprive Christians of nothing, since their hearts are set on heavenly things. Suffering and deprivation are part of their Christian instruction. The City of God alone is eternal, yet the two cities will coexist inseparably until the end of the world.

Augustine did appreciate the achievement of Rome, though it stood under judgement. Rome provided the just government needed for an ordered society and the control of evil. God gave Rome this authority and the Christian must obey such government unless commanded to do evil.

The end of the Roman Empire in the West

The sack of Rome was not a serious blow to the Empire as a whole, since the Visigoths returned to Gaul after Alaric's death and Rome had ceased to be the administrative centre of the West. The Emperor and his court were safe behind the marshes at the coastal city of Ravenna.

ULFILAS' GOTHIC BIBLE

"Ulfilas took very great care of the Goths in many ways. For instance, he reduced their language to writing and translated all the books of the Bible into their everyday speech, except for the books of Kings. He left them out because they are merely an account of military exploits, and the Gothic tribes were particularly devoted to war. They were in more need of checks on their warlike natures than of spurs to urge them on to acts of war."

PHILOSTORGIUS, History of the Church ii.5

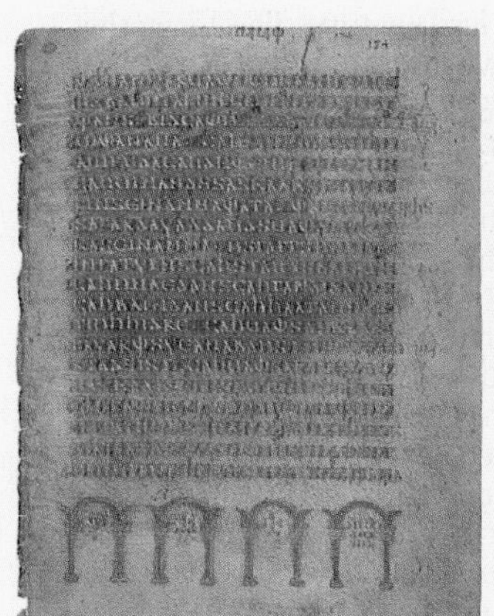

This magnificent sixth-century copy of Ulfilas' translation is the Codex Argenteus or Silver bible belonging to Uppsala university Library. It was written in gold and silver on a purple-painted parchment.

Safely protected at Ravenna, the imperial court continued to live in magnificence. This mausoleum was built in the fifth century to hold the remains of the Empress Galla Placidia.

The interior is richly decorated. Over the door is this colourful mosaic of the Good Shepherd.

Gaul, however, was in desperate straits, attacked by a new group of barbarian tribes—Vandals, Alans, Suevi, Franks and Burgundians. Britain was meanwhile occupied by Anglo-Saxons from northern Europe. The legendary Arthur, though certainly not the royal hero of the Round Table, may have been the last successful military leader of Christian Britain against the pagan invaders (490–510).

Attila the Hun is possibly the most famous of barbarian kings, but the Huns made a less permanent impact than the Visigoths, Vandals and some other barbarians. In 452 Attila invaded Italy but was persuaded to withdraw—according to tradition, by a Roman delegation led by Pope Leo I. Attila died the next year, his army dissolved, and the Huns were absorbed into the surrounding population.

By the mid-fifth century, the Frankish invaders held most of north and central Gaul. This helmet once belonged to a Frankish warrior.

Meanwhile another Germanic people, the Vandals led by Gaiseric, had crossed from Spain into North Africa in 429, and by 435 controlled much of the coast. They mastered the sea and in 455 dared to attack Rome itself. The Romans were unprepared and leaderless. It is reported that Leo again saved Rome by pleading with Gaiseric for restraint in his fourteen-day sack of the city.

The final act of the drama may be quickly told. The next two decades were filled with wars against the Vandals and complicated intrigues, in which puppet emperors were set up and deposed at will by barbarian generals. Eventually, the barbarian Roman army in Italy revolted—the army of true Romans had by this time completely disappeared—and elected as their king Odoacer, one of the barbarian officers of the imperial guard. In 476 Odoacer deposed the last Roman Emperor in the West, the little Romulus Augustulus, and sent his imperial regalia to the Eastern Emperor Zeno, affirming his allegiance to the government at Constantinople and seeking to be recognized as ruler of the West.

The church and the poor

Salvian, a presbyter of Marseilles, reveals something of life in Roman Gaul in the mid-fifth century. His book, *The Government of God*, tries to answer a question similar to that faced by Augustine—why God would bring suffering on a Christian people. He shows that the terrible experience of Christian Gaul does reflect God's just rule; it is his righteous judgement on a wicked people, particularly on wealthy aristocrats and greedy public officials who mercilessly ppress the poor. This sympathy for the common man sets off Salvian from most writers of the ancient world. Landowners, governors, municipal officials, and tax collectors, says Salvian, have all conspired to rob the poor, who can least afford to pay. No wonder that the poor prefer life among the barbarians or in the monasteries.

Salvian's picture is certainly overdrawn, for there were many prosperous peasants, merciful landlords, and honest officials in the mid-fifth century. Nevertheless, the peasant's life was usually hard and sometimes desperate; they were at the bottom of the pile when the crunch came, as in times of famine. Taxes were collected from the poor even when they were starving, while rich landowners were often able to arrange remission of their taxes.

Sometimes the church was part of the oppressive system, for example when its lands were managed by harsh or corrupt administrators. Such cases occurred on the estates of the Roman church in Sicily, in the time of Pope Gregory the Great, but were quickly rectified when they came to Gregory's attention.

The church was generally on the side of the poor and oppressed. Ambrose protested about the expulsion of non-residents from the city of Rome in time of famine, and eventually money was raised to buy grain for distribution. The same thing happened at Edessa at the urging of Ephraem the Syrian. In this case not only was bread distributed but an open-air hospital of 300 beds was set up. Sometimes church officials shared in the relief effort; the bishop was usually a conscientious shepherd of his flock. It was the church's care for its own poor and for outsiders that so impressed the pagan Emperor Julian.

Christians and morality

The success of the church in dealing with other social evils of the day is more debatable. It succeeded in ending gladiatorial combats, but chariot-races, wild beast hunts and an extremely immoral theatre continued in spite of Christian condemnations and, in some cases, imperial prohibition. The rigid sexual standards of the church (see article on *Christian Ascetics*) were not observed by most Christians, except for the many who fled to monasteries or desert hermitages, or the few who, like the women friends of Jerome and Ambrose, could afford to live privately as virgins in their own homes.

For many it was thought difficult to live a Christian life in the secular world. The Christian magistrate, for example, might have to order torture or execution. Thus Christians were often advised, for the sake of their souls, to leave public office. This attitude of the church probably contributed to the decline of public morality in the late Empire, as posts were often filled with people of lower ideals.

Although poverty was widespread, some Christians possessed extravagant objects. This ivory casket is covered with scenes drawn from the Old and New Testaments.

"A large part of public wealth was consecrated to the specious demands of charity and devotion; and the soldiers' pay was lavished on the useless multitudes of both sexes, who could only plead the merits of abstinence and chastity."

EDWARD GIBBON, The Fall of the Roman Empire

It is surprising that the harsh treatment of the lower classes in the late Empire did not produce more uprisings, like that of the Bagaudae in Gaul. Most of the peasants seemed not to care *who* ruled them. The Circumcellions of North Africa, a militant fringe of the Donatists, are a special case since they were inspired by both religious and social grievances. The Circumcellions were peasants who lived around the shrines of their martyrs, where they stored their food. They raided the country villas of catholic landlords, combining economic and religious protest.

Why Rome fell

Ever since Edward Gibbon concluded that his account of the fall of the Roman Empire had traced 'the triumph of Barbarism and Religion', there has been a special interest in trying to explain why it fell.

The immediate cause is, of course, the barbarian attacks on the Western Empire in the fifth century which resulted in the replacement of Roman government by Germanic kingdoms in the Western provinces. But it is surprising that the barbarian attacks, which had harassed the Empire since before the Christian era, should suddenly prove fatal in the fifth century.

Numerous unsatisfactory explanations have been given—change in climate, soil exhaustion, race mixture, for example. One popular idea is that the Empire fell because of a decline in morality. Immorality there certainly was in plenty in the Roman Empire—but throughout its history. The late Empire was probably no more immoral than any other period, except possibly in the area of public administration, where corruption and brutality seem to have increased. The church, while it preached against such abuses, contributed to the decline by discouraging good Christians from holding public office.

A much more important cause for the end of the Western Empire was a failure of human and material resources. The West had always been poorer than the East, and conditions had become worse in the two or three hundred years before the disastrous fifth century.

The basic problem was that too many non-productive members of the society had to be fed by too few productive labourers. The army had doubled in size since the third century and the bureaucracy had expanded considerably, while the number of producers had shrunk. In addition, the great senatorial landowners, who possessed a vastly disproportionate share of the wealth of the Empire, frustrated imperial attempts to make them pay a fair share of taxes or to conscript their agricultural labourers into the army. But whatever the causes that make the West weaker than the East, the most important reason for the fall of the Roman Empire in the West was the unprecedented severity of barbarian attacks in the fifth century.

Was Christianity to blame?

Gibbon complained that 'a large part of public and private wealth was consecrated to the specious demands of charity and devotion; and the soldiers' pay was lavished on the useless multitudes of both sexes, who could only plead the merits of abstinence and chastity.' Though Gibbon's anti-religious bias is evident, the numerous monks and clergy were certainly among those non-producers who had to be fed from the diminishing resources of the Empire.

The bulk of the Roman troops were withdrawn from Britain in 407, never to return. They abandoned the northern frontier marked by Hadrian's Wall.

Furthermore, the church, in ocusing attention on the heavenly 'City of God', encouraged neglect of the earthly 'City of Man'—the Empire. The church attracted he most creative minds and the nost capable leaders of the day. Athanasius, Ambrose, Augustine and Gregory the Great are only he most famous of hundreds of capable bishops who might have staffed the imperial civil service, so badly in need of leadership. Ambrose, Gregory and Sidonius Apollinaris were all magistrates before they responded to the call of God.

Christians in the West tended f not to welcome the barbarians, at least to accept them as God's judgement and to reach n understanding with them. For example, Pope Gregory the Great despaired about the decaying city of Rome and negotiated with he invading Lombards (without imperial authorization). But while submitting to barbarian political rule, the church converted he barbarians to orthodox Christianity.

Christians thus shared esponsibility for the fall of the Western Empire. But by the fifth entury was the Empire worth aving? It had proved itself unable to deal not only with the barbarian problem, but with political, social and economic problems as well. We may well regret the passing of 'the glory that was Greece and the grandeur that was Rome'. But the fall of the Western Empire was offset in the long run by the conversion of the barbarians of Western Europe to Christianity.

Italy under Theodoric and Justinian

Odoacer, the Gothic chief who had deposed the last Roman Emperor in the West, was himself overthrown in 493 by Theodoric, chief of a group of Ostrogoths, who had served previously in the Eastern Empire. Theodoric now ruled a Gothic kingdom in Italy, taking over all the old Roman administration including the Senate. His administration of both Romans and barbarians worked surprisingly well, at least until near the end of his reign, when harmony was destroyed in the intrigues that accompanied the death of the statesman Boethius.

The Ostrogoths were Arian Christians, but tolerant, like the Visigoths and Burgundians. Although Theodoric made the

The pagans' complaint

“*When we used to sacrifice to our gods, Rome was flourishing; but now when people sacrifice to your God everywhere, and our sacrifices are forbidden, see what is happening to Rome.*”

AUGUSTINE

A crude representation decorates the gravestone of a Frankish warrior.

popes do as he wanted, he attempted to maintain friendly re tions with his catholic (mainstrea Christian) subjects. In North Africa the church suffered more from the barbarians. Augustine's death in 430, during the siege of the Vandals, marked the end of t brilliant period in its history. The Vandals were intolerant Arians who sent nearly 5,000 Catholics the southern desert and shipped Catholic bishops to Corsica to cu timber for the fleet.

After the death of Theodoric in 526 the generals of the Eastern Emperor Justinian (527–65) temporarily reconquered Italy. B the imperial army was unable to defend Italy against the Lombard invasions after Justinian's death, and Italy was once more dominated by barbarians. Although th imperial army managed to hold Ravenna and some other parts of Italy, Rome itself was governed her bishop.

Clovis and the church Gaul

In Gaul, Clovis, pagan king of the Franks, married a Catholic Christian princess and was converted to orthodox Christianity in 496. This proved extremely significant for Christianity in the West. Legend makes Clovis a second Constantine, praying in battle to the Christian God and receiving baptism after his victory. But though Clovis' conversion broug to his side the Gallo-Roman church, it changed neither his character nor his reign, which co tinued to prosper on its treacher brutality and murder. Gregory of Tours reported that Clovis' reign was attended by miraculous sign of divine approval; the pious bish had to see the hand of God in a victory which meant the triumph Catholic Christianity in Gaul.

Clergy, bishops and pope

Richard A. Todd

The growth of the church in the third century had so increased the responsibilities of the bishop, at least in the cities and larger towns, that it was no longer possible for him to know all his flock. Theoretically a bishop could have been appointed for each small congregation, but the idea of dividing the church by having more than one bishop in a city seems never to have been considered in the West.

Instead, the number of presbyters (priests) assisting the bishop was increased and more minor clergy appointed. By the mid-third century in Rome exorcists had joined readers on the bishop's liturgical staff and sub-deacons and acolytes had become his personal and secretarial assistants. The bishop closely controlled this developing organization.

In the fourth century these clerical offices became a formal hierarchy, similar to the succession of posts held by the ambitious Roman aristocrat. The aspiring church leader began as a reader, often in childhood, proceeding to acolyte (assistant) and subdeacon, up to the age of thirty. Then followed five years as deacon and ten as priest, so that the minimum age for a bishop was set at forty-five. Although this was normal in the Western church, exceptions could still be made, as the career of Ambrose illustrates. Ambrose passed from baptism to bishop of Milan in a week.

All the churches of a city were under the direct pastoral care of its bishop. At Rome, for example, the bishop himself took all baptisms and the consecrated elements for the eucharist were carried around each Sunday by acolytes from the bishop to the various churches of the city. Although several priests

After Constantine, churches were built by each Christian community. These are at Sardis, Philippi, Ephesus and Jerash (Gerasa).

JERome

Bruce A. Demarest

Jerome's Latin Bible

“I am not so stupid as to think that any of the Lord's words either need correcting or are not divinely inspired; but the Latin manuscripts of the Scriptures are proved faulty by the variations which are found in all of them. My aim has been to restore them to the form of the Greek original, from which my critics do not deny that they have been translated.”

JEROME, Letters XXVII

Jerome (about 345–420), the leading biblical scholar of his time in the Western church, was born in a small town in north–east Italy. He studied the classical disciplines and was baptized at Rome and then journeyed through Gaul where he was converted to ascetic Christianity and joined an ascetic community near his home at Aquileia. Later at Antioch in 374, Jerome had a vision criticizing his preoccupation with secular learning and accusing him of being a 'follower of Cicero and not of Christ'. This led the learned scholar to withdraw to an ascetic life in the Syrian desert south–east of Antioch, where he mastered Hebrew and transcribed biblical manuscripts.

After ordination at Antioch, Jerome travelled to Constantinople where he studied with the Eastern theologian Gregory of Nazianzus in 380. He then acted as secretary to Pope Damasus in Rome in 382, where he also became involved in various experiments in monastic living by aristocrats. While at Rome, Jerome was commissioned by the pope to make an improved Latin translation of the Bible. Following the death of Pope Damasus Jerome visited Antioch, Egypt and the Holy Land, but finally setted down to monastic life in Bethlehem in 386. There he spent the rest of his days in seclusion completing his translation of the Scriptures into Latin and writing commentaries on the books of the Bible.

Jerome achieved distinction in his studies of the text of the Bible and his biblical exegesis, based on his unsurpassed skills with languages. Pope Damasus wanted a Latin version of the Scriptures to replace the confusion of corrupted 'Old Latin' manuscripts then in circulation. Jerome went back to the Greek version of the Old Testament (the *Septuagint*) and the Greek New Testament to prepare fresh Latin translations of the Psalms, other Old Testament books, and the Gospels. Later, convinced of the need to base his Old Testament translation on the Hebrew original rather than the Greek of the *Septuagint,* in his own words, to 'give my Latin readers the hidden treasures of Hebrew erudition', Jerome reworked his Latin translation of the Old Testament to conform more closely to the Hebrew Bible. After twenty-three years' labour, Jerome completed his revision of the Latin Scriptures (382–405). Known as the 'Vulgate Bible' it was eventually accepted as the authorized Latin version of the Western church, and although the text became corrupted during the Middle Ages, its supremacy was reaffirmed by the Council of Trent (1546).

Jerome, who was a biblical scholar not a theologian, wrote commentaries on most of the Bible. Because of his use of Hebrew and Greek, his profound knowledge of early church writings, and his familiarity with the Bible lands gained by much travel, Jerome's comments on Scripture are of considerable significance. He sought to steer a safe course between an allegorical and a woodenly literal interpretation of Scripture. Although he avoided the unrestrained use of allegory of many contemporaries, he commended a threefold interpretation (finding historical, symbolic and spiritual senses) which resulted in ıumerous arbitrary and mystical ɔxplanations.

Jerome's commentaries on Scripture were prepared with great speed. His exposition of Galatians was written at the rate of a thousand lines per day, and his Matthew commentary was completed within a fortnight. His exposition of Scripture leans heavily on Jewish tradition, and also involves extensive quotations of numerous authorities of the early church. Quite often Jerome's comments are indistinguishable from those of other interpreters. Nevertheless, Jerome ranks with Origen and Augustine as an early biblical interpreter of the first order. He also translated into Latin several works by Greek theologians, and engaged in one controversy after another with merciless passion.

One of the most cultured and learned of the Fathers, Jerome's reputation as a keen biblical scholar endures. 'The great hermit of Bethlehem had less genius than Augustine, less purity and loftiness of character than Ambrose, less sovereign good sense and steadfastness than Chrysostom, less keenness of insight and consistency of courage than Theodore of Mopsuestia; but in learning and versatile talent he was superior to them all' (Farrar).

Bethlehem: Jerome spent the last thirty-three years of his life here, though he remained very critical of Eastern Christianity.

were attached to each church, there was no parish priest, at least until the end of the fifth century.

Financing the churches

The bishop also controlled the finances of all the churches and clergy of the city. Churches had begun to acquire property by the third century, but it was the extraordinary growth of church wealth in the fourth century that changed the pattern of church support. After Constantine, endowments, supplemented by government subsidies, provided the major income, though voluntary offerings always remained an important part of church revenue. Earlier on the bishop alone allocated these revenues, which resulted in abuses. By the end of the fifth century the church at Rome had devised a system by which all income from rents and offerings was divided into four parts—for bishop, clergy, the poor, and for repair and lighting of the churches. Elsewhere the distribution varied.

Under this system the bishop received an income much greater than that of the priests and deacons—though he had to spend a considerable amount on hospitality. Another contrast was that between rich and poor churches. The wealth of the Roman bishop was enough to make the great pagan senator Praetextatus say, 'Make me bishop of Rome and I will become a Christian tomorrow.' The regular income of some country clergy was so small, on the other hand, that they had to rely primarily on the generosity of the Christians of their congregation.

Country churches

"Make me a bishop of Rome and I will become a Christian tomorrow."

PRAETEXTATUS

The Christian church was primarily a church of the cities for the first centuries of its existence. By the beginning of the fourth century, however, it had begun to move into the countryside in the West (earlier in the East), usually as a result of the preaching tours of bishops, who set up churches in the larger villages to care for their new converts. At first these churches were under the care of clergy sent out from the city. Only in the sixth century, and primarily in Gaul, did each country church come to have its own staff of clergy. Priests in these country parishes were still consecrated and controlled by the city bishop but could administer the sacraments. The church was beginning to take on the form of local parish ministry familiar in the Middle Ages and modern times.

Another kind of country church developed at the same time. This was the church building given by a landowner to benefit those on his private estate. The landowner would normally provide an endowment for the upkeep of the church and have the right to appoint the clergy. Such clergy, though subject to the bishop, were not to the same extent under his control.

Church organization grew in two ways: by the development of the authority of church councils, and that of certain bishops over other bishops. Councils developed out of the irregular meetings of bishops of neighbouring communities to discuss common problems. These meetings became more regular during the third century when some local and provincial councils began to meet annually.

Constantine called larger councils to settle matters that could not be resolved by local or provincial synods. Arles, in 314, was a general council of the Western church and Nicaea, in 325, the first general council of the whole church. The decrees of these and subsequent councils became the canon law of the church.

The bishop of Rome pre-eminent

Meanwhile the growth in the authority of the bishop of Rome was of vital significance. In theory bishops were all equal, but from earliest times some were more prominent than others because of the importance of their cities. The most important were Alexandria, Antioch, Rome and Carthage. The Council of Nicaea recognized the first three of these as pre-eminent in their own areas.

Constantinople was added in 381, when the church council meeting in that city declared it second only to Rome. The bishop of Rome objected to this because it implied that the position of church and bishop depended on the status of their city in the Empire. The pre-eminence of Rome did not depend on any such historical accident, nor on the decrees of any synod, declared a Council of Rome probably in 382, under Damasus' leadership. Rome's position was due to the pope's position as successor to Peter, the founder of the Roman church, on whom

Christ had promised he would build his church. This exalted view, though not for some time accepted even in the West, was the foundation for the eventual supremacy of the bishop of Rome in the church of the Middle Ages.

Constantine's reign as the first Christian emperor was immensely significant for the bishop of Rome. The Roman church suddenly found itself not only free of persecution but also gifted with churches and estates. Constantine ordered a basilica to be begun over the shrine of Peter on the Vatican hill, and another over the shrine of Paul on the Ostian Way; and the Lateran Palace of the Empress Fausta was given to the bishop of Rome as his official residence.

But Constantine was certainly not the emperor of later legend, prostrate before Pope Sylvester,

JOHN CHRYSOSTOM

Everett Ferguson

John, who became known as the greatest of Christian preachers, was born about 350 at Antioch. He was brought up by his devoted mother Anthusa, who at twenty was left a widow with an infant son. John's teacher, the pagan orator Libanius, paid Anthusa the tribute, 'God, what women these Christians have!'

John was baptized at the age of eighteen and became a reader in the church. His devotion to ascetic practices, including two years living alone in a mountain cave, ruined his health. Returning to the city, he was ordained a deacon in 381 and presbyter in 386. From the latter date he was appointed to preach in the principal church in Antioch, where he built up his reputation as a preacher.

In 397 John was chosen bishop of Constantinople against his will and consecrated to that position in 398. He was unsuited for the intrigues and pressures of Constantinople. His efforts to raise the moral climate of the capital met strong opposition. His enemies joined forces: the Empress Eudoxia, stung by his attacks on sin in high places; local clergy who found John too strict; and Theophilus, patriarch of Alexandria, jealous of a churchman from Antioch at the capital. They had John deposed at the 'synod of the Oak' in 403. The Emperor accepted the decision and exiled him. The people of Constantinople rioted in support of their bishop; the Emperor was frightened by the response and recalled John the next day.

John's brave, if tactless, preaching angered Eudoxia again, and his enemies now tried to banish him once more. The Emperor ordered him to cease his official church duties, which he refused to do. While gathering catechumens for baptism, he was driven out of the church by soldiers, and blood stained the baptismal waters. This exile (404) ended in his death in 407. His remains were brought back to Constantinople in 438 and buried in the Church of the Apostles.

John Chrysostom has been honoured for his courage and piety. From the sixth century he has been known as the 'Golden mouth', for he was a master of preaching. His insights into the meaning of the Greek Bible and skill in applying it practically to his hearers are the enduring contribution of his hundreds of surviving sermons.

"Again Herodias raves, again she dances, again she demands John's head on a charger."

JOHN CHRYSOSTOM attacks the Empress Eudoxia from the pulpit.

stripped of his imperial regalia, begging forgiveness for his sins—or handing over to the pope the rule of Rome, Italy and the West, as the forged *Donation of Constantine* has it.

Until Damasus (366–84) the popes of this period were at best undistinguished men who were unable and sometimes unwilling to stop the Emperor from dominating the church. The dramatic change at the end of the fourth century, when the church came to dominate the Emperor, was due to Ambrose, the great bishop of Milan.

A great basilica dedicated to Peter was built on the Vatican hill. The five aisles can be seen clearly in this seventeenth-century fresco of the church.

But it was Ambrose's contemporary Damasus who made the theory about Peter an essential part of papal doctrine. He was the first pope to refer consistently to the church of Rome as the 'apostolic see' and to address bishops of other churches as 'sons' rather than as 'brothers'.

Damasus' successor, Siricius (384–99) was the first to use the 'decretal', a letter of instruction modelled on the Emperor's decree sent to provincial governors. In using this kind of letter the pope was claiming the same kind of binding authority for himself in the church as the Emperor had in secular affairs.

The successors of Siricius, Innocent I (401–17), Zosimus (417–18) and Boniface I (418–22), continued and built on the claim to Peter's authority, although theory often ran ahead of practice. Innocent claimed universal authority for the bishop of Rome by declaring that nothing done in the provinces could be regarded as finished until it had come to his knowledge, and that the pope's decisions affected 'all the churches of the world'.

The ineffective Zosimus made just as exalted claims, but his success was meagre, for he fell foul of the Emperor, the strongly independent North African church and some strong-minded bishops in Gaul. He reversed Innocent's condemnation of Pelagius, but was forced to change his decision by pressure from the Emperor and the North African church.

Leo I and Gelasius I

Popes Leo I (440–61) and Gelasius I (492–96) were undoubtedly the most significant of the fifth century. The climax of barbarian attacks on the Empire made the imperial court at Ravenna desperate for the support of any authority that might help to hold the Empire together. This is the background to the decree of the Emperor Valentinian III (in 445) instructing Aëtius, the Roman commander in Gaul, to compel the attendance at the papal court of any bishop who refused to come voluntarily. An emperor's edict had turned the pope's claim into law.

The stories about Leo's intercession with Attila the Hun and Gaiseric the Vandal king suggest that the pope could now perform imperial services at a time when the civil government was disintegrating. Leo had a moment of triumph in the east when his skilful *Tome* (on the divine and human natures of Christ) was read before the fourth general Council of Chalcedon (451) and was received with the cry, 'St Peter has spoken through Leo!' But the Council of Chalcedon rejected the Petrine basis for the pope's supremacy, by declaring that a city's ecclesiastical status was determined by its civil status, and that the church of 'New Rome' (Constantinople) had a legal position similar to that of Old Rome. The Roman delegates refused to sign and left in protest.

Leo set out more clearly than any before him the concept that the papacy was Peter's own office, not only as founder but also as present ruler of the church through his servant, the pope. Leo claimed it did not matter how unworthy any particular pope might be, as long as he was the successor of Peter and was acting according to canon law.

Gelasius I completed the papal theory of the Middle Ages. He insisted that the Emperor must guard the church but submit himself to the guidance of the pope, who was himself guided by God and St Peter. It followed that clergy should not be judged in secular courts and that the pope himself could not be judged by any man. As Gelasius put it, 'Nobody at any time and for whatever human pretext may haughtily set himself above the office of the pope who by Christ's order was set above all and everyone and whom the universal church has always recognized as its head.'

For more than half a century after Gelasius the real position of the popes was very much less than their exalted claims. They were used, and sometimes abused, first by the Gothic kings in Italy and then, after Justinian reconquered the West, by the Eastern emperors. There were scenes of humiliation, as when Pope John

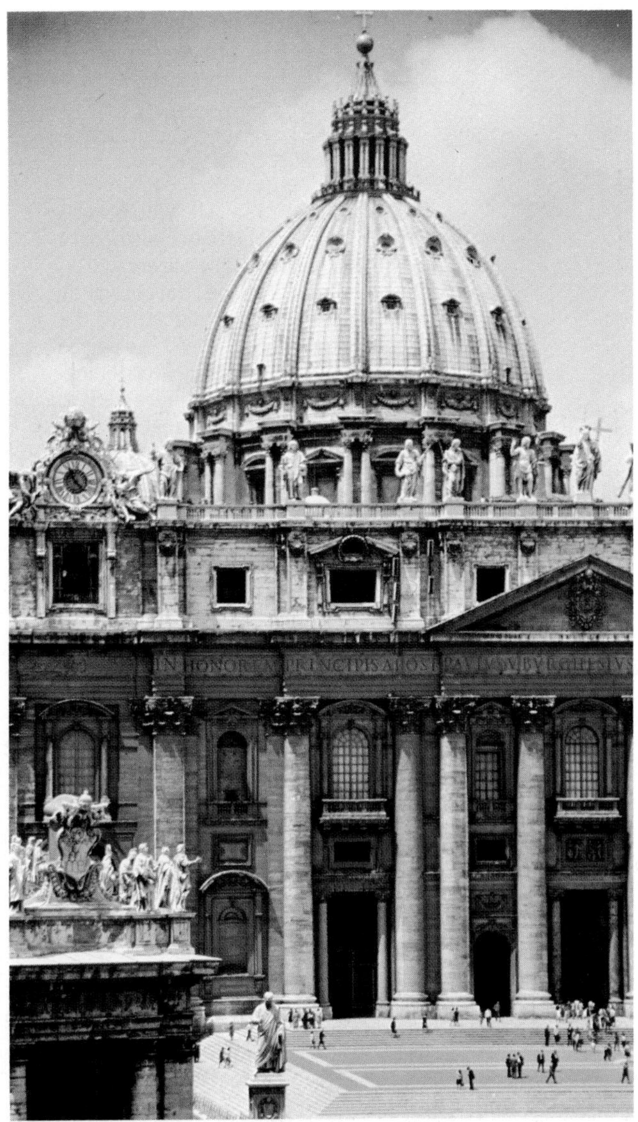

The Constantinian basilica of St Peter was demolished during the sixteenth century to make way for the present building.

COLUMBA

Robert G. Clouse

Columba (521–97), who became a famous abbot and missionary, was born of noble parents in Donegal, Ireland, the land of the 'Scots'. He was educated at the schools of Finbar at Moville and Finnian at Clonard. After being ordained, he preached widely and helped to establish churches and monasteries, such as those at Derry and Durrow.

In 563 Columba left Ireland, determined to 'go on pilgrimage for Christ'. There is some disagreement over why he left his homeland. He had been involved in a dispute over the possession of a manuscript he had copied out, and he fell into disfavour for his part in causing the civil war that followed between his clan and the High King Diarmid. His departure may have been partly a self-imposed penance.

With twelve companions Columba sailed to the island of Iona on the west coast of Scotland. There he established a monastery which served as a base for evangelism among his fellow Scots and among the Picts. A courageous man, almost warlike at times, Columba preached to people who were under the influence of Druid opponents of Christianity. His faithfulness was rewarded when rulers such as Brude, king of the Picts, were converted. Many churches were founded and much of the religious, political and social life of Scotland Christianized. The extent of Columba's influence beyond the west of Scotland is uncertain.

Columba combined deep visionary piety and a forceful involvement in the affairs of kings and chiefs with a concern for scholarship and a love of nature. He is a typical figure of the Celtic church. His achievements illustrate the importance of the Celtic church in bringing a revival of Christianity to Western Europe after the fall of the Roman Empire. An important early *Life of Columba* was written about 688–92 by Adamnan, the ninth abbot of Iona.

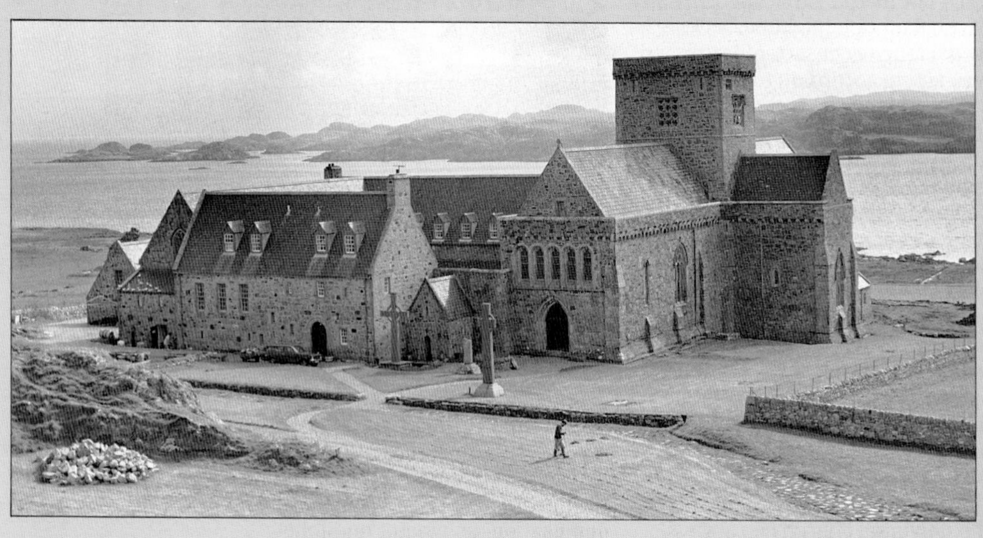

The monastery of Iona became the centre for the energetic spread of Christianity and Celtic monasticism throughout Scotland and northern England.

I, on the orders of Theodoric the Ostrogothic king of Italy, travelled to Constantinople to plead with the Emperor on behalf of Arian Christians. When he returned in failure he was thrown into prison. The papacy remained subservient to Constantinople long after the death of Justinian and the failure of Roman rule in Italy. Until 741 papal elections had to be confirmed by Constantinople, or the imperial exarch of Ravenna.

Gregory and the Lombards

The Lombard invasions ended Roman imperial domination of Italy and gave the pope a new independence, though they threatened to overwhelm the city of Rome in a barbarian flood. Fortunately for Rome, and the Roman church, Gregory the Great, pope during the critical last decade of the sixth century was equal to the challenge. Gregory was a Roman of noble birth who was prefect of the city about 573, but soon after gave up his wealth and estates to become a monk. A few years later he was recalled by the pope for administrative work in Rome, and then to serve as ambassador to Constantinople.

When Gregory became pope in 590 Rome's situation was desperate. The Romans faced the Lombard threat with no hope of help from the imperial exarch at Ravenna, and famine and plague were also in the land. Gregory took command without hesitation, provisioned the city and provided for its defence, sent orders to generals in the field, negotiated with the Lombards, and finally concluded peace without the Emperor's authorization. No pope before Gregory had dared half as much.

In the midst of all this Gregory was administering the estates of the church, caring for the spiritual needs of his flock, strengthening the churches in Gaul and Spain, defending the rights of the church of Rome against the claims of Constantinople, and sending missionaries to England. Gregory's period as pope, by its extension of the pope's authority, marks the transition from the ancient world of imperial Rome to medieval Christendom united by the Roman Catholic church.

Into the Middle Ages

The Roman church played a central role in the transition to the medieval world, since it was primarily the church, the principal surviving institution from the ancient world, that transmitted Roman culture to the Middle Ages. In many ways the Roman church had taken on the shape of the Roman world in which it had grown to maturity.

The most obvious example of this is the way in which the church's organization followed the pattern of the imperial administration. Each city was entitled to a bishop and each province to an archbishop. Within the bishop's diocese, the hierarchy of officers was virtually the same as that of the Roman civil administration. Church canon law was modelled on Roman law. At first it contained only decrees of church councils, but eventually included papal decretals, which paralleled imperial edicts. The Latin language gave a unity to the Christian world. Though little ancient literature joined the mainstream of medieval culture, Christian literature and learning were patterned on Latin models. Christian architecture was naturally Roman in origin. The obvious example of this is the development of the basilica-church, and later the medieval cathedral, from the Roman meeting-hall known as a basilica.

The church in North Africa

David F. Wright

The Great Persecution initiated by Diocletian affected Africa, directly and indirectly, more severely than anywhere else in the West. For example, during the persecution all forty-seven Christians from Abitina were martyred at Carthage. The African church had massively expanded during the third century. Moreover, response to the imperial decrees, and esteem for confessors and martyrs, caused conflict, resulting in the division between the Donatists and the catholics. Soon bishop was ranged against bishop in many a town and village.

The Donatists flourished despite and because of persecution by emperors. A protracted assembly in the latter years of Constantine gathered 270 Donatist bishops. Constantine had to acquiesce when they took over a basilica he had built in the Numidian city of Cirta (renamed Constantine), and granted the catholics another building. After Julian's reign the Donatists dominated the fourth-century church in North Africa. Social protest was expressed in religious dissent. In Donatus and Parmenian they had gifted leaders, and thus could even afford to expel the ablest African theologian of the years between Tertullian and Augustine—Tyconius, who lost an internal Donatist debate about the nature of the church.

In the early fourth century lived two African orators and apologists who were noted writers. Arnobius the Elder from Numidia was the teacher of Lactantius, who died around 320. Lactantius served

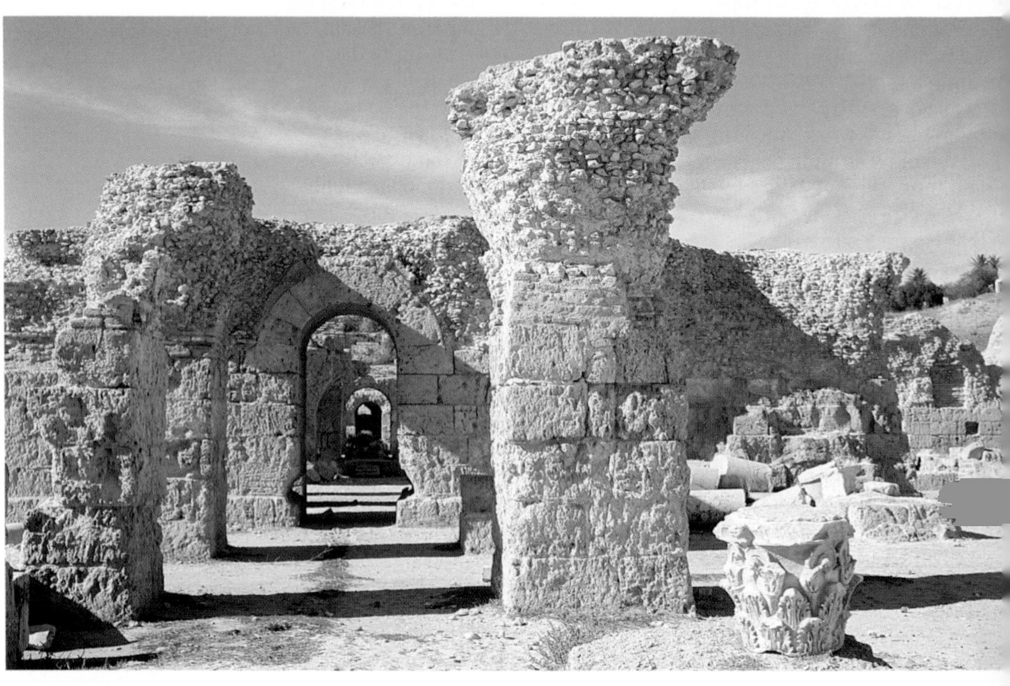

The ruins of ancient Carthage, near Cape Bon, Tunisia. Carthage was a great Christian centre in the early centuries.

The capitol building at Thucca (modern Dougga, Tunisia). The Romans imposed their system of government throughout the Empire.

;s a tutor in Diocletian's court ıt Nicomedia, and again later, ıfter becoming a Christian, in ;onstantine's. His elegant Latin ·arned him the title 'The Christian ;icero'. His book *The Deaths of the ʼersecutors* luridly demonstrates hat persecutors come to bad ·nds, and three other apologetic vorks, including *The Divine nstitutes*, commend Christianity o educated readers. His theol- ·gy was defective, being often ationalistic and moralistic in tone.

Manicheism was also successful ı Africa, despite being banned in round 302. It gathered up rem- ants of the Gnostic tradition, and s austerity and radicalism also ppealed to minds as distinguished s Augustine's, who recruited ther converts.

Augustine's appointment as pres- yter and bishop of Hippo marked ıe beginning of a catholic resur- ence, and hastened the downfall f the Donatists, who at their eak around 394 assembled 310 ishops. The Donatist Circum- ellions, who had easily been con- ısed with the aggressively ortho- ox roving monks of the East, had iscredited asceticism. Augustine timulated the monastic movement ithin the catholic church. From is cathedral chapter-cum-seminary merged several bishops for frican churches.

Above all, Augustine raised the elf-confidence and intellectual ·vel of African catholicism. (He ad himself encountered enlight- ıed catholic Christianity only ıtside Africa.) Under Aurelius, shop of Carthage 391/2 to about 30, councils of bishops again ecame influential in the church's e. The Councils of Hippo (393) ıd Carthage (397) published the rst complete canons of the New estament in the West. Councils ere important in uniting the bish- ɔs on issues such as Donatism.

The Donatists resisted reasoned argument, and managed to avoid the public debates in which Augustine routed leading Manicheans. But they felt the force of anti-heretical legislation in the late fourth and early fifth centuries. After the imperial enquiry under the commissioner Marcellinus at Carthage in 411, when 286 catholic bishops confronted 284 Donatists, they suffered harsh repression, especially in the better-policed cities nearer the coast. Donatist strength came to be concentrated in Numidia. In the process of defeating Donatism, African churchmen found themselves on the side of the Empire with untypical enthusiasm.

The African church had known close, but rarely subservient, relations with the church of Rome at least since Tertullian's time. The Donatists found it expedient to maintain a Roman congregation for a period. In their anti-Donatist campaign the African bishops sought Roman support, and the Pelagian controversy meant that they uncharacteristically became more dependent on Roman bishops.

Africa had taken the initiative in condemning Celestius in 411—the same year as the catholic-Donatist confrontation at Carthage. Issues of baptism and the doctrine of the church were involved in both cases. After acquittals in Palestine, Pelagius too was first condemned at councils of Carthage and Milevis, in 416. When Pope Zosimus lifted his predecessor's

AUGUSTINE OF HIPPO

David F. Wright

Augustine, whose influence was to dominate the medieval church in the West, was born to African parents of Romanized Berber origins in Tagaste in Numidia (modern Algeria) in 354. From childhood he was a catechumen, learning the Christian faith from his earnest mother Monnica, but his baptism was delayed until 387 by a lengthy religious and philosophical pilgrimage, described in his *Confessions*.

He excelled in the literary education of his time, except in Greek, and lectured in rhetoric at Carthage. In 373 a work by Cicero converted him to love the divine wisdom; but he was repelled by the Bible's apparent barbarity. He became a follower of Manicheism, a Gnostic religion with a dualistic mythology which encouraged asceticism and intense devotion to Christ. He persisted with Manicheism for nine years, although he soon began to distrust its claims to demonstrate the truth by rational means.

Disillusioned, he went to Rome, where for a time he shared the 'Academics" despair of reaching any certainty. He was even tempted to taste the pleasures of Epicureanism. But in 384 he was appointed imperial rhetorician at Milan and exposed to the influence of Bishop Ambrose and the ideas of Neoplatonism. Together they undermined the obstacles which had alienated him from the orthodox faith.

From Ambrose he discovered that Christianity could be eloquent and intelligent and learnt that the difficult stories of the Old Testament could be treated as allegories. The Neoplatonists revealed the spiritual perfection of

This aerial view of Hippo (Algeria) shows the remains of several of the Christian buildings. Around the basilica itself cluster a baptistery, chapels, courtyard, library and dwellings. This was probably where Augustine spent his years as a bishop.

God and sought insight and vision through inward contemplation. Augustine came to believe that the cause of evil, which preoccupied him all his days, lay in the absence of good, rather than being a power in itself as the Manichees believed.

He was now challenged to abandon 'the flesh and the world'. He had lived with a common-law wife for over ten years, and seemed destined for high office (which would gratify Monnica). The challenge to 'conversion from the world' came through repeated stories of heroic renunciations such as Antony's and Victorinus's. The chain finally snapped as he read Romans 13:13–14 in a garden in Milan.

Prior to baptism Augustine retired to Cassiciacum, where a few companions spent their disciplined leisure as Christian philosophers. On returning to Africa in 388 after Monnica's death, he formed a monastic community for study and contemplation at Tagaste. However, in 391 he was press-ganged into the priesthood at Hippo on the coast (modern Annata), and by 396 he was the catholic bishop. For the rest of his life he was preacher and pastor, minister of the sacraments, judge and intercessor, trustee and organizer of charity, as well as a tireless defender of catholic orthodoxy and a voluminous writer. Hippo's half-pagan catholics and stubborn Donatists rapidly turned him from the confident humanism of a Christian Neoplatonist to a more biblical and pessimistic view of human nature, society and history. The *Confessions* were an early fruit of this new outlook, *The City of God* a more mature one.

Augustine developed his influential principle, 'Believe in order to understand', as he opposed the rationalism of the Manicheans. He used the principle himself in numerous writings, above all in *The Trinity*. Against the Donatists he insisted that the church was a mixed field of wheat and tares, believers and unbelievers, growing together until the harvest. He undercut Donatist rebaptism by claiming that Christ is the chief minister of the sacraments, so that they remained true sacraments even if administered by unworthy people. Yet the sacraments brought no benefit as long as those receiving them remained outside the fold of the Spirit's unity and love. Augustine also justified the coercion of dissident Christians as being an act of loving correction.

Pelagian refugees from sacked Rome occupied Augustine's attention from 411. He attacked them only after Celestius questioned the grounds for infant baptism (which Augustine helped to make normal practice). The eventual condemnation of the Pelagians in the West came largely as the result of African pressure spearheaded by Augustine. They provoked him to develop further his doctrines of the fall and original sin, as both corruption and guilt; the necessity of grace to free the will in turning to God; and the predestination and perseverance of the 'fixed number of the elect'.

The Arian Vandal invaders were besieging Hippo when Augustine died in 430. Living amid the shocks and disruptions of the disintegrating Roman Empire, Augustine taught Christians to endure the world, where evil reigns invincibly, and to seek the peace of the heavenly city. He stood at the close of the creative era of Latin Christianity and was to dominate the minds of medieval and Reformation church leaders.

What is man?

"Can any praise be worthy of the Lord's majesty? How magnificent is his strength! How inscrutable his wisdom! Man is one of your creatures, Lord, and his instinct is to praise you. He bears about him the mark of death, the sign of his own sin, to remind him that you thwart the proud. But still, since he is part of your creation, he wishes to praise you. The thought of you stirs him so deeply that he cannot be content unless he praises you, because you made us for yourself and our hearts find no peace until they rest in you."

From AUGUSTINE's Confessions

AUGUSTINE DESCRIBES HIS CONVERSION

"I probed the hidden depths of my soul and wrung its pitiful secrets from it, and when I gathered them all before the eyes of my heart, a great storm broke within me, bringing with it a great deluge of tears . . . For I felt that I was still enslaved by my sins, and in my misery I kept crying, 'How long shall I go on saying "Tomorrow, tomorrow"? Why not now? Why not make an end of my ugly sins at this moment?'

I was asking myself these questions, weeping all the while with the most bitter sorrow in my heart, when all at once I heard the sing-song voice of a child in a nearby house. Whether it was the voice of a boy or a girl I cannot say, but again and again it repeated the chorus, 'Take it and read, take it and read.' At this I looked up, thinking hard whether there was any kind of game in which children used to chant words like these, but I could not remember ever hearing them before. I stemmed my flood of tears and stood up, telling myself that this could only be God's command to open my book of Scripture and read the first passage on which my eyes should fall. For I had heard the story of Antony, and I remembered how he had happened to go into a church while the Gospel was being read and had taken it as an instruction addressed to himself when he heard the words, 'Go home and sell all that belongs to you. Give it to the poor, and so the treasure you have shall be in heaven; then come back and follow me.' By this message from God he had at once been converted.

So I hurried back to the place where Alypius was sitting, for when I stood up to move away I had put down the book containing Paul's Letters. I seized it and opened it, and in silence I read the first passage on which my eyes fell: 'No orgies or drunkenness, no immorality or indecency, no fighting or jealousy. Take up the weapons of the Lord Jesus Christ; and stop giving attention to your sinful nature, to satisfy its desires.' I had no wish to read more and no need to do so. For in an instant, as I came to the end of the sentence, it was as though the light of faith flooded into my heart and all the darkness of doubt was dispelled."

AUGUSTINE's Confessions VIII.12

ban on the pair, another Council of Carthage in 418 weightily repeated earlier African verdicts. Zosimus bowed to the Africans, and the Pelagians' fate in the West was finally decided.

Not all African church leaders shared Augustine's keen opposition to Pelagian teachings. In the late 420s monks at Hadrumetum, in Byzacena (Tunisia), and Carthage suggested modifications to his anti-Pelagian doctrines that amounted to what was misleadingly called 'semi-Pelagianism'.

The case of Apiarius is an example of the African bishops asserting their traditional independence of Rome. Apiarius, a Numidian presbyter, had appealed to Zosimus against deposition by his bishop. Zosimus attempted to reinstate him—but this led to a decree by the Council of Carthage in 418 banning such appeals to authorities outside Africa. The

Roman bishop rested his authority n the canons of Sardica which his ollection of canons attributed to icaea. Africa knew better. When he situation was repeated a few ears later, the Africans insisted n African independence, while ecognizing that Rome had a prinacy of honour. Recently discovered letters of Augustine reveal imilar attitudes over the case of nthony of Fussala. Augustine early resigned.

The Vandals crossed to Africa rom Spain in 429, captured Carhage in 439, and ruled until 533. s a result, catholics and Donatists like were persecuted for a long eriod. The Vandals, who were rian Christians, sought church nity in time-honoured Roman ashion, and imposed rebaptism, xiled bishops and prevented their replacement, and dissolved monasteries. There were peaceful interludes, especially under Gunthamund (484–96), when Dracontius, Africa's only Christian poet of distinction, flourished at Carthage, and under Hilderic (523–30), during whose reign an all-African council met in the capital (525).

Arianism became an inevitable concern of catholic writers. They included Quodvultdeus, bishop of Carthage, whose exile in 456/7 was followed by a vacancy in the see for a quarter of a century. Another exile, Victor, bishop of Vita, compiled an invaluable history of the Arian persecution in about 485. Vigilius, bishop of Thapsus, fled to Constantinople around 484, where he wrote extensively against the Eastern heresies,

This Vandal has become a North African landowner, and is shown leaving his villa.

THE DONATISTS IN NORTH AFRICA

David F. Wright

The Donatists were a protest movement, standing for a holy church, purity of discipline and unflinching defiance of godless rulers. They were named after Donatus, their bishop in Carthage from 313 to about 355.

They elected their own first bishop of Carthage in 312 after rejecting Caecilian, the catholic bishop, because one man who consecrated him, Felix of Apthungi, had allegedly been guilty of *traditio,* the 'handing over' or 'betrayal' of the Scriptures during the Great Persecution. African Christianity, like Judaism, was a religion of the holy book, and the surrender of precious biblical manuscripts to persecutors was naturally viewed by many as apostasy.

The dissidents were motivated by a number of other grievances. The bishops of Numidia (some of whom were themselves guilty of *traditio* and similar compromises) felt slighted. Caecilian's hasty consecration had precluded their own archbishop from taking his traditional place in consecrating the bishop of Carthage. The ambitions of disappointed clerics, the greed of frustrated presbyters and the pique of a formidable lady rebuked by Caecilian for her superstitious devotion to a martyr's relic all played their part. Caecilian had been rather cool towards the confessors awaiting martyrdom, and his predecessor Mensurius had almost gone along with the authorities.

What Donatists believed

The Donatists believed that they constituted the true church, and that the catholics were apostate. When Constantine restricted his grants and immunities to Caecilian's party, the Donatists demanded adjudication of their cause. Repeated enquiries cleared Felix and Caecilian, and an impatient Constantine attempted, with catholic backing, to coerce the Donatists (317–21). Persecution and martyrdom, the

especially Monophysitism. Fulgentius was a monk and founder of monasteries before becoming bishop of Ruspe. He spent fifteen years in exile in Sardinia with numerous other bishops, and as a keen Augustinian wrote against both Arians and Pelagians. Exiled African clergy and monks contributed helpfully to church life in Spain, Italy and Gaul.

After Justinian's general Belisarius reconquered Africa in 533, catholic Christianity recovered much of its vigour. It was now directed more against the Eastern emperors' compromises with the Monophysites than against the Donatists, who were buoyant, especially in Numidia. Mutual toleration between catholics and Donatists under Arian persecution seems to have resulted in practice in each 'denomination' recognizing the other. Pope Gregory I repeatedly rebuked the African bishops for their slackness in opposing the Donatists.

In the seventh century African church leaders, reinforced by the great Eastern Theologian Maximus the Confessor, again resisted the imperial theology of Monotheletism (646). But fate of all the righteous, confirmed them in their convictions. Further oppression under the Emperor Constans in 347–48 left them depleted until Julian's tolerant reign in the 360s, and provoked Donatus' famous question 'What has the Emperor to do with the church?' The Circumcellions' violence provided one answer. They were wandering 'warriors of Christ' on the fringe of the Donatists, righting wrongs and intimidating Donatist waverers and catholic clergy. They were devoted to martyrdom.

The decline of the Donatists

Donatism had become the dominant church in North Africa, but after Parmenian (who succeeded Donatus) its fortunes declined. In the 370s and 390s some Donatists supported local revolts against Roman rule and suffered when they were put down. Above all, in Aurelius of Carthage and in Augustine the catholics at last had leaders who were a match for the Donatists. Augustine issued exhaustive historical and theological counter-arguments and a justification of coercion, while Aurelius' organizing ability produced effective action. Yet it took legal sanctions to check Donatism—especially the Edict of Unity (405) and the proscription which followed the convention in Carthage in 411.

Donatism was inspired by the traditions of African Christianity, as represented by Tertullian and Cyprian. It inevitably gathered up currents of popular social and economic discontent without being itself a nationalist or revolutionary movement.

Under Vandal rule (429–533) the catholics and Donatists suffered together—which probably encouraged mutual acceptance. Subsequently Donatism flourished again, apparently diverging less and less from the catholic body. It survived until North African Christianity was submerged by the invading Moors in the seventh century. Its repression in Augustine's time may have permanently weakened the African church's ability to withstand such a challenge.

“What has the Emperor to do with the church?”

me was running out for African hristianity. The Muslim Saracens egan their invasion in 642/3, took arthage in 698, and completed e conquest by 709. The decline the church is not easy to trace. y 1100 only a handful of bishopcs survived, but a Christian mmunity of some sort lived on in unis until the sixteenth century. nly literary remains and impresve archaeological monuments day bear witness to the life and dependence of early African hristianity.

CHRISTIAN ASCETICS AND MONKS

Michael A. Smith

> *"Antony would eat only once a day after sunset, and sometimes he did not taste food for two or frequently for four days. His food was bread and salt; he drank only water."*
>
> *ATHANASIUS*

Ascetic Christianity may be defined as a more rigorous practice of the faith than normal for the average Christian. It can involve a variety of practices: abstaining from certain things normally considered good (for example, marriage) and adding further requirements or routines (for example, extra set periods of prayer). Asceticism encourages the idea of a double standard, with a spiritual elite set above the general level of Christians. There can also be, in monasticism, the additional step of withdrawing from society and seeking solitude.

Asceticism and the Bible

Parts of the New Testament have been held to encourage asceticism; but there it is advocated for practical reasons, with no suggestion that it is especially praiseworthy. Jesus said that 'there are some who are eunuchs for the sake of the kingdom of God', but this was specifically 'for those who can receive it'. Similarly, Paul's preference for the single life was based on his feeling that Christ's return might come very soon and that marriage ties might impede evangelism.

On the other hand, the New Testament strongly condemns some types of asceticism. Jesus rejected the Pharisees' scruples over clean and unclean food, and Paul attacked the teaching that it was wrong to marry or to eat certain foods.

The Jews had traditions of asceticism, both individual and communal, reaching back into the Old Testament. The Nazirite vow involved temporary abstinence from wine and other restrictions. Later in Israelite history, prophets gathered into special groups for teaching and prayer, under the leadership of notable holy men such as Elisha.

Regular puritanical groups, such as the Rechabites, came into being later; they kept apart from normal Israelite life and aimed at a purer and more faithful devotion to God.

In New Testament times there were both individual and communal ascetics in Palestine. Josephus, the Jewish historian, mentions that he received some of his teaching from a hermit called Banus. John the Baptist, living a solitary ascetic life in the Judean desert, also represents this tradition. On the communal side, the best-known are the Essenes, of whom the group at Qumran who produced the Dead Sea Scrolls were the most prominent. But some Essenes lived ascetic lives in the community, as did some of the Pharisees.

None of the earliest Christians appears to have lived as a hermit or in an ascetic community. Individuals, however, were noted for their rigour of life and devotion to God. James the Lord's brother, for example, was admired by many non-Christian Jews for his constant fasting and prayer. Also, in the early period, any consistent Christian life was likely to be viewed as extremely ascetic by a morally lax society. Some noble Roman ladies, who may have been Christians, are reported by pagan sources to have lived in mourning and seclusion for years, presumably because they had no time for the pagan social life surrounding them.

While Christianity was under threat of persecution, congregations tended to be small, and to keep very high moral standards (even if there were some lapses, which were severely punished). Martyrdom was valued as the supreme example of devotion to God. Although some churches may have had church membership requirements that were ascetic (for instance, some Syriac-speaking churches appear to have accepted as baptized members only those who were celibate), there was no sign of an organized 'spiritual elite' inside the church apart from groups of widows and virgins. On the fringes of mainstream Christianity, for example among Jewish-Christian groups, Marcionites and Montanists, asceticism was very popular, often in the form of encratism (Greek for 'self-control'). Encratites rejected marriage, wine and meat. Clement of Alexandria and Origen laid the foundations for an orthodox theology of asceticism.

The first monks

The late third and early fourth centuries saw the beginnings of monastic asceticism in Christianity. General toleration of Christianity even before Constantine produced an influx of new members into the churches, and growth in numbers was accompanied by a lowering of standards. At the same time martyrdom became less and less frequent, and the martyrs and confessors were replaced as the spiritual elite by the first monks. The monks aimed to live the Christian life to the full, and felt that continued residence in the 'world' hindered this. They tried to achieve a pure Christianity and a deep communion with God which they considered unattainable in the existing churches.

There is considerable debate as to where monasticism began. The first monks were individuals who retreated to the desert in Egypt or Syria. Sometimes these retreats were only temporary, and may have been prompted by the need to flee persecution; often they became permanent. Although he may not have been the earliest, Antony (about 256–356), a Coptic peasant from Egypt, was the first famous hermit. His example was followed by others, and soon there were many hermits, living either singly or in loosely-associated groups on the edge of the desert.

The ascetics settled on the fringe of the desert, in their attempt to find solitude.

The main routine of the hermit was prayer and meditation, supplemented by reading of the Bible. Fasting was also important and they attempted many other rigorous feats such as standing for hours while praying. Some of the prayers were rather mechanical, involving the repetition of short set formulas.

The prolonged loneliness and the shortage of food and sleep fostered hallucinations as well as growth in spiritual awareness of God. Conflicts with demons were frequent. Many of the visions, trances and strange experiences of the desert hermits have obvious psychological explanations (for example, the appearance of the devil as a seductive woman could be the result of repressed sexual feelings). Those who retreated to the desert inevitably abandoned family life, and celibacy was the rule, although some married couples retreated together into the desert, but lived without sexual intercourse. Most hermits remained fairly stationary, but there were some wanderers especially in the regions of Syria including more extreme groups such as the unruly Messalians who wandered about, sleeping rough and keeping up a continual chanting.

Some hermits went to unnatural extremes, such as living at the top of pillars, or walling themselves up in caves. Early hermits were largely lay people. Occasionally they might meet to receive the eucharist, or a priest who was a hermit would minister to a group throughout an area. But the eucharist had little place in the routines of the early hermits.

Simeon Stylites gained fame for endurance, spending the last part of his life on top of a pillar. In time an extensive church was constructed over the site of his achievement. The base of his pillar can be seen in the middle of this picture of the remains of that church, in Syria.

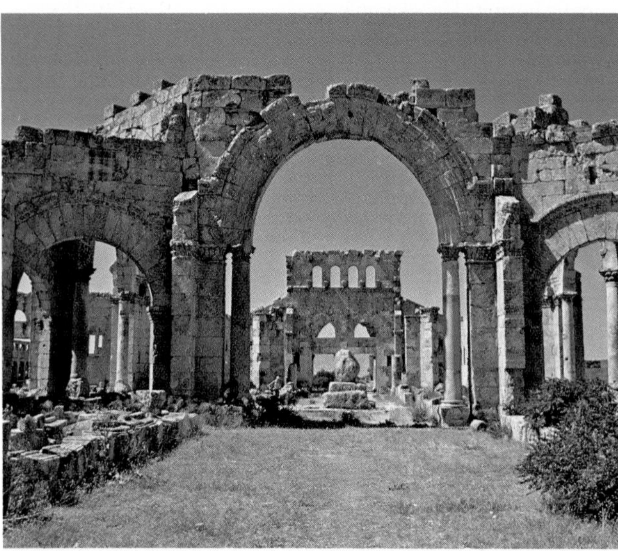

Pachomius starts a community

Communal monasticism was begu about 320 by Pachomius. He was a converted soldier, and after discharge he spent some time as a hermit before setting up his first ascetic community at Tabennisi, b the River Nile in Egypt. The rule for his community survives in a Latin translation made by Jerome.

Pachomius set his face against extremism. He insisted on regular meals and worship, and aimed to make his communities self-supporting through such industries as the weaving of palm-mats or growing fruit and vegetables for sale. Entrants to his community had to hand over their personal wealth to a commo fund, and were only admitted as full members after a period of probation. To prove their initial earnestness they were required to stand outside the monastery door for several days. Part of the qualification for full membership was to memorize parts of the Bible; and if the candidates were illiterate they were taught how to read and write. Although Pachomius' first communities were for men, before his death he supervised the establishment of the first communities for women as well. Pachomius created the basic framework which was followed by all later monastic communities.

Monasticism appeared first out of Eastern Christianity. It was first brought to the notice of the Western churches by Athanasius. While he was in exile in the West between 340 and 346, he was accompanied by two Egyptian monks. Athanasius spent parts o his later exiles hiding among the hermits of the Egyptian desert, and subsequently wrote the life c Antony. This biography provides almost all our knowledge about

Antony, and largely helped to spread the ideals of the ascetic movement. It was quickly translated into Latin, and among those influenced by it was Augustine of Hippo. In the West monasticism had the backing of church leaders such as Ambrose from the very beginning.

Bishops and monks

After Pachomius, Basil the Great (330–79) made the most important contribution to Eastern monasticism. After being educated at Constantinople and Athens, in 356 Basil returned to his home in Cappadocia, determined to renounce the world and live as a hermit. He visited many of the ascetics before setting up his own community with the help of Gregory of Nazianzus. His monastic planning comes from this period, but was influenced by the fact that he was ordained in 364 and became bishop of Caesarea (in Cappadocia) in 370. Basil was both a bishop and an ascetic.

Basil integrated the monastic communities more closely with the church. He believed the bishop should have ultimate authority over a monastery. At the same time, monasteries started to become more outward-looking. Basil's monastery provided medical treatment for the sick and relief for the poor, and also did some work in education. He disapproved strongly of individualistic piety which ran to extremes, and laid down set times of prayer, eight times daily.

Basil's ascetic theory was summed up in two monastic 'rules'. While these owe something to an older friend of his, Eustathius of Sebaste, and have also been modified later, they remain basically the work of Basil. The rule of Basil is still observed in Eastern monasteries today. Basil saw the monastic life as the climax of Christian achievement, with its aim of freeing the soul from the entanglements of the body through discipline. Basil stressed the need for self-examination, but believed that people could in fact fulfil the commandments of God.

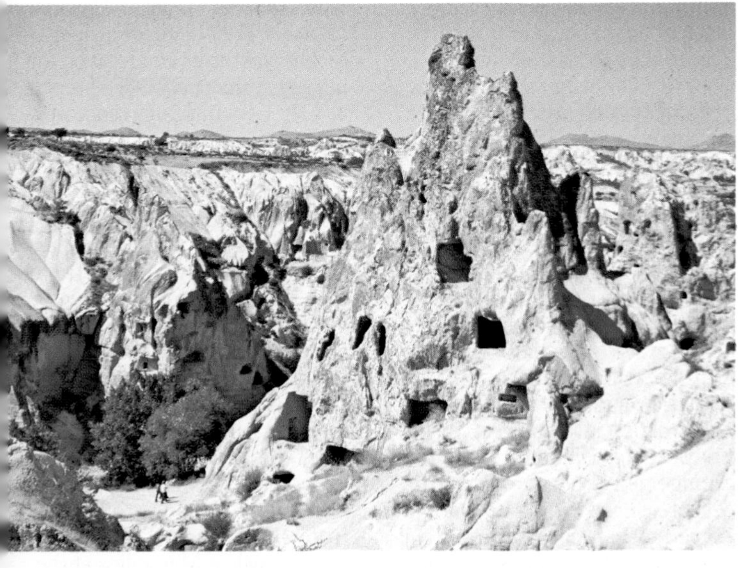

Monasteries and churches were constructed in the extraordinary rock formations of the Goreme valley in Cappadocia (Turkey). The rock was hollowed out to make domes, apses, naves and aisles. Complete underground monasteries were also built.

Monasticism in the West

In the West, monasticism was stimulated by Martin of Tours who died in 397. Martin took up the hermit's life after military service and lived in a solitary cell near Ligugé, in France. His sanctity resulted in many others coming to join him, and a form of community was set up. Rather against his will, he was persuaded to become bishop of Tours in 372, and for some time lived as a hermit in a cell next to the church. The continued distraction of his curious visitors compelled Martin to retreat to Marmoutier, where he set up a monastery as a spring-board for evangelizing much of the still-pagan rural France. His monastery was also a nursery for bishops, as a result of its rigour and sanctity. Most of our knowledge of Martin of Tours comes from a life of him written by Sulpicius Severus. This extremely popular biography helped spread Martin's example throughout the West. Many early churches were dedicated to him, and he is probably the first non-martyr to be venerated as a saint. Martin of Tours set the pattern for the Dark Age 'holy man'.

Augustine of Hippo introduced a new aspect to monasticism; the arrangement whereby a group of celibate clergy lived together and served a local church. Jerome and Rufinus had belonged to a similar group in north-east Italy. After his conversion and his return to North Africa in 388, Augustine gathered a group of his friends to live together in an ascetic community, devoting themselves mainly to study. They continued after Augustine was made bishop of Hippo in 395. Here were the roots of the later cathedral 'chapters' and the medieval practice of the bishop of a town surrounding himself with a 'family', comprising his subordinate clergy and often young men under training for ordination. The monastic rules circulating under his name in the Middle Ages originated in part with Augustine, but they had been worked over extensively by later writers.

Monks and learning

In Egypt, and to a lesser extent in Syria, monastic communities took part in political warfare. Organized and armed crowds of monks took sides in theological disputes and overawed church councils by their presence. Foremost in this activity was Schnoudi, the fierce abbot of the White Monastery in Egypt, who supported Cyril of Alexandria violently and effectively when he got Nestorius condemned for heresy at the council of Ephesus in 431. With the connivance of cynical bishops such as Theophilus of Alexandria, monks were also responsible for destroying pagan temples, and for harassing and even murdering pagans and heretics. In this they were no better than the pagan mobs of earlier periods who had often persecuted Christians savagely at Alexandria and elsewhere.

In the West in the fifth century, monasticism flourished in southern Gaul. Honoratus founded a monastery on the island of Lérins, which became the training ground for many monk-bishops. John Cassian began work at Marseilles at the same period. He had trained as a monk in Bethlehem and Egypt. After a period in Constantinople, he came west and in 415 founded a monastery and a convent at Marseilles.

Cassian is the West's great writer on monasticism, and his detailed instructions for monasteries served to promote the monastic movement widely. He went into great detail, covering not only subjects such as clothing ınd the form of monastery ;ervices, but also examining he temptations against which ı monk had to fight. He was an ·xceptionally keen observer and ›ainstaking administrator. Cassian ·eacted against what he felt to be ın over-emphasis on human weak-ıess in the theology of Augustine. Ie held that people are able to nake some response to God in heir own strength, even though hey cannot totally fulfil God's ·ommands. Cassian's viewpoint, ›robably brought from the East, vas especially common in the nonastic communities of south-·rn France, and is often called ,emi-Pelagianism. In addition to ;assian, its most notable teacher vas Vincent of Lérins. Semi-'elagianism became quite popular n southern France until it was con-lemned by the Synod of Orange in ;29.

The next great name in West-·rn monasticism is Cassiodorus 490–583), who came from a listinguished Roman senato-ial family, and held high office ınder Theodoric the Great, the)strogothic king of Italy. In 540 he retired to the monastery he had founded at Vivarium, in Calabria (southern Italy). He placed great emphasis on the copying of manu-scripts and the study of ancient writings, and some scholars believe that Benedict of Nursia derived his stress on study from Cassiodorus. This emphasis on monastic learning ensured that Greco-Roman culture survived into the Middle Ages.

Celtic monasticism

Monasticism seems to have begun among the Celts in the late fifth or early sixth century, but its origins are extremely obscure. Although its establishment was later attribu-ted to Patrick, there is no certain evidence from his writings that he founded monasteries or that he was a monk himself. Patrick him-self seems to have encouraged the private type of asceticism favoured before 325. However, in the late fifth century, monasticism seems to have taken root in Ireland in a form which owed much to the Egyptian pattern. Martin of Tours' monastic ideals may have reached

A monastery on the isolated island of the Skelligs, County Kerry, Ireland.

Ireland *via* Ninian's monastery at Whithorn in Scotland.

The extreme rigour of Irish hermits, and the arrangement of cells within an outer boundary wall, both reflect Egyptian influences. Irish monks also acquired a great enthusiasm for scholarship, which may have been encouraged by continental scholars who fled to Ireland from the barbarian invasions of the fifth century. Fifth-century Ireland was a tribal society without large towns, and the monasteries exerted a great influence on church life. Unlike Western monasticism in mainland Europe, Irish monks put little value on staying in one place, and from the sixth century onwards the wandering Celtic monk became a common figure on the continent. Such wandering monks founded some of the most famous of the early continental monasteries—including Luxeuil, St Gall and Bobbio; they promoted the evangelization of much of central Europe.

Benedict of Nursia provided the definitive rule for monasteries in the West; from the late sixth century his system gradually superseded other Western monastic rules.

Very little is known of the life

An expedition attempts to retrace the sixth-century voyage of Brendan, an Irish abbot believed by some to have discovered America. He set sail in a simple boat to try to rediscover paradise.

PATRICK

Robert G. Clouse

Patrick (about 389–461), the great missionary to the Irish, was probably born in Roman Britain. He was the son of a deacon and magistrate named Calpurnius.

The details of Patrick's life are disputed and overlaid with many pious legends. The small amount of definite information about him is found in his two writings: *The Confession* and *A Letter to the Soldiers of Coroticus,* a chief in north Britain.

At the age of sixteen, while staying on his father's farm, Patrick was seized by raiders and sold as a slave in Ireland. After six years of service as a shepherd he escaped and eventually reached home again. He also spent some time in Gaul. During his captivity his Christian faith had been decisively deepened and he became convinced that he must return and evangelize Ireland. Once in a dream he heard the voice of the Irish calling: 'We beseech you to come and walk among us once more.'

Patrick returned to Ireland as a bishop in 432 and spent the next thirty years ministering there. He had a great influence on several chieftains and special ties in the areas of Tara, Croagh Patrick and Armagh. Although he was not well educated, he encouraged learning and possibly through contact with strict monasteries in Gaul he began to emphasize the ascetic life and monasticism. In the later Irish church the basic unit became the monastery led by the abbot, rather than the bishop's diocese. Patrick also communicated the priority of mission to Celtic Christianity which produced great numbers of monks who evangelized Western Europe during the sixth and seventh centuries.

From Ireland came distinctive forms of monasticism. This round tower is at Ardmore, County Waterford.

of Benedict apart from the details given in a biography attributed to Gregory the Great. Only in the time of Charlemagne, and through the efforts of Witiza who called himself Benedict of Aniane, was the Benedictine rule widely published and imposed on monasteries. Benedict was born at Nursia, in Umbria (north-central Italy), and studied at Rome before withdrawing to live as a hermit. He founded several small monasteries, but had little success until he moved to the monastery at Monte Cassino. He wrote his rule during his early years as a monk, and died at Monte Cassino about 547. When the monastery there was destroyed by the Lombards, some of the monks fled to Rome and there brought his rule to the notice of Gregory the Great.

The Rule of Benedict is based on two activities, prayer and work. The individual monk had to show high moral character, and Benedict insisted that a monk should remain in the same monastery where he had taken his vows. The abbot was the spiritual head of the monastery and exercised all the normal

LIFE IN BENEDICT'S MONASTERY

In every aspect all shall follow the *Rule* as their guide: and let no one depart from it without good reason. Let no one in the monastery follow his own inclinations, or brazenly argue with his abbot . . . The abbot, for his part, should do everything in the fear of the Lord and in obedience to the *Rule*, knowing that he will have to account to God for all his decisions.

If a brother is insubordinate or disobedient, proud or a grumbler, or in any way acting contrary to the holy *Rule* and despising the orders of his seniors, let him, according to the Lord's commandment, be privately warned twice by his seniors. If he does not improve, let him be publicly rebuked before them all. But if even then he does not correct himself, he should be excommunicated, if he understands how severe this penalty is. If, however, he is beyond conviction, he should be physically punished.

The brothers shall take turns to wait on each other so that no one is excused from kitchen work, unless prevented by sickness or taken up with some vital business . . . An hour before each meal the week's servers are to receive a cup of drink and a piece of bread over and above their ration, so that they can wait on their brothers without grumbling or undue fatigue.

At the brothers' meal times there should always be a reading . . . There shall be complete silence at table, and no whispering or any voice except the reader's should be heard. The brethren should pass to each other in turn whatever food is needed so that no one needs to ask for anything. If anything should be wanted, ask for it by sign-language rather than by speech.

Above all, care must be taken of the sick . . . Baths should be available to the sick as often as necessary: to the healthy, and especially the young, less often. The eating of meat shall also be allowed to the sick and the delicate to aid recovery. But when they have got better, they shall all abstain from flesh, as is normal.

In winter, that is from 1 November until Easter, as far as possible discipline. The monasteries' stable, well-ordered communities, with their emphasis on worship, greatly helped to keep up spiritual standards during these centuries. Perhaps thanks to the influence of Cassiodorus the Benedictine monasteries also became centres of learning.

The Rule of Benedict observed in monasteries today is still largely that of the founder, although many copies of the rule have been enlarged and altered to fit later developments. Some historians now believe that Benedict's rule owes a great deal to another monastic rule of similar date, known as the *Regula Magistri,* the 'Rule of the Master'. Benedict's genius lay in making the harsher requirements of this older rule more human.

Celibate clergy

The idea that the clergy should remain unmarried developed only slowly. In the New Testament, it is reasonable to suppose that most of the apostles were married. Certainly this is true of Peter

they must get up at the eighth hour of the night, so that they rest for a little over half the night, and rise when they have had a good sleep. But the time that remains after 'vigils' shall be spent in study . . .

As the prophet says, 'Seven times in the day do I praise thee.' We will complete this sacred number seven if, at lauds, at the first, third, sixth, ninth hours, at vesper time and at compline we carry out the duties of our service.

Idleness is the enemy of the soul. Therefore, at fixed times, the brothers should be busy with manual work; and at other times in holy reading. We believe these ought to be arranged in ths way: from Easter until 1 October, on coming out of *Prime* they shall do the work needing attention until the fourth hour. From the fourth hour until about the sixth, they should concentrate on reading. After the meal on the sixth hour, they shall rest on their beds in complete silence; anyone who wishes may read to himself as long as he does not disturb anyone else. *None* shall be said a little early, about the middle of the eighth hour; after that they shall work at their tasks until evening.

A mattress, woollen blanket, woollen under-blanket, and a pillow shall be enough bedding. Beds are to be searched frequently by the abbot for private belongings. And, if anyone is found to possess anything he did not receive from the abbot, he shall be very severely disciplined. To abolish private property everything necessary shall be given by the abbot: a hood, tunic, shoes, long socks, belt, knife, pen, needle, handkerchief, tablets, so that they can have no excuses about needing things.

A monastery should, if possible, be built so that everything needed—water, mill, garden, bakery—is available, so that the monks do not need to wander about outside. For this is not at all good for their souls.

We intend to found a school to train men in the service of the Lord, but where we shall not make the rules too strict and heavy . . . If we seem to be severe, do not get frightened and run away. The entrance to the path of salvation must be narrow, but as you progress along the life of the Faith, the heart expands and speeds with love's sweetness along the pathway of God's commandments.

Selections from Benedict's *Rule*

"Seven times in the day do I praise thee."

(his mother-in-law is mentioned) and the brothers of Jesus; and it was regarded as normal that an apostle could take his wife with him on church work. At the same time, Paul recognized the practical advantages in being unmarried. Also, with sexual excesses all around them, it is likely that some Christians reacted against sex from a fairly early period. However, this was not formally set out or made a matter of special praise. In fact, special vows by younger women to abstain from marriage were discouraged by Paul.

During the period which followed, abstinence from marriage was left a matter of personal choice, although in most Gnostic sects marriage was actively discouraged on the grounds that it entangled the spiritual soul with the evil physical world. Some Jewish and Christian traditions blamed sexual differences on the fall, and believed that salvation included a return to 'unisex' life. In the mainstream churches, leaders such as Melito of Sardis became known for their austere personal lives; abstinence from marriage was part of this. In many churches, too, Christian women may have had difficulty in finding suitable husbands. Tertullian spells out the problem of a Christian woman with a pagan husband in a tract dedicated to his own wife! For such reasons some women remained unmarried, which could give them more time for prayer and devotion. In the same way, men who were free from family ties had more time to devote to church affairs, and were often obvious choices as leaders.

A remote monastery nestles among barren rocks in Lebanon.

By the third century, celibacy was beginning to be valued as a mark of holiness. Even so, extremes were frowned upon, and Origen earned considerable disapproval because he made himself a eunuch, believing this was commended in the Gospels. As martyrdom declined, asceticism began to become the measure of spirituality; the leaders regarded as more spiritual in the churches tended to be those who practised an ascetic way of life. However, the clergy were not generally obliged to be celibate and some important church leaders such as Hilary of Poitiers were married. In the fourth century also some men in public life were ordained later on in life, after they had married. In some cases they continued to live with their wives but abstained from sexual intercourse.

In the fourth century, moves were made to restrict marriage after ordination. The Council of Ancyra, about 315, declared that deacons had to choose between marriage and celibacy before ordination, and could not marry afterwards; the Council of Neocaesarea, about 320, ruled that presbyters who married after ordination were to be deposed. However, it is uncertain how far these rules were enforced. As the fourth century proceeded, the pressure for Christians to be celibate became very great. Jerome was the most enthusiastic supporter of celibacy, and was criticized because many of his pronouncements seemed to denigrate marriage. Some Western theologians believed that original guilt entered into the soul of the infant through the act of conception and thus cast doubt on sexual intercourse. In spite of protests that celibacy was Manichean (the Manichees held that all aspects of the physical world were evil), supporters of celibacy persuaded the churches that celibacy and holiness were closely connected.

Celibacy of the clergy introduced two great abuses. Many so-called celibate clergy in fact lived with women who were not their wives (called *subintroductae*), a practice repeatedly condemned by church councils and writers. Jerome was particularly biting about such disgraceful behaviour. Also, enthusiastic men were tempted to desert their wives in order to follow the celibate life. A Roman law of 420 expressly forbade this.

In the fifth century and after, two codes of practice evolved. In the Eastern churches, presbyters and deacons were allowed to marry before ordination, but bishops were always chosen from among the celibate clergy (very often they were monks). This practice was accepted as the norm by Justinian and remains in force in Eastern Christianity today. In the West there was strong pressure for complete clerical celibacy. Leo the Great wanted to forbid marriage even for subdeacons, but it is uncertain whether this was ever enforced during his time. Certainly, during the fifth and sixth centuries married men such as Sidonius Apollinaris became bishops. However, during these centuries the monasteries came to be regarded as the main centres of spirituality, which meant that increasingly the best bishops

CASSIODORUS

David F. Wright

This long-lived Roman aristocrat, who died around 583, forged lasting links between classical and early Christian civilization and the medieval world of monks and barbarians. Cassiodorus attained high office as a minister of Theodoric and other Ostrogothic rulers. In drafting official documents, collected and known as his *Variae,* he drew upon traditional Latin rhetoric to serve a barbarian court, and influenced later practice. He encouraged Theodoric's regard for the cultural legacy of Rome. *The History of the Goths,* his most original work, is now lost.

He wanted to create a Christian academy at Rome, but was frustrated by the Gothic wars—although a library was collected about 535 under Pope Agapetus. Cassiodorus fulfilled his ideals in the monastery he established on his estate at Vivarium ('fish-pond', from the landscaped gardens) near the southern Italian coast, where he settled after 540.

His *Introduction to Theological and Secular Studies* advocated a marriage of biblical study (part one, dealing with commentaries, versions, canon, textual criticism, manuscript production and so forth) and the liberal arts (part two), the basic educational curriculum of the period. His enthusiasm for secular learning, which was not shared by Benedict or Gregory the Great, strongly influenced later Benedictine practice. Vivarium's library and scriptorium (room set apart for writing) preserved and passed on manuscripts of the early Christian writers and the classics alike. Cassiodorus supervised the translation from Greek into Latin of works by such Christian writers as Clement of Alexandria, Didymus the Blind and the church historians, as well as Josephus. He also made earlier Latin theology more readily available, especially Augustine's commentary on the Psalms and Pelaguis on Paul's letters.

Cassiodorus' ideal was *civilitas,* 'humane values and order'. For the privileged it meant monastic culture, civilized study in a refined setting, welding together Roman and Christian, just as earlier he had reconciled the Gothic and the Roman.

Cassiodorus urged the pope:

"Seeing that the schools (are) swarming with students with a great longing for secular letters, collect subscriptions and . . . have Christian rather than secular schools in the city of Rome, with professors, just as there had been for so long in Alexandria."

tended to be celibate. Celibacy of the clergy continued to be praised as an ideal, although it was not enforced legally and effectively until the time of Hildebrand (Pope Gregory VII, 1073–85).

Daily prayer

Ascetic communities influenced the liturgy considerably, especially in the matter of daily services. Early in the second century the *Didache* had encouraged Christians to pray three times a day. Another early practice was for Christians to rise and pray at midnight—common by the time of Tertullian. Morning and evening prayer in church became customary during the fourth century, especially at centres of pilgrimage like Jerusalem. Egeria, a lady pilgrim to the Holy Land in the late fourth century, mentions four daily services attended by clergy and monks in Jerusalem. The seven-times-daily order of prayer evolved in the monasteries soon after, and was claimed to be sanctioned by the text from Psalm 119, 'Seven times a day will I praise thee.'

The routine was made up from the three hours of prayer (9 a.m., 12 noon, 3 p.m.), the morning and evening prayers, and two additional services. The complete cycle was:

Lauds (the old morning prayer)
Prime (to fill the gap between Lauds in the small hours and Terce)
Terce (at 9 a.m.)
Sext (12 noon)
None (3 p.m.)
Vespers (old evening prayer)
Compline (prayer just before bed-time).

These services varied in content, but included prayers and intercessions, reciting of psalms, the reading of the Bible and a certain amount of singing, mainly by a solo singer, with the congregation repeating a refrain at intervals. On occasions there was also antiphonal singing, where the congregation divided into two choirs and sang alternate halves of the verses of a psalm; but this only happened where the training of singers could be concentrated on. On the anniversaries of martyrs or saints, the Bible reading might be replaced by a reading from the account of the martyrdom or from the 'Life' of the particular saint.

SECTION 4
A CHRISTIAN SOCIETY 600–1500

A CHRISTIAN SOCIETY

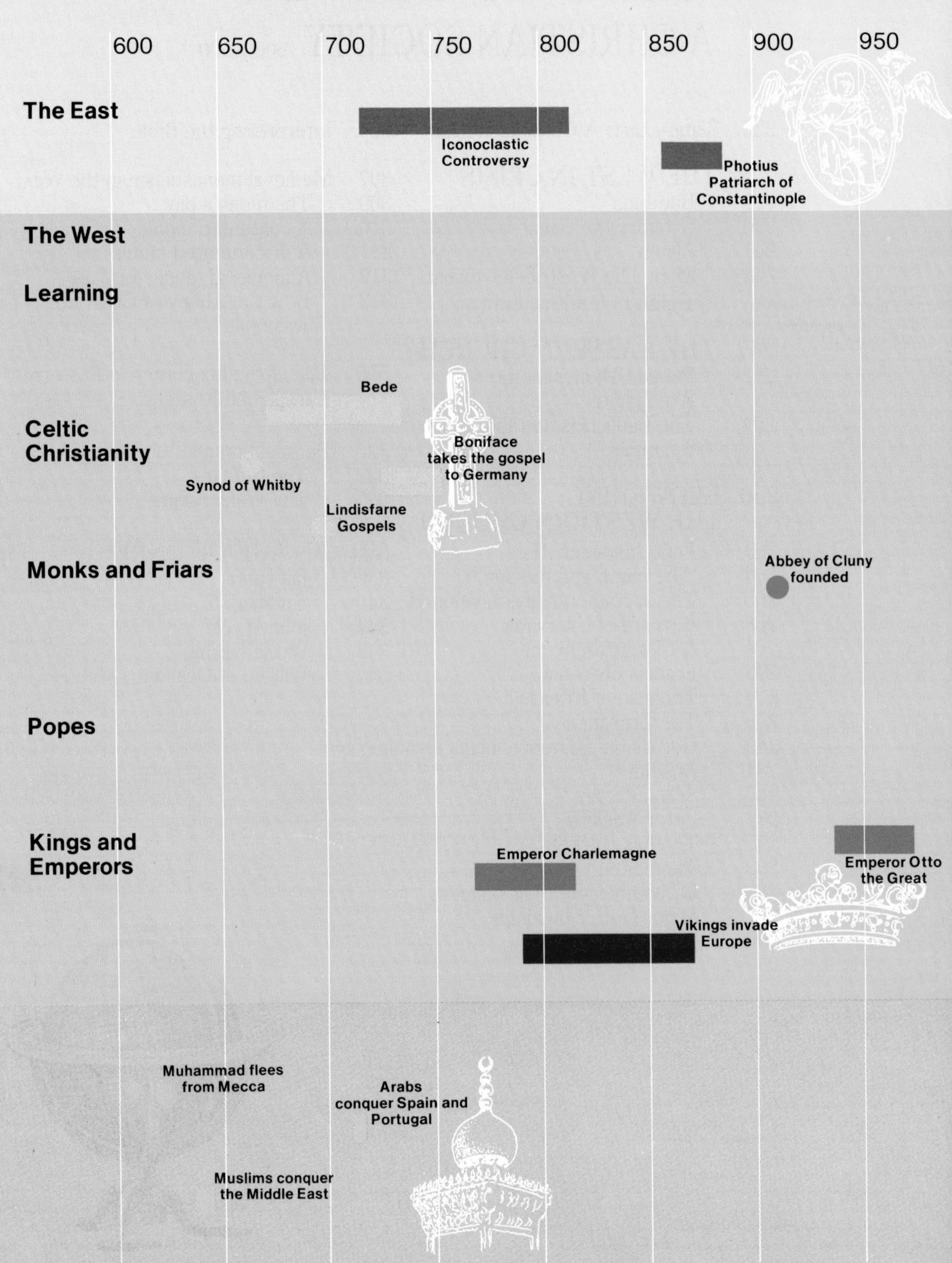
600
650
700
750
800
850
900
950
The East
Iconoclastic Controversy
Photius Patriarch of Constantinople
The West
Learning
Bede
Celtic Christianity
Boniface takes the gospel to Germany
Synod of Whitby
Lindisfarne Gospels
Monks and Friars
Abbey of Cluny founded
Popes
Kings and Emperors
Emperor Charlemagne
Emperor Otto the Great
Vikings invade Europe
Muhammad flees from Mecca
Arabs conquer Spain and Portugal
Muslims conquer the Middle East

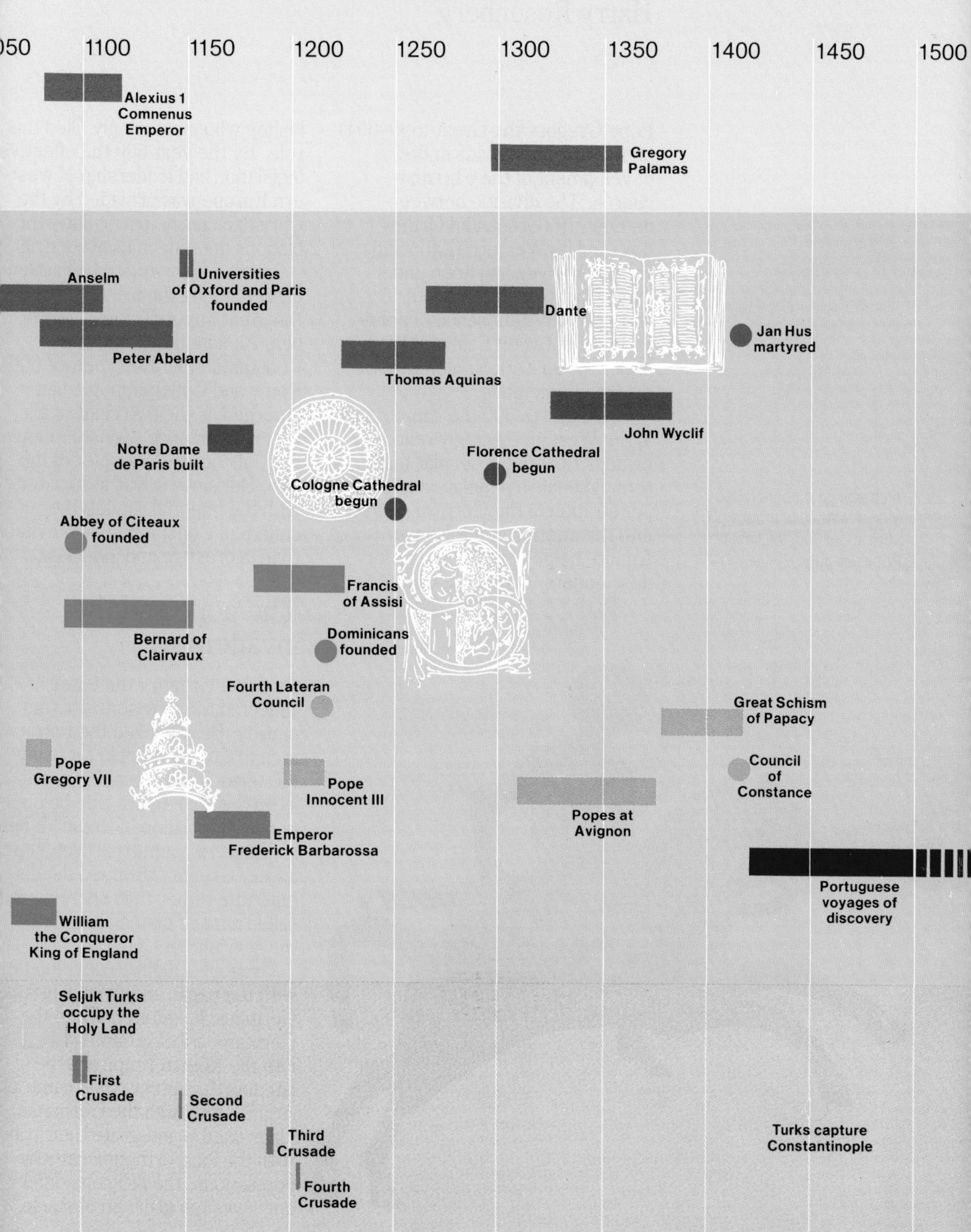

1050
1100
1150
1200
1250
1300
1350
1400
1450
1500
Alexius 1 Comnenus Emperor
Gregory Palamas
Anselm
Universities of Oxford and Paris founded
Dante
Peter Abelard
Jan Hus martyred
Thomas Aquinas
John Wyclif
Notre Dame de Paris built
Florence Cathedral begun
Cologne Cathedral begun
Abbey of Citeaux founded
Francis of Assisi
Bernard of Clairvaux
Dominicans founded
Fourth Lateran Council
Great Schism of Papacy
Pope Gregory VII
Pope Innocent III
Council of Constance
Popes at Avignon
Emperor Frederick Barbarossa
Portuguese voyages of discovery
William the Conqueror King of England
Seljuk Turks occupy the Holy Land
First Crusade
Second Crusade
Third Crusade
Fourth Crusade
Turks capture Constantinople

THE WEST IN CRISIS

Harry Rosenberg

Pope Gregory the Great (590–604) stands at a crossroads in the development of the Christian church. The division between its Eastern (Greek and Orthodox) and its Western (Latin and catholic) halves had been under way from at least the fourth century. Any semblance of political unity between East and West under the eastern Roman Empire was mere pretence.

From 400 to 600 the Emperors in the West increasingly relied on bishops to assist in secular matters. The fall in population and the penetration of the German peoples into the interior of the Roman Empire helped create a need for new leaders. It was the Christian bishop who increasingly filled this role. By the year 600 the effective legislation and leadership of western Europe was provided by the Christian clergy, particularly the bishops meeting in local councils.

Intense competition had arisen earlier among the bishops of the great imperial cities—Antioch, Alexandria, Rome and Constantinople. Long before 600 Rome and Constantinople had emerged as the two chief rivals for pre-eminence. Constantinople was, of course, the junior of the two. But since it was associated with the imperial capital, the church of Constantinople inevitabl rose in prestige and influence.

A charging Lombard horseman. A plaque of bronze gilt from about 600, the time of Pope Gregory.

The pope and the invaders

As pope, Gregory the Great reflected the new status of the papacy. He criticized the Patriarch of Constantinople for using the term 'Ecumenical Patriarch', asserting that such a title belonge only to the bishop of Rome. Wher his Eastern counterpart refused t agree, Gregory dropped the dispute title rather than share it, and called himself instead 'servant of the servants of God'.

Gregory sought to develop ties with the pagan and Arian Christia Germanic kingdoms. When the Germanic tribal groups pushed into the Roman Empire in the late fourth century, they came as Arians. Although the Germanic kings tried to integrate their tribe with the local orthodox catholic populations, the religious difference was too great an obstacle.

Catholic antagonism towards the heretical rulers resulted in constant tension between the ruling elite and the rest of the population.

The bishops of Rome had come to enjoy great power in Rome and in Italy as a result of the decline and the eventual disappearance of effective imperial authority in the West, and through their extensive landholdings. While the legal basis for the Papal States ('the Patrimony of St Peter') was probably not established until the eighth century, its origins clearly go back to the fourth century. The title 'Republic of St Peter' appears in papal documents as early as the late seventh century.

The last of the Germanic tribes to enter the Roman Empire, the Arian Lombards, arrived in Italy in 568. The ineffectiveness of the imperial governor at Ravenna in combating them, brought home to the papacy the need to find another protector. Conversion of the invaders to catholic Christianity was one possible solution—which Gregory did in fact try. He supported the Lombard Queen Theodelinda, who was a catholic Christian. Eventually the Lombards were weaned away from Arian to catholic Christianity, though this did not solve the political problems of the papacy. But Gregory pointed the way to the future solution, namely looking west and not east for protection.

Gregory wrote a series of important letters to Germanic rulers elsewhere in the West. By this time, the Arian Visigoths in Spain had accepted catholic Christianity. Gregory's letters to Reccared, the first catholic Visigoth king of Spain, demonstrate the pope's desire to make his influence felt there.

Clovis is converted

The Frankish kings in Gaul were the only Germanic tribes to enter

BOETHIUS

Robert G. Clouse

Boethius is ranked among the founders of the Middle Ages because of his great influence on medieval education and thought. A statesman and philosopher, Anicius Manlius Torquatus Severinus Boethius (about 480–524) was educated at Athens and Alexandria, and served the Arian king of the Ostrogoths in Italy, Theodoric the Great. Living in the twilight of the Roman Empire, he was the last Western scholar before the twelfth century to be thoroughly familiar with the Greek texts of Aristotle's philosophical works. He planned to translate the works of both Plato and Aristotle into Latin, but was able to complete only Aristotle's works on logic, together with some commentaries on them.

He also wrote five *Tractates (Opuscula Sacra)* in defence of orthodox theology. One of these books, which systematically applied Aristotle's logic to Christian theology, earned him the title of the 'first scholastic'—one who was attempting to harmonize faith and reason.

Towards the close of his life Boethius was accused of treason against Theodoric. He was imprisoned and executed. While in prison he wrote his best-known work *The Consolation of Philosophy*; a dialogue between Boethius and 'Philosophy', who leads him from despair over his situation to 'that true contentment which reason united with virtue can give'.

Boethius sits down to work—pictured here inside the initial letter of the first book of the *The Consolation of Philosophy*.

the Roman Empire as pagans and not as Arian Christians. About 500, Clovis—the first great ruler among the Franks—decided to accept catholic baptism, following his marriage to Clotild a catholic Burgundian princess. According to a Frankish history, Clovis agreed to accept Christ if the Christian God gave him victory over another tribe with whom he was at war. Clovis won his battle against the Alemanni; then, with three thousand of his warriors, he was baptized.

This event points up the general pattern of early medieval conversions. The change to Christianity was essentially a matter of royal policy. The ruler's conversion decided the religion of his subjects. Catholic queens and princesses did much to bring about the conversion of their husbands—and their kingdoms.

Clovis' conversion laid the foundations for an important alliance between the papacy and the Franks. Although the Franks showed great devotion to Peter and the Roman church from a very early stage, this did not mean that

GREGORY THE GREAT

Harry Rosenberg

Of the approximately 180 bishops of Rome between Constantine the Great and the Reformation, none was more influential than Gregory the Great. Indeed, the medieval papacy clearly makes its appearance with the career of this remarkably able churchman. Gregory, who came from a distinguished Roman aristocratic family with a long tradition of imperial service and, later, service to the church, also began his career in public administration.

But Gregory turned away from public life and became a monk. He was the first pope who had been a monk and he introduced monasticism to the papacy. Gregory stressed ascetic ideals – ideals associated with the rule of Benedict which became the prevailing style of monasticism by the ninth century.

Gregory marked his period as pope by his claim to 'universal' jurisdiction over Christendom, notably in a controversy with the Patriarch of Constantinople over the latter's right to use the title of 'Ecumenical Patriarch', and in Gregory's efforts to cultivate the rulers of Germanic kingdoms in western Europe. One matter of outstanding importance was Gregory's decision to send a team of monks to the kingdom of Kent in Britain. The Christianization of the Anglo-Saxons and the victory of Roman Christianity over the Celtic church were the long-term result of Gregory's missionary policy.

Gregory's prolific writing resulted in the production of a basic textbook for training the medieval clergy, and increased the popularity of allegorical interpretations of the Bible, and interest in saints' lives—the truly popular Christian literature of the Middle Ages. He gave to early medieval Catholicism its distinctive character, stressing the cult of saints and relics, demonology, and ascetic virtues. Finally, Gregory confirmed the authority and hierarchy of the papacy and the church, and he proclaimed the 'Christian Commonwealth' in which the pope and the clergy were to be responsible for ordering society.

the pope immediately had great influence on royal policy. The harsh, even barbaric, conditions of Gaul under the Merovingian dynasty of Frankish rulers proved very detrimental to the church during the sixth and seventh centuries.

Gregory, determined to revive the church in the West, attempted to launch reform in Gaul. He was thwarted by the Merovingian rulers, who indulged in such practices as appointing laymen as bishops and selling church appointments. These Frankish rulers simply assumed that the church was freely at their own disposal. Gregory's efforts pointed the way to the reform of the eighth century.

Angels—not Angles!

Gregory's relations with the Merovingian kings did have one positive result: the mission to England and the conversion of the Angles, Saxons and Jutes. This enterprise best demonstrates Gregory's vision to convert the 'barbarians' and to make them members of a 'Christian commonwealth' led by the pope. Gregory's vision became reality in medieval Europe.

The mission to England is described in a simple, perhaps apocryphal, story told by a pious papal biographer. Gregory, while still a monk in Rome, one day saw some attractive young children in the slave market. On inquiring who they were, Gregory learned that they were *Angli* from England, and that they were pagans. He replied that these young lads were not 'Angles' but 'Angels'!

It is certain that Gregory had such contacts, for in 595 he ordered his representative in Arles, in southern France, to purchase Anglo-Saxon slaves to be brought to Rome for training as clerics. Gregory also had very good information about the political and religious situation in England. In 596 he assembled a team of forty monks under Augustine, the prior of the pope's own monastery in Rome. With Frankish priests as interpreters, the team arrived in England just before Easter 597. Gregory's information indicated that the Jutish kingdom of Kent should be the target of the mission. Its king, Ethelbert, was married to a catholic Frankish princess, Bertha. Ethelbert accepted catholicism, and, since he was nominal overlord of the neighbouring Anglo-Saxon kingdoms of Essex and East Anglia, catholic Christianity came to three out of twelve Anglo-Saxon kingdoms.

By late 597, the pope appointed Augustine archbishop of the church in England. King Ethelbert gave the new archbishop his own palace in Canterbury, which became the first episcopal centre in England. Pope Gregory instructed the rather unimaginative Augustine on how to convert the pagans—they were to be weaned slowly away from their current religion.

Evangelistic efforts among the Angles and Saxons went slowly, and were directly affected by the intense political and religious competition among the kings. Archbishop Augustine was also concerned about the Celtic church—its attitude towards the Anglo-Saxon mission, and its practices, which differed from those of Rome. Bede, the historian, wrote that Augustine's attempts to unite the Celtic church and Rome failed on three basic issues; namely his requirement that the Celtic church adopt the Roman method of arriving at the date of Easter, adopt the Roman tradition of baptism, and join his mission to convert the Anglo-Saxons.

The seal of Childeric, one of the Frankish kings.

Mark, the Gospel-writer, has been drawn, along with his traditional symbol of the lion, on the opening page of his Gospel in the famous Celtic *Lindisfarne Gospels*.

Celtic Christians object

Relations between Augustine and the Celtic churchmen turned sour. The Celtic bishops took offence when the archbishop refused to stand to greet them. They refused to accept him as their archbishop.

The Celtic church already had a long history when Augustine arrived. British bishops were present at the Council of Arles convened by Constantine in 314. In the late fourth and early fifth centuries Christianity thrived in Britain. But in the face of the invasions of Britain by the Angles, Saxons and Jutes, from the mid-fifth century on, much of the Celtic-Roman British population, as well as the Celtic church, retreated to the south-west. British conservatism, caused by the long period of isolation from continental Christianity, together with hatred of the foreign invaders, were the major barriers to unity between Augustine and the British church.

The British church finally fused with Roman Christianity during the course of the following century. This occurred when the mission among the Anglo-Saxons succeeded; both Celtic-British and Roman Christians participated in this mission.

By the third quarter of the seventh century a generation of church leaders emerged who combined the order and authority of Rome with the emotional and imaginative vigour of Celtic Christianity. Aidan of Lindisfarne, the first Celtic churchman to take an active part in the mission to the Anglo-Saxons, with a number of other Anglo-Saxon churchmen, such as Wilfrid of York, took the lead in overcoming paganism and racism. Again with royal support, this time that of Oswy, king of Northumbria, this mission achieved success. The Synod of Whitby in 664 confirmed the Romanization of British Christianity.

Five years later two church leaders were sent to England by the pope to complete the reordering of the church in England. Theodore of Tarsus, a Greek who served the pope as Archbishop of Canterbury, and Hadrian, from North Africa, stand out as the real founders of the catholic church in England.

They built on the foundations laid by Pope Gregory and Archbishop Augustine, and drew on the spiritual and intellectual vigour of Celtic Christianity. The new leaders carried out effective administrative and educational work.

Theodore wisely followed a policy of reconciliation with Celtic Christianity. He and Hadrian brought Mediterranean Christian culture to Canterbury. They contributed a permanent framework to the Anglo-Saxon church. By establishing a 'national' body which transcended local boundaries and local patriotism, Theodore's reorganization of the church helped develop secular government as well as bringing order out of chaos. The church conveyed the concept

In 633 King Oswald of Northumbria asked the monks of Iona to send someone to teach his people the Christian faith. Aidan, the man who fulfilled this task, made his headquarters on the small island of Lindisfarne. He founded this monastery there.

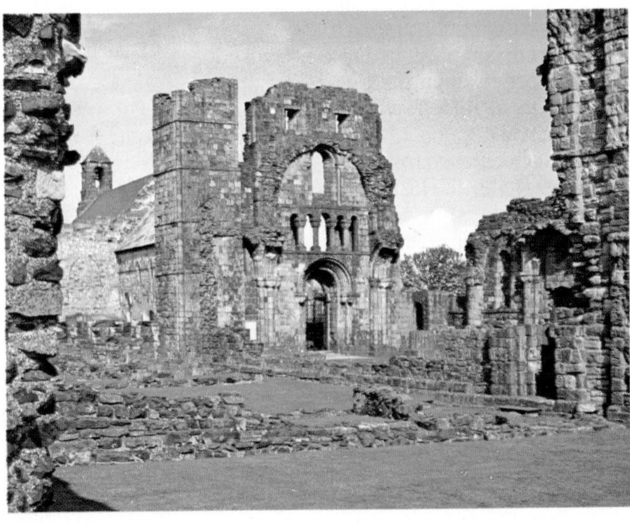

imago leonis
ACI
HA
R
US
CUS

"He would resort most commonly to those places and preach in those hamlets lying far away in steep and craggy hills, which other people had dreaded to visit, and which from their poverty as well as upland rudeness teachers shunned to approach. Tarrying in the hilly part, he would call the poor folk of the country to heavenly things with the word of preaching as well as work of virtuous example."

BEDE describes Cuthbert's work, in his History

of unity and centralization to the secular leaders.

Archbishop Theodore, who had studied in Athens, also contributed to the development of Anglo-Saxon culture. Assisted by Hadrian and Benedict Biscop, an Anglo-Saxon deeply interested in Christian learning, the archbishop founded at Canterbury a school where the cultures of British and Mediterranean Christianity were fused. The result was a remarkable intellectual flowering in the arts and humanities. The Venerable Bede is an outstanding example of the literary achievement of this rebirth of biblical and historical studies. The superb artistic skills of the Celts in illustrating manuscripts are seen in remarkable Bibles such as the *Lindisfarne Gospels* (now in the British Museum) and *The Book of Kells* (at Trinity College Library, Dublin). The culture and learning of the Anglo-Saxon church, as well as its fervour for the gospel, contributed directly to the revival of religious and intellectual life in Europe during the century after Theodore.

Cuthbert introduced Roman traditions to the monks at Lindisfarne when he was made prior there in 664. In 676 he withdrew to this lonely island, Farne, to be alone with God.

The rise of Islam

Meanwhile another development with far-reaching consequences for the history of Christianity and the medieval and modern world was taking place. At the very time when Gregory the Great was turning away from the eastern Mediterranean and seeking to extend papal influence throughout the West, there began in Arabia the career of a remarkable religious leader, Muhammad of Mecca (about 570–632). His teachings had an almost immediate impact. The movement of Islam was born, and spread with dramatic speed outside Arabia after the prophet's death.

The course of medieval history in both the Orthodox East and the Catholic West was drastically affected. The rise of Islam directly influenced the political and economic development of the two halves of Christendom. Islam became medieval Christianity's greatest opponent. By the tenth century the Islamic community, stretching from Baghdad to Cordova, had become the most prosperous of the early Middle Ages.

Although cradled in Arabia, with Arab cults and social habits somewhat limiting its outlook and influencing its ritual, the new religion was in many ways an offshoot of Judaism and Christianity. It was also influenced by Zoroastrianism, the religion of Persia. The culture associated with Islam was not simply Asian as distinct from Mediterranean. Islamic culture shared the same background as early Christian thought—the Jewish and Hellenistic cultures which prevailed in western Asia. Thus, medieval Islamic civilization shared a common basis with medieval Christian civilization and this made contacts between the two easier. (The later shift to Iraq as the centre of Islam, and its spread into

South and East Asia, resulted in increased oriental influences.)

The prophet's call

Following his religious call in 610, Muhammad proclaimed the message of Islam (Arabic for 'submission to the will of God'). His teachings included: the impending judgement of the world, with reward and punishment for each individual's actions, and the teachings of *Allah,* the creator and judge. In addition, the message of Muhammad imposed five main obligations upon Muslim believers: the confession of faith ('There is no god but *Allah,* and Muhammad is his prophet'), prayer five times a day, charitable gifts, fasting in the holy month of *Ramadan,* and the pilgrimage to Mecca.

The basic source of the divine revelation was the *Qur'an* (which was collected and committed to writing by Othman, the second leader after Muhammad). In addition there was the *Hadith,* which recorded the traditions of the habits and sayings of the prophet. Finally the *Ijma*; which consisted of the 'accord of the faithful', formed the body of law followed by devout Muslims. Taken together these three religious sources constitute the *Sunna* or 'The Path'. A subsequent division within Islam between the Sunnites and the Shiites left the *Sunna* in dispute. This schism was caused by the problem of choosing a successor to Muhammad; the division still persists.

When Muhammad's proclamation was ill-received in Mecca, he made the fateful decision to leave for Medina in June 622. This emigration to Medina, the city of the prophet, is known as the *Hegira.* It marked the beginning of a new era and achange in fortune for Muhammad. It also marked the beginning of the Islamic calendar. With Medina as his base of operations, Muhammad developed the rudiments of what became the major characteristics of Islam world-wide. Idol-worshippers had to accept Islam or the sword, but monotheists—Jews and Christians—enjoyed a special status; they were tolerated on condition that they paid a special tax. Eight years after leaving Mecca, Muhammad returned in triumph. He purified the city by removing the various idols in the ancient Arab shrine, the *Ka'ba.* By the time of his death, two years later, the whole of Arabia was committed to Islam.

A new world-religion

The Islamic community was now led by the caliphs, literally 'successors'. Although other factors contributed to the expansion of Islam outside Arabia, the chief force was the extraordinary religious enthusiasm generated by Muhammad and his immediate converts, the 'Companions'. Within a century of the prophet's death, Islam had reached the Atlantic (Morocco) and the River Indus (Pakistan). Within this vast area, there was created a theocratic empire led by the caliphs, who combined religious and political functions. Arab military commanders became the civil governors of the occupied areas, as representatives of the caliphs.

This new world empire soon divided into a series of caliphates based primarily upon Mecca, Baghdad, Damascus and Cairo, together with a number of separate states. But the Islamic states had a coherent and homogeneous civilization, thanks to their basic Arab core. This was due, in the first instance, to the fact that no translation of the *Qur'an* was allowed, and thus the Arabic language dominated

The seventh century saw the rise of a new religion – Islam. Mecca became a place of pilgrimage.

not only the religion of Islam but also the closely allied areas of law, language and education. Islam influenced a vast array of ethnic groups, cultures and religions. Contrary to the generally accepted view in the West, forced conversions were the exception.

By the beginning of the eighth century, Islam reached its northernmost limits of growth. Following a series of sieges of the great imperial stronghold of Constantinople, a Muslim-Byzantine frontier was established. In the west, the Muslims rapidly occupied Visigothic Spain. Raiding parties probed into Frankish Gaul, but were defeated by the Carolingian leader, Charles Martel, in 732. Although the Muslims were prevented from penetrating into the heart of Europe, they did succeed in gaining control over the Western Mediterranean.

In Spain, the mutual exchange of ideas among Arabs, Berbers, Jews and Christians produced a unique culture in the Middle Ages. But Catholic Europe was concerned above all about its religious differences with the Muslim community. This concern was expressed in unrelieved hostility. Islam and its prophet, Muhammad were identified with the beast in the book of Revelation, or with the Antichrist. Medieval Christian authors portrayed Muhammad as an imposter and Islam as a religion of violence and idolatry. The Muslim community believed that their civilization was superior to all others, since the revelation to Muhammad was the final one, supplanting all previous ones, such as the Old and New Testaments.

England and Ireland evangelize Europe

After Gregory the Great, Euro-

Devout Muslims pack the open square around the Ka'ba, in Mecca.

ean Catholicism went through difficult period. The papacy uffered at the hands of both he Lombards in Italy and the yzantine rulers. In Frankish Gaul he Merovingian kings became icreasingly ineffective, and the ioral, spiritual and intellectual uality of the clergy steadily eclined. Effective church governent was weakened as a result of onstant interference by secular ulers. In his writings Gregory, ishop of Tours, reveals a sordid icture of society. He shows too hat women were particularly nportant in sustaining sincere eligious endeavour, especially by upporting monasteries.

The revival of religious life in Gaul and, indeed, in all of Latin Christendom, came about in the ighth century. It was led by he Anglo-Saxon missionaries, vho came in great numbers, by a evitalized papacy, and a new royal house in Frankish Gaul.

Missionaries from the Irish-Celtic church had engaged in missions to Europe from the late sixth century. Outstanding among them was Columban, who was active in Gaul and Italy. Gallus, a member of his group, founded the monastery of St Gallen at an important junction along the road linking Italy and Germany. It remained a vital centre of monastic life and culture throughout the early Middle Ages. Celtic missionaries also found their way into Bavaria and central Germany.

Although vigorous and venturesome, these missionaries paid little attention to consolidating their work. Constant movement characterized Celtic Christianity. For this reason much of their work had to be done over again by the late seventh century. The Anglo-Saxons, themselves objects of a mission from Europe at the begin-

ning of the century, were in turn impelled to carry the gospel back into Europe. Unlike their Celtic predecessors, however, these new missionaries brought with them Roman church organization and sense of order. In addition, they had close ties with the papacy. Outstanding among these hardy and courageous missionaries was Wynfrith of Crediton (680–754)—better known as Boniface.

Boniface had consultations in Rome and received papal consecration as 'bishop of the German church'. He then evangelized among the Hessians of Bavaria and Thuringia. He established the famous monastery of Fulda and finally became Archbishop of Mainz. He is justly known as the 'Apostle to the Germans'. He brought Germany into Christian Europe under papal leadership.

A new royal house

In addition, Boniface played a critical role in the revival of the church in Gaul. Earlier Anglo-Saxon missionaries to Germany had received the support of Charles Martel, a member of the Carolingian family, the rising power in Frankish politics. He supported the missions because of his desire to expand his rule eastwards into Bavaria. The church and the papacy were grateful for his support, and for Charles' victory over the Muslims when they crossed the Pyrenees to invade Gaul. But Charles Martel incurred the wrath of the church because he took away church lands. Initially, the church had agreed to the use of its lands and incomes to help fight off the Muslim invaders. But Charles did not return the lands. In addition, he refused the papal request for an attack on the Lombards in Italy, because the Lombards had been his allies against the Muslims.

A new era began with the accession of Martel's heirs, Carloman and Pepin, who had been raised in the monastery of St Denis near Paris. These two Frankish rulers were helped by Boniface to carry out a major reform of the Frankish church. These reforms of the clergy and church organization, brought about a renewal of religious and intellectual life and made possible the educational revival associated with the greatest of the Carolingian rulers, Charlemagne.

After his brother entered a monastry, Pepin was in a posi-

Two cultures meet. Two contrasting scenes illustrate this Frankish casket, made of whalebone in the eighth century. *Left*, a scene from a popular pagan story; *right*, the wise men come to the baby Jesus.

tion to complete the Carolingian quest for legitimate authority. Negotiations between Pepin and Pope Zachary in 751 resulted in Boniface, the Pope's legate, anointing the new King Pepin at Soissons. Another milestone in church-state relations was passed when Pope Stephen II appealed to Pepin for aid against the Lombards. The pope placed Rome under the protection of Pepin and recognized him and his sons as 'protectors of the Romans'.

This sequence of events, together with the coronation of Charlemagne as emperor, gave the pope the opportunity he wanted of loosening ties to the Eastern Empire and Constantinople. Religious developments in the East provided the papacy with an opportunity finally to break free. The 'Iconoclastic controversy' engulfed the East after Emperor Leo III banned the use of icons (images of Christ, the Virgin Mary, or a saint) in 726. The supporters of icons ultimately prevailed after a century and a quarter of bitter, disruptive dispute. Meanwhile Pope Gregory II not only rejected the edict banning the use of icons, but went on bluntly to flaunt his disrespect for the Emperor's authority in the West. Gregory's bombastic letter included much bluffing, but also a dramatic statement which clearly reveals the differences between the state church of the Orthodox East, where the secular ruler always played a leading role in church affairs, and the papal church of the west, where the papacy was trying to eliminate secular influence. Gregory wrote: 'Listen! Dogmas are not the business of emperors but of pontiffs.'

The presence of what was regarded as a heretical dynasty in the East gave the pope the excuse he needed to separate from the East and to find a new, devoted and orthodox protector in the West. The alliance between the papacy and the Carolingians represents the culmination of the papal quest, and opened a new and momentous chapter in the history of medieval Christianity.

In response to Pope Stephen's appeal for help, Pepin recovered territories in north-east and central Italy from the Lombards and gave them to the pope, an action known as the 'Donation of Pepin'. This confirmed the legal foundation of the Papal States.

At about this time, the pope's claim to sovereign rule in Italy and independence from the Eastern Roman Empire was reinforced by the appearance of one of the great forgeries of the Middle Ages, the *Donation of Constantine.* This document alleged that Constantine had bequeathed Rome and the western part of the Empire to the bishop of Rome when he relocated the capital of the empire in the East. The *Donation* was not exposed as a forgery until the fifteenth century.

Charlemagne crowned Emperor

The concluding act in the papal attempt to free itself from Constantinople came on Christmas Day 800 when Pope Leo III revived the Empire in the West by crowning Charlemagne as emperor. However, Charlemagne did not relish the thought of owing his crown to the pope. In the last fourteen years of his reign he made the papacy subordinate in his Empire. He continued the largely educational reform of the church begun by his father Pepin and Boniface. His chief educational adviser was the Anglo-Saxon Alcuin of York. It was indeed an age that needed to go to school and in Alcuin it found a masterful

---

Charlemagne: God's deputy

"Always remember, my king, that you are the deputy of God, your king. You are set to guard and rule all his members, and you must render an account for them on the day of judgement. The bishop is on a secondary plane.

Our Lord Jesus Christ has set you up as the ruler of the Christian people, in power more excellent than the pope or the Emperor of Constantinople, in wisdom more distinguished, in the dignity of your rule more sublime. On you alone depends the whole safety of the churches of Christ."

EPISTOLAE KAROLINI AEVI, ii, 503; 288

---

teacher.

From the palace school at the royal court a generation of Alcuin's students went out to head monastic and cathedral schools throughout the Empire which Charlemagne created. Even though this Empire barely outlived its founder, the revival of education and religion associated with Alcuin and Charlemagne brightened European culture throughout the bleak and chaotic period that followed. This 'Carolingian Renaissance' turned to classical antiquity and also to early Christianity for its models. The emphasis was on Latin literature; the efforts at Greek were tentative and quite artificial. The Irishman John Scotus Erigena was the only accomplished Greek scholar in the Carolingian world. The activity in the copying rooms of Carolingian monasteries was of major importance for Western culture. The works of both pagan and Christian classical authors were copied. Many original texts have not survived: these manuscripts give us our only access to their original writings.

The present York Minster was built mainly between 1200 and 1400, but the first mention of a bishop of York is in 314. The see of York became an archbishopric in 735.

The intellectual vigour of the Carolingian Renaissance and the political dynamism of the revived Empire stimulated new theological activity. There was some discussion and writing about the continuing iconoclastic problem in the Orthodox East. Political antagonism between the Eastern and the Carolingian emperors also led to an attack by theologians in the West on the practices and beliefs of the Orthodox church. These controversial works on the 'Errors of the Greeks' proliferated during the ninth century as a result of the 'Photian Schism', when the Patriarch of Constantinople was deposed by the Eastern Emperor. The deposed Patriarch appealed to Pope Nicholas I (858–67), as did his replacement, Photius. But when Nicholas ordered the restoration of Ignatius as Patriarch, relations between Constantinople and Rome worsened.

By this time the icon supporters had triumphed at Constantinople. Latin theologians also criticized the Eastern church for its different method for deciding the date of Easter, the difference in clergymen's tonsure-style, and over the celibacy of the clergy. (The Eastern church allowed clergy to narry, but required monks to be :elibate.)

The major theological contro- ⁄ersy involved the *filioque* ques- ion. Did the Holy Spirit descend from the Father *through* the Son' or 'from the Father *and* the Son'? From the time of Photius Ortho- lox theologians bitterly attacked he Western church on this issue, leclaring that the Western position of 'and the Son' (*filioque*) was a late addition to the Nicene Creed (as ndeed it was). This issue further lienated the Eastern and Western :hurches. The Greek-speaking East and the Latin West were also divided in language. 'East nd West could not understand each other because they could not nderstand each other!'

Jew questions of belief

Carolingian theologians often nticipated later medieval theologi- al issues. The Adoptionist heresy, lleging that Christ in his human- y was only the 'adopted' Son f God, arose in Spain in the late ighth century and appeared again ater in the Carolingian Empire. lcuin combated it vigorously in is work, *Against Felix.* Several Carolingian monks disputed the uestion of the perpetual virginity f Mary, a view widely accepted om the fifth century. Carolingian oncern to protect the holiness and nlessness of Mary points toward ne later medieval emphasis on the 'irgin Mary.

A significant discussion arose ver the question of predestina- on. A Carolingian monk amed Gottschalk, who studied ugustine's theology carefully, ppears to have been the first to each 'double predestination'. This 'as the belief that some people re predestined to salvation, while thers are justly predestined to ternal judgement. He was tried nd condemned for his views by two synods and finally imprisoned by the Archbishop of Rheims. Gottschalk died twenty years later, holding his views to the end.

The other major theological issue of the Carolingian era concerned the Lord's Supper. The influential Abbot of Corbie, Paschasius Radbertus, wrote a treatise *On the Body and Blood of the Lord.* This was the first clear statement of a doctrine of

ALCUIN

W. Delius

Alcuin, an Anglo-Saxon scholar, became head tutor at the court of Charlemagne at Aachen, and in 796 Abbot of Tours. Previously he had for a time been master of the cathedral school in York. He died in 804.

He profoundly influenced the intellectual, cultural and religious direction of the Carolingian Empire, as revealed by his more than three hundred surviving letters. Alcuin's importance is best shown in the manuscripts of the school at Tours, in his educational writings, revision of the text of the Bible, biblical commentaries and in the completion of the Gregorian Sacramentary version of the Roman liturgy. He standardized spelling and the style of writing, reformed missionary practice, and contributed to the drawing up of collections of church regulations.

Alcuin was also the leading theologian in the struggle against Adoptionists in Spain, who believed that the man Christ was God's 'adopted son'. Alcuin upheld orthodox belief and the authority of the church, the eminence of the Holy Roman see and Charlemagne's sacred position as Emperor.

The decorated initial letter of the book of Wisdom, from Alcuin's Bible. He revised the text of the Latin *Vulgate* Bible in the ninth century.

the 'real presence' of Christ's body and blood in the eucharist, suggesting what was later called transubstantiation. Ordinary Christians readily accepted the idea that the actual body and blood of Christ were present in the sacrament of the mass.

Reforming the clergy

The reform synods of King Pepin and Boniface focussed attention on the lives of the non-monastic clergy. Priests must lead lives beyond reproach. The repetition of this requirement at synod after synod during the sixth, seventh and eighth centuries clearly witnessed to the need for reform among the clergy. Among the violations criticized were the rejection of celibacy, over-eating and drunkenness, unnecessary and unwise relationships with women, hunting (and keeping hunting-animals—dogs and hawks), carrying arms and frequenting taverns.

Chrodegang, bishop of Metz, did most to reform the clergy, by preparing a rule for his cathedral clergy. This rule eventually spread throughout the Carolingian empire. The spirit of reform was strongly supported by Pepin and Charlemagne themselves.

Monastic developments at this time were particularly significant. The emphasis was on standardization and centralization. Between 813 and 817 a revised Benedictine rule was adopted for the whole of the Carolingian Empire.

Another Benedict, a monk from Aniane in Burgundy, was responsible for an exceedingly strict regime based on the Benedictine rule. His model was soon copied in all the monasteries of Burgundy. Charlemagne's successor, Louis the Pious, appointed Benedict the overseer of all monasteries in the realm, and a few years later his revised Benedictine rule was made obligatory for all monasteries, but with little long-term effect.

When Louis the Pious succeeded Charlemagne, the pope was able to reassert his independence, following the long period of domination by Charlemagne. The new trend towards an imperial theocracy during Charlemagne's era would have yielded a 'state church' as in the Eastern Orthodox Empire. But the papacy stressed the superiority of the spiritual power over the secular. This was reinforced by the forged *Donation of Constantine* with its emphasis on papal pre-eminence in the governing of the western half of the Roman Empire. The pope's crowning of Charlemagne was a further demonstration of the pope's claim to decide who should wear the imperial crown.

After Charlemagne, the Carolingian Empire was torn by civil wars. The political chaos as well as the prevailing system of church control threatened the independence of the bishops. Laymen controlled churches by means of the 'proprietary' system, providing the land and erecting the church building. Increasingly the lay patrons felt free to choose the clergymen to serve in these churches. Associated with this system there arose the abuse of simony, the sale of church posts, often with little or no regard to the clerical qualifications of the purchaser. These arrangements persisted throughout succeeding centuries, the age of classic feudalism. The church was seriously compromised.

The Carolingian era did see a major effort to deal with this problem. In the diocese of Rheims between 845 and 853 clergymen produced another remarkable forgery, the *Pseudo-Isidorian Decretals* or *False Decretals*. This extraordinary fabrication, done with great inventiveness, was designed to provide 'law' which

In the ninth century the Vikings made successful raids on western Europe. They had great sea power. This is the head of the wooden stem-post of a Viking ship.

:ould protect the rights of the ›ishops.

In order to strengthen the .rgument, the authors invoked he principle of the supremacy of he pope. Their intent was not o aid the papacy, but in fact it vas the papacy which ultimately ›enefited most from the *False)ecretals*. This compendium of hurch law, which incorporated the *)onation of Constantine,* became . vital part of medieval canon law, ınd buttressed the papal claims o supremacy in the church and ›ver secular authority. The first ›ope to make use of this collec- ion was Nicholas I (858–67), the nost important pope in the period ›etween Gregory the Great and ;regory VII. Nicholas saw clearly he danger of a church dominated ›y civil rulers, and he was deter- nined to avert this possibility by tressing that the church's govern- nent was centred on Rome.

Despair and darkness

From the late ninth century until the mid-eleventh century, internal and external problems steadily weakened western Christendom. The Carolingian Empire frag- mented; no major military power existed in the West. The con- tinued attacks of the Muslims in the south, a new wave of attackers from central Asia, the Magyars (Hungarians), and the almost overwhelming movement of Norsemen from Scandinavia, brought yet more fragmentation and chaos. A contemporary chroni- cler lamented, 'Once we had a king, now we have kinglets!' The end of the world seemed at hand. It was seriously expected by many as the year 1000 approached.

For the papacy this was an era of despair; the pope no longer had Carolingian 'Protectors' to come to his assistance. The papacy was

The remains of the abbey church of Whitby, built on the site of the original seventh-century abbey.

In the ninth and tenth centuries the Norsemen sailed out of Scandinavia in boats such as this. This longship has been carefully reconstructed and preserved.

increasingly involved in the power struggle among the nobility for the rule of Italy. Popes became the captive partisans of one political faction or another, and the result was spiritual and moral decline. For example, Pope Stephen VI took vengeance by having his predecessor's body disinterred and brought before a synod, where it was propped up in a chair for a trial. Following conviction, the body was thrown into the River Tiber. Within a year Stephen was overthrown. He was strangled while in prison.

There was an almost total collapse of civil order and culture in Europe during the tenth century. Everywhere church property was either devastated and ransacked by foreign invaders, or fell into the hands of catholic nobility. Noblemen treated bishoprics and monasteries as their private property to dispose of as they wished. The clergy steadily became indifferent to duty, and their ignorance and immorality increased.

For the papacy the tenth century was indeed a dark age. Without imperial protection, the popes now became the helpless plaything of the Roman nobility, who fought to gain control by appointing relatives or political favourites. The fascinating chroni-cle by Liutprand, the German bishop of Cremona, presents a picture of sexual debauchery at the papal court; but it must be re with caution since the author was very anti-Roman.

Although there were incompet-ent and immoral popes during the tenth and the first half of the elev-enth century, the papal institution continued to operate and to be respected throughout the West. The papal administration continue to function, even though at a reduced level. The nerve centre papal government, the chancery, continued to issue letters to all

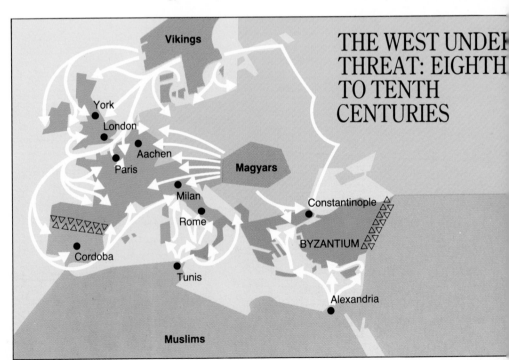

THE WEST UNDER THREAT: EIGHTH TO TENTH CENTURIES

Vikings
York
London
Aachen
Paris
Magyars
Milan
Rome
Constantinople
Cordoba
BYZANTIUM
Tunis
Alexandria
Muslims

parts of Europe dealing with a variety of issues. Bishoprics and abbeys were founded by laymen after they had obtained the approval of the papal court. Pilgrimages to Rome hardly slackened during this age, as Christians visited the most important shrines in the West, the tombs of Peter and Paul, as well as a host of other relics which could be venerated in the papal city.

Otto rescues the papacy

At the lowest ebb of the tenth-century papacy, during the reign of Pope John XII (955–64), a major change in Italian politics directly affected the position of the popes. A strong, independent German monarchy emerged. The Saxon dynasty began with the election of Henry I and was vigorously continued in his son, Otto I (936–73). Otto developed a very close relationship with the church in Germany. Bishops and abbots were given the rights and dignity of princes of the realm; the church was given generous grants of land. By means of his alliance with the church Otto sought to offset the power of the rebellious hereditary nobles of his kingdom.

The 'spiritual aristocracy' created by the Saxon kings was not hereditary. The loyalty of these men could therefore be counted on much more readily, and in fact the German bishops contributed money and arms to help the German kings expand into Italy, what is now East Germany, and Poland.

Otto the Great provided the desperately needed assistance to raise the papacy out of the mire of Roman and Italian politics. His entrance into papal and Italian affairs was indeed a fateful decision. Otto marched south into Italy to help Adelaide of Burgundy, to marry her and also to declare himself king of the Lombards. A decade later, he was again in Italy, this time invited by Pope John XII. In February 962, the papacy revived the empire in the West when John XII crowned Otto and Adelaide in St Peter's. The price paid by the papacy for the support of the secular state was interference in the internal affairs of the church.

The events of 962–63 initiated another decisive phase in church-state relations. Until 1250 each German ruler was to follow up his election as king by making the march to Rome to be crowned Emperor. German involvement in papal affairs meant emperors deciding who should be pope, or recognizing 'anti-popes'.

In 963 Otto returned to Rome and made the Romans promise not to elect a pope thereafter without his or his son's consent. Then he convened a synod which tried Pope John, found him guilty of a list of sordid crimes, and finally deposed him. In his place they chose a layman, who received all of his ecclesiastical orders in one day to become Pope Leo VIII.

THE EASTERN CHURCH

Harlie Kay Gallatin

Many of the characteristics that today distinguish Eastern Christianity developed very early in Christian history. As early as the fifth century, the legacy of unresolved differences separating East and West began gradually to mount up. By the end of the twelfth century, the Eastern and Western parts of the church had come to the point of thinking of each other as separated bodies. Unfortunately, but predictably, each area held the other responsible for having abandoned the true Christian tradition.

Making a tradition

The Christian message was, of course, first proclaimed in the context of the predominately Jewish culture of Palestine. But long before AD 100, through contacts with the dispersed Jews who were part of the 'hellenized' population influenced by Greek culture, Christianity made its way to regions far from Jerusalem. Christianity next moved to various hellenized Gentile cultures—in Egypt, Syria, Asia Minor, Greece and hellenistic outposts in the cities of the West. By the mid-second century AD, Christianity had begun to spread from the hellenized people of Egypt and Syria into the Coptic and Syriac sub-cultures. Similar developments in other regions of the Roman Empire brought Christianity into contact with a still wider range of cultures by the end of the second century.

The word 'catholic', meaning general or universal, as opposed to particular or local, began to be used regularly during the second century to refer to Christianity's common body of beliefs and practices. Although a large part of this catholic Christian tradition was shared by all Christians, no matter what their language or culture, many differences of interpretation, emphasis and practice emerged from the diverse cultural circumstances. Indeed, during the following centuries further differences developed, which caused new tensions and problems within the Christian community.

'New Rome'

By 324 Constantine the Great had made himself master of the Roman world, ushering in an epoch of general peace and prosperity. He established a new capital on the Bosphorus. A symbol of the new era, the city was originally designed as a Christian counterpart of Rome, and was called 'New Rome'. However, during its long and illustrious history, as the center of a thriving civilization and the seat of economic and political power, it has more often been known as Constantinople—the city of Constantine. It was to become and to remain for many centuries the greatest city in the Christian world, the cultural and political hub of the Byzantine or East Roman state. And it was the focus around which the Eastern Church took form.

By bringing about reconciliation between the Roman Empire and the Christian church, Constantine greatly influenced Christianity as

Opposite The artist has drawn this map of the world centred on Jerusalem. God is shown upholding the world. The map is from an English psalter of the early thirteenth century.

a whole, and the traditions of the Eastern Church in particular. His achievement was of pivotal importance for the cultural and political future of Western civilization,

Constantine found Christianity divided and torn over differences in doctrine and practice. He was superstitiously anxious that God would hold him personally responsible for these divisions and quarrels among the Christians. If Christianity lacked cohesion and unity, how could it be a proper religion for the Emperor? Constantine, and many later emperors, made every effort to lessen the divisions and increase agreement about the faith.

Constantine adopted a procedure already developed by the Christians to settle differences of opinion at a local or regional level. He called the leaders of the entire church to assemble in his presence in order to define and agree upon the correct tradition. This procedure itself became a part of the Christian tradition. From the first ecumenical council at Nicaea (325), to the seventh, also held at Nicaea, in 787, it was always the emperor who called the council and presided over it—either personally or by deputy. Eastern Christians today still place great emphasis on these seven ecumenical councils. They sometimes refer to themselves as 'The Church of the Seven Councils'.

The Emperor believed that it was just as important to achieve

The great city of Constantinople has become the modern city of Istanbul.

nd maintain a uniform tradition as was to decide what the correct radition was. Uniformity in the vhole church could be most easily ecured by controlling its leaders. Whatever the Christian leaders greed upon in an ecumenical ouncil was immediately pro- ounced as law by the Emperor. hurch leaders who dissented om the beliefs and practices dged by the council to be ortho- ox were labelled 'heretics' or schismatics', and deposed from ffice. The government then equently deported the deposed ader to some distant corner of e Empire, where his influence ould have little effect.

But this procedure was of little elp in dealing effectively with e widespread and deep-seated octrinal controversies which the hurch endured from the fourth to e seventh centuries, Arianism nd Monophysitism in particu- r. Even the most energetic mperors, such as Justinian I and Heraclius, were unable to avoid r to moderate such controver- ies. Statesmanlike emperors s Zeno or Constans II, who emanded that all debate on ontroversial issues should cease, nly stirred up the wrath of both arties against themselves.

A pattern of government

One reason why the emperors did ot achieve unity and uniformity y in the pattern of organization sed from very early times. This olity is still carefully maintained y the Orthodox Church today. Every bishop is bound to uphold cripture and the apostolic radition. But the actual govern- ent of the local church rests in e local synod or council. This onsists of the bishop together with the local clergy (priests and eacons) and influential laymen, who may be monks or scholars.

Each bishop was elected by the local synod and congregation, although he was often nominated by a neighbouring bishop. After his election, the neighbouring bishops (at least two) gathered to ordain their new colleague. Once consecrated, he normally served for life. He could be deposed only if charges against him were accepted by a synod of his fellow bishops in the same province. All bishops were in theory equal. But those in the larger cities easily came to exercise more influence than the bishops from smaller places in the province. As a result, the synod of bishops in the province recognized the bishop of the capital city, the 'metropolitan bishop', as their presiding officer. Normally the metropolitan bishop had the right to approve all candidates for bishop before they were consecrated, and the right to carry out any disciplinary actions voted by the provincial synod.

By Constantine's day the bishops of the cities of Rome, Alexandria and Antioch were recognized as 'chief metropoli- tans', reflecting the fact they were customarily called upon to approve the candidates for metropolitan bishop in adjoining provinces, and to preside at any synod which involved those metropolitans and their bishops. Eventually the chief metropolitans became known as 'patriarchs'. The bishops of Constantinople and Jerusalem were later recognized to make a total of five patriarchs, each representing a section of the total church called a patriarchate. Representatives from all five of the patriarchs had to be present in order for a council to be recognized as truly ecumenical. Any change in Christian teaching or practice required the approval of such an ecumenical council.

In theory, each patriarch's authority as a bishop was equal, as was his importance in relation to the clergy of his patriarchate. Each patriarch was also seen as equally responsible to the Emperor and to the decrees of the ecumenical councils. The patriarch bishop of Rome was regarded as first among equals at the first ecumenical council because of status of the ancient capital. At the next ecumenical council (381) it was agreed that the Patriarch of Constantinople was to rank second, because Constantinople was the 'New Rome'. It was the Patriarch of Constantinople, sometimes known as the 'Ecumenical Patriarch', who became the spokesman for Eastern Christianity. Though the Emperor's immediate presence was a powerful influence with which other patriarchs did not have to deal, the Patriarch of Constantinople never became simply an imperial agent in charge of religious affairs. Nor did his authority exceed that of the other patriarchs.

God's chosen deputy

The emperor, 'the living image of Christ', stood at the head of the church. The notion that his office was sacred, a mixture of priest and king, was not originally a Christian idea. Pagan emperors of Rome had carried the title of chief priest, and performed official religious duties as part of their office. Leading Christians saw Constantine as God's chosen deputy whose imperial power was an earthly reflection of God's heavenly sovereignty. The Emperor, as head of the church, presided over certain local synods at Constantinople, and over all general councils. He had the right to approve all candidates for the post of patriarch. Hence, in the Eastern Church, the ecclesiastical role of the imperial head of state became traditional, so that after Roman emperors ceased to exist in the fifteenth century the church conferred its attention on Russian emperors as a substitute. This helps to explain the strong national identity of modern orthodox churches.

During the pagan centuries the emperor had set out official religious policy. This principle remained basically unchanged. Certain forms of religious behavior were limited or prohibited, and selected cults were favoured and patronized. Constantine began by granting Christian priests and bishops the same sort of privileges as the pagan priesthoods had enjoyed. He also prohibited the most immoral of pagan rites. It was Theodosius I (379–95) who took the final step of totally outlawing paganism and establishing orthodox Christianity as the only official religion of the Roman Empire.

In imitation of the gifts of earlier emperors to pagan cults, Constantine granted funds for new furnishings and new church buildings to many Christian congregations. Later emperors did the same. But the most famous of all was Justinian I (527–65), whose extensive construction programme of church buildings across the Empire included the huge and impressive church of Saint Sophia. It was the largest and most elaborate of about twenty new churches he erected in or near Constantinople, and it still stands in modern Istanbul.

Combating decline

In time the church began to regard correct belief as much more important than correct behavior, even for the clergy. Correct behavior for the clergy was gradually narrowed down to a ritualistic life-style. It involved only the traditional duties of the priest and such superficial things as distinctive dress and special haircut.

Preaching was given great importance, especially in the fourth and fifth centuries. Through long, eloquent, but heavily theological sermons, Gregory of Nazianzus in Asia Minor and John Chrysostom (Golden Mouth) at Antioch and Constantinople, with a host of less celebrated preachers, instructed throngs of converts in Christian belief and behavior. Christian ideas were so popularized that they often became items of everyday conversation. But there was no immediate transformation of society.

The rich liturgical tradition, which forms part of the Eastern Orthodox Church's uniqueness, developed at Constantinople from the fourth century. The elaborate liturgy of Basil, bishop of Caesarea in Cappadocia (370–79), was brought to the capital shortly after it had been written. This liturgy is still used for ten special services during the Orthodox church year. During the rest of the year Orthodox worshippers use the shorter liturgy, which was introduced at Constantinople by John Chrysostom, patriarch 398–404. Some additions were made to Chrysostom's liturgy in the ninth century, on the basis of the liturgy then in use at Jerusalem. Also, most of the hymns that have survived with this liturgical tradition originated in Constantinople. Those written there in the sixth century by the Syrian, Romanus the Melodist, are particularly important.

Monasticism from its earliest stages made many important contributions to Eastern Christianity. It began in the eastern regions of the Empire in the fourth century and spread rapidly. Many pious people, both laymen and clergy, were troubled by the apparent failure of the church to escape worldly entanglements, and turned to asceticism and monasticism. Basil, the bishop of Caesarea in Cappadocia, provided a set of rules for those in his area that had chosen monastic life. This 'Basilian Rule' has remained the basic constitution for all monasteries connected with the Orthodox churches. In the Eastern church the great majority of monks were laymen. After the middle of the sixth century, it became customary to select and ordain monks to fill the highest posts in the church. Eastern monks were better known for their piety and contemplative prayer than for their scholarship. After the tenth century a group of monasteries on Mount Athos, near Thessalonica, became increasingly important. In the fourteenth century a movement of radical mysticism, based on the tradition of contemplative prayer, began.

Constantine and Justinian present their gifts to the Virgin and Child. This mosaic is found above one of the doors of St Sophia, Istanbul.

Gregory Palamas was the leader and theologian of this new movement, which the Orthodox church accepted.

Byzantium besieged

Since the Christian and political institutions of Byzantine society were closely related, secular events often directly influenced the development of Christianity. In the two hundred years following Justinian I's death (565), the Empire fell on evil times and was nearly obliterated. In the early seventh century Sassanid Persia in the east and the Avar kingdom of central Europe co-operated in a war effort. This culminated in a joint attack on Constantinople (626) that came very close to success. Emperor Heraclius (610–41) with the aid of wealth generously offered by the Church, led the imperial forces to victory over both Avars and Persians. But he was unable to check the advance of the Arabs into the imperial territories of Syria, Palestine and Egypt during his last years. Inspired by their new religion, Islam, the Arabs pushed on relentlessly to conquer all North Africa and a great part of Asia Minor. Twice their forces advanced to the bulwarks of Con-

PSEUDO-DIONYSIUS THE AREOPAGITE

David F. Wright

The name of Dionysius, Paul's convert in Athens, was borrowed by the unidentified early sixth-century Syrian who wrote *The Divine Names, Mystical Theology, The Celestial Hierarchy, The Ecclesiastical Hierarchy* and some letters. Although Monophysite Christians were the first to refer to them, they were soon accepted as authentic by Chalcedonians such as Leontius of Byzantium. Maximus the Confessor's paraphrases finally established their authority in the East, while in the West Gregory the Great and the Lateran Council of 649 accepted them as first-century writings.

Pseudo-Dionysius' writings depend closely on the Neoplatonists Plotinus and Proclus (died 485). He views the universe as a hierarchy, with the heavenly pattern reflected in the church. The 'triads' of angel choirs which mediate between God and humanity correspond to the 'triads' of sacraments, of orders of clergy and of classes of 'inferior Christians'. Moreover, three stages of spiritual life—purification, illumination and union—lead to the goal of becoming like God himself. The ascent through these stages consists of advances in 'unknowing'—by shedding sensible and rational perceptions; illumination is by a 'ray of divine darkness'. This 'mysticism of darkness' has secular Greek roots, identifying spirit with pure intelligence, rather than using biblical concepts.

This synthesis of Christian and Neoplatonist concepts enormously influenced Byzantine theologies of mysticism and liturgy, and Western mystics, scholastics and Renaissance Platonist thinkers. Dionysius' works were translated into Latin by Eriugena about 850. Lorenzo Valla first questioned their authenticity in the fifteenth century; this was widely doubted in the Reformation era, although not disproved until the end of the nineteenth century.

;tantinople, but without success. Che emperors also had to contend vith the expanding power of the ombards in Italy, the various ;lavic peoples in Greece and the 3ulgarians in the valley of the River Danube.

The Empire survived with only fraction of its former territory, ut Constantinople remained the ultural, political and economic ocus of its existence. Large umbers of orthodox Christians eft the regions which had been levastated by the Persians and hen the Arabs. These refugees ncluded many monks and clergy vho settled in the central and vestern parts of the Empire, specially around Constantinople, n southern Italy and near Rome.

By 800, four of the five patriar- hates of the church were in new ands. Alexandria, Antioch and erusalem were under Muslim ule, and their patriarchs, unable to naintain their positions or exercise heir powers, frequently chose to ve in exile at Constantinople. The ope, the new contemporary title or the patriarchal bishop of Rome, elt abandoned by Constantinople n the face of the Lombard menace nd after 750 forged a political lliance with the Frankish kings. n 800 he crowned the Frankish ing, Charlemagne, as 'Emperor of he Romans'. Thus, for all practi- al purposes, a separate Roman Empire was created in the West.

The increasing political, conomic and cultural fragmenta- ion of the Empire after 800 hallenged the unity of Christianity s never before. Paying lip-service o the ideal of unity, each isolated egion of the church became nore and more independent of, nd divergent from, the others. Eastern Christianity was now oncentrated more than ever t Constantinople, and its own radition was still developing. At he sixth ecumenical council held in Constantinople in 681, the long struggle with Monophysitism was laid to rest and the doctrine for which orthodox leaders had contended since the middle of the fifth century was affirmed. Monophysitism arose out of dissatisfaction with the doctrinal definitions of the Council of Chalcedon (451). Its greatest popular support had been in those regions of the East that were now conquered by the Arabs. In those areas, the Monophysites continued to enjoy freedom to create independent churches,

The Muslims quickly overran much of the Empire. They turned the Basilica of St John at Damascus into a mosque.

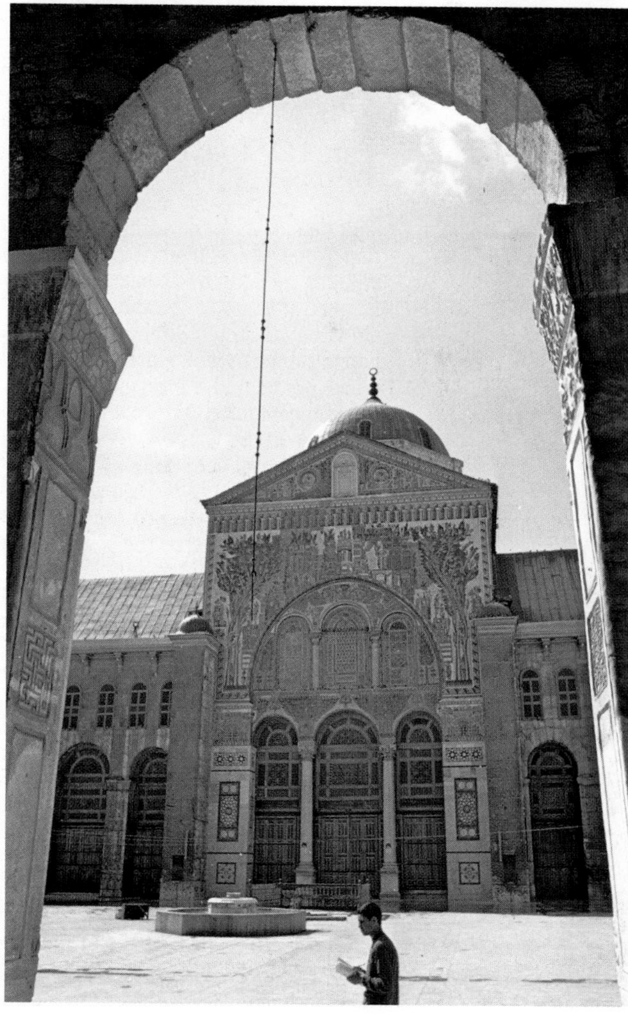

some of which have endured to the present.

What is 'holy'?

Soon yet another religious controversy began to rage across the Byzantine world. On the surface it was a disagreement over the use of icons, that is, images. But at a deeper level it was a disagreement over which things were sufficiently sacred or holy to deserve worship The Christian clergy are set apart by ordination; hence, they are holy. Church buildings are set apart by dedication; they are holy. The martyrs and heroes of the faith are set apart by their deeds, and they are normally called 'saints' (which means 'holy one'). Do they not deserve the same reverence as the clergy? And as the martyrs became holy by their self-sacrifice, so monks, sacrificed

THE PAULICIANS AND THE BOGOMILS

Paul D. Steeves

The Paulicians were a Christian group who appeared in the eastern parts of the Byzantine Empire after 650. Their founder, Constantine, rejected the formalism of the Orthodox state church which dominated the religious life of the Empire. He based his teaching on the written word of God alone, but held that only the Gospels and letters of Paul were divinely inspired. An evil deity, he declared, had inspired the rest of the New Testament and the Old Testament.

The Paulicians claimed that this evil deity was the creator and god of this world. The true God of heaven, they said, was opposed to all material things. In order to save people's spirits from the evil of the physical world, the true God sent an angel who appeared to be a man, Jesus. From this dualistic view came the Paulicians' ideas about the Scriptures and church.

Since the Old Testament both declared that God created the world and provided the basis for the theocratic principles of the Byzantine union of church and state, they believed that it must have been produced by the evil spirit. Since the Orthodox church involved so much that was physical and material, such as the sacraments, priesthood, images, liturgy and secular influence, it, too, must have come from the same evil spirit. The Paulicians also claimed that the church's appeal to the authority of the apostle Peter showed that he was a messenger of that spirit.

The origin of the Paulicians' ideas is unclear. They are similar to some of the earlier ideas of Marcion and especially the Manicheans, but not identical with either of these systems.

Constantine changed his name to Silvanus (Silas), which was the name of one of the associates of Paul. After Silvanus was stoned to death, the next leader of the sect took the name of Titus. He was burned alive. Other leaders adopted the names of Timothy and Tychicus. This attempt to associate themselves with the apostle Paul probably led to their name of 'Paulicians'.

During the 'Iconoclastic Controversy' of the eighth century, the persecution of the Paulicians eased. One emperor, Constantine ne normal routines of everyday fe. Do they, too, deserve vorship?

The holiness of the saints was upported by the miracles reported s taking place in connection with ne saint's tomb, relics, or even con. By the beginning of the eventh century many of the cities f the Empire had one or more ocal saints whose icons were evered as having special powers f intercession and protection. Examples include Saint Demetrius of Thessalonica, the miraculous Christ-icon of Edessa, and the miracle-working icon of Mary, the *Hodegetria,* of Constantinople.

From the sixth century, both the church and the imperial government encouraged the recognition given both to monastic holy men and Christian icons. The failed to realize that the uncontrolled multiplying of icons and holy men would encourage people to confine

Copronymus, may even have been a Paulician. But in the ninth century, the Empress Theodora ordered the massacre of tens of thousands of Paulicians, who were most numerous in the area of Armenia.

In response to persecutions, the Paulicians organized armies which proved skilful in battle. Therefore, the emperors moved many Paulicians from their Armenian homeland to the Balkans (present-day Bulgaria). They meant the Paulicians to defend the Empire against threats from the Slavs and Bulgars.

The Paulicians, it turned out, had a greater impact on the Bulgars in the religious than in the military field. They preached their beliefs to these recent converts to Christianity. Some of the Bulgars adopted Paulician ideas into a new religious system that acquired the name 'Bogomilism.'

The Bogomils

The organizer of the new movement, it appears, was a priest named Bogomil. His name means 'beloved of God'. Around the middle of the tenth century Bogomil began to teach that the first-born son of God was Satanael. Because of his pride, this deity was expelled from heaven. He made a new heaven and earth, in which he placed Adam and Eve. Satenael and Eve became the parents of Cain, who was the source of all evil among humans. Moses and John the Baptist, according to Bogomil teaching, were both servants of Satanael. But God sent the *Logos,* his second son, to save humanity from the control of Satanael. Although Satanael killed the incarnate *Logos,* Jesus, his spiritual body was resurrected and returned to the right hand of God. Satanael was in this way defeated.

In contrast to the Paulicians, the Bogomils adopted a rigidly ascetic life-style. They despised marriage, although they permitted it in the case of less-than-perfect believers. They condemned the eating of meat and drinking of wine. They rejected baptism and communion as Satanic rites, since they used material things.

Bogomilism flourished in Bulgaria while it was an independent country in the tenth, and again in the thirteenth centuries. Bogomil ideas probably spread to western Europe where they influenced the Cathars and Albigensians. When the Turks destroyed the Bulgarian Empire in 1393, the sect of the Bogomils disappeared. Paulicians continued to exist in Armenia into the nineteenth century.

their Christian devotion to unique local shrines and figures. Most ordinary Christians failed to distinguish between the holy object or holy person and the spiritual reality it stood for. They fell into idolatry.

This kind of idolatry had its precedents. In pagan Rome the icon of the Emperor was revered as if the Emperor himself were present. Special agents of the Emperor were also given royal treatment. Even after the emperors became Christian, the imperial image on coins, in court-houses, and in the most prominent places in the major cities continued to be an object of devotion. Constantine and his successors had the habit of erecting huge statues of themselves at Constantinople. It was Justinian who first broke with tradition and erected instead a huge statue of Christ over the main gate, 'the Bronze Gate', of the imperial palace at Constantinople. During the following century icons of Christ or Mary came to replace the imperial icon in many settings. Eventually, in the reign of Justinian II (685–95, 705–11), the icon of Christ began to appear on the reverse side of the coinage.

John the Baptist. A mosaic from the interior of Saint Sophia, modern Istanbul.

Leo the iconoclast

Emperor Leo III (717–41) launched an attack on the use of icons. Perhaps he was motivated by a sense of the nation's guilt. Christianity taught that God punished the children of Israel because of their idolatry. Perhap the humiliating defeats and losse of the previous century, as well a the calamitous earthquake early in Leo's reign, were intended to bring 'God's new chosen people' to their senses. Christian antago ism to the use of icons developed during the seventh century in the eastern regions next to the Arab frontier were Leo grew up. Befo becoming emperor, Leo served a governor-general of western Asi Minor where several bishops we beginning to speak out against icons.

After successfully repulsing th Muslim armies in their second major attack on Constantinople (717–718), in 726 Leo openly declared his opposition to icons f the first time. He ordered the ic of Christ over the Bronze Gate be replaced with a cross. In spite of angry rioting which spread to many cities, Leo called in 730 for the removal and destruction of al religious icons in public places an churches.

Under Leo III and his son Constantine V (741–75), those supporting icons were persecuted vigorously. The pope at Rome dared to officially condem iconoclasm, that is, the destructi of icons. The Emperor retaliated by removing Sicily, southern Ital and the entire western part of the Balkans and Greece from the patriarchate of Rome and into the patriarchate of Constantinople. This, as much as anything else, forced the bishop of Rome to see the support and protection of the Franks.

A synod of bishops met

t Hieria in 1753 and described ll use of icons as idolatry. ll remaining icons were estroyed. Supporters of icons n the area around Constantinople vere excommunicated, mutilated nd sent into exile. Constantine V eliberately destroyed the eputation and influence of monks n general and the popular, highly enerated ascetics in particular. n estimated 50,000 of these oly men fled from the region nmediately around onstantinople to escape ersecution and humiliation. The mperor also attempted to limit the ractice of saint-worship by estroying relics and condemning rayers made to saints.

The iconoclasts wanted to eplace the religious icons with ne traditional Christian symbols f the cross, the Book (Bible) and ne elements of the Lord's Supper. These objects alone were to e considered holy. Beyond this, nly ordained clergy and dedicated uildings possessed a kind of holiness. Constantine V argued that, hen consecrated, the elements f the Lord's Supper were the ue icon of Christ. He apparently elieved that the consecrated read and wine were identical in *ubstance* with the flesh and blood f the divine and human Christ. proper icon must consist of the ame *substance* as what it stands or.

defence of icons

he icon supporters consisted rgely of monks and other ascetics gether with their uneducated nd superstitious followers from ne general population. Although ot all monks were in favour of on usage, some monasteries vere in the lucrative business of aking and selling them. Reasoned efense of their position came from distant source. John Mansour (about 730–60), in a monastery in Arab-controlled Palestine, formulated the ideas that were eventually used to justify religious icons. Mansour, better known as John of Damascus (his birthplace) was the greatest theologian of the eighth century. He is recognized today by the Orthodox churches as the last of the great teachers of the early church, the so-called 'Fathers'.

John explained that an image was never of the same substance as its original, but merely imitated it. An icon's only significance is as a copy and reminder of the original. To deny, as the iconoclasts did, that any true icon could depict Christ, was, in effect, to deny the possibility of the incarnation. Although it was wrong to worship an icon, the presence of an icon of Christ could instruct and assist the believer in the worship of the true Christ. Icons should be honoured and venerated in much the same way as the Bible, or the cross. It also came to be accepted that icons of Mary, the apostles, the saints and even the angles could be used. But the pictures themselves were no more than reminders to help the faithful give proper respect and reverence.

Constantine V's son and successor, Leo IV (775–80), was not an energetic iconoclast. His widow Irene, regent for their son Constantine VI (780–97), overturned the dynasty's iconoclastic policy. Under her instigation the seventh ecumenical council assembled at Nicaea in 787 and condemned the whole iconoclastic movement, affirming the position taken by John of Damascus.

But that was not the end of iconoclasm. An influential block of support developed in the professional military class, partly as a reaction to the series of military disasters, diplomatic humiliations, and economic problems the state

The Virgin and Child, from St Sophia, Istanbul.

experienced in the quarter century after Nicaea. Finally, Emperor Leo V, the Armenian (813–20), decided that iconoclasm should again become the official policy of his government. A synod of church leaders in 815 reaffirmed the position taken by the anti-icon synod of 754—except that they no longer regarded the icons as idols. Key leaders of the opposition, such as the deposed Patriarch Nicephorus and Theodore the abbot of the Studios monastery in Constantinople, were imprisoned. A few other unbending church leaders were deposed, and several monks gained notoriety by openly and violently confessing pro-icon views.

With Leo V's death, active persecution of the pro-icon party waned for seventeen years before bursting out again in 837 under the leadership of John Grammaticus, patriarch of Constantinople. Under John's influence Emperor Theophilus (829–842) decreed exile or capital punishment for all who openly supported the use of icons.

This ivory carving was made in tenth-century Byzantium (Constantinople). It shows John the Baptist with (*above*) Saints Philip and Stephen, and (*below*) Saints Andrew and Thomas.

Theodora, widow of Theophilus and regent for their son Michael III (842–67), determined that her son must abandon the iconoclastic policy to retain the widest support for his rule. A synod early in 843 condemned all iconoclasts (except Theophilus), deposed patriarch John Grammaticus, and confirmed the decrees of the seventh council. Thereafter the relationship of the Orthodox church and the Byzantine government became more one of harmony and cooperation. Each year Orthodox churches still celebrate the first Sunday in Lent as the 'Feast of Orthodoxy', to commemorate the end of the iconoclastic controversy. In today's Orthodox church buildings paintings and mosaics frequently fill spaces on ceilings and walls. A screen or low partition called the *iconostasis* stretches across the front of the church, between the congregation and the altar area, for the purpose of displaying all the special icons pertaining to the liturgy, the Holy days and seasons

The church divided

In the period from the sixth to the eleventh centuries the widen-

Byzantium produced distinctive forms of art. This gold enamel container (reliquary) was made to hold a saint's relic. St George is portrayed on the cover.

g cultural divide between the ıstern and western regions d not prevent the faithful from ›ntinuing to think of the Church ; a single, universal body. Epi- ›des of intense disagreement ere relatively infrequent, and harmony more apparent than :al, based perhaps on frail human ;sumptions and the enormous fficulty of maintaining regular ›mmunication, masked the ct that a growing number controversial issues stood ıresolved. The western church's clusion, and the eastern church's leged exclusion, of a phrase in e Nicene Creed was the basis of charge and counter-charge on more than one occasion. The controversial insertion, the Latin word *filioque* meaning 'and the Son', remains today one of the significant points of disagreement between Eastern and Western churches. In 1054, an angry rift between the agents of the Roman pope, Leo IX (1049–1054), and the patriarch of Constantinople, Michael Cerularius (1043–58), proved to be the final one. Repeated initiatives to heal the schism and reunite the Roman Catholic and Eastern Orthodox parts of the church have so far failed.

FLOWERING: THE WESTERN CHURCH

Robert G. Clouse

A great struggle developed in this period between lay people and clergy over the control of the church. During the ninth and tenth centuries when the Carolingian Empire was declining, feudal nobles had gone far beyond their historic rights in selecting candidates for church posts and controlling church affairs. This was one symptom of a general crisis through which Europe passed due to the invasion of the Magyars, Saracens and Vikings, which destroyed both morale and property. Examples of the sorry state of the church included untrained clergy, simony (purchase of church posts), general sexual laxity, and lay investiture (control of the appointment and allegiance of abbots, bishops and popes).

Monastic reform

Sometimes it is darkest before the dawn, and in the case of the medieval church this proved to be the case. Growing out of the reform movement of the monastery at Cluny a great renewal cam to eleventh-century Christianity which helped the church gain control over medieval Europe. The Cluniac order, founded in 910 in France, reinvigorated monasticism. A new method of organization developed to promot the reform movement; each new monastery that was founded was tied to the mother house. They were exempt from any local control, and responsible only to the pope. Eventually the Cluniac ord came to include 300 priories, whi turned out a host of prominent church leaders, and inspired man institutions and individuals who were not members of the order.

One of these men, Hildebrand (Pope Gregory VII), has given his name to the papal reform of the eleventh century, called the

The order at Cluny, France, played an important part in monastic reform in the tenth century. The picture shows the abbey complex at Cluny as it is today.

Iildebrandine' or 'Gregorian' ·form. Actually several individ-ıls in the court of Pope Leo IX .048–54) were responsible for ·forming the church. Eventually ıey were to engage in a bitter ruggle with the Holy Roman nperors, but at first this was ɔt apparent. In fact it was the mperor Henry III (1039–56), who ded the reformers in gaining con-'ol of the papacy.

In addition to Hildebrand, ·ominent leaders of this move-ıent included Humbert of Ioyenmoutier, Peter Damian, rederick of Lorraine, and Otto f Lagery (Pope Urban II). These ıen desired the freedom of the ıurch—that the church should be ıbject only to the commands of od as revealed through canon law ıd the Scriptures. The church, hich meant in effect the whole f society, viewed as Christian ɜople, was to be governed by ıe hierarchy of clergy. The pope 'as superior to secular rulers and veryone was to obey him.

Although this programme ɜemed revolutionary in its day, ıe reformers claimed that they 'ished to restore the ancient and ue law of the church which had ɜen neglected and perverted y their time. As they examined ınon law, they learned that ıe initiative for choosing a pope ıould lie with the clergy and the ɜople rather than with a king or nperor. The canons also stated ıat buying and selling of church ffices (simony) was wrong, and ɔ must stop. In a similar manner ıurch law taught that clerics ıould not be married, so that ɜlibacy should be enforced for ergy.

The main controversy between ıe reformers and the emperors ıme to be lay investiture (choice f important clergymen). In 1059 ıe reform position was laid out in decree of Pope Nicholas II, which included the statement that the election of future popes was to be by the vote of the College of Cardinals. In addition, the papal legate's job was made more important and through his office the power of Rome could be felt throughout western Europe. Under Pope Gregory VII the conflict with the secular forces came to open warfare. In 1075, he drew up a considered statement of clerical power, the *Dictatus Papae*. Simony, clerical marriage, lay investiture were all forbidden and papal power was declared absolute. All secular forces owed him submission, and he could depose emperors and kings.

The struggle which followed between the Emperor Henry IV and Pope Gregory VII was marked by a dramatic incident at Canossa. Because of rebellion in his Empire and his own excommunication, Henry went to Italy (1077) and stood in the snow for three days in front of a fortress where Gregory was staying, thus forcing the pope to forgive him. Although regarded as a humiliation for Henry, it actually enabled him to carry on his fight against the reformers. The popes allied themselves variously with German rivals to the Emperor, the Normans of south Italy, and the cities of north Italy and gradually wore down imperial power.

Kings versus popes

Eventually the papacy came to stand for the reform programme in the minds of Christians. Each of the major areas of western Europe—England, France and the Holy Roman Empire—accepted the pope as supreme in the church. When Duke William of Normandy decided to conquer England the reformers had an opportunity to control the church there more

"King William . . . was a man of great wisdom and power . . . Though stern beyond measure to those who opposed his will, he was kind to those good men who loved God. On the very spot where God granted him the conquest of England he caused a great abbey to be built; and settled monks in it and richly endowed it. During his reign was built the great cathedral at Canterbury, and many others throughout England."

Anglo Saxon Chronicle, 1086

effectively. The pope sanctioned this invasion; William was not a disappointment and Lanfranc, one of the reformers, became Archbishop of Canterbury.

Although he retained the right to lay investiture, William the Conqueror never questioned the spiritual superiority of the pope, and the need for obedience. The king worked to separate church courts from secular courts, but he ordered that the pope could exercise authority in England only with royal approval. The reformers thus made significant gains under William I.

William II, who became king on the death of the Conqueror in 1093, appointed Anselm as Archbishop of Canterbury. A dedicated reformer, the new archbishop struggled with the king and it was not until the reign of King Henry I (1110–35) that an agreement was reached. Bishops were to be elected by the cathedral chapter in the king's presence and, after election, the bishop was to do homage for his temporal possessions to the king and then be invested with his spiritual dignity by the archbishop.

Other lands of western Europe reached a similar settlement over this question. In France, King Philip I approved a settlement by which the king would invest the bishop with the temporal powers of the office and the church would give the spiritual authority. In the Empire, the agreement reached between Emperor Henry V and the church was called the Concordat of Worms (1122). The Emperor agreed to cease the traditional investiture with the ring and staff (which symbolized the conferring of ecclesiastical power) and in exchange the pope recognized the Emperor's right to confer the *regalia* (temporal rights) by investiture with the sceptre.

Seeking God

“*Yield room for some little time to God; and rest for a little time in him. Enter the inner chamber of your mind; shut out all thoughts except that of God, and such as can help you in seeking him; close your door and seek him. Speak now, my whole heart! Speak now to God, saying, I seek your face; your face, Lord, will I seek. And come now, Lord my God, teach my heart where and how it may seek you, where and how it may find you.*”

ANSELM, Proslogion, Chapter 1

The pope and the emperor

The struggle between the Empire and the papacy was not finally settled by the agreement reached in the twelfth century. This was only a compromise, which left each side feeling that an opportunity would come to gain the upper hand. By the second half of the century the German electors had chosen a new emperor, Frederick I of Hohenstaufen (*Barbarossa,* who ruled 1152–90), who turned out to be a man of great ability. He aimed to establish peace in Germany and lead an army into Italy to make imperial control effective there.

After several warlike campaigns Frederick I realized that force would not solve the situation, and he resorted to diplomacy. Once the north Italian towns had acknowledged his control, he agreed to allow them to govern themselves. He also made peace with the south Italians and his heir married the aunt of the king of Sicily. When Frederick died, his son, Emperor Henry VI, became ruler of Germany, north Italy, Sicily, and south Italy. If the Hohenstaufen emperors could control these lands effectively, the pope would be caught in a pincer. As events unfolded this was not possible, because Henry died in 1197 while in his early thirties, leaving his possessions to a three-year-old son, Frederick (1194–1250). Anarchy became the order of the day in both Germany and Italy.

The imperial weakness worked to the advantage of the papacy, since a very competent pope acceded—Innocent III (who ruled 1198–1216). The son of a noble Roman family, he was trained in both theology and law. Innocent was determined to build a strong papal state in Italy, so that secular rulers could not so easily use naterial means to force the papacy o do their bidding. Frederick ecame Innocent's ward and was stablished as Emperor Frederick I with the pope's help.

However, after Innocent's leath, Frederick turned out to e a disappointment to the pope's ause. He attempted to control oth northern and southern Italy, vhich resulted in a life-and-death truggle with the pope, who tried o crush his power. Frederick's own character complicated this struggle, for he combined a Western outlook with the style of an oriental sultan. He organized southern Italy into a kingdom that set an example for later Renaissance states. He was himself a linguist, a physician, a hunter and a poet. Although a persecutor of heretics, he shared many of the ideas of his Muslim subjects, including a fatalist outlook and a belief in astrology. An insatiably

POPE INNOCENT III

Harry Rosenberg

The medieval papacy attained the peak of its authority and influence under Innocent, who was pope 1198–1216. He had a unique ability to apply abstract concepts to concrete situations. His aristocratic background together with his outstanding personal abilities, sharpened by a precise training in canon and civil law as well as theology, fitted him to become a cardinal. In papal service he demonstrated unusual skill in dealing with the enormous variety of religious and secular problems which arose.

Innocent's diplomatic skills enabled him to wield papal authority to a remarkable degree throughout Christendom, although not always with the success he desired. He successfully upheld papal political power in Italy when it was gravely threatened by the union of the kingdom of Sicily with the German Empire. But Pope Innocent was unable to rescue King John from his rebellious English barons.

Because he believed the pope had unique authority as the 'Vicar of Christ' and as the successor of Peter, Innocent claimed the right to set aside any human actions since these were contaminated by sin and therefore came within his competence. Consequently he decreed an election for the German kingship null and void because, while one candidate had the majority of the votes, Innocent's candidate had the 'saner' votes.

The Fourth Lateran Council, called by Innocent in 1215, was the fitting climax to his career. This general council symbolized the mastery of the papacy over every feature of Latin Christendom (and seemingly over Greek Christendom, since the fourth Crusade had led to a short-lived Latin Empire of Constantinople between 1204 and 1261). Innocent's council confirmed the shameful isolation of Jews from society at large, requiring among other things that they wear a special badge. Sadly the Jews were increasingly confined to living in ghettos.

curious person, he kept a zoo of exotic animals as well as a harem.

While on a crusade, Frederick II made a treaty with the Muslims, and visited the church of the Holy Sepulchre and the Islamic Shrine of Omar with equal zeal. Though successful in Italy, he gained for his heirs the hatred of the papacy, causing the extinction of his line.

The peak of papal power

Innocent III also led the papacy to victory over the kings of France and England. In 1205 King John argued with the pope over the appointment of the Archbishop of Canterbury, and Innocent arranged the election of Stephen Langton to the post. John refused to accept him, so England was placed under an interdict in 1208, with the result that the church refused to marry, baptize or bury people. John retaliated by seizing church lands and forcing most of the bishops out of England. In 120 Innocent excommunicated the English king and in 1212 declared the throne of England vacant, inviting the French to invade the land. This proved effective, and John agreed to accept Langton and return church property. He resigned the crown of England, to receive it back as a feudal retaine of the pope. Although the indignit inflicted on the king was not realized at first by the English, taxes exacted by the pope in the thirtee century caused a bitter hatred of the papacy in England.

Innocent was just as successful against the king of France, with whom he quarrelled over a moral issue. With the permission of a synod of French bishops, King Philip Augustus left his wife for another woman, on the grounds that the queen was a distant relative. She appealed to Rome, and Innocent ordered Philip to take her back. France was placed under an interdict and after a long struggle the queen was restored.

The leadership of the clergy and pope over society was affirmed under Innocent's direction at the Fourth Lateran Council of 1215. The power of the church was demonstrated by the wide range of participants in this convocation—including archbishops, bishops, abbots, priors, the heads of the religious orders, and representatives of the secular rulers.

The Council demanded that each archbishop hold a council each year

'THE MOON AND THE SUN'

"The Creator of the universe set up two great luminaries in the firmament of heaven; the greater light to rule the day, the lesser light to rule the night. In the same way for the firmament of the universal church, which is spoken of as heaven, he appointed two great dignities; the greater to bear rule over souls (these being, as it were, days), the lesser to bear rule over bodies (these being, as it were, nights). These dignities are the pontifical authority and the royal power. Furthermore, the moon derives her light from the sun, and is in truth inferior to the sun in both size and quality, in position as well as effect. In the same way the royal power derives its dignity from the pontifical authority: and the more closely it cleaves to the sphere of that authority the less is the light with which it is adorned; the further it is removed, the more it increases in splendour."

Innocent III writes on the Emperor and the papacy in Sicut universitatis conditor, October 1198

THE SACRAMENTS ARE DEVELOPED

Colin Buchanan

During the second five hundred years of the Christian era in the West the doctrines of baptism and of communion developed considerably—both in a slightly 'magical' direction. Baptism was greatly affected by Augustine's controversy with Pelagius and his followers. The doctrine of original sin, which Augustine set out, made it vital for the church to believe in the absolute necessity of baptism for salvation. People took this to imply that unbaptized infants who died went to hell, or at least to 'limbo' on the borders of hell. The high rate of infant mortality at this period led to baptism being carried out within minutes of birth, often by midwives. (A carry-over survives to this day when newborn infants are in danger of death.)

During this same period western Europe came to be regarded as 'Christendom'—a Christian society. As a result virtually all baptisms were of infants, with this enormous pressure to baptize quickly. The older tradition of Easter baptisms ceased. It also became impossible for the bishop to lay on hands (or anoint) at baptism. Indeed, in the larger dioceses of France and Britain, this practice was often neglected entirely, so that many people were never 'confirmed' at all. Aquinas even argued that confirmation was not necessary for ordination.

By 1000, more and more people believed that, at the communion, the sign is itself that which it signifies (the 'realist' position). A controversy concerning the use of unleavened bread *(azymes)* in the eighth century standardized the use of wafers at communion in the Western church. Ratramnus in the ninth century was one of the last writers to describe the elements at the eucharist as 'symbols', but his book was condemned in 1050. He opposed Paschasius who took the 'realist' doctrine a long step further towards transubstantiation. The last opponent of this trend was Berengar of Tours in the eleventh century. His denials of 'realism' provoked further definitions (for example, by Lanfranc who opposed him). Finally, transubstantiation was adopted as orthodox at the Fourth Lateran Council in 1215. It taught that the underlying, permanent reality of the bread and wine are changed at consecration into Christ's body and blood.

The sacraments systematized

Meanwhile the sacraments were increasingly organized as a system. Hugh of St Victor in the early twelfth century still listed thirty sacraments, following Augustine's pattern. But his contemporary, Peter Lombard, in his *Sentences*, produced a tightly organized scheme of seven sacraments (which he divided off from the lesser 'sacramentals'). Lombard's views were pronounced orthodox by the Fourth Lateran Council and his system finally entrenched by Aquinas who expounded it in his *Summa Theologiae.*

The seven sacraments are baptism, confirmation, eucharist, penance, extreme unction, ordination and matrimony. Their distinctive mark is that they are outward signs of inward grace, and were instituted by Christ. Lombard

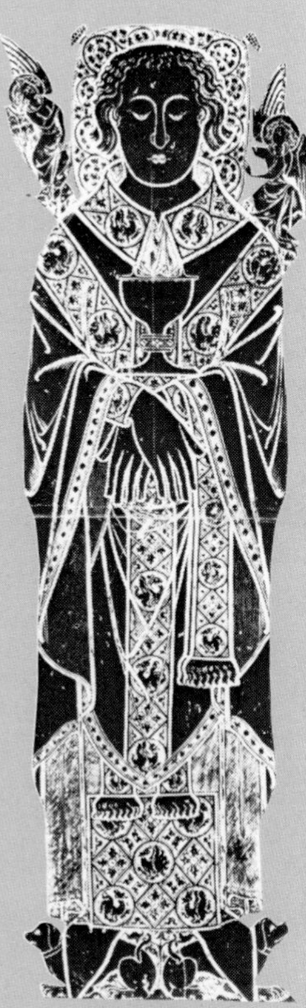

This fourteenth-century priest is shown holding a communion cup. A brass-rubbing from a church memorial in northern England.

and Aquinas taught that the sacraments confer grace simply by being performed *(ex opere operato)*. People receiving them can, through unbelief, put up a barrier to grace—though this is of course impossible for an unconscious infant or a dying person.

The new system left many problems unsolved. The question as to where and how Christ had instituted these seven sacraments was left to the Reformers to discuss. Meanwhile the nature of the outward sign of the sacraments came under discussion. The Council of Florence (1438–45) defined the outward sign at ordination as the handing on of the paten and chalice to candidates for priest's orders.

During this period, too, came the idea that a 'seal' was made indelibly on the soul by the sacraments of baptism, confirmation and ordination; this was held to make them unrepeatable. This was a logical conclusion from Augustine's claim that Donatist baptism was valid, and thus did not need repeating when Donatists were reconciled to the catholic church.

The doctrine of the eucharist was developed after the Fourth Lateran Council. Aquinas discussed it in terms of Aristotelian categories, and the doctrine of transubstantiation itself gave rise to new emphases: the building up to a climax of adoration in the rite; an increase in devotions outside the liturgy; the new feast of Corpus Christi; the barring of lay people from the wine (lest the spilling of transubstantiated wine should occur and cause scandal). Theories were developed that, through the offering of Christ himself under the forms of bread and wine in the sacrifice of the mass, atonement was made for both living and dead. This in turn led to the later medieval proliferation of masses for the dead.

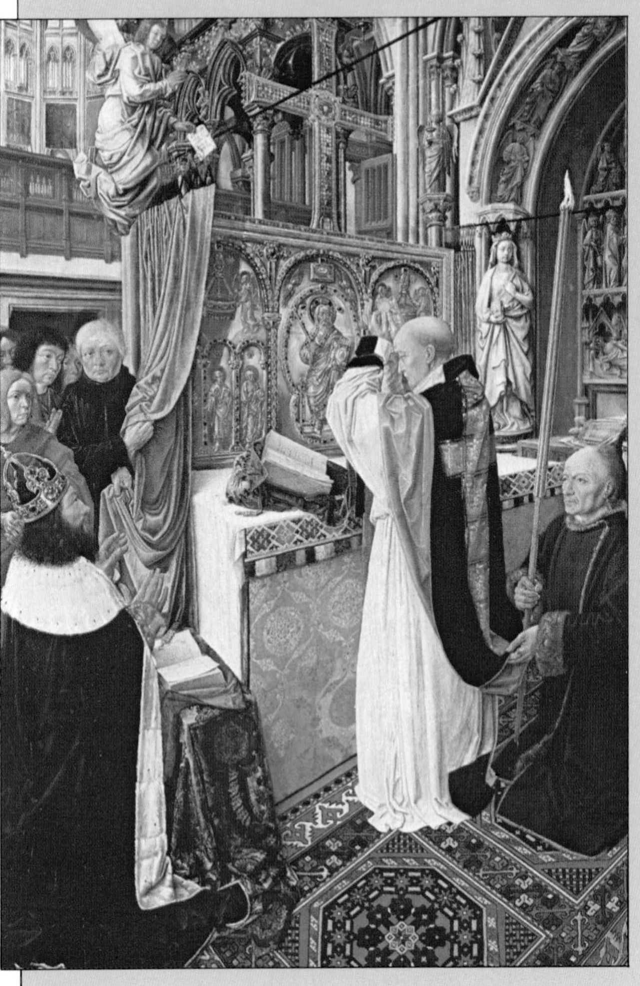

The extravagant splendour of the late medieval mass. From a painting by the Master of St Giles.

o make certain that the bishops were doing their duty. Provincial meetings of monks were to be held annually to see that each community adhered to its rule. Ignorance and heresy were to be crushed by the setting up of an efficient educational system. The bishops were to inspect the churches of the diocese to make certain that they supported schools where the children of the rich could pay to be taught and where the sons of the poor could receive a free education. Lay people were commanded to respect church property, to obey church courts, and to observe the Christian rules of marriage. The clergy were warned to abstain from sexual disorder, fighting and drunkenness, and procedures were established for the trial of erring clerics.

Although the church reached the height of its power in the early thirteenth century the seeds of its subsequent decline had been sown. To defeat the emperors, the church strengthened other European royal houses. It was one of these, the Capetians in France, who would defeat the papacy and bring about its removal from Rome to Avignon in the fourteenth century.

New monastic orders

The spirit of revival or renewal in the church expressed itself not only in organizational change by the papacy but also in the formation of new monastic orders. The success of the reformed papacy and the growth of culture led to a crisis in Benedictine monasticism in the later eleventh century. The monastic role of handing on order and culture was superseded by the rise in the power of popes, bishops and kings. Education now became centred in the bishops' schools rather than in the monasteries. Non-monastic clergy and civil government guaranteed an order in society that made obsolete the monasteries' function as oases of culture. New monastic movements emphasized the spirit of prophecy rather than the spirit of power.

The most influential of the new groups was the Cistercians, founded in 1097 at Cîteaux as an offshoot from a Benedictine house at Molesme. Stephen Harding, third abbot of the new group, drew up a rule for the order. It emphasized manual labour instead of scholarship, and private rather than corporate prayer. They were to construct their own community houses in the most desolate places, while accepting no titles, gifts or lay patrons. Hiring no servants and believing that 'to work is to pray', they took upon themselves the tasks of farming, cooking, weaving, carpentry, and the many other duties of life. Their churches were plain, with no ornaments or treasures, and they owned no personal possessions. They were allowed seven hours of sleep in the winter and six in the summer. Gathering for communal prayer periodically, the brothers spent the rest of the day in manual work, meditation, reading and divine service. Cistercians ate sparingly of vegetables, fish and cheese—this only once a day in summer, and twice a day in winter. Even in the coldest regions, a fire was allowed only on Christmas Day.

This strict rule met with a phenomenal success, and by the end of the twelfth century there were hundreds of Cistercian monastic houses. The ethos of this movement appealed to medieval people, and the group was doubly fortunate in having a remarkable leader in the person of Bernard of Clairvaux (1090–1153). Bernard arrived at Cîteaux in 1112. Later, at Clairvaux, he founded the first of more than sixty-five new monasteries and as an abbot was able to

Benedictine monks

wield a Europe-wide influence. He was so persuasive in convincing men to enter the monastery that it is said that mothers hid their sons, and wives their husbands, when he came fishing for the souls of men. His sermons on the *Song of Solomon* and his work *Why and How God is to be Loved* demonstrate the appeal of his thought. Bernard described the Christian life as an experience of progress in love, and it is easy to understand how an age that was moved by the adventures of knights searching for the Holy Grail would respond to his teachings.

Despite Bernard's success, by the end of the twelfth century the Cistercians had already become la and ineffective. They had grown wealthy and had become as famou for their agricultural skills as for their spiritual life.

The preaching monks

The decline of the Cistercian Order coincided with the passing of the importance of cloistered monasteries. During the twelfth and thirteenth centuries Europe

BERNARD OF CLAIRVAUX

Caroline T. Marshall

Bernard (1090–1153), the Abbot of Clairvaux, was the most influential Christian of his age. He bridged two worlds: the ages of feudal values and of the rise of towns and universities. He was the first of the great medieval mystics, and a leader of a new spirit of ascetic simplicity and personal devotion.

Born near Dijon to a noble family, Bernard took on the ideals of feudalism and chivalry characteristic of his class. However, he was also moulded by the Gregorian and Cluniac reforms, and was educated in the studies of the *trivium* (rhetoric, grammar and logic). At the age of twenty-one he entered the monastery of Cîteaux, the centre of the Cistercian order, in the wild valley of the River Saône. In 1115 he led a dozen Cistercians to found the new house of Clairvaux in the Champagne region.

Bernard wished to turn his back on the world and its comforts, and lead a life of prayer and self-denial. He emphasized God's love and believed that Christians come to know God by loving him. Bernard preached that physical love, which was natural to man, could be transformed by prayer and discipline into a redeeming spiritual love, the passion for Christ.

He was so exceptional that the world he wished to escape constantly sought him out. Aggressively self-righteous, he did not hesitate to criticize and correct the powerful leaders of his age. In 1130 he intervened in a controversy over the selection of a new pope. Bernard unhesitatingly backed the claimant he considered morally more worthy, and scolded the rest of Europe into doing likewise. He made peace between King Louis VII and his feudal subjects, wrote a rule for the order of Knights Templar, condemned the scholastic rationalism of Peter Abelard and preached the second Crusade.

Privately Bernard practised the most rigorous self-denial until, in August 1153, worn out by strenuous asceticism, he died. His writings remain a source of comfort and inspiration to thousands of modern Christians.

The Abbot of Evesham, Worcestershire, England, had a Psalter made for his abbey about 1280. This page illustrates the crucifixion. The abbot can be seen kneeling in devotion at the foot of the cross.

vas more settled and the secu-ity of the monastery was less ıecessary. Towns and cities were leveloping and offered a new chal-enge to the church. Traditional xpressions of faith were failing o cope with worldliness and the rowth of population.

Many clergymen recognized he need to bring a new form of pirituality to the people and found method that would enable them o work in the world but at the ame time live under a spiritual ule. A group of clergy would live ogether under a strict rule but go ut to work among the ordinary opulation. Among the orders that perated in this fashion were the 'remonstratensians, who had a ule resembling the Cistercians', and the Augustinians or Austin monks, who used the Rule of Augustine. They followed as much of the monastic life as was possible, while carrying out their duties of preaching and teaching in the world.

At the beginning of the thirteenth century new groups of preaching monks, the friars, arose. Extremely ascetic, working in

A CISTERCIAN HYMN

O sacred Head, now wounded,
With grief and shame weighed down,
Now scornfully surrounded
With thorns, thine only crown!
O sacred Head, what glory,
What bliss, till now was thine!
Yet though despised and gory,
I joy to call thee mine.

What thou, my Lord, hast suffered
Was all for sinners' gain:
Mine, mine was the transgression,
But thine the deadly pain.
Lo, here I fall, my Saviour!
'Tis I deserve thy place;
Look on me with thy favour,
Vouchsafe to me thy grace.

What language shall I borrow,
To thank thee, dearest Friend,
For this thy dying sorrow,
Thy pity without end?
O make me thine for ever;
And should I fainting be,
Lord, let me never, never
Outlive my love to thee.

Be near when I am dying,
O show thy cross to me;
And for my succour flying,
Come, Lord, and set me free.
These eyes, new faith receiving,
From Jesus shall not move;
For he who dies believing,
Dies safely through thy love.

Translated by Paul Gerhardt, 1656, and James W. Alexander, 1830

Medieval nuns

›wns and cities, they commanded ıe respect of society. The friars reached in the parishes and town quare, taught in the schools, nd eventually dominated many f the universities. One group, ıe Franciscans, developed from ıe teachings of Francis of Assisi 1182–1226) who gave up his ʼealth, renounced his inheritance, nd settled outside his native town › live a life of prayer and poverty. athering a band of followers, he andered the hills of Tuscany, orked at part-time jobs, and erved others by preaching and ursing the sick. Francis taught ıat complete poverty relieved ıe brothers from cares and made ıem joyous before God. Approved y the pope in 1209, the brothers ere known as the Minor Friars *ratres minores)*, wore dark grey nd so were called the Grey riars) and went barefoot. As ıe organization grew it became ıore difficult to continue a life of overty. In time the order was ermitted to own property. However, some wanted to continue to ve according to the teachings of rancis, insisting upon a life of poverty and a renunciation of endowments. They became known as the piritual Franciscans (or *Fraticelli*). ecause they refused to obey the ›pe's order to alter their rule, this roup was persecuted and became ssociated with several other suppressed movements. The brothers ho accepted the changes to ıe order were known as the onventuals'.

Watchdogs of the Lord'

he second great order of medieval friars, the Dominicans, was unded by Dominic de Guzman 1170–1221), a studious cleric om Castile who was sent to rovence to preach against the lbigensians. He realized the eed for an educated clergy able to communicate with the people through sermons. He founded the new order, recognized in 1220, which emphasized the friar's calling to teach and preach. Hence the Dominicans' official title was the Order of Preachers and, wearing a white habit and black cloak (scapular), and so known as the Black Friars they spread throughout Europe as 'the watchdogs of the Lord' (a pun on the Latin name *Dominicanus=domini canis*) to hunt down heresy and ignorance.

The academic emphasis of the Dominicans contrasted with Franciscan anti-intellectualism. The friar preachers established colleges and seminaries not only for their own members but also for other clergy who might care to attend. They produced leading medieval theologians such as Albert the Great and Thomas Aquinas. However, the two orders gradually became more alike, because the Franciscans found it necessary to train young friars, and thus also set up educational foundations.

The friars accomplished social, pastoral, educational and missionary work. As Francis and the early brothers had done, they continued to serve lepers and other sick, a practice which encouraged the study of medicine. They showed courage and loving care while working with the sick during the frequent medieval plagues. Friars were also effective preachers, although they frequently met difficulties with the local clergy. More thoroughly trained than the parish ministers, encouraged by their wider contact with brothers of their order, and burning with the zeal of first love, the friars made a notable impression on their audiences. Their sermons were marked by humour, and effectively used rhyme and stories from everyday life. Their devotional books, paraphrases of Scripture

Each order of monks and friars had its own form of dress. Some of them are illustrated here. *Left to right*: Cistercian, Dominican, Premonstratensian, Austin Friar

FRANCIS OF ASSISI

Robert G. Clouse

Francis of Assisi (1182–1226), a popular youth who led a carefree life, was destined for a career as a knight, until converted through illness, a pilgrimage to Rome, a vision and the words of Jesus in Matthew 10: 7–10. He was the son of a wealthy Italian cloth merchant, and his father was angry because Francis interpreted the gospel to mean that goods should be freely given to the poor. Leaving home in a ragged cloak and a rope-belt taken from a scarecrow, he wandered the countryside with a few followers, begging from the rich, giving to the poor, and preaching. His charm, humility, and kindly manner attracted many followers.

In 1210 Francis obtained approval from Pope Innocent III for his simple rule devoted to apostolic poverty and began to call his associates the Friars Minor ('Lesser Brothers'). The new group, which followed its founder in preaching and caring for the poor and sick, met yearly at Portiuncula near Assisi. A society for women, the poor Clares, began in 1212 when Clare, an heiress of Assisi, was converted and commissioned.

To encourage missionary activities, Francis tried to go to Syria (1212) and to Morocco (1213–14) but was thwarted by misfortune. In 1219 he travelled to the Middle East, where he tried unsuccessfully to convert the Sultan of Egypt.

While Francis was absent, problems arose among the members of his order in Italy; upon his return he was forced to deal with them. Cardinal Ugolino was asked to be the protector of the order, and the appointment of a politically-minded brother, Elias of Cortona, as vicar-general led to a change in the character of the movement. In 1223, Pope Honorius III confirmed a new rule which allowed for an elaborate organization. Francis, holding to his original ideals, laid down his leadership and retired to a hermitage on Monte Alvernia, where he allegedly received the *stigmata* (bodily representations of the wounds of Christ). In spite of illness, pain and blindness he composed his 'Canticle to the Sun', his *Admonitions* and his *Testament* before submitting gladly to 'Brother Death' in 1226.

Francis did not turn to nature as a refuge from the world, as many monks did, but rather saw in created things objects of love that pointed to their Creator. For this reason he enjoyed the solitary life, and it is reported that even birds and animals enjoyed his sermons. However, his major concern was the growing cities, where he spent

Francis of Assisi turned his back on worldly goods. Ironically, this great church was built to commemorate him. It is at Perugia, Assisi.

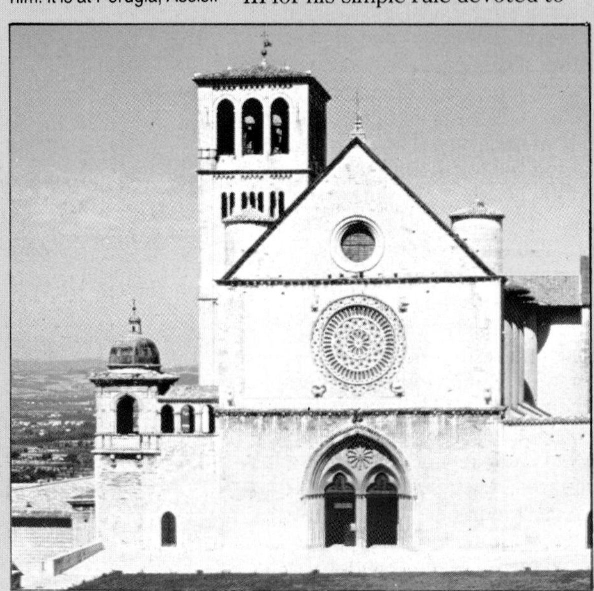

most of his time preaching the gospel while living in utter poverty among ordinary people. He is revered by many Christians as one of the most noble, Christ-like figures who ever lived.

Francis of Assisi, surrounded by scenes from his life. In the lower left-hand corner he is preaching to the Sultan; above that, he is addressing the birds.

THE RULE OF FRANCIS

Franciscans.

"1. *This is the rule and way of life of the Brothers Minor: to observe the holy gospel of our Lord Jesus Christ, living in obedience, without personal belongings and in chastity . . .*
2. If any wish to take up this way of life and join our brothers, they shall send them to the provincial ministers; to them alone, and to no others, permission is given to receive brothers. And the ministers shall carefully examine them in the Catholic faith and the sacraments of the church. And if they believe all these, and will confess them faithfully and observe them steadfastly to the end; and if they have no wives, or if they have them and the wives have already entered a convent . . . the ministers shall tell them, in the words of the gospel, to go and sell all they have and give it carefully to the poor. But if they are not able to do this, their good intention is enough . . . After that they shall be given the garments of the probationers: two gowns without hoods and a belt, and stockings and a cape reaching the belt . . . And, when the probationary year is over, they shall be received into obedience, promising always to observe this way of life and the rule . . . And those who have now promised obedience shall have one gown with a hood and another, if they wish it, without a hood. And those who really need them may wear shoes. And all the brothers shall wear humble garments, and may repair them with sackcloth and other remnants, with God's blessing . . .
3. The clerical brothers shall perform the divine service according to the order of the holy Roman church . . . And they shall fast from the feast of All Saints to the Nativity of the Lord; but as to the holy season of Lent . . . those who fast during this time shall be blessed of the Lord, and those who do not wish to fast shall not be bound to do so. At other times the brothers shall not be bound to fast except on Friday; but when there is a compelling reason the brothers shall not be bound to observe a physical fast. But I advise, warn and exhort my brothers in the Lord Jesus Christ that, when they go into the world, they shall not quarrel, nor contend with words, nor judge each other. But let them be gentle, peaceable, modest, merciful and humble, as is fitting. They ought not to ride, except when infirmity or necessity clearly compels them to do so . . .
4. I strictly command all the brothers never to receive coins or money either directly or through an intermediary. The ministers and guardians alone shall make provision, through spiritual friends, for the needs of the infirm and for other brothers who need clothing.
6. The brothers shall possess nothing, neither a house, nor a place, nor anything. But, as pilgrims and strangers in this world, serving God in poverty and humility, they shall

"*Lord, make me an instrument of thy peace.*
Where there is hatred, let me sow love;
Where there is injury, pardon;
Where there is doubt, faith;
Where there is despair, hope;
Where there is darkness, light;
Where there is sadness, joy.

O Divine Master, grant that I may not so much seek
To be consoled, as to console;
Not so much to be understood as
To understand;
Not so much to be loved
As to love;
For it is in giving that we receive;
It is in pardoning that we are pardoned;
It is in dying that we awaken to eternal life."

FRANCIS OF ASSISI

ontinually seek alms, and not be 'shamed, for the Lord made himself oor in this world for us . . . And f any of them fall sick, the other rothers are bound to minister to hem as they themselves would wish o be ministered to . . .

'1. I strictly charge all the brethen not to hold conversation with vomen so as to arouse suspicion, ior to take counsel with them . . .

'2. Whoever of the brothers by livine inspiration may wish to o among the Saracens and other nfidels shall seek permission from heir provincial ministers. But the ninisters shall give permission to go o none but those whom they see to e fit for the mission.

Furthermore I charge the minisers on their obedience that they lemand from the lord pope one of he cardinals of the holy Roman hurch, who shall be the governor, orrector and protector of the fraterity, so that, always submissive and ying at the feet of that same holy hurch, steadfast in the Catholic aith, we may observe poverty and umility, and the holy gospel of ur Lord Jesus Christ, as we have irmly promised.»

'he original Rule of Francis consisted of a few instructions from ne Gospels. When the Order xpanded a new rule was prouced, but this was felt too strict, nd was never used. The final ersion of the rule, quoted above, ras approved by Pope Honorius II in 1223, three years before 'rancis' death.

into local languages, and religious poetry still convey the message of Christ today.

The friars were also busy in education, establishing a school at each house for young men entering their orders. Houses were also founded at the universities of Paris, Oxford, Cambridge and Bologna. The Franciscans could boast of such famous scholars as Bonaventura (1221–74), Alexander of Hales (1170–1245), William of Ockham, and Roger Bacon (about 1214–92).

The missionary activity of the friars also adds a challenging chapter to their work. Francis himself had preached the gospel abroad, and sent friars to Spain, Hungary and the East. The orders encouraged the study of eastern languages so that missionaries could communicate with the Muslims. During the thirteenth century they preached and founded houses in North Africa, the Middle East, and Eastern Europe.

East and West divided

The preaching of the friars in the East might have resulted in a more peaceful penetration of the area by Latin Christianity had it not been for a breakdown of relations between Byzantium and the West. At the beginning of the eleventh century the Greek church was not obviously separated from the Western church, but the position was to change during the next two centuries. After the crusaders' conquests in the Middle East there came to be two rival claimants for each of the major Eastern Sees—one a Latin and the other a Greek.

The Eastern Orthodox church had been drifting apart from the Roman Catholic church for centuries. Certain distinctive features of the two churches can be listed—such as a different ritual, the use of a different type of communion bread, a different version of the Nicene Creed, and different attitudes towards the use of statues in the church—but none of these problems marked a *decisive* break between the two communions. For centuries contact between western Europe and the East had been limited. However, with the Crusades, commerce and communication between the two were reawakened. Paradoxically, the final break came at the time of this new closeness—because of the new attitude of the reformed papacy and the behaviour of the crusaders.

The eleventh-century popes, as described, wanted effectively to control Christianity. The Patriarch of Constantinople was not willing to accept the pope's mandates and legates. When Humbert of Moyenmoutier arrived in Constantinople in 1054 as a representative of the pope, the patriarch refused to submit to him. Humbert then published a document excommunicating the patriarch. As the pope's control of the Western church tightened, the split with the East grew wider. Eastern theory emphasized control of the church by a council of the five important leaders of the Christian world, while the papal reformers believed the church should be ruled by the pope alone.

A new enemy

The Crusades also contributed much to the schism between East and West. These were religious wars fought by western Europeans to recover the Holy Land from the Muslims. The remarkable growth of the new religion of Islam threatened to engulf Byzantium (Constantinople). Threatened on all sides by enemies, the Eastern emperors of the tenth century fought a series of wars, defeating in turn the Muslims, the Bulgars and the Armenians. A new foe appeared, however, in the form of the fierce Seljuk Turks who defeated the forces of Byzantium at the Battle of Manzikert (1071) and invaded Asia Minor, depriving the Eastern Empire of more than half its realm.

After repeated appeals to the West for aid, it was a message from the Eastern Emperor Alexius Comnenus to Pope Urban II (1095) that finally attracted the attention of Latin ears. The pope responded with a sermon to a convocation at Clermont in southern France, where church dignitaries as well as the common people heard Urban

The famous Crac des Chevaliers in Syria, one of the formidable fortresses built by the crusaders, in their attempt to hold their territories in the East.

xplain:

'From the confines of Jerusalem nd from the city of Constantinople horrible tale has gone forth . . . n accursed race, a race utterly lienated from God . . . has ıvaded the lands of those Chrisians and depopulated them by the word, plundering and fire.' The ope proceeded to list the Turkish trocities, mentioning the desecraion of churches, the rape of Chrisan women, and the torture and ıurder of men. He also appealed ɔ French honour with the words:

'Recall the greatness of :harlemagne. O most valiant oldiers, descendants of invincible ncestors, be not degenerate. Let ll hatred between you depart, ll quarrels end, all wars cease. tart upon the road to the Holy epulchre, to tear that land from ıe wicked race and subject it to ourselves.' At the conclusion of is address a shout rose from the rowd, *'Deus Vult! Deus Vult!'* 3od wills it). Obviously pleased ith this response Urban made *eus Vult* the battle-cry of the rusades, and suggested that each 'arrior wear the sign of the cross pon his clothing.

In the months that followed, ıe pope's representatives travlled throughout Europe enlisting ecruits to go to the Holy Land to ght the Turks. The leaders of this rst Crusade represent a medieval urope's *Who's Who* and include obert of Normandy, Raymond of 'oulouse, Bohemond of Taranto, obert of Flanders, Godfrey of ouillon, Baldwin of Boulogne and tephen of Blois. The imaginations f many who romanticize medieval urope have conjured a picture of ıe crusaders as great, armourlad warriors who rode forth on ıge steeds. In reality, the averge knight stood about five feet ıree inches tall and wore a haubrk and a leather coat protected y chain mail.

The crusaders fail

When they arrived in Constantinople the crusaders misbehaved and the Emperor Alexius was frightened. He had imagined that Urban would help him recruit mercenaries for his own armies; now a religious horde of 50,000 had descended on his

The crusading knights set out with high ideals. They saw their task as a holy mission.

THE CRUSADES

John Clare

In 1095 Pope Urban II appealed at Clermont for aid to the Eastern Christians against the Turks. They had conquered Jerusalem and threatened Constantinople itself. He received an enthusiastic response, and the first Crusade soon set out overland via Constantinople. Despite immense difficulties, the crusaders eventually reached the Holy Land and captured Jerusalem in 1099. Four crusader states were established, including the 'Latin Kingdom' of Jerusalem.

The Crusades joined together two themes which were developing strongly in eleventh-century Europe; the holy war, or military expedition blessed by the church, and the pilgrimage to a holy place. The journey of a Christian army to recover the Holy Land from the Muslims fulfilled both of these. There is little doubt that the crusaders were largely driven by religious motives.

The first Crusade was far more successful than later expeditions, even though the twelfth and thirteenth centuries saw a great development in the theology and organization of crusades. From the beginning the papacy was prominently involved in the movement. It issued incentives to go on crusade, such as immunity from taxes and debt payment, protection of crusaders' property and families, and especially the indulgence, which guaranteed the crusader's entry into heaven and reduced or abolished his time in purgatory. The popes sent out crusade preachers, organized financial support, and sought to provide

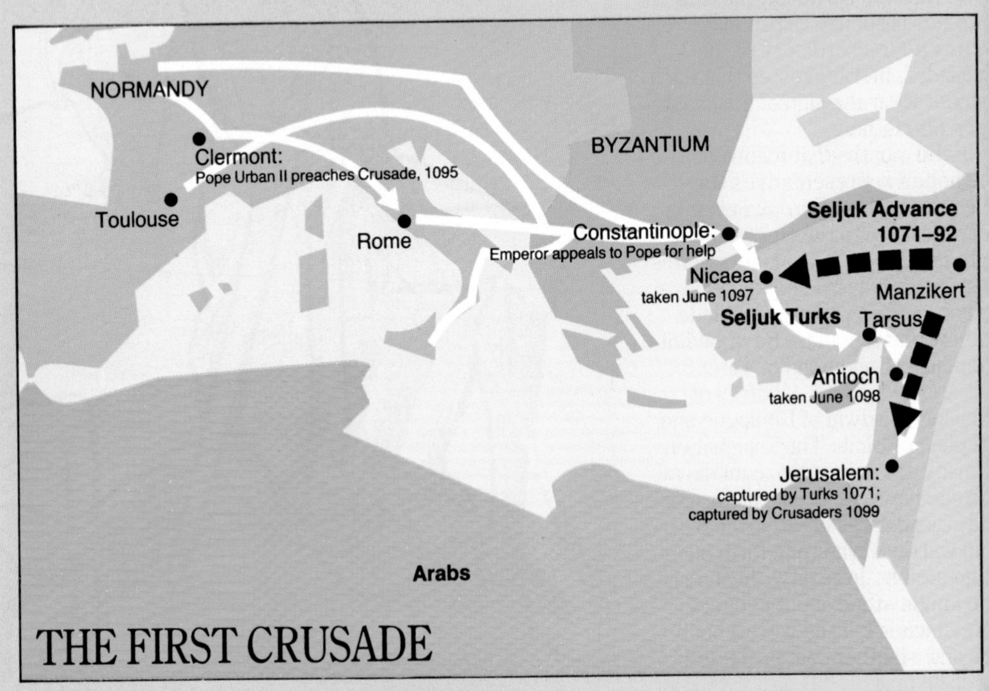

THE FIRST CRUSADE

transport, which from the early twelfth century was usually by sea.

The Crusades may be seen as part of the expansion of Christian Europe after centuries of being on the defensive against Islam and paganism. Crusading enthusiasm remained strong in Europe until at least 1250. The number of Crusades is normally given as seven or eight, but this gives the misleading impression of a few expeditions with long gaps in between. It is better to see the Crusades as a continuous movement, featuring many smaller expeditions in addition to the larger ones, and after about 1150 there was a regular stream of soldiers, pilgrims and merchants from Europe to Syria.

One of the original crusader states, Edessa, fell to the Muslims in 1144, and the second Crusade led by the kings of France and Germany in 1147–49 failed to recover it. The Christian hold on the Holy Land depended on Muslim disunity; but after 1150 the Islamic leaders Nureddin and Saladin united the Near East and Egypt under one dynasty. In 1187 Saladin defeated the crusaders at Hattin, captured Jerusalem and overran the crusaders' lands. The third Crusade, led by King Richard Lionheart of England and the rulers of France and Germany, recovered part of the lost territory but not Jerusalem itself.

In the thirteenth century the crusaders were restricted to a coastal strip, and the seaport Acre replaced Jerusalem as their capital. Egypt now became the target of the major Crusades, as it was believed that it held the key to the recovery of the whole of Palestine. But of the thirteenth-century Crusades the only one to achieve success was that of the Emperor Frederick II in 1228–29, which regained Jerusalem by negotiation, and which was repudiated by the pope, since Frederick had been excommunicated. Jerusalem was lost again in 1244, and even the great Crusade of the French King Louis IX in 1248–54 could not recover it. After 1250 the Mameluke Sultans of Egypt gradually wore down the crusader states, until they ended Christian rule in Syria by capturing Acre in 1291.

The Crusades failed in their aims. The crusaders were a small minority in the East, and those who had settled there for two or three generations tended to adopt Eastern customs, to the disgust of new arrivals from Europe. Crusader society was poised between East and West, having characteristics of both, yet different from either.

As time went on the crusading movement was increasingly diverted from the Holy Land and in the thirteenth century the popes launched crusades not only against European heretics such as the Albigensians, but also against Catholic rulers such as Frederick II. In the thirteenth century, too, there arose criticism of the crusading principle; people such as Raymond Lull argued for peaceful missions to convert the Muslims, rather than armed expeditions to subdue them. Nevertheless the Crusades, attracting people from all the countries of Europe, were a striking example of both the unity and the religious zeal of medieval Europe.

“When men are hot with drinking wine
And idly by the fire recline,
They take the cross with eager boast
To make a great crusading host.
But with first glow of morning light
The whole Crusade dissolves in flight.”

city. He provisioned them well, surrounded them with guards, extracted an oath of allegiance from their commanders and got them safely across the Bosphorus into Asia Minor.

The Emperor displeased his new Western allies by making treaties with the Turks while they were fighting. This seeming treachery on the part of the Eastern Empire caused the crusaders to defend the carving out of their own states in the Middle East. They had invaded at a fortunate time, because Islam was divided between the caliphates of Baghdad, Cairo and Cordova into rival factions and sects. Driving south through Syria and Palestine, the crusaders took Jerusalem in 1099.

The conquests of the crusaders extended along a strip of eastern Mediterranean coastline and were divided into the kingdom of Jerusalem, the county of Edessa, the principality of Antioch and the county of Tripoli. For almost 200 years they were to represent a toehold of Western Christianity in the East; but these territories were the areas where the clash between Greek Orthodox and Catholic had resulted in total alienation. For example, Antioch in Syria, captured by the crusaders, had a Greek bishop (John of Antioch) who was in communion with the Patriarch of Constantinople. When Alexius wanted the city restored to the Eastern Empire and the crusaders refused, the bishop's position became untenable and he left the city and moved to Constantinople. The westerners chose another church leader, who was a Latin, but John refused to resign, leaving two claimants to the Patriarchate of Antioch. A similar situation arose when Jerusalem was conquered, and in Constantinople when it fell to the fourth Crusade.

The hold of the Europeans on the Middle East was always fragile. The Italian maritime cities such as Venice, Genoa and Pisa provided a lifeline—not only helping streams of pilgrims to get to the Holy Land, but also sending supplies and recruits to fight the Muslims. Two new religious orders were formed for the purpose of defending the Holy Land; the Knights Templar and the Knights Hospitaller. The young men who formed these orders served as soldier-monks but, despite their efforts, the county of Edessa fell to the Muslims.

A second Crusade (1147) was encouraged by the preaching of Bernard of Clairvaux, and was led by King Louis VII of France and Conrad III, the Holy Roman Emperor. The expedition was marked by a series of disasters which culminated in the gardens of Damascus, where the crusaders were ambushed and prevented from taking the city. After two years their forces melted away. A crusade preached by the man with the greatest name for sanctity in Europe and led by royalty had failed. This defeat astounded and angered medieval Christians and, as they tried to understand the situation, the treachery of the Greeks began to appear to them

The Byzantine Emperor at Constantinople tried desperately to protect his subjects from the undisciplined soldiers of the Second Crusade. The crusaders marched through Greece and Asia Minor on their way to Palestine.

he main reason. Consequently, Bernard began to suggest that campaign be mounted against Constantinople.

He got his wish in 1204 when the Doge of Venice persuaded an expedition of knights (the fourth Crusade) to besiege and conquer the great Eastern city. The rape of Constantinople made an indelible impression on the Orthodox people and whatever ties still existed between them and Rome were severed. A Latin Empire set up in Byzantium lasted from 1204–61, with the lands of the Empire divided into feudal holdings and presented to the crusaders. A Latin patriarch was appointed, but the Western church made little impression on the Greek population.

There were other crusades, some pathetic, like the Children's Crusade, others militarily effective, such as the one Frederick II embarked upon when he was excommunicated. But with the fall of the crusader states in 1291 the movement lost its impetus. As well as alienating the Eastern Christians, two centuries of contact with the East caused cultural changes which in turn had a lasting effect on life in the West.

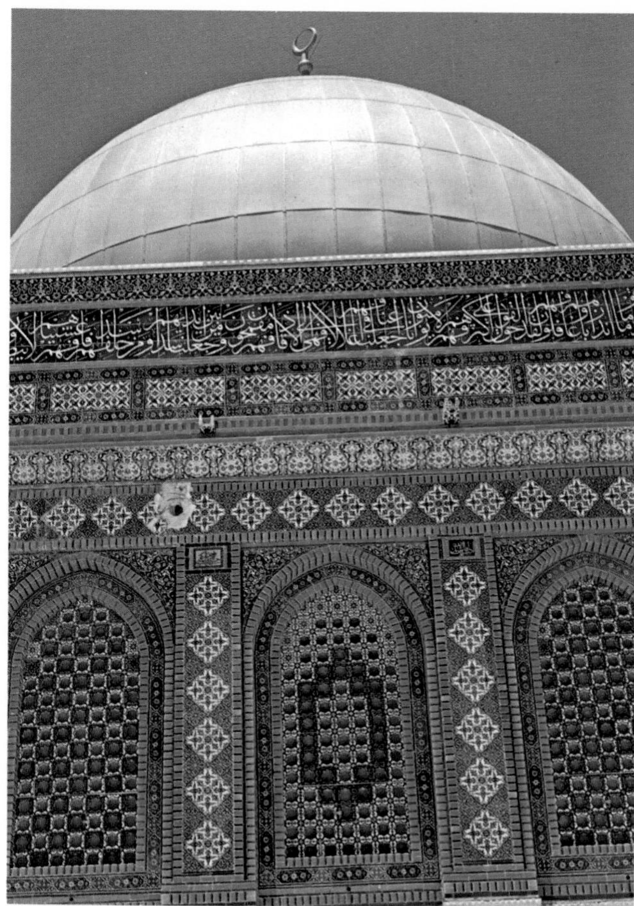

The Muslim Dome of the Rock, Jerusalem. The crusaders set out to recapture the 'Holy Places' from the Muslims.

The growth of learning

The stability and optimism reflected in the papal reform movement also resulted in the growth of learning and of the universities. Education during the age of Charlemagne and the tenth and eleventh centuries was carried on mainly by the monasteries and cathedral schools, the former being more famous until the eleventh century.

A learned monk was appointed to teach novices (new monks) and when he was a famous scholar, adult monks from other houses would come to study with him. Other young men from well-to-do families would also be sent to study under the monastic tutor and many of these would join the clergy or take up secular work.

By the twelfth century the cathedral schools had surpassed the monastic establishments, and the chief cathedral dignitary after the bishop and dean was the chancellor, who taught the seven liberal arts and theology to the advanced students. Other teachers would instruct the younger scholars in Latin grammar. Students in these schools were generally destined for service as clerics. A licence to teach, given by the chancellor, was the predecessor of a university degree.

During the eleventh century the leading cathedral schools in northern Europe were at Laon, Paris, Chartres and Cologne. Debates were carried on which reawakened intellectual life in Europe and helped to expand the vocabulary and depth of Christian thought. One of the significant controversies involved Berengar, a pupil of Fulbert of Chartres, who became the teacher in the cathedral school of Tours.

Discussion revolved around the meaning of the words of consecration in the mass: 'This is my body, this is my blood.' Berengar held that a real and true change takes place in these elements, but that the change is spiritual, and that the bread and wine remain of the same substance. Lanfranc and other theologians debated with him, believing that the underlying substance of the bread and wine was changed to Christ's blood and body, while the 'accidents' (touch, taste, sight and smell) of the bread and wine remained the same. During a long and bitter controversy (1045–80) the term 'transubstantiation' emerged and took on Lanfranc's definition. Berengar was condemned and forced to disown his views.

> *"I do not seek to understand that I may believe, but I believe that I may understand: for this I also believe, that unless I believe I will not understand."*
>
> *ANSELM of Canterbury*

The great debate

Another controversy concerned Christ's work on the cross. How was it that the death of Christ could work a reconciliation between God and man? Before the eleventh century the dominant teaching on this subject was as old as Origen, who believed that through sin mankind had made itself subject to the devil. The mark of this subjection was death. God in his grace wished to free men, but he was unable to because the devil's claim was just. Consequently, to neutralize Satan's claim, a ransom had to be paid in the form of a valuable person over whom Satan had no right—a sinless person. Thus the devil was tricked when Christ was crucified, because the Son of God was sinless; now God can with justice save whomsoever he pleases.

This theory was challenged by Anselm of Canterbury in *Cur Deus Homo?* He believed that when a person sins he breaks the right order of the universe and is alienated from God. Because he is just God must be given a satisfaction for sin before he can forgive the sinner. Christ was sinless, sent by the mercy of God; he was able to offer to God the satisfaction owed by the human race. This explanation was widely accepted in Europe and changed the whole outlook concerning the incarnation and the atonement.

Perhaps the leading figure of the schools of Europe in the period just before the founding of the universities was Peter Abelard. He studied in Paris with two teachers of logic—Roscelin, the leading Nominalist, and William of Champeaux, a Realist philosopher. Later he left Paris temporarily for Laon where he studied theology with Anselm.

It was probably Abelard's methods more than his conclusions that upset many important medieval church leaders. As he stated: 'The first key to wisdom is this constant and frequent questioning . . . For by doubting we are led to question, by questioning we arrive at the truth.' Using this approach, Abelard wrote *Sic et Non (Yes and No)* in which he demonstrated that tradition and authority alone were not sufficient to answer such questions as: 'Is God omnipotent?' 'Do we sin without willing it?' and, 'Is faith based upon reason?' He quoted authorities on both sides and left the contradictions unresolved.

A pupil of Abelard, Peter

ombard (1100–60), used reason
answer many of the same ques-
ons in his book *The Sentences*, a
opular theological textbook of the
liddle Ages. The scholastic tech-
que of setting up contradictory
atements concerning a problem,
nd then resolving them by reason,
as also used by Thomas Aquinas.
The scholastic method was also
opularized in the twelfth century
y Gratian in his systematizing of
anon law in the *Decretum*. In this
reat work he would state a law
nd, if it was not contradicted, it
as allowed to stand. But if there
ere opposing statements he tried
reconcile them through logic.
his law code, as applied by church
ourts, was to guide the Christian
n earth. Certain cases involving
ersonal offences were to be tried
church courts, and any crime
ommitted by a clergyman was to
e punished by canon law courts.
here was a large area of overlap between secular and church courts which led to much tension between monarchs and the church during the Middle Ages.

The universities arise

The cathedral schools culminated in the foundation of universities. The term *universitas* was used to describe a guild or corporation of either teachers or scholars who might band together in self-defence against the town in which they were located, or to discipline lazy or profligate students (or professors). A city with a well-known cathedral might become the centre for a great number of schools. At first scholars would rent rooms and students would pay to come and listen to lectures. Guilds of professors organized the universities of northern Europe, while in Italy it was the students who formed the guilds. The first universities

GOD'S NON-EXISTENCE INCONCEIVABLE

"This proposition is indeed so true that its negation is inconceivable. For it is quite conceivable that there is something whose non-existence is inconceivable, and this must be greater than that whose non-existence is conceivable. Wherefore, if that thing than which no greater thing is conceivable can be conceived as non-existent; then, that very thing than which a greater is inconceivable is not that than which a greater is inconceivable; which is a contradiction.

So true is that there exits something than which a greater is inconceivable, that its non-existence is inconceivable: and this thing you are, O Lord our God!

So truly therefore do you exist, O Lord my God, that your non-existence is inconceivable; and with good reason; for if a man's mind could conceive anything better than you, the creature would rise above the Creator and judge him; which is utterly absurd. And in truth whatever else there be beside you may be conceived as non-existent. You alone, therefore, most truly of all, and therefore most of all, have exist ence: because whatever else there is, is not so truly existent, and therefore has less the prerogative of existence."

ANSELM 'Ontological Proof,'
Proslogion, iii and iv

obtained a charter from the pope; those established later applied to the secular ruler.

The gradual development of universities makes it difficult to date them, but a list of the first universities would certainly include Bologna, Paris, Salerno, Oxford, Cambridge, Montpellier, Padua, Salamanca and Toulouse. The universities taught the seven liberal arts—a late Roman system of knowledge thought necessary to make an educated person. Although these included grammar, logic and rhetoric (together the 'three ways', *trivium*) as well as arithmetic, geometry, astronomy, and music (the 'four ways', *quadrivium*), the teaching of logic or philosophy tended to dominate the undergraduate curriculum. The graduate faculties taught medicine, law and theology.

Medieval universities were relatively small by modern standards, the largest having between 3,000 and 4,000 students. At

This plan of the precinct and waterworks of Canterbury Cathedral Priory survives from the twelfth century. The fishpond (*upper left*) and cloisters (*upper right*), as well as the other buildings making up the priory, can be clearly picked out.

ANSELM

Colin Brown

Anselm (1033–1109), one of the great archbishops of Canterbury, is today remembered chiefly as a philosopher and a theologian. Anselm was part of the Norman conquest of England. Taking monastic vows in 1060, he succeeded Lanfranc as prior of Bec, in Normandy, in 1063. Thirty years later he succeeded Lanfranc as Archbishop of Canterbury. His time as archbishop was marked by conflict with King Rufus and his successor King Henry I. He was exiled more than once. As archbishop, he was known as a reformer, encouraging regular church synods, enforcing clerical celibacy and suppressing the slave trade.

Anselm was one of the early scholastic theologians. He taught that faith must lead to the right use of reason: 'I believe, in order that I may understand.'

It was Anselm who first put forward the 'ontological argument' for the existence of God. This was an attempt to prove God's existence by reason alone, starting with the idea of the most perfect being . . . God is 'that than which no greater can be conceived'. But if 'that than which no greater can be conceived' is greatest in every respect except for existence, then clearly it would be inferior to the greatest being which did actually exist.

Anselm himself expressed the argument in several different forms. Even today it is the subject of intense debate among the philosophers. But most thinkers agree that it contains something of a conjuring trick. For it treats existence as if it were a quality which a thing might or might not have. The thing is either there or not there. And the only way of knowing is to ask for some tangible evidence.

Anselm's greatest work in theology was his *Cur Deus Homo (Why God Became Man)*. Anselm replied that sin runs up a debt with God which humans can never themselves repay. But Christ's death was of such worth that it 'satisfied' God's offended majesty and earned a reward. Hence the Father gives humanity salvation on account of the merits of Christ. Anselm's work showed deep insight into humanity's need of atonement. But he expressed it in terms of the thinking of his day. The New Testament speaks of Christ dying for us; Anselm tried to explain it by means of medieval ideas of merit and rewards.

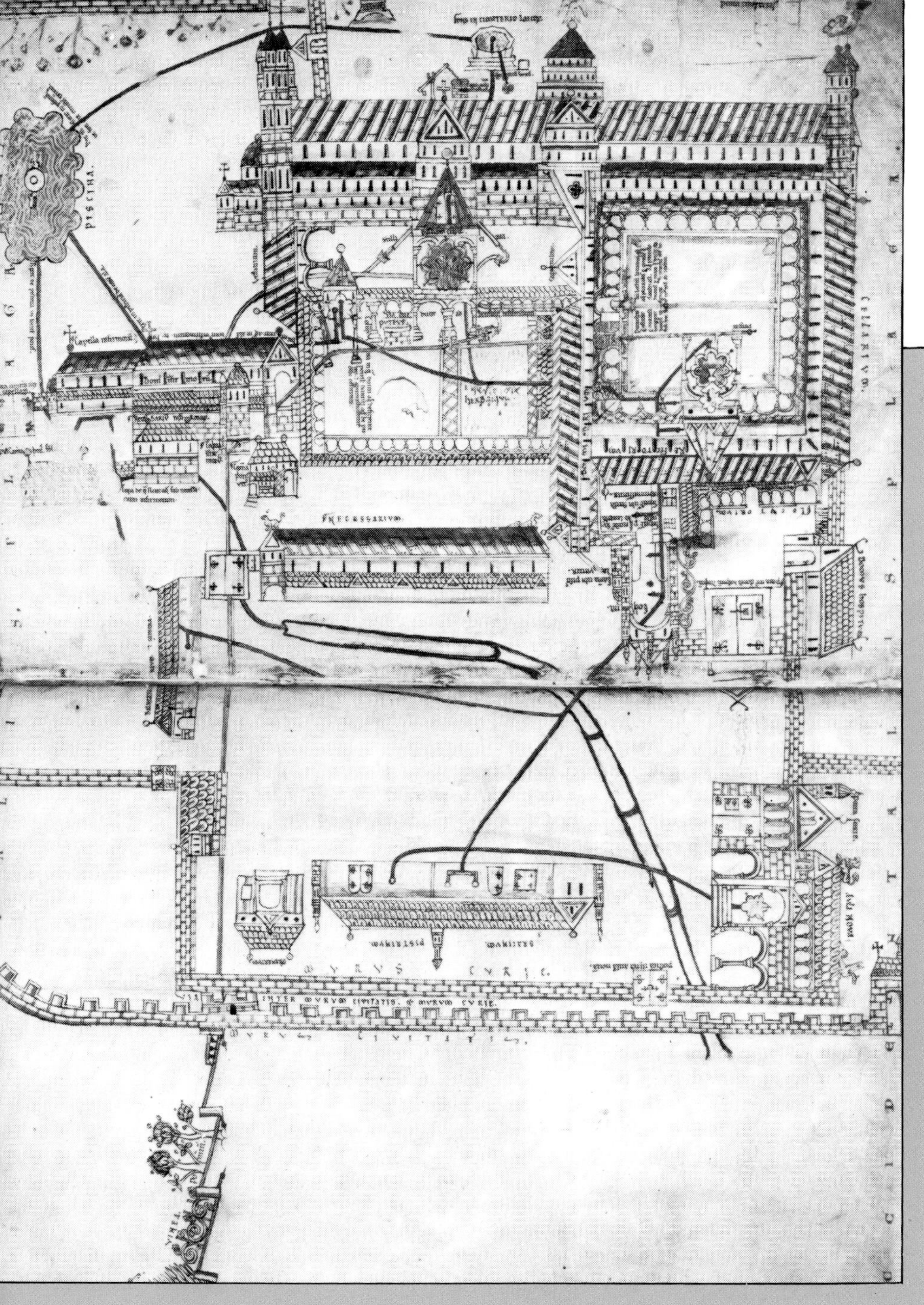
PISCINA
CELLARIUM
NECESSARIUM
MURUS CURIE
INTER MURUM CIVITATIS ET MURUM CURIE
MURUS CIVITATIS

Paris, the most famous, a boy could begin his studies at the age of twelve, but the privilege of lecturing in theology was not granted until a person was thirty-five. The only entrance requirement was a knowledge of Latin; the first four years' studies consisted of the liberal arts. The next two years' work consisted of study, a teaching assistantship, thesis defence and culminated in the MA degree. This enabled a student to go on to study law, medicine, or theology. At Paris, if he decided to earn the DD (Doctor of Divinity) degree in theology he would spend six years studying the Bible and Peter Lombard's systematic theology (*The Sentences*). Finally, three years' study of the writings of the early church theologians and the Bible led to the STD (Doctor of Sacred Theology)—which qualified the scholar to teach theology the same way as the MA entitled him to teach the arts.

Students paid their fees to each professor as they left his class. What they received in return was the reading of a text and the teacher's comments upon the book. This method was necessary because hand-copied books were rare and expensive. It could take over a year to copy the Bible. As a result most students could own only one or two books and the lecturer had to dictate their textbooks to them. Later, comments on the outstanding lecturers were incorporated into the dictated materials. Since parchment was expensive the student was often forced to remember the lesson. Students at first settled in rented rooms but, beginning in the thirteenth century, colleges were founded where they could live cheaply, with some regulation by the older students and professors.

At Paris the most famous college was the Sorbonne, founded in 1256. England modelled its univer sities, Oxford and Cambridge, on Paris. The colleges at these two universities resembled the group of canons of a cathedral, where clerics lived together under a rule The religious origins of the colleges at Oxford and Cambridge ar evident in the way their chapels are arranged in a similar manner t

SCHOLASTICISM

Colin Brown

In western Europe at the height o the Middle Ages all education was in the hands of the church, and th great thinkers were all monks and clergy. Their thinking was carried on against the background of what had gone before—the classical philosophy of ancient Greece, the Bible and the teaching of the early Christian writers. What the scholastics or 'schoolmen' did was to put it into a logical system. Their quest of faith was a quest fo logical formulation.

Scholasticism gets its name fro the medieval monastery and cath dral schools. It covers the period from the ninth century to the end of the fourteenth—from Eriugena to William of Ockham. Anselm, Peter Abelard, Hugh of St Victor, Peter Lombard, Albert the Great Thomas Aquinas and Duns Scotus are among the great schoolmen. The *Sentences* of Lombard was one of the most popular scholastic works. Often the schoolmen disagreed violently among themselves. The 'Nominalists' were opposed to the 'Realists'; and Thomas Aquinas who became *the* great philosophical theologian of the Catholic church was regarded in his own day as a dangerous innovator.

What the schoolmen had in

a monastic chapel, with facing choir stalls.

Although the professors and students at medieval universities were supposed to be clerics, their conduct suggests that their minds were often on other matters.

Aristotle re-discovered

Scholastics tried by means of reason to reconcile the Christian revelation with Aristotle's philosophy, which was transmitted to western Europe through the Muslims and Jews of Spain and south Italy. One of the earlier controversies resulting from the

common was not so much a monochrome set of beliefs—although all belonged to the church—as a certain style and way of thinking. It has been said that there was no such thing as philosophy in the Middle Ages—only logic and theology. But it could equally be said that the theology which interested the schoolmen was basically philosophical. Moreover, their way of doing it was to examine the logical links and implications of ideas.

The work of Thomas Aquinas has been compared to a lake into which many streams flowed and from which many drew, but which was not itself a water-source. His originality lay in two things: the way in which he drew together what had gone before, and the rigorous way in which he explored question after question.

Aquinas would start with a problem. He then would quote his authority. This could be a text of Scripture, a passage from one of the early Christian writers or a quotation from 'the philosopher'. The latter was never named; he did not need to be. It was Aristotle, the Greek philosopher from the fourth century BC, whose writings had been rediscovered and translated into Latin in the twelfth century. From now on his ideas set the tone. The Islamic philosophies of Avicenna and Averroes, as well as contemporary Jewish thinkers, were also taken into account. Only when he had taken note of all the relevant points both for and against would Aquinas give his own answer.

Anyone who has attempted to work his way through a passage of Aquinas (or any of the other great medieval writers) cannot fail to be impressed by the rigour, complexity and subtlety of the thought. The schoolmen were no fools; they belong to the intellectual giants of the human race. At the same time they were often attempting the impossible. Much of their work was devoted to reconciling what cannot be reconciled. For the early Christian authorities to whom they appealed were by no means infallible. And Greek philosophy could at times only be harmonized with biblical theology by trimming the one to fit the other. But, perhaps above all, they sometimes operated with out-dated concepts. So many of the questions that they wrestled with have turned out to be pseudo-questions, in the light of our scientific view of the world, and modern critical philosophy.

In one sense the Middle Ages were an age of faith. The questions that the schoolmen asked all had a theological bearing. But ironically the questions which so preoccupied them were a hindrance to hearing the message of the Bible about God and his love in Christ.

rediscovery of Aristotle concerned the problem of universals. In the early Middle Ages Platonic idealism prevailed—the view that in God's mind there are 'ideas', perfect forms or essences, such as chair, man, honour and tree, and that the individual things which people actually perceive correspond to these 'ideas'. Defenders of the Platonic position were called 'realists' because they believed in the reality of these 'ideas' or 'universals'; they were challenged by 'nominalists' who maintained that 'universals' were only useful 'names' for talking about the world.

Abelard worked out a middle position between these two, stating that universals are ideas formed in the mind by abstracting characteristics which really do apply to the objects sensed. This view enabled Western minds to appreciate the more advanced work of Aristotle (*On the Soul, Physics,* and *Metaphysics*) which became available by 1200. The shock of these new ideas is difficult to exaggerate, and can be compared with the impact of Darwin's theories in the nineteenth century. Aristotle presented a complete explanation of reality, without any reference to a personal God. He challenged Christian and Muslim theology and strained Jewish faith as well. All of these beliefs were confronted by a system which taught that matter and form were

PETER ABELARD

Robert D. Linder

A dynamic, popular teacher, Peter Abelard's life was one of constant personal turmoil and confrontation with authority. His stormy career in many ways reflects the public and personal turbulence of the world in which be lived. Contrary to the stereotype of the medieval philosopher and theologian, he did not live in the proverbial ivory tower, nor make his important intellectual contributions to Christianity in a saintly manner.

Born in Brittany in 1079, Abelard studied as a young man with some of the most respected theologians of his day. However, he soon became convinced that he knew more than his teachers. He arrogantly challenged and quarrelled with them on a variety of subjects. He finally withdrew to set up his own lectures, to which large numbers of enthusiastic students flocked in order to hear the young, rebellious upstart.

A brilliant lecturer and slashing debater, Abelard's reputation grew until he became known as Paris's brightest intellectual star. However, his celebrated love affair with the beautiful and talented Héloise almost shattered his academic career and cut short his intellectual influence. In 1115, at the age of thirty-six, Abelard agreed to tutor the teenage niece of Fulbert, a canon of Notre Dame Cathedral in Paris. A tender relationship developed—which resulted in a son whom they called Astrolabe. Later, to pacify her irate uncle, Abelard agreed to marry Héloise secretly. (This was possible since he was at this time only in minor orders, which permitted him to take a wife, though this practice was frowned upon for those in his position).

Despite all of their precautions, ugly rumours circulated. Héloise agreed to retire to a local convent rather than further damage her lover's academic reputation. Fulbert considered this an evasion of responsibility, and retaliated by hiring a band of thugs who broke into Abelard's chambers one night

Students at a lecture, from a tomb in Bologna, Italy. The university of Bologna is one of the oldest in Europe.

and castrated him.

Following this humiliation, Abelard became a Benedictine monk. He soon resumed his teaching and once again became involved in bitter controversy. In 1121, the Council of Soissons condemned his views on the Trinity without a hearing. For the next twenty years he lived a harassed existence as he moved from place to place, followed hither and yon by both the authorities and large numbers of students. Finally, around 1136, he returned to Paris for the last time, where he enjoyed renewed popularity and wrote several important works. He helped to make Paris one of the intellectual capitals of Europe.

During this last period in Paris, Bernard of Clairvaux accused Abelard of polluting the minds of his students with heretical ideas. In 1141, several statements selected from his writings were condemned at the Council of Sens. He decided to appeal to the pope, but died near Cluny on his way to Rome in 1142.

Abelard was the major Christian thinker of his period. Particularly after becoming a monk, he struggled with many of the problems which were to emerge as the major theological issues of the next centuries.

For example, Abelard's book *Sic et Non (Yes and No)* (1122) set the stage for discussing the relationship between faith and reason in Christian theology. Also, by pointing out that established authorities often conflicted, Abelard called attention to the fact that they needed to be sorted out, clarified and reconciled. He believed that genuine Christianity was both reasonable and consistent. He began a search for the ultimate authority in the faith and practice of the church, which was to culminate in Luther's return to Scripture in the early sixteenth century. Moreover, his desire to reconcile faith and reason in the context of Christian theology set the stage for the work of Thomas Aquinas in the thirteenth century. He was one of the pioneers of Scholasticism, but also wrote poems, hymns and an autobiography.

> *"Faith has no merit with God when it is not the testimony of divine authority that leads us to it, but the evidence of human reason."*
>
> *PETER ABELARD*

> *"Will no one rid me of this turbulent priest?"*
>
> *HENRY II*

This late-twelfth-century illumination is probably the earliest surviving illustration of the murder of Thomas Becket at Canterbury.

THOMAS BECKET

Caroline T. Marshall

Thomas Becket, Archbishop of Canterbury 1162–70, struggled with King Henry II (1154–89) over the conflicting claims of church and stage in England. Becket had been nominated by Henry who hoped to make good the crown's superior rights over those of the church.

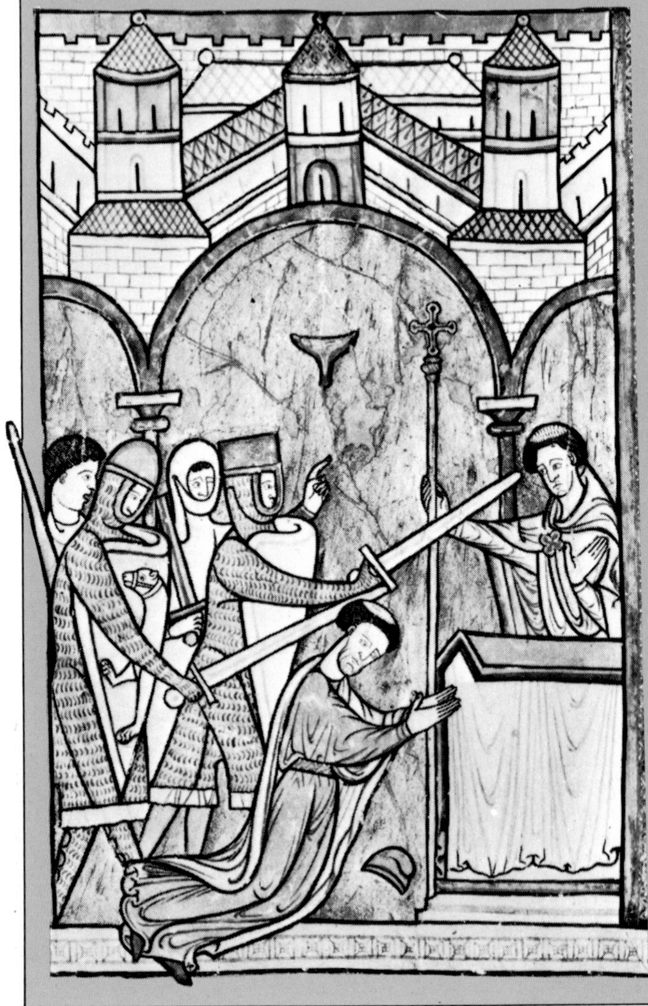

From being the king's dutiful minister he became the uncompromising champion of the church.

The issues were the independence of the church courts, which claimed exclusive authority over anyone in holy orders, the right of appeals to Rome, and the alienation of church lands. Henry II attempted to establish his jurisdiction over clergy guilty of criminal offences, and to forbid appeals to Rome in the famous *Constitutions of Clarendon* in 1164. The resulting conflict drove Becket into exile in France.

A truce was finally arranged in 1170, and Becket returned to Canterbury for Christmas. Immediately upon his return, he excommunicated several English bishops who had supported the king, who in turn violently criticized Becket. Four royal knights, impelled by the king's anger, appeared at Canterbury on 29 December, and murdered the archbishop before his own high altar.

Christian society throughout Europe was shocked and at once a cult developed around the martyred Becket. In 1173 he was canonized by Pope Alexander III, and Canterbury became one of the three great Western shrines for pilgrims. The king did a public penance.

Becket's courage and defiance in the face of armed knights, and his commitment to 'the liberty of the church', which he felt he had been called upon to defend in the face of a weak pope and a rapacious king, were remarkable. From Chaucer's *Canterbury Tales* to T.S. Eliot's *Murder in the Cathedral,* Thomas of Canterbury remains a central figure in the story of the Christian conscience.

ternal, that there was no individ-ial immortality apart from the ody, and that no cosmic progress vas possible—rather, history vas an endless cycle of existence, triving to be like the 'Unmoved Aover', but never reaching its oal.

Muslims had to come to terms vith Aristotle earlier than the Vest. Since the work of Islamic cholars like Averroes (Ibn-Rushd) ccompanied Aristotle to western Europe it is important to notice he intellectual agony caused y his thought in Islam. Among Auslim scholars one of the most amous who tried to come to terms vith Aristotle was Ghazali (who ied in 1111). Although at first Ghazali tried to reconcile faith nd reason, later he interpreted hilosophical concerns as basically ntagonistic to religious belief nd wrote a book entitled *The Destruction of the Philosophers*, ondemning Aristotle's theory of nowledge. Averroes (1126–98) eplied to Ghazali and proposed 'double-truth' outlook—that hilosophy is one category of truth nd theology deals in quite another ind of reality. Some Christian cholars, among them Siger of Brabant (about 1240–84), followed Averroes, while others felt that Aristotle should be banned.

A new basis for thought

Most Christian schoolmen tried come to terms with the new nowledge. Two of the most mous of these were Albert e Great and his pupil Thomas quinas. Impressed by Aristotle's ilosophy, yet a profound Chris-an, Thomas harmonized, at least his own satisfaction, faith and ason. Accepting Aristotle as a uide in reason and Scripture as e rule of faith, Aquinas believed at there was a meaningful relationship between the two. Revelation, he felt, supplements but never contradicts reason.

A sample of Aquinas' application of this method to the problem suggested by Aristotelian logic is his discussion concerning the providence of God. Aristotle had stated that God (or the 'Unmoved Mover') neither knows nor cares about the world; yet the Bible states frequently that God is intimately concerned with his creation. Thomas explained that this was not a real contradiction because God as the Maker of the world is its ultimate cause, and knows of the effects of this creation. Since he knows everything in himself, he knows of the whole creation. Also, because he created time, his knowledge of his work is eternal.

Proceeding in this fashion, Thomas explained in as logical a way as possible the doctrines of immortality, creation and judgement. He made a clear distinction between the way knowledge is gained in the present world, and what an individual learns after death. In this world knowledge is gained through experience, either directly or indirectly; but in heaven an individual will learn through mystic knowledge. He stated that the apostles and prophets were privileged individuals, who could experience God in a mystic fashion before their death, but that this knowledge was limited to them. By distinguishing in this way between sense experience and heavenly knowledge, Thomas made a clear difference between science and the Christian hope.

Not all medieval scholastics followed the method of Aquinas. Bonaventura (1221–74), governor-general of the Franciscans and professor of theology at Paris, taught that rational knowledge of God is impossible, because God is different from a human being in

The dining hall of an Oxford college

THOMAS AQUINAS

Robert G. Clouse

Thomas Aquinas (1225–74), the greatest scholastic theologian of the Middle Ages, was born into a wealthy noble family in Aquino, Italy. Thomas was a fat, slow, pious boy who at the age of five was sent to the abbey of Monte Cassino. He was brought up there until the age of fourteen when he went to study at the University of Naples. Impressed by his Dominican teacher, he decided to enter that order. His family was angered by his decision, and tried to dissuade him by tempting him with a prostitute, kidnapping him and offering to buy him the post of Archbishop of Naples. All of these attempts were unsuccessful and he went to study at Paris, the centre of theological learning.

Although nicknamed the 'Dumb Ox' because of his bulk, seriousness and slowness, Thomas demonstrated his brilliance in public disputation. He studied under Albert the Great in Paris and Cologne, returning to Paris in 1252. He spent the rest of his life teaching there and in Italy.

A prolific writer, Thomas's works fill eighteen large volumes. They include commentaries on most of the books of the Bible and on Peter Lombard's *Sentences*, discussions of thirteen works of Aristotle, and a variety of disputations and sermons. His two most important works are the *Summa Theologiae* and the *Summa Contra Gentiles*. Together they represent an encyclopedic summary of Christian thought, the first based on revelation, and the second designed to support Christian belief with human reason. Both works use Aristotelian logic in unfolding the connections and implications of revealed truth.

Thomas was challenged by secular Aristotelian thought which came to western Europe through the Muslims in Spain. Although an enthusiastic student of the new knowledge, he insisted on separating what was acceptable to Christianity from what was not. Following Aristotle, Thomas emphasized that all human knowledge originates in the senses. Aquinas emphasized that philosophy is based on data accessible to all men; theology only on revelation and logical deduction from revelation. His famous 'Five Ways' were attempts to prove God's existence by reasoning based on what can be known from the world. But this 'natural theology' teaches very little about God, and nothing that is not also clear in Scripture. He developed one of the most internally-consistent systems of thought ever devised, but it did not receive universal acceptance even in his own day. Some of his statements were condemned by the University of Paris in 1277, and a group of scholars, including Duns Scotus and William of Ockham, criticized him for not recognizing that reason and revelation often contradict one another.

Years later, however, Thomas's work gained the prominence in Roman Catholic thought which it has retained to the present time. At the Council of Trent (1545–63) the Roman Catholic reformers used the works of Aquinas in drafting their decrees; and in 1879 the pope declared Thomism (Aquinas's theology) eternally valid.

uality as well as quantity. Thus, nowledge of God can only be quivocal, hazy and by analogy. ;od is experienced by an individual vhen he or she withdraws from he world and seeks reflections or hadows of God in material things.

Another group of Franciscans, ed by Roger Bacon (about 214–92) and Robert Grosseteste about 1168–1253), resisted quinas' method and laid the roundwork for modern science in heir experimental studies of the ehaviour of light, prisms, rainows and mirrors. These scholars mphasized observation, experiment and the use of measurement or understanding the world. Bacon ame to recognize the practical ossibilities of his studies. He reamed of a world in which the ope would have an army equipped vith new types of weapon that vould be able to destroy with one low the Islamic armies and bring eace to the world.

:hurch-building boom

'he most important area of artistic chievement during the Middle ges was the churches—and the culpture and painting associated vith them. Two building styles redominated during this period, ne Romanesque and the Gothic.

The Romanesque style, named fter the Romans, appeared in a reat burst of church building uring the eleventh century, which roduced an estimated 1,587 new uildings in France alone. These nassive churches were richly ecorated. The wooden roof (a re hazard) was replaced by a hick half-cylinder of stone called a arrel vault, whose weight forced he builders to construct uniform, eavy walls. Because of the need o support the roof, windows had o be few and small, and the strucures tended to be dark inside. In n attempt to brighten the interior, churches were hung with tapestries or painted bright colours, with gilding or jewels used on statues, chalices and reliquaries. Freestanding stone sculpture, which had not been used in the West since the fifth century, was re-introduced to lighten the heavy effect of Romanesque construction. The desire to develop a free and less monotonous effect led architects to use cross-vaulting down the nave, which transferred the weight of the roof to a series of posts or pilasters. The Romanesque style emphasized horizontal lines, and tended to give the worshipper a feeling of repose and solidity.

The shift in style from Romanesque to Gothic is not essentially a matter of dates. The forms overlap. Romanesque reached its peak in 1150 and continued into the thirteenth century; while Gothic originated in 1137 and reached its climax about 1250. Gothic first appeared in the construction of the church of St Denis in Paris (1137–44) under the direction of Suger, the adviser to kings Louis VI and Louis VII of France. Wishing to build a fitting tribute both to the Franks and to Dionysius (Denis), the supposed founder of the monastery, Suger created a building of great beauty and originality.

Characterized by delicacy, detail and light, the Gothic style places the support needed for the structure outside the walls, in the form of flying-buttresses. The pointed arch, another innovation of Gothic construction, made it possible to build a very tall structure which emphasized vertical lines, and caused people who entered to share a feeling of striving upwards towards heaven. The builders of Gothic churches, like the medieval theologians who set up their arguments in a very straight-forward manner, aimed for a structural

Flying buttresses similar to these supported the soaring nave of Gothic cathedrals built in the Middle Ages.

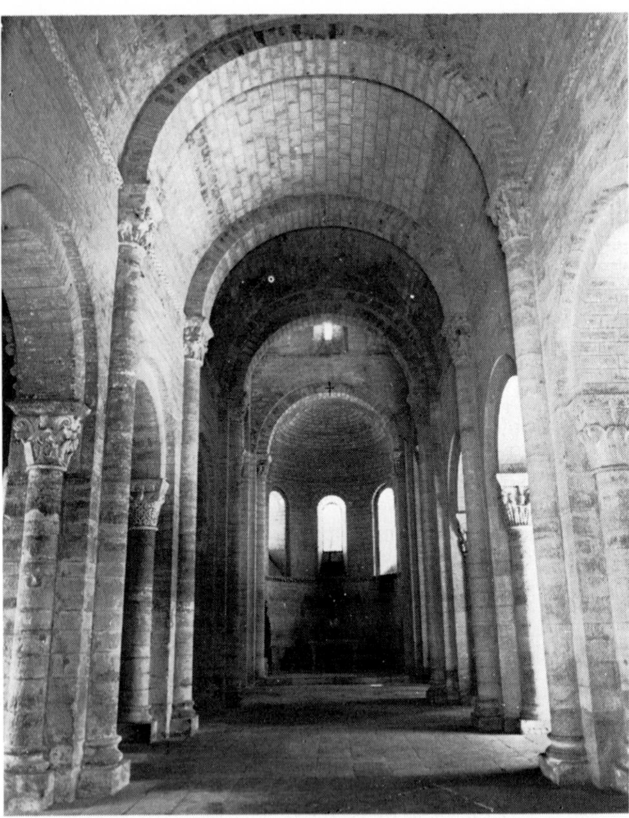

Massive pillars were needed to support the heavy barrel-vault arch of a Romanesque church built in the Middle Ages. This is St Martins, Promista, Spain.

explicitness; that is, they wanted all to see how their buildings were constructed.

In the following century rivalry sprang up to see which city could build the highest cathedral structure. Notre Dame de Paris soared to 114ft/34.8m; Chartres, to 123ft/37.5m; and Amiens, to 138ft/42.1m. Beauvais tried to reach 157ft/47.9m but the vault collapsed and the city ran out of money trying to rebuild it. These churches were light in two ways; because of the design, the stone-work seemed to lose its massive weightiness; and the stained-glass windows constituted a vast wall of colour, dispelling darkness. Not only the windows were works of art; the pillars, doors and every possible part of the cathedral were sculpted. The church was built according to a specific design—though, since it took generations to build, the plans would often be altered. The plan was drawn by professional architects who hired labourers an people skilled in various crafts.

Mirror of a Christian society

Medieval artistic expression was basically different from modern art. Today there is no generally accepted coherent system of goal and values, and the language of ar is largely personal. Medieval art expressed a coherent system of values and a view of the universe based on an understanding of Christianity. Its purpose was to point to the spiritual reality that underlay the material world. Med eval artists used symbolism and allegory to present their ideas.

William Durand remarked in th thirteenth century: 'Pictures and ornaments in churches are the lessons and scripture of the laity. Pictures, statues, architecture, poetry, hymns, legends and the theatre were all needed to teach those who could not read. These artists created a highly developec system of symbols in which most things had a spiritual as well as a literal meaning. For example, fire represented martyrdom or religious fervour; a lily stood for chastity; an owl, the bird of darkness, often represented Satan; and a lamb stood for Christ, as th sacrifice for sin.

Medieval artistic achievement reached its height in the Gothic cathedral. It combined the medieval version of a place of worship, theatre, art gallery, school and library. The market would be est ablished in the area of the cathedral, plays were staged on its steps, strangers slept there, and townsfolk would meet in the side aisles.

CATHEDRALS AND THEIR BUILDERS

Henry Sefton

Cathedrals stand as a symbol of the Christian society which formed the ideal of the Middle Ages. Technically a cathedral is merely a church which contains a bishop's *cathedra,* or chair, and as such can be quite a humble building. But to most people the word cathedral suggests a structure of great size and splendour. This is largely due to what has been called 'the cathedral crusade'—the enormous spate of cathedral building undertaken during the Middle Ages. In France alone, eighty cathedrals were built in a period of two hundred years, along with some five hundred other churches of considerable size. The major force behind this movement was the religious fervour of the times. Other elements such as civic pride and rivalry were also present.

How cathedrals were used

The original purpose of a cathedral was to provide a church in which the bishop and his household of priests could celebrate the mass and sing the daily services. Gradually the bishop became taken up with the administration of his diocese and often he was also employed on the king's business. He visited his cathedral only on special occasions. The household of priests became the "chapter" of the cathedral, and took over its administration and services.

The cathedral itself was developed in size and magnificence far beyond what was needed for its original purpose. The bishop's church became a screened enclosure within a very much larger structure. The cathedral came to be a house of many rooms. There was the room known as the chancel or choir, containing the high altar, the bishop's *cathedra,* and stalls for the clergy, who sang the daily services. The other main room, known as the nave, provided for the religious needs of the people: a nave altar for mass, a font for baptisms, and a pulpit for sermons. But there were many smaller rooms, in which side-altars were set up and at which masses were said for the dead. These were endowed either by wealthy individuals or by guilds of merchants and craftsmen.

But the cathedral was not only used for religious purposes. As the largest building in the town it was a natural meeting-place for social activity and even trade. At Chartres the transepts of the cathedral served as a kind of labour exchange, and the crypt beneath the church was always open for the shelter of pilgrims and the sick. The sounds of services often mingled with the greetings of friends and the haggling of traders.

The decoration of the cathedrals reflects the unified view of the world held in the Middle Ages. Religious subjects abound in the carvings and stained glass, but the world of nature is also well represented. So too is the world of what we would call 'secular humanity'. Kings and great nobles have their place, but so also do merchants, craftsmen and peasants. In the windows of Chartres cathedral, no less than forty-three trades of the city are

Cross-section of Rheims Cathedral: flying buttress.

represented, while at Wells there is a vivid carving of a person with toothache!

It was right that every class of society should be portrayed. All classes made their contribution to the building of the cathedrals. The accounts of the building of Milan cathedral record the lavish gifts of the duke, but also the donations of cheese, grain, poultry and animal-skins made by the citizens. Some women staged the story of Jason and the Golden Fleece, and, using the pretext of the Golden Fleece, appealed for a real fleece. The clergy of Laon raised a considerable amount of money for the repair of their cathedral by a tour of England with their most sacred relics.

The cathedral builders

The belief that the great cathedrals necessarily took hundreds of years to complete is untrue. When building funds were available progress could be quite rapid. The idea that building operations were carried out by pious volunteers is equally untrue. A complex building such as medieval cathedral had to be entrusted to professionals. The bishop acted as the patron or sponsor of the new cathedral, but practical oversight of the building was the task of the chapter. They had to arrange for adequate supplies of stone and timber. They also had to engage the services of a 'master', who acted as both architect and clerk of works. The master was generally a stone-mason with a practical knowledge of his craft, who had also learnt some geometry and how to draw up plans. He supervised not only the masons but also the work of the master-carpenter, the master-smith and the other skilled workers. Capable masters were much in demand and therefore in a position to bargain.

Surprisingly the construction of a great cathedral was seldom regarded as a subject worth an artist depicting. But when an event such as the building of the Tower of Babel was depicted, the artist often showed the building methods of his own day. A thirteenth-century French Bible shows a mason chiselling stone, while another checks a right-angle with a set square. Two labourers carry stone in a hand-barrow, a third mounts a ladder with a basket of mortar. On the tower a stone-setter works, with a trowel identical to those in use today. The stone-setter's companion steadies a basketful of stone, hoisted by means of a crane operated by a treadmill.

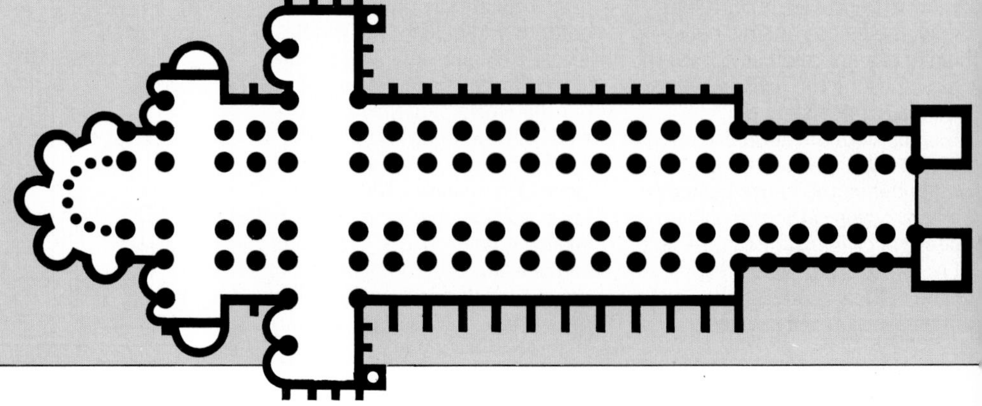

Plan of the third Abbey Church of Cluny, 1088–1130.

MAJOR GOTHIC BUILDINGS

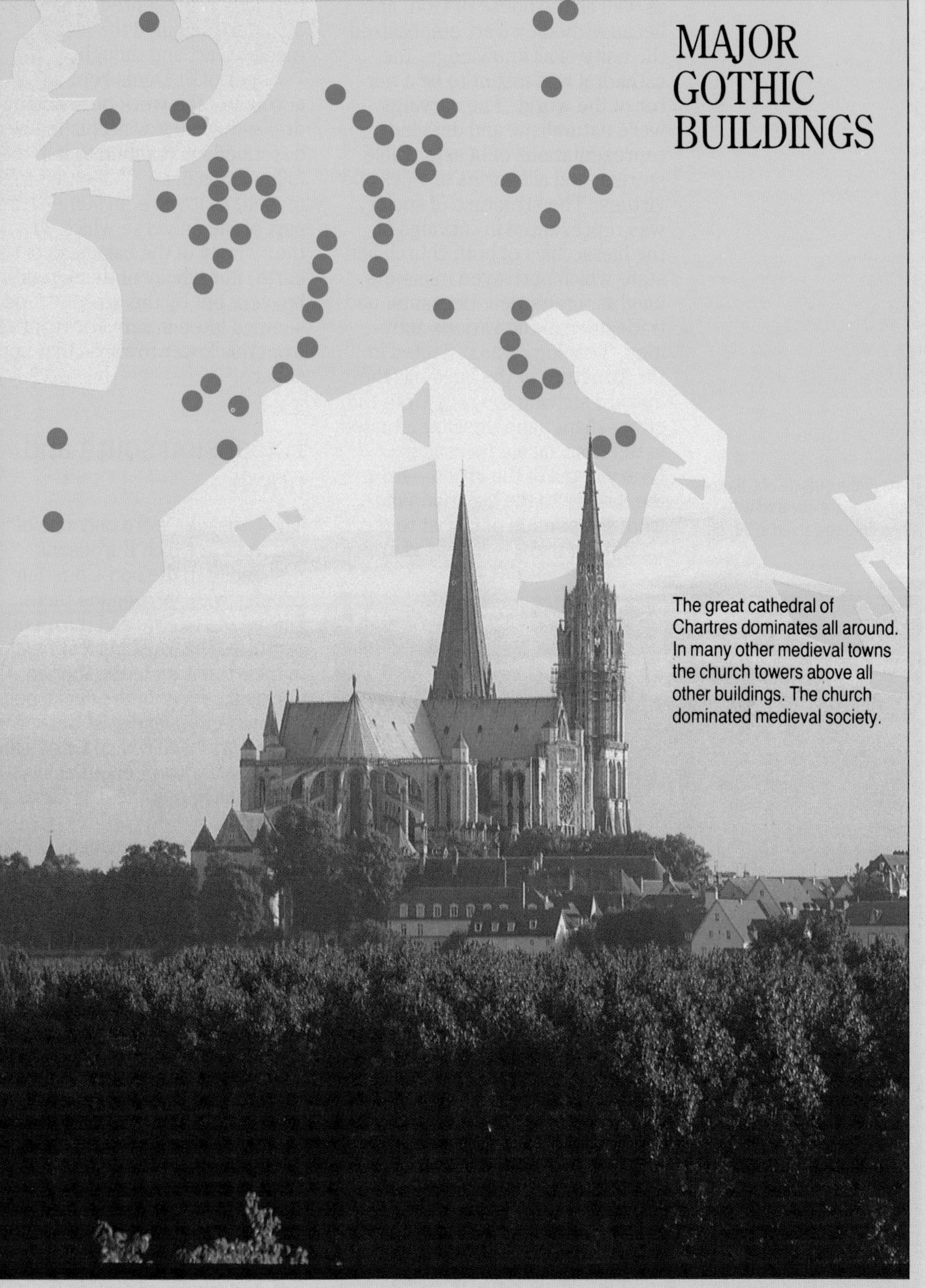

The great cathedral of Chartres dominates all around. In many other medieval towns the church towers above all other buildings. The church dominated medieval society.

Since it was the house of people as well as the house of God, and because medieval art emphasized the unity of all knowledge, the cathedral was meant to be a mirror of the world. The carvings were naturalistic and detailed representations of beasts, Bible stories, and allegories of vices and virtues. The structure of society was represented in carvings of the hierarchies of both church and state which portrayed ministers, knights, craftsmen, peasants, and tradesmen in the various activities. Theology was reflected in the structure of the building; the upward striving towards God; the cross-shape; and the altar situated in the east, facing Jerusalem. Every detail of the creed—from the Trinity to the creation, and from the passion of Christ to the Last Judgement—appeared in sculpture and stained glass. The harmony represented by such a structure signified the ideals of medieval art and thought.

Suger of St Denis kept an account of the work on his cathedral and when it was finished he described his reaction to it in the following manner: 'I seemed to fi myself, as it were, in some strang part of the universe which was ne ther wholly of the baseness of the earth, nor wholly of the serenity heaven, but by the grace of God I seemed lifted in a mystic manner from this lower towards that upp sphere.'

Parts of the outside of Chartres Cathedral are covered with stone figures carved in intricate detail.

Expansion south and north

The Crusades were only one of the ways in which Europeans responded to the non-Christian peoples who surrounded them. During the twelfth and thirteenth centuries the Muslims lost much of their territory in the Iberian peninsula, most of the pagan peoples in the remainder of Europe were Christianized and Christian missionaries went on preaching tours which took them as far as East Asia.

In Spain, at the beginning of the eleventh century, Christian rule was confined to a narrow strip of states in the north while the rest c the area was held by the Muslims. With the collapse of the Caliphate of Cordova (1034), Islamic power there came to an end. The tide of the Christian reconquest ebbed and flowed, but by the middle of the thirteenth century Muslims controlled only the small state of Granada in the far south. In the reconquered territories Muslims were treated in a similar way to th Christians under Islamic control. They were free to practise their own religion and culture, but they suffered from civil disabilities,

Cologne Cathedral, the largest church in Germany. Construction began in 1248. It is 144 metres/472 feet long, and the west tower reaches a height of 156 metres/512 feet.

including the payment of special tithes and taxes. Under these circumstances Islam declined and many of its adherents migrated to Africa, while others became Christians. The Franciscans and Dominicans were especially successful in winning Muslims to the church.

Even before the flowering of medieval Christianity, attempts had been made to reach the Scandinavians for Christ. In Denmark, Norway and Sweden conversion occurred as a community affair, following the royal lead, and resulted in greater control over the nobles by the kings. The impetus for missionary work in northern Europe came chiefly from England; the Viking conquests brought closer contact with the English, and the Scandinavians feared German political power. King Knut (Canute) of Denmark (1018–35), King Olaf I Tryggvason of Norway (969–1000), and Olaf Skötkonung (about 995–1021) of Sweden were responsible for introducing Christianity into their respective lands.

Although these peoples were officially Christianized by their rulers' actions, the church took several generations to instruct them in the faith and develop an organization. Monks and secular priests from abroad, the scalds (bards), and respected lay converts all helped spread the gospel.

POPULAR RELIGION

Caroline T. Marshall

Geoffrey Chaucer (about 1340–1400), the English poet, whose best-known work, *The Canterbury Tales*, focuses on a pilgrimage.

In the Middle Ages, popular religion concentrated on the least abstract expressions of faith. Particularly popular were veneration of the saints, especially the Virgin Mary, emphasis on relics and their shrines, pilgrimages, and heroic efforts to recapture the Holy Land.

The ordinary Christian kept much of his pagan heritage, translated into Christian terms. The old spirit-shrines and pagan festivals became the new holy relics and holy days. Sophisticated theologians understood the absolute difference between the saints and the Trinity, but it is doubtful whether most lay people did. In the effort to achieve mass conversions during the Christianizing of Europe the church made ready use of festivals of pagan religion. It was easy to transfer the powerful character of pagan gods to Christian saints. Often the pagan temples became Christian churches.

The growth of popular devotion in the twelfth century greatly advanced the role of the Virgin Mary. She became the 'universal mother', the great intercessor with her divine son, almost his rival. The universal authority of the Virgin was heightened by the belief that she was taken up body and soul into heaven at the end of her earthly life. This belief made it impossible to confine her cult in time and space in the same way as that of other saints. The introduction from the East of the rosary with its prayers to the Virgin gave additional support to her cult in the West.

During the central Middle Ages emphasis was given to the humanity of Christ. The waves of devotion and emotion which swept Europe from the twelfth century onwards were fed by an increased interest in the life and death of the human Jesus. In this drama his mother became the central figure;

> *"There was a Knight; a most distinguished man,*
> *Who from the day in which he first began*
> *To ride abroad had followed chivalry,*
> *Truth, honour, generous thought and courtesy."*

This woodcut of the Knight was made for an early edition of *The Canterbury Tales*.

the story of mother and son had great human appeal. Mary's appeal was as the beloved mother and protectress of all men. No sin was too dreadful, no transgression too vile to escape her compassionate pleading with her son on behalf of the sinner.

Peasants, knights and kings begged her help, and she became a romantic obsession. With the rise of the tradition of chivalry, she became the focus of a romantic cult that it is difficult for the modern mind to appreciate. The great Gothic cathedrals cannot be fully understood until it is recalled that they were built partly as trophies for a beautiful woman, for ever young, for ever kind.

With the growth of popular devotion the traffic in holy relics swelled. The desire to own a memento of a revered and powerful religious figure was universal. Every new church building needed a relic for its altar, and the official church kept a vast stock of them. Merchants carried splinters of the true cross to protect them from thieves. Knights concealed saints' teeth, bones or hair in their sword-hilts. Peasants bought drops of the Saviour's bloody sweat and the Virgin's milk at local fairs. Cities cherished and stole from one another the bodies of famous saints. Martin Luther's patron, Frederick the Wise of Saxony, had a huge and valuable collection of relics. The Reformation saw the destruction of millions of such relics.

Closely related to the adoration of relics and the cult of the saints was the passion for pilgrimage. The impulse to travel was fed partly by a belief that a visit to the great shrines could bring physical and spiritual healing. But there was also a new and restless desire to explore the mystical holy places and to experience the sights and smells of foreign places.

Pilgrimages to the Holy Land were hard and dangerous, and, consequently, were restricted to the most devout and those obliged to do particularly serious penances. The most popular Western shrines included Rome, Canterbury (Thomas Becket) and St James of Compostela in north-west Spain. Most pilgrimage routes were carefully arranged, with hostels spaced along the way. A pilgrimage could be a very light-hearted affair (witness Chaucer's *Canterbury Tales*). Like modern tourists, the pilgrims tended to travel in groups, gossiping, singing and stopping at minor shrines along the way. The pilgrimage gave the faithful a combination of religious duty and holiday relaxation.

"When in April the sweet
showers fall
And pierce the drought
of March to the root,
and all . . .
Then people long to go
on pilgrimages
And palmers long to see
the stranger strands
Of far-off saints,
hallowed in sundry
lands,
And specially, from
every shire's end
In England, down to
Canterbury they wend
To seek the holy blissful
martyr, quick
To give his help to
them when they were
sick."

CHAUCER, The Canterbury Tales

The pilgrims' routes to Santiago de Compostela, one of the most popular shrines.

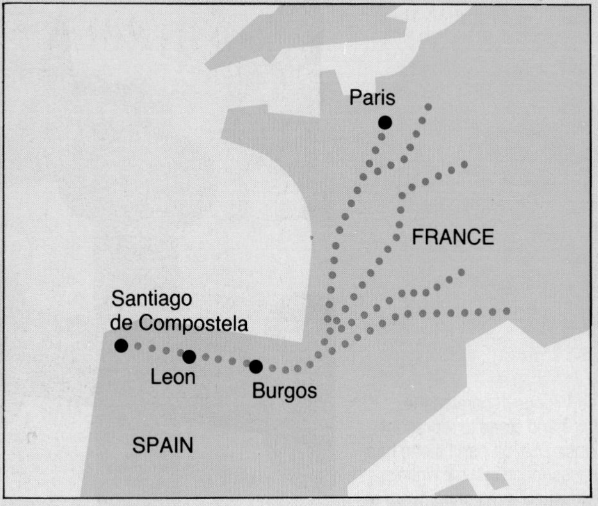

Diocesan boundaries usually paralleled political divisions, and by the close of the twelfth century each country had its own archbishop.

Christianity revolutionized the Scandinavians' way of life. Many resisted the new faith because marriage customs had to change, horsemeat (a Viking delicacy) could no longer be eaten, and church duties such as fasting, penance and tithing were considered too burdensome. Despite pagan-inspired civil wars fought in opposition to both the monarchy and clergy, old customs gradually disappeared. The Viking fleets ceased to terrorize Europe and more humane attitudes became characteristic of the descendants of the Norsemen.

Into eastern Europe

Another area that challenged Christian missionary enthusiasm was eastern Europe. The Russiar were converted through their contact with Constantinople and the Orthodox church. The Poles, Hungarians and Bohemians were won to Latin Christianity. As in Scandinavia, it was the action of rulers that gave the gospel its opportunity. Wenceslas of Bohemia (about 907–29), Boleslaus I o Poland (992–1025), and Stephen of Hungary (about 975–1038), encouraged by the German churc based their rule on Christianity. A result there was a band of states depending on Germany for their culture all along her eastern fronti

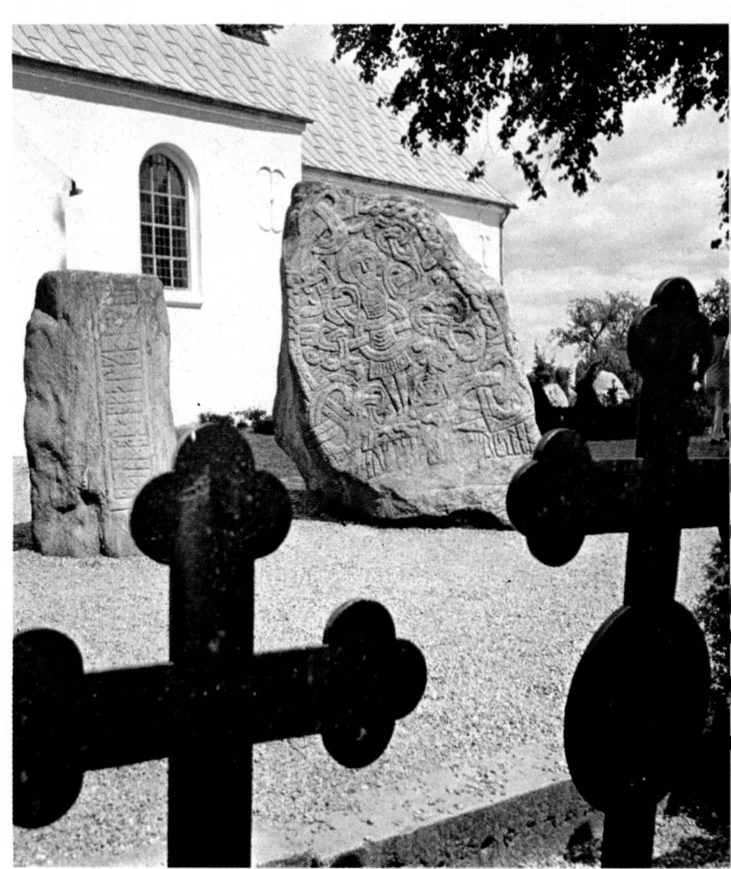

The Vikings decorated the right-hand stone to represent Christ. The left-hand stone has an inscription in runic writings. Both stand in the churchyard at Jelling, Denmark.

Many of the native people were oppressed farmers, who resented Christianity and the immigrant Germans who settled in the cities. These rural folk only gradually adopted Christianity, following decades of instruction, recruiting and training of clergy, the development of dioceses and parishes, and the administration of the sacraments. By the early fourteenth century not only the Bohemians, Poles and Hungarians but also the Wends (Slavs east of the River Elbe), Pomeranians, Lithuanians, Prussians and the Baltic peoples had adopted the Christian faith. The German-inspired push to the east might even have included the Russians if the Teutonic knights, who were one of the agents of the conversion process, had not been defeated at the Battle of the Ice (1242) by the forces of Novgorod.

By this time Russia was invaded by the Mongols and cut off from the West and the creative ferment of early modern Europe. But the vast Mongol Empire, which extended from China to the Caucasus and from the frozen north to the Himalayas, provided opportunity for many Franciscan friars. Two Franciscans, John of Planocarpini and William of Rubriquis, travelled to the court of the Mongol Khan in China (about 1250). Others followed them to the East, preaching in Persia and India, as well as China.

Their journeys met with such success that early in the fourteenth century a chain of Christian missions extended from Constantinople to Peking, and it seemed at one time as if even the Mongol rulers might accept the Christian faith. This promising beginning did not lead to permanent results, however, since the western Mongols became Muslims and prevented the missionaries from travelling through their territories. Travel was made even more dangerous when the Mongol Empire broke up into many quarrelling states. Western Europe itself lost its enthusiasm for mission during the fourteenth century as a result of wars, plague and renewed arguments between secular and church power.

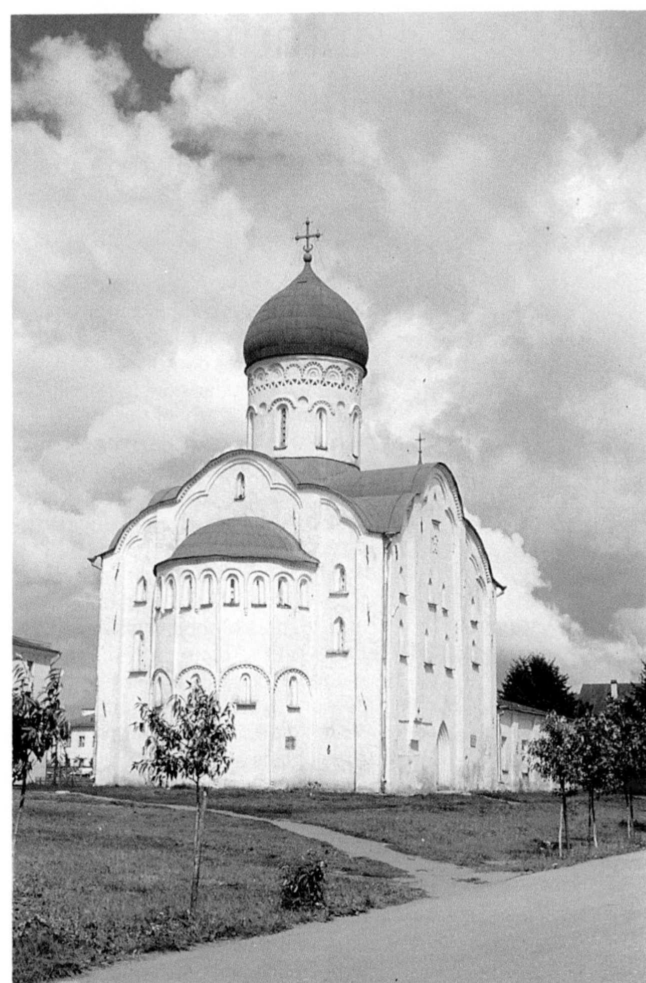

The medieval church at Novgorod, in Russia.

Interpreting the Bible

Bruce A. Demarest

"The sense of God's work is infinitely varied, and like a peacock's feather glows with many colours."

The fall of the Roman Empire led to widespread illiteracy and ignorance. For centuries, in the absence of public education, all learning and study of the Scriptures was restricted to the monasteries. Medieval theologians held that Scripture could be interpreted only by the learned few, under the direction of the church.

The medieval church believed it should uphold the traditions and dogmas of the early Christian writers. Thus, in general, medieval biblical scholars were content to collect and synthesize the traditional explanations of theologians as far back as Origen. One scholar of the period wrote: 'It is better not to be taken up with supposedly new ideas, but to be filled from the fountain of the ancients.' Thus medieval scholars produced massive volumes of dogma and morality which claim to explain Scripture but which in reality have hardly any connection with the biblical text.

Following the methods of many early Greek and Latin Christian writers, medieval interpreters for nearly a thousand years used a fourfold scheme of biblical interpretation: 'The literal teaches the events, allegory what you are to believe, the moral sense what you are to do, the anagogical (spiritual) where you are to aim.' The literal, historical sense of the biblical text was smothered by a swarm of mystical interpretations. Thus, for example, the word 'water' in Scripture was often interpreted in the following fourfo way: literally, water, the physical element; allegorically, baptism, tl nations or grace; morally, sorrow wisdom, heresy or prosperity; spiritually, eternal happiness. An unbridled sense of imagination wa a prime requisite for interpreting Scripture.

Never has biblical interpretatio been made so obscure as during the Dark Ages. Few interpreters paid attention to the historical and literal sense of the biblical text; still fewer had more than an elementary knowledge of Hebrew and Greek. For about four hundre years priests and monks tediously compiled early Christian writings, characterized by rigid dogmatic sentences, moral platitudes, mystical play on numbers and fals word-meanings.

Bede, the English historian and theologian, devoted his entire life to the study of Scripture in a monastery. Following Philo and Origen, he tried to extract the spiritual kernel of truth from the Bible, using an allegorical interpretation. Bede's comments on Scripture are little more than a patchwork quilt fashioned from Ambrose, Jerome, Augustine and Gregory. Alcuin and Walafrid Strabo (who died in 849) similarly produced highly allegorical commentaries on Scripture, compiled largely from excerpts from earlier writers.

The fanciful allegorical interpretation of the period is illustrated by a comment by Haymo of Halberstadt (who died in 856) on Joel 2:16 ('let the bridegroom leave his room, and the bride her chamber'). The text means, 'let Christ go out of the bosom of the Father and the flesh of Christ from the virgin's womb.' John Scotus Erigena (died about 875), summed up the medieval attitude towards the Word of God: 'The sense of God's work is infinitely aried, and like a peacock's feather glows with many colours.'

Scholastic theologians continued o bypass the biblical languages of Greek and Hebrew and perpetuated the multi-sense interpretation of the Bible, while striving to einforce the traditions of the church.

Peter Lombard, a pupil of Abelard, and later bishop of Paris, produced a theological extbook of scholasticism entitled he *Book of Sentences* (1158). This well-organized one-volume system of medieval dogma was primarily a collection of the opinions of previous writers—for example, Hilary, Ambrose and Augustine. Lombard's numerous commentaries on Scripture were similarly an unimaginative collection of the moral and spiritual opinions of earlier writers.

Reacting to the sterile formalism and traditionalism of the scholastics, there arose important mystical interpreters and theologians. They stressed the devotional tudy of the Bible aided by the free use of allegory. They replaced dialectical reasoning with ecstasy and intuition as the accepted yardtick for interpreting.

Bernard of Clairvaux, regarded s the father of medieval mysticism, wrote eighty-six sermons on the Song of Solomon, which re characterized not by the ogical subtleties of scholasticism, out by highly esoteric mystical xplanations.

Hugh (who died in 1141), head of a theological academy at the monastery of St Victor in Paris the principal centre of medieval mysticism), while allowing certain mystical meanings, emphasized he literal sense of Scripture. But Hugh adhered to the dogmatism f his time by affirming that the cholar first decides what he ought o believe and then goes to Scripure to confirm his judgement. The Franciscan mystic Bonaventura (died in 1274) was influenced by the scholasticism of his day. The book of seven seals in Revelation allows the sevenfold sense of Scripture: the historical, anagogical, allegorical, tropological, symbolical, synechdochical and hyperbolical. Only a learned monk could fathom the depths of wisdom contained in such a book!

Thomas Aquinas, the master of scholastic theology, has a much less distinguished reputation as an interpreter of Scripture. His *catena* (a stringing together of observations from the ancient authorities) on the Gospels quotes no less than twenty-two Greek and twenty Latin writers. Furthermore, Thomas rigorously allegorizes even the most simple texts. For example, he interprets Genesis 1:3, 'Let there be light', thus: historically, it refers to the act of creation; allegorically, 'let Christ be love'; morally, 'may we be mentally illuminated by Christ'; anagogically, 'may we be led to glory by Christ'.

Meanwhile the plain sense of the Bible was being revived by certain Jewish commentators. Writing on the Pentateuch, Rashi (Rabbi Solomon ben Isaac, from Troyes, who died in 1105) concentrates on 'the simple sense of the Bible'. His Old Testament commentaries devote unusual attention to philology, grammar and sentence construction. The Spanish scholar, Abraham ibn Ezra (who died in 1167), wrote commentaries on most of the Old Testament, and strengthened the Jewish shift towards a modern historical and grammatical interpretation. He identified five traditional methods of biblical interpretation, but preferred the plain approach, which explains the meaning intended by the biblical writer.

Nicholas of Lyra (1265–1349), a Franciscan at the University of

Jewish scholars studied the Hebrew text of the Old Testament. This fourteenth-century Old Testament manuscript shows a teacher driving on his pupil.

Paris, was primarily responsible for bringing the approach of Rashi and his followers to Christian scholarship. Lyra wrote about eighty-five volumes covering the whole of the Bible. A master of Old Testament Hebrew, he prepared the first Bible commentary to be printed. The commentary was printed in Rome in 1471–2 and was widely consulted. While repeating the common medieval definition of the fourhold sense of Scripture, Lyra claimed that the plain sense of the text had priority: 'I intend to insist upon the literal sense and sometimes to insert brief mystical expositions, though rarely.' Lyra's contribution towards a responsible method of interpretation and the dissolution of the iron grip of church tradition led to the proverb 'Had Lyra not played his lyre, Luther would not have danced.' The Reformer in reality did lean heavily upon the biblical interpretation of the French scholar.

The early English reformer Wyclif claimed that 'the whole error in the knowledge of Scripture, and the source of its debasement and falsification by incompetent persons, was the ignorance of grammar and logic'. For such reasons the Bible lay buried and obscured for centuries. With the Renaissance revival of the study of the languages and literature of Greece and Rome, scholasticism finally toppled.

Medieval monasticism in the West

Ronald Finucane

In the centuries after 600 the monastic rule established by Benedict was gradually accepted throughout western Europe. In the earlier centuries, however, it always existed alongside other types of monastic life. The most important of these was Celtic monasticism which, from its centres in Ireland, sent out missions to Britain and Europe. Irish monasticism was distinguished by an ascetic rigour, a high level of cultural attainment and, in organization, by the very subordinate position of the bishop. The great Irish missionary figures were Columba in Scotland and Columbanus (about 543–615), whose missionary work took place in the Rhineland and the Alps. Columbanus founded the abbeys of Luxeuil in Gaul (about 590) and Bobbio in north Italy (612), cultural centres of great importance. He was responsible for the introduction of much Celtic influence into continental monasticism.

English missions to mainland Europe

However, it was monasticism based on the Benedictine rule that was to become the normal and, indeed, official form. In 600 this rule was simply one of many. The monasteries of Gaul, for example, were influenced by Eastern, Celtic and Italian models. By the reign of Charlemagne (768–814), however, the Benedictine rule was universal within his domains. The rule had been taken to England by Wilfrid (634–709) and ultimately replaced the earlier influence of Celtic monasticism.

From England missionary monks such as Boniface evangelized the pagan Germans. Boniface used the Benedictine monastery as the base for his work. The abbey of Fulda, founded under Boniface's influence in 744, became a great cultural and

Cuthbert busily writing in his monastery.

A page from the *Lindisfarne Gospels*, one of the masterpieces of the Celtic church.

religious centre in the following centuries. Later missionary work among the Slavs and Scandinavians made use of the monastery as a centre in a similar way.

The form of Benedictine monasticism widespread in Europe by the eighth century showed many differences from its early days. Increasingly monks were drawn from the nobility. It was a common practice for nobles to 'devote' their sons and daughters to a monastery while still children. As a result of such changes the monks' share of manual work had been gradually reduced and replaced by liturgical and cultural activities. This concentration on scholarly and artistic work made the great monasteries of the eighth to the tenth centuries, such as Reichenau, St Gallen and Corbie, the cultural and educational centre of Europe. They possessed large libraries and their monks copied the manuscripts which were to transmit ancient literature and learning to later centuries. In fact, the great majority of ancient Latin prose and poetry comes down to us only via early medieval monastic manuscripts. The monks' creative achievements were in the development of script and the illumination of manuscripts. In Ireland and Britain these beautiful works are best represented by the *Book of Kells* and the *Lindisfarne Gospels* respectively.

Between the sixth and eighth centuries, too, the monasteries became far more closely linked with the society within which they existed. Their abbots and monks were related to local noble families; lands were granted to them by kings and magnates; they achieved both economic and political importance. Instead of a group of individuals fleeing from the world to live a life of perfection, the monastic community was becoming a religious corporation which served a definite function in society. Its duty consisted of keeping up a continual sequence of praise and prayer. The monks, in a sense, prayed on behalf of the rest of humankind. In the never-ending battle with the forces of evil, the monks undertook penance and intercession for others, and thereby increased the chances of salvation. They were seen as spiritual counterparts of the feudal knights.

This close connection with society aroused some criticism. Much of the history of monasticism from the ninth century onwards revolves around repeated attempts at reform. These reforms had varying goals. Already in 817 Benedict of Aniane had attempted to reform the monasteries in the irection of greater severity, nore manual labour and less tudy, greater central control, nd a curtailment of the outside ctivities of monks. This attempt vas stillborn and, in the next entury and a half, the monasteries ared badly. Renewed barbarian ttacks from Vikings, Saracens and Magyars destroyed many of the reat abbeys and dispersed the nonks and their cultural treasures. By 950 the destruction or decay f many monasteries and the onfusion caused by their relative independence led to a determined attempt at reform.

Cluny restores dignity

The tenth-century reform is closely associated with the abbey of Cluny in central France, founded about 909. Cluny's long-ruling abbots (Odo, 927–42; Odilo, 994–1049; Hugh the Great, 1049–1109), spiritual and political figures of European importance, led the movement. The 'Cluniac' reform had both a religious and

THE MONK'S DAY

Monks all over western Europe practised a daily routine similar to this. There were slight variations according to the season of the year or the tradition of the order.

The monastery of Monte Cassino

“They come and find, the tired travellers,
Green herbs and ample bread,
Quiet and brothers' love and humbleness,
Christ's peace on every head.”

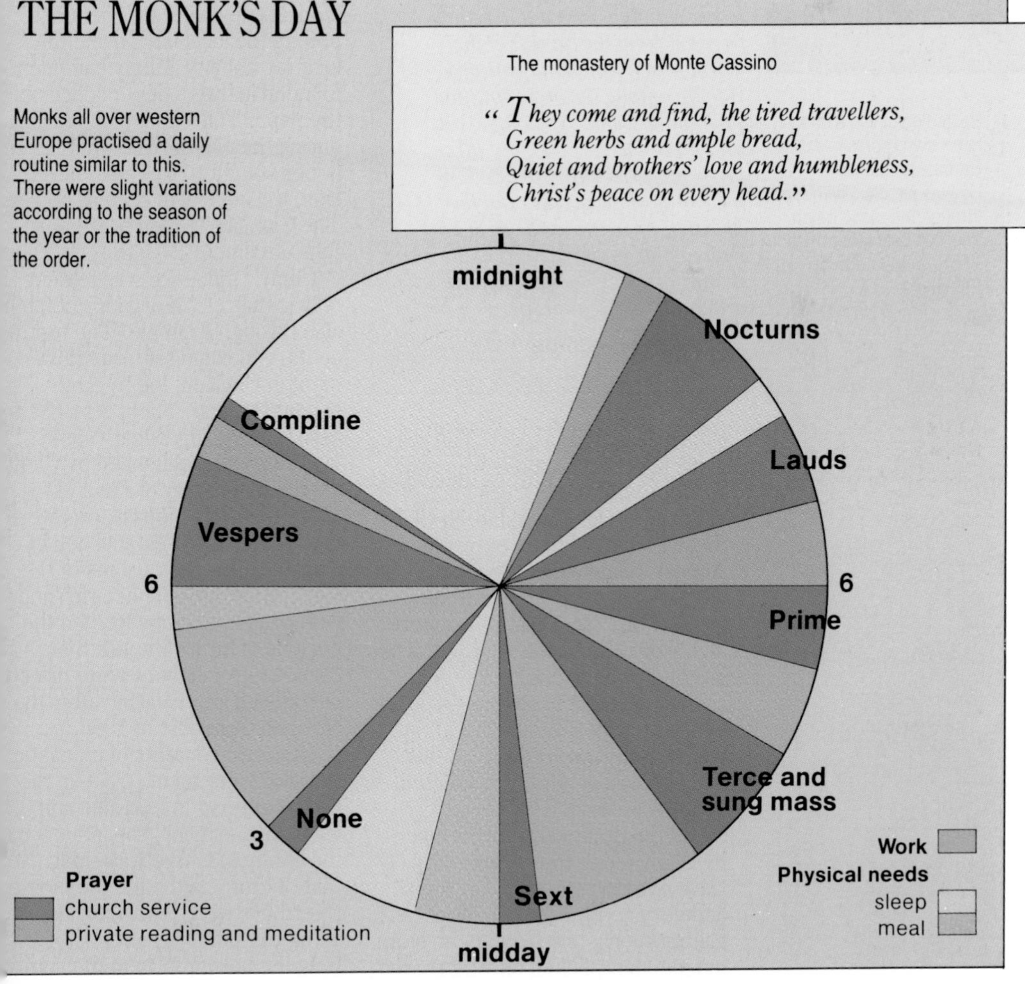

Each monk lived alone in his own rooms in this Carthusian monastery. He was supplied with food through the stone hatch. This cell is at Mount Grace Priory, in the north of England.

A CONTENTED MONK

“*Our food is scanty, our garments rough; our drink is from the stream and our sleep often upon our book. Under our tired limbs there is but a hard mat; when sleep is sweetest we must rise at a bell's bidding . . . Self-will has no scope; there is no moment for idleness or dissipation . . . Everywhere peace, everywhere serenity, and a marvellous freedom from the tumult of the world. Such unity and concord is there among the brethren, that each thing seems to belong to all, and all to each . . . To put all in brief, no perfection expressed in the words of the gospel or of the apostles, or in the writings of the Fathers, or in the sayings of the monks of old, is lacking to our order and our way of life.*”

AILRED, Speculum Caritatis, 1.17

an organizational aspect. The religious task of the monks was seen as, above all, the performance of the daily cycle of worship. In Cluny this was carried to its extreme. Almost the whole of the monks' day was taken up with church services. The Cluniac churches were highly decorated and adorned. The intention was to create a service as magnificent and solemn as possible. The widespread admiration which Cluny inspired shows that this aim was generally respected, in both church and lay society.

The institutional reforms made by Cluny led to the creation, by the eleventh century, of a complex and very centralized organization. Earlier monasteries had been quite independent, linked only by shared emphases, such as the form of their observance, or by historical association, such as that between a founding abbey and its 'daughter houses. The abbots of Cluny, especially Odilo, actually created a large chain of dependent houses. Instead of an abbot, these houses had a prior appointed by the abbot of Cluny. The obedience of a monk to his abbot, a central feature of Benedict's rule, was extended to all the monks of the dependent houses, who were regarded as 'monks of Cluny' too.

One of the advantages of being a Cluniac monk was that Cluniac monasteries were independent both of the local bishop and the local lay nobility. Cluny had been founded in direct dependence on the pope. This became important during the eleventh century, as the popes sought to free the church from the control of secular powers. The Cluniacs tended to support this movement.

Cluny's influence was felt not only in matters of organization but also through example. The tenth-century monastic reform movement in England, led by Archbishop Dunstan (about 909–88) and assisted by King Edgar (959–75), was indirectly influenced by Cluny via the monastery of Fleury. More than fifty monasteries were established or re-established in England after the ravages of the Viking invasions. These rich and cultured foundations formed the nucleus of future English monasticism. Cluniac houses were directly introduced into England after the Norman Conquest of 1066.

Other movements of monastic renewal were taking place in the tenth century. In Lorraine and western Germany, the influence of the abbey of Gorze was similar to that of Cluny, although the Gorze reformers were less rigorous about excluding lay authority. In Italy the hermit form of monasti-

A DISCONTENTED MONK

"Everything here and in my nature are opposed to each other. I cannot endure the daily tasks. The sight of it all revolts me. I am tormented and crushed down by the length of the vigils, I often succumb to the manual labour. The food cleaves to my mouth, more bitter than wormwood. The rough clothing cuts through my skin and flesh down to my very bones. More than this, my will is always hankering after other things, it longs for the delights of the world and sighs unceasingly for its loves and affections and pleasures."

WALTER DANIEL'S *Life of Ailred*

The monks of Eberbach slept in this vaulted room. Theirs was one of the first Cistercian monasteries to be built in Germany.

ism was renewed. Monks of his type lived together inside an nclosure, and might meet for ommon meals and services, but therwise lived solitary lives. This vas an attempt to return to the ype of organization of the first ıonastics in the deserts of Egypt. 'he eleventh century foundation f Camaldoli by Romuald, and of 'allombrosa by John Gualbert both imed at solitariness and severity.

The activities of the monastic eformers of the tenth century nd their alliance with the new xpansionist papacy of the elevnth century made these the lassic centuries of Benedictine ıonasticism. But already a new 'ave of reform was imminent. The vealth of the Cluniac monasteries, heir easy relations with the world t large and their emphasis on the hurch service led some reformers o seek a more austere and primiive path.

Some, for example, Bruno of Cologne, who founded La Grande Chartreuse in southern France in 1084, turned to the hermit type of monastery. The Carthusian order, which arose from this, remained one of the most rigorous throughout the Middle Ages. Their proud claim was that they were never reformed because their original ideals were never lost. The alleged laxity of some of the great Cluniac houses led to the foundation of several strict Benedictine orders around 1100: those of Grandmont, Fontevrault (a distinctive 'double order' of monks and nuns) and Savigny.

Escaping this world

But the most important and successful of the orders seeking to revive the primitive Benedictine life was that of the Cistercians or 'White Monks'. Their mother

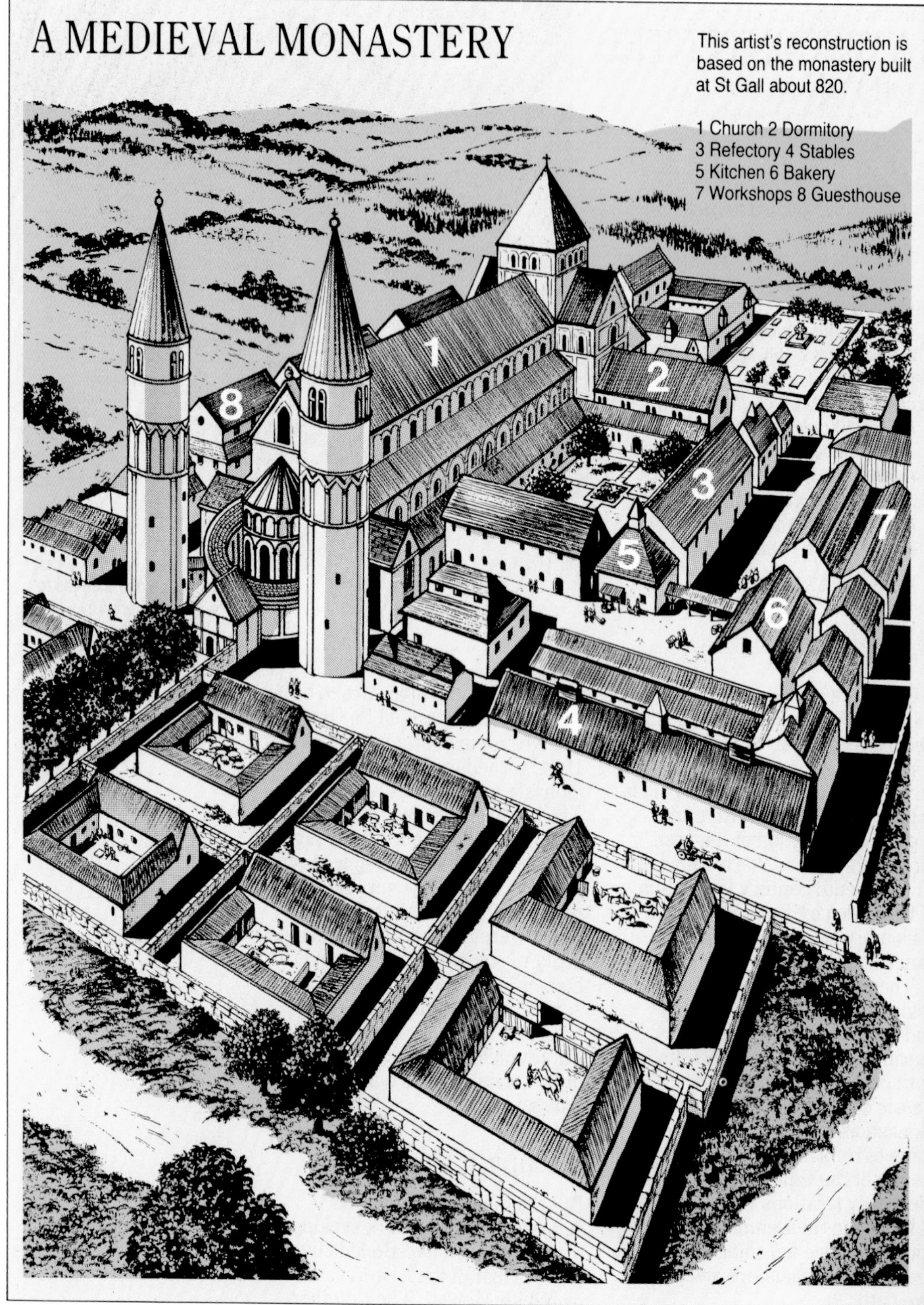
A MEDIEVAL MONASTERY
This artist's reconstruction is based on the monastery built at St Gall about 820.
1 Church 2 Dormitory
3 Refectory 4 Stables
5 Kitchen 6 Bakery
7 Workshops 8 Guesthouse
1
2
3
4
5
6
7
8

house was Cîteaux in Burgundy, founded in 1098 by Robert of Molesme, with Stephen Harding and other reforming monks. While Englishman Stephen Harding (about 1110–34) was abbot, Cistercian houses spread throughout western Europe. They aimed at a complete break with the Cluniac past. Their churches and their services were to be simple and unadorned. Their abbeys were founded in remote and desolate regions, again recalling the ideal of the earlier Christian monastics, who fled to 'the wilderness'. Silence and austerity were stressed and a renewed emphasis was placed on manual work. The constitution of the order was set out in the *Carta Caritatis* of 1119. Each house had to be visited annually by the abbot of its mother house. Every year a general assembly (chapter) of all the abbots was to be held at Cîteaux, to lay down ordinances for the whole order. The severity and organization of the Cistercians proved remarkably successful. By 1300 over 600 monasteries and nunneries were in existence.

The Cistercians soon came under attack, however, on unexpected grounds. As their houses had to be founded in remote wastes because of their flight from the world, they were gradually forced to develop techniques of survival in such regions. They learned how to turn the wastes into productive agricultural

A monastery on top of a volcano. Monks still work and pray today at Maria Laach, a Benedictine monastery in the Rhineland, Germany. It was founded in the eleventh century, and is in the Romanesque style of architecture.

HOW THE ABBEY OF CLAIRVAUX WAS BUILT

“The bishops of the region, noblemen and merchants of the land heard of it, and joyfully offered rich aid in God's work. Supplies were abundant, workmen quickly hired, the brothers themselves joined in the work in every way: some cut timbers, others shaped stones, others built walls, others divided the river, set it in new channels and lifted the leaping waters to the mill-wheels; fullers and bakers and tanners and smiths and other artificers prepared suitable machines for their tasks, that the river might flow fast and do good wherever it was needed in every building, flowing freely in underground conduits; the streams performed suitable tasks in every office and cleansed the abbey and at length returned to the main course and restored to the river what it had lost. The walls which gave the abbey a spacious enclosure were finished with unlooked-for speed. The abbey rose; the new-born church, as if it had a living soul that moves, quickly developed and grew.”

Vita prima, II.5

land. Their economic activities, especially sheep-farming, made them a wealthy order. The monks withdrew from manual work, leaving this to the 'lay brothers', normally illiterate folk who joined the order but were not offered full membership, and lived in separate buildings on monastic lands. Because of the wealth derived from their wide estates and the labour of the lay brothers (known as the *conversi*), the Cistercians were soon accused of the sin of greed. Spoiled by worldly success, their initial aim of austerity was ironically reversed.

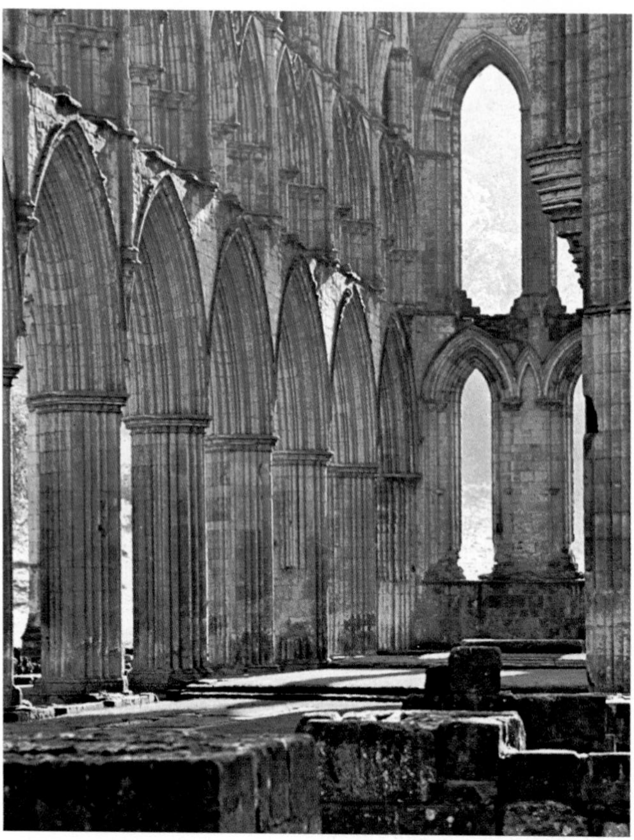

The great age of the monasteries had passed. These are the remains of the once-magnificent Rievaulx Abbey, in northern England.

Before this stage was reached, however, the Cistercian ideal was generally admired and had been imitated by other strict orders. The Premonstratensians, founded by Norbert in northern France around 1120, and the Gilbertines, founded by Gilbert of Sempringham in Lincolnshire (about 1083–1189) were deeply influenced by the Cistercian ideal. The Gilbertines, a double order of monks and nuns, was the only new order established by an English person within England in the monastic movement of the later medieval period. These two orders took as their rule, not that of Benedict, but the more flexible Augustinian rule which, although based on advice given by Augustine, only came into practical use in the eleventh century. They were canons, clergy living in community, rather than monks. The adaptability of their rule meant that the Augustinian canons not only included more cloistered orders, such as the Premonstratensian and Gilbertine but also included many houses where canons took up teaching or hospital work in the towns. The founding of a house of Augustinian canons was generally less expensive than a Benedictine abbey, and so benefactors found a new outlet in endowing such houses rather than Benedictine abbeys—now largely declining in public favour.

The military orders were also affected by monastic ideals. These orders consisted of monk-knights, who originally intended to fight in the Holy Land, and were a logical extension of monastic involvement in the Crusades. The chief crusading orders adopted forms of the Cistercian regulations. The Knights Templar (founded about 1118, and suppressed in the early fourteenth century), the Hospitallers (late eleventh century) and the Teutonic Knights (late twelfth century) came to wield great political and economic power for several centuries.

The friars take over

By 1200, however, monasticism had passed the peak of its appeal and influence. The initiative was taken by the new begging orders of friars, especially the Dominicans and Franciscans, or by the universities. Although new monasteries were indeed founded, the total number of monks began to decline. Standards of monastic life fell as strictness was relaxed. Ingenious means were sometimes found to keep to the letter of monastic constitutions, while deviating greatly from the spirit of those early rules. Community life was gradually modified, and divisions appeared within abbeys between the abbot, the monastic officials and the monks. Increasingly, abbots and priors came to live and eat apart from the monks. Religious houses became more and more involved in the running of their estates and in legal squabbles. Many monks spent much of their time in supervising estates, collecting revenues and battling for property rights. In Europe the 'commendatory' system brought in lay people to take over the income and administration of monasteries. Everywhere the system of allowing 'corrodies'—virtually supporting lay people out of monastic income in exchange for a lay grant—took the monk farther and farther away from the life of prayer and into the world.

Nevertheless, attempts at reform continued throughout the later centuries of the Middle Ages. Some were initiated by popes, such as Innocent III in 1215, or Benedict XII in 1336. Others took the familiar form of a return to strict observance of the Benedictine rule. The Sylvestrines (1231), Celestinians (later thirteenth century), and Olivetans (1319) adopted this approach. The general attempt at church reform in the fifteenth century, associated with the great Councils, also saw further attempts at monastic reform. In the German lands Kastl, Melk and Bursfeld were centres of reform, while St Justina in Padua provided an example for Italy and Spain. Other new movements were the Brethren of the Common Life, the Brigittines, a Swedish order of the fourteenth century, and the Minims, a fifteenth-century order which combined certain aspects of monasticism with the Franciscan rule.

The over-all picture of late medieval monasticism, however, is one in which the monks have become an established and integrated part of society but are no longer respected and attractive as their predecessors had been before 1200. It is significant that many monastic-type movements in the last two medieval centuries were based rather upon lay participation and were in effect a result of lay devotion. Growing criticism of monastic abuses and even of the very principle of monasticism itself foreshadowed the great attack that the institution was to experience in the Protestant Reformation.

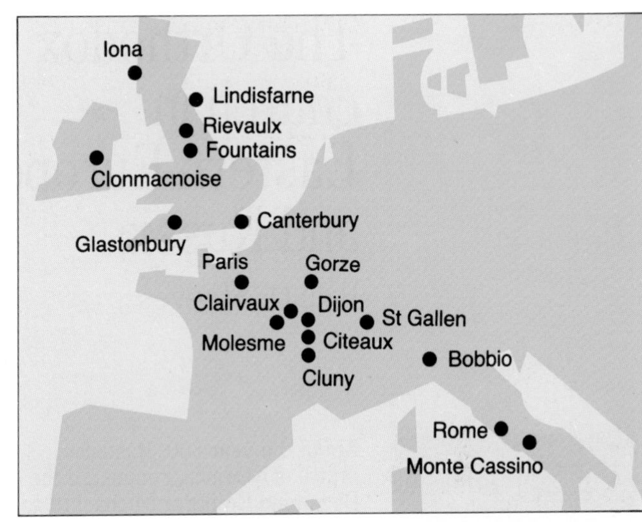

Leading Western monasteries of the Middle Ages

The Orthodox church in Eastern Europe and Russia

Paul D. Steeves

Characteristic 'onion dome' church towers in Sofia, Bulgaria.

About the year 860, Rastislav, prince of Moravia, requested the Byzantine Emperor Michael III to send missionaries to instruct his people in the ways of Christ. The Moravians, ancestors of the modern Czechs, belonged to the Slavic race which had come from Asia and spread throughout the eastern plains of Europe. In response, Patriarch Photius provided two Greek brothers who were to be among the most influential of Christian missionaries.

Mission to Moravia

The two brothers Cyril and Methodius had grown up near Slavs who had settled in Macedonia and therefore they knew the Slavic language. Before embarking upon their mission, the evangelists began to prepare an alphabet for the hitherto unwritten language, so that the converts could have the Scriptures and liturgy in their native tongue This script, known as Glagolitic, was the forerunner of the form of writing now used in south-eastern Europe and Russia, which is called Cyrillic, after the younger brother. By this means, Orthodox Christianity, and with it the culture of Byzantium, spread among the Slavic tribes. This Byzantine culture determined the main lines of development for these peoples, especially the Russians, for centuries. Thus Cyril and Methodius rightfully earned the title of 'The Apostles of the Slavs'.

The Moravian mission of Cyril and Methodius met with success in its first three years. But any long-term results were lost when the invading Magyars destroyed the state of Moravia. The church of this area eventually developed along Western Catholic lines. The brothers' work did not disappear, however, because their followers carried their message and Slavonic books southward to the Bulgarians, who became fervently attached to Byzantine Orthodoxy.

The Bulgarian Czar Boris, who accepted Christianity for his people, prevailed upon the Emperor and Patriarch of Constantinople to recognize, in 870, the Bulgarians' right to have an independent church organization, under the Ecumenical Patriarch. The Bulgarians also won approval for their liturgy to be conducted in the Slavonic language. In this way a distinctive form of Orthodoxy was established in Eastern Europe: state churches employing local languages. In 927, the chief bishop of the Bulgarian church was raised to the rank of patriarch.

From Bulgaria, the Old Church Slavonic liturgical language and Byzantine Christianity were transplanted to Serbia, the third Slavic nation to be Christianized in the second half of the ninth century. The Serbian church remained in the shadow of the Bulgarians until the time of the most celebrated Serbian Christian, Sava. In 1219, he was consecrated Archbishop of Serbia. The Serbian archbishopric was promoted to a patriarchate in 1346, at the height of the Serbian Empire under King Stefan Dushan. Bulgarian influence also drew the church of Romania into the Orthodox fold.

'ladimir's choice

he most illustrious fruit of the ·others' Slavonic influence ›peared when the pagan prince of iev, Vladimir, officially adopted rthodoxy as the religion of his ate. The magnificent legend of e conversion of the Russians nar- ıtes how Vladimir, around 988, ecided that the interests of his ·alm required that he take up one the major religions. According the *Russian Chronicle,* Vladimir ·nt envoys to investigate Islam, daism, Latin and Byzantine hristianity. The first three failed suit Vladimir, but he was won ver by the report of those who ·turned from Constantinople, ho declared that when they tended the mass in the great urch of St Sophia they could not ll whether they were on earth or heaven. Vladimir then ordered e mass baptism of the Russians cording to the Orthodox form. rthodoxy thus became the state ligion of Russia, which it was to main until 1917.

Although the details of the leg- d probably do not record actual story, they do reflect one of the ost significant features of Russian ıristianity. The forms of worship ve always been more impor- nt than other aspects—such as eology or ethics. The primary peal of Orthodoxy was aesthetic ther than intellectual or moral. deed, the name of the religion in avonic, *Pravoslavie,* means 'true ›rship' or 'right glory', reflecting e pre-eminence of the liturgy to e Russian mind.

After Vladimir's conversion, e Slavonic books of Cyril and ethodius were brought to Kiev. ıe Russians received a benefit ıich Christians of the Latin-using estern church did not enjoy. ıeir religious liturgy and writings isted in a language which was elligible to all of them. Thus the church both civilized the Russian tribes and stimulated the growth of their native culture.

Vladimir's son and successor, Yaroslav the Wise, who began to rule in 1019, cemented the bonds between the Russian church and Byzantine Orthodoxy by accepting for his realm a bishop appointed by the Ecumenical Patriarch. In this way he acknowledged Constantinople as the overseer of the Russian church. Yaroslav provided the bishop, consecrated as the Metropolitan of Kiev, with

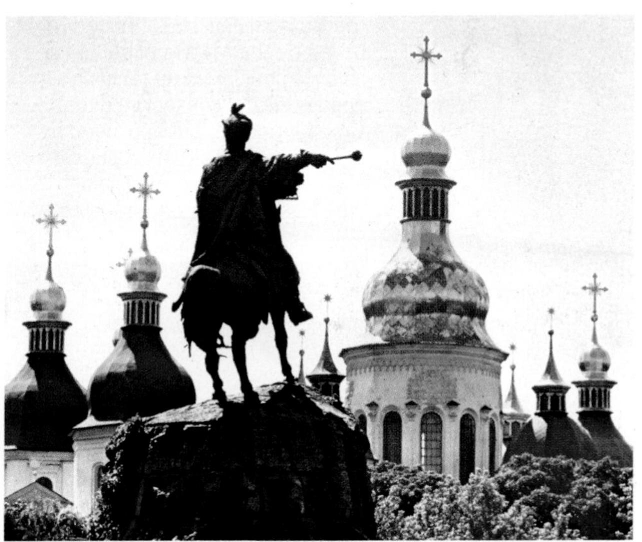

Saint Sophia cathedral Kiev—named after Saint Sophia, Constantinople.

a cathedral which he dedicated as St Sophia's in imitation of the mother church. For most of the next four hundred years, the head of the Russian church was a Greek appointed by the Patriarch of Constantinople.

Yaroslav's death coincided with the year traditionally regarded as marking the final rupture between the Latin and Greek churches (1054). The newly-converted Russians quickly learned to despise the Catholics as 'heretics'. Their hatred of the Latin Christians was greatly reinforced when German knights tried to take advantage of the chaos caused by the invasion of Russia by Genghis Khan's Mongol hordes in the thirteenth century and launched a Catholic Crusade against the northern Russians. The Western invaders were repulsed by the heroic leadership of Alexander Nevsky in 1242. He was later recognized as a saint for his achievements.

Nevsky established an important precedent for the Russians by submitting voluntarily to the rule of the Khan. For over two hundred years the Russians lived under the 'Mongol Yoke'. During this period, the Russian church continued to be led by the Metropolitan of Kiev and Vladimir, who was usually appointed and consecrated by Constantinople, but approved by the Khan. This situation goes a long way towards explaining why Russia never experienced a Renaissance and Reformation as western Europe did.

The Russian tradition

The period under the Mongol Yoke included the life of one of the greatest of Russian Christians, Sergius of Radonezh. In search of solitude, Sergius withdrew around 1350 into the forest about twenty-five miles north of Moscow where he soon became the elder of the monastic community of the Holy Trinity, which is now the headquarters of the Russian Orthodox church (*Zagorsk*). From the monastic tradition begun by Sergius, Russian spirituality began to penetrate in an unprecedented manner to the lower levels of Russian society.

At the same time, Sergius' monastery inspired the emergence of the Russian artistic

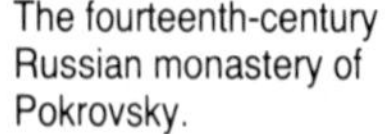

The fourteenth-century Russian monastery of Pokrovsky.

genius expressed in the creation of magnificent icons. The greatest icon painters, Andrei Rublev and Daniel Chorney, flourished in the years around 1400, decorating the churches in Sergius' Holy Trinity monastery, and in Moscow and the surrounding principalities. In their works distinctively Russian art forms appeared.

Sergius influenced Russian society in a third important way. He kindled the spirit of Russian national resistance to Mongol overlordship. In 1380 he inspired Dmitry, prince of Moscow, to lead a Russian allied army against the Khan's forces. Dmitry's troops won a significant battle on Kulikovo Field. Although the Mongol yoke was not immediately cast off, the prince of Moscow had demonstrated that the Mongols were not invincible, and the hope of final liberation smouldered in the Russian breast. It was amidst these events that Moscow rose to the leading position among Russian cities. Moscow's prestige was heightened by Dmitry's achievements, Sergius' reputation, and the transfer of the Russian Metropolitan to the city.

'The Third Rome'

By the second half of the fifteenth century, conditions were right for Moscow to emerge as the world's leading Orthodox city. Late in the fourteenth century, the Ottoman Turks occupied Bulgaria and Serbia, placing these Orthodox states under Islamic authority. In 1453, they captured Constantinople itself, killing the Byzantine emperor and making the Ecumenical Patriarch the virtual prisoner of the Muslim conquerors. Shortly after, Ivan III of Moscow married Sophia Paleologue, niece of the last emperor, and subsequently repudiated Mongol domination. Ivan took the Byzantine double-headed eagle as the symbol of his power.

Russian church theorists saw profound theological significance in these events. Moscow, they declared, had become 'The Third Rome'. They claimed that the church of Rome fell because of its heresy and was succeeded by Constantinople, the Second Rome. But this city, too, was punished by God by means of the infidel Turks. The monk Philotheus wrote to Ivan's son: 'The church of Moscow, the new 'third Rome', shines throughout the entire world more brightly than the sun . . . Two Romes have fallen, but the third stands and a fourth can never be.' The now thoroughly national Russian church thus claimed to be chief protector of Eastern Christianity.

Andrei Rublev was one of the greatest Russian icon-painters. This example represents the Trinity.

Persecution and Inquisition

Ronald Finucane

The exercise of choice (Latin, *haeresis*) in religious doctrine has posed a problem in Christianity since the days of the apostles; by the fifth century Augustine could list no fewer than eighty-eight different heresies. Yet throughout the early Middle Ages, heretics were mainly individual intellectuals or idiosyncratic rabble-rousers, and the response of the church was localized and sporadic. From the twelfth century, however, the problem of heresy became far more marked, and the reaction of the church correspondingly more rigorous. During the thirteenth century a strong papacy directed this response.

Dissident movements arise

During the twelfth century, whole areas of Europe began to show tendencies either to purify (for example, the Waldensians), or to provide alternatives to (for example, the Cathars), the established church. Both of these movements were persecuted by lay rulers as well as diocesan authorities. By the end of the twelfth century, the papacy had entered the battle against such disruptive groups. Pope Alexander III in 1162–63 suggested that lay and clerical

St Peter's, Rome.

nformers who brought reports of eretics should be supplemented y officials who went out to iscover evidence of heresy. He alled upon lay rulers to combat eresy, and in the Third Lateran ouncil of 1179 announced a rusade against the Cathars of rance. These efforts were not articularly effective.

His successor, Lucius III, ecreed in 1184 that bishops hould take action against her- tics such as the Cathars, Patari, Iumiliati, Waldensians and rnoldists. A special characteristic f this decree, establishing the ishops' inquisition, which was choed in a contemporary imperial dict, was that a suspect, once onvicted of being a heretic, was to e handed over to the secular arm or punishment. The death penalty vas not yet official, although medi- val heretics had been burned at he stake—often by mobs of lay eople—at least from the early leventh century.

Innocent III further defined and xtended the attitude of the papacy owards heresy. For example, nnocent was the first pope to talk bout heresy in terms of 'treason' 1199). By his time the Cathars ad spread widely in France and taly, and he found it difficult to ouse local bishops to stamp out heir dualistic doctrines. He sent istercians into the Midi region f France, with little success. He hen sent others, more devoted o preaching and exemplary living, ıcluding Dominic Guzman, whose ollowers—the Dominicans—were o become the foremost order of he Inquisition.

His successor, Pope Honorius I, allowed the Albigensian Cru- ade to intensify, assisted by the rench King Louis VIII, who in 226 issued an ordinance under vhich bishops would judge, and rench law punish, heretics. mperor Frederick II had issued a similar decree in 1220, and in 1224 he ordered the burning of heretics. When in 1231 another great pope, Gregory IX, in *Excommunicamus,* issued further decrees against heretics, he repeated this law of 1224. Execution by the secular authorities had finally and officially become papal policy. Under Gregory the Inquisition as a church institution was practically completed, and the new orders of friars, especially Dominicans, had become the favoured papal agents of the Inquisition. The finishing touches were supplied by Pope Innocent IV who, in the bull *Ad extirpanda* (1252), incorporated all earlier papal statements about the organization of the Inquisition, as well as condoning the use of torture.

What was the Inquisition?

The Inquisition was a special court with a peculiar power to judge intentions as well as actions. It was made up of several officials who assisted inquisitors in various ways: delegates—examiners who handled preliminary investigations and formalities; the *socius* —a personal adviser and companion to the inquisitor; familiars—guards, prison visitors and secret agents; and notaries, who carefully collected evidence and filed it efficiently for present and future instances of suspected heresy. Usually a few dozen councillors were present, but since the inquisitor was not bound to follow their advice, their role was often merely formal. The bishop, too, would be represented, even though there was not always co-operation between bishops and inquisitors.

As to classifying suspected heretics, the widest and most vague description would be applied in the first instance, and

THE CATHARS

John Clare

The church and the papacy were naturally alarmed by the rapid growth of the Cathars, a heretical sect. In 1208 Pope Innocent III launched a crusade against it in Southern France. The crusade was successful, destroying Cathar political power by 1250, and ruining the civilization of the area in the process. After the crusade, the Inquisition was established in 1231–33 to root out heresy by relentless persecution. However, the preaching of the newly-established friars was also effective in winning people from Catharism, and in Italy this was probably the chief cause of its disappearance in the late fourteenth century. The Cathars should in no sense be regarded as medieval Protestants, as writers have sometimes mistakenly suggested.

The Cathars (Greek *Katharoi,* 'Puritans') flourished in western Europe in the twelfth and thirteenth centuries and, like the earlier Manicheans, they believed in two gods, a good god who created the invisible spiritual world, and an evil god who created the visible material world. Matter, including the human body, was evil and was ruled by the evil god, whom the Cathars identified with the God of the Old Testament. He had, they claimed, imprisoned the human soul in its earthly body, and death merely caused the soul to migrate to another body, human or animal. Salvation could be attained only by breaking free from this miserable cycle, and Christ, the Son of the good God, had been sent by him to reveal to the human race the way of this salvation. Christ was a life-giving Spirit, whose earthly body was only an appearance.

The Cathars accepted the New Testament and various Christian teachings, but of course they rejected the incarnation and the sacraments since they completely separated spirit and matter. The one Cathar sacrament, which

Cathars were so strong around Albi in southern France that the French called them Albigensians. This night-time scene shows the cathedral and bishop's palace at Albi.

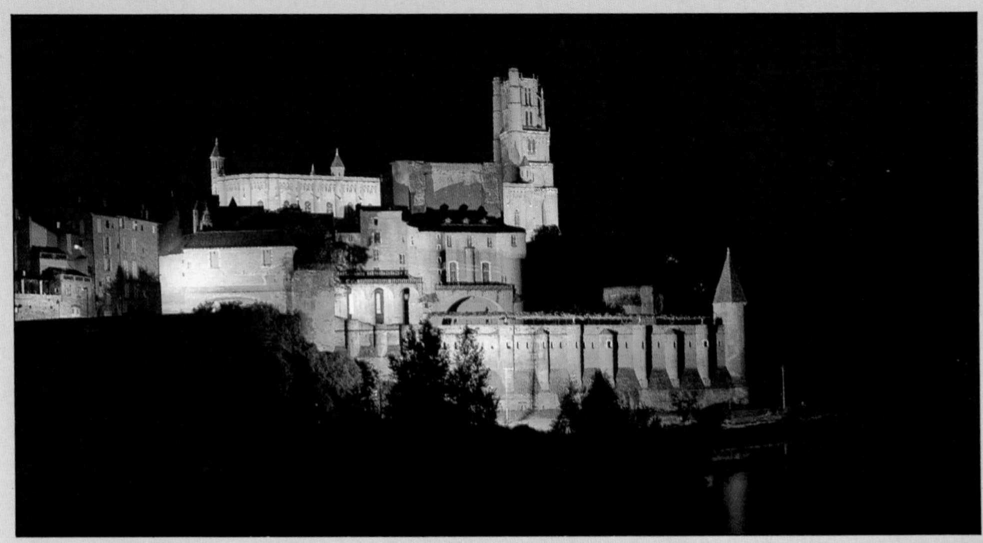

they believed enabled the soul to escape from the evil material world, was the *consolamentum,* or spiritual baptism, administered by the laying-on-of-hands. This they held was the baptism instituted by Christ, which gave to recipients the Holy Spirit, removed their original sin, and enabled them on death to enter the pure world of spirit and be united with the good God. The *consolamentum* had been handed down from the apostles by a succession of 'good men', but the church had perverted Christ's teachings and ordinances, and was enslaved by the evil god of matter.

The Cathars were divided into two classes, the Perfect, who had received the *consolamentum,* and the Believers, who had not. The former lived in strict poverty as ascetics, involving chastity, frequent fasts, vegetarianism and the renunciation of marriage and oaths. They received unquestioning obedience and great veneration from the Believers, as the Perfect alone could pray directly to God. Most Believers delayed receiving the *consolamentum* until they were in danger of death, as the rigour necessary among the Perfect was too much for them.

After 1100, and especially after 1140, Catharism spread through western Europe, gaining its greatest strength in northern Italy and southern France, where it developed an advanced organization. The French Cathars were called 'Albigensians', being most numerous in the district of Albi. The holiness and simplicity of the Perfect undoubtedly contrasted with the riches of the Catholic church and the corruptions of many of its clergy, and large numbers must have found that Catharism answered their spiritual needs in a way that Catholicism did not. By 1200 it seemed possible that southern France might become entirely Cathar, as the Cathars were protected by the sophisticated and anti-clerical merchants and nobles, notably the Count of Toulouse. It was this threat that provoked Innocent's crusade.

The massive cathedral dominates the town of Albi today.

eventually specialized phrases came to be used. Distinctions were made between heretics who had additional beliefs and those who denied orthodox beliefs, and between perfected and imperfect heretics; or again, since mere suspicion was sufficient cause to be summoned, individuals were classified as lightly suspect, vehemently suspect, or violently suspect. The web was carefully woven, and it was often simpler to confess than to try to defend oneself.

The inquisitor or his vicar would arrive suddenly, deliver a sermon to the townspeople calling for reports of anyone suspected of heresy, and for all who felt heresy within themselves to come forth and confess, within a period of grace. This was the 'general inquisition'. When the period of grace expired, the 'special inquisition' began, with a summons to suspected heretics who were detained until trial.

At this trial the inquisitor had complete control as judge, prosecutor and jury. The proceedings were not public, evidence from two witnesses was sufficient, and it was usually possible to learn only the general nature of the charges. The names of witnesses, who might be of most questionable character, were equally difficult to discover. The suspect was not allowed a defence lawyer or, rather, lawyers quickly discovered that defence of a suspected heretic might result in their own summons to the Holy tribunal. Certain pleas might be accepted as an alternative to admitting the charges; for example, ignorance, or that the charge was brought by malice—but since the suspect did not know the names of his accusers, he could at best merely provide the court with a list of individuals whom he suspected of such hatred towards him. Trials might continue for years, during which the suspect could languish in prison. Torture was a most effective means to secure repentance. Though it could not be *repeated*, torture cou be *continued*, and though torture of children and old people had to be relatively light, only pregnant women were exempt—until after delivery.

'Penance' following confession might be light, such as the hearin of a number of masses or, more commonly, pilgrimage to specific local or distant shrines, where scourging might be prescribed. Confessed heretics were sometimes forced to wear symbols denoting their fallen state, such as crosses of special design and colour. Penitents might instead (in addition) be fined or have their property confiscated. In some countries, heirs who were not heretics might subsequently recover these lands. A sentence to the inquisitorial prison was among th heaviest of penances, and degree of detention were specified as op or strict. Besides loss of liberty heretics suffered civil 'death', and were disqualified from holding office or making legal contracts. I many cases sentences could be c for a price. But the papacy found this and many of the other penances too harsh or extortionate, and at times particular inquisitors were directed to cool their ardou

For a final group of heretics, the 'unreconciled'—classified as insubordinate, impenitent, or relapsed—a much more terrible fate was in store. The first two categories could still save themselves from the flames, to suffer less severe punishment. But for the last, especially after the midd of the thirteenth century, the onl possibility was death at the stake This the Inquisition entrusted to the secular authorities, which pronounced and carried out the sentence, since the church could not shed blood.

Did the Inquisition succeed?

The success of the Inquisition varied from one region to another, depending upon political relations with the papacy and the amount of co-operation given by local church dignitaries. Its influence was affected by events such as the Avignon 'Captivity' and the papal Schism. In Spain the Inquisition had come under secular control as early as 1230, but it was not until 1480 that the Catholic monarchs Ferdinand and Isabella made the Spanish Inquisition a royal instrument with its centre at Madrid. This near-independence in Spain produced a unique institution which was very influential until the nineteenth century.

In Germany, papal and imperial feuds meant that the course of the Inquisition never ran smoothly. Conrad of Marburg is perhaps the best-known of thirteenth-century inquisitors; his reign of terror resulted in his murder. In the middle of the fourteenth century further attempts to enforce inquisitorial procedure in Germany met with little success, and by the end of the fifteenth century the papacy allowed German church dignitaries to oversee the Inquisition.

France was the scene of

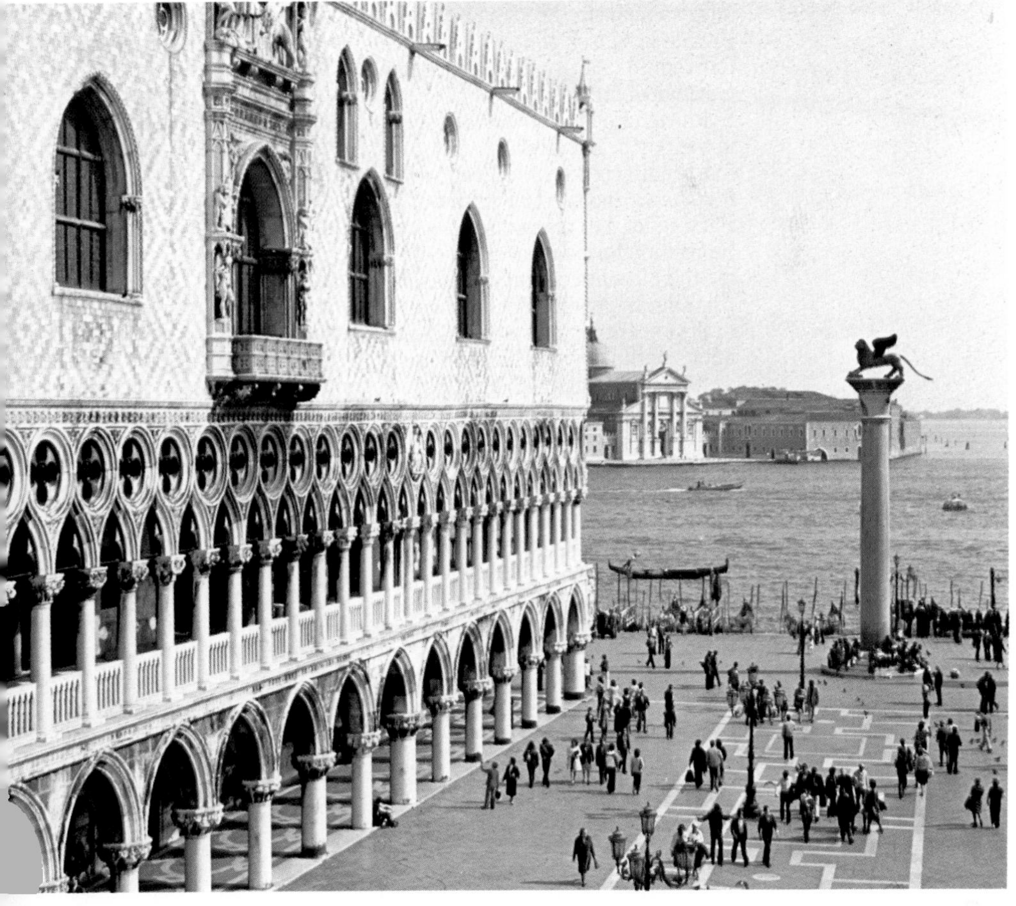

The city-state of Venice controlled much of the Mediterranean in the late Middle Ages.

extensive activity by the Inquisition. Though the Cathars were of little importance after the mid-fourteenth century, constant demands were made upon the Inquisition. For example, after the condemnation of the Franciscan Spirituals in 1317, the Inquisition in Languedoc directed its energies against them and in 1318 four Spirituals were executed at Marseilles. The Beguines, too, came under attack and some were executed about 1320; but the Waldensians proved more elusive.

Northern France, too, saw some inquisitorial activity. The Inquisitor Robert le Bougre, active during the 1230s, was imprisoned by the pope for an excess of zeal after rampaging through northern France in search of heretics. In the fourteenth century the Flemish-German doctrines of the Free Spirit resulted in some executions in the north, but after the mid-fourteenth century the French *Parlement* and the University of Paris tended to manipulate the Inquisition for political ends. During the fifteenth century, pressure from the Inquisition declined generally except for sporadic condemnations of those with Hussite views.

Italy, too, had much business for the Inquisition, particularly against the Cathars who were strong in the north. After the assassination of the Inquisitor Peter Martyr in 1252, the Dominican inquisitors in Lombardy were increased from four to eight. There was much local resistance to this papal institution in those states which had a tradition of political independence. Venice especially resented the intrusion of the Inquisition, and heresy remained a matter for the civil government of that powerful city-state. In the Papal States themselves, inquisitors found that any enemy of the pope was automatically suspected of heresy, but, on the other hand, in the Alps the Waldensians managed to survive through the fourteenth and fifteenth centuries in spite of harassment.

In two countries, England and Bohemia, the Inquisition made little impact. Heresy became a problem in England with Wyclif's doctrinal and the Lollard's political social movements of the fourteent and early fifteenth centuries. But the fact that Parliament passed a statute in 1401 for the burning of heretics indicates how little reference there was to the Inquisition. According to church law such a statute was superfluous. Though inquisitors entered Bohemia in 1318, little headway was made during the fourteenth and fifteentl centuries in the independent atmosphere before the Hussites. In both England and Bohemia the political situation clearly restricte the effectiveness of the Inquisitior

Inquisitors were not all agitated zealots such as Conrad of Marburg. Most were well-educated and devoted to what they considered their duty. Some of them produced treatises for the use of othe inquisitors. Of these, perhaps the best-known were by Bernard Gui, inquisitor in southern France in the early fourteenth century, and Nicholas Eymeric in Aragon in the later fourteenth century. With the publication of *Malleus Maleficarur (Hammer of Witches)* by Kramer and Sprenger in Germany in the late fifteenth century, in which sorcery became a terrible heresy and the main purpose of the inquisitor to detect and eradicate witchcraft, there arose a different and in some ways far more siniste world of persecution.

THE WALDENSIANS

Ronald Finucane

A wealthy merchant of Lyons, who came to be known as Peter Waldo or Valdes, experienced conversion about 1175 or 1176. He gave away his worldly goods and decided to follow the example of Christ by leading a simple life of poverty and preaching. He had translations made from the Latin New Testament into the vernacular, which formed the basis of his evangelism.

Similarly dedicated men and women rallied to him, and this ideal of illiterate lay folk living in simple poverty was given the approval of Pope Alexander III at the Third Lateran Council (1179). The pope added a condition, however, that they must first obtain the permission and supervision of local church authorities before engaging in preaching. The Waldensians spread the message of the Bible and exalted the virtues of poverty. By so doing they were a living condemnation of the wealth and laxity of the established church. Waldo's original aims were entirely orthodox.

When the Archbishop of Lyons prohibited their scriptural preaching around 1181, the Waldensians responded by preaching even more zealously. In taking upon themselves the role of the church, by expounding the Bible, they shared a trait common to many other medieval dissenters. By living lives of poverty they only emphasized the worldliness of many clergy. The 1181 condemnation was echoed in an excommunication of 1184 at Verona, this time by Pope Lucius III, who also directed that the Waldensians and other similar groups should be eliminated by episcopal inquisition and secular punishment. In not much more than a decade, what had begun as an enthusiastic popular movement had been branded as heresy. Before long Waldo himself faded from the picture, although the movement he founded went on increasing in membership and self-confidence, to survive both medieval and modern persecution.

The Waldensians fled from Lyons rather than submit. They started to organize the movement as a church with bishops, priests and deacons. Eventually they began to claim to be the 'true' church. They spread throughout two regions of Europe notorious for unorthodox beliefs, Lombardy and Provence. These were also regions of Cathar strength; their growth was something the reigning pope, the powerful Innocent III, would not allow.

Although some Waldensians were re-converted to the established church following a debate in 1207, and Innocent readily received them back and gave them his special protection, this success was not to be repeated. In 1214 he described the Waldensians as heretics and schismatics, and in 1215, at the great Fourth Lateran Council, Innocent III repeated the general denunciation of heretics, including Waldensians.

As for the Waldensians, such outbursts by the pope only tended to convince them that the Catholic church was the 'Whore of Babylon', and need not to be acknowledged. The Waldensians had expanded so far geographically and doctrinally, that in 1218 they called a general council at Bergamo (Italy) where certain doctrinal differences between the Waldensians of Lombardy and France were

> *"They go about in twos, barefoot, in woollen garments, owning nothing, holding all things in common like the apostles."*
>
> *The Waldensians appear in Rome in 1179*

discussed. By the end of the thirteenth century, though hounded by the newly-strengthened Inquisition, the Waldensians had infiltrated practically the whole of Europe except for Britain, and had become one of the most common and widespread persecuted movements.

The Charles Bridge and Powder Tower, Prague – a city where the Waldensians were subject to fierce persecution.

What Waldensians believed

The doctrines which distinguished the Waldensians and which the church considered heretical were—however simple in origin—many and varied; and some altered during the later Middle Ages. The greatest objection to the Waldensians, who began within the church, was that they ended by rejecting that church altogether. The unauthorized preaching of the Bible, and the rejection of the intermediary role of the clergy were the two fundamental issues which gained the Waldensians the description of heretics.

One of the most convenient sources of their doctrines is a treatise written about 1320 by Bernard Gui, a famous inquisitor of Southern France, at a time when the Waldensians were still among the strongest of dissident movements. Obviously, he writes as a critical outsider. Gui emphasized that the Waldensians rejected ecclesiastical authority, especially by their conviction that they were not subject to the pope or his decrees of excommunication. They rejected or re-interpreted for themselves all the Catholic sacraments except confession and absolution and the eucharist. In theory all Waldensian men or women could administer these sacraments, and the eucharist was usually held only once a year. There seems also to have been some kind of Waldensian baptism.

All Catholic feast-days, festivals and prayers were rejected as human creations and not based upon the New Testament. They made exceptions in the case of Sundays, the feast-day of Mary the mother of Christ, and the Lord's Prayer. Gui accused them of setting themselves up as an alternative church in which the 'priest' was simply the good individual, rather than someone in clerical orders. This seemed to him somewhat more serious than that other great Waldensian hallmark, missionary preaching in the local language with a strong New Testament emphasis.

Gui also noted the refusal on the part of Waldensians to take oaths, except under very special circumstances, since they said that the Bible prohibited this. The Waldensians denied purgatory, for which they could find no basis in the New Testament. This led them to reject the Catholic belief in the value of alms and prayers for the dead. For the Waldensians, if the dead were in hell they were beyond hope and, if in heaven, they had no need of prayer. Similar reasoning led them to reject as well prayers to images of the saints.

As to organization, Gui found the Waldensians to be divided into superiors and ordinary believers, a distinction similar to that found among the Cathars. The superiors were expected to lead more austere lives, to depend on the alms of their followers, and to evangelize as ceaselessly wandering preachers in the tradition of the apostles.

The points noted by Inquisitor Gui in the fourteenth century were again and again brought out by other later inquisitors well into the fifteenth century, with certain features apparently becoming more radical. For example, by 1398 the Waldensians were accused of rejecting the entire physical paraphernalia traditionally associated with the church: buildings themselves, cemeteries, altars, holy water, liturgies, pilgrimages, indulgences—all were deemed unnecessary. The trend towards radicalism also appears in their rejection of all 'saints' not named in the New Testament. The Waldensians meanwhile elaborated their organization. The Waldensian 'clergy' continued to devote themselves to the single distinctive feature of preaching in the local dialect.

Where Waldensians prospered

Although the Waldensians spread throughout Europe, they had greater influence in some regions than in others. They were strongest in central and eastern Europe. Waldensian beliefs themselves were sometimes influenced by contact with other dissident movements. In southern France, for example, the inquisitors often discovered that Cathar rejection of the created world was combined with the traditional Waldensian rejection of the established church. French Waldensians continued to be harassed to the end of the Middle Ages. This culminated in a crusade against them in 1488 in the Dauphiné. In Italy they likewise continued to hold out against the Inquisition, taking refuge especially in Piedmont, where they were also attacked in 1488.

In their main region, central and eastern Europe, their work was later to influence the course of the Reformation. The inquisitors were active and—at least when papal-imperial politics allowed it—successful in seeking out Waldensians throughout these areas in the later Middle Ages. Peter Zwicker and Martin of Prague, for example, were the leading persecutors in Bohemia, Moravia, Brandenburg, Pomerania, and Austria in the decades round about 1400. Other regions of central and eastern Europe, including northern Germany, Poland and Hungary, were similarly scoured by inquisitors in the later fourteenth century.

During the fifteenth century, in spite of repeated campaigns against them, there was much coming and going of Waldensians in central Europe, and some interchange of ideas between the Bohemian Hussites, the English Wyclifites who were also to be found in this area, and the Waldensians. Though there were sporadic attempts to unite Hussites and Waldensians, these failed because of fundamental differences in doctrine. Nevertheless, such activity provided the charged atmosphere in which the great religious changes of the sixteenth century would occur, when many Waldensian beliefs entered the mainstream of the Protestant movement.

AN AGE OF UNREST

Ronald Finucane

Many important changes affected European society in the later Middle Ages. During the fourteenth and fifteenth centuries new economic and political conditions altered the outlines of medieval society. There was a decline in the importance of landed wealth; agriculture became less profitable for many reasons. The fourteenth-century decline in population was made far worse by the Black Death of 1348–49 and by later epidemics. Towards the end of the Middle Ages growth in commerce tended to draw more workers into towns and ports, where a new set of economic principles guided human relationships. The older, traditional medieval social patterns were beginning to dissolve.

Politically, this was an age of growing community self-consciousness. It is too early to speak of 'nations'; but, more and more, men were getting used to considering themselves 'English' or 'French' whenever their thoughts went beyond their own town or region. Monarchs were growing efficient in the business of governing. This in itself helped their subjects to see themselves as belonging to a wider political 'state'.

In every century of the Middle Ages, from about 400 to about 1500, the church was a dominant element in society. Just as there were changes in later medieval society, so too there were many important changes in the church in the years between 1300 and 1500. These changes tended to bring disunity and unrest, pointing to the Reformation. Such changes involved the papacy itself, monasticism, lay people's faith and heresy and missions.

The thirteenth century closed with the election and unheard-of abdication of Pope Celestine V in 1294. His resignation posed problems for his successors. It could always be argued that no pope had the right to give up his office. This threw the first pope of the fourteenth century, Boniface VIII (1294–1303), under a cloud of uncertainty and foreboding.

A political pope

Boniface was quite different from Celestine, who was a feeble ascetic. Boniface, a canon-lawyer with wide experience, set to work immediately, reforming papal finances and bringing peace to the Papal States and Rome. His programme brought him into conflict with the crowned heads of Europe. For example, his bull *Clericis laicos* (1296) limited the power of kings to tax their clergy. In retaliation France prohibited the export of bullion and in England King Edward I threatened to remove royal protection from the clergy. At the very beginning of the period, papal and royal policies came into conflict. These unseemly squabbles recurred again and again until the end of the Middle Ages.

Boniface later modified his views, though the French found his leniency too grudging. They put pressure on him by supporting an Italian family, the Colonna, who were his greatest rivals. This escalated until Boniface agreed to disregard *Clericis laicos* and to give in to other French demands, including the canonization of King Louis IX, in 1297.

The pope won a victory of sorts by announcing a plenary indulgence (ensuring immediate entry into heaven after death) for pilgrims to Rome in the Jubilee Year of 1300. This enhanced his prestige at least for the moment. By 1301 he was again in difficulties with the French. A bishop had been arrested in France and charged with treason. The pope demanded his release, which was refused. Boniface reactivated *Clericis laicos,* and issued another bull—*Ausculta fili* —emphasizing the pope's superiority over secular rulers. In reply, the French King Philip IV stirred up public opinion against the pope. Boniface answered with yet another bull, *Unam sanctam,* in 1302, summing up extreme papal claims. Finally, the French took direct action. Nogaret, the king's agent, went to Italy to bring back the pope. The issues were to be heard in France, and the pope's fate decided. Meanwhile Boniface excommunicated the French king. Finally, in September 1303, Nogaret with help from the Colonna family, attacked the pope at Anagni. With the aid of the townsfolk Boniface escaped to Rome. He died at the Vatican a month later.

The problems arising between Boniface and the French have tended to overshadow all other aspects of this pope's reign. Though he was arrogant and guilty of nepotism, he had less unfortunate traits. He added to canon law in the *Liber Sextus,* arranged more efficient papal administration, helped establish a university in Rome, and laid the foundations for an effective archives department. He even took an interest in the current battle between the friars and non-monastic clergy. In the end, however, his pontificate was ominous for the future, a future very much involved in secular politics.

When Boniface died, the French were still determined to exert pressure on the papacy to bring it into line. The new French monarchical state was prospering under the astute control of Philip the Fair (Philip IV). Much pressure was exerted on the College of Cardinals to elect a docile pope. In 1303 Benedict XI was elected, but his rather weak policy of conciliation had no time to develop before he died in 1304. By the time of the next election, the cardinals were split into a pro- and an anti-French faction.

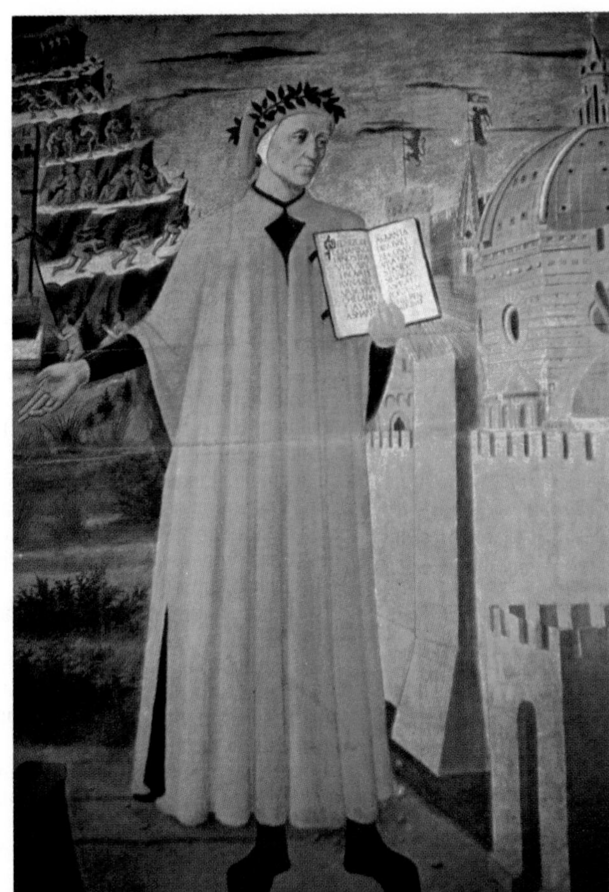

Dante Alighieri (1265–1321), the Italian poet, creator of one of the world's great classics, *The Divine Comedy*. This book consists of three parts: The inferno, The Purgatory and The Paradise. It is a Christian allegory about the soul's vision of sin, its cleansing from guilt, and its rising in newness of life.

The pope moves to Avignon

Eventually, by 1305, the Archbishop of Bordeaux was elected pope as a result of French pressure. He took the name of Clement V (1305–14). Clement, from Gascony in south-west France, never went to Rome. This was partly because of his own unwillingness to leave his native country, partly because of pressure from the French king. Clement also created French cardinals to balance the earlier predominantly Italian element in the College of Cardinals. Finally, the pope fixed on Avignon in southern France as his residence though he continued to travel widely throughout Philip the Fair's kingdom.

The papal palace at Avignon, France, residence of the popes in the fourteenth century.

Hence, Clement V became the first Avignon pope; the first to live under what was known as the 'Avignon Captivity'. There were protest against this from all sides. Among the loudest was that of Petrarch (who died in 1374), one of the greatest figures of the Italian Renaissance. For most of the fourteenth century no pope lived in Rome. This divorce between the head of the Western Christian world and Rome itself caused great scandal and unrest in many circles. Clement V died in 1314, still wandering about his beloved Gascony.

Clement is remembered because of the Avignon papacy. He also approved the French plan to destroy the Order of the Knights of the Temple, or 'Templars'. This military crusading order came to an end while he was pope. Various charges, such as sacrilege, sodomy and idolatry, were hurled at the Templars, especially in France. Torture was used to obtain 'confessions'. Those working to destroy them were aiming partly to disendow this very wealthy and influential order. By the fourteenth century it had become practically a European banking corporation. England and other kingdoms, as well as France, went along with papal directives, though to a lesser degree. The property of the order passed to the Hospitallers, or occasionally to other organizations. In France, however, the greatest benefactor was the king. In France the destruction of the Templars included the execution of the Templar Grand Master, Jacques de Molay, and others, in 1314. It was yet another incident among many gradually bringing the papacy into disrepute.

The popes favour France

For the moment, however, the papacy at Avignon received a vigorous infusion of new blood in Pope John XXII (1316–34). He was one of the most efficient—and ruthless—of fourteenth-century popes. He was a decidedly French pope, but also independent to an unusual degree. John was well versed in papal and secular politics and took a great interest in the affairs of Europe from the papal headquarters at Avignon. Among his many schemes was a reform in papal administration. His other interests included a controversy with the Franciscan Spirituals, certain aspects of speculative theology, compiling sermons, and tireless devotion to reading and making summaries of what he had read.

John was among the greatest of papal financiers, very interested in discovering better ways to increased papal income. At the same time he wished to make his power felt throughout the Christian West. In a sense he was president of a giant corporation with varied financial and political interests. He saw the papacy in administrative far more than spiritual terms.

Pope Benedict XII (1334–42), who followed him, was a theologian, a Cistercian, and also a Frenchman. He was greatly interested in the ever-increasing problems of heresy. Benedict began the construction of the papal palace archives at Avignon, and saw to it that the papal archives still in Rome were sent to him in France. He worked in co-operation with the French king. From time to time he did what he could for France during the Hundred Years' War which began while he was pope. The pope wished to make his influence felt among the religious orders of the church; but they were not particularly enthusiastic. In addition, he saw to it that recognition of the pope's supreme power percolated more effectively through all other levels of church government.

His successor, Pope Clement VI (1342–52), also supported France against the English during the Hundred Years' War. He himself had been a French cardinal, once Archbishop of Rouen. Clement was experienced in affairs at the papal court. He now used his expertise to the utmost to provide revenue for the French. It was while he was pope that, in 1348, the city of Avignon was officially purchased by the papacy. Clement was a forerunner of the great Renaissance popes, lavish in expenditure on pomp and ceremony, and open in his support of members of his own family. His own personal life left much to be desired from the moral standpoint. Observers, though impressed by his magnificent court, were very aware of the vast amounts of money spent on such display.

This waste of money was discontinued by the next Avignon pope, Innocent VI (1352–62). He paid more attention to the reformation of abuses within the church, and to regaining papal control in Italy. Ever since the popes had left, and indeed before this, local Italian families and princes had created difficulties. With the pope far away in Avignon, these inter-family quarrels and battles for control of parts of Italy grew worse. Among the areas to suffer were the Papal States. In addition to the pope's wish to resume power over these areas, there was by now growing pressure on the popes to return to Rome. It seems that Innocent VI seriously attempted to do what he could to bring this about.

By now, too, the situation around Avignon itself was dangerous. Roving bands of mercenaries, a by-product of the Hundred Years' War, brought trouble to the very gates of the pope's residence. Great walls were built around Avignon in 1357, and are still impressive today. As part off his programme of protecting the Papal States and Rome, the pope sent Cardinal Albornoz to Italy. This very capable papal agent remained there thirteen years (1353–66), during which time he succeeded, at least temporarily, in re-organizing control. Albornoz succeeded in carrying out many of the pope's plans in preparation for a return to Rome. Before he could move from Avignon, however, the pope died. The move back to the Holy City would be left to his successor, Urban V (1362–70).

Return to Rome

Pope Urban V was a canon-lawyer who led a simple life and wanted to see reform in the church. He reduced expenditure on non-essentials. He wished for peace in Italy and hoped to be able to dismiss his mercenaries. He also planned to call a crusade, and to achieve union with the Greek Church. In 1367 Urban at last returned to Rome, where he successfully imposed his authority on the various factions. A great deal of the ancient city was restored. In spite of this encouraging beginning, the pope failed to achieve many of his political aims. In 1368 he fell back into the tradition of the Avignon popes by appointing several French cardinals. Finally, in 1370, he gave up and went back to Avignon, where he died in the same year.

Urbans's successor, Gregory XI (1370–78), realized it was necessary to return to Rome. After gaining the upper hand against Italian city-state factions he left Avignon in 1376, perhaps influenced by the mystic Catherine of Siena, who urged a return to Rome. He was in Italy by late 1376, and entered Rome itself early in 1377. Peace moves were made towards Florence and Milan, but before anything could come of these, Gregory died. The papacy had at last returned to the Eternal City.

In a sense that Avignon papacy marked an advance in papal affairs. It was during the fourteenth century that the papal court became more bureaucratic. A more centralized, effective, but more complicated papacy developed. A more expensive papacy, too. The papacy of the fourteenth century, a kind of international corporation, employed about five hundred people in the papal palace alone. On average, about a hundred honorary papal chaplains were created each year of the Avignon papacy. The French continued to dominate papal government. About 82 per cent of all cardinals created in the Avignon period were French, 13 per cent Italian, and 5 per cent other nationalities.

The papal machine

Papal government became more efficient, especially in financial matters. The *Camera Apostolica,* or financial and political office, was one of the most highly bureaucratic. Other officers, such as the Apostolic Chancery and Rota, also had numerous officials assigned to them. The archives increased with this growth of 'red tape'. For the popes from John XXII to Gregory XI over a quarte of a million 'business' documents remain in the archives, many still unexamined. New sources of income were developed to suppor this gigantic machine, such as special taxes (annates) from the clergy. The average annual incom under John XXII, a pope much concerned with financial matters, was about a quarter of a million gold florins. For Pope Gregory XI, it amounted to half a million. John's average running costs, however, were about the same as his income. Even so, he was able to leave a surplus of one million florins at his death.

The financial activities of the papacy were more often than anything else attacked by those wanting reform. But in the fourteenth century the growing costs of the papal courts, and of Italian wars, aroused more and more clamour for reform. The spiritual role of the papacy seemed forgotten in the mad rush to collect income in exchange for some privilege or favour. This increase papal interference was sometime objected to by other European powers. In 1351, for example, England made it illegal for the pop to give foreign clergy positions in the English church. In 1353, England limited appeals from her clergy to the papal court.

Even with the best organizatio in the world, however, the papac could not mend its own inner divi-ions. These were evident follow-ng the death of Pope Gregory XI n 1387. Now the papacy was back n Rome. Angry crowds gathered lemanding a Roman, or at least n Italian, pope. Eventually the ardinals went along with them y electing Urban VI (1378–89). Jrban soon proved to be too much f a dictator for the cardinals. Jsing the disorderly behaviour at is election as an excuse, some of he cardinals gathered and elected nother pope, Clement VII. The cardinals had become very ndependent-minded.

The papacy splits

After armed battles for control of Rome between the forces of the ival popes, Clement VII retired to Avignon in 1381. This marked the eginning of the Great Schism, a plit at the very top of the govern-nent of the church. It had political s well as religious repercussions. ome countries, such as Italy, the Empire, the eastern and Scandina-ian areas, Hungary and England, upported Urban VI of Rome. rance and its territories, Spain nd Scotland supported Clement 'II in Avignon. In the earlier medi-val period two and even three opes had occasionally co-existed. ut this Schism was far more seri-us. Unlike earlier schisms, the roblem originated within the papal ourt itself, among cardinals.

This division affected all levels f the clergy, although changes f allegiance from one pope to the ther were not unheard of. Non-ionastic clergy, cathedral and ollege chapters and even religious rders sometimes found their alle-iance split. Urban's stubbornness nade an easy solution impossible. was a very real stubbornness: he ad some of his unbending cardi-als tortured to death. Even after rban's death in 1389 the problem continued, with parallel elections continuing into the next century.

By now, the embarrassment of the situation was clear even to the king of France. He attempted to heal the Schism, even at the cost of abandoning the Avignon pope. Various solutions were suggested, of which the three most important were for one pope to give way to the other; for one to conquer the other; or for both to compromise.

The farcical situation continued in Rome when Innocent VII became pope from 1404 to 1406 and was succeeded by Gregory XII (1406–15), in spite of general protests from church leaders and theologians. Meanwhile the rival colleges of cardinals—one at Rome, the other at Avignon—be-gan to compromise and discuss ways of ending the Schism. Finally, since neither pope would agree to give way, some of their cardinals called a council to meet in Pisa in 1409. Here, it was hoped, the Schism would be ended.

The popes refused to attend. The cardinals deposed both of them and elected in their place Alexander V (1409–10). Neither the Avignon nor the Roman pope recognized this new choice, so the result of the council was the crea-tion of three popes, where there had been two. More significantly, the Council of Pisa raised an impor-tant principle by its actions: a council may be superior in power to a pope. This in effect called papal supremacy into question.

A busy council

The issues were not settled at Pisa. At the greatest council of the period, the Council of Constance (1414–18), it was hoped that they would be. Another pope now reigned—John XXIII who in 1410 had succeeded Alexander V. The Council attracted wide interest,

The nave of the great cathedral of Pisa, Italy.

and by 1415 scholars, church dignitaries and various secular officials had arrived. Even the Greek Orthodox sent representatives. Over the next three years some forty-five main sessions were held, with scores of lesser committee meetings. Eventually, after a trial in 1415, John XXIII was forced to give up his claim to the papacy. In the same year Gregory XII resigned, leaving but one pope, the Spanish Benedict XIII. He too was tried and deposed in 1417. He went on living in Spain under the delusion that he was the only true pope, until his death in 1422.

No council had accomplished so much in healing breaches within the church since the very early general councils. The way was clear to elect one pope who would once again represent all Western Christians. This was done in 1417 and the new pope was Martin V. The problem was raised, however as to whether the council which had created him was superior to the pope who claimed supremacy. For the moment the claim of the council lapsed.

Other problems considered at Constance included the administration of the eucharist. The Hussites, especially after the execution of Jan Hus at the Coun

JAN HUS

Caroline T. Marshall

Jan Hus (1374–1415) achieved fame as a martyr to the cause of church reform and Czech nationalism. Jan was ordained a priest in 1401, and spent much of his career teaching at the Charles University in Prague, and as preacher in the Bethlehem Chapel, close to the university.

In his writing and public preaching, Hus emphasized personal piety and purity of life. He was heavily indebted to the works of Wyclif. He stressed the role of Scripture as an authority in the church and consequently lifted preaching to an important status in church services. In the process he became a national hero. In his chief work, *On the Church*, he defined the church as the body of Christ, with Christ its only head. Although he defended the traditional authority of the clergy, he taught that only God can forgive sin.

Hus believed that neither popes nor cardinals could establish doctrine which was contrary to Scripture, nor should any Christian obey an order from them which was plainly wrong. He condemned the corruptness of the clergy and criticized his people for worshipping images, belief in false miracles, and undertaking ‘superstitious pilgrimages’. He criticized the church for withholding the cup of wine from the people during communion, and condemned the sale of indulgences.

Hus was at the centre of lengthy struggles in Prague, and his case was referred to Rome. In 1415 Hus attended the Council of Constance in order to defend his beliefs. Although he was travelling under the Emperor’s safe-conduct, he was tried and condemned to be burnt at the stake, without a real opportunity to explain his views. However, his heroic death aroused the national feelings of the Czech people, who established the Hussite church in Bohemia until the Hapsburgs conquered in 1620 and restored the Roman Catholic church. The Hussite reform was closely associated with the resistance of the Czechs to German domination.

ı 1415, held that all Christians hould receive both bread and vine. The Council prohibited it. Vyclif was condemned for heresy y the Council in 1415, and his ody disinterred from holy ground ı 1427.

Besides a few other issues, ıainly political, the Council initi-ted reforms. It was decreed in 417 and 1418 that further coun-ıls should be held. In addition, ertain changes should be made ı the College of Cardinals, in the ureaucracy of the papacy, and in buses of tithes and indulgences. 'he real issue, however, was apal power.

Martin V showed himself to be a pope of the 'old school' after his return to Rome in 1420, which he finally subdued in 1424. He started a renovation scheme in Rome. The Papal States were reorganized under his direction, and he made good use of his extensive blood-ties with the Colonna family. He was only interested in administrative reform; he let religious reform take second place.

Martin V died in 1431, having brought peace to the Papal States. He was succeeded by Eugene IV (1431–39). His tactlessness provoked discontent among the cardinals, who wished to regain

Glass-makers at work. Several processes in medieval glass-making are illustrated in this scene from fifteenth-century Bohemia (Czechoslovakia).

control of papal government. As a result of a decree issued by Martin V before his death, a council met at Basle in 1431. The new pope was not interested in attending. He ordered the Council to dissolve. This was disregarded by the assembled members. Most of the College of Cardinals favoured the Council, as a continuation of the spirit of Constance. One of the major issues at Basle was the question of union with the Greek church, officially separated from Rome since the eleventh century. From 1433 envoys were exchanged between the Council and Constantinople, but the pope too sent his own representatives to the East. The question of union was lost in the competition between pope and council for 'credit' in achieving the reunion.

The pope got the Council transferred to Ferrara. At Basle, reforms were difficult to carry through in the face of papal hostility. In Ferrara from 1438 the reassembled Council again dealt with the union of East and West. But little interest was shown by the Western powers, and the Council was again moved, to Florence, in 1439.

Ever since 1438, when the pope transferred the Council, a Basle contingent continued to sit. In effect, there were two rival councils, one at Basle, and another, first at Ferrara and then at Florence. Schism seemed about to return. The Basle Council deposed Eugene IV and elected Felix V (1439–49). Once again there were two popes. As to Eugene IV, his death in 1447 was followed by the election of Nicholas V (1447–55). The crisis ended only when, in 1449, largely because of political pressures, Felix V resigned. The Basle Council broke up and dispersed. Its end marks the end of counciliarism, the reform movement within a framework of church councils. Obviously reform would have to come from some other source. Meanwhile the papacy withdrew into itself, becoming an Italian power with Italian interest The age of the Renaissance pope began.

Humanists as popes

Pope Nicholas V set the tone for his successors. He was concerne with the architectural adornment of Rome, and with promoting humanism, especially the study c Greek. This aspect of scholarshi was prominent following the sack of Constantinople in 1453 and the flight of Byzantine refugees to th West. The Vatican Library was r organized and many manuscripts added. The ideal, but not the rea ity, of a crusade also attracted hi attention.

The next pope, Alfonso Borgia (Calixtus III), who died in 1458, actually engineered schemes leading to a crusade, and spent a great deal of money towards it. The results were hardly worth the effort. His successor, Pius II (1438–64), was one of the more interesting Renaissance figures i his own right. One of the greates of humanist church leaders, he w widely travelled and fully experienced in affairs of the Empire, papal court and councils. He too worked conscientiously for a crusade against the Turks, but agair this came to nothing. Pius left many writings, including an exte sive collection of memoirs, from which the lifestyle of a Renaissan pope can be reconstructed. His successor, Paul II (1464–71), wa not on friendly terms with the humanists. Paul was interested i lavish processions and pompous display, and in his own reputatio rather than that of the office and dignity of the pope.

With Sixtus IV (1471–84) the papacy is sometimes said to have eached a new low. Although e was the general of the ranciscans, Sixtus, when elected, cted in a most un-Franciscan nanner. He was guilty of the nost flagrant nepotism. Of the hirty-four cardinals he elevated, ix were his own nephews. He vas involved in political intrigues. or example, he interfered in the ffairs of Florence, even being nplicated in the assassination of wo de Medicis in 1478. As to the rusade, Sixtus at first expressed iterest in the venture, but was nable to draw together enough naterial support. This was true ven after the Turks landed on talian soil, in Apulia.

The infamous Borgias

he need for greater amounts of ioney, in the form of 'gifts', led further bureaucratization of ie papal court. Sixtus exploited ie sale of offices and peddling of idulgences. He required more ioney partly for his patronage f humanistic studies, art and rchitecture. He was a man of omplex motives and interests; iis was the pope who built ie Sistine chapel in Rome. He stablished a hospital for deserted hildren; he cancelled the decrees f the Council of Constance. He eorganized the Vatican Library; e condemned the excesses of ie Spanish Inquisition. Such was ie anxiety aroused by this high enaissance pope that there was ven talk of another general council to bring him under control. This ame to nothing.

Pope Alexander VI (1492–1503) as one of the most controversial f all the popes. He was Rodrigo orgia, the wily politician, rich, ell-connected and careless of iorals. Born in Spain about 1430, odrigo studied at Bologna and ioved on to become a cardinal and ien vice-chancellor in the papal court of his uncle, Calixtus III. The many children of Rodrigo, born before his election as pope (for example, Isabella, Jeronima, John and Peter, Geoffrey, Caesar and perhaps the best-remembered, Lucretia—born in 1480), were all well provided for from church revenues, both before and after their

The Renaissance cathedral at Florence was built in the fifteenth century. Part of its famous dome can be seen (far left) in the painting overleaf.

father became pope.

Alexander was a careful and efficient manager of the Papal States. He wished to avoid foreign intrigues and entanglements in Italy. In this he was not above using even Turkish help, for example against the French. In the midst of these political skirmishes the preacher Savonarola was executed at Florence because of his opposition to Borgia, and his friendship with the French, whom he saw as the hope of Italy.

The pope was called upon to act as mediator between Spain and Portugal, dividing the 'new world' between them. It is fitting that his reign, which closed the fifteenth century, should witness the discoveries which opened up a new chapter in world history, and in the history of the church.

The character of the papacy was changing during the later Middle Ages, as was the attitude of many Christians towards it. The Avignon episode and especially the Schism brought about popular estrangement from the popes. Eventually the idea of 'national churches' would emerge, opposed to a universal papal church. The papacy grew in wealth and complexity. The prestige of the office was lowered by its political involvement and increased bureaucracy. In addition, the important church councils challenged papal superiority. The tastes and morals of some fifteenth-century popes also left much to be desired. In the midst of all these cross-currents, certain problems continued to intrude. One of these was the split between the Western church and the Byzantine or Orthodox church centred on Constantinople.

SAVONAROLA

Robert G. Clouse

> *"At the carnival in Florence in 1496, Savonarola inspired the 'burning of the vanities' when the people made a great bonfire of cosmetics, false hair, pornographic books and gambling equipment."*

Girolamo Savonarola (1452–98) was an Italian preacher of reform who was executed for his activities. Born in Ferrara, Italy, he studied humanism and medicine, but renounced these pursuits to become a Dominican in 1474. He served in several north Italian cities and by 1491 was Prior of San Marco and a popular preacher in Florence. His sermons warned of a great judgement coming on the city, after which a golden age would arrive, when Florence would unite all Italy in a just commonwealth. These predictions seemed to be fulfilled when Charles VIII, king of France, invaded Italy and the Medici rulers of Florence fled.

Under the new government, Savonarola rose to a position of power through his preaching. He initiated tax reforms, aided the poor, reformed the courts, and changed the city from a lax, corrupt, pleasure-loving place into a virtual monastery. Having reformed Florence, he next denounced Pope Alexander VI and the corrupt papal court. The quarrel which followed resulted in his excommunication and the threat of an interdict against Florence. This frightened the people and led to his execution.

Savonarola became a hero to many of the early Protestants, even though he retained a Catholic theology. They saw in his opposition to the papacy a useful example for them to follow. His success came at the height of the Italian Renaissance; it demonstrates a deeply religious attitude among the people of that era which is often overlooked.

The West looks East

A special relationship had growth up in Constantinople between the Eastern Emperor and the Patriarch. Secular influence over the spiritual power was far more acceptable in the East than in the West. This meant, among other things, that political considerations more directly affected the attitudes of the Eastern church. This relationship, or 'Caesaro-papism', as it was called in the West, was not acceptable to the Western papacy. There were also complex theological differences between the two churches.

In addition, the whole cultural background in which each church followed Christian traditions was different. The Latin-speaking Western church had its own customs and history, and the Greek-speaking Eastern church similarly had a tradition of which it was proud. The rift between the two was not helped by the fourth Crusade, when the Western crusaders, transported by Venice

A great crowd attended the burning of Savonarola in the *Piazza della Signoria*, Florence. The artist has thinned it out to a few small groups.

and at the mercy of her sea-power, were diverted to Constantinople itself. They captured and looted the city in 1204. For much of the thirteenth century the power of the Greek Emperor was replaced by the so-called Latin Kingdom of Constantinople, under Western leadership. By 1261 the Greeks had retaken their capital city and ousted the uncouth Westerners. The thirteenth century, then, was hardly a promising era in which to improve relationships between the churches of East and West.

Clement V, the first Avignonese pope, renewed the call to crusaders to recapture Constantinople, but with little response. The French King Charles IV (1322–28) expressed some interest in the scheme, but nothing lasting came of this. Meanwhile a new development in the East was eventually to alter papal as well as Byzantine policy. This was the rise of the Ottoman Turks. By the middle of the fourteenth century these 'savage hordes' seemed to pose a real threat not only to the East but to the West too. United in fear, East and West began to grow closer together for mutual protection.

As early as 1339, faced with the Ottoman Turks, the Greeks expressed an interest in a union with the West. Under Emperor John VI (1347–54), several missions were sent to Avignon to test the attitude of the papacy. Eventually it was accepted that an ecumenical council would be the best way to go about considering the union of Greek Orthodox and Roman Catholic Christianity. Unfortunately the outbreak of the Western Schism after 1378, and subsequent rivalry between popes and councils, ruined these prospects. Competing popes and councils appealed to the Eastern Emperor for recognition. These were political moves, and in the process the real issues were brushed aside. The East's response varied. On the one hand the Byzantines had no wish to get disagreebly involved in Western religious politics. On the other hand the Ottomans were menacing them.

Finally, Emperor Manuel II Palaeologus (1391–1425) journeyed to the West to try to resolve the issues. His reception was mixed, even lukewarm, and promises of armed assistance were not encouraging. His efforts were, in the event, unnecessary since immediately disaster was averted in the East. The Ottoman threat was quelled by the rise of a new intervening force, Tamberlaine, in 1402. For the moment, the Ottoman scourge seemed tamed. It was still discussed in the West, but with little real concern. For example, though the Turkish threat was raised at the Council of Constance in 1415, it was quickly pushed aside as a secondary issue.

The papacy was once again battling for independence, at the councils of Basle and Ferrara-Florence. This led each side, council and pope, to appeal to the Eastern Emperor for political support. Each side worked towards union with the Greeks. Whichever side achieved this could thereby claim the greater glory and prestige. In 1439 the papacy scored the victory, and a decree of union was agreed upon. This news was not well received back in Constantinople itself. There was much popular resistance to a religious union with the West, whatever the political advantages might be. It was not until 1452 that the decree of union was officially published in Constantinople. This was too little, too late. In the very next year, 1453, Constantinople, the ancient capital of Byzantium ınd stronghold of Orthodox :hristianity, was captured ›y the Muslim Turks. The :onflict between Roman and ;reek Christianity was thus esolved.

;hould the Franciscans 'emain poor?

The dispute with the Greek)rthodox church was only one ımong many problems of the later nedieval papacy. Other conflicts vere internal. One concerned the 'ranciscan Order, founded in the ·arly thirteenth century with papal .pproval. The father of the order, 'rancis of Assisi, died in 1226. As ·arly as 1245 difficulties which lso involved the papacy had arisen vithin his organization of friars.

The question was, should the 'ranciscans be allowed to own ›roperty, or should they keep to he original ideal of poverty, as 'rancis had directed? Franciscans vho favoured poverty discovered justification in the writings of he mystic Joachim of Fiore (who lied in 1202). The other camp ound a champion in Pope Innocent V (1243–54). He declared that 'ranciscan property belonged to he church, and then allowed it to e re-allocated to the order. This vas obviously a mere technical voidance of the rule of poverty.

The split within the Franciscans videned. Another papal decree of 279, along much the same lines, lso failed to unite the order. By he end of the thirteenth century he Franciscans had divided into a ;roup of 'Spiritual' who supported he ideal of poverty, and one of Conventuals' who tried to find a ompromise solution. They wished ı theory to maintain the spirit of heir order but in practice to avoid he burdens of poverty. Although n agreement of sorts was reached ınder the early Avignon popes, or example at the Council of Vienne (1311–12), the Spirituals began to move to a radical position. Ultimately they wished to cut all links with the order as such. In 1317 John XXII ordered them to rejoin the other Franciscans. Some Spirituals who continued to refuse fell under the judgement of the Inquisition. Four Spirituals, or 'Fraticelli', were executed in 1318.

The controversy involved basic problems for the papacy. In general the Franciscans accepted that poverty was an ideal practised by Christ and the apostles. From this arose the idea that the church hierarchy should remain aloof from entanglements in the world. If extended to the papacy, this put in question the position of the pope as ruler of the princes of Christendom. In addition, the massive wealth of the church as a whole came under scrutiny.

Eventually Pope John XXII condemned the Franciscan doctrine of poverty in 1323. Some Franciscan leaders were excommunicated. This problem continued to trouble fifteenth-century popes. By then the Spirituals were known as 'Observants'. In effect they had become a separate order from the Conventuals, though in theory still under a single rule.

In 1517 the division was formally recognized. The Observants then constituted the larger party, the Conventuals the minor. It cannot be said that the conflict among the Franciscans, which began in the thirteenth century, was successfully resolved by the medieval papacy.

Critics of the papacy

This period witnessed the decline in prestige of the papacy. At the same time there was a rise in various dissident religious movements. Some Spirituals were burnt by the Inquisition, declaring clearly their discontent with the church. The

Francis of Assisi

> *"We ask God then of his supreme goodness to reform our church, as being entirely out of joint, to the perfectness of its first beginning."*
>
> The Lollard Conclusions, *1394*

JOHN WYCLIF

Tim Dowley

John Wyclif (about 1329–84) was a prominent English reformer of the later Middle Ages. He came from the north of England, and became a leading philosopher at Oxford University. He was invited to serve at court by John of Gaunt, who was acting a ruler at this time. Wyclif offended the church by backing the right of the government to seize the property of corrupt clergymen. His views were condemned by the pope in 1377, but Wyclif's influential friends protected him.

Wyclif pushed his anti-clerical views further, and began to attack some of the central doctrines of the medieval church. He opposed the doctrine of transubstantiation. He claimed rather that Christ was spiritually present in the eucharist. He held that the church consisted of God's chosen people, who did not need a priest to mediate with God for them.

The reformer was gradually deserted by his friends in high places, and the church authorities forced him and his followers out of Oxford. In 1382 Wyclif, a sick man, went to live at Lutterworth, in the Midlands, where he died in 1384.

Wyclif wrote many books, including a *Summa Theologica*. He initiated a new translation of the Latin *Vulgate* Bible into English (*The Wyclif Bible*).

A group of followers soon arose around Wyclif at Oxford. He attracted support by his energetic preaching and lecturing. His followers spread to Leicestershire, and became known as 'Lollards'—which may mean 'Mutterer' or 'mumbler'. By 1395 the Lollards had developed into an organized group, with their own ministers and popular support.

The Lollards stood for any for the ideas set out by Wyclif. They believed particularly that the main task of a priest was to preach, and that the Bible should be available to all in their own language. From the beginning of the fifteenth century, the Lollards were suppressed, particularly when their protest became linked with political unrest. But Lollardy continued to thrive in some parts of England, and prepared the way for the coming of Lutheranism in the next century.

Inquisition, however, had been active from the early thirteenth century. Waldensians were hunted down, though sheltered groups survived until after the Middle Ages. During the fourteenth century one particularly bizarre movement was the Flagellants, with their practice of whipping themselves. There were other lesser groups which fell outside the lines of orthodoxy, for example the Brothers of the Free Spirit. The Black Death of the mid-fourteenth century brought hysteria as well as havoc and death to most of Europe.

The two most troublesome movements were those initiated by Hus and by Wyclif, whose followers came to be called Lollards. By the end of the Middle Ages they had come to attack the very foundations of the medieval hierarchy, including the papacy itself.

The attack came not only in the sophisticated Latin writings of professional theologians. Much of the vernacular literature of the later medieval centuries reveals discontent with the condition of the church and papacy. Examples occur in anti-clerical asides of the writer Boccaccio, and the condemnation of church wealth by the English writer Langland. Certainly Geoffrey Chaucer shows no love for the materialism of the church in fourteenth century England. Everywhere more and more people began to question the basic tenets of the church. Society was changing, and the church was not changing with it. The critics attacked the hierarchy and its wealth, and the doctrine and dogma of the sacramental system as well. In the universities, an Aristotelian philosophical basic for Christian theology (scholasticism) had been developed by Aquinas in the thirteenth century. Now these assumptions were being questioned by such men as William of Ockham (about 1280–1349) and Duns Scotus (about 1266–1308) in England, and the Frenchmen Jean Buridan (who died in 1358) and Nicholas Oresme (who died in 1382).

The later Middle Ages show an obvious change in yet another

WYCLIF'S BIBLE

“These thingis Jesus spak; and whanne he hadde cast up hise eyen into hevene, he seide: ‘Fadir, the our cometh; clarifie thi sone, that thi sone clarifie thee; as thou hast yovun to hym power on ech fleische, that al thing that thou hast yovun to hym, he yyve to hem everlastynge liif. And this is everlastynge liif, that thei knowe thee very God aloone, and whom thou hast sent, Jesu Christ. Y have clarified thee on the erthe; Y have endid the werk that thou hast yovun to me to do. And now, Fadir, clarifie thou me as thisilf, with the clereness that Y hadde at thee bifor the world was maad. Y have schewid thi name to the men whiche thou hast yovun to me of the world; thei weren thine, and thou has yovun hem to me, and thei han kept thi word.’”

John 17: 1–6, from the second version of Wyclif's Bible, 1388

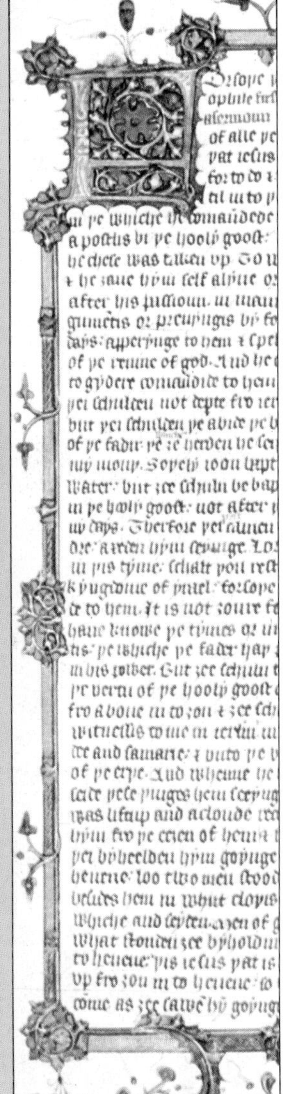

A page from *The Wyclif Bible*. This manuscript once belonged to the younger son of King Edward III of England.

The Earl of Warwick pictured with the chantry chapel he founded. His soul was to be remembered there in prayer by monks. On his left arm is a royal prince Warwick was responsible for educating. On his right arm is the chapel which was to house the Earl's tomb at Warwick.

sphere of Christian activity. During the eleventh and twelfth centuries the founding of monasteries was one of the more praiseworthy acts of piety among wealthy lords and ladies. But in the later medieval period this enthusiasm for foundation, reform and growth had died out. New houses of monks and nuns were seldom built. Endowments were less easy to obtain. Monasteries had fallen on evil times. For example, some were forced to sell room and board to private individuals and families. This meant in effect that some monasteries became a form of retirement home for those who could afford the fees. This was not the case everywhere. Some larger houses managed to carry on, so extensive were their lands. The smaller ones had the worst time of it, as changes in the agrarian economy and inflation lowered the value of their landed properties. Even before the end of the Middle Ages, smaller monasteries occasionally had to be closed down.

But people still wished to give towards establishing havens for holy men. Now, however, they would more often endow smaller places run by Augustinian canons, rather than Benedictine monks. The canons required a smaller endowment of land, worked in smaller groups, and seemed to contribute to the new town-dwelling society in which they settled. Canons worked in and with society; monks turned their backs on it, or so it appeared. Society was no longer tolerant of the exclusiveness of monks.

Another way the pious lay people tried to reassure themselves of their chances of salvation was by establishing private chantries. During the fourteenth and fifteenth centuries more and more of these chantries were endowed. The idea was simple enough: a wealthy individual or family, even a guild, provided a sum of money for a priest to sing a mass periodically and, in 'perpetual chantries', for ever, for the soul of the benefactor. Sometimes special chantry-altars were built—private chapels licensed by the local church authority. It was an easy way for poor priests to make a bit of money, and was one of the things the more conscientious reformers disliked.

Religion becomes more personal

Private chantries represent a break with the institutional, official and distant mediation on the part of the church. They satisfied the

WILLIAM OF OCKHAM

H. Dermot McDonald

William of Ockham was a thinker of first-rate importance. He was born around 1290, probably in the village of Ockham in Surrey, England, and died in Munich around 1349. After entering the Franciscan order he began theological study at Oxford around 1309, and completed the requirements for the status of Master with his lectures on Peter Lombard's *Book of Sentences* (about 1318–20).

Apparently denounced as heretic to Pope John XXII by the university's former chancellor, William was summoned to Avignon in 1324. While there, he was embroiled in a controversy about apostolic poverty, which made him more critical of the papacy. He called for a college of popes to rule the church, and claimed that Christ was the church's only head—teachings which looked forward to the conciliar movement. Ockham entirely rejected papal authority in secular matters. In 1328 he fled to the service of the Emperor, Louis of Bavaria, supporting him in his struggles with the papacy.

In philosophy, William elaborated a new form of Nominalist theory. He rejected the prevailing view that 'universals' really exist. He argued that they are simply artificial products of the human mind, necessary for communicating by means of language. Only individual or 'particular' things have real existence. William's Nominalism became known as the 'the modern way' (*via moderna*) over against 'the old way' (*via antiqua*) of Aquinas. Since knowledge was based on experience of individual things, natural science took a new significance.

In his many writings, William discussed with masterly logical skill the great themes of philosophy and theology. By the principle known as 'Ockham's razor' he insisted that 'What can be done with fewer (assumptions) is done in vain with more'; the mind should not multiply things without necessity. William made an elaborate criticism of philosophical proofs for the existence of God, although he himself had a strong, positive theology. He stressed that God was known by faith alone, not by reason or illumination, and that God's will was absolutely supreme. In these and other respects William of Ockham paved the way for Reformation theology.

One of the earliest surviving detailed maps of Britain. It was drawn about 1250 by Matthew Paris, a historian and monk at St Albans, Hertfordshire.

This extravagant object was made to contain a holy relic—a piece of 'holy thorn' claimed to come from the crown of thorns the soldiers placed on the head of Christ. It is enamelled with gold, and set with jewels. It was made for the Duke of Orleans in the late fourteenth century.

> *"Our Lord shewed me a little thing, the quantity of an hazel-nut, in the palm of my hand; and it was as round as a ball. I looked thereupon with the eye of my understanding, and thought, 'What may this be?' And it was answered generally thus: 'It is all that is made.' I marvelled how it might last, for methought it might suddenly have fallen to naught for littleness. And I was answered in my understanding: 'It lasteth and ever shall last for that God loveth it. And so All-thing hath Being by the love of God.'*
>
> *In this Little Thing I saw three properties. The first is that God made it, the second that God loveth it, the third that God keepeth it."*
>
> *JULIAN OF NORWICH,*
> *Revelations of Divine Love, V,*
> *late fourteenth century*

need for direct contact with one's own priest who said one's own mass for one's own soul. Religion had become more personal, more individual. Church art and the liturgy also suggested this. The suffering Christ replaced God the stern judge. The pitiful Virgin Mary was made more human. The cult of the Virgin became very popular in later medieval Christianity. Shrine after shrine was dedicated to her throughout Europe. The use of the rosary, the 'Hail, Mary', and feasts of the Virgin became increasingly common.

In art, the pierced and bleeding heart of Christ began to take its place more often among the other motifs. 'Miracles of the eucharist' became more frequent after the thirteenth century. Christ was worshipped in a way which replaced older saint-veneration: the 'monstrance' in which the eucharist was put on display was merely a newer-style saint's reliquary.

The standard of saintliness seems to have been changing. Joan of Arc was an ignorant peasant, unlike most of the saints revered earlier in the Middle Age Obviously, in her case, political considerations were important. The older approaches to popular religion still survived; for exampl the credulous belief in relics and i astounding miracles. Behind all th there was a profound swing away from an institutional, towards a personal, religion.

This change is even more clear documented in another area. The last two medieval centuries were noted for mysticism. This was perhaps the most personal form of expressed relationship betwee an individual and God to be found in medieval Christianity. If there was any philosophical basis to late mysticism, it was Neoplatonism. was occasionally non-intellectual, n the sense that the scholastic or Aristotelian view of the world was disregarded.

Mystics flourish

Mysticism continued to flourish. This tradition was strong in the Dominican order. Eckhart and Suso, for example, stimulated the mystical outpourings of John Nider (who died in 1438). In his entertaining book *Formicarius*, though, Nider proved himself to be as aware of the real world as of the mystical. Nicholas of Cusa (1401–64) was another well-known mystic; his empirical studies in science and languages produced a unique mystical vocabulary. Using Neoplatonic ideas to approach the Unknowable God, Cusa created similes based upon optics and mathematics. Germany was the foremost land of mysticism. Other regions also produced fine examples. Catherine of Siena (1374–80) as a well-known mystic from Italy. In England, an anonymous author contributed the *Cloud of Unknowing* to mystical literature. Richard Rolle (about 1293–1349), Walter Hilton (who died in 1396) and the late fourteenth-century Lady Julian of Norwich also wrote English mystical works.

Missions to Mongols and Muslims

Christianity was expanding to hitherto non-Christian parts of the world. The periods of greatest missionary activity in the Middle and Far East were the thirteenth and fourteenth centuries. The Franciscans and Dominicans were particularly concerned in these ventures. Francis himself went to Egypt in a fruitless effort to convert the Muslims. Further missions to North Africa followed, occasionally ending in martyrdom. Two sees, Fez and Morocco, were

Islam provided the great stimulus for the waves of Arab expansion. This is the Great Mosque, Mecca, today.

established, at least temporarily.

In addition, missionaries were also sent to central Asia. One of the motives behind this was to convert the Mongols and bring them into alliance with the Christians against the Muslims. An incidental effect of the movement was a new interest in oriental languages, which began to be studied in the West. Among the most important Franciscan and Dominican missionaries were Raymond Lull, Lawrence of Portugal, John of Plano Carpini, and William of Ruysbroeck.

> *"Missionaries will convert the world by preaching, but also through the shedding of tears and blood and with great labour, and through a bitter death."*
>
> *RAYMOND LULL*

Eventually the Franciscans established six mission fields or 'vicariates', three for the Mongols, one for North Africa, and two for Russia and south-east Europe. Pope John XXII also sent the Dominicans to govern other Eastern sees, for example, in southern India and Samarkand. Ultimately the attempt to convert the Mongols to Christianity failed. Muslim missionaries succeeded before the Christians. The Mongol Khan Uzbek (who died in 1340) was converted to Islam, and his 'Golden Horde' followed his example.

In the Far East, the thirteenth-century merchant family of the Polos was among the earliest messengers of the pope. The Franciscans followed up these preliminary steps. From 1289 John of Montecorvino worked in China, founding a see at Peking after he was created archbishop in 1307. Six suffragan or junior bishops were established in the area under his control.

Ultimately these missionary activities in the Middle and Far East, among the Mongols and the Chinese, declined and died out after the middle of the fourteenth century. This was probably partly because of the Black Death, which came into western Europe at this time. It disrupted both church and secular life. The failure was also due to the growth of Islamic influence among the Mongol people, and the confusion following Tamberlaine's rise to power. In China itself, a change to the new Ming dynasty in 1368 brought anti-Christian powers to the fore. These spelled the virtual end of eastward expansion for Christianity, and of Christian missionary activities, for some centuries.

During the fifteenth century in Portugal, at the other extremity of Europe, a strong royal house came to power, with an interest in overseas exploration. Under Prince Henry 'The Navigator' (who died in 1460), Portuguese ships nosed south along the west coast of Africa in search of commerce and converts. At the end of the Middle Ages, Catholic Christianity had retreated in the Orient. Now a new field of mission was about to open up. It was to be the Portuguese and the Spaniards who would take their religion and their missionaries to the newly found lands of the west, to South and Central America, to Mexico, in one last great burst of missionary activity.

SECTION 5

REFORM 1500–1650

SEEDS OF RENEWAL

Philip McNair

The great religious revolution called the Reformation broke out in 1517, but it is necessary to go back at least one hundred years to understand what caused it. Although the seeds of renewal had been sown in prepared soil, the roots of abuse were very old and deep. Martin Luther reckoned that things began to go badly wrong with the Christian church in the eighth century. Today most Catholics and Protestants alike would say that several generations before Luther's protest against indulgences it was evident that there was something radically wrong with the Roman Catholic church.

How corrupt was the church?

It is difficult to form an objective picture of the corruption of the clergy in the century before the Reformation. By most accounts, negligence, ignorance, absentee-ism and sexual immortality were widespread among the clergy and taken for granted by lay people. But not every lurid contempo-rary description should be taken at its face value. Just as in the heat of a love-quarrel, a jealous husband might accuse his wife of unfaithfulness he could not prove, so some high-minded Catholics of the time may have painted a blacker portrait of their church than was warranted by the facts. Nor was later mud-slinging always as accurate as it pretended, for exaggeration is all too easy in depicting human sin, folly and weakness. But corruption is one thing, official sanction of corruptio is quite another. The heart of the rotten condition of the Catholic church lay in papal protection and promotion of abuses.

The political writer, Machiavelli said that the nearer one got to Rome the more corruption one found; and, in 1510, seven years before his public protest, Luther was shocked by what he saw when he visited the Holy City. But just as today it is vice that hits the headlines while virtue goes unsung, so in the pre-Reformation church the scandals tend to be remembered and the piety forgot-ten. No doubt there much hidden devotion in all ranks of society in the fifteenth century and pockets of piety even in Rome. There wer probably many parish priests, like Chaucer's 'poor parson of a town' who lived useful lives of dedicated godliness: but they did not make history.

Europe under threat

The period of the Reformation was rich in conflicting personal-ities, institutions and events, and involved factors other than church practice and abuse. The lives of ordinary people in the Catholic West who were contemporaries of Luther, Luther's father, grandfather and great grandfather were threatened by two major menaces from outside the Chris-tian church: the plague and the Turk. Both suddenly appeared on the scene about the middle of the fourteenth century, and both wer regarded by popular preachers as the scourge of God to punish he failings of Catholicism.

Bubonic plague first struck ¡urope in 1347 in an epidemic nown as the Black Death, which n three years killed about one hird of the inhabitants of the Catholic West. After that, it emained endemic for centuries, ausing many deaths from time to ime (in London, for example, in 1665). People lived in the shadow of this pestilence, and during the ifteenth century Europe could be lescribed as a death-orientated ociety.

The Muslim Ottoman Turks ecame a political threat when hey captured Gallipoli in 1354 nd began their advance into Europe. Throughout the fifteenth entury they continued their areer of conquest to the north nd west. The reign of their Sultan Mohammed II (1451–81), who lied two years before Luther was orn, saw spectacular territorial ains. Constantinople fell to him in 1453, Negroponte in 1470. In 1480 is forces even made a landing at Otranto on the heel of Italy.

All through Luther's lifetime nd beyond, the Turks were as eal a menace as the plague—indeed more real to coast-dwellers outh of Rome, for Turkish aiding-parties would pounce in he night from the sea and carry off retty girls for the Sultan's harem. The writer Tasso's sister was early abducted from Sorento. In Machiavelli's comedy *Mandragola*, vritten within months of Luther's rotest, a woman asks her confessor: 'Do you think the Turk will ome into Italy this year?' It was a vorry never far from the minds of hose living near the Mediterranean.

New lands, new nations

Europe (this title is itself a ifteenth-century concept) was neanwhile finding new outlets for expansion overseas by exploration. For this was the age of navigation and geological discoveries. Martin Luther was five years old when Bartholomeu Díaz rounded the Cape of Good Hope, nine years old when Columbus discovered America, and fifteen when Vasco da Gama opened up the sea-route to India. In fact, the voyages and exploits of Cabot, Cortés, Magellan and Pizarro all fell within the lifetime of Luther; practically every year some new horizon was disclosed.

At the same time, great political developments at home matched great geological discoveries abroad. This was the age of emerging national consciousness in Europe. The three most powerful western monarchies were all growing in confidence with greater royal authority in provincial life. In England the new monarchy dates from 1485, in France from 1491, and in Spain from 1492.

Jan Brueghel painted the wise men visiting the infant Jesus, using the setting of his own time and country—sixteenth-century Netherlands. He depicted with characteristic detail the costumes, buildings and feeling of that period.

But it was in the field of church politics that the conflict of the Reformation was joined, and the most powerful and pretentious contestant was the pope. When the fifteenth century began, there were two rival popes in the West, each seeking to undo the work of the other, and from 1409 there were three. This unhappy state in the leadership of the western church reflected a blight which affected the quality of Christian life at almost every level.

For all its ideals, piety and art, Catholicism differed from the church of the New Testament in doctrine, morals and administration. Most men and women of conscience realized this, and called with increasing urgency for 'reform in head and members'. Some—such as Jan Hus the Bohemian disciple of John Wyclif—would not wait for Rome to reform herself, but separated from the unity of the Roman Catholic church for the honour of Christ and his gospel.

The Renaissance

The words 'Renaissance' and 'humanist' have been used in referring to some of the fifteenth century popes. *Renaissance* is a term which nineteenth-century historians began to apply to the broad cultural change which cam over western Europe in the fifteenth and sixteenth centuries. It means *re-birth*, and it is used to describe the reviving of the values of classical Greek and Roman civilization in the arts, politics and habits of mind, which originated in Italy and spread ove most of western Europe. Meanwhile, many of the attitudes and institutions which are thought of as 'medieval' persisted througho this period even in centres of the new culture.

The Renaissance began with the revival of classical learning by scholars who have come to be called 'humanists'. A *humanist* was originally someone who taught Latin grammar, but the

In this bronze, Donatello (1386–1466) the sculptor from Florence, expresses the grief of the disciples over the death of Christ.

word later came to a mean a student of Latin and Greek who not only read classical writings but moulded his life on what he read. Thus humanists stand in contrast to the *schoolmen,* and *humanism* in contrast to *scholasticism.* But although Renaissance humanists read non-Christian authors, such as Cicero and Plato, they were not necessarily opposed to Christianity; in fact most of the early humanists professed faith in Christ. Only later, in the heyday of the classical revival, did many Renaissance thinkers reject or ignore Christianity to admire pagan virtues and practise pagan vices. For example, anyone reading *The Prince* by Niccolò Machiavelli (1469–1527)—written four years before Luther's protest—might be tempted to suppose that Christianity had never existed.

Back to the classics

The home of humanism was Italy, and the first known humanist was Lovato Lovati (1241–1309). He was a judge in Padua who introduced a new way of treating the Latin classics by attempting to imitate their spirit as well as their letter. Besides composing Latin verse and cultivating literary friendships, he discovered manuscripts of forgotten classics in the library of the Benedictine abbey of Pomposa, thus launching a search for the hidden treasures of antiquity which became one of the hallmarks of humanism.

The Italian with whom humanism came of age was Francesco Petrarca, or Petrarch (1304–74), whose writings have had an enormous effect on European literature. Petrarch was a sensitive writer and a Christian by conviction (his favourite reading was Augustine), who reacted against the Aristotelian form in which Christianity was presented by the medieval schoolmen. He was not a speculative thinker, and hated the logic-chopping of the schools, the sterility of medieval rhetoric and the 'barbarism' of scholastic Latin.

The importance of Petrarch in the history of the church is that he polarized Christian opinion between the old scholasticism and the new humanism, between authoritarian tradition and the cult of original texts. In the next two centuries both the Reformation and the Counter-Reformation occurred in the context of this polarization. Petrarch has been called 'the first modern man', and it is true that some of his activities and attitudes (such as climbing a mountain to enjoy the view from the top) are more typical of our own day than of his. But in fact he shared with his contemporaries many of the medieval prejudices and limitations. His Christian humanism agonized between Augustine and Cicero, yet the inheritance which he left for his successors was the ideal of a world of classical values recaptured and displayed within the context of a restored Christianity.

Apart from his friend and admirer, Giovanni Boccaccio (1313–75), a fellow-humanist who wrote voluminously in Latin and Italian (the *Decameron* is his masterpiece), Petrarch's immediate heir was Coluccio Salutati (1331–1406). This Tuscan notary was for more than thirty years chancellor of the Florence City Council, and in that office introduced classical eloquence into city correspondence. He continued the quest to find hidden manuscripts and subject them to critical examination, and was himself the author of Latin works modelled on the classics of antiquity. Two of his most eminent followers, Leonardo Bruni (1374–1444) and Poggio Bracciolini (1380–1459), left Florence and found jobs in the papal chancery at Rome, which,

Major cities of Renaissance Italy

after the election of Pope Martin V in 1417, became the most important centre of humanism in Italy.

The Conciliar Movement, which looked for the reform of the church by the calling of a general council, was inextricably bound up with the history of the Renaissance and the expansion of humanism. While attending the Council of Constance as a papal secretary, Poggio Bracciolini found time to explore the surrounding German and Swiss monasteries for classical texts, and his searches were richly rewarded. At St Gall and elsewhere he discovered invaluable works by Cicero, Lucretius, Quintilian, Statius, Vitruvius and other Latin authors. These were the most notable manuscript finds of the century.

The council which was transferred from Ferrara to Florence gave classical studies another stimulus since it was attended by several learned Greeks. Among them was Cardinal Bessarion (1395–1472), the leading collector of Greek manuscripts in the fifteenth century. For the cult of ancient Rome led to the cult of ancient Greece.

One of the foremost aims of Italian humanists was to read classical Greek literature in the original. The knowledge of Greek had never entirely died out in the West, but before the fifteenth century it was confined to a mere handful of scholars in any one generation. Petrarch owned a tex of Homer, but could not read it. Boccaccio tried to learn the language but made little headway. It was Salutati who most effectively championed the cause of Greek studies in Italy. Through his effor a professorship of Greek was created at Florence in 1396, and the post was filled the following year by Emanuel Chrysoloras (about 1350–1415), a distinguishe Byzantine scholar and a diplomat

One of the most important centres of the Renaissance was Florence. In the foreground of this view is the famous *Ponte Vecchio*, the bridge over the River Arno.

brought over from Constantinople. A succession of learned Greeks occupied the position until 1480, when an Italian humanist—Angelo Poliziano (1454–94)—was appointed. By that time Greek studies were firmly established in the West.

Greek is the language of the New Testament as well as of the classics. Inevitably the humanists extended their attention from texts of profane literature to the texts of sacred literature. The pioneer in this field was Lorenzo Valla (1405–57), a Roman who deserves to be called the father of modern biblical criticism. In 1444 he published a daring comparison between the Latin *Vulgate* translation and the Greek original in his *Annotations on the New Testament.*

For Valla everything was subjected to the same scholarly investigation. Jerome's *Vulgate* Bible was a text to be examined on the same principles of criticism as the *Annals* of Tacitus. Four years earlier he had proved from historical and linguistic evidence that the *Donation of Constantine* was a forgery. In another work he mocked the methods of scholasticism. By meticulous scholarship and comparison of text with text he undermined the medieval tradition which was based on authority. In many ways he foreshadowed Erasmus. His writings deeply influenced the German Reformers of the next century, and were especially prized by Luther.

Other humanists were meanwhile encouraging new development in education. For this was the age of the first humanist educators, such as Guarino Guarini of Verona (1374–1450), tutor of Lionello d'Este, and Vittorino da Feltre (1378–1446), the herald of modern educational practice. In 1423 at Mantua, where he tutored the children of Gianfrancesco Gonzaga, Vittorino founded the *Casa Gioiosa* (the 'Happy House'). This was a school dedicated to the ideal of 'a sound mind in a healthy body' (*mens sana in corpore sano*). Its curriculum included music, philosophy and physical training as well as the *Trivium and Quadrivium* of traditional medieval education. Like many other innovations of this time—such as the introduction of the clock in the home, and the table-fork—the reforms in the schooling of boys initiated by these humanist educators began to be imitated far and wide and heralded the modern world.

It has been well said that medieval thought means Aristotle, and Renaissance thought means Plato. The revival of Platonism in the West owes much to Petrarch, Chrysoloras and Bruni, but still more to the council of Florence. One of the Greeks who attended it was George Gemistos Pletho (about 1355–1452), whose life was devoted to the cult of Plato. He influenced Cosimo de' Medici (1389–1464), the banker who virtually ruled Florence. Cosimo in turn was able to encourage Marsilio Ficino (1433–99), the Italian philosopher by whose efforts the enthusiasm for Plato as a forerunner of Christ caught fire in Italy.

Ficino translated all Plato's known writings into Latin, a daunting enterprise begun in 1463 and completed in 1477. He also founded the Platonic Academy, which became the focus of the cultural life of Florence in the golden age of Lorenzo de' Medici (1449–92), called 'the Magnificent'. The most remarkable member of this Academy was Giovanni Pico della Mirandola (1463–94), who represents Renaissance thinking at its brilliant best. In his writings he sought to harmonize Plato with Aristotle, the Jewish mystic doctrines (Cabbala) with Christianity, and eloquently proclaimed the

"When I portrayed the Lord God as a child, you cast me in prison; if I now portray him as a man, you'll do me worse."

LEONARDO DA VINCI

dignity of men and women in the universe of God.

A new world of learning

Neoplatonism (as this revival of Platonic thought in the context of Christianity is known) invaded the art and poetry of Florence. Examples include the paintings of Sandro Botticelli (1444–1510) and the *Stanze* of the poet Poliziano. It also affected some of the Italian reformers of the sixteenth century, such as Bernardino Ochino of Siena (1487–1564), making Calvin and other Protestants suspicious of them.

Papal diplomacy and the Conciliar Movement gave many varied opportunities for social and intellectual exchange. It was not long before the Renaissance was exported from its country of origin and humanists began to multiply in France, Germany, Holland, Spain and England. The two leading French humanists were Jacques Lefèvre d'Étaples (1450–1536) and Guillaume Budé (1468–1540), whose exact and penetrating scholarship paved the way for the Reformation in their country. Of particular importance in Germany were Cardinal Nicholas of Cusa (about 1400–64), the foremost speculative thinker of his age and Johann Reuchlin (1455–1522), whose *Rudimenta linguae hebraicae* of 1506 established the study of Hebrew in the West.

From Holland came Erasmus, the greatest of all humanists. Spain produced the *Complutensian Polyglot* Bible, a unique humanist project promoted by Cardinal Francisco Ximénez of Cisneros (1436–1517) with contributions by scholars such as Elio Antonio de Nebrija (about 1444 to about 1522). In England the new learning flowered in such Christian humanists as John Colet (1467–1519), Dean of St Paul's, whose Oxford lectures on Paul's letters broke new ground. Sir Thomas More (about 1478–1535), the author of *Utopia,* was martyred for his Catholic constancy by Henry VIII

Whether by cause or effect, the fifteenth century also saw the foundation of more than two doze new universities in Europe, amon them those of Alcalá, Bordeaux, Louvain, St Andrews, Tübingen and Uppsala. (The University of Wittenberg, in which Luther taught, was opened in 1502.) In the wake of humanism came the founding or development of some of the greatest non-monastic libraries in western Europe, such as the Vatican in Rome, the Laurentian in Florence and the Bodleian in Oxford.

Gutenberg's revolutio

A completely new dimension in the history of books, scholarship and education opened up with the invention of printing—sometimes called Germany's chief contribution to the Renaissance. The art of printing from handcut wooden blocks was invented in Asia in about the fifth century AD, and the first known printed book was produced by this means in China in 868. But Europe had to wait until the middle of the fifteenth century for the art to be rediscovered and developed. About 1445 Johann Gutenberg (1400–68) began to pioneer with movable metal type at Mainz in Germany, and—significantly—the first complete book known to have been printed in the Christian world was the Bible (1456).

Until 1462 the new art remaine a closely guarded trade secret in Mainz but in that year the city was plundered and the printers dispersed. Within two decades the invention spread north, south east and west: printing-presses were set up in Rome in 1467, aris in 1470, Cracow in 1474 and Vestminster in 1476. By the time uther was born, in 1483, printing s well established throughout urope. It was the most momenous invention since the stirrup, nd a revolutionary step forward in echnology. Like the invention of unpowder (rediscovered at about he same time), the application of rinting to book-production held a remendous potential for good and vil in subsequent history.

The printing-press was imporant in the early spread of the eformation. The writings of the rst German reformers (Luther nd Melanchthon) reached comparatively wide public in rinted form within weeks, and vere soon read in Paris and Rome. t the height of the Reformation, n the last years of Luther's life, usy printers enabled the anonynous work *Beneficio di Christo* which more than any other book pread the doctrine of justification y faith in Italy) to sell 40,000 opies in Venice alone after its ublication there in 1543. But even efore the Reformation, printing ad helped to create a wider and nore critical reading-public than ad ever been known in the Chrisan world. It also met the new emand for reading material with vorks such as the religious satires f Erasmus, which were a big ommercial success. On hearing rumour that the Sorbonne was bout to condemn it, one Paris rinter rushed through an edition f 24,000 copies of Erasmus' *olloquies*. Thus printing helped repare the way for the Reformaion.

The modern way of erving God'

ven more important in preparing he way for the Reformation was he rise of a movement called the *Devotio Moderna* ('the modern way of serving God') in northern Europe. This was a spiritual revival within the Catholic church, which strongly emphasized both personal devotion and social involvement, especially in education. It began in the late fourteenth century. At the time when humanism was beginning to flower in Italy, seeds of spiritual renewal were germinating north of the Alps.

Their most industrious sower was Geert Groote (1340–84), a native of Deventer in Holland who had studied at Paris and taught at Cologne. He lived a life of self-indulgent luxury before being brought to repentance and commitment to Christ in 1374 (the year Petrarch died). The change in his life was total: from that time forward he devoted himself to

Johann Gutenberg developed printing into a mass-production industry. As a result more books were printed in a few decades than had been copied by hand in several previous centuries. This is the title page of a book of grammar printed about 1491.

practical piety in the service of God and man. He joined the Carthusians and spent three years in their monastery of Munnikhuizen. He left the order in 1379 to undertake a strenuous travelling mission in the diocese of Utrecht, preaching with deep effect on the townspeople in Flanders, Guelders and Holland. He had such an exalted view of Christian priesthood that he never advanced beyond the rank of deacon. At the same time, he wrote tracts against simony and the immorality of the clergy, and condemned prevailing clerical abuses so sharply that his licence to preach was revoked in 1383.

In the year of his conversion, Groote gathered a community of devout women in his house at Deventer to live the common life together without taking the vows of a convent. Religion, he said, is to love God and worship him, not the taking of special vows. Jan van Ruysbroeck (1293–1381), the aged Flemish mystic, and Florens Radewijns (about 1350–1400) an ordained priest with organizing genius who had studied at Prague were both associated with him.

Mathis Grünewald painted this anguished crucifixion for the altarpiece at Isenheim. It reflects the deep mystical devotion of such movements as the *Devotio Moderna*.

Later a community of men, both ay and clergy (mainly like-minded riends and followers of Groote) ormed around Radewijns in his)eventer house, and became nown as the 'Brethren of the Common Life'. It was a semi-nonastic group, observing the hreefold rule of poverty, chastity nd obedience, but bound by no ormal vow. Thus any member vas free to quit the brotherhood nd return to secular life if he so leased. The Brethren did not beg or alms like the mendicant friars, ut studied to be quiet, to do heir own business and work with heir own hands, according to the nstruction of the apostle Paul.

When Groote died of the plague, Radewijns took over the leadership f the *Devotio Moderna* move-nent, and in 1387 founded its most nfluential house at Windesheim, lear Zwolle, in Holland. Here the Brethren of the Common Life ecame Augustinian canons, and heir constitutions were approved y Pope Boniface IX in 1395. A ew years later they combined with ther houses in Holland to form the Congregation of Windesheim.

They dedicated themselves ot only to spiritual discipline and enouncing the world, but also to he whole process of education. They taught in the local schools nd founded schools of their wn. In order to support their ommunity they busied them-selves with every aspect of ook-production: writing, copy-ng manuscripts, binding and narketing volumes, and—with he advent of printing—operating heir own press. Windesheim and ts daughter-houses were soon nown as hives of pious industry. n time the movement set on foot y Groote gathered momentum nd spread. During the fifteenth entury the 'Windesheim Canons' set up communities in Germany nd Switzerland.

Deventer in the Netherlands, was a centre of the mystical movement of the fifteenth century. It was here that Geert Groote and his companions formed the 'Brethren of the Common Life'.

THE IMITATION OF CHRIST

“ On friendship with Jesus

What can the world offer you, without Jesus? To be without Jesus is hell most grievous; to be with Jesus is to know the sweetness of heaven. If Jesus is with you, no enemy can harm you. Whoever finds Jesus, finds a rich treasure, and a good above every good. He who loses Jesus loses much indeed, and more than the whole world. Poorest of all men is he who lives without Jesus, and richest of all is he who stands in favour with Jesus.

On death

Of what use to us is a long life, if we amend so little? Alas, a long life often adds to our sins rather than to our virtue! Would to God that we might spend a single day really well! Many recount the years since their conversion, but their lives show little sign of improvement. If it is dreadful to die, it is perhaps more dangerous to live long. Blessed is the man who keeps the hour of his death always in mind, and daily prepares himself to die.

On the true lovers of Jesus

Jesus has many who love his kingdom in heaven, but few who bear his cross. He has many who desire comfort, but few who desire suffering. He finds many to share his feast, but few his fasting. All desire to rejoice with him, but few are willing to suffer for his sake. Many follow Jesus to the breaking of bread, but few to the drinking of the cup of his passion. Many admire his miracles, but few follow him to the humiliation of his cross. Many love Jesus as long as no hardship touches them . . .

They who love Jesus for his own sake, and not for the sake of comfort for themselves, bless him in every trial and anguish of heart, no less than in the greatest joy. And were he never willing to bestow comfort on them, they would still always praise him and give him thanks.

A prayer

Grant me, Lord, to know all that I should know, to love what I should love, to esteem what most pleases you, and to reject all that is evil in your sight. Let me not judge superficially by what I see, nor be influenced by what I hear from ignorant men, but with true judgement to discern between things spiritual and material, and to seek your will and good pleasure at all times and above all else. ”

THOMAS À KEMPIS

Many of the Brethren of the ;ommon Life and those educated y them left their mark on the ;hristian world. The foremost of hese were Nicholas of Cusa and ;rasmus himself. Gabriel Biel about 1420–95), the philosopher nown as 'the last German school-nan', and the humanist Rudolf gricola (1444–85) were both nembers of the community, for he finest elements of scholasti-ism and humanism co-existed in he *Devotio Moderna.*

Second only to the Bible

'erhaps the individual who best ums up the faith of the *Devotio Moderna* is Thomas Haemerken about 1380–1471), better known s Thomas à Kempis, the author f the *Imitation of Christ,* the hoicest devotional handbook of he Middle Ages. From the age f twelve, when he attended the hapter school at Deventer and ame under the spiritual guidance f Radewijns, to the end of his long fe, Thomas à Kempis was wholly nmersed in the movement begun y Groote. In 1406 he became an ugustinian canon in the daughter-ouse of St Agnietenberg, near ;wolle, which he had entered 1 1399 and where—apart from hree years—he remained until e died. He wrote books, copied nanuscripts, preached Christ and ounselled others. His life and orks reveal the fine flower of he spirituality of the late medieval hurch.

The *Imitation of Christ* is ritten in Latin and divided into our parts: the first contains Some thoughts to help with the piritual life'; the second 'Some dvice on the inner life'; the third nd longest provides 'Spiritual omfort'; and the fourth is 'A everent recommendation to holy ommunion'. As its title suggests, ne purpose of the book is to teach the Christian the way of perfection through following Christ's example. It began to circulate anonymously in the second quarter of the fifteenth century, and within a few decades it was read and loved throughout western Europe. Since it was first printed at Augsburg in 1471 it has appeared in thousands of editions, and is one of the most widely read books in the world.

If this handbook of the *Devotio Moderna* has influenced the lives of millions, the reasons is not far to seek: it is searching, scriptural and utterly centred on Christ. Indeed it is not until the fourth section that the reader is reminded of the sacrament-based Catholicism from which it sprang. Although it teaches justification by works, the *Imitation* focuses the mind and heart on Jesus Christ:

'If a man knows what it is to love Jesus, and to disregard himself for the sake of Jesus, then he is really blessed. We have to abandon all we love for the one we love, for Jesus wants us to love him only above all other things. The love of creatures is fickle and unreliable, but the love of Jesus is trustworthy and enduring. The man who clings to created things will fall with them when they fall, but a man who embraces Jesus will be upheld for ever. It is Jesus whom you must love and keep to be your friend; when all else fades away, he will not leave you, nor let you perish at the end. Whether you will or no, you must one day leave everything behind. Keep yourself close to Jesus in life as well as death; com-mit yourself to his faithfulness, for he only can help you when every-thing else will fail.'

The *Devotio Moderna* condi-tioned many hearts and minds in northern Europe to receive the teaching of the Reformers. No great revolution, such as the Protestant Reformation,

True wisdom

"*For though thou didst know the whole Bible by heart and by sayings of the philosophers, what doth it profit thee with-out the love of God? . . . Surely a humble hus-bandman that serveth God is better than a proud philosopher who, neglecting himself, labours to understand the movements of the heavens.*"

THOMAS À KEMPIS

happens without rumblings and warnings. Luther had his heralds and prophets: before him came many lesser Luthers. Four of them deserve mention because their writings either anticipated the Reformer or helped form his views.

Meister Eckhart (1260–1327) was a German Dominican mystic whose teaching was condemned by the pope after his death. He is now recognized as the most dynamic force in the religious life of Germany before the Reformation.

His pupil, Johann Tauler (about 1300–61), also a German Dominican mystic, was a powerful preacher who stressed human nothingness in the presence of God: his sermons helped to moul Luther's thinking at a critical stag in his spiritual experience.

John of Wesel (about 1400–81) from the Rhineland, foreshadowe the German Reformers in much of his teaching. He rejected many of the distinctive doctrines and practices of the medieval Catholi church, and declared that the Bib alone is the ultimate authority in matters of faith. He wrote agains indulgences in 1475, was tried by the Inquisition in 1479 and condemned to lifetime's confinement

IMAGO · ERASMI · ROTERODA
MI · AB · ALBERTO · DVRERO · AD
VIVAM · EFFIGIEM · DELINIATA ·
ΤΗΝ · ΚΡΕΙΤΤΩ · ΤΑ · ΣΥΓΓΡΑΜ
ΜΑΤΑ · ΔΕΙΞΕΙ
· MDXXVI ·
AD

The famous fifteenth-century scholar, Erasmus of Rotterdam, drawn by the great artist Albrecht Dürer. Erasmus, who published the first printed edition of the Greek New Testament, is shown characteristically at work with pen and paper, surrounded by books.

ı the Augustinian monastery at 1ainz.

Wessel Gansfort (1419–89), a)utch theologian educated by the Brethren of the Common Life at)eventer, has been called the first f the biblical humanists. He, too, vrote against indulgences and ook up much of the same position s Luther in attacking the pope's retensions and denouncing church rrors of his day.

The 'journalist of scholarship'

'he last and most effective fore-unner of the Reformation lived ong enough to be embarrassed by s challenge. Desiderius Erasmus f Rotterdam (1467–1536), the reatest humanist after Petrach, ıade the Reformation almost ıevitable, for (as the monks omplained) he laid the egg which ,uther hatched. Educated by ıe Brethren of the Common ife in Holland, he became an ugustinian canon in 1487, and vas ordained priest in 1492. He eft the monastery because he felt imself unsuited to the life of a ıonk. In 1495 he went to study ı Paris, but found the Nominalist ıeology of the schools distasteful, referring the classics of antiquity nd the circle of French humanists.)uring his first visit to England 1499–1500) he enjoyed the friend-hip of Colet and More, who drew im towards their own form of 'hristian humanism.

Back in Holland and France, rasmus began to publish a eries of best-selling satires vhich ridiculed monasticism and cholasticism, contrasted the)ld Ignorance' with the 'New earning', and used enlightened ommon sense to examine the ractice of Christianity. The first of ıese was the *Christian Soldier's 1anual* and the most widely read, ıe *Colloquies,* which appeared in over six hundred editions. A second visit to England (1505–06) was followed by three years in Italy, which deepened his humanist sympathies and contempt for the corruption of Rome. He expressed his contempt devastatingly in his *Praise of Folly,* written in seven days while staying with More in London.

Erasmus has been called the 'journalist of scholarship', and certainly he wrote with easy elegance and biting wit as he spread the ideals of Christian humanism. But he was also a serious editor of Latin and Greek texts. His edition of Jerome's works was a major piece of patient scholarship. But his most important contribution to the history of the church was his epoch-making edition of the Greek New Testament (the first ever published) which was printed at Basle in 1516—the year before the Reformation began.

Never had official religion been a lower ebb, or the public image of Christianity more defaced, than in the second decade of the sixteenth century. It seemed as though all opposition to the unreformed Catholic church from within and without was dying away. The Fifth Lateran Council met in Rome in 1512 and heard the orator declare: 'Now nobody contradicts, no one opposes.' The Medici Pope Leo X ascended the papal throne in 1513 with the quip: 'Now that we have attained the papacy, let us enjoy it!' The Lateran Council ended on a note of complacent self-congratulation in March 1517. The peace of the Christian world seemed assured. But the seeds of renewal had been sown, the harvest of Reformation was at hand. In October of that same year, in an obscure province of the Empire, one roused German conscience was stung into protest—and the great revolution began.

> *"I wish that the Scriptures might be translated into all languages, so that not only the Scots and the Irish, but also the Turk and the Saracen might read and understand them. I long that the farm-labourer might sing them as he follows his plough, the weaver hum them to the tune of his shuttle, the traveller beguile the weariness of his journey with their stories."*
>
> *ERASMUS*

REFORM

James Atkinson

> “*A Christian man is free from all things; he needs no work in order to be justified and saved, but receives these gifts in abundance from his faith alone.*”
>
> *MARTIN LUTHER*

The Reformation began on the eve of All Saints’ Day, 31 October 1517. On that day Martin Luther (1483–1546), professor of biblical studies at the newly founded University of Wittenberg in Germany, announced a disputation on indulgences. He stated his argument in *95 Theses*. Though they were heavily academic, and moderate in tone, news of them spread like wildfire throughout Europe. Within a fortnight every university and religious centre was agog with excitement. All marvelled that one obscure monk from an unknown university had stirred the whole of Europe.

Martin Luther protests

But the *95 Theses* were not by any means intended as a call to reformation. They were simply the proposal of an earnest university professor to discuss the theology of indulgences, in the light of the errors and abuses that had growr up over the centuries.

The dealings in indulgences (‘tł holy trade’ as it was unblushingly called), had grown into scandal. Luther did not oppose indulgence in their true and original sense— the merciful release of a penitent sinner from a penance imposed earlier by a priest. What Luther opposed was all the additions and perversions of indulgences, whic were harmful to human salvation and infected the everyday practic of the church.

Medieval people had a very re dread of the period of punishmen in purgatory which was portrayed in detail by the church. They had no great fear of hell, because the believed that, if they died forgive and blessed by the priest, they were guaranteed access through heaven’s gates, whose key was held by the church. But they feared purgatory’s pains; for the church taught that before they reached heaven they had to be cleansed of every sin committed in mortal life. Once penance was made a sacrament, the ordinary person believed (as even Dante did) that an indulgence assured the shortening of the punishments to be endured after death in purgatory. The relics of the Castle Church, on whose door Luther nailed his *95 Theses*, were reckoned to earn a remission for pilgrims of 1,902,202 years and 270 days!

Luther saw that the trade in indulgences was wholly unwarranted by Scripture, reaso or tradition. It encouraged people in their sin, and tended to turn

A scandal of the medieval church was the selling of indulgences. Clergymen and bankers’ agents collect money in return for absolving the purchaser of his sins. The banner is a symbol of the pope’s authorization.

heir mind away from Christ and rom God's forgiveness. It was at his point that Luther's theology contrasted sharply with that of he church. The pope claimed uthority 'to shut the gates of hell and open the door to paradise'. An obscure monk challenged that uthority. His contemporaries new at once that Luther had ouched the exposed nerve of both he hierarchy of the church and the everyday practice of Christianity. Christian Europe was never the ame again.

Ordered to recant in 1520, Luther was eventually excommunicated on 3 January 1521, and inally outlawed by the Emperor Charles V at Worms in 1521. He ad already had disputations with is own Augustinian order (in Heidelberg, 1518), and with papal uthorities (in Augsburg, 1518, and Leipzig, 1519). Luther's dramatic stand against both pope and Emperor fired the imagination of Europe. He found his sole support n his faith in God.

Luther published book after book over the next twenty-five ears. Those written for ordinary Christians were in powerful and vivid German. He translated the Bible, which enabled people to see for themselves the truth of is arguments. He published and account of each of his disputes with Rome, so that people could judge or themselves. He put the ordinary Christian on his theological eet. His followers multiplied.

In 1529, at the Diet of Speyer, he Emperor Charles V attempted o curb Luther's movement by orce. But some of the princes of the German states stood up in protest'. The movement found tself with the title 'Protestant'. From this moment the movement, which had all along been intended o reform Catholicism from within, eparated off, to become known as the Reformation'.

In 1530, Luther put forward the beliefs of the new movement at the Diet of Augsberg. It was a cool and non-controversial explanation, peace-seeking, comprehensive, Catholic and conservative. But Luther's movement split Christian Europe in two, and gave rise to the churches known as evangelical or Protestant. Three main traditions emerged: the Lutheran (in Germany and Scandinavia); the Zwinglian and Calvinist (in Switzerland, France, Holland and Scotland); and the Church of England.

Lasting social, political and economic changes followed the Reformation, and to some extent shaped it. But the Reformation was primarily a rediscovery of the gospel of God's saving work in Christ. This truth liberated the mind and heart from any theology which obscured it, and any practice or custom which corrupted it.

"Good works do not make a man good, but a good man does good works."

MARTIN LUTHER

31 October 1517, Martin Luther posted his *95 Theses* on the north door of the Castle Church in Wittenberg. The church doors were frequently used as a notice board.

MARTIN LUTHER

R. Stupperich

More books have been written about Luther, the great German Reformer, than about any other figure in history, except Christ. Martin Luther (1483–1546), born in Eisleben, studied law at the University of Erfurt. In 1505 he joined the Augustinian Hermits in Erfurt, after taking a dramatic vow during a thunderstorm. Luther was ordained in 1507, and after studying theology he was sent by his order to the University of Wittenberg to teach moral theology. In 1510–11 he visited Rome on business for his order, and in 1512 became a doctor of theology and professor of biblical studies at Wittenberg.

After a long spiritual crisis, Luther finally came to understand the nature of the righteousness of God. He now rejected all theology based solely on tradition, and emphasized personal understanding and experience of God's Word. He believed that all our actions stem from God. The discovery that God spares the sinner was always decisive for him. We are justified not by our deeds, but by faith alone.

Luther's views became widely known when he posted the *95 Theses* on the church door at Wittenberg. He attacked the teaching behind the sale of indulgences and the church's material preoccupations. But he also contrasted the treasures of the church with its true wealth, the gospel.

In December 1517 the Archbishop of Mainz complained to Rome about Luther. Faced with opposition, Luther's stand became even firmer. He refused to recant, confronted Cardinal Cajetan in Augsburg, and fled the town when summoned to Rome. In July 1519, during a disputation at Leipzig with Eck, his sharpest opponent, Luther denied the supremacy of the pope and the infallibility of general councils. He burned the papal bull which threatened his excommunication. Excommunication finally came in 1521.

Luther again refused to recant

before the Diet of Worms in April 1521—unless his ideas were refuted on scriptural grounds. For his own safety he was seized and taken to the Wartburg Castle under the protection of Frederick of Saxony. There he devoted his energies to translating the New Testament into German, so that the Bible might be read by all.

Eight months later, in 1522, Luther returned to Wittenberg to put a brake on the more radical reformers there. He set about reforming public worship by freeing the mass from rigid forms. He stressed preaching the Word, the communion and congregational singing.

In debate with Erasmus, Luther argued that salvation is entirely in the hands of God. During the Peasants' Revolts (1524–25) Luther opposed the 'murderous hordes of peasants' and alienated many of them. He combated Zwingli's interpretation of the communion service as simply a remembrance meal rather than 'a real presence' of Christ.

In 1530 Luther approved the *Augsburg Confession* drawn up by Melanchthon. This led him into conflict with the Emperor, but he believed the gospel must be defended whenever it was attacked. In 1537 Luther wrote the *Schmalkald Articles*, a doctrinal statement signed by many Lutheran theologians. His final pamphlet *Against the Roman Papacy, instituted by the Devil* repeated his old attack on Catholicism.

Luther's teaching and personal experience are closely connected. He always proceeds in the same way: from Scripture to personal conviction to declaration and preaching. For Luther there was no 'natural' understanding of God. God's only communication with mankind is through His Word. Christ is the essence of Scripture, and in Christ the Word becomes flesh. The Bible, and God, speaks only to those who have faith. Faith is God's gift, not our achievement.

Luther saw God behind everything in the world. He dismissed the problem of how to reconcile God's love and justice with the doctrine of predestination. God is always just. He is beyond human reason, mysterious and inconceivable. If we could comprehend him, he would not be God.

While in hiding at the Wartburg, Luther used his time to continue his writing. It was in this room in the fortress that he translated the New Testament from Greek into German.

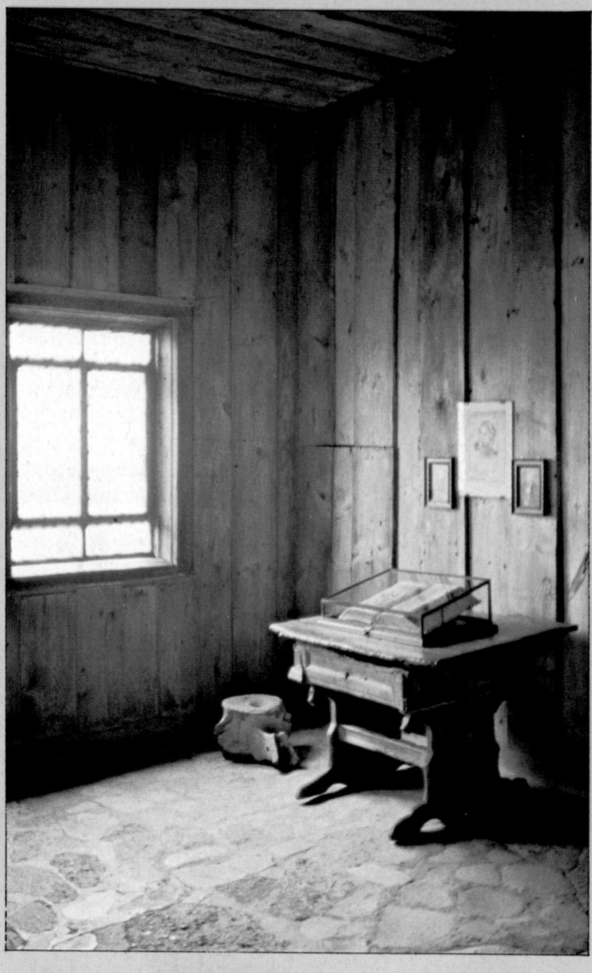

The Diet of Worms

“*Your Imperial Majesty and Your Lordships demand a simple answer. Here it is, plain and unvarnished. Unless I am convicted of error by the testimony of Scripture or (since I put no trust in the unsupported authority of pope or of councils, since it is plain that they have often erred and often contradicted themselves) by manifest reasoning I stand convicted by the Scriptures to which I have appealed, and my conscience is taken captive by God's word, I cannot and will not recant anything. For to act against our con science is neither safe for us nor open to us.*

On this I take my stand. I can do no other. God help me. Amen . . .”

MARTIN LUTHER

Luther's diagnosis

When, as a monk, Luther diagnosed the disease of Christian Europe to be the same as his own spiritual disease, he broke through to the gospel, and then offered it to Europe. In his monastery Luther had been searching for God's pardon and his peace. He faithfully obeyed his order, and observed punctiliously the spiritual techniques. Yet he found himself no nearer to God. He began to see that the way of the monk was merely a long discipline of religious duty and effort. Mysticism was an attempt to climb up to heaven. Academic theology was little more than speculation about God, his nature and his character.

Luther found one basic error in all these techniques of finding God. Ultimately they trusted in our own human ability to get us to God, or at least take us near enough for God to accept us. Luther realized that it was not a matter of God being far from everyone, and people having to strive to reach him. The reverse was true. Humanity, created and sinful, was distant from God; God in Christ had come all the way to find us. This was no new truth, but simply the old gospel of grace, which had been overlaid.

Luther's discovery did not represent a break with traditional doctrines. The Reformers held —as did the Roman church—all the orthodox doctrines stated in the general creeds of the early church. But the Reformers understood these doctrines in the particular context of salvation in Christ alone.

The Reformers held that the believer came into direct relation and union with Christ, as the one, only and all-sufficient source of grace. His grace is available to the penitent believer by the power of the Holy Spirit, through the preaching of the Word of God. This did away with the need for th Virgin as mediator, the clergy as priests, and the departed saints a intercessors.

In fact, the Reformers were never *in*novators, as the papacy w so often to allege, but *re*novators. What they removed were the medieval innovations of Rome, in favour of the doctrines of the Bibl and the early Christian theologian

From Luther's rediscovery of the direct and personal relationsh between Christ and the believer came the three great principles o the Reformation.

God's Word of authorit

Luther, and all the Reformers, believed that God had spoken to humanity, and acted on behalf of humanity, throughout history. The account of how God had dealt with people was given in Scriptur They believed that God continue to speak through the words spoke to prophets and apostles. In this personal revelation, God himself spoke in love to created humanity and renewed people heard and answered in faith.

The Reformers did not feel tha *they* were handling and interpretin Scripture; but that God was handling them through Scripture. This is what the Reformers mean by the Word of God: the living Word speaking to them in their own situation. Beliefs and church practice could not be justified if they were other than, outside of, or apart from the Word of God. These truths could be expressed non-biblical words, or non-biblical form, as they were in later creeds and statements of belief. But wha is being expressed must be biblic truth.

It is not true to say that the Reformation set up an infallible Bible instead of an infallible pope. The Roman church, too, accepte the authority of Scripture, but in

SAFE STRONGHOLD

A safe stronghold our God is still,
A trusty shield and weapon;
He'll help us clear from all the ill
That hath us now o'ertaken.
The ancient prince of hell
Hath risen with purpose fell;
Strong mail of craft and power
He weareth in this hour,
On earth is not his fellow.

With force of arms we nothing can,
Full soon were we down-ridden;
But for us fights the proper Man,
Whom God himself hath bidden.
Ask ye who is this same?
Christ Jesus is his name,
The Lord Sabaoth's Son;
He, and no other one,
Shall conquer in the battle.

And were this world all devils o'er,
And watching to devour us,
We lay it not to heart so sore;
Not they can overpower us.
And let the prince of ill
Look grim as e'er he will,
He harms us not a whit;
For why his doom is writ;
A word shall quickly slay him.

God's word, for all their craft and force,
One moment will not linger,
But, spite of hell, shall have its course;
'Tis written by his finger.
And, though they take our life,
Goods, honour, children, wife,
Yet is their profit small;
These things shall vanish all:
The city of God remaineth."

MARTIN LUTHER (1483–1546),
translated by Thomas Carlyle (1795–1881)

The Wartburg, a mountain fortress near Eisenach. It was here that Luther sheltered for seven months after he had been outlawed.

> "*I greatly longed to understand Paul's Epistle to the Romans, and nothing stood in the way but that one expression, 'the righteousness of God', because I took it to mean that righteousness whereby God is righteous and deals righteously in punishing the unrighteous . . . Night and day I pondered until . . . I grasped the truth that the righteousness of God is that righteousness whereby, through grace and sheer mercy, he justifies us by faith. Thereupon I felt myself to be reborn and to have gone through open doors into paradise. The whole of Scripture took on a new meaning, and whereas before 'the righteousness of God' had filled me with hate, now it became to me inexpressibly sweet in greater love. This passage of Paul became to me a gateway to heaven.*"
>
> *MARTIN LUTHER*

practice claimed that both the Bible *and* tradition were sources and rules of faith. The Roman church also made tradition, as it was expressed in the decrees of popes and councils, the only permissible, legitimate and infallible interpreter of the Bible. Roman Catholics appealed to Scripture to support views and positions arrived at on other grounds.

The Bible was hardly ever read. When it was, it was interpreted at four levels—the literal, spiritual, allegorical and anagogical (that is, its heavenly meaning). Hardly anybody knew what the Bible really said or meant. Faith was regarded largely as a matter of agreeing to statements about God, the soul, grace and other subjects. Medieval theologians had tended to put the church (in the shape of opinions of the early Fathers confirmed by popes and councils) between the believer and his Bible.

Many of the Reformers were linguists and scholars. Protestants produced biblical criticism, believing the Bible spoke to intellectuals of their age as well as common people of every period. The Reformers reasserted the ancient creeds as well as formulating their own statements. They rejected only those doctrines and ceremonies for which there was no clear basis in Scripture.

The Calvinists went further than the Lutherans in their opposition to traditions which had been handed down. They rejected a good deal of church music, art, architecture, and many more superficial matters such as the use of the ring in marriage, and signs of devotional practice.

But the Reformers rejected the authority of the pope, the merit of good works, indulgences, the mediation of the Virgin Mary and the saints, and all sacraments which had not been instituted by Christ. They rejected the doctrine of transubstantiation (the teaching that the bread and wine of communion became the body and blood of Christ when the priest consecrated them), the view of the mass as a sacrifice, purgatory and prayers for the dead, private confession of sin to a priest, celibacy of the clergy, and the use of Latin in the services. They also rejected all the paraphernalia that expressed these ideas—such as holy water, shrines, chantries, wonder-working images, rosaries, paternoster stones, images and candles.

By grace alone

The second great principle of the Reformation was salvation by the free and undeserved grace of Christ. This came to be known as 'justification by faith only'. The Protestants believed that by the action of God alone, in the death and resurrection of Christ, they were called from their sin to a new life in Christ. From this proceeded the fruits of the Spirit in loving acts.

The Catholics equally believed they were saved by Christ. But they made good works parallel faith, and laid stress on the merit of good works. The Protestants were 'justified'—made acceptable to God—solely by Christ. The Catholics modified this, by placing their own good works alongside. The Protestant did not disapprove of good works, but denied their value as a condition of justification. They saw them as the product and evidence of justification.

Every believer a priest

The third great Reformation principle was termed the 'priesthood of believers'. The Reformers argued that there was no precedent in the early church for the priest as mediator. Such a role was not part of the gospel. They also argued that nothing in Scripture supports the secular power of the clergy.

This doctrine meant that there were no longer two levels of Christian, spiritual and lay. There was one gospel, one justification by faith, one status before God common to all men and women, clergy and laity. Protestants opposed the idea that authority rested in an exclusive priesthood. People were freed from their vague fear of priests in this massive liberation movement.

The Reformers held that God called people to different occupations—father or farmer, scholar or pastor, servant or soldier. In and through his or her calling, the Christian served God. The Reformation demanded much from every Christian. Believers had both the right and the duty to read the newly-translated Bible. Every lay person was expected to take a responsible part in the government and public affairs of both church and society. Such thinking eventually helped give rise to the democratic states of Europe and North America.

The Reformers sometimes used words such as the 'invisible' church, or the 'latent' church, to distinguish between the true church known only to God, and the organization visible in the world. The church consisted of all those called by God to salvation.

Protestant ministers were recruited from the godly and learned. The Church of England, and large parts of the Lutheran church, particularly in Sweden, tried to keep the outward structure and ministry of their national church. They were attacked by both conservative Catholics and radical Protestants. Calvinists held an exalted and biblical view of the church as the chosen people of God. But they broke away completely from the traditional church structures as well as the Roman ministry. In this the free churches later followed them.

Germany

The movement initiated by Luther soon spread throughout Germany. Luther provided its chief source of energy and vision. But he received powerful academic support, notably from the brilliant and moderate young Philip Melanchthon. Luther also received support from some of the princes and from the German people. He was opposed by the pope, bishops and the Emperor.

Luther had aimed only at reform within the church. Ordered to recant in 1520, he burnt the papal bull publicly, and as a result was excommunicated by the pope on 3 January 1521. Later that same year, he fearlessly withstood the Emperor at Worms with his famous words, 'Here I stand'. Almost the whole of north Germany and almost every German free city was on Luther's side.

Luther virtually created and sustained the German Reformation single-handed. This he achieved by an immense output of books, by fearless preaching and teaching, by putting the Bible in German into the heart and mind of every man, woman and child, and by writing many biblical hymns. The 1526 Diet of Speyer had to allow his movement free course, but another in 1529 tried to prohibit further advance. It was at this Diet that a row of evangelical princes stood their ground and resisted this unacceptable legislation, following the example of their great teacher, Luther. Their brave protest gave history the word 'Protestantism'.

At the Diet of Augsburg (1530) the Protestants submitted their statement of belief. But the Catholics refused to accept it, so the

An illustration from the title page of the *Coverdale Bible*. Jesus sends out his disciples: 'Go throughout the whole world and preach the gospel to all mankind.'

THE FAITH OF THE PROTESTANTS

J. I. Packer

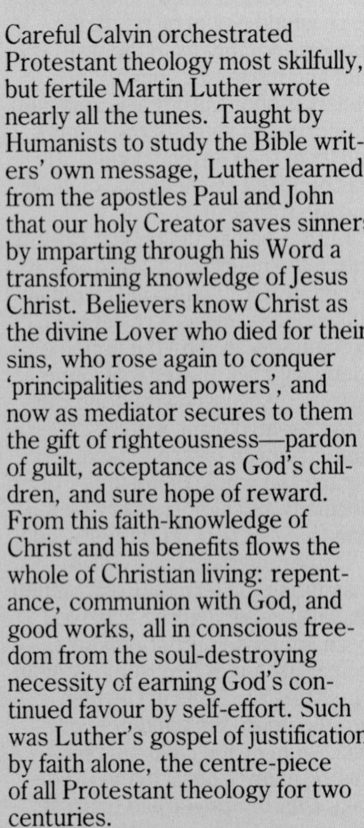

Peter preaches on the day of Pentecost. A detail from the title page of the Coverdale Bible.

Careful Calvin orchestrated Protestant theology most skilfully, but fertile Martin Luther wrote nearly all the tunes. Taught by Humanists to study the Bible writers' own message, Luther learned from the apostles Paul and John that our holy Creator saves sinners by imparting through his Word a transforming knowledge of Jesus Christ. Believers know Christ as the divine Lover who died for their sins, who rose again to conquer 'principalities and powers', and now as mediator secures to them the gift of righteousness—pardon of guilt, acceptance as God's children, and sure hope of reward. From this faith-knowledge of Christ and his benefits flows the whole of Christian living: repentance, communion with God, and good works, all in conscious freedom from the soul-destroying necessity of earning God's continued favour by self-effort. Such was Luther's gospel of justification by faith alone, the centre-piece of all Protestant theology for two centuries.

What Luther taught

Luther affirmed the final authority of a self-interpreted Bible, and rejected non-scriptural beliefs. He taught a 'spiritual' doctrine of the church. He depicted it as a serving priesthood of believers, as against the medieval idea of the church as a hierarchical institution under the bishop of Rome, administering salvation through sacraments. Here, too, all Protestants agreed.

The Lutheran churches of Germany and Scandinavia developed in isolation from the reformed churches of Switzerland, Holland, the Rhineland and Britain. But this was an accident of geography and politics, rather than a sign of major theological differences. Yet each tradition seemed at points eccentric to the other. Luther taught that infants were regenerated in baptism (through infant faith!). He also affirmed the 'real presence' of Christ's body 'in, with and under' the eucharistic bread. To buttress this idea he maintained the 'ubiquity', or capacity for 'multipresence', of Jesus' glorified flesh. Lutherans followed him, but Calvin and Reformed theologians generally rejected these ideas, holding that Christ's body is 'in Heaven, and not here', and that Christ encounters his people at the communion table, not by bodily presence in the elements, but by the Spirit's presence and power in their hearts. Lutherans have always found this view irreverently 'low'.

Changes to worship

For pastoral reasons Luther retained much medieval ceremony in worship, urging that when doctrine was sound ceremonies were 'things indifferent' *(adiaphora)*, which the church was free to use or not as it thought best. Reformed leaders, however, wanted worship to be as simple and scriptural as possible, and their liturgies were plainer than those of their Lutheran counterparts. From this standpoint the English *Prayer Book* was a half-way house. It came to be argued that features in worship not prescribed in Scripture should be seen as forbidden. This so-called 'puritan' or 'regulative' principle became the rule in Scotland and was basic to the further purfying of worship and ministry in England for which Elizabethan Puritans unsuccessfully called.

Meantime, in Germany in 1548, two years after Luther's death, mild Melanchthon, his successor as leader, accepted an agreement (the *Leipzig Interim*) re-establishing, among other things, the Latin mass, Corpus Christi Day, and extreme unction. He claimed these were 'things indifferent'. But fierce Flacius denounced him, and the Lutheran theological world was convulsed.

The doctrine of grace

Melanchthon made the doctrine of grace another storm-centre in Lutheranism. Luther had stressed the sinner's total spiritual impotence and made God's sovereign grace the sole source of faith. Now Melanchthon ascribed to fallen humanity free will in the sense of 'power of applying oneself to grace'. This phrase from Erasmus, which Luther had abhorred, Melanchthon explicitly approved. So my faith ceases to be God's work in me, and becomes my work. Flacius and followers attacked his position. A generation of conflict was ended by the pan-Lutheran *Formula of Concord* (1595), which reaffirmed the sinner's total spiritual inability and God's unconditional predestination of the elect to faith—but stated also that an external call to salvation reaches all people and that final falling from grace is possible.

Melanchthon's modification of the doctrine of sovereign grace had its Reformed parallel. Beza, Calvin's scholastic successor at Geneva, developed belief in sovereign grace into 'supralapsarianism'; the view that God decreed the fall as a means to the end of saving the elect from sin. Most Reformed theologians at the turn of the seventeenth century agreed, but Jacob Arminius, a gifted Dutchman, once Beza's pupil, did not. In 1610 his disciples produced their manifesto, the *Remonstrance*, affirming that election to salvation rests on faith foreseen; that Christ died for all, though only believers benefit (Beza said he died only for the elect); that grace is not irresistible; and that perseverance depends on one's own action over and above God's help. Against this the pan-Reformed Synod of Dort (1618) formulated the so-called 'five points of Calvinism'—total depravity, unconditional election, limited atonement (that is, limited in efficacy to the elect), irresistible grace in effectual calling, and final preservation of the saints (easily memorized by the mnemonic t-u-l-i-p).

Dutch Arminianism was rationalistic in spirit, and subsequently drifted into querying Jesus' full deity. Some High Church Anglicans came independently to an essentially Arminian view of grace, not from rationalism, but from deference to the Greek Fathers.

Meanwhile, Johann Arndt (1555–1621) in Lutheran Germany and the English Puritans, following William Perkins (1558–1602), developed an impressive devotional theology of regeneration, sanctification and the inner life, as being what the times most needed. One suspects they were right! From this seed the later Pietist movement grew.

"Question: *What is the chief end of man?*
Answer: *Man's chief end is to glorify God, and to enjoy him for ever.*"

The Shorter Catechism *of the Westminster Assembly (1643)*

Emperor ordered a recess.

The Protestant princes realized at Augsburg that the Emperor intended to make war on Protestantism. They formed the Schmalkald league, as a kind of defensive alliance. After several conferences designed to find some form of compromise between Catholic and Protestant, the tragic Schmalkald War broke out in 1547, shortly after Luther's death in 1546. The Emperor defeated the Protestant forces and imprisoned their leaders. But the Protestant Maurice of Saxony fought back successfully and by the Treaty of Passau (1552) Protestantism was legally recognized. This settlement was confirmed in the 'Interim' of 1555.

Once Luther had passed from the scene, a period of bitter theological warfare occured within Protestantism. There was controversy over such matters as the difference between justification and sanctification; what doctrine was essential or non-essential; faith and works; and the nature of the 'real presence' at the eucharist.

This is the period when Lutheran*ism* developed—something which Luther foresaw and condemned. The *Book of Concord,* which sets out what we now understand as Lutheranism, was published in 1580. It included Melanchthon's *Augsburg Confession* and *Augsburg Apology*; Luther's two catechisms and the *Schmalkald Articles* (drawn up in 1537); and the *Formula of Concord.* Some of the Lutheran theologians drove large numbers of people over to the Calvinist church through their dogmatism. The Calvinists in Germany adopte the *Heidelberg Confession* as their statement of faith.

The tragic Thirty Years' War perpetuated political strife in Germany in the seventeenth century, until by the Treaty of Westphalia (1648) the Lutherans and Calvinists won equal rights with the Catholics.

Reformation studies have traditionally focused on the religious debates. But in 1965 Bernd Meoller protested against this obsession with the theology of Luther and neglect of secular movements. During the last thirty years fresh emphases and insights have emerged from psychological, political and sociological research of the period. In this way the Reformation can be seen as a whole, with other fields of study (such as urban history, humanism and education, witchcraft and occult, trade and commerce, science and art) broadening previous accounts. The setting of the Reformation within secular history has now become a whole new field of research in itself. It must be watched with a critical eye, but it is demanding fresh assessments of the Reformation, viewed as a much larger movement and

Philip Melanchthon's study in his home in Wittenberg. He followed Luther as theological leader of the Reformation in Germany.

PHILIP MELANCHTHON

R. Stupperich

On Luther's death Philip Melanchthon (1497–1560) took over the theological leadership of the movement he had begun. Melanchthon taught Greek, first in Tübingen, then at the University of Wittenberg. There, in 1518, he met Luther. This decisive encounter changed Melanchthon from a humanist into a theologian and reformer. With his gift for logical consistency and wide knowledge of history, Melanchthon's influence on Protestantism was in certain ways even greater than Luther's.

Melanchthon publicly supported Luther at the Leipzig Disputation (1519). When Luther was away from Wittenberg, Melanchthon represented and defended him. In 1521, he wrote the *Commonplaces (Loci communes)*, the first book which described clearly the teachings of the Reformation. He also contributed to Luther's German translation of the Bible.

At Marburg (1529) Melanchthon opposed Zwingli. He claimed that the service of holy communion was more than a memorial. Melanchthon was responsible for the *Augsburg Confession* (1530), which remains the chief statement of faith in the Lutheran churches.

Melanchthon, however, often seemed too prepared to concede matters of doctrine to the Roman Catholics for the sake of peace. He believed that reunion was essential. The theological struggles in his own camp with other Lutherans deeply troubled him. Melanchthon remained the only Protestant theologian of his day to represent the views of the people at large.

"What are these new doctrines? The gospel? Why, that is 1,522 years old. The teaching of the apostles? Why, they are almost as old as the gospel. . . We will try everything by the touchstone of the gospel and the fire of Paul."

not exclusively as a religious phenomenon.

Switzerland

The Reformation broke out in Zürich at the same time as in Germany, but independently of it. Its theology was similar to Luther's, except in the doctrine of the eucharist. But Zwingli, the Swiss Reformer, had patriotic ideals. He determined that the discipline and worship in his church should follow a non-Roman Catholic line.

The battle of Kappel brought the Reformation in Switzerland to a halt. But in 1536 John Calvin (1509–64) was unwillingly pressed to lead the cause in French-speaking Geneva. Calvin was an exiled Frenchman. His theological writings, especially the *Institutes of the Christian Religion* and numerous commentaries on the Bible, did much to shape the Reformed churches and their confessions of faith. He developed the Presbyterian form of church government in which all ministers served at the same level, and the people were represented by lay elders.

Calvin is often remembered for his severe doctrine of election, particularly that some people are predestined to destruction. But Calvin also set out the way of repentance, faith and sanctification. Calvin intended that his theology should interpret Scripture faithfully, rather than develop his own ideas.

Zwingli in Zurich and Calvin in Geneva were succeeded respectively by Johann Heinrich Bullinger (1504–75) and Theodore Beza (1519–1605), who both kept alive the Reformed tradition. They exercised great influence in France, Holland, Germany, England and Scotland by their teaching and by their hospitality to the many exiles from persecution in their native lands.

MARTIN BUCER

R. Stupperich

Martin Bucer (or Butzer; 1491–1551) was the Reformer at Strasbourg. He had been a Dominican friar but left the order, and in 1522 married a former nun. He went to Strasbourg in 1523 and took over leadership of the reform. He became one of the chief statesmen among the Reformers, and was present at most of the important conferences of the Reformers.

Bucer tried to mediate between the divided Zwingli and Luther, in an effort to unite the German and Swiss Reformed churches. His discussions with Melanchthon led to peace in the debate over the sacraments at the Concord of Wittenberg. Bucer took part in the unsuccessful conferences with Roman Catholics at Hagenau, Worms and Ratisbon.

Bucer resisted the Emperor's religious settlement (the Augsburg Interim). In 1549 he was forced to leave Strasbourg for Cambridge. While in England, he advised Cranmer on *The Book of Common Prayer*. He had a great impact on the Church of England, pointing the way towards Puritanism. Although he died in 1551 his body was exhumed and burned during the Catholic reaction under Queen Mary.

Bucer wrote a large number of commentaries on the Bible and worked strenuously for reconciliation between various religious parties.

HULDREICH ZWINGLI

Robert V. Schnucker

Ulrich Zwingli, the reformer of Zürich. He died at the battle of Kappel, which halted the progress of the Reformation in German-speaking Switzerland.

Huldreich Zwingli (1484–1531), the Swiss Reformer, died in battle against the Catholics. He was educated in Basle, Berne and Vienna, and became vicar at Glarus until 1516. At Glarus he learned Greek, possibly Hebrew, and studied the church Fathers. He acted as chaplain to Swiss mercenary forces at the battle of Novara (1513) and at Marignano (1515), and as a result came to reject the current use of mercenary soldiers.

Zwingli met Erasmus in 1515 and was deeply influenced by him. After his forced transfer to Einsiedeln, he began to develop evangelical beliefs as he reflected upon the abuses of the church. In 1518 he was made peoples' priest at the Great Minster in Zürich. He lectured on the New Testament and began to reform Zürich, working carefully with the city council. In 1522 he secretly married Anna Meyer who bore him four children.

The Catholic bishop of Constance attempted to stop Zwingli, but Zwingli overcame him in two public debates in 1523. The reform movement was then challenged by Zwingli's former colleagues, Grebel and Manx; the latter was sentenced to death by drowning. When Zwingli won a further disputation at Berne in 1528, Basle, Gall, Schaffhausen and Constance all joined the reform movement. When Zwingli and Luther reached deadlock in their debate over the eucharist at Marburg (1529), the Swiss reform movement lost the support of the German princes. The five Catholic Forest Cantons of Switzerland sent an army against Zürich, and Zwingli died at the battle of Kappel.

Most of Zwingli's writings were born out of controversy. His *Commentary on True and False Religion* (1528), a systematic theology, had considerable impact upon Protestantism. Zwingli was the first of the Reformed theologians. He held that Christ was spiritually present at the Eucharist and that the secular ruler had a right to act in church matters.

In 1518 Ulrich Zwingli was called to be the people's priest in the Great Church at Zürich.

> “*Wherever we find the Word of God surely preached and heard, and the sacraments administered according to the institution of Christ, there, it is not to be doubted, is a church of God.*”
>
> *JOHN CALVIN, in The Institutes*

France

In France the pattern of reform was very different. Whereas in Germany and Switzerland there was solid support for the Reformation from the people, in France people, court and church provided less support. As a result the first Protestants suffered death or exile. But once the Reformed faith had been established in French-speaking Switzerland, Calvinists formed a congregation in Paris in 1555. Over seventy churches were represented at a national synod in Paris in 1559.

Reform took on the nature of a political movement in this hostile environment. A series of civil wars followed. Protestants were shamelessly massacred in cold blood on St Bartholomew's Day in 1572. This shattered, but did not destroyed, Protestantism in France. When the Protestant Henry IV succeeded to the French throne in 1589 Protestant hopes ran high. But the French Catholics formed an alliance with the king of Spain and threatened to plunge the country in blood if Henry remained a Protestant. Henry yielded for the sake of peace and to preserve his throne, and gave up his Protestantism. But in 1598 he had Protestantism legally recognized, and granted the freedom to practise Reformed Christianity, under the terms of the *Edict of Nantes*.

The French statesman, Cardinal Richelieu, played havoc with Protestantism in the seventeenth century. Finally King Louis XIV revoked the *Edict of Nantes* in 1685, after which French Protestants suffered bitter persecution.

The Low Countries

In the Netherlands reform was inspired by Luther. People were martyred for Lutheran beliefs

JOHN CALVIN

A. Lindt

John Calvin (1509–64), the Ger
evan Reformer, created and
systematized the Reformed tra
tion in Protestantism. A Frencl
man, he was born at Noyon,
Picardy. In contrast to Luther,
Calvin was a quiet, sensitive m
He said little about his inner life
he was content to trace God's h
controlling him. He inherited fr
his father an immovable will, w
stood him in good stead in turb
lent Geneva.

Calvin was always a conscien
tious student—at Orléans,
Bourges and the University of
Paris. He soon took up the met
ods of humanism, which he late
used 'to combat humanism'.

In Paris, the young Calvin m
the teachings of Luther. About
1533 he experienced a sudden
conversion: 'God subdued and
brought my heart to docility. It
was more hardened against suc
matters than was to be expecte
in such a young man.' He next
broke with Roman Catholicism,
left France and lived as an exile
Basle. He began to formulate h
theology, and in 1536 published
the first edition of *The Instituti
of the Christian Religion* (bette
known as the *Institutes*). It was
brief, clear defence of Reforma
beliefs.

Guillaume Farel, the Reform
of Geneva, persuaded Calvin to
help consolidate the Reformatio
there. In 1537 all the townspeo
were called upon to swear loyal
to a Protestant statement of
belief. But Genevans opposed
Calvin strongly, and disputes in
town, together with a quarrel w
the city of Berne, resulted in th

expulsion of both Calvin and Farel.

Calvin went to Strasbourg, where he made contact with Bucer, who encouraged and influenced him greatly. In 1539 Calvin published his commentary on the book of Romans. Many other commentaries followed. Calvin also produced a new, enlarged version of the *Institutes*. The French Reformer led the congregation of French refugees in Strasbourg, an experience which matured him for his task on returning to Geneva.

He was invited back to Geneva in September 1541. The town council accepted his revision of the city laws, but many bitter disputes followed. Calvin tried to bring every citizen under the moral discipline of the church. Many naturally resented such restrictions—especially when imposed by a foreigner. He now set about attaining his aim of a mature church—by preaching daily to the people.

Calvin devoted much energy to settling differences within Protestantism. The *Consensus Tigurinus,* on the Lord's Supper (1949), resulted in the German- and French-speaking churches of Switzerland moving closer together. In 1553 Michael Servetus, a notorious critic of Calvin, and of the doctrine of the Trinity, was arrested and burnt in Geneva. Servetus was already on the run from the Inquisition, and was regarded by all to be a heretic. The Protestant reformers could not afford to be seen to be soft on heresy.

Calvin was in a way trying to build a more visible 'City of God' in Europe—with Geneva as a starting-point. In his later years Calvin's authority in Geneva was less disputed. He founded the Geneva Academy, to which students of theology came from all parts of western and central Europe, particularly France.

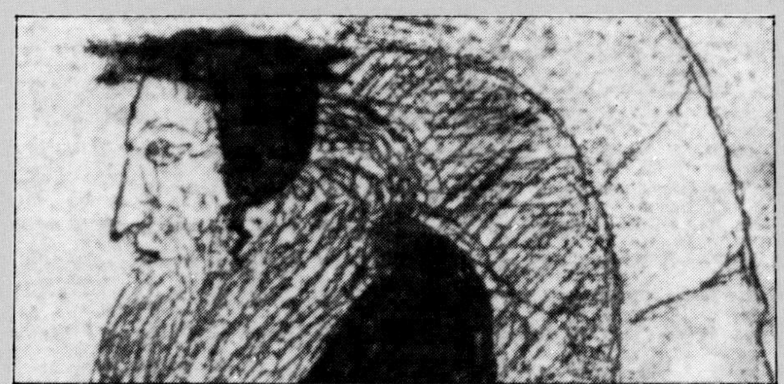

John Calvin, caricatured by one of his students during an idle moment in a lecture.

Calvin was the great systematizer. He took up and reapplied the ideas of the first generation of Reformers. His work was characterized by intellectual discipline and practical application. His *Institutes* have been a classic statement of Reformation theology for centuries. He was also a careful interpreter of the Bible.

Lutheranism strongly influenced Calvin's doctrine. For Calvin, all knowledge of God is to be found only in the Word of God. We can only know God if he chooses to be known. Pardon and salvation are possible only through the free working of the grace of God. Calvin claimed that even before the creation, God chose some of his creatures for salvation and others for destruction.

For Calvin, the church was supreme. It should not be restricted in any way by the state. He gave greater importance than Luther to the external organization of the church. Calvin regarded only baptism and communion as sacraments. Baptism was the individual's initiation into the new community of Christ. Calvin rejected Zwingli's idea that the sacrament of communion was merely a symbol; but he also warned against a magical belief in the real presence of Christ in the sacrament.

"We declare that by God's providence, not only heaven and earth and inanimate creatures, but also the counsels and wills of men are governed so as to move precisely to that end destined by him."

JOHN CALVIN

Theodore Beza—a pen and ink sketch by one of his students in Geneva.

THEODORE BEZA

Robert V. Schnucker

Theodore Beza (1519–1605) succeeded Calvin in Geneva as leader of Reformed Protestantism.

He had been trained as a lawyer, and a book of love poetry gained him a reputation as a Latin poet. He secretly married Claude Desnoz in 1544 but had no children. After a severe illness, in 1548 Beza went to Geneva and announced that he had become a Protestant. He was made professor of Greek at Lausanne University.

In 1559 Beza became the first rector of the Genevan Academy. He remained in Geneva, intimately involved in its affairs, and became Calvin's successor, and one of the leading advisors to the Huguenots in France. He participated in their conferences (Poissy, 1561, New Rochelle, 1571) and defended the purity of the Reformed faith. He produced new versions of the Greek and Latin New Testament, a source for the Geneva and King James' Bibles. Theodore Beza also completed the translation of the psalms begun by Marot—and wrote a biography of Calvin, *De jure magistratuum,* an important Protestant political work, as well as other political, polemical, and theological tracts.

Beza was an important figure for the Reformed churches. His political activities aimed to establish the Reformed faith throughout Europe, and particularly in France. Beza's theological method made the Reformed position more rigid. Under his leadership Geneva became the centre of Reformed Protestantism.

French Protestants at a service in Lyons *temple*, which was converted from an ordinary house. The hatted preacher is timed by an hourglass, and the two sexes are seated in separate parts of the building.

as early as 1523. Later the reformation came under Calvin's influence.

At this time the Low Countries were ruled by Spain. The reform movement was bitterly opposed by the Emperor Charles V, as well as by his successor King Philip II of Spain. The reform movement developed a strong political commitment to independence. It was claimed that the Spanish Duke of Alva was responsible for the deaths, of 100,000 Protestants between 1567 and 1573. In 1584 the northern Netherlands formed a federation under William the Silent. After a long and bitter struggle, they freed themselves from the Roman church and the Spanish crown. The first Reformed synod was held at Dort in 1574, and within a year the refomers founded the University of Leiden. The new Reformed church adopte the *Heidelberg Confession* and the *Belgic Confession* as statements o belief, and drew up its own pattern of organization.

The Dutch church now went through a very bitter theological struggle concerning the nature of predestination. Arminius (1560–1609), professor of theolog at Leiden, rejected the logical conclusions of the doctrine that the elect were determined by the sovereign will of God alone, as Calvin taught. Arminius insisted it was possible to believe in God's sovereignty while allowing for rea free will in an individual. God wille *all* to be saved and not merely the chosen. Arminius insisted that his views were biblical and not mere speculation. His doctrines were condemned at the Synod of Dort (1618–19), tolerated later in the

century, and officially recognized in 1795.

Central Europe

In Bohemia the Reformation had still earlier beginnings, under Jan Hus and Jerome of Prague. Hus's followers, the Hussites, supported Luther when the Reformation broke out, but most of them later became Calvinists. The cause of reform in Bohemia suffered severely during the Thirty Year's War, as well as under the Counter-Reformation. Bohemia was left a wilderness of desolation.

In Hungary, students of Luther and Melanchthon from the University of Wittenberg took back to their homeland the message of the Reformation in about 1524. As in Bohemia, Calvinist theology later took hold. The first Lutheran synod took place in 1545, the first Calvinist synod in 1557. Religious liberty was supressed by Rudolph II but regained by force by Prince Stephen of Transylvania, in the treaties of Nikolsburg (1622) and Linz (1645).

The Hussites, encouraged by Luther's writings, originated the reform movement in Poland. King Sigismund Augustus (1548–72) was a friend of the Reformation and corresponded with Calvin. The most distinguished Polish theologian was the Calvinist John Lasco, who later went to England as a professor and helped shape the English Reformation during the reign of King Edward VI. In Poland, general understanding was arrived at between Lutherans and Calvinists by 1570. But reform was marred by internal dissention created by Socinianism. This was a movement founded by Socinus, who denied the Trinity, the deity of Christ, his work on the cross, and that human beings are fallen. The reform movement was later hindered by the activities of the Jesuits.

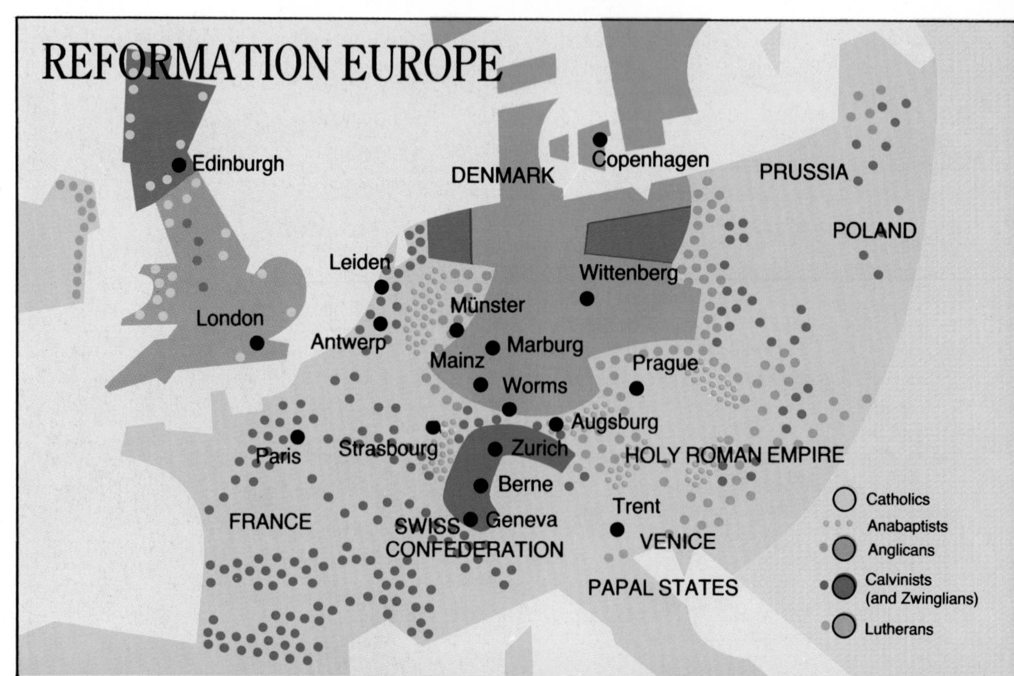

ʖcandinavia

ʼwo brothers, Olav and Lars ʼetri, both disciples of Luther, naugurated the Reformation n Sweden. Aided by Lorenz Anderson, they brought the berating evangelical theology of uther to the Swedish church. ʼhe courageous King Gustavus /asa, who eventually delivered ʖweden from the Danes in 1523, reatly favoured Protestantism. ʼhe whole country became utheran, with bishops of the ld church incorporated into the ew. In 1527 the Reformation vas established by Swedish law. n 1593, at the Synod of Uppsala, eform was completed, when the utheran *Augsburg Confession* vas adopted as the sole basis of aith. Sweden kept the traditional hurch structures and bishops, in a haracteristic church-state union. ʖwedes fought fiercely for the ʼrotestant cause during the Thirty ʼears' War.

Denmark's story is different, hough the Danish church, oo, went over completely to ʼrotestantism. Some Danes, hief among them Hans Tausen nd Jörgen Sadolin, studied under uther at Wittenberg. They then egan to preach irregularly but ffectively in Denmark. A Danish ersion of the New Testament was roduced in 1524. King Frederick pressed strongly for church eform, particularly by appointing eforming bishops and preachers. As a result there was an alarming efection of Catholics and, in some laces, no preaching at all, or a ervice only two or three times a ear.

After this period of disorder, King Christian III succeeded to he Danish throne in 1536 and the ransition to Protestantism was irtually completed. He stripped he bishops of their lands and property at the Diet of Copenhagen (1536), and transferred the church's wealth to the state.

Christian III then turned to Luther for help. In 1537 Luther sent Bugenhagen—the only Lutheran theologian at Wittenberg who could speak the dialects of Denmark and the German border. Bugenhagen crowned the king and appointed seven superintendents. This severed the old line of bishops and established a new line of presbyters. At the synods which followed church ordinances were published, and the reformation recognized in Danish law. The

Heddal Stave church, Norway. This form of construction is characteristic of this part of Scandinavia.

decayed University of Copenhagen was enlarged and revitalized. A new liturgy was drawn up, a new translation of the Bible completed, and a modified version of the *Augsburg Confession* eventually adopted.

The Reformation spread from Denmark to Norway in 1536. The pattern was similar to that of Denmark. Most of the bishops fled and, as the older clergy died, they were replaced with Reformed ministers. War between Denmark and Norway worsened political and social conditions. When the Danish Lutherans went to instruct the Norwegians, they found that many of the Norwegians spoke incomprehensible ancient Norse, and communications broke down.

In Iceland things were worse. Attempts to impose the Danish ecclesiastical system brought about a revolt. This was eventually quelled and the Reformation imposed. A New Testament in Icelandic was published in 1540.

England

The struggle between the old and the new lasted longer in England and Scotland than in the rest of Europe. As early as the thirteenth century a strong anti-papal and anti-clerical movement developed in Britain. Under Wyclif, a strong evangelical protest movement originated. This was strengthened early in the sixteenth century when Luther's writings and English Bibles were smuggled into England.

At first the reform movement was Lutheran and was supported by the older Lollard movement. But the Reformation, though religious in origin, became entangled with politics by corrupt and scheming opportunists concerned only to do well for themselves in a turbulent situation.

In 1534 King Henry VIII proclaimed himself the head of the Church of England. His quarrel with the pope was not on religious grounds, but merely on the selfish grounds that the pope would not sanction Henry's proposed divorce of Queen Catherine. Henr himself (though excommunicated) remained a Catholic in doctrine and practice all his days. The pope entitled him 'Defender of the Faith for a book he wrote against Luther in 1521. In 1539 Henry issued the *Six Articles* which aimed to restore the traditional Catholic faith.

Henry did destroy the power of the pope and end monasticism in England. But a powerful religious movement towards reform among his people was going on at the same time.

Under King Edward VI (1547–5 the Reformation was positively and effectively introduced. The leading figure was the Archbishop of Canterbury, Thomas Cranmer, supported by the scholar, Nichola Ridley, and the preacher, Hugh Latimer. Several European Reformers also contributed, notably Martin Bucer from Strasbourg, Peter Martyr from Italy and John à Lasco from Poland. These men, Calvinists rather than Lutherans, became professors at the Universities of Oxford and Cambridge.

Queen Mary (1553–58), a bigoted and intolerant Catholic, yet a religious woman, attempted to restore Catholicism and the authority of the pope to Britain, with the help of Cardinal Pole. Pole was an enlightened humanist. He was a Catholic sympathetic to evangelical doctrines, particularly justification by faith. He had a genuine ecumenical concern for the unity of the Church, and was bold enough to censure Henry VI with his book *On the Defence of th Unity of the Church* (1534–36). H was appointed to a commission by Paul III to draw up a report on the eformation of the church (1537), nd very nearly succeeded Paul II as pope. In company with the ke-minded Contarini, he took an nlightened line at Regensburg 1541), and played an important ole at the Council of Trent (1545 nwards). He was a man of ure morals and deep piety; he as holy and ascetic. As Cardinal rchbishop of Canterbury, it as Pole who carried out Queen lary's attempted restoration f Catholicism. But Mary's emperamental inability to understand Protestantism actually did more to strengthen the Reformation movement than weaken it. About two hundred bishops, scholars and other men and women were burnt at the stake, including the major leaders of Protestantism—Cranmer, Latimer and Ridley. Many people fled to the Continent. Mary died a hated woman. All hopes now centred on Elizabeth, her half-sister.

Queen Elizabeth restored and permanently established Protestantism in England during

The course of the English Reformation is pictured here graphically, with King Henry VIII pointing to his son and successor, Edward VI. The pope is languishing, and Thomas Cranmer, the reforming Archbishop, sits by the side of the prince as an adviser.

PURITANS AND SEPARATISTS

Keith L. Sprunger

> *"The Lord has more truth yet to break forth out of his holy Word."*
>
> *JOHN ROBINSON to the Pilgrims, as they set sail for America.*

People often complained about abuses in English religion. The Church of England, as established by Elizabeth I, was quite unsatisfactory to Roman Catholics and also to more extreme Protestants. The second group desired a fully Reformed church, more on the lines of Calvin's at Geneva. Those who worked to purify and reform the church beyond what the government had established were called 'Puritans'.

The first Puritans

The Elizabethan Puritans, working from within the Church of England, mostly wanted to abolish religious ceremonies thought to be remnants from Roman Catholicism—the use of the cross in baptism, the surplice, kneeling at communion. Many of the Puritans questioned whether there was any biblical authority for bishops. They wanted the Reformed pattern of church government, by elders and synods, with stricter discipline.

During the first years of Elizabeth's reign, the Puritan-minded clergy and lay members of the Church of England had strong support in Parliament, and high hopes of achieving their reforms. Their leaders included Thomas Cartwright (1535–1603) and William Perkins (1558–1602).

Elizabeth I was unwilling to allow changes along Puritan lines, and King James I was equally adamant against Puritans. 'I will make them conform themselves,' he threatened, 'or I will harry them out of the land, or else do worse.' The main part of the Puritan movement still survived within the Church of England. Many Puritans only marginally conformed to Anglicanism: they were very much on the defensive.

The Orthodox true Minifter,
the Seducer and falfe Prophet.

A pro-Anglican drawing contrasts the 'Orthodox true Minister' preaching in church, with the separatist 'Seducer and false Prophet' preaching from a tavern window.

A modern replica of the *Mayflower*, the tiny ship which carried the Pilgrim Fathers from Leiden via Plymouth to New England.

In the face of these discouragements, a small separatist movement grew up alongside the main Puritan group. The Separatist Puritans were led by Robert Browne (about 1550–1633) and Robert Harrison (died about 1585). These Separatists no longer regarded the Church of England as a true church, and in 1581 with their followers (often called Brownists) they formed an independent congregation at Norwich. Browne acted as pastor and Harrison as teacher of the church. They withdrew completely from the Anglican church, which they believed to be polluted and false, and set up their own congregation, based on a church covenant. This step marked the beginnings of the English Independent or Congregationalist movement. The English government and bishops lost all patience, and severely repressed the Brownists by imprisonment, harassment, and by driving them abroad to the Low Countries.

The Netherlands played an increasingly important role in the life of English dissent. As the English authorities repressed Puritanism more severely and systematically, the dissenters were often forced to find refuge abroad. The Dutch were tolerant of religious nonconformity, and allowed English refugees to come in freely. Browne and Harrison took their small church to Middelburg, in Zeeland, where it survived for a few years. Browne, however, later returned to England, where he eventually renounced his separation and resumed a ministry in the Church of England. Other leaders took over in the Separatist movement: Henry Barrow, John Greenwood, Francis Johnson, Henry Ainsworth, John Robinson and others.

The 'Pilgrim Fathers' led by John Robinson (about 1576–1625) after living in Leiden, eventually emigrated to New England. One of the Separatist groups in Amsterdam, led by John Smyth (died 1612) and Thomas Helwys (about 1550 to about 1616) became Anabaptist.

John Knox (about 1514–72), the Scots reformer, who spent several years as a French galley-slave. He was largely responsible for directing the Scots reformation, but alienated many by his rigid and censorious attitude.

"... the maist perfyt schoole of Chryst that ever was in the erth since the dayis of the Apostillis."

JOHN KNOX, on Calvin's Geneva

her long reign (1558–1603). She faced considerable difficulties: the threat of civil war; the theological and political threat of the Catholic powers; the hostility of France and Spain; and finally the doubts about her own claim to the throne.

Elizabeth gradually replaced the Catholic church leaders with Protestants. She restored the church *Articles* and the *Prayer Book* of Edward VI, and took the title of 'supreme governor' (not head) of the Church of England.

As re-established by Elizabeth, the Anglican church kept episcopal government and a liturgy. This offended many strict Calvinist Protestants—particularly the religious refugees who were returning from Switzerland. Meanwhile Roman Catholics plotted and intrigued. Virtually every Catholic appeared to be a traitor, since the pope had ordered them to oppose Elizabeth.

Bishop John Jewel's magnificent *Apology* (1560) and the writings of Richard Hooker (1554–1600), following Cranmer's position, attempted to demonstrate that Elizabeth's church was scriptural, catholic and reasonable. On the other hand the early Stuart Kings, James I (1603–25) and Charles I (1625–49), emphasized that the king received his powers directly from God, and could not be called to account by his subjects (the divine right of kings).

Following the English Civil War, Charles was eventually beheaded and the Commonwealth established. When King Charles II was restored to the throne in 1660, the bishops, the *Prayer Book* and Anglican system were all re-established; but the Stuarts themselves became Catholics and eventually were overthrown in 1688.

Scotland

At the opening of the sixteenth century Scotland was still a feudal country with a corrupt church. Scotland was awakened to Lutheranism by Patrick Hamilton, a student of Luther, who was burned for his faith in 1528. George Wishart and John Knox (1505–72) continued Hamilton's work, but Knox was taken prisoner by the French in 1547 and forced to serve as a galley-slave. When freed, he studied under Calvin in Geneva and Bullinger in Zürich. From the vantage point of Europe, and as an observer of events rather thar a participant, he realized that the future of the Reformation lay in a protestant England united with a protestant Scotland. In 1557 the Scottish Protestants covenanted to effect reformation, and wrote to Calvin and Knox urging the return of Knox to Scotland. Knox responded, and set out for Scotland. But he was stopped at Dieppe because of the hostile activities of Mary Tudor and Mar of Guise. It was at this moment he wrote his *First Blast... agains the monstrous Regiment of Wome* (1558).

He reached Scotland the next year. Fearlessly he launched the Reformation, attacking the papac the mass and Catholic idolatry. The Catholic Mary Queen of Sco opposed Knox. Knox clearly saw that if he could prevail in Scotlan and if Cecil could keep England Protestant, then the Reformatio was won for all Britain, and a new Protestant united nation would be born. As the Scottish historia Lindsay expressed it, 'Elizabeth' crown and Parke's mitre depend on the victory of Knox in Scotlan With the help of the English army and navy, the French were drive out, and Scotland was left to sett her own affairs.

THOMAS CRANMER

James Atkinson

Thomas Cranmer, the man largely responsible for shaping the Church of England after the Reformation.

Thomas Cranmer (1489–1556) was largely responsible for shaping the Protestant Church of England. He was born at Asclacton, Nottinghamshire, and educated at Cambridge University. He remained a quiet scholar until he was suddenly summoned to Canterbury as archbishop in 1532, following advice he had given earlier about Henry VIII's divorce. Cranmer remained archbishop throughout Henry's turbulent reign, and kept Henry's respect to the end. He then piloted the Reformation through the reign of King Edward VI; but he was deposed by Mary, and burnt as a heretic at Oxford in 1556.

Cranmer was a godly man, Lutheran in his theology, well read in the church Fathers, a gifted liturgist, and had a superb command of English. He was sensitive and brave, cautious and slow to decide in a period of transition bedevilled by turbulence and treachery. He preferred reformation by gentle persuasion, rather than by force. Like Luther, he believed firmly in the role of the 'godly prince', who had a God-given task to uphold a just society, and give free scope to the gospel.

Archbishop Cranmer was responsible for the *Great Bible* (1538) and its prefaces; the *Litany* of 1545 and the two *Prayer Books* of 1549 and 1552. He also produced the *Reformation of Church Laws* (published in 1571) and a defence of the doctrine of the sacrament, 1550. He was largely responsible for the *Articles* of the Church of England, the *Homilies* and the *Institution of a Christian man*.

The driving force of Cranmer's life was to restore to the church of the West the catholic faith it had so long lost. When the church of Rome refused to be reformed, Cranmer took it upon himself to reform his own province of Canterbury. He sought an ecumenical council with the Lutherans and the Calvinists of Europe, but Melanchthon proved too timid.

Cranmer's second great concern was to restore a living theology based on the experience of the person and work of Christ. From his doctrine of Christ came Cranmer's theology of justification by faith and of Christ's presence in the sacraments. His third emphasis was the doctrine of the Holy Spirit —which lay behind his high view of scripture and tradition, and the meaning of union with Christ.

At the end he experienced a long solitary confinement, and was brain-washed into recanting. But at his final trial in 1556 he put up a magnificent defence, and died bravely at the stake. He first thrust into the flames the hand that had once written the recantations. The Martyrs' Memorial at Oxford commemorates his death, together with those of Ridley and Latimer, whose deaths he had witnessed from prison a year earlier.

At this time Knox's one and only theological work appeared in Geneva (1560), his *Treatise on Predestination*. Through his preaching at St Giles, Edinburgh, Knox grew in stature. At the request of Parliament, he drew up a *Confession of Faith and Doctrine* (1560, displaced in 1647 by the *Westminster Confession*). Knox's warm document confirmed the four ecumenical councils. He emphasized the evangelical doctrines of grace and forgiveness, the Word and Scripture, and the Holy Spirit and the Church. He urged the distinctive necessity of discipline. The General Assembly was called in 1560, a date which settled the Reformation in Scotland. The Book of Discipline followed (1561), a new liturgy in the *Book of Common Order* (1564) and a translation of Calvin's *Catechism*. Knox had now consolidated the Reformation in Scotland, where it reigns to this day.

Mary, the autocratic and despotic queen, now faced Knox, a prophet of religious truth who maintained the spiritual and civil rights of the common people. Knox prevailed. After disreputable plots, sordid intrigues and even war, Mary was eventually beaten in battle. She was tried and imprisoned. She displayed supreme courage and regal dignity, but in the end she was executed in 1587. On the death of Elizabeth, it was Mary's son to Lord Darnley who united the two kingdoms—as James VI of Scotland and James I of England.

Ireland

The Reformation in Ireland is a story of misunderstanding and bitterness. The new ideas were imposed from outside and Ireland became a land of intrigue and counter-intrigue.

The Celtic church of Ireland existed before the time of Patrick (432). The Danes began to invade Ireland in 795, and by the eleventh century Danish bishops had brought the Irish largely under the church of Rome. This transfer was completed by Lanfranc and Anselm, Norman archbishops of

JOHN BUNYAN

Tim Dowley

John Bunyan (1628–88) is widely known as the writer of the English classic, *The Pilgrim's Progress*.

Bunyan was born at Elstow, Bedfordshire, the son of a poor brazier or tinker. In the 1650s he served for a time in the Parliamentary army during the Civil War. His first wife, whom he married in 1649, caused him to try to reform his way of life.

In 1651 he came into contact with an independent congregation meeting at Bedford. Bunyan despaired over his spiritual state for several years. Finally he experienced assurance of God's saving work in him. He joined the Bedford congregation, and soon began to preach successfully for them. This led his imprisonment in Bedford jail after the Restoration (1660). John spent much of the period 1660–72 as a prisoner, and was again in jail around 1676.

It was during these jail years that his books began to appear. *Grace Abounding to the Chief of Sinners* (1666) was an account of Bunyan's own spiritual pilgrimage. In it, he described God's working and speaking to him through every aspect of life.

The Pilgrim's Progress was first published in 1678. It is an allegory based on Bunyan's spiritual life. In the book Christian meets such well-known characters as anterbury. King Henry II of ngland gained the permission of e pope to bring Ireland within his phere, landed in Ireland in 1171, nd appointed English bishops. his attempt at anglicization alienated the Irish chieftains and many of their people.

When Henry VIII rejected the papacy in England he also compelled the Irish to do the same thing in 1537. But no change of doctrine was made. The low level of education, absence of any

> “*Then Mr Valiant-for-Truth said: ‘I am going to my fathers, and though with great difficulty I am got hither, yet now I do not repent me of all the trouble I have been at to arrive where I am. My sword I give to him that shall succeed me in my pilgrimage, and my courage and skill, to him that can get it. My marks and scars I carry with me, to be a witness for me that I have fought his battles who will now be my rewarder.’ When the day that he must go hence was come, many accompanied him to the river side, unto which as he went he said, ‘Death, where is thy sting?’ And as he went down deeper he said, ‘Grave, where is thy victory?’ So he passed over and the trumpets sounded for him on the other side.*”
>
> JOHN BUNYAN, *The Pilgrim's Progress*

Evangelist, Faithful, Pliable and Giant Despair. His hazardous journey takes him from the City of Destruction, through the Slough of Despond, to the foot of the cross; then on through the Valley of the Shadow, Vanity Fair, Doubting Castle and many other places till he finally crosses the river to reach the shining city.

Bunyan's language is a happy mixture of homespun phrases and echoes of the English Bible. His beliefs come straight from the pages of his Bible, and are shaped by his own Calvinist and Independent position.

His other well-known work, *The Holy War* (1682), uses warfare images to construct another allegory. The book is very complex, and mixes personal and cosmic events. But it was *The Pilgrim's Progress* which soon established itself as a perennial classic.

John Bunyan, from an eighteenth-century engraving. He is dreaming of the beginning of *The Pilgrim's Progress*, with Christian fleeing the City of Destruction.

printed books in Irish, and lack of Irish reformers made any doctrinal change virtually impossible. Under King Edward VI a reformed liturgy was introduced from England. In fact, the English *Prayer Book*, published in Dublin in 1551, was the first book printed in Ireland. Queen Mary re-established Roman Catholicism in Ireland, deposed the reforming bishops and punished married clergy.

Queen Elizabeth, in her turn, restored the English liturgy. In 1560 the Irish parliament again repudiated the authority of the pope and passed the Act of Uniformity which set up Anglicanism as the national religion. It was a great tragedy that the Reformation was imposed on Ireland by the English, for in this way Protestantism became inseparably linked with foreign rule. Under King James I many Presbyterian Scots settled in northern Ireland (Ulster).

Under Charles II and James II church life in Ireland went from bad to worse. William of Orange tried to change matters in 1689, but the church had been so long treated as a department of state that a deadness prevailed in spiritual lif which sank lower and lower duri the eighteenth century.

Conflict in the sixteenth century, a woodcut by Albrecht Dürer.

The radicals

Luther experienced more oppos tion from radical reformers than he did from Catholics. The radic wanted more wide-ranging changes than Luther. While Lutl was a prisoner in the Wartburg (1521–22), Andreas Karlstadt took over the leadership of the reform movement in Wittenberg itself. Assisted by a few fiery monks he set the church in Witte berg in a more extreme directio

Luther believed that it was necessary only to preach the Wo of God, teach the Bible, and allo the Holy Spirit to create fresh ways through the old forms for a believing church to emerge. He always hoped for a reformation of doctrine and morality within an undivided church. Inevitably he clashed with the radicals, some of whom expressed their theology in terms of the political and revolutionary hopes of the age. The clash came to a head in the disastrous Peasants' War of 1525. Luther bitterly opposed the peasants' uprising, which wa supported by many, and led by t able and learned Thomas Müntz During its course 100,000 perished, and indescribable misery followed the destruction of farms agricultural implements and catt

Luther always attempted to work with a 'godly prince'. He made a clear-cut division betwee the concerns and responsibilities of church and state. The radicals sometimes called 'enthusiasts', wanted to carry a complete spiritual reformation of the churc and expected Christians to live by the standards and teaching of Scripture. Their reform programme was more far-reaching than most people would accept.

A flood of Bibles

Tony Lane

Throughout the Middle Ages the Bible was known almost exclusively in the Latin translation known as the *Vulgate*. But the humanist scholars of the Renaissance period had a new concern to recover the original Hebrew and Greek texts of the Bible.

The Hebrew text

The Jews were the first to print a complete Hebrew Old Testament, at Soncino (north Italy) in 1488. In the next few years two further editions appeared, probably from the same group of Jews. The first Christian contribution came some years later. Early in the sixteenth century the Catholic university at Alcalá in Spain produced a massive work known as the *Complutensian Polyglot*. This consisted of the Hebrew and Greek *(Septuagint)* Old Testament, the Greek New Testament and the Latin *Vulgate*. It was printed between 1514 and 1517 but the pope delayed authorization and it was not issued until about 1522.

In the meantime, in 1516–17, a Christian, Daniel Bomberg, printed the Rabbinical Bible (the Hebrew Old Testament together with the Targums (paraphrases) and the rabbinical commentaries), which had been edited by a Christian Jew, Felix Pratensis. In 1524–25 Bomberg printed a second edition, with the aid of a Jew, Jacob ben Chayim. This edition is important: Chayim went to great pains to consult as many different Hebrew manuscripts as possible. Further editions of the Hebrew Old Testament appeared, notably from Sebastian Münster (1535), Robert Estienne (1539–44) and Christopher Plantin (1569–72), but these did nothing to help recover the original text.

The Greek text

Although Volume 5 of the *Complutensian Polyglot*, which contained the Greek text of the New Testament, was printed in 1514, it was not issued for some years. This gave an opportunity for the Basle printer, Froben, to be the first to publish. He persuaded Erasmus to complete his own edition of the Greek text in great haste, which resulted in many errors. This was then rushed through the press and appeared in 1516. Conservatives reacted with hostility. Erasmus had had the effrontery to include his own Latin translation, rather than the traditional *Vulgate*. Furthermore he had omitted the famous 'Johannine comma' of 1 John 5:7, 8 (the reference to the Trinity found in the King James' Version but in neither the original Greek nor modern translations).

Erasmus' New Testament went through many editions and was improved, though under pressure he restored the Johannine comma. The first serious attempt to produce a critical edition of the Greek New Testament (attempting to get back to the original text by comparing surviving manuscripts) was that of Simon Collines, a Parisian printer, in 1534. This work was continued by his step-son Robert Estienne, who produced several editions from 1546, first at Paris and later at Geneva, where he had fled because of his Protestant beliefs. Estienne's work was continued by Theodore Beza, Calvin's successor at Geneva, who produced a series of editions of the Greek New Testament, beginning in 1565. This text came to be known as the *textus receptus,* or the text which was universally accepted; the attempt to get back to the original text was abandoned for some time.

The Latin Bible

The *Vulgate* was the authentic text of the Bible for the Roman Catholic church and this was confirmed by the Council of Trent in 1546. Various attempts were made by individual printers and scholars to produce an accurate edition of the *Vulgate,* either by revising it against the Hebrew and Greek, or by consulting early manuscripts of the *Vulgate.* In 1590 Pope Sixtus V issued an official edition of the *Vulgate,* together with severe penalties for those who dared to alter it. But, two years later, his successor Clement VIII was forced to revise it and produce a more accurate edition. This then became the standard text of the *Vulgate.*

Translations

The invention of printing allowed the Bible to be circulated more widely than ever before. With this possibility came the desire of the Reformers to make the Word of God available to all people in their own language. This came at a period when it was unusual to write in the vernacular languages, and works such as the *Luther Bible* contributed greatly to growth of the European languages.

The Reformers did not accept the Old Testament *Apocrypha* (which is not part of the Hebrew Bible, but is accepted by the Roman Catholic church) as inspired Scripture. But they recognized it as profitable to read, and it was included in the great majority of Bibles during this period.

German The major German translation of the sixteenth centur is Luther's. All the other German translations are dependent upon it. Luther translated the New Testament early in 1522, in two-and-a-half months, and the Old Testament in stages between 1522 and 1532. The first complet *Luther Bible* (with the *Apocrypha*) appeared at Wittenberg in 1534. Earlier that year it had been translated into Low German. The *Luther Bible* was frequently revised and the last revision befor Luther's death (1545) later came to be regarded as the definitive version. It has been said that 'Luther's Bible was a literary eve of the first magnitude, for it is the first work of art in German prose.

French No one French Bible has the exalted status of the *Luth Bible.* The humanist Jacques Lefèvre d'Étaples was the pionee with his New Testament (1523), followed by the Old Testament and *Apocrypha* (1528). These were produced together in 1530 a the *Antwerp Bible.* Although this translation kept close to both the text and the Latin words of the *Vulgate* it was used as a basis for later translations.

In 1535 Calvin's cousin, Pierre Robert Olivetan, produced the *Neuchâtel Bible,* which had been sponsored mainly by the Waldensian church. This translation drew upon Lefèvre's, especially for the New Testamen and *Apocrypha.* The pastors of Geneva (including Calvin and Theodore Beza) produced many revisions of this translation. The 1588 revision became the definiti *Geneva Bible.*

Less influential, but no less skilful, was the translation by Sebastian Castellio, which appeared at Basle in 1555. In 1550, a Roman Catholic revision of Lefèvre's translation had been produced at Louvain. This was

The title page of the *Great Bible* (1539). King Henry VIII is pictured giving copies to Archbishop Cranmer and Chancellor Thomas Cromwell, who in turn distribute them to the people, who are loyally shouting *'Vivat Rex!'*

> "*If God spare my life, ere many years pass I will cause a boy that driveth the plough shall know more of the Scriptures than thou dost.*"
>
> WILLIAM TYNDALE

evised a number of times to ecome, in 1578, the definitive *Louvain Bible*.

English The pioneer of the English Bible is William Tyndale, who published the New Testament (1525 and later revisions) and part of the Old Testament. Complete Bibles began to appear: Miles Coverdale's in 1535 and the *Matthew Bible* in 1537. With the backing of Thomas Cranmer and Thomas Cromwell the *Matthew Bible* was revised by Coverdale to become the *Great Bible* (1539).

During the reign of Queen Mary (1553–58) many leading Protestants went into exile. Those at Geneva determined to produce a new translation of the Bible. The New Testament and Psalms appeared in 1557 and finally the

WILLIAM TYNDALE AND THE ENGLISH BIBLE

Tony Lane

The title page of the first Bible to be printed in English; Miles Coverdale's translation (1535). Coverdale had helped Tyndale to revise his translation of the Pentateuch.

William Tyndale is celebrated for his English translation of the New Testament. He was educated at Magdalen Hall, Oxford, and possibly later at Cambridge. He then became tutor to the family of Sir John Walsh. While living in his household Tyndale saw at first hand the ignorance of the local clergy. To one cleric he is reported to have declared that: if God spare my life, ere many years pass, I will cause a boy that driveth the plough shall know more of the Scriptures than thou dost.' This task became his life's work.

> *"Euangelio (that we cal gospel) is a greke word, and signifyth good, mery, glad and joyful tydings, that maketh a mannes hert glad, and maketh hym synge, daunce and leepe for joye."*
>
> *WILLIAM TYNDALE*

William Tyndale suffered shipwreck, loss of manuscripts, pursuit by secret agents, betrayal by friends and pirated edition in his efforts to publish the Bible in English.

The bishops had banned the English Bible since 1408 because they feared the Lollards, who had their own translation (the *Wyclif Bible*). As this translation had been made only from the Latin *Vulgate* and was inaccurate, Tyndale set out to make a translation from the Hebrew and Greek. He hoped to win the support of the learned bishop of London, Cuthbert Tunstall. But the bishops were more concerned to prevent the spread of Lutheran ideas than to promote the study of Scripture. In due course Tyndale obtained financial support from a number of London merchants, especially Humphrey Monmouth.

It was clear that England was no safe place to translate the Bible, so Tyndale left for Europe, never to return. By early 1525 his New Testament was ready for the press. Tyndale narrowly escaped arrest at Cologne, but managed to see the book published later the same year at Worms.

Tyndale's translation has had an immense influence, and rightly earned him the title of the 'father of the English Bible'. It could almost be said that every English New Testament until this century was simply a revision of Tyndale's. Some 90 per cent of his words passed into the King James' Version and about 75 per cent into the Revised Standard Version. Tyndale also translated parts of the Old Testament, including the first five books. He was unable to complete the Old Testament because he was betrayed and arrested near Brussels in 1535. In October 1536 he was strangled and burnt, it is reported that his last words were: 'Lord, open the king of England's eyes.'

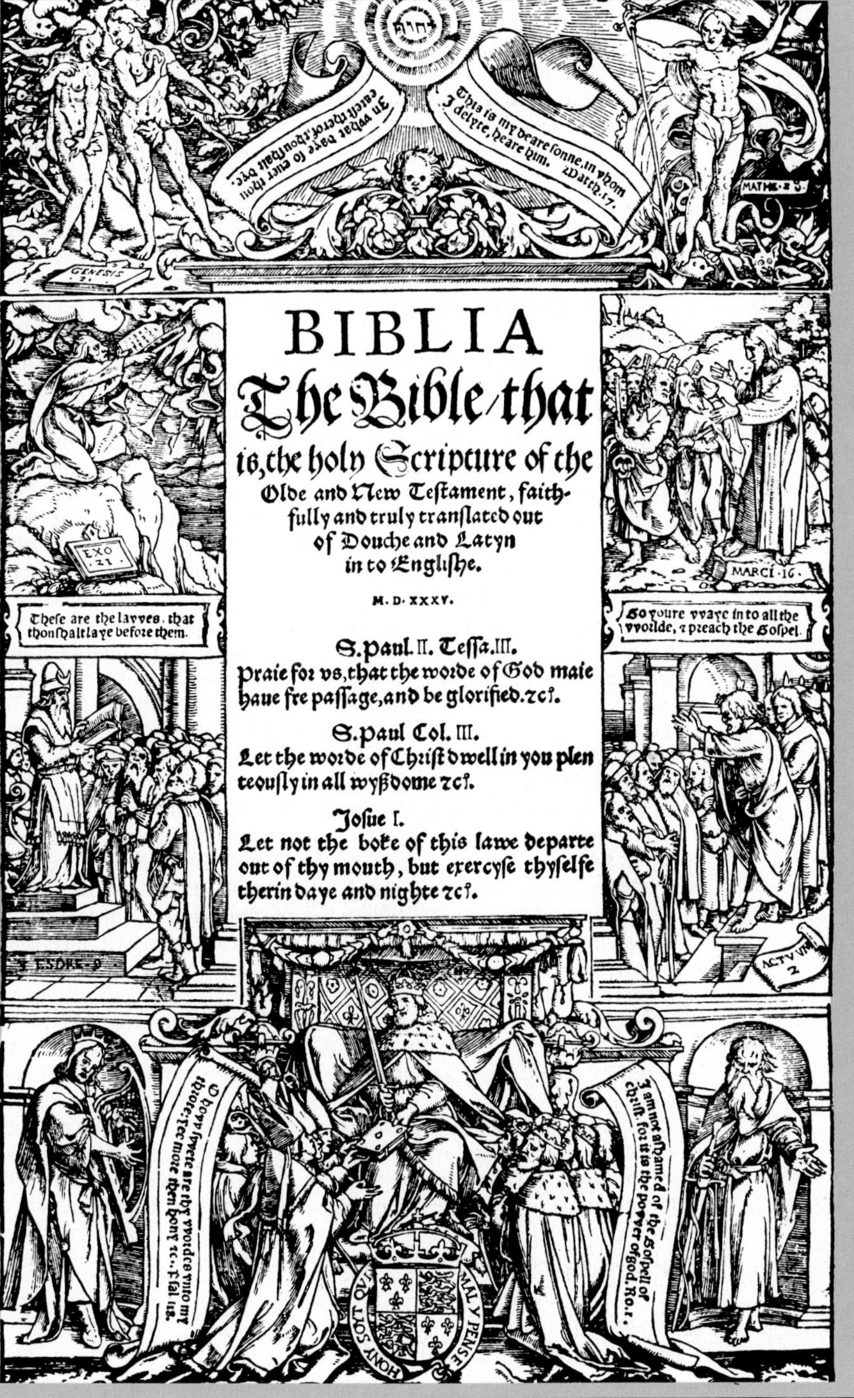
In what daye so euer thou eatest therof, thou shalt dye.
This is my deare sonne, in whom I delyte, heare him. Matth. 17.
GENESIS 2.
MATHE. 28.
BIBLIA
The Bible/that
is, the holy Scripture of the
Olde and New Teſtament, faith-
fully and truly tranſlated out
of Douche and Latyn
in to Engliſhe.
M.D.XXXV.
EXO. 21.
These are the lawes, that thou ſhalt laye before them.
MARCI. 16.
Go youre waye in to all the worlde, & preach the Goſpel.
S.paul. II. Teſſa. III.
Praie for vs, that the worde of God maie
haue fre paſſage, and be glorified. &c.
S.paul Col. III.
Let the worde of Chriſt dwell in you plen
teouſly in all wyſdome &c.
Joſue I.
Let not the boke of this lawe departe
out of thy mouth, but exercyſe thyſelfe
therin daye and nighte &c.
ESDRE. 9.
ACTUUM 2.
O how ſwete are thy wordes vnto my throte: yee more then hony &c. Pſal. 118.
I am not aſhamed of the Goſpell of Chriſt, for it is the power of god. Ro. I.
HONY SOIT QUI MAL Y PENSE

complete *Geneva Bible* in 1560. The New Testament was revised in later editions. This translation became immensely popular. The bishops attempted to undermine it with their *Bishops' Bible* (1568) but this never became popular. The one major Roman Catholic translation at this time is the *Rheims-Douai Bible.* This was translated from the *Vulgate* and appeared in 1582 (New Testament, Rheims) and 1609–10 (Old Testament, Douai).

King James I sponsored a new translation of the Bible following a request by the Puritans in 1604. It appeared in 1611, and drew heavily on all that was good in previous translations. This translation, often inaccurately called the *Authorized Version,* only gradually replaced the *Geneva Bible,* which remained popular for another fifty years.

Dutch Translations of parts of the Bible, and one complete Bible, were printed in Dutch in the fifteenth century. The Reformation led to an increase in such printings, but it was some time before widely-accepted versions appeared. The earliest of these was the *Mennonite Bible,* first printed at Emden in 1558, but later known as the *Biestkens Bible,* after the person who printed it from 1560.

Calvinists mainly used a translation which was heavily dependent upon the *Luther Bible* and which first appeared in 1561–62. This was replaced in 1637 by the *Statenvertaling* or 'States' translation' which was produced at the expense of the states. This became the standard version, and was adopted by the Mennonites in the seventeenth century. The Catholics had their own translation, made by Nicolaas van Winghe in 1548 from the *Vulgate.* This translation, wit revisions, remained in use for several centuries.

Italian Work on an Italian Bib began in the 1530s, pioneered by Antonio Brucioli. Others followe in his footsteps. But the first Protestant Italian Bible did not appear until 1562 at Geneva, and this was only a revision of earlier translations. The greatest was th of the Italian emigrant, Giovanni Diodati, who was Beza's success at Geneva. He produced a transla tion of the Bible in 1607 which was further revised in 1641. This translation was unchallenged unti the end of the eighteenth century and remained in use much longer

Spanish In Spain the Inquisition was more effective than elsewhere, and work on Bible translation had to take place mainly outside the country. Two translations of the New Testame appeared in the middle of the sixteenth century: those of Francisc de Enzinas (Antwerp, 1543) and Juan Pérez de Pineda (Geneva, 1556). The first complete Spanis Bible was that of Cassiodoro de Reyna, a former monk, which appeared at Basle in 1569.

Swedish Sweden early had a standard translation in the form of the 1541 *Uppsala Bible.* This was translated by Laurentius Petri, possibly with the help of hi brother.

Danish In Denmark the standard translation was the *Christian III Bible,* printed in 1550 at Copenhagen. This was revised in 1589 and 1633, the revisions also being named after kings. Thi indicates the extent to which the Reformation in Scandinavia was firmly controlled by the state.

The Anabaptists

John H. Yoder and Alan Kreider

The Anabaptists made the most radical attempt of the Reformation era to renew the church. They did not consist of a single, coherent organizing, but a loose grouping of movements. All rejected infant baptism and practised the baptism of adults upon confession of faith. They never accepted the label 'Anabaptist' (meaning 'rebaptizer')—a term of reproach which was coined by their opponents. They objected to the implication that the ceremonial sprinkling which they had received as infants had in fact been a valid baptism. They denied that their baptism of believing adults was arrogant and superfluous. To their grief, they also soon discovered that the term 'Anabaptist' gave the authorities a legal precedent—harking back to the fifth-century Roman laws against the Donatists—to persecute and execute them.

A split in Zürich

To the Anabaptists, however, the fundamental issue was not baptism. More basic was their growing conviction about the role the civil government should play in the reformation of the church. Late in 1523 intense debate on this issue broke out in Zürich. At that time it became clear that the Zürich city council was unwilling to bring about the religious changes that the theologians believed were called for by Scripture.

The Anabaptists issue was a subject of hot debate in sixteenth-century Zürich.

What then? Should one wait, and attempt to persuade the authorities by preaching? This was the view of the Zürich Reformer, Zwingli. Or should the community of Christians, led by the Holy Spirit, initiate Scripture-backed reforms regardless of the views of the council? So argued Zwingli's radical disciples. Despite continuing attempts to discuss the matters in dispute (the mass, baptism and tithes), the gap between the two parties widened.

"No one can truly know Christ except he follow him in life."

Finally, on 21 January 1525, came a complete rupture. On that day the Zürich city council forbade the radicals to assemble or disseminate their views. That evening, in the neighbouring village of Zollikon, 'praying that God would grant them to do his divine will and that he would show them mercy,' the radicals met, baptized each other, and so became the first free church of modern times.

Despite the fact that it was illegal from the outset, the Anabaptist movement spread rapidly throughout German-speaking Europe. Unlike the other Reformers, the Anabaptists were not committed to the notion that 'Christendom' was Christian. From the beginning they saw themselves as missionaries to people of lukewarm piety, only partly obedient to the gospel.

The Anabaptists systematically divided Europe into sectors for evangelistic outreach and sent missionaries out into them in twos and threes. Many people were bewildered by their message; and others pulled back when the cost of Anabaptist discipleship became clear. But others heard them gladly. Mysticism, late-medieval asceticism, and the disillusionment which followed the peasants' revolts of 1524–25 had prepared the way for the Anabaptists. Almost simultaneously with events in Switzerland, Anabaptist-type groups sprang up spontaneously in various parts of Europe. By the late 1520s Anabaptism was to be found as far afield as Holland and Moravia, the Tyrol and Mecklenburg.

Anabaptist beliefs

What did these Anabaptists believe? There was a considerable variety of opinion among them. Their rapid growth, the diverse backgrounds of their able leaders, and the absence of any ecclesiastical authority to control them were enough to ensure that.

But they did attempt to agree upon a common basis. In 1527 at Schleitheim (on today's Swiss-German border, near Schaffhausen) the Anabaptists called the first 'synod' of the Protestant Reformation. The leading figure at this meeting was the former Benedictine prior, Michael Sattler who, four months later, was burne[d] at the stake in nearby Rottenburg-am-Neckar. The 'Brotherly Union[']' adopted at Schleitheim was to be a highly significant document. Durin[g] the next decade most Anabaptists in all parts of Europe came to agree with the beliefs which it laid down.

By 1540 there was a body of beliefs which broadly characterized the movement as a whole. Important among these conviction[s] was what the Anabaptists called 'discipleship'. The Christian's relationship with Jesus Christ mus[t] go beyond inner experience and acceptance of doctrines. It must involve a daily walk with God, in which Christ's teaching and example shaped a transformed style of life. As one Anabaptist put it, 'No one can truly know Christ except he follow him in life.' This meant resolutely obeying the 'bright and clear words of the Son of God, whose word is truth and whose commandment is eternal life'.

The consequences of being

ı disciple, as the Anabaptists ealized, were wide-ranging. To :hoose only one, the Anabaptists ·ejected the swearing of oaths, ›ecause of Jesus' clear command n the Sermon on the Mount. For hem there could be no gradation ›f levels of truth-telling.

A second Anabaptist principle —the principle of love—grew ogically out of the first. In their lealings with non-Anabaptists, hey acted as pacifists. They would ıeither go to war, defend themselves against their persecutors, ıor take part in coercion by the state.

The love ethic was also expressed within the Anabaptist communities, in mutual aid and the redistribution of wealth. Among Moravian Anabaptists it even led to Christian communism.

Restoring the church

Anabaptist beliefs about the church were very distinctive. They were ıot interested in simply reforming he church; they were committed o *restoring* it to the vigour and aithfulness of its earliest centuies. In the Scriptures they read of a church which was not a wealthy and powerful institution—but a family of brothers and sisters in Christ. It existed, not because it was recognized by some outside ecclesiastical or political organization, but because God was at work among his people.

The Anabaptists came to elaborate upon the 'congregational' view of church authority, towards which Luther and Zwingli had inclined in their earliest reforming years. In their congregations, all members were to be believers, baptized voluntarily as adults upon confession of faith. Decision-making was to be by the entire membership. In deciding matters of doctrine, the authority of Scripture was to be interpreted, not by a dogmatic tradition or by an ecclesiastical leader, but by the consensus of the local gathering—in which all could speak, and listen critically. In matters of church discipline, the believers were also to act corporately. They were to assist each other to live out faithfully the meaning of their baptismal commitments.

A fourth major Anabaptist conviction was the insistence upon

Ferryman Pieter Pietersz was burned to death in Amsterdam in 1569, because he had made his boat available for Christians to hold services. In an age of intolerance, many Anabaptists suffered for their faith.

the separation of church and state. Christians, they claimed, were a 'free, unforced, uncompelled people'. Faith is a free gift of God, and the authorities exceed their competence when they 'champion the Word of God with a fist'. The Anabaptists also believed that the church was distinct from society, even if society claimed to be Christian. Christ's true followers were a pilgrim people; and his church was an association of perpetual aliens.

> "*The regenerated do not go to war, nor engage in strife. They are the children of peace who have beaten their swords into plowshares and their spears into pruning hooks, and know of no war . . . Since we are to be conformed to the image of Christ, how can we then fight our enemies with the sword? . . . Spears and swords of iron we leave to whose who, alas, consider human blood and swine's blood of well-nigh equal value . . .*"
>
> *MENNO SIMONS, 1539*

Twenty-five years' persecution

To the established leaders of Protestant and Catholic Europe, these beliefs (and the personalities and movements which gave rise to them) were alarming indeed. The Reformers were understandably dismayed when news spread of Anabaptists interrupting Protestant sermons or attracting the most earnest of their parishoners. They were also concerned that the Anabaptists' emphasis upon life as well as belief seemed to challenge the basic Reformation principle of 'by faith alone'.

In vain did the Anabaptists protest that their ethical teachings were not a means of obtaining salvation—but rather a necessary expression of the new life in Christ which resulted from salvation. In fact, the Anabaptists argued, these teachings stemmed from specific scriptural commandments.

The Reformers were not impressed by this reasoning. By 1527 they had determined to use all necessary means to root out Anabaptism. They were joined in this determination by the Catholic authorities. To Protestants and Catholics alike, the Anabaptists seemed not only to be dangerous heretics; they also seemed to threaten the religious and social stability of Christian Europe. In the carnage of the next quarter of a century thousands of Anabaptis were put to death (by fire in the Catholic territories, by drowning and the sword under Protestant regimes). Thousands more saved their skins by recanting.

The authorities' persecution of the Anabaptists seemed to be jus fied by the upheaval at Münster in the mid-1530s. In 1534 a group of Anabaptists who expected the millennium came to power in Münster, an episcopal city in Westphalia. When the bishop massed his troops to besiege the city, these Anabaptists defended themselves by arms. As the siege progressed, even more extreme leaders gained control. Some of the Münsterite leaders claimed prophetic authority to received new revelations. They claimed that Old Testament ethics still applied, and thus they felt justified in reintroducing polygamy. They even crowned a 'King David'.

For centuries churches and governments have exploited the excesses of these months prior to the fall of the city in June 1535 to make 'Anabaptism' an all-embracing by-word for fanaticism and disorder. It is striking, however, that many of the major principles of the Münsterites (for example, the linking of church and state, the validity of Old Testament social patterns and the right of Christians to take part in violence) were more typical of the official churches than they were c other Anabaptists.

War no more

In the aftermath of the suppressio of Münster, the dispirited Anabap tists of the lower-Rhine area were given new heart by the ministry o Menno Simons (about 1496–1561 This former priest travelled widely, although always in great personal danger. He visited the cattered Anabaptist groups of orthern Europe and inspired them vith his night-time preaching. Aenno was unswerving in ommanding pacifism. As a result, is name in time came to stand or the movement's repudiation f violence. Although Menno was ot the founder of the movement, nost of the twentieth-century escendants of the Anabaptists are alled 'Mennonite'.

Anabaptists had also spread in rge numbers eastwards to the yrol and Moravia. The early nissioner who took the message astwards along the Alps to he Tyrol was Jörg Cajacob Blaurock'), who had been the rst adult to be baptized, in 1525. Vhen the Tyrolean Catholic uthorities began to persecute hem intensely, many of the nabaptists found refuge on the nds of some exceptionally tolerent princes in Moravia. There they ounded a very long-lasting form f economic community called he *Bruderhof*. In part they aimed o follow the pattern of the early postolic community. But they ought community for practical easons too—as a means of group urvival under persecution. Their ommunities attempted to show hat commitment to others comes efore self in the kingdom of God. Consolidated under the leadership of Jakob Hutter (died 1536), hese groups came to be known as Hutterites'.

With the passage of time, and nder the pressure of persecution, nost of the extravagant variety f views, leaders, and separate novements of Anabaptism's earliest years soon sifted out. Only hree groups were able to survive eyond the mid-sixteenth century as ordered communities: the 'brethren' in Switzerland and south Germany; the Mennonites in the Netherlands and north Germany; and the Hutterites in Moravia.

Over the centuries, these descendants lost many of their Anabaptist characteristics. Seeking purity, they became legalistic. In the interests of sheer survival, they lost evangelistic zeal. They became know as excellent farmers, good people, and the 'Quiet in the Land'. Not until the late nineteenth century did they experience revival. But by the 1970s they were experiencing rapid growth; between 1950 and 1988 their worldwide membership more than trebled to a total of 750,000. Whether the mass of the Mennonites can rediscover the spiritual vitality, the evangelistic fervour, and the radical discipleship that made their forefathers such unique actors in the drama of the Reformation is a question that remains to be answered.

A family of sixteenth-century Hutterites, the Anabaptist community in Moravia, from the title page of a book defending the Anabaptists (1589).

EARLY ENGLISH BAPTISTS

John Briggs

In 1608, John Smyth baptized himself in Amsterdam. He had been a fellow of Christ's College, Cambridge, but as a Separatist fled from the harsh rule of James I's England. After his death one of his associates, Thomas Helwys, led back to England a group that had split from Smyth's former congregation. They formed the first General or Arminian Baptist congregation in England at Spitalfields, London, in 1612.

Part of seventeenth-century London from the south side of the River Thames. (*Left to right*) Parliament House, Westminster Hall and Westminster Abbey.

Believers' baptism

By 1638 at the latest there were also congregations holding a Calvinistic theology in London who practised believers' baptism ('Particular Baptists'). These Baptists grew out of the first congregation of English Independents; although it is not known exactly when they adopted full Baptist views. A radical look at church principles, in the Puritan manner, led first to the understanding of the church as a gathered community, and then to a realization that only the baptism of believers fitted such a view.

The extent to which the early Baptists were influenced by European ideas and the thinking of the Radical Reformation is still hotly contested. The links with the Dutch Mennonites in the very earliest days are clear. But it is equally clear that the English Baptist movement came out of a conscientious search among the English Separatists for the pattern of apostolic churches. They believed this could be discovered from the pages of the New Testament, and that it was the only pattern of church organization for all succeeding generations.

These youthful Baptist churches were hurled into the current debate about the relationship between church and state. They championed their own particular answers to that controversy at great personal cost. They soon also became involved, to varying degrees, in the millenarian speculations of the mid-seventeenth century. Like many others, the Baptists eagerly thumbed through the pages of Daniel and Revelation, seeking the signs of the times and looking for guidance about their proper Christian obedience.

At the same time parliamentary opposition to King Charles I hardened and led on relentlessly to the outbreak of the Civil War, or 'English Revolution'. Cromwell's victorious New Model Army held religions opinions which differed from the State-Presbyterianism of Parliament. Independents and Baptists were dominant in the army's leadership and amongst the rank and file. Cromwell allowed an established church to continue but let Baptists, Independents, Presbyterians and non-royalist Anglicans to act as ministers in it. Those who wanted to worship apart from a state church were permitted to continue a separate existence as long as they did not disturb the peace. Some Baptists accepted office in the state church, but the majority chose to continue independently.

What Baptists stood for

The Baptists achieved an early peak of numerical strength and national influence during the interregnum. But even before the Restoration their position was seriously compromised by the loss of members to more radical sects such as the Quakers and the widespread adoption of the revolutionary views of the Fifth Monarchists in many places. Vavasor Powell, a committed Fifth-Monarchist, saw two stark alternatives. He asked his congregation whether God would have 'Oliver Cromwell or Jesus Christ to reign over us?'

When these Baptist congregations claimed local independence, it was freedom from state interference they were seeking. They were not claiming total competence for the local congregation. The need for mutual assistance from congregation to congregation led very early to the setting up of a General Assembly amongst the General Baptists, and of regional 'associations' amongst the Particular Baptists. Both structures became important tools for expanding the work. They also became forums for discussing theological and disciplinary queries, and so for establishing a 'Baptist viewpoint'. Particular Baptist association meetings discussed such issues as 'the gathering of churches, believer's baptism, communion with the unbaptized, the ordination of ministers, the maintenance of the ministry, the place of the magistrate, missionary activity, liturgical usages—such as vocal ministry, breaking bread, psalm-singing, foot-washing, anointing the sick—ecclesiastical discipline, the grounds and manner of exclusion, domestic duties and relationships'.

Persecuted then tolerated

It has been estimated that by 1660 there were roughly 300 General and Particular Baptist churches. The Restoration brought a quarter of a century of intermittent persecution by the state. Local evidence, such as that in *The Broadmead Records* for Bristol, gives graphic details of the price of dissent in these years. When King

One of the old gates of the city of London, from a contemporary illustration. The Baptists formed many congregations in and around the capital in the seventeenth century.

Charles II was restored in 1660 'then Satan stirred up adversaryes against us, and our Trouble or Persecution began'. It was not until 1687 that the churches felt able to look back on 'ye Times of our late Troubles'.

The accession of William and Mary brought only limited toleration. The oppressive laws remained, though Protestant dissenters of Trinitarian faith, who subscribed to the main points of the Thirty-nine Articles, were exempted from penalty. But with toleration came a tolerance for a wider range of theological views. Dissenters and Anglicans both suffered a decline in religious vitality.

On the one hand, the General Baptists, like the Presbyterians, fell prey to the spread of Arianism, which denied the divinity of Christ. By the end of the eighteenth century many General Baptist congregations were calling themselves Unitarians or, at any rate, holding a Unitarian theology. On the other hand, some Particular Baptists, especially those who looked to the London leadership of Gill and Brine, overreacted against theological liberalism. They tended so to stress the sovereignty of God that both individual moral action and evangelism were inhibited in what is known as 'hyper-Calvinism'.

A slow awakening

Consequently Baptists were in no position to benefit immediately from the new life represented by the Great Awakening. But several distinct movements brought the impact of the Awakening to the Baptists. First, a group of working folk in some villages in Leicestershire who had been evangelized by one of the Countess of Huntingdon's servants came, independently, to Baptist convictions in 1755. Dan Taylor, a Yorkshire miner, converted among the Methodists, similarly came to Baptist convictions by his own study of the subject. He sought out the General Baptists of Lincolnshire to be baptized.

Eventually the Leicestershire group and Dan Taylor's church, together with a few General Baptist churches that remained orthodox, formed the 'New Connexion of General Baptists' in 1770. These churches prospered in the emerging industrial communities of central England, the textile communities of Lancashire and Yorkshire, and the hosiery and lace-making areas of the east midlands.

New life came to the Particular Baptists when, in 1785, Andrew Fuller of Kettering published *The Gospel Worthy of all Acceptation*. He 'proved that Calvinism itself, as distinct from the "false Calvinism" which was common in the eighteenth century, was essentially a missionary theology'. This expressed systematically the doubts that a number of ministers had about the prevailing hyper-Calvinism.

The Baptists went through a form of rebirth in the eighteenth century. Their life from that time represents a debate between puritanism and Evangelicalism. The General Baptists who opposed Dan Taylor's enthusiasm lapsed into Unitarianism; the Particular Baptists who rejected the correcting force of the Evangelical Revival and allowed only their own members to the communion table, became the 'Strict Baptists'.

Call to mission

Fuller completed his book in 1781 but hesitated four years before publishing it. In 1784 he was able to apply the thought of the American theologian Jonathan Edwards to the English religious scene. Others too were influenced by the Awakening. Fuller's colleague, John Sutcliffe, issued a 'Call to Prayer' to the Northamptonshire Baptists: 'Let the whole interest of the Redeemer be affectionately remembered and the spread of the Gospel to the most distant parts of the habitable globe be the object of your most fervent requests.'

Out of this renewal of Baptist life came the founding of the Baptist Missionary Society in 1792. William Carey and John Thomas became the Society's first representatives abroad. Fuller, with John Ryland of Bristol, John Sutcliffe of Olney, and Samuel Pearce of Birmingham, supported them at home. The message of *The Gospel Worthy of All Acceptation* not only revived the churches at home, it gave British Baptists a world-wide vision.

In 1812 it was agreed that a more general union of Particular Baptists was desirable, particularly, though not exclusively, to support the work of 'the Baptist Mission'. In such a way revival gave birth to mission and mission to denominational organization. But a further twenty years passed before the Baptist Union was founded.

William Carey, the untiring English Baptist pioneer missionary. His many-sided work in India included Bible translation and production, evangelism, church-planting, education and medical relief, as well as social reform, and linguistic and horticultural research.

THE CATHOLIC REFORMATION

Robert D. Linder

The response of the church of Rome to Martin Luther's '95 Theses' and his attack upon its authority is both curious and revealing. It is curious because the Roman church seemed unaware of the widespread unrest among the faithful which Luther's protest represented. It is revealing in that the first response to the rumblings in northern Europe was low-key and almost nonchalant. Yet the way in which the church of Rome reacted to Luther and his cause was to have far-reaching consequences.

Leo and Luther

Leo X (1513–21), pope at the time of the circulation of Luther's '95 Theses', had other things on his mind. Leo was in many ways a typical Renaissance pope: elegant, worldly, sophisticated, intelligent, consumed with political and family ambition, more of an administrator than 'a servant of the servants of God'. He was also an enthusiastic patron of Renaissance art and ideals. He aimed to advance the fortunes of his own family—the Medicis of Florence—and to increase the political power of the Papal States in central Italy, of which he was ruler. He revelled in Renaissance activities and spent a great deal of money on the arts and gambling. In addition, the day-to-day routine of managing the large and corrupt papal bureaucracy took much of his time and energy. All of this sapped his ability to give any kind of moral leadership over Christian Europe at a critical point in its history.

When Leo first saw a copy of Luther's Theses in 1518, he is supposed to have made two comments. Probably neither of them is authentic but both are in keepin with his known initial response to Luther. The first was: 'Luther is a drunken German. He will feel different when he is sober.' The second: 'friar Martin is a brilliant chap. The whole row is due to the envy of the monks.' He concluded that it was probably 'only a monks quarrel'.

Two important points emerge about the short-term response of church and papacy to Luther. First, the negative and disdainful attitude of the Roman church towards Luther's initial pronounce ments helped make the Wittenber professor a major public figure, especially in Germany. Second, it showed that the church was not aware of the significance of the threat it was facing. Indeed, the great irony and danger of the situation was that the pope was in no position to provide the kind of inspiring leadership necessary to head off Luther's challenge. Nor was he able to provide a constructive channel for this new force.

Relations between Luther and the papacy deteriorated badly afte 1519, as leaders of the church began to realize what Luther was in fact saying. When they saw that he was calling for a spiritual autho ity other than the one established and accepted by the late medieval church and for a major overhaul of the institution of the church itself—a threat to vested interest —they came to regard Luther as a 'son of iniquity'. By 1520 the die vas cast. Following his reading of .uther's *Babylonian Captivity of he Church* in that year, Erasmus adly noted: 'The Breach is irreparable.' And so it was. The Diet of Vorms in 1521 confirmed Luther's xcommunication and declared him political outlaw.

But through all of this there vere some who remained within he church of Rome, many in high laces, who readily acknowledged he truth of Luther's accusations f misplaced spiritual authority and nstitutional corruption. Many of hese, troubled about the situation or a variety of reasons, did not eave the church. Instead, these ious individuals worked in many lifferent ways to reform the hurch of Rome from within. This arge number of devout Catholics ontributed to the long-term esponse to the Protestant challenge, now known as the Catholic Reformation. This movement was n part a direct reaction to the xternal threat of the Protestant novement, and in part an effort to orrect internal abuses and restore genuine piety to the Roman Church.

Among the various outworkings f the Catholic Reformation were: he establishment of the Oratory f Divine Love; the reform of the apacy; the founding of the Society f Jesus and several other new nonastic orders; the meeting of n ecumenical council at Trent; he rejuvenation and reorganization of the Inquisition; the issuing f an 'index' of books which the aithful were not permitted to ead; the resurgence of Catholic nysticism in Spain; and 'wars of eligion' which led to the forced e-conversion of certain areas of Europe from Protestantism to Roman Catholicism. Each of these eatures helped revitalize the hurch of Rome, so that by 1650 it tood at the threshold of a new era f expansion and spiritual vigour.

A society of reformers

In 1517, the same year that Luther posted his Theses at Wittenberg, the Oratory of Divine Love appeared in Rome. An informal society of about fifty clergy and lay people, the Oratory stressed reform along liberal lines similar to the ideas of Erasmus. The group met frequently in the church of Saints Sylvester and Dorothea for prayer, meditation, mutual encouragement and discussions about reforming the institutional church through love and moral improvement. Few of the members favoured radical doctrinal or structural changes. The society included in its ranks some of the most influential leaders in the Roman hierarchy.

St Peter's, Rome. The basic design of the new basilica was by Donato Bramante, but in 1546 Michelangelo was put in charge of its completion.

Among those who identified with the Oratory were Jacopo Sadoleto, Gian Matteo Gilberti, Gaetano da Thiene, Reginald Pole, Gian Pietro Caraffa (who later became Pope Paul IV) and Gasparo Contarini (1483–1542). Of these, Contarini was the most deeply committed to reform on the lines of Erasmus' ideas, and the most openly sympathetic with the Protestant point of view.

Contarini was an experienced politician and diplomat, and a Christian humanist. He was a layman in 1517 but later took holy orders and was made a cardinal in 1535. He was by temperament a peacemaker and apparently shared some views with the evangelicals. Philip Melanchthon, from the Lutheran camp, is often compared with him, because of their similar personalities, conciliatory natures and humanism. Contarini influenced Pope Paul III in the direction of reform. He presided over a papal reform commission, supported attempts at reconciliation with the Protestants, and advocated a return to the faith of the apostles by the church-at-large.

Perhaps Contarini's supreme attempt to bring real and lasting reform to the church of Rome occurred in 1541 when he was a papal legate (or delegate) at the Colloquy of Regensburg. At that meeting the last major effort was made to work out a compromise statement of theology acceptable to both the evangelical Reformers and the Roman leaders. Basing their discussions upon about twenty articles largely drawn up by Protestants, Melanchthon and Contarini hammered out a verbal statement of the doctrine of justification by faith acceptable to both men. However, they were less successful in reaching agreement on questions regarding transubstantiation and the authority of the papacy. After reaching an impasse on these and related points, Melanchthon and Contarini returned to their respective parties only to have their views repudiated in the areas where they had reached agreement.

Luther adamantly refused to accept the compromise formula on faith. When Contarini returned to Italy, he was accused of heresy and associating with enemies of the church. He died the next year, before these charges could be pressed further. The failure of Contarini and other liberals to work out a peaceful solution to the split in the church opened the way for the militant programme of the Catholic hardliners. But before the militants gained contro of the papacy, the positive spiritu momentum created by the Orator of Divine Love led to its reform.

Popes stimulate reforn

A reformed papacy made possible both the positive and negative sides of the vigorous Catholic Reformation. The popes most responsible for reforming the papal office were Clement VII (1523–34), Paul III (1534–49) and Paul VI (1555–59). In so doing, they had to deal with several monumental problems. For one thing, there were serious division among those who remained faithfu to Rome over which course of action to take in order to meet the Protestant threat. Another difficulty facing these popes was the complex political situation in Europe at the time. For example, rulers holding a common Roman Catholic faith were often military and diplomatic rivals. The political situation was muddied further by the fact that the pope was himself the temporal ruler of the Papal States as well as the spiritual leader of the international Roman Catholic church. Finally, those wh had a vested interest in a corrupt church were reluctant to give a reform-minded pope a free hand t cleanse the church of abuses.

Pope Clement VII accomplishe little in the way of reform despite sincere efforts. The political manoeuvrings of the Emperor Charles V and King Francis I

(1515–47) of France often put Clement in an utterly hopeless situation. Each monarch exerted enormous pressure on the pope to side with him. In the end, Clement suffered the wrath of both, and experienced the worst of all possible worlds.

An illustration of the political vice in which Clement found himself was the dilemma he faced following Henry VIII of England's request in 1527 for an annulment of his marriage to Catherine of Aragon. Henry's plea arrived in Rome at a most untimely moment. The city was surrounded by the troops of Charles V, who happened also to be Catherine's nephew. In this situation, no matter what the pope decided, he had to lose. Thus, when he refused Henry's request, the first step towards the English Reformation was taken.

Perhaps the best thing Clement might have done would have been to call an ecumenical council to seek a solution to the problems besetting the church. He did in fact seriously consider such a move, but finally gave up the idea because of the political pincers in which he found himself, as the king of France and the Holy Roman Emperor struggled for supremacy in Europe. He could suggest no venue for the proposed council which was acceptable to both rulers.

Paul III: reformer

Clement made some attempts to end corruption in the church. However, his major contribution to reform was probably his recommendation that the highly gifted Alessandro Farnese should succeed him. Farnese became Pope Paul III, the most sincere reformer to mount the papal throne in the sixteenth century.

GASPARO CONTARINI

John P. Donnelly

Cardinal Contarini (1483–1542) was a leader of reform in the Roman Catholic church. He belonged to a leading family in Venice and studied at the University of Padua. He became well known both for his scientific studies and for defending the doctrine of the immortality of the soul against Pietro Pomponazzi. He served Venice as ambassador to the Emperor Charles V and in other important posts. His study of the constitution of Venice long remained a classic.

But Contarini was also deeply concerned with religious reform. In 1511 he underwent a religious conversion similar to Luther's. He wrote tracts on the ideal bishop, the papacy, the sacraments and Lutheranism. In 1535 Pope Paul III made Contarini a cardinal and a year later named him chairman of a reform commission. Contarini helped win approval for the Jesuits and urged reconciliation with the Protestants.

He tried to achieve this as papal legate to the Regensburg Colloquy of 1541. But he could reach no agreement with the Protestants on the sacraments. When Contarini returned to Italy, Rome refused to approve his views on justification and Luther attacked them too.

Contarini died shortly after this. His life reflects, better than that of any other contemporary, the political, intellectual and religious crisis of Italy during the early sixteenth century.

Cardinal Contarini, the great Catholic reformer. He experienced conversion in 1511 and strove to achieve understanding with the Reformers in 1530s.

Under Paul III many positive steps were taken to correct abuses and bring about needed change. Perhaps the most outstanding of these were his appointment of reformers to the College of Cardinals, the setting up of a papal reform commission, and the calling of the Council of Trent in 1545.

The Castle of Trent, depicted by Albrecht Dürer. Trent was selected as the venue for the great Council of the Roman Catholic church which opened 13 December 1545. The city was inside the Holy Roman Empire—but not too far from Rome.

Among those made cardinals by Paul III were such dedicated reformers as Contarini, Caraffa, Pole, Sadoleto (all former members of the Oratory of Divine Love—the Oratory at Rome was disbanded in 1527), Pietro Bembo and Jean du Bellay. The appointments revealed Paul's determination to rid the College of Cardinals of its moral laxity and to make it more international.

More important was the papal reform commission which Paul appointed in 1536. The pope named nine leading cardinals to serve on it and made Contarini its head. Its task was to recommend reforms for the church and to prepare the way for a council. It made a wide-ranging study of conditions in the church—especially in the papal bureaucracy—and issued a formal report entitled *Advice . . . Concerning the Reform of the Church.* The commission submitted the document to the pope in February 1537.

The report analysed the causes of the disorder in the church and recommended immediate action to correct the worst offences and to remove the worst offenders. The language of the document was painfully blunt. The papal office had become too secular. Both popes and cardinals needed to give more attention to spiritual matters and stop flirting with the world. It gave concrete examples of the kind of problems which needed attention: bribery in high places, abuses of papal power, the evasion of church law by lay people and clergy alike, laxity in the monastic orders, the abuse of indulgences, and the high number of prostitutes operating in Rome itself.

Despite the opposition of a number of powerful older cardinals, Paul took action to end several of these problems. He reformed the papal bureaucracy, ordered an end to the taking of money for spiritual favours, and forbade the buying and selling of church appointments. Unfortunately, the pope put into practice only a few of the commission's recommendations. Moreover, the Protestants obtained a copy of the commission's report and published it as documentary evidence of the corrupt state of the Roman church.

The Council of Trent is called

Paul III's most significant action was to call an ecumenical church council to deal with reform and the growing menace of Protestantism. After intense negotiations with

:he Emperor and the French king, Paul finally named Trent as the venue for the council. It was a compromise location. Trent is a city in present-day northern Italy, but at the time was just inside the area of the Italian peninsula ruled by the Emperor. The French were offended by this choice and only a handful of French church leaders attended the council.

As it turned out, Trent was the most important ecumenical council between Nicaea in 325 and Vatican II in 1962–65. It was to deal with the monumental problems posed by the split in the church and with the renewal of the church of Rome. In this it was only partly successful. Despite this failure to achieve all its goals, the council shaped the response of Rome to the Protestant Reformation.

The council met in three main sessions: 1545–47, 1551–52 and 1562–63. It was not a continuous meeting, but really three different gatherings attended by three different, but overlapping, groups of representatives of the Roman church. Attendance was scanty and irregular for an enterprise of such significance. The first session opened with only four archbishops, twenty bishops, four generals of monastic orders, and a few theologians present. The largest number of delegates to attend the second session was fifty-nine. The third session was the largest of all, with as many as 255 at one of its meetings.

The Italians were the best represented throughout the council, with many bishops attending from Spain and the Empire. Other

The final meeting of the Council of Trent (1563) in the cathedral of Trent. The great Council settled the course of the Roman Catholic church for many years to come.

areas, including France, were noticeably under-represented. It proved most difficult to bring the Spanish into agreement with the decisions of the majority. They were not only doctrinal hardliners, but also sensitive to the Emperor's wishes (Charles V, Holy Roman Emperor, was also Charles I, king of Spain) and held that councils were superior to popes, a view repulsive to the papacy. Sometimes feelings ran so high that there were physical struggles between delegates. Despite all these difficulties, the council persevered and accomplished much.

Perhaps the most interesting session of the council was the second, when a number of Protestants were present. The Emperor held back the German bishops from this session until the pope agreed to allow Protestants to attend. However, the pope did not agree to the Emperor's demand that the Protestants should also be allowed to vote. Consequently, not one leading Lutheran theologian came, nor did any Calvinists show up. However, at least three delegations of Protestants arrived late in 1551: one from Brandenburg, one from Württemberg, and one from Strasbourg. In January 1552, they were joined by representatives of Maurice of Saxony.

The Württembergers wanted to discuss their own confession of faith and not a statement imposed by the papal legate. Johann Sleidan, the distinguished Protestant historian, led the Strasbourg delegation in maintaining their doctrinal position. They refused to compromise. When the group from Saxony arrived, the Protestants drew up a list of demands which included a chance to re-examine all decrees on doctrine previously accepted by the council. They started by declaring in effect that the pope was the servant of the council and not its master. But they also indicated that these points were negotiable.

Nothing came of the Protestant presence at the second session. Informal talks were held, but nothing appeared on the formal agenda concerning the points they raised. So they left in March 1552, convinced that there was nothing to be gained by remaining any longer at Trent. The inability or unwillingness of the two sides to come to some sort of understanding illustrated how great the theological chasm between them now was.

Catholic doctrine clarified

As far as the Roman church was concerned, the third session proved to be the most productive. A number of issues debated in earlier meetings were resolved. Medieval orthodoxy was reaffirmed as it related to most of the doctrines under dispute in the Reformation. For example, transubstantiation, justification by faith *and* works, and established medieval practices connected with the mass were all upheld. The seven sacraments were once again insisted upon. The celibacy of the clergy, the existence of purgatory, and indulgences were all reaffirmed. However, the post of indulgence-seller was abolished and abuses connected with the distribution of indulgences were condemned. In short, the council clarified and reasserted most of the doctrines of the late medieval Roman church. In addition, papal power generally was increased by giving the pope the authority to enforce the decrees of the council and by again requiring that church officials had to promise him obedience.

Protestants were bitterly disappointed—though not surprised. Most shared Luther's initial

cepticism concerning the 'irre-
ɔrmability of the church'. The
ouncil ruled out any possibility of
Christian reconciliation in the
nmediate future. The scholastic-
tyle definitions, with the accom-
anying curses on anyone who
id not agree with them, killed
ny lingering Protestant hopes
f restored unity. But by elevat-
ıg the papacy once more, by im-
roving church organization, by
ealing with the most flagrant of
ıe abuses pointed out by the Prot-
stant Reformers, and by clarifying
octrine and dogma, the Council of
'rent gave the church of Rome a
lear position to uphold in the next
ɔur centuries. The work of Trent
ould stand the church in good stead during the wars of religion and the period of missionary expansion which lay ahead.

Loyola founds the Jesuits

Present at the Council of Trent were two suave, intelligent and highly influential members of the Society of Jesus—a new monastic order which Pope Paul III had approved in 1540. The two 'Jesuits', as the fledgling order soon became popularly known, were Diego Laynez and Alfonso Salmerón. The founder and leader of their order was one of the most dramatic and powerful figures in Christian history, Ignatius of

IGNATIUS OF LOYOLA

J. I. Packer

Ignatius of Loyola founded the dedicated and powerful Society of Jesus (the Jesuits). Ignatius, a Spanish nobleman, was born in 1491 or 1495 at the castle of Loyola near the Pyrenees. His career as a professional soldier ended with a leg wound in 1521. Through reading lives of Christ and the saints while convalescing, Loyola resolved to become Christ's soldier. He hung up his sword at the altar of Mary in Montserrat. Ignatius then spent a year (1522–23) in prayer and meditation at Manresa monastery, seeking total consecration to Christ. He was much blessed. Here he drafted his *Spiritual Exercises*.

Between 1524 and 1534 Loyola studied at Barcelona, Alcalá, Salamanca and Paris, preparing for service. Then he and six friends vowed to practice poverty and celibacy, to make a pilgrimage to Jerusalem (this never came off), and to give the rest of their lives to apostolic labours. In this way the Society of Jesus began. 'Jesuits', as its members were called, vowed total obedience to the pope as, in effect, Commander-in-chief, and under him to the general of the order. Ignatius, a fine organizer, was general till his death in 1556.

All Roman Catholic ordinands still go at least once through Ignatius' *Spiritual Exercises*. These form a four-week retreat programme and devotional meditations and instructions. Week one is on sin, week two on Christ's kingship, week three on his passion and week four on his risen life. The aim is to achieve complete and realistic consecration. The *Exercises* appeal to the will through understanding, imagination and conscience. They remain a potent aid to self-knowledge and devotion to the Lord Jesus, even for those outside the Catholicism in which they are so strongly rooted.

> *"Teach us, good Lord, to serve thee as thou deservest; to give and not to count the cost; to fight and not to heed the wounds; to toil and not to ask for rest; to labour and not to ask for any reward save knowing that we do thy will. Through Jesus Christ our Lord."*
>
> *IGNATIUS OF LOYOLA*

Loyola. Loyola is often taken as the embodiment of the Catholic Reformation.

Loyola had been a professional soldier, but a serious wound cut short his military career. While recovering, he had time to think about his rough-and-tumble past and his future. During this period of sober reflection Loyola read a number of books about the saints. He was challenged by their holiness and their achievements as 'soldier of Christ'. Finally, he decided that, like the knights of old, he would dedicate his weapons and armour of God and take up the cross of Christ. He waited on God, to know what he should do.

A diagram of the seven deadly sins from an illustrated edition of Loyola's classic *Spiritual Exercises*.

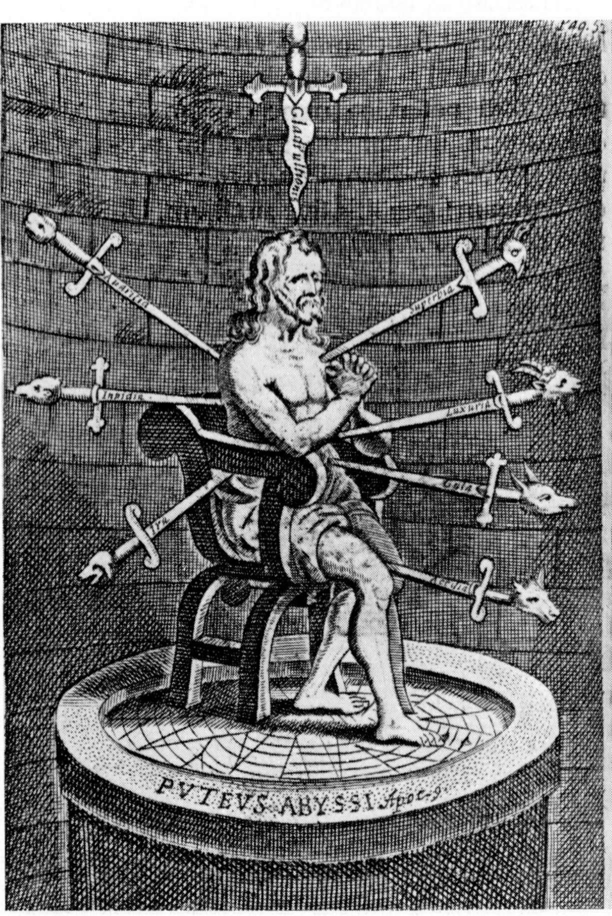

Loyola's period waiting for God's guidance was immensely important and has been compared to Luther's monastic experience. But whereas Luther finally found his peace by rejecting the traditions of the medieval church in favour of the biblical basics of primitive Christianity, Loyola finally found his peace by rededicating himself to the conventions of the medieval church. Loyola emerged from his convalescence a curious mixture of soldier, mystic and monk. He wrote up his own spiritual pilgrimage and circulated it as a book entitled *The Spiritual Exercises*. The book, with its powerful appeal to the imagination and its great emphasis on obedience to Christ and his church (meaning the church of Rome) provided the cornerstone for the new ascetic order which Loyola founded.

After many initial setbacks and discouragements, Loyola finally gathered about him a small group of young men wholly dedicated to serving Christ through the church of Rome. As the new order took shape, it bore the indelible stamp of its founder. The Jesuits were to become a new spiritual élite, at the disposal of the pope to use in whatever way he thought appropriate for spreading the 'true church'. Absolute, unquestioning, military-style obedience became the hallmark of the new society. The famous Jesuit dictum was that every member of the society would obey the pope and the general of the order as unquestioningly 'as a corpse'.

After some hesitation, Paul III gave papal approval to the Society of Jesus in 1540. The constitution of the new order insisted on a fourth vow in addition to the traditional ones of poverty, chastity and obedience: a special oath of absolute obedience to the pope. The purpose of the society was to propagate the faith by every

THE JESUITS

John P. Donnelly

The Jesuits, or Society of Jesus, were founded by Ignatius of Loyola. They were approved by the papacy in 1540 as an order of Catholic priests depending solely on charity (mendicants).

In 1535, in Paris, Loyola and six remarkable disciples took vows of poverty and chastity and promised to go as missionaries to Palestine. When war between Venice and the Turks blocked their passage, they began work in the north Italian cities. They gathered new recruits and sought direction and approval from Pope Paul III. Loyola was elected their general. He devoted the rest of his life to writing the Jesuit *Constitutions* at Rome, and to directing the rapidly spreading order.

The new order had several distinctive features. It was highly centralized. All of its leaders were appointed by the general, who was elected for life. The *Constitutions* imposed no special religious uniform, no bodily penances or fasts, and no choral recitation of the daily liturgy (Divine Office). But Loyola insisted that recruits be carefully selected and arduously trained. Later fifteen years' training became quite normal. He also stressed obedience and a close link with the papacy. Above all, the Jesuit was to cultivate an inner life based on meditation and Loyola's *Spiritual Exercises*. Prayer was to mould him into an effective apostle to others.

Loyola wanted quality rather than numbers, but the order grew rapidly. By 1556 there were over a thousand Jesuits—mainly in Spain, Portugal and Italy, but also in France, Germany, the Low Countries, India, Brazil and Africa. By 1626 there were 15,544, and during the next 130 years the Jesuits grew slowly but steadily. Jesuits were working in almost every corner of the globe.

In 1773 the Bourbon monarchs of France and Spain forced the pope to suppress the Jesuits. A few Jesuits survived in Prussia and Russia. In 1814 the papacy restored the Jesuits throughout the world. Jesuits reached a peak of 36,038 members in 1964. In the unrest following Vatican II, membership fell to 24,924 in 1988.

Education quickly became the most important Jesuit emphasis. Within a decade of their foundation the Jesuits had a dozen colleges. By 1626 there were 400 colleges, and by 1749 about 800, including seminaries. These schools were open to all classes of people and generally charged nothing for tuition. During the seventeenth and early eighteenth century a high percentage of the educated people of Catholic Europe passed through Jesuit schools.

Jesuit education was based on the *Plan of Studies* of 1599. It purified and simplified Renaissance humanism. Jesuits insisted on pupils attending classes. A carefully planned curriculum took students forward step by step. The Jesuits used friendly rivalry instead of the rod to stimulate their students. Philosophy in their schools generally followed Aristotle. Theology was freely adapted from Thomas Aquinas, as in the system of Francisco Suarez (1548–1617). Jesuit schools were famous for their drama. Moral and religious values were taught through a pageantry that rivalled early opera. Today the Jesuits run about 4,000 schools, including

> *"I can find God wherever I will."*
>
> *IGNATIUS OF LOYOLA, founder of the Jesuits*

▶▶

nineteen universities in the United States.

The foreign missions were always the most highly regarded of Jesuit activities. Francis Xavier (1506–52), who worked in India, Indonesia and Japan, was the first and greatest Jesuit missionary. Matteo Ricci (1552–1610) founded modern mission work in China and adapted the gospel to Chinese traditions and thought-forms. The Jesuits used their western scientific knowledge to gain entry to court circles in Peking. But they never succeeded in converting a Chinese ruler. Robert De Nobili (1577–1656) applied Ricci's methods of adapting the gospel to the local culture in India. Isaac Joques, Jacques Marquette and many other French Jesuits worked with mixed success among the Canadian Indians. Eusebio Kino (1644–1711) built mission stations and introduced advanced agriculture among the Indians of northern Mexico and the south-western United States. Other Jesuits organized towns (or *reductions*) to convert and civilize the Indians of Paraguay and Brazil.

Loyola did not found the Jesuits in order to combat Protestantism. But this became a Jesuit goal, increasingly, during the sixteenth century. Several Jesuits served as papal representatives (legates) in complex negotiations to link various countries more firmly to Rome—for instance Ireland, Sweden and Russia. Other Jesuits served as court preachers or confessors to the Emperor, the kings of France and Poland, and the dukes of Bavaria. Peter Canisius and Robert Bellarmine wrote catechisms and anti-Protestant works of theology which were influential for centuries. Many Jesuits lost their lives for their cause. In all the Jesuits list over 1,000 martyrs, mostly in mission countries.

Francis Xavier, one of the founding members of the Society of Jesus. He went to Goa in 1542 to preach the gospel. Many of the Goan pearl-fishers were subsequently baptized. Xavier later went on to Japan and China.

neans at the order's disposal. 'he approach taken was that 'the nd justifies the means'. Recruits or the Jesuits were to reflect .oyola's spirituality and his stress n military-style organization and bedience. They were to be of obust health, handsome in appear- nce, intelligent and eloquent in peech. No one of bad character r with even the slightest hint of northodox belief was admitted.

The growth of the Jesuit order vas extraordinarily rapid. When .oyola died in 1556, there were nembers of the society in Japan, Brazil, Ethiopia and the coast of entral Africa, as well as in nearly very country in Europe. Many ad reached high positions in the hurch. Two served as the pope's mbassadors in Poland and Ireland espectively. A number were rofessors in the largest and best niversities in Europe. By 1556 he half-dozen original followers f Loyola had grown to more than ,500.

The Jesuits' work centred n three main tasks: education, ounteracting the Protestants, and nissionary expansion in new areas.

The Jesuits provided high- uality education and by this means pgraded the training of Catholic elievers as well as winning the pinion-makers of society for the Roman church. Their schools soon ecame famous for high standards nd attainments. Many individuals rom the élite were won to Roman Catholicism by this means. Chil- ren were given special attention. Before long the now-familiar Jesuit aying was coined: 'Give me a hild until he is seven, and he will emain a Catholic the rest of his fe.'

Counter-reform was a second najor Jesuit preoccupation in he second half of the sixteenth entury and throughout the seven- eenth century. In France, in what today Belgium, in southern Germany, and most noticeably in eastern Europe, the Jesuits led the counter-attack against the Protestants. Using literally almost any means at their disposal, they recaptured large areas for the church of Rome. They earned a reputation as 'the feared and formidable storm-troops of the Counter Reformation'. Only in England did their onslaught fail.

The third task at which the Jesuits excelled was missionary activity in new lands. Increasingly, Jesuit priests travelled in the ships of Spain and Portugal as they sailed the seven seas in search of new colonies and new riches. Jesuit missionaries travelled to America, Africa and Asia in search of converts. As they went, they helped counterbalance the greedy imperialism of the European merchants and soldiers. They also produced scholarly accounts of the history and geography of the new places they visited. But most of all they left their converts with an enthusiastic brand of Catholicism and produced devout, tough Catholics, on their own model.

The Jesuits played a leading role in the conversion of Brazil and Paraguay. They were not as successful in Africa, where native peoples often resisted their efforts. The greatest stories of Jesuit heroism come from Asia. There, the incredibly courageous Francis Xavier (1506–52) towered above all the rest as the 'apostle to the Indies and to Japan'.

Xavier was born into the Spanish nobility and was one of the original members of the Society of Jesus. Loyola early recognized that this handsome, bright and cheerful young man would make a powerful servant of God. He became the most widely-acclaimed Jesuit missionary of all time. He was appointed the pope's ambassador and sent to evangelize the East Indies in 1542. He spent three

---

"On Sundays I assemble all the people, men and women, young and old, and get them to repeat the prayers in their language. They take much pleasure in doing so, and come to the meetings gladly . . . I give out the First Commandment, which they repeat, and then we say all together, Jesus Christ, Son of God, grant us grace to love thee above all things. When we have asked for this grace, we recite the Pater Noster *together, and then cry with one accord, Holy Mary, Mother of Jesus Christ, obtain for us grace from thy son to enable us to keep the First Commandment. Next we say an* Ave Maria, *and proceed in the same manner through each of the remaining nine Commandments. And just as we say twelve* Paters *and* Aves *in honour of the twelve articles of the Creed, so we say ten* Paters *and ten* Aves *in honour of the Ten Commandments, asking God to give us grace to keep them well."*

FRANCIS XAVIER, Jesuit missionary, describing his methods in South India

---

years there, followed by preaching and baptizing in present-day Malaysia, Vietnam and Japan. His most remarkable mission was in Japan where he established a Christian community which has survived to this day, despite numerous periods of severe persecution. Xavier died of a fever when he was only forty-six years old, while he was attempting to take the Christian message to China.

The Jesuits, together with the Dominicans, Franciscans and Augustinians, led the church of Rome in a new period of rapid overseas expansion between 1550 and 1650. By this means nearly all of Mexico, Central America and South America, along with a large part of the population of the Philippines and smaller numbers of people in Africa, India, the East Indies and the Far East, became adherents of the church of Rome.

The Inquisition is revived

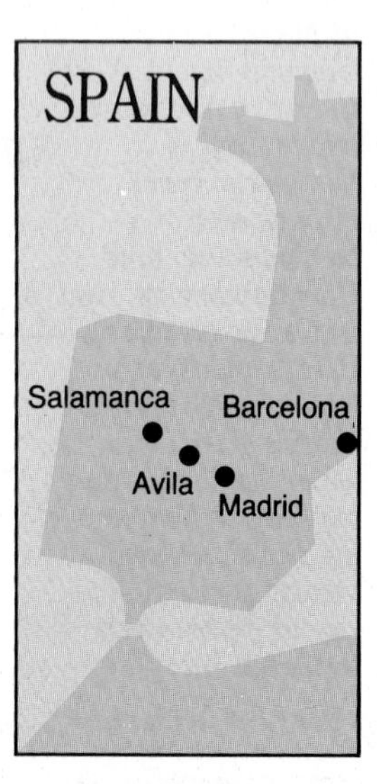

The Jesuits were most active in the border areas of Europe and in the newly-discovered lands overseas. In the traditionally Roman Catholic countries such as Italy, Spain and France, the Inquisition became the major instrument of the Catholic Reformation. The Inquisition, or the Supreme Sacred Congregation of the Holy Office, as it was officially called, was not an invention of the sixteenth century. The so-called Roman Inquisition begun in 1542 was child and grandchild of the medieval and Spanish Inquisitions which had gone before it in the thirteenth and fifteenth centuries respectively.

The rejuvenation of the Inquisition as a means of reform and counter-reform was largely the work of Cardinal Caraffa. Originally a theological moderate, Caraffa became increasingly conservative as the Protestant Reformation progressed. By 1542, he was an outspoken critic of those who sought reconciliation with the Protestants and, instead, advocated fighting them with the weapons of coercion, censorship and propaganda. It was at his urging that the new Roman Inquisition was established. It was 'Roman' because it was to be controlled by the papacy from Rome.

Caraffa was one of the six cardinals, appointed as Inquisitors General. In this capacity, and later as pope, he supported the Inquisition as the most effective means of dealing with heretics. Caraffa and his fellow inquisitors regarded heretics as traitors against God, and the foulest of criminals. It was for their own good, and for the good of the church, that they had to be sought out and dealt with by the Inquisition. If the Holy Office could not return these benighted individuals to the church, then they must be eradicated before they contaminated other immortal souls with their spiritual disease. Thus, they were removed from the body of Christian society in much the same way that surgeons remove cancer tissue from the human body in order to save a person's life.

The Inquisition commonly used terror and torture to obtain confessions. If the death penalty was required, the convicted heretic was handed over to the civil authorities for execution, since canon law forbade the church to shed blood.

The Inquisition was used widely and effectively in Italy, except in Venice. In Spain, it was fused with the older Spanish Inquisition and produced substantial results. In France, it was modified and kept under quite close control by the French monarchs. It was not widely used in Germany, where there was no inquisitorial tradition. In England, common law prevented its introduction. It was most effective where the population was still largely Roman Catholic. With wide popular support, it became a major deterrent to the further spread of the Protestant faith.

Books prohibited

Associated with the concept of coercion by the Inquisition was the idea of a list of prohibited books. Actually, the practice of maintaining a catalogue of heretical and dangerous books was an old one. It had been used in the Middle Ages with varying degrees of success. In the early sixteenth century, several theological faculties and the Holy Office itself circulated lists of books pronounced unfit for the eyes of the faithful. The first real papal 'index' of prohibited books was issued by Pope Paul IV in 1559. It was extensive, naming books, parts of books, authors and printers.

The last major session of the Council of Trent issued the most authoritative index of prohibited books of the period. Their list, the so-called *Tridentine Index,* was handed over to Pope Pius IV (1559–65) to enforce. He published this *Index* in 1564 and called on true Christians everywhere to observe it. In effect it censored nearly three-quarters of all the books that were being printed in Europe at the time. Almost the only books allowed were Catholic devotional literature and the Latin *Vulgate* Bible. The pope also appointed a Congregation of the Index to update the list periodically. The practice of keeping up the *Index* lasted until 1966, when it was finally abolished. Both in the sixteenth century, and in the centuries following, it was largely a failure.

Mystics in Spain

One expression of the Catholic Reformation which was not particularly welcomed by the church of Rome was the revival of Catholic mysticism in Spain. Mysticism makes the institutional church nervous because, carried to its logical conclusion, it does away with the need for the priesthood and the sacraments. The mystic emphasizes personal religion and his or her direct relationship to God. The ultimate goal of the

Bernini's famous sculpture of the *Ecstasy of Saint Teresa,* in Rome. The story of the reforming nun Teresa is far removed from the extravagant spirit of this baroque sculpture. The sculptor was not concerned to give an accurate picture of the saint commemorated.

TERESA OF AVILA

Caroline Marshall

> *"Let everyone understand that real love of God does not consist in tear-shedding, nor in that sweetness and tenderness for which we usually long, just because they console us, but in serving God in justice, fortitude of soul and humility."*
>
> *TERESA OF AVILA*

Teresa of Avila (1515–82) was one of the most famous mystics of sixteenth-century Spain. Teresa was born in Avila into a Spanish noble family. As a young woman she committed herself to converting the heathen and to healing the division with Protestants. In 1536 she entered the Carmelite Convent of the Incarnation in Avila. Her religious career was interrupted for a time by severe illness. But she was able to return to the convent in 1540.

Teresa was deeply moved by the need to reform the lax, often scandalous, condition of the Spanish monasteries. Supported by wealthy relatives and friends she founded a reformed Carmelite convent, St Joseph's of Avila. In the years that followed she founded sixteen more religious houses. Meanwhile she travelled the length and breadth of Spain inspecting monasteries, encouraging monks and nuns, and preaching reform.

Teresa was familiar with the great religious literature and epics of the Spanish Golden Age. She herself wrote *El Libro de su Vida (The Book of Her Life), Camino de Perfeccion (The Road of Perfection), Conceptos del Amor de Dios (Concepts of the Love of God),* and *El Castillo Interior (The Interior Castle).* The central theme of her best writing is the mystical life.

The religious ecstasy of Teresa can appear embarrassing, and even erotic. She sought oneness with God through contemplation and prayer. This led to a profound experience and personal knowledge of God through love. She described this as 'mystical marriage'. She spoke of a second conversion, and of union through love. In her *Life* Teresa describes an ecstasy in which a seraphim appeared to her carrying a spear tipped with fire. He plunged the spear into her heart, straight through to her innermost being. She was left aflame with a great love for God. The experience, she says, was both painful and sweet beyond description. It symbolized the mystical union of the believer with God.

Teresa and her companions represent the Catholic Reformation's emphasis on emotion and religious passion. The scholastics' emphasis on reason had failed to satisfy the deep-felt need of men and women for a personal experience of God.

mystic is to lose himself or herself in the essence of God. The Christian mystic usually stresses the personal reality of Christ and seeks personal union with God through the Son. Often this ultimate union comes in a blinding flash of supreme ecstasy. In short, Christian mysticism is contemplative, personal and usually practical. Such was the case with Teresa of Avila (1515–82), the best-known of the sixteenth-century Spanish mystics (see feature article).

Teresa and her devoted follower, John of the Cross, revitalized a large part of the spiritual life of Spain through their practical mysticism. Teresa was a Carmelite nun who searched for the life of perfection. Ill-health caused her great anguish and threatened her career as a nun. Finally, in the 1550s, while in a period of intense prayer, she experienced the first of her many heavenly visions. She wrote of her mystical experiences but did not stress them, because she recognized their dangers as well as their value.

Spurred on by her personal relationship with God, Teresa became the great reformer of the Carmelite Order. She proved that mysticism could stimulate practical reform. Because she and John of the Cross spread Catholic mysticism throughout the country, many of the faithful experienced spiritual satisfaction. This filled a void which in other parts of Europe formed the basis for the spread of Protestantism, with its emphasis on a personal, biblical faith. The reform of the Spanish monasteries and convents begun under Teresa also helped to head off the criticism of those religious houses in other parts of Europe which made the Protestant case for reform so compelling.

Europe divided

The intensity and scope of the Catholic Reformation helped set the stage for the wars of religion which broke out in many parts of Europe following the failure of the Lutherans and Roman Catholics to achieve reconciliation at Regensburg in 1541. Major fighting between the Lutheran princes and the imperial forces in the 1540s and early 1550s finally came to an end with the compromise Peace of Augsburg in 1555. The Augsburg agreement provided for the co-existence of Lutheran and Roman Catholic expressions of Christianity in Germany on the basis of 'whose the rule, his the religion'. That is, the prince could decide the faith of his subjects.

In France, a series of civil wars involving both religious and political considerations raged intermittently

Teresa came from the town of Avila in central Spain. John of the Cross was confessor at the Convent of the Incarnation at Avila 1572–77.

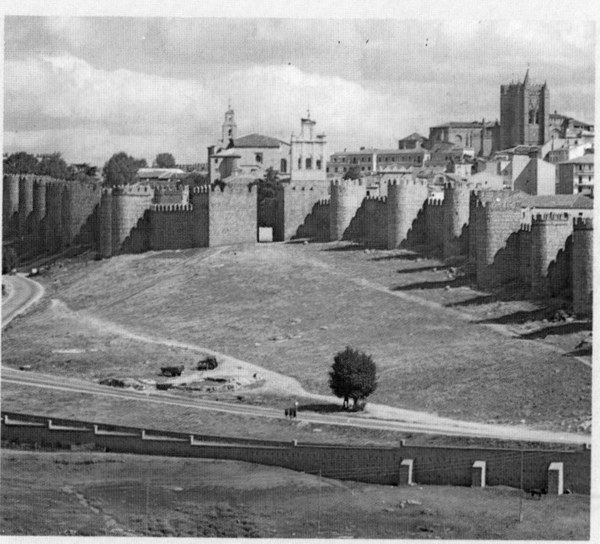

"A beginner in prayer must look on himself as one setting out to make a garden for his Lord's pleasure, on most unfruitful soil which abounds in weeds. His Majesty roots up the weeds and will put in good plants instead. Let us reckon that this is already done when a soul decides to practise prayer and has begun to do so. We have, then, as good gardeners, with God's help to make these plants grow, and to water them carefully so that they will not die, but produce flowers which give out a good smell, to delight this Lord of ours. Then he will often come to take his pleasure in this garden and enjoy these virtues."

TERESA OF AVILA, The Interior Castle

JOHN OF THE CROSS

Robert G. Clouse

> *"If we are guided by divine Scripture, we shall not be able to err, for he who speaks in it is the Holy Spirit."*
>
> *Spanish mystic, JOHN OF THE CROSS*

John of the Cross (1542–91) was a Spanish mystic. He helped found the reformed or barefoot (*Discalced*) Carmelite Order. John came from a noble but poor background. He joined the Carmelites at their monastery at Medina (1563) and then studied theology at the University of Salamanca. After he had been ordained a priest, Teresa of Avila persuaded him to join in the reform of the Carmelites. Later he became confessor at the Convent of the Incarnation of Avila (1572–77).

Opposition arose against the austerity and simplicity of the new Carmelite movement. This led to John's imprisonment at Toledo (1578). He expressed his experience in *The Spiritual Canticle*. After escaping from prison, John spent the rest of his life in monastic administration and in elaborating his mystical theology. He was a prior on several occasions, rector of the college at Baeza, and vicar of the southern province of the Carmelite order.

During these years he wrote *The Ascent of Mount Carmel, The Dark Night of the Soul, and The Living Flame of Love*. These consist of poems with commentaries, which instruct the soul on how to achieve union with God. John made contact with Muslim mystics, and studied Scripture and the writings of Aquinas. These and his personal experiences are all reflected in his works. He died amidst a controversy over the reform movement.

from 1562 and 1598. The conflict was basically between the Huguenots (Calvinist Protestants) and the Roman Catholics, with political issues often complicating the picture. Finally, a third force appeared when the *politiques* (politically-inspired) announced that it was immaterial which religion dominated France. All that mattered was the political well-being of the nation.

After such devastation, and with all parties on the point of total exhaustion, a compromise was reached by partitioning the country. This settlement, expressed in the royal Edict of Nantes in 1598, gave the Huguenots religious freedom and political control of certain parts of the country, while Roman Catholicism remained the official religion of the realm and retained by far the larger portion of the nation.

This compromise lasted on an increasingly precarious foundation until it was revoked by King Louis XIV (1643–1715) in 1685. Interestingly enough, the Jesuits were partly responsible for the revocation. Louis' act was the signal for hundreds of Protestants to reconvert to Catholicism, and thousands of others to flee. Many Huguenots left France in 1685 and made their way to Geneva, Germany, England and America. Others remained and either suffered persecution or fled to the mountains of central France in order to avoid it. Most of the Protestants who left France in this period were professional people or skilled craftsmen. Their exodus may not have crippled the French economy, as some historians in the past have claimed, but it was certainly significant socially and economically. France lost many of its most intelligent and hardworking citizens as a result of this act of religious bigotry.

The Dutch war for independence, 1560–1618, is also an example of fighting in this period which had an important religious dimension. Along with political, economic and racial considerations, religion was a major motivation in the Protestant Dutch struggle for independence from Catholic Spain. Likewise, the English Civil War, 1642–49, involved a large element of religious conflict.

The Thirty Years' War

The last of the so-called wars of religion was the Thirty Years' War, 1618–48. This conflict began as a basically religious struggle with political overtones, and ended as a basically political struggle with religious overtones—heralding the modern era.

The build-up of tension between Protestants and Catholics in Germany in the period from the Peace of Augsburg in 1555 to the outbreak of the Thirty Years' War in 1618 reflects in part the vitality of the Catholic Reformation in that area. When the Jesuit-educated Ferdinand II became Emperor and king of Bohemia, growing religious tensions came to a head. Anti-Protestant religious violence broke out in 1618, and the Bohemian nobles, mostly Protestants, appealed to the Emperor for protection and a guarantee of their religious liberties. Receiving no satisfaction, they rose in revolt.

The war began as a conflict between the Calvinists and the Catholics. Calvinism had not been recognized as a legal religion in the Empire in the treaty of Augsburg in 1555. This posed a continuing problem for those German princes who became Calvinists after 1555. The situation became even more complicated when in 1618 the Bohemian nobles declared their king, Ferdinand II, deposed, and offered the crown to the Calvinist ruler of the Palatinate, one of the major German states. His acceptance of the crown of Bohemia touched off fighting between Calvinists and Catholics all over Germany. Finally, the German Lutherans, Danes, Swedes and even the French became involved in the warfare in Germany.

The war dragged on sporadically for nearly thirty years. Finally, a peace was hammered out between the belligerents in a series of conferences held in the German province of Westphalia in the years 1643–48. The resultant agreements are known, together, as the Peace of Westphalia.

The royal chapel at the Palace of Versailles, near Paris. Louis XIV built this enormous palace, which symbolizes the splendours of his reign. The darker side was his revocation of the Edict of Nantes which had given the Huguenots religious freedom.

The war left Germany culturally, politically, economically and physically devastated. Only the principality of Brandenburg escaped major destruction. But the peace signalled the end of the religious wars in Europe. Ironically, the treaty in essence provided for a return to the religious situation of 1529, when certain German princes and representatives of various imperial free cities made their first famous 'protestation' on behalf of the Lutheran faith at the Diet of Speyer. All the bloodshed and misery had brought the religious settlement full circle in that tormented land. In 1648, the religious lines were in general drawn much as they were in 1529—and much as they remain to this day.

Results of the Catholic Reformation

What then were the results of the response of Rome to the Protestant Reformation? Out of the rubble of the medieval church arose a new Roman Catholic piety and a better-defined Roman Catholic orthodoxy. The Council of Trent and the leadership of reform-minded popes provided a solid basis for this new piety and renewed orthodoxy. The beliefs of the church of Rome were better understood, even by the rank and file. Differences between Roman orthodoxy and Protestant doctrine now stood out more clearly. To be sure, the Catholic Reformation retained a great many non-apostolic, medieval practices and beliefs.

Roman Catholic missionary expansion overseas in this period was fuelled as a response to the Protestant Reformation. Partly in order to make up for the loss of large areas of Europe, the rejuvenated church turned its attention to the newly-discovered lands overseas as a means of recoupin its fortunes. Thanks mainly to th Jesuits and other monastic missi aries, many people in other parts of the world embraced the Roma faith during this period. Even tod large numbers of people in the Americas, Africa, India, Japan an Sri Lanka owe their affiliation to the Roman church to the Catholi Reformation.

The political and cultural consequences of the Catholic Ref mation were far-reaching. The resurgence of the church of Rom in countries such as Germany an France kept them from becomin Protestant as England, Scotland and Sweden had done. The political development of France and Germany over the years has reflected these religious division The Catholic Reformation also helped Italy and Spain to retain their particular Catholic religious and cultural identities. Most important, the success of the Catholic Reformation in stopping the spread of the Protestant faith meant that Europe developed fro that time without a shared cultur base. Once again, the irony is striking. The success of the Cath lic response to the Protestant Reformation eventually ended th cultural and religious unity of me eval Europe.

Art and the spirit

I. R. Rookmaaker

'he transition from the Middle
ages to the early modern world
vas accompanied by tensions.
n the arts these tensions were
esolved, particularly in Italy, in
he new approach of the High
Renaissance, around 1500.

An exalted art

'he greatest examples of High
Renaissance Roman Catholic art
re to be found in Rome in the
vork of Raphael and Michelangelo
n the Vatican Palace, and above
ll in the the new St Peter's. All
ne outstanding artists of the
ay contributed to what was
ntended to be the greatest of all
Christian churches. Bramante
nd Michelangelo (who designed
ne cupola) both took a share. In
ne second half of the sixteenth
entury, following the spiritual
enewal, della Porta and Maderna
vorked on the façade of St Peter's.

In Venice a similar High Renais-
ance movement took place.
'itian, and, in the second half of
ne sixteenth century, the great
'intoretto both worked there.
'intoretto's art expressed an
ntense Roman Catholic piety.

As the Roman Catholic church
lowly recovered from the shock
f the Reformation, and gained
ew strength through the Counter
Reformation, a new art gradually
merged. It was founded on the
vork of the High Renaissance,
articularly that of Raphael and
ne Venetian artists. One of the
rst examples of the new style
was the *Gesu,* the mother church of the Jesuit order in Rome. This building was begun in 1568 by Vignola and set the style for many churches built in the following centuries. The painters of Bologna, particularly the Caraccis, and Caravaggio, working around 1600, created the new style we know as 'baroque'.

Reformation spirit

Meanwhile, in Germany, Albrecht Dürer pointed the way towards a

Raphael was one of the greatest of the Renaissance painters. This study is of the Madonna and Child, a frequent subject. His portraits of Bible characters have had such great influence that to the present day the popular image of these figures is largely derived from them.

new style which combined the best elements of earlier German and Flemish art with strong influences from the Italian Renaissance. His art breathed the spirit of the Reformation. We find this spirit as clearly as 1498 in his famous series of woodcuts, illustrating the book of Revelation. As soon as Luther made his stand, Dürer followed him.

Dürer's art strives to depict reality in all its aspects. He has never been equalled in the field of engravings and woodcuts. He was also a very great and prolific draughtsman and a good painter. No other artist has covered quite such a wide range of subjects: fro simple animals and plants to figur studies, portraits, buildings (with accurate perspective), biblical an classical stories, and even fantasy scenes and dreams. Although the painters Cranach and Holbein we also Lutheran Protestants, few other great artists came from tha tradition in the following centurie In Germany the Protestant spirit expressed itself mainly in music.

Calvinist refugees from the southern Netherlands settled in Holland in the late sixteenth century. There, after a while, a new art emerged, with biblical and Calvinist roots. Many churches were built in this tradition, for example by Hendrick de Keyser in A sterdam, and many older churche were given new furnishings.

Albrecht Dürer's powerful woodcut *The Four Horsemen of the Apocalypse*. Death is on a bony horse, Want flourishes scales, Sickness waves his sword and War draws his bow. The people are trodden underfoot.

Love of reality

But Protestantism found its supreme expression in painting. After some experiment, the new art emerged around 1600 in Haarlem. It was quite different from the baroque of southern Europe. The Dutch painters were mainly based in Haarlem, Amsterdam, Delft and Dordrecht. They included world famous masters: Frans Hals (portraits), Solomon and Jacob van Ruysdael, Jan van Goyen (landscapes), Heda and Peter Claesz (still-lifes), Brouwer and van Ostade (*genre*-painting), Gerard Dou (interiors), Simon de Vlieger (seascapes), the Delft school—Vermeer, Pieter de Hoogh—and of course Rembrand (biblical and historical themes, portraits and etchings). Rembran was the exception, since he painted many biblical subjects.

The Dutch painters concentrated on depicting everyday reality in a variety of ways. Historical and biblical scenes are quite rare; their most characteristic subjects were everyday life—in the house, the fields, the tavern, landscapes, seascapes and still-lifes.

The Dutch painters' art expressed a deep love for reality. But it was not a mere naturalism. Through their use of 'emblems' and other kinds of visual metaphors, through their carefully constructed compositions, and through their choice of subject they were 'preaching' in their art. They were pointing morals: the vanity of everything; redemption with its full cosmic and human implications; the positive and negative sides to life; and the beauties of the created world. Their art was imbued with the wisdom of the Bible and of common sense.

Masters of the baroque

Two geniuses appeared after 1600 and used the baroque style of Roman Catholic art of the Counter Reformation. The first was Rubens, who worked mainly in Antwerp, but also occasionally in Italy, England, France and Spain. The altarpieces he painted are unsurpassed. They portray the Madonna and lives and martyrdoms of saints. He also painted historical and classical subjects, portraits and landscapes and exerted an immense influence.

The second genius was the sculptor and architect Lorenzo Bernini. He was responsible for some of the principal statues inside St Peter's in Rome, as well as the great square in front. All later baroque sculpture can almost be called the 'school of Bernini'. Borromini, another great Roman architect, worked out the inward

Rembrandt's painting of the disciples from Emmaus (1648).

and outward curved façades and oval-shaped plans characteristic of baroque churches.

The baroque is recognized as the art of the Counter Reformation. It expressed the aims and served the goals of Catholic renewal. The baroque church had to overwhelm the visitor. It was designed to impress him with its display of riches and power, and convince him of the value, importance and truth of the doctrines upheld. All the means of salvation had to be represented dramatically: the Madonna, the saints and revered relics, the mass and the host. Baroque churches displayed many images. Some showed Christ the Redeemer. His suffering on the cross was often directly linked with the host on the altar.

Other images stressed the Trinity. But, above all, the images exalted the Virgin, as the Madonna, as Queen of heaven, as the Immaculate Conception, assumed up into heaven. Other images portrayed the mystic fervour of the saints, whose piety and asceticism provided examples for the faithful. The great events of the Bible and of church history were celebrated. Finally, allegorical figures and scenes spoke in more general terms of theological truth or more directly of human and natural reality and values. Meanwhile, in palaces and other secular buildings, classical themes testified to the same truths and values in an allegorical but more humanistic way.

Baroque art built on the style of the Renaissance, but added the effects of light and darkness. It can be called a 'naturalism of the supernatural'. It stressed that we live in an open world, where communication is possible between earth and heaven, with the Virgin and saints interceding.

A remarkable painter, Pietro da Cortona, was at work in Rome in the mid-seventeenth century. His painted ceilings mark the final stage of the fantastic art of 'sotto in su'—painting the supernatural world as seen from below. (Examples in Rome include Palazzo Barberini and Chiesa Nuova.) Pozzo, who followed Cortona, painted the ceiling of St Ignatio in Rome. Pozzo took this style to Austria at the end of the seventeenth century.

The other main centre of the

The cathedral of Santiago de Compostela in Spain, in all its baroque extravagance.

Counter Reformation was Spain. Here too we find great painters. Zurbaran, Ribera and Murillo all excelled in altarpieces and religious art, and Velasquez was a portraitist. But perhaps the most characteristic expression of burning Spanish piety is found in architecture. This was based on the examples in Rome, amazingly developed with a profusion of detailed statues and ornaments. This style was to spread all over the Spanish-speaking world, including South and Central America.

In eighteenth-century Italy the centre of the baroque shifted north. The great Tiepolo painted baroque altarpieces, frescoes in palaces, and ceilings of unsurpassed lyrical fluency. His style was both naturalistic and idealized.

Baroque in Bavaria

The last great flowering of baroque Counter Reformation art was in Austria and southern Germany. The architect Fischer von Erlach was working in Vienna and Salzburg early in the eighteenth century. He and his followers were responsible for the magnificent architecture of eighteenth-century Austria—which still today dictates the appearance of Vienna and other Austrian cities.

In Bavaria this style of architecture was taken to great heights by the Asam brothers in their Weltenburg church, about 1720, and by Balthasar Neumann in the Vierzehnheiligen, about 1750. J. M. Fischer also built many churches and monasteries, the most important being Ottobeuren. The church at Wies (about 1750), designed by Dom. Zimmermann, is regarded as the best example of this amazing late baroque, or 'religious rococo', art.

This art is worked out very elaborately. The imagery is complex and was carefully designed, down to the smallest detail. A theologian would draw up a plan for decorating a church. But the baroque also had a popular, dramatic character, which gave it appeal to the masses.

The baroque church is one rich, festive whole. Altars, paintings, sculptures, furnishings, organ, stucco-work and other ornaments all contribute, with their gilding and soft but magnificent colouring. There is play with light and shade, a unity of style and content.

The Spanish cathedral at Murcia displays a fine baroque façade.

The whole church really comes to life when filled with Mozart's music performed by the organ, orchestra and choir, and when packed full of priests and people for a religious festival. The many artists who decorated these churches remained relatively anonymous. Their art was part of the whole—they depended on each other's work.

While these churches were being built, magnificent palaces were being constructed for the absolute rulers of Europe. Princes, bishops and abbots all built their palaces. The palace of

Versailles provided their model. They designed and decorated their palaces in a similar style to the churches. One example is the *Residenz* at Würzburg. This was begun in 1720 by Balthasar Neumann and its great ceilings painted by Tiepolo in 1750.

Death of an era

The Counter Reformation, with its exalted piety and worship, found its ultimate expression in these baroque churches. Yet a visitor to them will often find the dead body of a saint, exposed on or under the altar. Death seems to be at the centre. The whole show is meant to reassure us in the face of the death that will surely come. These shrines are often too much geared towards a superstition in which the saints and their relics play a magical and protective role. The system—the rich and powerful church—rather than Christ, is at the centre. Sometimes there is a feeling of light and of beauty—but at the same time a sense of superficiality.

The inner spirit disappeared from this eighteenth-century baroque art, leaving behind a more worldly emphasis. The beautiful forms were becoming a façade. This may explain the sudden end of this art. Around 1780, just when the best works were completed, the tradition stopped. Nothing more was attempted in this style. Neo-classicism, with its 'rationality' and almost totally secular expression, took over. The age of reason and the Enlightenment had won the battle. Soon the revolutionary wars would bring about the suppression of the monasteries and closing of the churches. The Roman Catholic church would lose its power.

The interior of the church at Odenwald in Germany is a glorious extravaganza of baroque decoration.

SECTION 6
REASON, REVIVAL AND REVOLUTION 1650–1789

AWAKENING

A. Skevington Wood

In the English-speaking churches the age of reason became the age of renewal. The tide of rationalism was stemmed. Deadening formality was replaced by a fresh wind of the Spirit. This rebirth took place in the 1730s and 40s. Its roots lay in the Pietist movement in Europe as well as in the lively force of Puritanism.

In Britain the movement was known as the Evangelical or Methodist Revival (the terms were interchangeable). In the North American colonies it was called the Great Awakening. It began in Northampton, Massachusetts, under Jonathan Edwards in 1734. This preceded the conversions of both George Whitefield and the brothers John and Charles Wesley, and can be regarded as feeding the Evangelical Revival in Britain. The movement came to fruition in New England between 1740 and 1743, the time of George Whitefield's whirlwind visit.

An early log-cabin church at Hartford, Connecticut.

The first American Protestants

It is a striking fact that the Reformation was launched only twenty-five years after Columbus had sailed to the American continent. Early in the seventeenth century Protestants began to colonize North America, starting with settlements on the Atlantic coast. It has been claimed that one of the most powerful side-effects of the Reformation, was to give oppressed people a spiritual motive for emigration. The first colonists combined missionary zeal with a desire for freedom of worship; at the same time they certainly had commercial motives too.

Successive waves of immigrants from Britain and Europe came to the east coast. All but one of the thirteen English colonies had Protestant beginnings, and it was here that the Great Awakening occured. Almost all the newcomers were Calvinists.

Calvinism in its most direct form was carried across the Atlantic by the Scots and the Dutch, who set up both Presbyterian and Reformed churches. But the earliest settlers also brought the modified Calvinism of the English Puritans and Separatists. Their beliefs were to have a notable influence. Groups which traced their origin to other Reformation movements—Dunkers, Lutherans, Moravians, Mennonites—came later and in smaller numbers.

The earliest American Protestants were Anglican. In 1607 a community was set up at Jamestown, Virginia, with Robert Hunt acting as chaplain. Anglicanism was never popular either in Virginia or in the other colonies. The church authorities failed to provide a bishop for New England; this helped weaken the Episcopalian church during the colonial period.

The Congregational churches, together with the Presbyterians, formed the largest group in the English colonies. American Congregationalism arose from a merging of Separatists and Puritans. The Pilgrim Fathers who disembarked at Plymouth, New England, in 1620, were Independents who had already left the English national church to seek ecclesiastical asylum in Holland. The much larger group who migrated from 1628 onwards were Puritans in the strict sense of the term; those who desired reform from within the Anglican church. Driven from England by repressive measures in the reign of Charles I, they settled in Massachusetts. The Separatists and Puritans eventually joined forces. In 1648 they expressed their agreement in the *Cambridge Platform*—the charter of American Congregationalism.

Dartmouth, where the *Mayflower* and *Speedwell* had to put in after setting sail for New England in 1620. The *Speedwell* was 'open and leaky as a sieve'. Eventually she had to be abandoned at Plymouth, and 102 people crowded on to the *Mayflower* for the voyage to Plymouth, Massachusetts.

The Presbyterians arrive

Presbyterianism first appeared in America in the Dutch Reformed church. In 1626 the Dutch East India Company founded a colony on the Hudson River, renaming Manhattan Island as New Amsterdam. Two years later a minister was appointed. The Dutch Reformed church continued to flourish after the colony was handed over to England in 1664. By 1700 the church held a strong position in New York.

The form of Presbyterianism which was to play such a prominent part in American Christianity came from Britain. It was founded by Francis Makemie who was commissioned to work in the American colonies by an Irish presbytery. Churches were planted in Maryland as early as 1683. In 1706 the presbytery of Philadelphia was formed with

Makemie as its moderator. He encouraged many Scottish and Irish Presbyterians to seek refuge in America from the oppression of the Stuarts. From 1710, the flow of immigrants increased dramatically when England imposed economic sanctions on Ireland.

The American Baptists trace their ancestry to a congregation at Providence, Rhode Island. They were first gathered in 1639 by Roger Williams, a Separatist from London, who had been ejected from the Puritan colony in Massachusetts Bay. Most of those making up the first congregations were English or Welsh Baptists who already shared Williams' beliefs. The Baptists grew slowly until after the Great Awakening. Meanwhile the Quakers launched their 'holy experiment' in Pennsylvania.

In 1690 the total population of the colonies—some 250,000—was almost exclusively British. European Protestants had already begun to arrive—Huguenots and Mennonites, as well as the Dutch Calvinists. This movement intensified at the opening of the eighteenth century. There was a large-scale influx of German Protestants belonging chiefly to the Lutheran church. Most of them were fleeing persecution in the Palatinate. When William Penn invited them to his colony, Pennsylvania, they crossed the Atlantic in their thousands. By the middle of the eighteenth century there were 70,000 Germans in Pennsylvania alone and almost 200,000 in North America as a whole. Among them were not only Lutherans but Moravians, Dunkers and Schwenkfelders.

These German settlers introduced a new element into American Christianity, which hitherto had been dominated by the Calvinist tradition. Other Reformation streams made their contribution. The German groups had already been touched by the Pietist movement which itself directly fed the fires of the Revival in England.

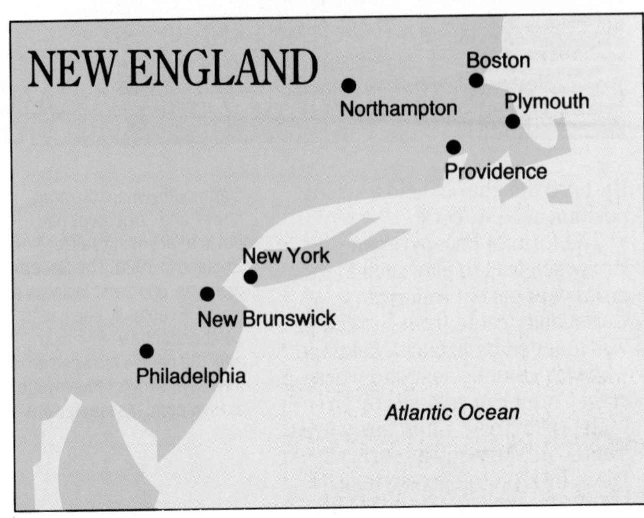

'As dead a sleep as ever'

By the beginning of the eighteenth century the American churches had been overtaken by a creeping paralysis. The evangelical enthusiasm of the pioneering generation of colonists had not been maintained. The reasons for decline are clear. The development of commerce, and with it the increase of wealth, bred a materialism which blunted the keen edge of Protestant witness. The fervour of the fathers was not reproduced in their children.

The Puritan ideal of a society ruled by God faded from view. Previously believers had had to assent to a church covenant to qualify for church membership; now this was seriously compromised. The notorious Half Way Covenant allowed the children of uncommitted parents to be received in baptism. Previously only those who could testify to a saving experience of Christ were admitted as members. Now any 'persons not scandalous in life' could be included. Moral respectability, rather than spiritual rebirth, had become the criterion.

A Presbyterian Synod held at Boston in 1679 discussed 'the necessity of reformation' and described in detail the evils which had 'provoked the Lord to turn His judgements on New England'. For the next thirty years zealous ministers bemoaned the worsening situation and called on their congregations to repent. In 1727 an earthquake which disturbed much of New England and neighbouring provinces was interpreted as a sign of God's judgement. There was a temporary rush to the churches but little lasting improvement. A few years later, a Boston preacher could report, sadly: 'Alas, as though nothing but the most amazing thunders and lightnings, and the most terrible earthquakes could awaken us, we are at this time fallen into as dead a sleep as ever.' It was obvious that something more than reform was required. By the 1730s people were calling for revival. It began in Northampton in 1734.

There had already been early signs elsewhere. Whitefield believed that Theodore Jacobus Frelinghuysen was the initiator. 'He is a worthy soldier of Jesus Christ and was the beginner of the great work which I trust the Lord is carrying on in these parts.' Frelinghuysen was a minister in the Dutch Reformed church. Born in Germany, he was revived by Pietism both in his homeland and while in Holland studying. When he arrived in America he was shocked by the lifeless orthodoxy of his denomination and launched a campaign of evangelism and reform. In 1720 he embarked on a mission in the Raritan Valley in New Jersey. His impassioned preaching produced many conversions, but earned the disapproval of the Amsterdam church authorities, who still controlled the American congregations. By 1726 the revival was spreading to the Presbyterian churches of the district.

In the same year, Gilbert Tennent was ordained as a Presbyterian minister and placed at New Brunswick. Here he was influenced by Frelinghuysen and was used to bring revival to his own denomination. He saw encouraging signs among his congregation, which was composed mainly of Ulster refugees, who brought over a revival tradition from their own land. Tennent was to follow in the steps of Whitefield as one of the great itinerant figures of the

A typical New England church of the eighteenth century.

JONATHAN EDWARDS

Howard J. Sainsbury

Jonathan Edwards, the great American philosopher and theologian. Under his preaching the Awakening broke out in Northampton, Massachusetts.

"On January 12 1723, I made a solemn dedication of myself to God, and wrote it down; giving up myself, and all that I had to God; to be for the future, in no respect, my own; to act as one that had no right to be himself, in any respect. And solemnly vowed to take God for my whole portion and felicity; looking on nothing else, as any part of my happiness."

JONATHAN EDWARDS, Personal Narrative

Jonathan Edwards (1703–58), whose name is inseparably linked with the Great Awakening, was born in Connecticut, New England, the son of the local pastor. He was a precocious child, fluent in Latin, Greek and Hebrew at thirteen. He wrote essays on natural science which showed rare powers of observation and analysis and, at sixteen, while at the Collegiate School of Connecticut (afterwards Yale) worked out a speculative philosophy on Being. This anticipated the thinking of the British philosopher, Bishop Berkeley.

Edwards graduated head of his class in 1720, then studied divinity and after a short period as a Presbyterian minister in New York City, became a senior tutor at Yale in 1724.

In 1727 Edwards had an experience which gave him a new awareness of God's absolute sovereignty, and of his own dependence on God. He described this in his *Personal Narrative* (1739). In 1727, too, he became the associate pastor of the Congregational church at Northampton, Massachusetts. Here, in 1735, under his preaching came the Awakening. Edwards described and analysed in minute detail what happened. He spent thirteen or fourteen hours each day in his study and was a prolific writer. Edwards believed that the Awakening was a genuine work of grace, expressing itself in both mental and physical excitement.

Edwards was dismissed from his pastorate in 1750 after a long controversy about admitting unbelievers to the church ordinances (especially the Lord's Supper). He then went as a missionary to the little frontier hamlet of Stockbridge, preaching to Housatonic Indians and to the white settlers.

Despite various difficulties, Edwards produced his most important work at Stockbridge, on the *Freedom of the Will* (1754). In it he denies that human beings are free to choose. This viewpoint fitted with his Calvinistic doctrines of election, predestination and the fallenness of humanity in every aspect.

In January 1758 Edwards, reluctantly, became President of the College of New Jersey at Princeton. But, after being inoculated against smallpox in February, he died of the disease in March.

Edwards' arguments for a clear, Calvinistic position delayed the liberal theology which was to dominate New England in the nineteenth century. He brought together evangelistic zeal and a powerful intellectual curiosity.

Awakening. He created a furore with his sermon 'On the Dangers of an Unconverted Ministry'.

The Great Awakening

But these and other scattered events were merely oases of spiritual life in a desert of increasing religious indifference. One further local revival may well be regarded as inaugurating the Great Awakening. It occurred in Northampton, Massachusetts, under Jonathan Edwards. It had a profound effect not only elsewhere in America, but in Britain as well through the circulation of Edwards' account of what happened, the *Narrative.*

Edwards followed his grandfather, Solomon Stoddard, as pastor of the Congregational church at Northampton. Stoddard has been called the first great revivalist in New England. In his sixty years as a minister he reaped five successive 'harvests', as he called them. But when Edwards took over, he found the people 'very insensible of the things of religion.'

In 1733 he began to see a change. The next year he preached a series of sermons on justification by faith, and towards the end of December 'the Spirit of God began extraordinarily to set in'. The revival grew and 'souls did as it were come by flocks to Jesus Christ'. 'The town never was so full of love, nor of joy, and yet so full of distress, as it was then,' Edwards declared afterwards. The effect was felt in the surrounding area and even in neighbouring Connecticut. Although the excitement in Northampton subsided within a couple of years, Edwards was convinced that a work of the Spirit had begun which would have widespread repercussions.

When the Awakening reached

"There was scarcely a single person in the town, old or young, left unconcerned about the great things of the eternal world. Those who were wont to be the vainest, and loosest; and those who had been most disposed to think, and speak slightly of vital and experimental religion, were now generally subject to great awakenings. And the work of conversion was carried on in a most astonishing manner, and increased more and more; souls did, as it were, come by flocks to Jesus Christ. From day to day, for many months together, might be seen evident instances of sinners brought out of darkness into marvellous light, and delivered out of a horrible pit, and from the miry clay, and set upon a rock with a new song of praise to God in their mouths.

This work of God, as it was carried on, and the number of true saints multiplied, soon made a glorious alteration in the town; so that in the spring and summer following, anno *1735, the town seemed to be full of the presence of God: it never was so full of love, nor of joy, and yet so full of distress, as it was then. There were remarkable tokens of God's presence in almost every house. It was a time of joy in families on account of salvation being brought unto them; parents rejoicing over their children as new born, and husbands over their wives, and wives over their husbands."*

JONATHAN EDWARDS,
A Faithful Narrative of the Surprising Work of God

George Whitefield, the great preacher of the English Awakening. His first sermon in his native town of Gloucester was of such fervour that someone complained to his bishop that he had driven fifteen people mad. The famous actor David Garrick once said: 'I would give a hundred guineas if I could say "Oh" like Mr Whitefield.'

This building was erected at Moorfields, just outside the City of London, to accommodate Whitefield's congregation.

GEORGE WHITEFIELD

Ian Sellers

George Whitefield was an outstanding preacher during the Revival. Born in Gloucester in 1714 he was educated at Pembroke College, Oxford, and became associated with the Wesleys and others in the 'Holy Club'. Converted in 1735, he was ordained deacon in 1736 and set sail for Georgia the following year. In America he engaged in a variety of charitable and church work. He returned to England briefly between 1738 and 1739 in order to be ordained priest and to collect money for his new orphanages and schools. It was on this visit that he first discovered his talent for open-air evangelism and made contact with Howell Harris and the Welsh revival. He returned to Georgia and in 1740 his Calvinistic form of Methodism came into sharp conflict with the Wesleys' Arminianism, thus opening up a breach which was never healed.

Returning to England in 1741, Whitefield embarked on a round of missionary tours which took him enormous distances and were to continue almost to the end of his life. He paid fourteen visits to Scotland, and on the second of which (1742) he helped during the famous Cambuslang revival. He visited America seven times and travelled all over England and Wales. He became closely associated with the Welsh Calvinistic Methodists and toured South Wales several times with Howell Harris, Whitefield preaching in English, Harris in Welsh. He preached in many chapels owned by the Countess of Huntingdon, whose preachers' college at Trevecca he opened in 1768. George Whitefield died in America in 1770.

Whitefield is generally thought

of as a fervent persuader, who left others to build churches out of his converts. Certainly his letters to Wesley, and his entrusting the care of his English societies to Harris in 1749, underline his lack of interest in the administrative task of raising and caring for infant churches. But he founded the English Calvinistic Methodist Connexion, whose first conference met in 1743. This boasted important London chapels, such as Moorfields and the Tabernacle, Tottenham Court Road. These churches, known as 'the Countess of Huntingdon's Connexion', mainly in the south and west of England, kept up a separate existence until they were absorbed into Congregationalism in the nineteenth century.

Whitefield centred his theology on the old English Puritan themes of original sin, justification by faith and regeneration. Sometimes he was militantly Calvinist, but he preached with a rare passion for souls. 'Calvinistic Methodist' was indeed a term with real meaning when applied to him.

His preaching style was dynamic and compelling; he spoke with fervour, yet in a style plain, unadorned and often colloquial. His physical bearing commanded attention and the range of his voice was astonishing. Anglican pulpits were often barred to him: his open-air services were often interrupted, and he was a favourite target for anti-Methodist propaganda. In many ways his work complements that of Wesleyan Methodism. In some respects he was a forerunner of the Wesley brothers: for example, in his choice of Bristol as a base for evangelism, in publishing a magazine, founding a school, daring to preach in the open air and summoning a conference of preachers.

its peak in 1740, Northampton was once again a centre and Edwards a key figure. But the major influence was that of George Whitefield. Converted in 1735, Whitefield had proved to be a pioneer in the English Revival. He arrived in New England in September 1740, for his second visit to America, and set off on a six-week tour which resulted in the most general awakening the American colonies had yet experienced.

In Boston the crowds soon grew too large to be accommodated in any of the churches and Whitefield took to the open air, as he had previously done in England. He preached his farewell sermon to a congregation estimated at 20,000. Before leaving he invited Gilbert Tennent to Boston 'in order to blow up the divine fire lately kindled there.' The revival continued in Boston with equal success for a period of eighteen months. Thirty 'religious societies' were formed. Churches were packed. Services were regularly held in homes. It was said that even the very face of Boston seemed to be strangely altered. A similar tale was told as Whitefield continued his triumphal journey.

Within the next three years around one hundred and fifty churches were affected by the Awakening, not only in New England but also in New York, New Jersey, Pennsylvania, Maryland and Virginia. In the latter colony revival started in Hanover county under William Robinson. This paved the way for the outstanding preaching of Samuel Davies and the building up of the Presbyterian church there. Now the Baptists began to expand too—through evangelists such as Daniel Marshall and Shubal Stearns. Soon they began reviving the revival. Devereux Jarrett attempted to arouse the established church, but it proved largely unresponsive.

Boston Common. Whitefield preached here during the Great Awakening.

The Awakening was not forwarded solely through the campaigns of itinerant preachers. One effect of Whitefield's visits was to rouse the ministers. 'The reason why congregations have been so dead,' he explained bluntly, 'is because dead men preach to them.' During the Awakening 'dead men' came alive and were themselves used to revive their people.

Renewed churches began to show an uncustomary concern for evangelism. Missionary enterprise was stimulated. David Brainerd, a product of the revival, became the apostle to the Red Indians. As the movement gained support or provoked opposition, parties tended to polarize. Denominational barriers were nevertheless broken down and a new spirit of co-operation prevailed among those sympathetic to the Awakening. Higher education was encouraged; major institutions like Princeton College opened as result of the revival. Spiritual liberation paved the way for political liberation, and contributed indirectly to the American revolution. Christianity acquired such a hold that it expanded with the American frontier and ensured that the independent nation would rest on a reliable foundation.

New life in Germany

The Great Awakening in America was a distinctively Protestant revival. Its principal channels were churches in the Calvinist tradition, although it was also represented in churches deriving from both the Lutheran and Radical Reformation. In England, revival was focussed largely on the established church and groups which eventually broke away from it. On the continent of Europe it had its source in the Pietist movement.

Pietism was cradled in the Dutch Reformed church in the early seventeenth century. It was probably Theodore Untereyk who introduced it in Germany. It flowered in the Lutheran church. It breathed new life into a country exhausted by the Thirty Years' War. This was an age of Protestant scholasticism. The vital insights of the Reformers had hardened into rigid formulas. The Pietist revival re-emphasized the importance of the new birth, personal faith and the warmth of Christian experience as a spur to effective mission.

Philip Jacob Spener, a Frankfurt pastor, was a central figure. He wanted to recover Luther's appeal to the heart, and set up house meetings for prayer, Bible study and the sharing of Christian experience. August Herrman Francke, professor of Hebrew at the University of Leipzig, founded a Bible school which led to an awakening among the undergraduates and local citizens. When he was appointed to Halle in 1692, he made it a centre of Pietist influence. He founded a poor school, a orphanage and other institutions.

Pietism restored the vitality of the German church. It had its weaknesses, which opponents were not slow to expose. Some adherents left Lutheranism to join or form other denominations. Some, such as Paulus Gerhardt, Joachim Neander and Gerhard Tersteegen, were inspired to write many new hymns. One of the more obvious links between German Pietism and the Evangelical Revival lies in the fact that these hymns, many of which were translated by the Wesleys, were widely used in England. Pietism also stimulated a missionary concern, which became a prominent feature of the revival both in Britain and America. Through Spener's godson, Nikolaus Ludwig Count von Zinzendorf, Pietism made its impact on the Moravian community. It was partly by this route that the Pietist influence reached England

The Moravians were the piritual descendants of Jan Hus.)riven from their homeland during he Thirty Years' War, they were cattered throughout Europe nd lost many members. But a ew remained, to hold services n secret and pray for the rebirth f their church of the United Brethren. In 1722 a little company f Moravians settled in Saxony, on Zinzendorf's estate. The party was ed by Christian David, a convert rom Roman Catholicism, who is aid to have 'burned with zeal like n oven'.

Johann Andreas Rothe, a Pietist, vas installed as pastor in the utheran church at Bertholdsdorf. At his induction the preacher, Melchior Schäfer, prophesied that God will place a light on these hills which will illumine the whole land.' Zinzendorf's steward suggested name for this Moravian colony. Since the plot of land lay on the *Hutberg* or Watch Hill, it was called Herrnhut ('The Lord's Watch'). It became a haven for Protestant refugees from all parts of Germany as well as from Moravia and Bohemia. By no means all belonged to the United Brethren. Lutherans, Reformed, Separatists, Anabaptists and Schwenkfelders were all represented.

At first it seemed unlikely that people from such an assortment of traditions could co-operate. A malicious fanatic named Kruger threatened to wreck the whole project. 'It looks as if the devil will turn everything upside down,' wrote Schäfer in 1727. Yet it was in this very year that the fire of Pentecost was to fall. In May the whole community agreed to accept an apostolic rule drawn up in forty-two statutes. The future of Herrnhut was then decided: it was no longer to be a hive of sectarians but a living congregation of Christ.

PHILIP JACOB SPENER

Philip Spener (1635–1705) was the founder of Lutheran Pietism. He studied history and theology in Strasbourg, and was appointed a senior member of the Lutheran clergy in Frankfurt in 1666. In his sermons Spener stressed the value of a life of devotion rather than correct dogma. He began to hold devotional meetings, known as *Collegia pietatis,* which quickly multiplied and formed a basis for the Pietist movement.

In 1675 Spener published his *Pia Desideria (Holy Desires)*, a plan intended to remedy the spiritual decay within the church at every level. He believed that the reason for the decay was the absence of a true, living faith. Spener sought to spread the Word of God by promoting Bible-reading. He also wanted to put into practice the doctrine of the priesthood of all believers, and to shift the emphasis from the theory to the practice of Christianity. The *Pia Desideria* was completely in line with Lutheran theology, except for Spener's belief that there will be a millennium on earth.

In spite of this, Spener could not prevent the separation of Pietists from the Lutheran church, and the persecution of Francke's group of Pietists in Leipzig. In 1991 Spener moved to Berlin. The state there was more tolerant and he was able to secure positions in church and academic life for Pietist friends, most importantly at the University of Halle, which had become the centre of Pietism by the time of his death.

At a communion service on 13 August the Holy Spirit himself made them one. According to Arvid Gradin, who was present, they 'were so convinced and affected that their hearts were set on fire with new faith and love towards the Saviour, and likewise with burning love towards one another; which moved them so far that of their own accord they embraced one another in tears, and grew together into a holy union among themselves, so raising again as it were out of its ashes that ancient Unity of Moravian Brethren'. In this way the Moravians became 'the vital leaven of European Protestantism'.

There are clear links between the renewed Moravian community and the Evangelical Revival in England. A London bookseller named James Hutton became the first English member of the Moravian church, and was to play a leading role in the English Revival. In his house met the religious society from which both the Moravian and the Methodist witness in England sprang. Other similar groups soon appeared, some of which attracted German exiles. A centre was eventually opened in Yorkshire, and in the period of intense evangelization produced by the Revival itself the Moravians were unusually active.

But of more importance still was the fact that it was a Moravia leader who steered John Wesley towards his dynamic conversion i 1738. The Wesley brothers first met a group of Moravian missionaries on a voyage to Georgia. The were greatly impressed by their spirituality.

It was another Moravian, Peter Böhler, who was eventuall responsible for counselling John Wesley as he searched for the assurance of saving faith in Chris When Wesley wanted to conside the implications of his revolutionary experience, it was to Herrnh that he went. Many of the features of the Moravian community were taken up by the Methodist societies—for example the love feast, the watch night and the class-meeting. Wesley was soon to part company from the Londor Moravians and take a line of his own, but he owed an incalculable debt. He could say of Böhler: 'Oh what a work hath God begun sinc his coming to England! Such a one as shall never come to an en till heaven and earth pass away!' Wesley and Whitefield were then selves greatly used in the Reviva but much of its inspiration can be traced back to the Moravians.

'The decay of vital religion'

The Anglican church of the eighteenth century, though not so bla as it has sometimes been painted stood in urgent need of revitaliza tion. Several causes had contributed to its decline. The seeds of decay had been sown in the prev ous century. Anglicans had a fea of extremes (both Roman Cathol

and Puritan) which resulted in a moderation which frowned on passionate convictions of any kind. Preaching lacked punch, since sermons tended to be no more than polished moral essays.

The political situation also helped to stifle spirituality. King George I and his son were both indifferent to Christianity. Sir Robert Walpole, Prime Minister for twenty-one years, openly aimed to put a stop to the progress of the gospel. The cynicism of the age was reflected in a rumour that there was 'a bill cooking up . . . to have "not" taken out of the commandments and clapped into the creed'.

The collapse of personal faith led to a slide in moral standards. Permissiveness was the order of the day. The orthodox theologians scored an intellectual victory in the fight against Deism. It was sadly ironical that, although the central doctrines of Christianity had been defended, the new life in Christ they were intended to encourage was no longer in evidence. A new dynamic was needed. It was precisely this that the Revival supplied, as it reminded the church of its inner resources.

Wesley himself spoke candidly about the irreligion of his time. 'What is the present characteristic of the English nation?' he enquired. 'It is ungodliness . . . Ungodliness is our universal, our constant, our peculiar character.' Wesley's assessment is repeated by many others. The hymn-writer, Isaac Watts, regretted 'the decay of vital religion in the hearts and lives of men'. The philosopher, Bishop Berkeley, declared that morality and religion in Britain had collapsed 'to a degree that was never known in any Christian country'. It was 'just at this time . . .' explained Wesley, 'that two or three clergymen of the church of England began vehemently to "call sinners

William Hogarth illustrates the lifelessness of a sermon: a vivid caricature of the state of the eighteenth-century Church of England.

HOWELL HARRIS

Ian Sellers

Howell Harris, the tireless Welsh evangelist. In 1752 he retired to a house at Trevecca which became a centre of Revival activities.

Howell Harris (1714–73), the Welsh revivalist, was born in Talgarth, the son of a farmer. He was converted in 1735 and resolved to enter the Anglican ministry. However, he was four times refused ordination, and remained a lay preacher to the end of his life. His preaching inspired revivals throughout South Wales. In 1739 he moved to North Wales and carried out a work of evangelism comparable to that of Whitefield and Wesley in England. In 1752 he turned his New House at Trevecca into a centre for revivalist activity.

Harris later became associated with the Countess of Huntingdon, who after 1768 sent her own students for the ministry to Trevecca for training. Harris was devoted to the Church of England, and deplored any tendency to break away. None the less, along with Daniel Rowland, he was the leading promoter of the Welsh revival and the founder of the Welsh Calvinistic Methodists.

Harris could be awkward and dictatorial—yet shy and diffident in the presence of other evangelical leaders. He was an impressive figure, with a powerful voice and magnetic personality. He was no theologian, but his enthusiasm won many to Christ, and there were signs of the Holy Spirit's blessing wherever he preached.

to repentance". In two or three years they had sounded the alarm to the utmost borders of the land. Many thousands gathered to hear them, and in every place where they came, many began to show such a concern for religion as they had never done before.'

Revival reaches Wales

It is usual to regard the Revival as running from 1738 to 1742. But, as in America, there were earlier signs of it. They first appeared almost simultaneously at Talgarth and Llangeitho in Wales in the summer of 1735. Griffith Jones had been preaching the evangelical message in Llandowror for the past twenty years. He well deserves his title 'morning star of the Methodist Revival'.

Howell Harris, a schoolmaster at Talgarth, had been moved by reading books published by the Society for Promoting Christian Knowledge, with which Griffith Jones was prominently associated. Harris was converted at a communion service on Whitsunday 1735; his heart was filled with 'the fire of the love of God'. He witnessed to his new-found experience and soon gathered a little society of fellow believers. They were the beginnings of the Welsh Calvinistic Methodist church. Although not ordained, Harris began to preach in private houses. People were transformed; the district was transformed; and further societies were started. The Welsh Revival had begun.

Meanwhile, Daniel Rowland of Llangeitho had been spiritually awakened through a sermon by Griffith Jones. His preaching in turn brought about an awakening in his own parish. Harris and Rowland met and from that point worked together for the spiritual welfare of Wales.

In the year of the Welsh Revival George Whitefield was converted. The son of a Gloucester innkeeper, he had once hoped to become an actor. Instead he was ɪrdained as an Anglican clergyman nd became the impassioned orator f the new movement. Whitefield vas the pioneer in England. His onverts in London and Bristol in 737 were the first of the Great Awakening. It was he who started ield-preaching, who first recruited ay preachers, who first travelled o and fro as 'one of God's run-bouts', as he described himself. He was also the first to make con-act with both the American and Scottish awakenings. His conver-ion heralded the English Revival. t was with him that the prepara-ions began.

The apostle of England

The culmination of the prepara-ions was the strange 'warming' f John Wesley's heart on 24 May 738. Here, without question, the novement received its most vital timulus. The dapper little Oxford cholar was transformed by the race of God into the 'apostle of England'. The Revival had found s true genius. 'If one man had to e picked out as *the* reviver, that nan's name would assuredly be ohn Wesley.'

On 1 January 1739 a remark-ble love feast was held at Fetter ane in London. There the lead-rs of the Revival were welded nto a fellowship of the Spirit in way similar to what had hap-ened at Herrnhut in 1727. The Vesleys were present, along with Vhitefield and Benjamin Ingham, who was to become an outstanding vangelist among the Moravians. About three in the morning, as ve were continuing instant in rayer,' John Wesley recorded n his *Journal*, 'the power of God ame mightily upon us insomuch hat many cried out for exceeding oy and many fell to the ground. As soon as were recovered a little rom that awe and amazement at he presence of His majesty, we broke out with one voice, "We praise Thee, O God, we acknowl-edge Thee to be the Lord".' This Pentecost on New Year's Day confirmed that the Awakening had come and launched the campaign of extensive evangelization which sprang from it.

The eighteenth-century Revival in England was a work of the Holy Spirit. It is important to realize, too, that it developed through various channels. There was the Moravian mission led by men such as Ingham and Cennick. There was the Calvinistic mission, in which Whitefield was the key figure. There was the Wesleyan mission, which produced the societies which were eventually to evolve into the Methodist church.

In addition to these three strands of the Revival, there was a movement within the Church of England which gave rise to what is now known as Anglican Evangelicalism. At first, all who were caught up in the spiritual renewal were dubbed either 'Methodists' or 'Evangelicals', irrespective of their church membership. But gradually the Evangelicals were recognized as a party within the Church of England who were seeking to achieve their aims within its existing framework.

Cornwall was the cradle of Anglican Evangelicalism. Samuel Walker of Truro emerged as leader of the party until his death in 1763. James Hervey, whose books attempted to bring the evangelical message to polite soci-ety, began his ministry in the west of England before moving to the midlands. The scholarly William Romaine was the first evangeli-cal to have a parish in London. Henry Venn at Huddersfield and William Grimshaw at Haworth were evangelical stalwarts in the north. John Berridge's parish at Everton, Cambridgeshire, was the scene of a local awakening in

1759. John Newton, the one-time slave trader turned preacher and hymn-writer, was curate of Olney in Buckinghamshire. The Anglican Evangelicals witnessed particularly effectively at the universities of Oxford and Cambridge.

Selina, Countess of Huntingdon, was the patroness of the Revival. Horace Walpole nicknamed her 'St Teresa of the Methodists'. When evangelical preachers were banned from other pulpits she found them a place in her domestic chapels and drawing-rooms. She made possible the proclamation of the gospel to the aristocracy. In 1768 she founded a theological training college at Trevecca in South Wales. In 1779 she was compelled by law to register her chapels as 'nonconformist meeting-houses'; they became known as 'the Countess of Huntingdon's Connexion'.

The Scots church transformed

No account of the Evangelical Revival is complete without reference to the transformation in Scotland. Its impact on the national church there was even more marked than in England. It is no exaggeration to say that the history of Scottish Presbyterianism was radically altered. The eighteenth century was once described as 'the dark age of the Scottish Church'. A debate about patrons had drained its energies and left it incapable of facing the more damaging challenge of theological scepticism.

John Simpson, professor of Divinity in Glasgow, was accused of teaching heretical views about the person of Christ, similar to those voiced in England by the deists. One of his students, Francis Hutchinson, set out to 'put a new face upon theology in Scotland'. In his ideas, known as 'Moderatism', the gospel was reduced to a system of morality which offered only a flimsy hope to those who wanted assurance about eternity. Ministers were more concerned about culture than conversions, and dismissed their heritage, which included the persecuted Covenanters, with derision.

A group of objectors, led by Ebenezer Erskine of Stirling, set up an independent presbytery and were forced to leave the national church in 1740. They themselves insisted that they were only withdrawing from 'the prevailing party', not from the church. The 'Seceders' gained some support, and their breakaway might have spread; but revival broke out in the parish of Cambuslang in 1742.

There had already been stirrings of revival in Easter Ross and Sutherland in the north of Scotland. John Balfour emerged as a leader of the movement in the northern Highlands which reached its peak in 1739. All this happened before ever Whitefield crossed the border, although he is often regarded as the bringer of revival to Scotland. As in America, he sowed the seed on prepared soil. Whitefield was first invited to Scotland in 1741 by the Seceders, but when he refused to confine his activities to their churches they disowned him. Immediately he found an opportunity to work within the Church of Scotland.

In 1742 William McCulloch was used to spread the revival known as the 'Cambuslang Wark'. It was under way when Whitefield visited the parish of Cambuslang during his second Scottish tour. He shared in two memorable open-air communion services. Commenting on the second of these, McCulloch described 'the spiritual glory of the solemnity . . . the gracious and sensible presence of God'.

Revival quickly spread to the surrounding area. Soon another outbreak occurred at Kilsyth. James Robe had preached there for over thirty years without obvious effect. In 1740 he began a series of sermons on the new birth. Two years later he was able to report that 'while pressing all the unregenerate to seek to have Christ formed within them, an extraordinary power of the divine Spirit accompanied the word preached'. Similar scenes were repeated for eighteen months or more.

Cambuslang and Kilsyth were the highlights of the Scottish Revival. The excitement subsided but the benefits remained. The Evangelical party, mocked as 'Zealots' or 'High-flyers' by their opponents, took over from the moderates and shaped the outlook of the church.

England aroused

What were the overall effects of the eighteenth-century Awakening? The most important are in fact the most difficult to quantify. Revival is a work of the Holy Spirit in human lives and cannot be mathematically measured. Nominal members of the church, who had 'the form of godliness without the power', were turned into New Testament Christians. Many thousands who before had made no claim to be Christians were swept into the kingdom of heaven; for revival and evangelism go hand in hand. The clergy were reformed. They set a new and high standard of pastoral care. The revival was not confined to the Anglican church. Nonconformists shared in the renewal.

The Awakening led to the creation of agencies aimed at promoting Christian work. Foremost among these were the missionary organizations which multiplied at the close of the century—the Baptist Missionary Society (1792), the London Missionary Society—an interdenominational venture (1795)—and the Church Missionary Society (1799). In 1786 the Wesleyan Conference approved the plan of Thomas Coke to take the gospel to India and took on the task of overseas extension.

It was not only missionary societies that owed their inspiration to the Revival. Both the Religious Tract Society (1799) (now the United Society for Christian Literature) and the British and Foreign Bible Society (1804) sprang from the Revival. Christian education

The Scottish Highlands saw revival in the eighteenth century.

gained a new dimension with the introduction of Sunday schools. They were started in 1769 by a Methodist, Hannah Ball, and then developed and popularized by Robert Raikes, an Anglican layman. The Church of England Sunday School Society was founded in 1786 by William Richardson, the evangelical vicar of St Michael-le-Belfrey, York, and the Sunday School Union was founded in 1803. The Sunday school movement in Britain marked a step towards free education for all.

The Revival encouraged a passion for social justice. The campaign to banish slavery from British colonies was led by people of evangelical convictions. In 1767 Grenville Sharp fought a case in the law courts to ensure that a slave should be freed whenever he set foot on English territory. Thomas Clarkson submitted a prize-winning essay on slavery in 1785, while still at St John's College, Cambridge, where he had been influenced by evangelicals. It was Clarkson who persuaded William Wilberforce to take up the issue of slavery in Parliament.

Wilberforce himself had been converted while on a tour of Europe with Isaac Milner, 'the Evangelical Dr Johnson', who became President of Queens' College, Cambridge. John Wesley published his *Thoughts on Slavery* in 1774; and only four days before his death penned a now-famous letter to Wilberforce urging him to 'go on, in the name of God, and in the power of His might, till even American slavery (the vilest that ever saw the sun) shall vanish away before it'.

Wesley also advocated prison reform and encouraged John Howard in his crusade for reform. Wesley had a practical concern for the poor and contributed personally to their relief as well as raising funds. He saw to it that through his societies clothing was distributed and food provided for the needy. Dispensaries were set up to treat the sick. In London one Methodist meeting-room was turned into a workshop for carding and spinning cotton. Other jobs were created for the unemployed.

A lending bank was opened by Christians in 1746. Legal advice and aid was made available. Widows and orphans were housed. This Christian concern for the under-privileged led to the birth of the Benevolent or Strangers' Friend Societies in 1787. They quickly established themselves as agencies of poor relief and bridged the gap until finally the state took over. The Evangelical Revival made England aware of its social obligations.

George Whitefield, the great preacher of the English Awakening.

The Methodists

A. Skevington Wood

What Charles Wesley described as 'the harmless nickname of Methodist' was originally applied in 1729 to a group at Oxford University also known as the Holy Club. The group was led by his brother John and aimed to provide a disciplined method of spiritual improvement. Members pledged themselves to have regular private devotions and to meet each evening to read the Bible and pray. Several labels were invented for them by jeering undergraduates—Enthusiasts, Bible Moths, Sacramentarians—but 'Methodist' was the one that caught on.

John Wesley traced the 'first rise' of Methodism to these years. The second stage, he explained, was in 1736 when 'the rudiments of a Methodist society' appeared in Georgia. Then, in 1738, Wesley helped to reframe the rules for an Anglican society which met in Fetter Lane, London. All this came before his revolutionizing conversion.

A new society

When, as a result of his conversion, John Wesley became 'an apostle to the nation', he was soon faced with the problem of caring for the converts. To meet this need, Methodist organization was called into being. Wesley found such societies already operating in Bristol, but in London he was pressed to devise one of his own for those who had listened to his outdoor preaching at Moorfields. When numbers increased to about a hundred, Wesley noted their names and addresses, intending to visit them in their homes. 'Thus, without any previous plan or design, began the Methodist society in England—a company of people associating together to help each other work out their own salvation.' The early successes of the Methodist preachers are to be explained both by the carelessness of many Anglican clergymen, and the fact that the Church of England had very little strength in the industrial towns and cities.

Methodism, then, began not as a church or a sect, but as a society. It was born, and expected to remain, within the Church of England. From the start, Wesley assumed that Methodists would attend Anglican services and sacraments. He himself had no desire to leave the Anglican church, despite the opposition he met, especially in

Love divine, all loves excelling,
Joy of heaven, to earth come down,
Fix in us thy humble dwelling,
All thy faithful mercies crown.
Jesu, thou art all compassion,
Pure, unbounded love thou art;
Visit us with thy salvation,
Enter every trembling heart.

Come, almighty to deliver,
Let us all thy life receive;
Suddenly return, and never,
Never more thy temples leave.
Thee we would be always blessing,
Serve thee as thy hosts above,
Pray, and praise thee, without ceasing,
Glory in thy perfect love.

Finish then thy new creation:
Pure and spotless may we be;
Let us see thy great salvation,
Perfectly restored in thee.
Changed from glory into glory,
Till in heaven we take our place,
Till we cast our crowns before thee,
Lost in wonder, love and praise.

CHARLES WESLEY (1707–88)

JOHN AND CHARLES WESLEY

A. Skevington Wood

The Wesley brothers are jointly commemorated in Westminster Abbey. A wall medallion displays their twin profiles. They were partners in evangelism and in the care of the Methodist societies. Both were powerful preachers. Each made his own special contribution: John was the organizer and administrator of a rapidly expanding movement, and Charles was the 'sweet singer' of Methodism. His hymns are a legacy to the world-wide church.

John and Charles were born at the rectory at Epworth in Lincolnshire. Their father, Samuel Wesley, was a staunch high churchman but their grandparents were nonconformists. Susanna Wesley, their mother, was a remarkable woman whose influence on her sons was exceptionally strong. John was born in 1703 and Charles four years later.

John Wesley, the itinerant evangelist. He declared that he had in only 'one point in view—to promote, so far as I am able, vital, practical religion; and by the grace of God, beget, preserve and increase the life of God in the soul of men.'

After attending different schools, each went up to Oxford University. Charles entered Christ Church in 1726, just when John had completed his course there and had been elected a fellow at Lincoln College. While John was away from Oxford for a period, serving as his father's curate, Charles started the Holy Club. On his return, John took over as leader. It was Charles who guided the devotional reading of George Whitefield before his conversion.

In 1737 the Wesley brothers sailed for Georgia to undertake a mission on behalf of the Society for the Propagation of the Gospel. Charles acted as secretary to the governor of the colony, James Oglethorpe. During the voyage to America, and in Georgia itself, the Wesleys met some Moravian Christians. They were dissatisfied with the result of their mission, and returned to England in 1738.

Both were influenced by another Moravian, Peter Böhler. Within three days each had a vital Christian experience—Charles on Whitsunday, and John on 24 May 1738, when his heart was 'strangely warmed'. This was at a meeting in Aldersgate Street, London, when a passage from Luther's *Preface to Romans* was being read. It proved to be the turning-point of the Evangelical Revival. 'What happened in that little room was of more importance to England than all the victories of Pitt by land or sea.'

The Wesleys were convinced that at all costs the people of Britain must hear the good news of salvation. While others might confine themselves to their parishes, the Wesleys believed that their call was to travel from place to place. They preached in churches whenever pulpits were made available to them. But more often, as opposition grew, the only possibility was to go out into the market-place or on to the common, so that the crowds might hear. The result was that the working classes were drawn to Christianity as the industrial revolution approached.

In 1749 Charles Wesley married Sarah (Sally) Gwynne, the daughter of a Welsh magistrate, and made his home in Bristol. For twenty years he supervised the Methodist society which met at the New Room there. He moved to London in 1771 and shared the preaching at City Road Chapel. He has been described as the most gifted and untiring hymn writer that England has ever known. He produced over 7,000 sacred songs and poems. It is remarkable that so many reached such a high standard.

Hymn singing made an enormous contribution to the Evangelical Revival. The songs had at least as great an effect as the sermons. They not only expressed the joys of Christian experience but also taught the truths of Scripture. John Wesley called the *Methodist Hymn Book* of 1780 'a little body of experimental and practical divinity'.

John Wesley's *Journal* is a classic of terse, shrewd and revealing comment. It records the journeys of someone who covered over 250,000 miles in the cause of the gospel. Wesley virtually invented the religious tract. He edited the *Christian Library,* which brought a rich selection of theological and devotional books within reach of the non-specialist reader. He also pioneered a new type of publication—the monthly magazine. His major printed sermons, along with his expository *Notes on the New Testament,* form the distinctive doctrinal standard of the Methodist church.

the early years of his ministry. He consistently advised his people to stand by the established church.

The title 'United Society' was probably borrowed from the Moravians. It indicated that, even though societies multipled throughout the county, they were regarded as one body. By 1743 Wesley was referring to the 'United Societies' in the plural; they were soon organized in a Connexion. Only after his death did the Methodist church emerge.

The parent society in London was gathered late in 1739, and met in a disused cannon-foundry. This was the headquarters of Methodism until the opening of City Road Chapel in 1778. The society included 'voluntary bands'—select groups of up to ten Christians supervised by a leader.

In one aspect the foundry society was unique. The sole condition for prospective members was 'a desire to flee from the wrath to come, to be saved from their sins'. The existing religious societies were restricted to those already attached to the Anglican church, or in full communion with it such as the Moravians). Wesley refused to impose any such ecclesiastical test, and opened his new society to nonconformists too. This openness was a mark of Methodism from the start.

In 1742 the class-meeting was introduced. This turned out to be of 'unspeakable usefulness', as Wesley recognized. (The name was simply the English form of the Latin *classic,* division, and carried with it no overtones of school.) The classes were rather larger in size than the bands and involved every member of the society. Their original purpose was to encourage Christian stewardship, since each member gave a penny a week to the funds. Then Wesley realized that the leaders were 'the persons who may not

“I fear, wherever riches have increased the essence of religion has decreased in the same proportion. Therefore I do not see how it is possible, in the nature of things for any revival of true religion to continue long. For religion must necessarily produce both industry and frugality, and these cannot but produce riches. But as riches increase, so will pride, anger and love of the world in all its branches.”

JOHN WESLEY

only receive the contributions, but also watch over the souls of their brethren'. The class system secured discipline as well as providing fellowship and pastoral care.

A nationwide movement

Wesley took another step in 1743. He drew up a common set of rules for all his societies, for Methodism was by then a nationwide organization. In 1744 the first Conference was held to consider 'the best method of carrying on the work of God' throughout the land. The Connexion was arranged in a series of circuits, or preachers' rounds. The earliest printed list of circuits, published in 1746, included seven: London, Bristol, Cornwall, Evesham, Yorkshire (covering six other counties), Newcastle and Wales.

The circuits were placed under the control of Assistants (that is, assistants to Wesley himself). They were recruited from the more experienced travelling preachers (or itinerants). They were responsible 'in the absence of the [parish] Minister, to feed and guide, to teach and govern the flock', and to lead the team of preachers (or Helpers) in the circuit. From the beginning the oversight of Methodism was entrusted to the Assistants (later called Superintendents), although their authority was always subject to that of Wesley and the Conference.

The Assistants were sometimes backed up by a limited number of Anglican clergymen who were prepared to devote some part of their time to itinerating for Wesley. Of these the most notable was John Fletcher of Madeley (1729–85). In addition to the travelling preachers (clergy and laymen), others on the spot shared in proclaiming the Word as local preachers (laymen—and in a few cases laywomen).

Preachers and members alike were committed to what Wesley referred to as 'our doctrines'. The basic theological conviction of the Methodists was 'that justification by faith is the doctrine of the Church as well as of the Bible'. To this was added a specific emphasis that salvation is for all, and a stress on the assurance of the Holy Spirit and scriptural holiness.

Whitefield disagreed with Wesley's belief that salvation is for all, and went his separate way. But the two men kept in touch and helped one another from time to time. From 1741 on, 'Arminian Methodists' allied with Wesley and 'Calvinistic Methodists' followed Whitefield. Wesley's Arminianism was that of the evangelical and reformed Arminius.

Methodism spread rapidly. Much of England was covered within ten years. Ireland, first visited by Wesley, in 1747, became a stronghold. In Wales the Calvinistic Methodists prevailed, except in some English-speaking areas. Only in Scotland did Methodism fail to gain much ground—although it left its mark on the Presbyterian church.

Into America

Methodism in America owed its beginnings to immigrants from Ireland. Robert Strawbridge, a Methodist local preacher from Drumsna, Ireland, settled at Sam's Creek in Maryland. He opened his log cabin for services and formed a society not long after his arrival in 1760. Soon he began to evangelize the district and further societies were started. About the same time another local preacher from Ireland, Philip Embury, arrived in New York and joined the Lutheran church. In 1765 his cousin,

Mrs Barbara Heck, prodded him to preach again and start a Methodist society. A British army officer, Thomas Webb, also lent a hand. He sent Wesley an account of what was happening and appealed for help. Volunteers were asked for at the Conference of 1769. Richard Boardman, and Joseph Pilmoor offered to go.

The major figure in the founding of American Methodism was Francis Asbury. He came from Handsworth near Birmingham, and had been apprenticed to an iron smelter before joining the ranks of Wesley's itinerants preachers. In 1771 he responded to another call to help in America. He urged his colleagues in America to press to the frontiers in their evangelism. Wesley's others preachers returned to base in England during the Revolutionary War; Asbury alone remained.

In 1784 Wesley appointed Asbury and Coke as joint superintendents for America. Contrary to his wishes, the title of Methodist Episcopal church was adopted by the Christmas Conference in Baltimore; Asbury and Coke were made bishops. This amounted to a declaration of independence; American Methodism now stood on its own feet as a separate body.

When he set apart Thomas Coke for America, Wesley authorized him to ordain Asbury. The two superintendents were then to ordain presbyters from among the American preachers. Later, Wesley broke with Anglican practice by himself laying hands on men who were to minister in Scotland and overseas as missionaries. Shortly before his death, he began to make similar provision for areas in England where the Methodists could not receive the sacraments. These steps inevitably hastened the departure of his followers from the established church, although Wesley insisted to the end that he did not aim at separation.

A legal *Deed of Declaration* in 1784 ensured that on Wesley's death his authority would pass to the Methodist Conference, represented by one hundred of its members. In 1787 Methodist preaching-places were licensed under the *Toleration Act.* In 1795 Methodism seceded from the Anglican church: this was agreed in the *Plan of Pacification.* By the close of the century the Methodist church was ready to spread across the world.

HYMNS AND CHURCH MUSIC

John S. Andrews

A Christian hymn is a song, normally in metre and in stanza-form, which is used in worship. An ideal hymn has something definite to say, is scriptural, poetic, yet simple and singable; it is God- (or Christ-) centred, orthodox and non-sectarian.

The first hymn-books in Britain

For two centuries after the Reformation there was no book of hymns for use in the Church of England. Metrical psalms were often sung, especially the so-called *Old Version* (1562). In 1696 *A New Version* of metrical psalms, by Nahum Tate and Nicholas Brady was published. To this book we owe paraphrases such as, 'As pants the hart for cooling streams' (Psalm 42) and 'Through all the changing scenes of life' (Psalm 34). Both books continued in use until about 1870. *The Scottish Psalter,* still used by Scottish Presbyterians, dates from 1650.

In 1623 George Wither's *Hymnes and Songs of the Church* was published. It was the first attempt at a comprehensive English hymn-book, but had little success. In the seventeenth century, hymns were taken or adapted from the work of poets such as George Herbert and John Milton, and writers such as Richard Baxter and John Bunyan. The essayist, Joseph Addison, is also remembered for his hymns: 'When all thy mercies, O my God' and 'The spacious firmament on high'.

Bishop Thomas Ken's best-known hymns are those for morning and evening, written for the scholars of Winchester College, 'Awake, my soul, and with the sun', and 'Glory to thee, my God, this night'.

Late in the seventeenth century, hymns began to be freely written. Dissenters began to use them in congregational worship, the Baptists being the pioneers.

A new kind of hymn-writing

Isaac Watts gave a great boost to the movement for using 'man-made' hymns—as distinct from the inspired hymns (mainly psalms) in Scripture. His best-seller, *Hymns and Spiritual Songs,* appeared in 1707. He followed this in 1715 with *Divine Songs* for children and in 1719 with *The Psalms of David.* In this book he made 'David speak like a Christian'. For example he transformed Psalm 72 into the missionary fervour of 'Jesus shall reign where'er the sun'. In over

JESU

Jesu is in my heart, his sacred name
Is deeply carved there: but th'other week
A great affliction broke the little frame,
Ev'n all to pieces: which I went to seek:
And first I found the corner, where was *J*,
After, where *ES*, and next where *U* was graved.
When I had got these parcels, instantly
I sat me down to spell them, and perceived
That to my broken heart he was *I ease you*,
And to my whole is JESU.

GEORGE HERBERT

600 hymns, many still sung, Isaac Watts expressed wonder, praise and adoration covering the whole and adoration covering the whole range of Christian experience. Another dissenter, Philip Doddridge, composed about 370 hymns, including 'Hark, the glad sound, the Saviour comes' and 'O God of Bethel'. The staunch Calvinist, Augustus Toplady, wrote 'Rock of Ages', lines that have been sung by Christians of all persuasions. This hymn first appeared in a magazine article calculating the 'National Debt' in terms of sin.

A movement 'born in song'

Overshadowing all other eighteenth-century hymnwriters were the Wesley brothers. *The Collection of Psalms and Hymns* (1737), compiled by John Wesley and published in Charleston, South Carolina, was the first successful hymn-book compiled for use in the Church of England. John Wesley later edited collections for the Methodists, notably the definitive *Collection* (1780). This book contained many of his brother's compositions and of his own paraphrases from German writers such as Zinzendorf.

Methodism, like Lutheranism, was 'born in song'. Charles Wesley's hymns are marked by a constant note of praise—for example 'O for a thousand tongues to sing' and, 'Rejoice, the Lord is King'. He praised God because he was amazed at his love: 'And can it be that I should gain . . .?'; 'Jesu, Lover of my soul'. Watts and Doddridge freely paraphrased Scripture. Charles Wesley in addition paraphrased the *Prayer Book,* and versified Christian doctrine and experience. He wrote hymns that are still sung at all the major Christian festivals.

The Olney Hymns

In 1779 the fiery, converted slave-trader, John Newton, and the gentle, retiring, melancholic poet, William Cowper, produced a hymn-book for the village of Olney, where they lived. Newton wrote such hymns as 'Glorious things of thee are spoken' and 'Amazing grace! how sweet the sound'. Cowper was more inward-looking; even his hymn of assurance, 'God moves in a mysterious way' had its 'fearful saints' dreading the storm-clouds.

American writers

The earliest book known to have been printed in English in the British North American colonies was *The Whole Book of Psalmes Faithfully Translated into English Metre* (1640), which became known as *The Bay Psalm Book* because it was used by the Massachusetts Bay Colony. It was compiled by, among others, John

Glorious things of thee are spoken,
Zion, city of our God!
He whose word cannot be broken
Formed thee for his own abode.
On the Rock of Ages founded,
What can shake thy sure repose?
With salvation's walls surrounded,
Thou mayst smile at all thy foes.

Saviour, if of Zion's city
I, through grace, a member am,
Let the world deride or pity,
I will glory in thy name:
Fading is the worldling's pleasure,
All his boasted pomp and show,
Solid joys and lasting treasure
None but Zion's children know.

JOHN NEWTON (1725–1807)

William Cowper (1731–1800) the English poet. Although he suffered severe depression, he wrote a number of hymns which achieved lasting recognition.

Eliot, the 'apostle to the Indians', who was famous for his learning, piety, zeal and practical wisdom.

American hymns of the eighteenth century were similar to English hymns of that period. Hymns of only two of these authors are still in common use: Samuel Davies ('Great God of wonders, all thy ways') and Timothy Dwight ('I love thy kingdom, Lord'). Davies was President of the New Jersey Presbyterian College, Princeton; Dwight was President of Yale.

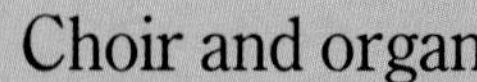

Choir and organ

In countries where Luther's influence was strongest, a great tradition of singing by both choir and congregation was laid down. A large treasury of organ music, largely based on the melodies from chorales, reached its peak in the genius of Johann Sebastian Bach (1685–1750). Bach's many cantatas written for different periods in the church's year include the *Christmas Oratorio*. His most ambitious works were the *Mass in B Minor* and the *St Matthew Passion*. Since the time of Bach the major German Protestant churches have tended to regard their repertory of hymn-tunes as complete. Few new tunes have been composed.

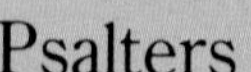

Psalters

Church music developed differently in countries dominated

When I survey the wondrous Cross
On which the Prince of Glory dy'd,
My richest Gain I count but loss,
And pour Contempt on all my Pride.

Forbid it, Lord, that I should boast
Save in the Death of Christ my God;
All the vain things that charm me most,
I sacrifice them to his Blood.

See from his Head, his Hands, his Feet,
Sorrow and Love flow mingled down;
Did e'er such Love and Sorrow meet?
Or Thorns compose so rich a Crown?

His dying Crimson like a Robe
Spreads o'er his Body on the Tree,
Then am I dead to all the Globe,
And all the Globe is dead to me.

Were the whole Realm of nature mine,
That were a Present far too small;
Love so amazing, so divine
Demands my Soul, my Life, my All.

ISAAC WATTS, 1709

by Calvin's teachings. *The Genevan Psalter* (1562), a volume of metrical psalms in French, with music edited by Louis Bourgeois and others, was translated into German and Dutch. For a long time it was the only tune-book of the Reformed churches in continental Europe. Unaccompanied unison singing was the rule, except in Holland where the organ continued in use.

England and Scotland followed Geneva's lead. But although the psalters contained some excellent tunes, many were inferior to those in the *Genevan Psalter*. Each psalm was 'lined out'. This practice, necessary when few could read and books were expensive, meant that each line in turn was first read by a precentor before being slowly sung by the congregation.

Anthems

Although metrical psalms long prevailed in parish churches, in Anglican cathedrals they began to sing anthems. Henry Purcell wrote fine anthems, especially 'Rejoice in the Lord alway'.

George Frederick Handel's church music consisted mostly of passion music, Latin psalms and cantata-like anthems. He wrote a number of oratorios—above all *Messiah*. Haydn followed with *The Creation*, and Mendelssohn with *Elijah*. With a few exceptions, little really good music appeared in England for church choirs before the end of the nineteenth century.

The Wesleys popularized congregational hymn-singing in Britain; but early Methodism lacked a really outstanding composer. Their tunes were borrowed or adapted from many sources, particularly German ones.

In Europe, the Roman Catholics revived hymns in the sixteenth and seventeenth centuries. The French diocesan prayer books of 1675–1800 provided admirable tunes modified from plainsong and known as French church melodies.

Johann Sebastian Bach, the greatest composer of all time for the organ. Most of his musical writing was for the Lutheran church, and included about 300 cantatas for the church year, as well as the great B Minor Mass and St Matthew Passion.

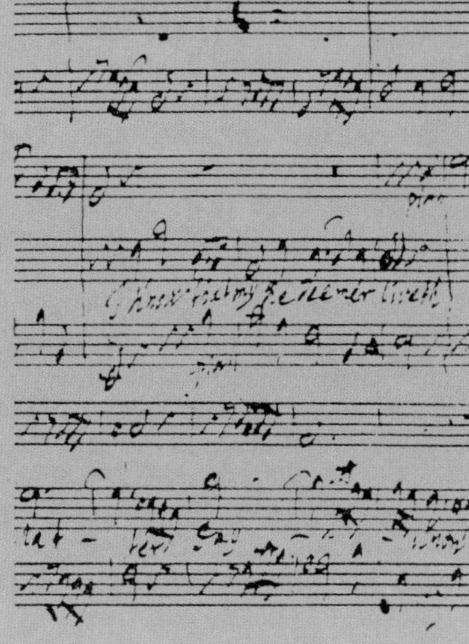

Handel's original manuscript for his famous *aria* 'I know that my Redeemer liveth', from *Messiah*.

The Russian Church

Paul D. Steeves

The alliance between the Russian church and the state, which was close from the time of Prince Vladimir's conversion in 988, became especially strong after 1500. As the sixteenth century opened, controversy raged within the church regarding its role in society. On the one hand, Nil Sorsky called on the church to minister to society from a position of poverty, independent of secular, political concerns. On the other hand, Joseph of Volokolamsk wanted church and state united, with the rich church supporting, and supported by, the ruler. Nil's supporters were known as 'Non-Possessers'; Joseph's as 'Possessers'.

For obvious reasons, the state favoured the Possessers and severely persecuted the mystical Non-Possessers. But in doing so it created fateful consequences for the Russian church. The intense devotional emphasis of Nil and his 'Transvolga Hermits' receded into the background. The church, following Joseph, became a wealthy landowner, holding as much as one-third of all property in Russia.

In line with the claim of 'Moscow, The Third Rome', the prince of Muscovy assumed the title 'Czar', a variation of 'Caesar'. Ivan IV, the Terrible, was the first ruler to be formally crowned as successor to the Roman emperors, 'Czar of all the Russians'. Consistent with the theory which assumed that there could be only one Christian emperor, the Russians asserted that Moscow deserved to have a patriarch, the highest office in the Orthodox church. Consequently, in 1589, the head of the Russian church was raised to the rank of patriarch, equal to the patriarchs of Antioch, Alexandria, Jerusalem and Constantinople.

The first decades of the Moscow patriarchate coincided with a period of political disorder in Muscovy. The dynasty came to an end with the death of Ivan IV's son. Russia plunged into the terrible 'Time of Troubles' (1598–1613), which ended with the election of the Romanov royal house. The patriarchs played a leading role in shepherding Russia through the chaos. Patriarch Germogen inspired national unity in the worst years of the 'Troubles', until he was murdered by the Polish conquerors of Moscow. His successor, Filaret, father of the first Romanov Czar, Michael, completely dominated his weak son. The patriarch called himself 'The Great Sovereign' and sat on the throne beside his son, signing all state papers jointly with the Czar. Thus the Russian church and state became as one.

Material concerns sorely sapped the spiritual vitality of the Russian church. Several sensitive, devout young men became disturbed by this condition. Soon a circle of 'Zealots of Faith' formed around Michael's son, the future Czar Alexis. Travelling throughout the land they called clergy and lay people alike to sincere spiritual devotion. Although united by the desire to see error and corruption rooted out of the church, the circle of Zealots was soon broken by disputes over the way to correct the abuses.

When Alexis became Czar, he arranged for the election of his fellow-Zealot, Nikon, as patriarch. Nikon immediately used the power of his office to order changes in the forms of ritual which, he thought, the Russians mistakenly employed. For example, he declared that the sign of the cross must be made with three fingers raised, not two, as had been the Russian Practice; the three-fold *Alleluia* was to be sung in worship, not the two-fold.

Nikon's former associates objected that his reforms were not what was needed to purify the church. They called, instead, for reform of the moral and spiritual laxness which had crept into all levels of the church, from parishioners up to bishops. Moreover, they accused Nikon of introducing further error into the church, rather than correction. Led by the archpriest Avvakum, they rejected Nikon's liturgical reforms. When the patriarch used the power of the state to enforce his changes, the Russian church split into two parts. Avvakum and his followers were imprisoned and exiled. From prison, Avvakum wrote his *Autobiography,* a magnificent landmark in Russian literature, which deserves a place second only to Augustine's *Confessions*.

When Avvakum was finally burned at the stake in 1682, the schism was complete. Large numbers of ordinary believers who had been spiritually awakened by the fervent preaching of the Zealots readily followed their leaders into openly opposing the official church. Thousands of these 'Old Ritualists', or 'Old Believers', died in fires lit by state agents or by themselves. They were ready to die in this way because they believed that the end of the world was near. The liturgical changes clearly proved to them that this was the case. Was not Moscow the third, and last, Rome? If it deserted Orthodoxy, that is 'true worship', had not the reign of Antichrist begun? To understand the extreme reactions of the schismatics it is important to remember that the Russians attached great significance to the external forms of worship.

Russian liturgical practices had diverged from those in the Orthodox churches that lay under the political sway of the Ottoman Empire. Nikon declared that the Greeks, not the Russians, had preserved the original, and therefore correct, forms of worship. Moreover, he reckoned that if Russian practice was made to conform with that of the subjugated churches it would allow the Russians to lead all Orthodoxy and perhaps even permit Russia to liberate the suppressed peoples.

The schism profoundly weakened the power of the church over against that of the state. When Patriarch Nikon attempted to claim

St Basil's cathedral, Red Square, Moscow. This wooden church was built in the sixteenth century. With its strident colours, rich decoration and nine onion-domes it contrasts sharply with west European styles of architecture.

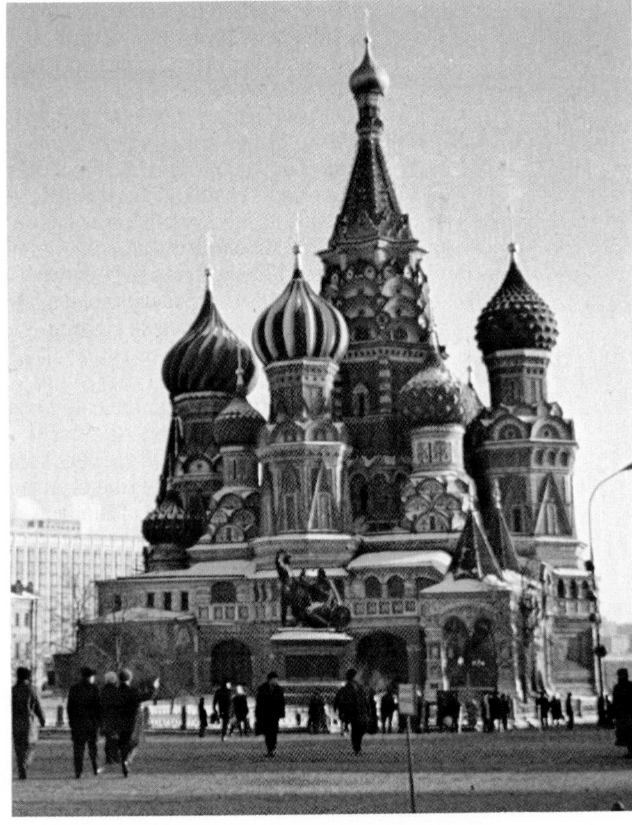

the title of 'Great Sovereign', as his predecessors had done, Czar Alexis had him removed from office in order to ensure that the church remained under the state. Alexis' son, Peter the Great, abolished the office of patriarch altogether. In place of the patriarchate, Peter introduced in 1721 the Most Holy Synod. The Synod consisted of a board of bishops which supervised church affairs and which was, in turn, supervised by a secular government official, the Procurator General, appointed by the Czar.

The Russian Orthodox church thus became little more than a department of state for the remaining two hundred years of the existence of the Czarist state. The 'Ecclesiastical Regulation' creating the Synod obliged any priest who discovered, in the confessional, evidence of treason or of anti-government plans, to pass on such information to the police.

Peter's innovations made significant changes in Russian religious life. They confirmed Old Ritualists' suspicions that Antichrist ruled in Russia. As a result some Old Believers withdrew into communities of like-minded believers. Because of their discipline, frugality and industry, these communities soon became prosperous and created an important part of the basis of Russian economic development and expansion to the north and east. Some Old Believers concluded that under the rule of Antichrist the succession of the true priesthood had ceased on earth. Thus the schismatics divided into 'priestly' and 'priest-less' groups, both of which continue to exist to the present. Peasant revolts in Russia, notably that led by Pugachev (1773–75), were fuelled by Old Ritualist opposition to the Czarist state and church.

The Synodal church, by pressing its claim as leader of Orthodox Christianity, became an instrument of Russian imperialism. Under Catherine the Great, the treaty ending Russia's aggressive war against the Turks in 1774 recognized the Czar's right to intervene in the internal affairs of the Ottoman Empire on behalf of the Orthodox subjects of the Sultan.

As a result of Peter the Great's innovations, a split appeared in the official Orthodox church between the upper, 'black' clergy, bishops and monks, and the lower, 'white' parish clergy. The former, who sometimes received lavish support from the state, became enmeshed in politics. The latter were frequently extremely poor. They were compelled to earn their living either through working in the fields or charging fees for the sacraments and prayers. Generally they were poorly educated, and they were obliged to report social discontent to the state. As a result, the Russian clergy gained a miserable reputation.

The church suffered yet further at the hands of the state when Catherine ordered that church and monastery lands should became state property. The church thereby lost most of its property to the state and, subsequently, over three-quarters of its annual income.

In these circumstances, Russian society became a fertile field for the growth of sectarian movements. Many Russians sought satisfaction for their religious needs outside the church, which they saw to be unspiritual, and even hostile, to their interests. Some turned to mystical Protestantism and freemasonry. Opposition to Orthodoxy often assumed bizarre forms: *Khlysty* ('Flagellants'), *Skoptsy* ('Castrates'), *Dukhobors* ('Spirit-Wrestlers'), *Molokany* ('Milk Drinkers').

It is perhaps surprising that

any religious devotion could survive in Russian Orthodoxy. Nevertheless, the church can proudly point to leaders such as Tikhon Zadonsky (1724–83) and Serafim (1759–1832). Tikhon's humility and wisdom have been immortalized in Dostoevsky's portrait of Father Zosima in *The Brothers Karamazov*. Serafim revived monasticism in Russia as a source of godly advice and aid for ordinary Russian believers. The most notable outpost of spirituality in Russia was the famous hermitage of Optino, to which, among the thousands of pilgrims, the great writers Gogol, Dostoevsky and Tolstoy went. There was a great revival in the nineteenth-century Russian church. It was accompanied by a mushrooming of church-backed educational institutions and by a new enthusiasm for missionary work, particularly in China, Japan and North America.

The devout Czar Alexander I sponsored the creation, in 1812, of the Russian Bible Society which began to translate the Scriptures into the ordinary Russian language. Although the Society's work was temporarily interrupted by Nicholas I's prohibition of the circulation of Russian Scriptures, after 1863 the written Word of God became widely available to the Russian people.

It was also in the nineteenth century that two of Russia's greatest original religious thinkers appeared. Both were laymen. Alexis Khomiakov put forward a doctrine of Christian community which suggested that religious authority rested in the entire body of the church rather than in the papacy or the Bible. Vladimir Soloviev proclaimed the idea of 'Godmanhood', that God and man were united through spiritual participation in the incarnated *Logos*. Both men viewed Russia as God's appointed teacher for the world, pointing the way to the ecumenical unity of all Christians.

Czar Peter the Great had considerable influence on the Russian church. He set in motion the expansion of the Orthodox church into Siberia.

EXPANSION WORLD-WIDE

James A. De Jong

For some decades before 1650, much of Europe had been embroiled in warfare. The nations were fighting for the control of Europe—and of world-wide commerce. The powerful Habsburg rulers of Austria and Spain, usually backed by the pope, had been pitted against the kings and princes of north-west Europe, most of whom were Protestants.

The last religious war

With the Peace of Westphalia (1648) an era came to an end. Wars of religion now belonged to the past. A variety of churches and denominations were recognized in Europe, though religious discrimination and persecution persisted. In the same year, by the Treaty of Münster, Dutch independence was recognized. The German principalities, Denmark and Sweden all turned away from war.

The nations which had avoided total involvement in the Thirty Years' War reaped the benefits. France, England and the Netherlands had used the opportunity to expand their fleets, establish trading colonies overseas and manoeuvre themselves into dominant positions in Europe. By 1650 the tide had turned in their favour. Spain, weak in armies and finance, continued to be a major colonial power, but lost the ability to keep up with her northern neighbours. Portugal's population was too small, her grip on her colonies too weak, and the colonies themselves too far-flung to protect them adequately.

England increased in power and influence until 1789. France's colonial growth was halted only by the first Peace of Paris (1763) when she was forced to give up some colonies to England. For a time the Dutch, and even the Danes, did not lag far behind. But the fortunes of Catholic Spain and Portugal steadily declined.

In the East, Christianity, whether Catholic, Orthodox or Protestant, was on the defensive. It was facing Islamic Turkey's penetration into Europe. In 1529, and again in 1683, Turkish armies put Vienna under siege. The minarets to be found in Eastern Europe today are witness to the Turkish occupation of much of the Balkan territories.

As Russia expanded to the east—in 1648 Russians stood on the shores of the Pacific Ocean for the first time—Orthodox missions began. These Russian missions, some state-sponsored, others voluntary, began to claim the Eastern territories for the Orthodox church. They tended to develop in a sporadic way—but displayed apostolic simplicity and zeal, and there were many martyrs.

Europe colonizes the world

Christian missions form part of the story of European colonization. Their history must be seen in that context. Friars and missionaries followed merchants and colonial administrators to remote, exotic lands. Sometimes the missionaries arrived first.

Spain sustained her earlier control of the Philippines, Central and South America. In some areas she extended her control; for example on the coast of California and in the semi-arid stretches north and east of Old Mexico.

In the Caribbean and along the Gulf coast Spain suffered losses. The British repeatedly fought Spain for the possession of Florida. French explorers also claimed this area, as they did Louisiana, which became a French territory after 1682. England occupied the Caribbean islands of Barbados and Trinidad, and in 1655 took Jamaica. To her colonies of Martinique, Guadeloupe and Saint Christophe, France added Haiti in 1697. The Dutch, French and English each carved out their respective Guianas on the north-east coast of South America, to form buffers between the Spanish and Portuguese colonies. One by one the islands of the West Indies, colonial jewels, were contested by the new powers. By the eighteenth century the Caribbean had become the most cosmopolitan sea in the world.

Portuguese colonies in Africa and the Far East came off even worse. As the northern colonial powers increased their shipping around the Cape of Good Hope, they established settlements on both the west and the east coasts of Africa. The French, who had founded a post in Senegal in 1626, gained Madagascar in 1686 and took Mauritius from the Dutch in 1715. After 1652 the Dutch held tenaciously to the tip of Africa, and Netherlanders gradually began to colonize this area. Not to be outdone, the English settled a colony at the mouth of the River Gambia, in West Africa.

By the eighteenth century Portugal had rivals for the rich, prized trade with India. Although she retained Goa, other European nations made their colonies in India too. The French had Surat, Calicut, Pondicherry and Chandarnagar; the British had Bombay, Madras and Calcutta; the Danes could be found in Tranquebar. Although in general the Dutch ignored India, they wrested Malacca from the Portuguese in 1641, and took Sri

This map of the new world was drawn in 1570 in Antwerp. Some parts of the map have few named places: at that time these areas were unexplored.

Jesuit missionaries crucified at Nagasaki, Japan, in 1597. Christians were subjected to several waves of persecution. But even when the Jesuits were expelled, some Japanese congregations survived into the nineteenth century.

Lanka in 1655. They also increased their holdings in the Spice Islands, particularly after winning land and trade from a Javanese ruler in 1677 in exchange for military assistance.

With few exceptions, the Europeans went to Africa and Asia mainly to trade. Yet even this was suspect in China and Japan. The Manchu rulers in China cut short trade, and the Tokugawas in Japan virtually stopped it. Chinese bandits drove the Dutch from Formosa in 1661.

Not until the nineteenth century did further huge chunks of Africa and Asia come under Western domination. Meanwhile European missionaries, both Roman Catholic and Protestant, followed the trade routes, taking with them the Christian gospel.

The 'Propaganda'

Catholic missions were shaped by the new policies and organizational structures introduced by Pope Gregory XV. In 1622 Gregory founded the 'Sacred Congregation for the Propagation of the Faith,' usually referred to simply as the *Propaganda*. This was an attempt to bring Catholic missions more directly under Vatican control.

This new policy aimed to replace the patronage system, which had been used in missions since the end of the fifteenth century. Patronage had been granted by the pope to the monarchs of Spain and Portugal. It gave them responsibility for Christianizing natives, establishing dioceses and appointing clergy in their colonies. Because these responsibilities had been neglected in many instances, Gregory set up the *Propaganda*, a body of clergy charged with spreading the Catholic faith. It was to work in countries where the faith was either unknown or under attack from heretics.

Under the direction of its first secretary, Francesco Ingoli, the *Propaganda* made a series of investigations into the condition of Catholic missions. It documented many evils: rivalry between the religious orders; political interests taking priority over the spread of the gospel; and the abuse and alienation of native populations. As a result, the *Propaganda* in 1627 persuaded Pope Urban VIII to found the College of Urban for the training of missionaries. The *Propaganda* also found missionary recruits, gave financial aid to missions, printed liturgies and catechisms for use overseas and requested reports from its agents to guide its work. By the time of Ingoli's death in 1649, the *Propaganda* had become the most important force in Roman Catholic expansion.

The *Propaganda* made great use of the office of vicar-apostolic. This was designed to overcome the evils of patronage, and to establish bishoprics in areas not held by Spain or Portugal. The vicar-apostolic was given the full authority of a bishop and was directly responsible to Rome. He was chosen from the non-monastic clergy, to avoid getting entangled with the religious orders. Although he was known by the name of a diocese, he was not limited to one area. He was in fact a roving missionary. The vicar-apostolic was often instructed to keep his title and mission secret until he arrived at his destination. He met the stiffest opposition from the clergy still working under the patronage system.

In 1637 Matthew de Castro, a Brahmin convert who had been an outstanding student in Rome, and Franciscus de Santo Felice were named the first vicars-apostolic. The latter was appointed Archbishop of Myra and sent to Japan, although he never arrived there. Castro was named bishop of

Chrysopolis and sent to Idalkan, an area of India free of Portuguese control, though not entirely free of its influence. The Portuguese clergy in Goa obstructed Castro's work so successfully that he was forced to give up. The *Propaganda* next sent him to Golconda, a kingdom recently taken from Portugal by the Mogul rulers of India. Here Castro still met with opposition from Goa, but he won a number of converts. He began training native clergy, and handed over his work to two successors—like himself Hindu converts acting as vicars-apostolic.

Mission to Vietnam

The *Propaganda* turned increasingly to France for vicars-apostolic and for finances. The French clergy were free from the ties of patronage. France's rise as a commercial power was accompanied by a growing sense of missionary obligation, which was fostered by widely-circulated missionary journals and accounts. Both the nobility and the clergy made generous gifts and promoted foreign missions. Organizations such as the Capuchins, and the Company of the Blessed Sacrament

Two Jesuits at the court of a Muslim prince in India. They are suggesting a test of religions: they will walk into the fire holding the Bible if the Muslims will do the same carrying the Qur'an.

and the Lazarists became deeply committed to mission.

A veteran French Jesuit, Alexander de Rhodes, was the man mainly responsible for bringing together the *Propaganda* and French missionary concerns. He laboured in the Far East from 1623 until 1645. About half his time was spent in Macao. But his most effective work was done in Vietnam before 1630, and between 1640 and 1645. He quickly mastered the Vietnamese language and reduced it to writing. He trained a group of native catechists, who continued his work when he was banished from Vietnam in 1645. The catechists were organized as a celibate lay order. They showed dedication and knowledge of the faith and were given medical instruction by de Rhodes. By the mid-seventeenth century the mission had resulted in a flourishing Vietnamese church numbering about 30,000.

Portuguese missionaries brought Christianity to Macao in the seventeenth and eighteenth centuries. This early Portuguese-style Roman Catholic church still stands in modern Macao.

When he returned to Rome, de Rhodes urged the *Propaganda* to appoint vicars-apostolic to train and ordain native clergy in the Far East. The *Propaganda* was initially cool to his idea. They suggested that he should recruit missionaries in his homeland. He found ready volunteers among his French Jesuit brothers. But de Rhodes desperately wanted men from the secular clergy, who could take a vow directly from the *Propaganda*. He found the priests he was looking for among a small group called the 'Good Friends'; they had already committed themselves to foreign service.

'Good Friends' in Asia

Out of this group grew the Society of Foreign Missions (Société des Missions Étrangères) in Paris. In 1663 this society dedicated its seminary to the training of missionaries. The papacy and *Propaganda* finally accepted de Rhodes' suggestion, after prodding by the Assembly of the French Clergy in 1655. In 1658 two 'Good Friends', François Pallu and Pierre Lambert de la Motte, were appointed vicars-apostolic. De la Motte was entitled bishop of Beirut, for service in Cochin, and Pallu entitled bishop of Heliopolis, for service in Tonkin. They were followed by Pallu's friend, Ignazio Cotolendi, who was sent as bishop of Metallopolis to central and northern China (which included Peking).

Cotolendi died soon after reaching Asia, and the other two were strongly opposed by Portuguese clergy. But their work marked a new departure for Catholic missions in the Far East. For the first time Rome had direct rule over all areas in the Far East that were not subject to Portuguese patronage. In 1665 the first native seminary was opened in Ayuthia. The earlier work of de Rhodes was consolidated on a firm local basis. The future of Catholic missions seemed bright.

Questioning the instructions

But in 1659 the *Propaganda* issued a set of instructions to its vicars-apostolic. They touched on an issue that was ultimately to divide. The instructions dealt partly with missionary attitudes towards native culture. Until this date there had been two opposite theories on this subject. Most Catholics demanded that converts should make a complete break with their ethnic culture. They held that local customs and practices were rooted in non-Christian religion. They should be tested by the gospel, and cleansed of any trace of paganism. But a minority of Catholics had followed a different policy. Missionaries such as Robert de Nobili in south India and Matthew Ricci in China had adopted the native dress and customs. They studied local literature and beliefs and lived in the style of their adopted country.

The instructions of 1659 opted for the approach of de Nobili and Ricci. Vicars-apostolic were advised to learn the local language. They were warned not to revolutionize the habits, customs and culture of the people to whom they had been sent. The instructions claimed that it was absurd to attempt to turn Asians into Europeans. The *Propaganda* felt that the mission would be undermined if local customs were constantly criticized. If some things were obviously incompatible with Christianity, any changes undertaken must be gradual and gentle.

The two methods clashed most sharply in China. As the century wore on, the controversy developed into a battle between the religious orders. Vicars-apostolic found it difficult to work out exactly what the instructions meant. The debate on method became heated and parties were formed. The *Propaganda* found itself caught between the Jesuits on the one hand and the Franciscans and Dominicans on the other.

The Jesuits had held a favoured position in China since the days of Ricci. They impressed the Chinese with such skills as clock-making, mathematics, map-making, canonry and astronomy. They also gained access to the imperial court, where they acted as advisers to the Chinese government. When the Ming dynasty toppled, between 1644 and 1662, the German Jesuit, Johann Adam Schall, weathered the crisis. When the new rulers took over, he was appointed chairman of the board to regulate the Chinese calendar. His younger colleague, a Belgian named Ferdinand Verbiest, was befriended by the emperor, Kang Hsi, who held the Chinese throne until 1722.

A church in China

The Jesuits used their prestige to win an edict of toleration for Chinese Christians in 1692. By 1700 a flourishing Chinese church existed, with as many as 300,000 converts. But such gains had not come without a price. The Jesuits had studied Confucius. They concluded that Confucius was not a Chinese god, and that Confucian temples were merely meeting-places for scholars. They decided that incense burned, and prayers offered, for the dead were not idolatry, but healthy respect for ancestors. They also claimed that Confucian terms such as *Tien* (heaven) and *Chang-ti* (sovereign lord) were Chinese names for the God of whom the Jesuits themselves spoke. The Jesuits strongly advocated that the Chinese language be used in worship. They translated the liturgy into Chinese as early as the 1660s.

Issues such as these were

"Do not regard it as your task, and do not bring any pressure to bear on the peoples, to change their manners, customs and uses, unless they are evidently contrary to religion and sound morals. What could be more absurd than to transport France, Spain, Italy or some other European country to China? Do not introduce all that to them, but only the faith, which does not despise or destroy the manners and customs of any people, always supposing they are not evil, but rather wishes to see them preserved unharmed . . ."

Part of the Instructions *sent out by the* Propaganda, *1659* called into question, particularly by religious orders whose ranks were filled by Spaniards from the Philippines. The problem became known as the 'rites controversy'. Differences in the missionaries' national backgrounds, and differences between their orders, unquestionably sharpened differences over the Chinese rites. Ultimately the *Propaganda*, caught in the middle, had to make a choice.

Gradually both the *Propaganda* and the vicars-apostolic began to question the Jesuit approach. As early as 1684, Charles Maigrot, Pallu's successor, voiced his opposition. By 1704 Pope Clement XI banned Jesuit missionary methods and ordered Charles de Tournon to enforce his decision. The emperor of China himself appealed to Rome but was ignored. Angered by this, Kang Hsi, the Emperor, delivered an edict which forbade evangelism. Seven years later every missionary, except a few Jesuit advisers, was expelled from China. Christians suddenly found themselves persecuted, and believers were martyred. The mission effort, which by 1684 had produced a native vicar-apostolic named Lo Wen-Tsao, lost all its power. The Chinese church shrivelled. Not until the mid-nineteenth century would the Chinese Catholic church again flourish. But the Vatican did not take this opportunity to rethink the question of missionary methods.

Mission to Asia

Meanwhile the Vietnamese mission continued fruitfully even if it never repeated the dramatic results of de Rhodes' time. In the Philippines, Spanish orders worked without interruption. They were impeded only by the remoteness of unreached tribes, and the low level of Philippino morale.

The Philippines themselves became a base from which missions were launched to other parts of Asia. The northern and central regions of India remained closed to missionaries. But in southern India, John de Britto, a Portuguese nobleman, used de Nobili's methods as he evangelized the lower castes. His work was short-lived, lasting only from 1685 until 1693, when he was martyred. De Britto was succeeded by Constantine Beschi, who used his fluency in the Tamil language as he built a native church between 1711 and 1742. Along India's narrow coast the Catholic church grew more rapidly. By 1750 it was led by many native priests and bishops. In Sri Lanka, Joseph Vaz, a half-caste priest, proclaimed the faith with great piety and dedication. Despite Dutch control of the island, he founded scores of churches and made tens of thousands of converts.

The Middle East, though not impenetrable by Europeans, was not fertile mission territory. It was dominated by the Ottoman Turks, who allowed occasional French and Italian explorer-missionaries to pass through on the old overland route to China and the northern slopes of the Himalayas. Catholic trading consuls sometimes brought Christian influence to the area, too. French missions in Persia were able to win Armenians to the Catholic faith. But such examples are exceptional. The Middle East belonged to Islam.

In Africa, Christianity had by 1789 lost the ground gained in the sixteenth and early seventeenth centuries. The Capuchin order's work on the coasts of modern Zaïre and Angola claimed over half a million converts in the later seventeenth century. But these gains were weakened by European rivalry for Africa, by the instability of the tribes and by the slave

Jesuit missionaries worked extensively in South America in the sixteenth and seventeenth centuries. This church in Quito, Ecuador, was built by them.

rade. Slaving reached its peak uring this period. It undermined ny chance of Christianity being lanted effectively in West Africa efore 1800.

French religious orders made poradic efforts to do mission work Madagascar. Their approach vas feeble, and thwarted by native ostility. Islam was reviving in Iorth Africa and easily withstood Roman Catholicism. European Christianity was at this time being radually weakened by the secular hinking of the eighteenth-century hilosophers.

Evangelizing America

n Canada, Catholic Christianity grew primarily through French olonization. The church there ncreased from 3,000 believers in 650 to over 75,000 by 1763. A andful of courageous priests, such s Jean de Brebeuf, made early ttempts to convert the Hurons nd the Iroquois. They paid with heir lives. In 1658 the *Propaganda* ent François de Montigny-Laval o New France as vicar-apostolic. Less than twenty years later, Quebec was made a diocese. Canada was no longer technically onsidered a mission territory by Rome. The notable expedition of he trapper Louis Jolliet and Father Marquette, begun in 1673, which ed them to the Mississippi valley, vas, in fact, more interested in xploration than evangelization.

The fur trade soon began to oom in Canada. The alcohol nd venereal disease brought by Europeans first debased and then laughtered the Indian peoples. Self-sacrificing missionary service vas the exception. The moral limate was hardly conducive to he planting of a flourishing Indian hurch.

In Latin America, the patron-ge system remained intact. This vas in spite of pressure from the

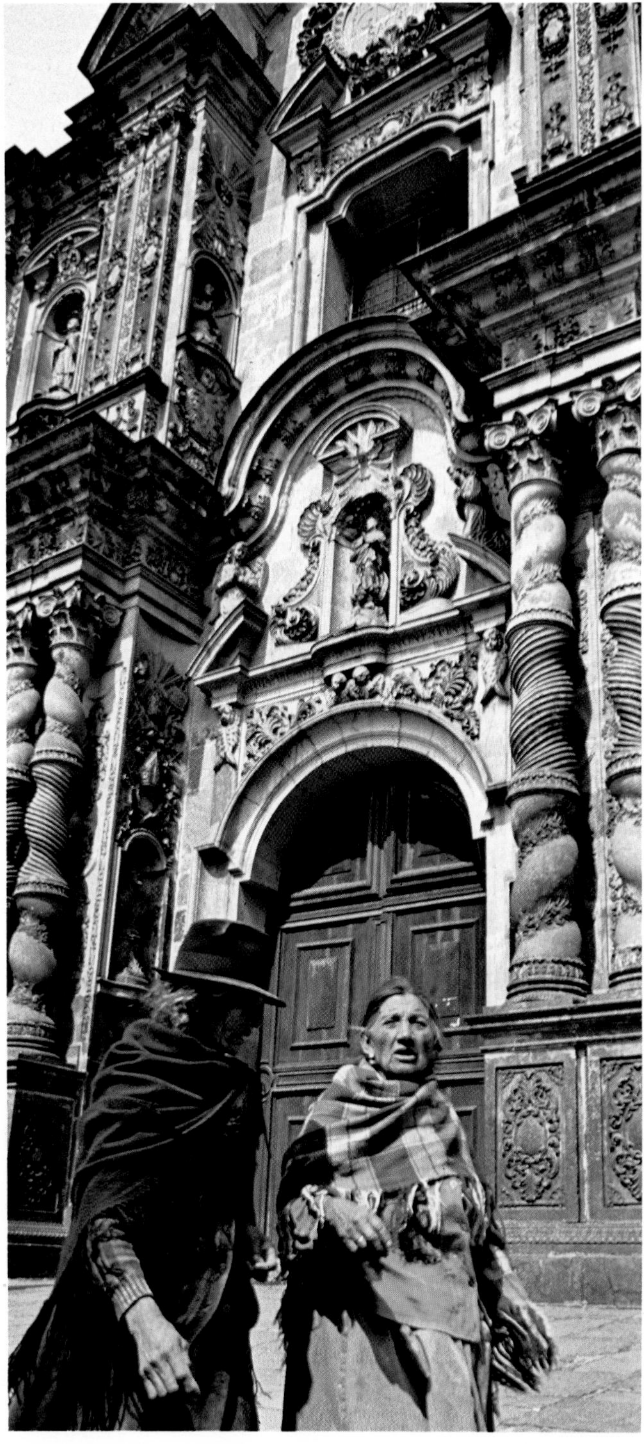

pope. The cross and the crown were more closely linked in this area than anywhere else in the Catholic world. The 'Council of the Indies' in Madrid continued to control important appointments in the Latin American church. All the major religious orders—tens of thousands of priests—contributed to the almost complete—but superficial—Christianization of Latin America. Mission annals are filled with inspiring accounts of dedicated people, who often fought against the political and economic oppression suffered by native populations. In the mid-seventeenth century, for example, Antonio Vieira, a Portuguese ambassador who later entered the Jesuit order, won concessions for Brazilian Indians and blacks from the Portuguese government.

The Jesuit experiment

The Jesuits tried a new experiment in missionary methods in the vast, uncolonized areas of Paraguay. To protect and defend the Indians, as well as to Christianize them, the fathers gathered them into self-contained and self-sustaining villages called *reductions*. Their experiment flourished between 165(and 1720. Natives were instructe in the basics of Christianity. Their lives were organized into times for prayer, work in the fields or at trades, religious festivals and recreation. At the peak there wer approximately sixty *reductions*, involving a total of over 100,000 people. The controversial experiment collapsed in the eighteenth century. Spanish-Portuguese boundary disputes over the area, and increased opposition to the Jesuit order, contributed to its failure.

In Spanish North America, mor permanent gains were made. Afte a hundred years of missionary progress among New Mexico's Indians (1580–1680), a revolt drove out the Spanish in the early 1680s. By 1692 they had retaken New Mexico and their mission cer tres had been rebuilt.

Meanwhile, in 1686, the Jesuit Father Kino entered southern Arizona. He then used his skills as explorer, physician, architect and astronomer to educate and Christianize in Pima Indians of the area. In 1690, Franciscans under Father Damian Massanet founded short-lived missions in east Texas Thirty years later, Franciscans constructed six flourishing settlements along the San Antonio river These missions were similar to th *reductions* of South America. Fror this base the Catholics expanded i Texas.

In the mid-eighteenth century, Father Junipero Serra, a Majorcan, erected a chain of missions along the coast of northern California. The original church buildings of many of these early missionaries still stand today. Regrettably, the Spanish missions

The eighteenth-century Spanish missionaries to California built defensible centres for their work. This is *Mission San Carlos,* near Monterey, one of a chain of such centres.

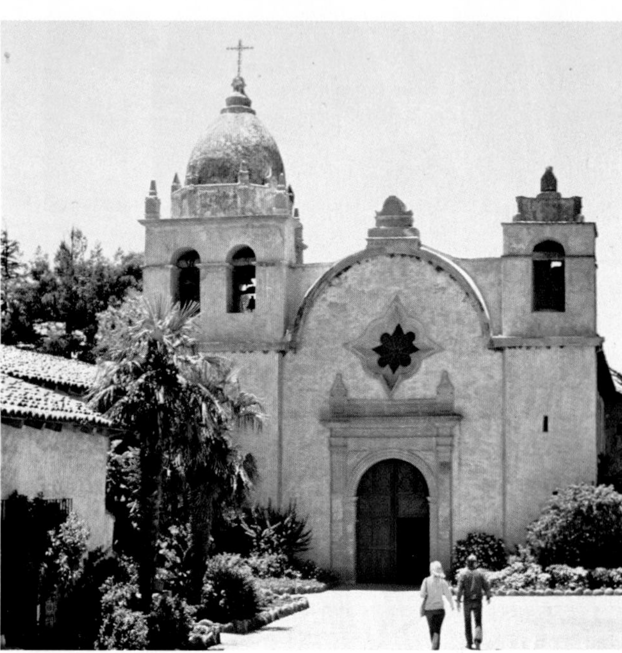

ıll stubbornly refused to train local .ndian clergy.

By 1789 Catholic missionaries ıad traversed the globe and organ-ized about sixty dioceses outside Europe. In the Americas and parts of Asia they had founded a Catholic church which still survives today. The missionaries experienced policy differences, friction between rival orders, political tensions and obstacles of travel and climate. But they were people with faith, vision and dedication.

Through colonies and companies

Protestant Christianity expanded during this period along two different, but not unrelated, lines. The first approach rested on the assumption that all the citizens of a nation formed the Christian church of that country. Such a view of society was later undermined by religious dissent. But it shaped missions of two types during the early part of this period. The first type of mission worked through the national trading companies. The second type worked through the overseas colonies of European emigrants. Both the companies and the colonies were chartered by the crown. Thus both bodies were expected by the state to promote the form of Protestantism prac-tised in the homeland.

The second approach used by Protestants was by voluntary societies and denominations, which regarded mission as their duty. A number of societies were formed specifically to evangelize peoples outside western Europe. Their vision was fuelled by movements such as Pietism in Germany and the awakenings in England and America. In time, denominations such as the Moravians and the Quakers became directly involved in spreading Christianity overseas. The missionary vision is clearly

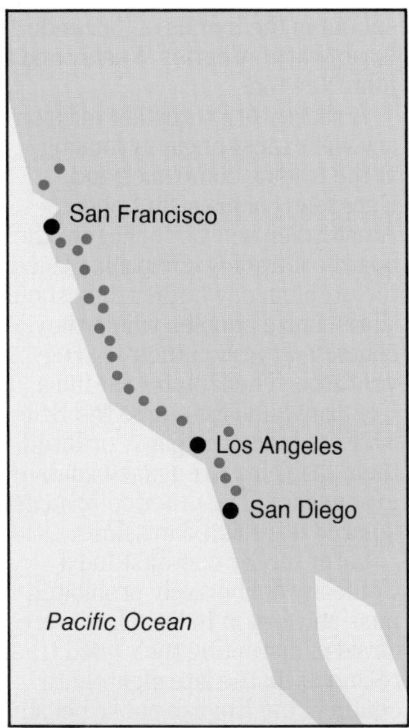

California missions founded 1769–1823

Junipero Serra, a Jesuit from Majorca, founded the first nine missions in California. They formed part of the attempt to convert the Indians of this area.

set out in the hymns of Zinzendorf, Isaac Watts, Charles Wesley and John Newton.

A survey of Protestant missionary work must begin by looking at the trading companies and European colonies. In London, Amsterdam and Copenhagen, the boards of trading companies faced the problem of whether they should Christianize peoples whom they contacted through their trading ventures. The Dutch East India Company, and for a time the British East India Company, ordered their chaplains to engage in native evangelism. The other companies ignored or resisted missions.

Later the British East India Company deliberately prohibited mission work in India. They were afraid of disrupting their good trade relations. In the late eighteenth century, the English public became outraged at the inhumane policies of colonial governors such as Clive and Hastings. The company was forced to change its policy and to send out chaplains such as Claudius Buchanan (1796) and Henry Martyn (1805).

Amsterdam became one of the centres of the Dutch colonial empire in the seventeenth century. The Dutch East India Company sent ministers to Indonesia and Sri Lanka as missionaries.

The Dutch go east

The Dutch East India Company had been established in 1602. It supported the training of twelve men at a missionary training centre in Leiden from 1622 to 1633. Although the college collapsed for lack of finance, the company continued to support mission work. Its chaplains in South Africa, Sri Lanka and the Malay Archipelago were paid a sum of money for every native converted and baptized. The company filled missionary posts, established schools, encouraged Bible translation and the pastoral care of converts.

An interesting relationship developed between Classis Amsterdam and the Dutch East India Company. The Classis, a regional division of the Dutch Reformed church, controlled the theological education and the ordination of the chaplain-missionaries and the company paid their salaries.

The results of the Dutch work were often superficial. But most of the Calvinist churches founded still exist today. By 1800 a native church, estimated at 200,000, existed in the East Indies. The New Testament (1688) and, by 1734, the entire Bible, were translated into the Malay language. The Dutch tried unsuccessfully to root out Portuguese Catholicism in Sri Lanka. They founded a network of schools, and translated the Bible into the native dialects of the island. In 1690 they opened two seminaries for training Sinhalese catechists and teachers. By the mid-eighteenth century, there were well over 300,000 Protestants on Sri Lanka.

In South Africa, minister-chaplains concentrated their evangelism on Dutch and Huguenot refugees. Some slaves were baptized and instructed in the faith and formed a small, local church.

The fortunes of the Dutch East India Company waned after 1750, and the number of missionary-chaplains fell. In 1798 the company was disbanded.

'Praying towns'

The best example of Protestant expansion through colonies is in Puritan New England. When Charles I granted the Massachusetts Bay Company a charter as a colony, the document contained a clause concerning missions: 'The people from England may be so religiously, peaceably, and civilly governed, as their good life and orderly conversation may win and incite the natives of the country to the knowledge and obedience of the only true God and Saviour of mankind, and the Christian faith.'

In the 1640s, Thomas Mayhew took the gospel to Martha's Vineyard, an island just off the coast of Massachusetts. His work was continued by the next four generations of Mayhews. About the same time John Eliot, a Puritan minister at Roxbury, Massachusetts, began to evangelize the Indians of the Pequot tribe. He gathered New England Indians into 'praying towns'. There he taught them trades, agriculture and academic subjects. He believed that he had to civilize them before he could Christianize them. He mastered their language, into which he translated the Bible by 1663. Eliot was familiar with Catholic missionary methods, and seems to have borrowed some of his ideas from the Jesuits. Eliot sent several Indians to Harvard College for training as pastors. In 1675, war between the Indians and the colonists virtually destroyed his work. In that year there were two dozen Indian evangelists at work, fourteen 'praying towns', and about 4,000 Christian Indians.

News of Mayhew's and Eliot's work reached England through

One of the oldest surviving buildings of Harvard University. John Harvard (1607–38) was an early Puritan emigrant to New England. By his will he left half his estate, and about 400 books, towards founding the new college.

The New England town of Stourbridge has been restored to its early colonial appearance.

printed reports known as the *Eliot Tracts*. These generated interest that led to the formation of the 'Society for the Propagation of the Gospel in New England' in 1649. This was the first Protestant missionary society. It supported the work of both Eliot and Mayhew, and continued to finance Indian missions until the American Revolution, when it channelled its resources to missions among Canadian tribes.

European colonists on the Atlantic coast and in the Caribbean began to evangelize Indians and blacks early in the eighteenth century. Earlier pioneers include[d] Roger Williams in Rhode Island, Swedes in Delaware and Quakers throughout the colonies. But Eur[o]peans did not colonize the New World for the express purpose of evangelizing non-Christians, although some contemporary writ[ers] suggested that they should do so.

A burning fire

Towards the end of the seventeenth century a warm, evangelic[al]

THE FIRST ENGLISH MISSIONS

Leonard W. Cowie

A revolution took place in English preaching during the later years of the seventeenth century. It was largely brought about by John Tillotson, Archbishop of Canterbury 1691–94. It changed from theological interpretation and magnificent eloquence to moral argument and practical simplicity. One effect was that 'groups of serious men' formed voluntary societies for religious and social purposes, influenced by some of the great preachers in London. Most of these societies were small and short-lived. But two became of great importance and have survived to the present time. These are the Society for Promoting Christian Knowledge (SPCK) and the Society for the Propagation of the Gospel (SPG). Both of these owe their foundation to the initiative of a small group of lay people and clergy under the leadership of Dr Thomas Bray (1656–1730).

Bray was the rector, first of a parish in Warwickshire, then of a parish in London. He was seriously concerned by 'the gross ignorance of the Christian religion', which was so prevalent. In 1696 he drew up a plan for 'a Protestant Congregation or Society', which was to work in a similar way to the *Propaganda* of the Roman Catholic church.

In 1698, with four laymen, Bray set up the SPCK. Its objects were 'to promote and encourage the erection of charity schools in all parts of England and Wales; to disperse, both at home and abroad, Bibles and tracts of religion; and in general to advance the honour of God and the good of mankind by promoting Christian knowledge both at home and in the other parts of the world by the best methods that should offer'.

The SPCK gave much of its attention to education during the first half of the eighteenth century. It helped found charity schools, where poor children were given an elementary education and religious instruction. The SPCK also published books and tracts, encouraged the forming of libraries for the clergy, corresponded iety began to appear among 'rotestants. It crossed denomina-ional and political boundaries. 'rotestants again emphasized the nportance of personal conver-ion, holy living and the need to ell non-Christians about Christ's aving work. They believed that he entrance of Jews and Gentiles nto the church, and the kingdom of 'hrist, would fulfil promises in the Bible.

English Puritans and dissent-ers, and Dutch Calvinists, had shown this form of piety early in he seventeenth century. Philip Spener's *Pia Desideria* gave it a new name and a new direction, in the form of German Pietism, after 1675. It caught fire among Anglicans in the early eighteenth century in the Great Awakening. It burned in virtually every church in the American colonies. Wherever it appeared it generated a practical interest in mission.

In Britain, Thomas Bray adopted the use of the society for Christian missions. He was appointed commissary for the colony of Maryland by the bishop of London in 1695. Bray recruited evangelists for the

with Protestant churches on the continent of Europe, assisted Protestant refugees and provided religious books for settlers in the American colonies.

When the SPCK had become active in so many fields, Bray decided to found a separate society to engage in overseas mission. This was the SPG, founded in 1701. Its object was to provide an Anglican ministry for British people overseas, and to evangelize the non-Christian subjects of the British monarch. It had a more official position within the Anglican church than the SPCK. It was authorized by the English clergy in Convocation and incorporated by royal charter. It was a body corporate, and had the power (which the SPCK lacked) to receive, invest and administer funds.

In 1699 Bray had made a brief visit to Maryland as the bishop of London's representative (Commissary). He had become aware of the weakness of the Church of England in the American colonies. For this reason the society at first concentrated upon raising money to provide 'a sufficient maintenance for an orthodox clergy' to care for the spiritual needs of the colonists. But in 1710 the SPG agreed to concern itself also with the 'conversion of heathens and infidels'. During the eighteenth century SPG missionaries worked in the North American colonies, Canada and the West Indies. The SPG was the first missionary society of the Church of England.

The official seal of the Society for the Propagation of the Gospel. On the left, people are calling for help, which is arriving in the shape of an English warship carrying a clergyman.

colonies and collected funds to establish parish libraries. Out of these efforts grew the Society for Promoting Christian Knowledge (SPCK) in 1698.

Bray next helped to found the Society for the Propagation of the Gospel in Foreign Parts (SPG) in 1701. This society had specifically missionary aims. During the eighteenth century it supported several hundred men working among British colonists, Indians and Negroes in North America and the Caribbean. In 1709 the Scottish SPCK was founded. All three agencies, together with the older New England Company, supported missionaries who had a zeal sparked by evangelical piety.

The Danes depart

Much of the religious fervour of the eighteenth century began in Germany. Spener, and after him August Francke, founded several projects and institutions in Halle. These provided a stream of foreign missionaries. When King Frederick IV of Denmark wanted missionaries for his colony in Tranquebar, he found them among the Pietists in Halle. Bartholomäus Ziegenbalg and Heinrich Plütschau responded to his appeal in 1705. This marked the beginnings of the Danish-Halle mission.

These two missionaries arrived in India the following year, but met harsh criticism from Lutherans in both Denmark and Germany. The Danish governor of Tranquebar opposed them too. Plütschau died five years later, but Ziegenbalg continued the work for fifteen years. Their example aroused wide interest in missions in Europe. They concentrated on educating children, translating the Bible into the native language, preaching a gospel of personal conversion and training a local clergy. All these became hallmarks of evangelical Protestant missions.

In 1714 a royal authority was established in Copenhagen. This guaranteed missionaries official Danish sanction and support in further areas. Hans Egede started a missionary colony in Greenland in 1722. Other missionaries went to the West Indies. By 1800 Halle had contributed approximately sixty people to the Danish-Halle enterprise.

The English also became involved in the Danish-Halle mission. Anton Wilhelm Boehme, a former student of Francke, persuaded the SPCK to support Danish-Halle missionaries in British holdings in India. These evangelicals from Germany used Anglican church practices and ministered to British troops in India for decades, in spite of their links with Halle and Copenhagen. One of the most successful of these missionaries was Christian

Modern Copenhagen. In 1714 a missionary college was established in the city, guaranteeing official support.

EXPANSION WORLD-WIDE

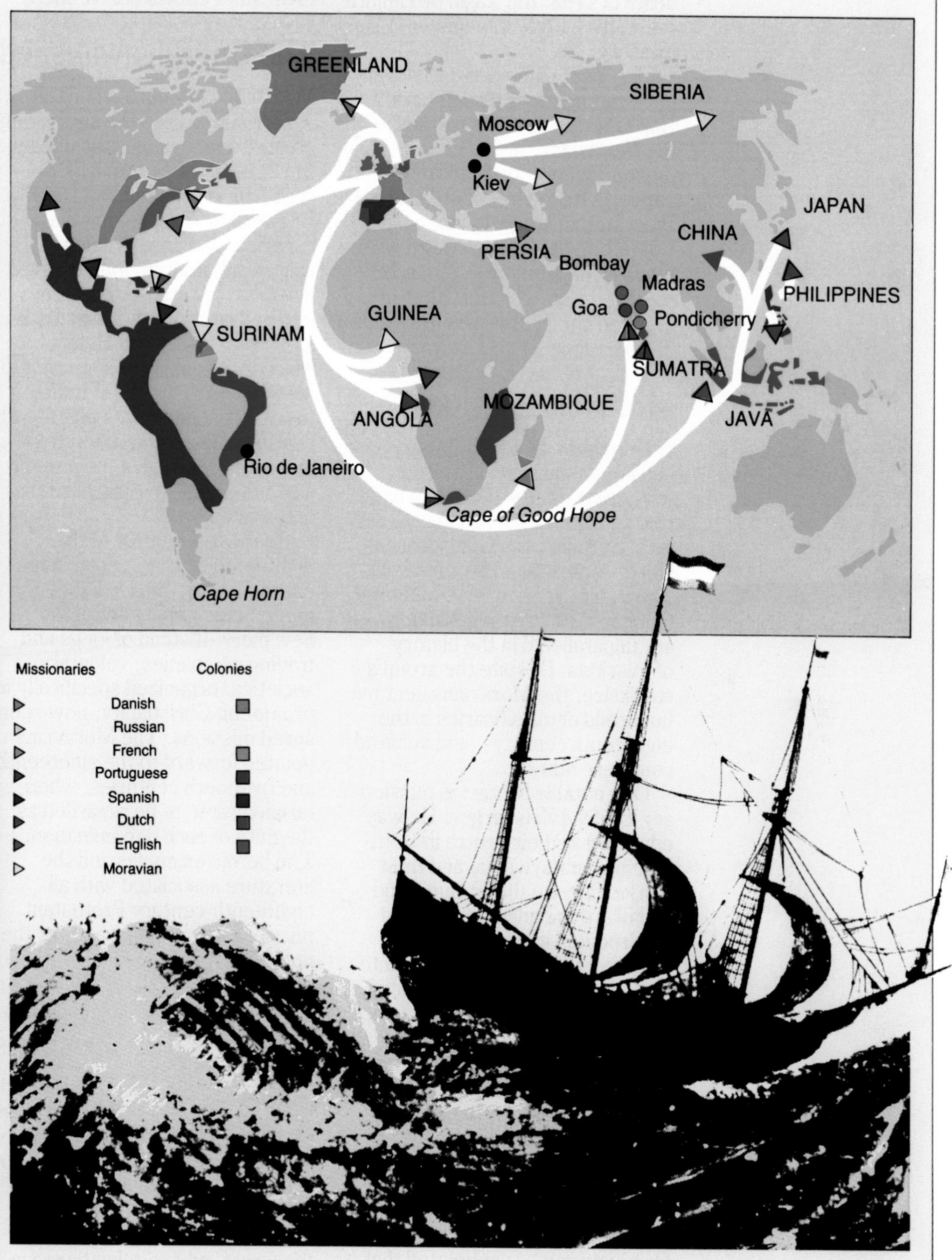

Friedrich Schwartz. He served with such distinction that, upon his death in 1798, the Rajah of Tanjore erected a marble monument in his memory.

The most significant missionary movement arising directly from Halle Pietism was the work of the Moravians. In 1731 Count Zinzendorf met two Eskimo converts from Greenland and a West Indian Christian in Copenhagen. They pleaded with him for missionaries. When he returned home to Herrnhut he inspired the Moravians to respond to this appeal.

Moravian missions

Within thirty years the Moravians had begun missions in at least ten countries. By 1740 they had reached the Virgin Islands, Greenland, Surinam, the Gold Coast, North America and South Africa. Their self-sacrifice, love and total commitment to evangelization are unparalleled in the history of missions. Despite the group's small size, the Moravians sent out hundreds of missionaries in the eighteenth century—and inspired countless others.

One notable Moravian missionary is David Zeisberger. He was educated at their centre in Bethlehem, Pennsylvania, and then worked among the Iroquois and Delaware Indians. He followed the Iroquois when European colonizers pushed their tribe into eastern Ohio. There he founded several Indian settlements, which were later ruthlessly exterminated by white colonists during the American Revolution. But wherever the Moravians went with the gospel, their loving spirit, strong faith and total commitment conveyed the true nature of Christianity so clearly that hundreds of converts were made. One historian has estimated that the Moravian missions achieved more in this period than all the Protestant efforts before them.

The English awakened

Meanwhile in England and the American colonies the awakenings created new evangelistic efforts. In 1741–42 the Scottish SPCK sent Azariah Horton and David Brainerd to work among the American Indians. Brainerd's diaries and journals long outlived his short, ascetic service. They inspired later missionaries such as William Carey and Henry Martyn. Thomas Coke promoted Methodism in the West Indies towards the end of the eighteenth century. He is remembered for giving the Methodist movement a commitment to evangelize the non-whites.

By the last quarter of the eighteenth century, Protestant expansion was largely led by movements arising out of the new piety. Instead of kings and trading companies, voluntary societies, organized specifically for promoting Christianity, now sponsored missions. The Moravians pointed forward to the nineteenth and twentieth centuries, when mission came to be regarded as the duty of each denomination. The heroic examples and the literature associated with all eighteenth-century Protestant missions formed the basis for the numerically greater achievements of the next 150 years.

Tax-cuts for Christians

Christian expansion in this period cannot be recorded solely in terms of Western Christianity. The Eastern churches were intimidated and repressed by Islam. But the Russian church contributed to missionary outreach. Czar Peter the Great, whose reign began in

COUNT VON ZINZENDORF

A. Skevington Wood

The key figure in the renewal of Moravianism in the eighteenth century was a Lutheran nobleman, Nikolaus Ludwig Count von Zinzendorf (1700–60). His father, a cabinet minister in Saxony, died when Zinzendorf was only six weeks old. The Count was brought up his grandmother, Baroness von Gersdorf, who was a friend of Spener and a devotee of Pietism.

At the age of ten, Zinzendorf was sent to Francke's grammar school at Halle. He and five other Christian boys founded 'the Order of the Grain of Mustard Seed'. They pledged themselves to 'love the whole human family' and to spread the gospel. Zinzendorf went on to study law at the universities of Wittenberg and Utrecht, and entered the civil service in 1721.

On a grand tour of Europe in 1719 he had been moved by a painting in the art gallery at Düsseldorf. It was Domenico Feti's *Ecce Homo,* showing Christ wearing the crown of thorns. Its inscription read: 'All this I did for you. What are you doing for me?' It was then that Zinzendorf offered himself for Christ's service, instead of service to the state of Saxony.

In 1722 he brought about the settlement of a company of Moravian refugees on his estate at Berthesdorf. With Baron Frederick von Watteville and the pastors Rothe and Schäfer he subscribed to the so-called 'Covenant of the Four Brethren'. It sought to promote world-wide evangelization. After the coming of the Holy Spirit at Herrnhut in 1727, Zinzendorf became aware that his missionary vision was to be realized through the Moravian Brethren. He emerged as their acknowledged leader and was consecrated as a bishop in 1737. He travelled extensively in Europe, visiting England and also North America.

Zinzendorf was a leader of many talents—pastor, teacher, theologian, missionary, hymn-writer, liturgist and administrator. He was a pioneer of ecumenism, and indeed was the first to employ the term 'ecumenical' in its modern sense. His aim was to unite all Christians in evangelism. The goal has not yet been reached; but Zinzendorf led the way to its recognition.

Zinzendorf, the founder of the Moravian church laid great stress on the importance of the emotions in religious expression, and wrote many hymns, some of which have been translated into English.

1682, encouraged the expansion of Christianity into his eastern territories as part of his overall policy.

Filofei Leshchinskii, Metropolitan of Tobolsk, 1702–9, gained the Czar's permission to promise tax concessions to new Christians. He gained 40,000 converts and planted about 300 new churches in western Siberia. But this work declined after his death in 1727. In the early 1700s Peter excused from military service men of the middle Volga region who were baptized as Christians. But the Christianization of tribes in this area was not completed until the mid-eighteenth century by Bishop Konashevich.

Czar Peter the Great campaigned to raise religious and moral standards among both clergy and people in 1720. But missionary efforts remained sporadic and were often politically motivated. In 1721 the Russian Orthodox church in effect became a section of the imperial bureaucracy, as a result of the *Ecclesiastical Regulation*.

Some missionary work may have been achieved by the Russian diplomatic delegation in Peking. There was also mission work among the Kalmucks, and missions to eastern Siberia and the peninsula of Kamchatka. But the poor state of Russian Orthodoxy, the political situation and the geographical vastness and ethnic diversity of Russia all helped to discourage missionary outreach. It is amazing that as much Christian expansion occurred as did in Russian territories.

Compared to what followed in the nineteenth century, Christian expansion between 1650 and 1800 was limited. But from its achievement the next generations of mission leaders gained inspiration and guidance. Mistakes were made. The missionary vision did not pervade the Christian West as in the next century. But issues such as the relationship between Christianity and indigenous culture, the need to train local Christian leaders, and the importance of translating the Bible were grappled with by Protestants, Orthodox and Roman Catholics. In this era, their Christian faith became global.

REASON AND UNREASON

Colin Brown

Archbishop William Temple once remarked that the most disastrous moment in European history was perhaps the bitterly cold day in the winter of 1619–20 when the French philosopher René Descartes climbed into the alcove of a stove and resolved to search for a new kind of philosophy. The resolve led in due course to the formulation of Descartes' Rationalism, which took as its first principle *Cogito ergo sum* 'I think, therefore I am.'

Doubt comes first

To Temple it was disastrous because it was a symptom of the dilemma of the modern mind. Descartes' new thinking began with a resolve to doubt everything that could be doubted. Doubt is put first. The individual self becomes the ultimate reference-point in thought. What Descartes did on that day began a trend that has not yet been reversed.

Temple saw a theological counterpart to this in Luther's stand before the Holy Roman Emperor at the Diet of Worms a hundred years earlier. Luther took his stand against the most powerful ruler in Europe, the might of the church and centuries of tradition, declaring that his conscience was captive to the Word of God. Here again Temple saw the beginnings of an individualism which was to become characteristic of the modern mind.

But, in fact, the two cases were not parallel. Descartes was seeking a self-evident idea which any rational thinker could see was true. This would form the basis of his view of reality. Luther was not, as Temple imagined, making his individual conscience the test of truth. Rather the Word of God was his authority; his conscience was simply that part of him which called him to submit.

The larger-than-life figures of Descartes and Luther typify the forces that were at work in the seventeenth and eighteenth centuries. They had in common the awareness that we must each make up our own mind. It is useless to accept anyone else's answer as true unless we have proved it for ourselves. But there the ways part.

On the one hand; there was a quest for rationality. In some cases it meant trying to show the rational

Galileo Galilei (1564–1642) the Italian astronomer and physicist. By observation and reasoning he argued that the planets revolve around the sun. This led him to support Copernicus' theory of the solar system. But Galileo came into conflict with the Inquisition for writing on Copernicus' theory, after which time he lived under house arrest until his death.

basis of Christianity. In others it meant looking for a rational alternative religion. In yet other cases it meant discarding religion altogether in favour of a view of life based on reason.

On the other hand, there was a retreat from reason. There were those who had a horror not only of secular thinkers but also of those in the church who set out their doctrines in a rational way. To the 'Pietists' what mattered was the personal devotional life. To the Quakers even reformed theology, with its stress on the Bible, and the ordered worship of the community, went too far. What mattered to them was the 'inner light' of the Spirit. The seventeenth and eighteenth centuries were an era of conflict, during which reason vied with unreason. And at the end of the day there was no agreement.

Three great rationalists

In everyday language rationalism means that everything is judged by reason. Bound up with this is the idea that, when this is done, belief in God and the supernatural will be swept away; we shall be left with nature and hard facts. But in the seventeenth century rationalism was not necessarily hostile to belief in God. There were various rationalist systems of thought. But common to all was the belief in the rationality of the universe, and the power of reason to grasp it.

The first of the great rationalists was René Descartes (1596–1650), who was a mathematician of the first rank and a Roman Catholic. His ideal in philosophy was to think rationally from first principles. He lived at a time when modern science was beginning to transform our picture of the world. But this in itself presented a problem. Science relies on the evidence of our senses—what can be touched, seen and measured. But how do we know that our senses can be relied upon? To answer this question Descartes turned to the formula *Cogito ergo sum.*

What Descartes was doing was to devise a philosophy which would answer the sceptics of his time. The 'New Pyrrhonists' (named after the ancient philosopher Pyrrho) were students of classical scepticism who applied the arguments of ancient scepticism to the great questions of their own day in the fields of science, religion, and philosophy. They made doubt the basic principle in philosophy. When Descartes, too, resolved to doubt everything that he possibly could, he was playing the Pyrrhonists at their own game. He readily saw that there was one thing that he could not doubt. It was the fact that he was doubting. And if he was doubting, he must actually exist in order to doubt. In other words, 'I think, therefore I am.'

The formula *Cogito ergo sum* was not exactly new. It had been used by Augustine in answering the sceptics of *his* day. What was new was Descartes' use of it as the first principle of his philosophy. From there Descartes went on to prove the existence of God, and to show that God, being good, would not allow us to be deceived in the right use of our minds and senses.

Although Descartes is widely regarded as the first modern philosopher, he took over the medieval proofs of the existence of God. He adapted Anselm's 'ontological argument'. Just as the sum of the three angles of a triangle equalling two right angles is included in the very area of a triangle, so the existence of God is included in the idea of God. Descartes also took over Aquinas' 'Cosmological argument' which argued back to a first cause. But whereas Aquinas had used the world to show the existence of

God, Descartes used God to argue for the validity of our perceptions of the world.

From that day to this philosophers have argued over the *Cogito ergo sum*. Some have seen it as an attempt to deduce the existence of a person from the fact of thinking. But if so, it is like the rabbit in the conjuror's hat. The rabbit has to be there to begin with. The premise of the argument already contains the conclusion. However, the argument is best seen as an affirmation of personal existence. Some things in life cannot be doubted – even by the doubters. Among them is the fact that we exist. It is a basic, irremovable intuition.

Pyrrhonian scepticism left its mark on many thinkers of the age, including the sceptical Scottish philosopher David Hume. But attracted as he was to scepticism, Hume pronounced thorough-going Pyrrhonism to be unworkable. In the meantime Blaise Pascal produced a Christian answer to it in France, and in Holland Spinoza turned rationalism into a form of pantheism.

René Descartes, the French philosopher, who died while in Sweden as a guest of Queen Christiana.

'A hideous atheist'

Whereas Descartes remained an orthodox Catholic, Baruch Spinoza (1632–77) came of Jewish stock. His parents had migrated to Holland, which in the seventeenth century was a haven of toleration for intellectual refugees. But Spinoza soon found himself in conflict with his own Jewish rabbis, and was expelled from the synagogue for his unorthodoxy. In 1663 Spinoza published a restatement of Descartes, set out in geometrical fashion; his posthumously published *Ethics* took the same form.

Spinoza has been described by turn as a hideous atheist and as God-intoxicated. In fact, he was a pantheist who combined features of both. He emphatically denied the existence of God over and above the world. At the same time, he believed that there was only one substance—God, or nature. All reality is the manifestation of God. Whether we say God or nature we are really talking about the same thing. To speak of God emphasizes the cause; to speak of nature emphasizes the end product.

Spinoza's pantheism was not the same as that of the later romantic poets, although some of them drew intellectual inspiration from it. Rather, it was an elaborate system worked out in a geometrical manner from what he alleged were self-evident first principles.

BLAISE PASCAL

Paul Bechtel

> *"What a vast distance there is between knowing God and loving him!"*
>
> *BLAISE PASCAL*

Blaise Pascal (1623–62), one of the great thinkers of the West, excelled as mathematician, physicist, inventor, writer and religious thinker. He was born in Claremont, France, and at an early age he made original contributions to geometry and the calculus. Later he worked out the theory of probability. At nineteen Pascal invented the first workable calculating machine, based on a system of rotating discs—the basis of arithmetical machines until modern times. In physics 'Pascal's law' stated the principle which makes possible all modern hydraulic operations. Some people credit Pascal with having created the first wrist-watch, and having set up the first bus route in Paris.

In 1654 Pascal became a Christian as the result of a mystical vision. He inscribed the details of his experience on a piece of parchment which he sewed into his coat. Through his sister, Pascal became associated with the Jansenists. In 1657 he published his *Provincial Letters*, a masterpiece of irony and satire written to support the Jansenists' demand for a re-emphasis on Augustine's doctrine of grace within the Catholic church.

About 1658, Pascal set out to prepare an *Apology for the Christian Religion*. This work was never completed, for Pascal died at the age of thirty-nine. He left only a series of remarkable notes, later published as *Pensées (Thoughts)*. The work is a classic of literature and apologetics. It puts the case for vital Christianity, against the rationalism of Descartes and the scepticism of the French writer Montaigne.

Pascal wrote that God can be known through Jesus Christ by an act of faith, itself given by God. People's need for God is made evident by their misery apart from God. God may only be known by faith. Though there is plentiful evidence to support belief: fulfilled prophecies, miracles, the witness of history, the self-authentication of Scripture, 'The heart has its reasons, which the reason does not know,' wrote Pascal.

> *"Do not be surprised at the sight of simple people who believe without argument. God makes them love him and hate themselves. He inclines their hearts to believe. We shall never believe with a vigorous and unquestioning faith unless God touches our hearts; and we shall believe as soon as he does so."*
>
> *BLAISE PASCAL*

Blaise Pascal, the religious thinker, believed that, in the search for truth, reason was neutral. A rational proof of God, or Christianity, would never displace the gift of faith. 'We come to know truth not only by reason, but still more so through our hearts.'

Whether it was as rational as Spinoza imagined it to be is another matter. The first principles might have been clear definitions. But philosophers now recognize that it is not enough to start with a clear definition, unless there is something that actually corresponds with it.

The rationalists made a double mistake. On the one hand, they thought that if their first principles were rational enough, they were sound. On the other hand, they thought that it was enough to proceed by rationally deducing one point from another. But in both instances—as the British empiricists pointed out—reality is not known by reason alone. Our knowledge has to be based on our experience of it.

The third great thinker in the rationalist tradition was the German Protestant, G.W. Leibniz (1646–1716). His scientific work earned him honorary membership of the Royal Society in England. His view of reality was different again. He held that the universe is made up of an infinite number of *monads,* or simple substances without parts and which are eternally active. The *monads* form an ascending series, from the lowest which is next to nothing, to the highest which is God. Leibniz used the ontological argument to prove the existence of God—the original simple substance from which all others come.

Emphasizing experience

Rationalism dominated continental European philosophy, but in Britain empiricism was the most significant philosophical movement. The term derives from the Greek word for experience. Though they had many differences, the empiricists all stressed the part played by experience in knowledge. In this they were reacting to, and correcting, European rationalism. The three leading British figures were Locke, Berkeley and Hume.

John Locke (1632–1704) studied medicine at the University of Oxford in the heyday of the Puritans. When the Commonwealth collapsed and Charles II was brought back as king, Locke found it prudent to live in Holland. He wrote various works on politics and apologetics. But his main philosophical work was his *Essay Concerning Human Understanding* (1690).

Locke pictured the human mind as a blank sheet. How does it get its ideas and knowledge? Locke replied that there is only one way—through the experience of our senses. Reason has its part to play in judging ideas, and in interpreting the data fed to it by the senses. But reason cannot operate independently. It is what we see, touch, taste, hear and smell that provides the basis of all knowledge.

If this is so, then Christian faith must likewise be based on experience. The world around us points to its origin in a wise, loving and all-powerful God. The gospel is vindicated by the way in which Old Testament prophecy is fulfilled by Jesus and by the miracles that he performed.

Miracles are like the credentials of an ambassador. They are proof of his authority. Because we accept the miracles of Jesus we can trust the truth of his teaching about God. There are some things which accord with reason (for example, the existence of God). Other things are contrary to reason (for example, the existence of more than one God). But there are also things which are above reason (for example, the resurrection of Jesus). There are grounds for believing it, but human reason just cannot grasp it.

G.W. Leibniz is often regarded as the founder of the German philosophic tradition. Repelled by the excesses of the Thirty Years' War, he attempted to achieve some understanding between divided Christians.

George Berkeley, bishop of Cloyne in Ireland, was both a brilliant philosopher and a missionary enthusiast. He tried to get a missionary college founded in Bermuda.

Is reality 'all in the mind'?

George Berkeley (1685–1753), who went to Bermuda to establish a missionary college for the evangelism of America, was later made bishop of Cloyne in Ireland. Like Locke, he was interested in the problem of knowledge. But he gave it a novel twist. He claimed that to exist means either to perceive or to be perceived. In other words, all reality is in the mind. It is not material. Berkeley's views have been caricatured in Ronald Knox's pair of limericks:

There was a young man who
said, 'God
Must think it exceedingly odd
If he finds that this tree
Continues to be
When there's no-one about in
the Quad.'

REPLY

Dear Sir:
Your astonishment's odd:
I am always about in the Quad.
And that's why the tree
Will continue to be,
Since observed by
Yours faithfully,
GOD.

> *"The existence of one God is according to reason; the existence of more than one God contrary to reason; the resurrection of the dead, above reason."*
>
> *JOHN LOCKE,* An Essay Concerning Human Understanding

Few thinkers have followed Berkeley in his non-material position. Dr Johnson's reply was to kick a stone and remark: 'Thus I refute Dr Berkeley.' But Berkeley would not have seen this as a refutation. For all it would mean was that, in his mind, Dr Johnson was performing the act of kicking the stone.

Most thinkers have regarded Berkeley's position as too improbable to be taken seriously. It makes the objects we perceive hollow. There is nothing behind them. It is difficult to see what is the difference between an imaginary stone and a real stone.

Berkeley's argument contains a novel proof of the existence of God. The continued existence of objects requires the continued existence of God in order that he can perceive them and thus give them reality. On the other hand, it is not clear whether the objects that we perceive are the same as the objects that God perceives. For it could be argued that the tree in the college courtyard ('quad') exists only in our minds as part of our own thought-world, but does not have any other existence.

David Hume

Both Locke and Berkeley believed in God. Scepticism in Britain began with David Hume (1711–76). In his lifetime he was perhaps best known for his *History of England,* but today he is remembered for the scepticism which Bertrand Russell claimed showed the bankruptcy of eighteenth-century reasonableness. Hume's sceptical thought was embodied in such works as *Treatise of Human Nature* (1739–40), *Philosophical Essays Concerning Human Understanding* (1748) and *Dialogues Concerning Natural Religion* (1752).

Hume's scepticism extended to the whole range of human knowledge. He claimed that it was impossible to demonstrate the existence of the soul or self. For whenever we look into ourselves we see only some feeling of pleasure or pain, but never the *self* as such.

Hume questioned the logic of speaking about cause and effect. He insisted that all we can see is one event following another. We do not see the cause as such, but only the sequence of events.

In religion he cast doubt on the old proofs for the existence of God, pronouncing the idea of a first cause to be useless. Miracles violate the laws of nature and are therefore improbable. For, since 'a firm and unalterable experience' has established the laws of nature, the proof against miracles is as complete as any proof can be.

Hume has influenced many thinkers, from Kant in the eighteenth century to the logical positivists in the twentieth. He has become a kind of patron saint of scepticism. But it is worthwhile pausing to ask how valid were Hume's arguments.

There is a sense in which what Hume says about the self is true. It cannot be seen directly, like an arm, a leg or even a brain. But this is not the same as saying that Hume gets rid of the self altogether. For when we try to look into ourselves the self is active as the organizing subject of the action. In other words, in order to refute the self as an object, Hume has to make use of the self as a subject. What the argument shows is something of the peculiar nature of the self.

Similarly, Hume did not dispose of the idea of causation. The whole of our everyday experience of things and the whole fabric of modern science rest upon the principle that when certain things always follow other things under given conditions, then it is proper to say that one causes the other. The idea of a law of science depends on the fact that things just do not happen at random, but that some things are causes and other things are effects. It was this very thing that Hume appealed to in his rejection of miracles!

Does God exist?

Some of Hume's criticism of the arguments for the existence of God were just. A cause cannot be wholly known from its effect, and the first cause is hidden from us by myriads of other causes. Moreover, if we have an argument

David Hume, the Scottish philosopher, made one of the most fundamental attacks on natural theology in the modern age.

for God's existence from causation and another from design, we need another argument to show that the God in each case is one and the same. And we need a further argument to show that this God is the same as the God of Christian faith.

But to say all this is only to spotlight certain flaws in the way in which the existence of God has been argued. It does not settle once and for all the question whether God exists. Still less does it settle the question of who God is.

Hume's critique of miracles made some telling points, but it was far from watertight. For when Hume talked about 'a firm and unalterable experience' establishing the laws of nature, he omitted to ask the question, 'Whose experience?' If we take a sample selection of experience only from those who have no experience of miracles, then we are bound to conclude that miracles have not been experienced. But if we include evidence of contrary cases, we cannot say that miracles are automatically ruled out. They may be unusual and contrary to common experience. But we cannot rule them out on the grounds

fire as fast as he could. He argued that religion was not true because the apostles taught it; they taught it because it was true. He wrote that 'The accidental truths of history can never become proof for the necessary truths of reason.' Both points were in fact truisms. We cannot prove that two and two make four by appealing to history. But history does not give the same kind of truth as mathematics. Therefore Lessing was unwilling to base faith on history. At best history might embody truths; it does not provide the basis for truth.

In his play, *Nathan the Wise,* Lessing expressed his ideas through the parable of the three rings: There was once a ring which gave its owner the gift of being loved by God and people. The owner of this ring had three sons whom he loved equally dearly. To resolve the dilemma of who should receive the ring on his death, the owner had two exact replicas made. The three sons quarrelled as to who had the true ring. But a wise judge told them each to behave as if they possessed the authentic ring. Their behaviour would show which one had the gift of being loved by God and people.

The three sons represent Judaism, Christianity and Islam. Lessing's point is that the truth of religion cannot be settled by appeals to history. All religions are relative, and will be superseded one day by a universal religion. In the meantime the enlightened person realizes all this, and proceeds to live according to good sense, in tolerance and harmony.

One of the difficulties about this enlightened position is that it is smug. It blithely assumes that all religions are saying more or less the same thing. It assumes that what happened in history is either relatively unimportant or unknowable. The enlightened thinkers imagined that they had superior knowledge—or that what they di not know was not worth knowing

Enlightened thought reached its climax in the philosophy of Immanuel Kant, whose ideas dictated the course of a great dea of philosophy and theology in the nineteenth century. To Kant, the human race's emergence from a self-imposed immaturity represented enlightenment. It was humanity come of age, casting aside all outside authorities and bringing everything to the bar of human reason. The motto of enlightenment was, said Kant, *Sapere aude—'Dare to be wise.'*

Self-evident truths

Although Kant wrote this some time after the American *Declaration of Independence,* those who framed the *Declaration* were strongly inclined in the same direction. They were not prepar to renounce God altogether. Indeed, they appeal to God as the ultimate source of justificatio for the liberties they demanded. But their political philosophy had much in common with Rousseau. (The principal author, Thomas Jefferson, was a deist at heart, ar owed much to English and Frencl political theory.)

The appeal to self-evident trut in order to justify the basis of the *Declaration,* had an ancestry whi went back to Descartes. 'We hol these truths to be self-evident, that all men are created equal, th they are endowed by their Creat with certain unalienable Rights, that among these are Life, Libert and the pursuit of Happiness. Th to secure these rights, Governments are instituted among men, deriving their just powers from the consent of the governed. Tha whenever any Form of Government becomes destructive of the ends, it is the Right of the People to alter or to abolish it, and to institute new Government, laying its foundation on such principles and organizing its powers in such form, as to them shall seem most likely to effect their Safety and Happiness.'

The ideals which led to the separation of the United States of America from Great Britain came back into a French setting in the *Statement of Human and Civil Rights* agreed by the revolutionary French National Assembly in 1789. This, too, contains references to God but perhaps less strongly. Karl Barth observed that the *Declaration of Independence* represents a Calvinism gone to seed, whereas the *Statement of Human and Civil Rights* represents a Catholicism gone to seed.

Be that as it may, the two respective governments broke with religion. The First Amendment to the *American Constitution* (1791) laid down that there should be neutrality in religion. It allowed free speech and right of assembly, but laid down that 'Congress shall make no law respecting an establishment of religion'. The *Constitution* rejected all religious tests for office-holders. The United States of America were the first modern secular state. Christianity (and other religions) flourished in America because of—or, as some would say, in spite of—the neutral position of the government and Constitution.

Liberty, Equality, Fraternity

In France it was different. It soon became clear that the liberties granted to all in the *Statement* did not extend to the church. 'Liberty, Equality, Fraternity' did not include those who had supported the old regime. For a time the church was outlawed and a 'religion of reason' was introduced. But, although the religious orders were suppressed and church property was confiscated, the Catholic church was too strong to be crushed.

When Napoleon came to power, a 'Concordat' was negotiated in 1801 by which the church surrendered its former property and the state undertook to subsidize the clergy. The history of relations between church and state in France continued to be turbulent throughout the nineteenth century. Within the Catholic church there were deep divisions over policy. The old 'Gallican movement' wanted to keep the church both Catholic and French, with as little interference as possible from Rome. Ultramontanists (they got their name from the latin *ultra montes,* 'beyond the mountains', that is the Alps) thought the only solution lay in bringing the French church further under the authority of the papacy in Rome.

In the often bitter relations of church and state, freemasonry played a crucial part. The Catholic church and freemasons were deadly rivals; both sides saw it as

"Congress shall make no law respecting an establishment of religion or prohibiting the free exercise thereof."

First Amendment, US Constitution

Life in colonial America is recaptured at Williamsburg, Virginia. Many of the eighteenth-century buildings have been restored to their original state.

a duel to the death. This antagonism between freemasonry and Christianity was by no means confined to France. Many of the most enlightened people who wanted to escape from the old ways and find a new outlook, guided by reason and humanity, were enthusiastic freemasons. Perhaps it is understandable that the ideals of enlightenment should coincide with those of freemasonry. Figures as diverse as Lessing and George Washington were freemasons. But it is ironic that many who rejected the rites of the church in the name of reason found it necessary to resort to the secret mysteries of freemasonry.

The other side of the coin

So far we have been looking at attempts to find truth and to frame a world view by placing great reliance upon reason. Even if reason was not the be-all and end-all, it played a major part. But alongside those who stressed the role of reason, there were others who sought meaning and reality elsewhere.

In seventeenth-century France the Quietists, Monsieur de Molinos, Madame Guyon and Archbishop Fénelon, condemned human effort. They believed that, to attain perfection, people must be passive. They must abandon themselves to God to the extent that they do not even care for their own salvation. This state can be reached in prayer. When it is truly achieved, sin is impossible. Temptation may come, and even compel the Quietists to perform actions which would be sinful in others. But because they no longer have wills of their own, the actions are not sins. Quietism was condemned by Pope Innocent XI in 1687.

Jansenism, another seventeenth-century movement in the Roman Catholic church, was also condemned. It was named after Cornelius Jansen whose work, *Augustinus* (1640), revived a form of Augustine's theology. It is impossible to obey God's commandments without special grace. On the other hand, it is impossible to resist God's grace. Logically, man is a victim of natural or supernatural determinism. His actions are determined either by nature or by grace.

Jansenist teachings were accompanied by a harsh, moral rigorism. They were first condemned by Pope Innocent X in 1653. But the Jansenists claimed that they had been condemned for ideas which they did not in fact hold. In 1668 they were persuaded to modify their position. Final condemnation came in 1713; many French Jansenists found refuge from persecution in Holland.

A questing age

All ages are ages of transition, and most of them contain extremes. The period between 1650 and 1789 was no exception. It opened just after the Civil War in England and ended with the beginning of the French Revolution. Protestantism was already well established when the period began. But no movement can ever remain static. Fresh questions are always begin asked.

The period saw many quests. In philosophy there was the quest for truth and rationality. In religion there were quests for greater doctrinal clarity and deeper personal knowledge of God.

The reasonableness of Christianity

James R. Moore

Sir Isaac Newton, the great English scientist, is best remembered for his law of gravity and work on the physics of light. He believed that his scientific discoveries were communicated to him by the Holy Spirit, and regarded the understanding of Scripture as more important than his scientific work. Although many of his personal beliefs were unorthodox, he did not allow this to become widely known.

Beginning with the speeches of Peter and Paul in the book of Acts, Christians have engaged in apologetics. They have defended their faith from hostile attacks, and commended it through argument to unbelievers in general. At the same time, in giving 'a reason for the hope' that is in them, Christians have often appealed to natural theology. They have looked for a basis in innate or 'natural' human reason for accepting specific theological beliefs. Origen, Anselm and Aquinas are among the better-known apologists who used natural theology in their arguments.

At no time in history was natural theology more widely used to defend the Christian faith than in the eighteenth century. At no time did it seem so important to make Christianity appear 'reasonable'. There were three main causes for this.

First, Descartes, Spinoza and Leibniz had exalted reason and doubt in building their influential philosophies. Historians such as Simon and Bayle had also stimulated scepticism by criticizing the Bible. Second, Isaac Newton in his *Principia Mathematica* (1687) had set out laws which appeared to prove that the universe was divinely ordered. This encouraged the belief that human enquiries into nature, unaided by Scripture, could demonstrate the power and wisdom of the Creator. Third, a century of appalling religious conflicts—the Thirty Years' War in Germany, the persecution of Jansenists and Huguenots in France, the Puritan Revolution, and the Glorious Revolution of 1688 in England—had created a thirst for tolerance and a desire to find doctrines on which everyone could agree.

'The reasonableness of Christianity' (the title of John Locke's revolutionary book, published in 1695) became the central theme of theology for more than a century. The fundamental truths of the Christian religion were claimed to be few and simple, intelligible to the plainest of people. The immense size of the universe, the stability of its bodies and the simplicity of its laws; the position of the earth, the usefulness of its resources and the variety of its inhabitants; and the detail, order and symmetry of every form of life—all witnessed clearly to God's existence, his wisdom and goodness, his purposes, providence and power. They witnessed, in other words, to a God of whom it was probable that a special revelation had been given. And this revelation—the Bible—confirmed that Christianity was basically reasonable.

From the outset, the English specialized in using natural theology in apologetics. The 'Cambridge Platonists'—among whom were Ralph Cudworth, Henry More and John Wilkins—made important contributions in the last decades of the seventeenth century. Their followers, the so-called 'Latitudinarians' (including Edward Stillingfleet, bishop of Worcester, and John Tillotson, Archbishop of Canterbury), wrote in a rather more rationalistic manner. In 1691 Robert Boyle, a chemist and natural theologian, founded a lectureship 'for proving the Christian Religion, against notorious Infidels, viz. Atheists, Theists, Pagans, Jews, and Mahometans, not descending lower to any Controversies, that are among Christians themselves.' The Boyle Lectures continued for many years.

But the natural theologians neglected the teaching of the Bible so much that in time some came to argue that its distinctive doctrines were either superfluous or false. They claimed that the parts of the Bible that agree with natural theology are simply unnecessary; the parts that contradict natural theology—the myths, miracles, and priestly mumbo-jumbo—are simply untrue. The Christian religion consists solely of what nature and reason teach unaided: the belief in and worship of God, the repentance of sin, the practice of virtue, and the expectation of punishment and rewards after death.

Those who held such views were known as deists. Their number greatly increased in England and continental Europe during the first half of the eighteenth century. John Toland, the author of *Christianity Not Mysterious* (1696), was patronized by German nobility. Lord Bolingbroke, a witty and frivolous popularizer, won the admiration of Voltaire. And when Anthony Collins and the 'doubting Thomases', Woolston, Morgan and Chubb, had published their free-thinking works, Matthew Tindal gave deists everywhere a new 'Bible': his *Christianity as Old as the Creation* (1730).

Orthodox Christians responded to the deists in various ways. Many continued with ever more detailed elaborations of natural theology. They particularly used the argument from design. In England, John Ray's *Wisdom of God Manifested in the Works of Creation* (1691) passed through numerous editions. In France, Abbé Pluche and J.B. Bullet produced similar works between 1730 and 1770. Meanwhile, in Germany, the arguments were taken to extraordinary lengths by J.A. Fabricius in his *Water-Theology* (1734) and by F.C. Lesser in his *Stone-Theology*(1735), *Insect Theology* (1740), and *Shell-Theology* (1744).

Other Christians more appropriately chose to defend the Bible by showing that its authors were reliable and honest. They then used the evidence of miracle and prophecy to show that orthodox beliefs were reasonable. The older work of Hugo Grotius was useful in this regard. The controversy also produced some classics of its own—for example, Thomas Sherlock's *Trial of the Witnesses of the Resurrection* (1729), and Nathaniel Lardner's fourteen-volume masterpiece, *The Credibility of the Gospel History* (1727–55). The literature on 'Christian evidences' grew and remained in fashion until the mid-nineteenth century.

The deists were best combated by writers who questioned and reinterpreted the role of 'reason'. In the *The Case of Reason* (1731) William Law showed that it was false to suppose that God always behaves according to strictly human rationality. George Berkeley, in *Alciphron* (1732), argued that God's ideas, not matter, are what really exist. Therefore all beliefs which separate the human reason from the divine are faulty. Joseph Butler all but ended the controversy with his famous *Analogy of Religion* (1736). He argued that reason justifies only probable inferences about the world; and that both nature and revelation are beset with difficulties which make inferences about them merely probable. Therefore both natural and revealed religion can be accepted on the same grounds as from the same Author.

The difficulties which Butler highlighted could become the grounds for *denying* the divine authorship of both nature and the Bible. But this was not yet so obvious as it would be later. The sceptical philosopher David Hume had little effect on his own century. His *Dialogues Concerning Natural Religion* appeared only after he died, in 1777. Similarly Kant's critical philosophy, contained in his *Critique of Pure Reason* (1781) and *Critique of Practical Reason* (1788), influenced the nineteenth rather than the eighteenth century. Writers of natural theology, cautioned by Butler, continued to follow the lines laid down in the deistic controversy. Their work culminated in the most popular apologetics texts ever written: William Paley's *View of the Evidences of Christianity* (1794) and *Natural Theology* (1802).

George Fox and the Quakers

Arthur O. Roberts

George Fox, who, after years of painful searching for truth, began to gather the Society of Friends. He wrote a detailed account of his experiences, published as his *Journal*.

In 1650 a judge sentenced a young man to six months in jail in Derby, England, on charges of blasphemy. The youth had claimed that Christ, the Saviour, had taken away his sin; and in Christ there was no sin. Before he was sentenced, George Fox told Judge Bennett to tremble in the fear of God. Professing Christ was not enough. Everyone must follow him.

At that, the judge laughed. He knew about the meetings of George Fox and his followers. People sometimes shook with emotion. So he told Fox, 'You folk are the tremblers, you are the quakers.'

'Quaker' was a derisive nickname, and it stuck—like 'Christian' at Antioch sixteen hundred years earlier. Those people to whom the name was applied referred to themselves as 'Children of the Light' or 'publishers of Truth', or 'the people of God in scorn called Quakers'. Or simply 'Friends'—following the words of Jesus, 'You are my friends, if you do what I command you.'

Later, when dissent from the Church of England was made legal, Quakers called themselves the 'Society of Friends'. That is what they are called today, although in many parts of the world 'Friends' Church' is the name. Friends are scattered throughout the world and about half of them are of non-European origin.

George Fox was weary of formal religion. The English church had been Roman, Anglican, Presbyterian and Independent, but always under state control. This bothered Fox. It seemed as if the church had given up spirituality in exchange for protection. The church had become a kind of public service managed by state-appointed officials. Fox called them all 'priests' —whether Catholic or Protestant. The liturgy might vary; the system never. The church had become apostate. But Christ was not a commodity to be bought and sold.

Second-hand answers left Fox empty. It wasn't enough to *read about* Spirit-led people in the book of Acts. Irrelevant advice in his spiritual search frustrated him further. 'Try tobacco,' said one minister, 'and sing psalms.' 'Get married,' advised another. 'Bloodletting may help,' said a third.

George Fox tried spiritual advisers, and asked them theological questions until they were uncomfortable. All was second-hand. Then one day he heard a voice which said: 'There is one, even Christ Jesus, who can speak to thy condition.' Christ was revealed to him in immediate experience.

Theory became reality.

People sensed the power of God when Fox preached. Sometimes he would speak after the minister had finished; sometimes he preached outside the church. People argued with him. One even hit him on the head with a brass-bound Bible, upset because the brash Fox knew the Bible so well.

One day George Fox climbed Pendle Hill, in the north of England. It is still a place where wind sweeps grey mists across grassy slopes and rocky crags. At the top of Pendle Hill, George Fox had a vision of 'a people to be gathered to the Lord'. He saw Christ gathering people into victory over Satan. The need was to proclaim Christ who *liberates* people from the power of sin in their lives.

Now Fox began preaching in the open air to thousands. 'Christ has been too long locked up in the Mass or in the Book,' he said, 'let him be your prophet, priest and king. Obey him.' This appealed to the yeomen of north-west England.

A band of young men and women became the evangelists of the Quaker movement. Known as the 'valiant sixty', they fanned out across England and wherever ships would take them. Many 'seekers' joined the movement as well as those who had previously belonged to other denominations. Three years after the Pendle Hill vision there were fifty thousand Quakers and, before the end of the seventeenth century, double that number. The movement crossed

An early Quaker meeting. The first Quakers called churches 'steeplehouses'. They termed clergymen 'hirelings', and gave any Friend freedom to speak.

cultural barriers. Servant girls took part in worship with aristocrats such as the scholar Robert Barclay.

James Nayler, who at one time led the London Quakers, illustrates how hard it was to be Spirit-filled without becoming fanatical. A powerful preacher whose images still speak ('join the *Lamb's* war'), he got carried away by his own charisma. Once he tried to illustrate the inward coming of Christ into the heart by staging a 'triumphant entry' into Bristol, complete with donkey and hosannas. This shocked the townspeople and scandalized Friends. They questioned his symbolism. He was branded on the forehead, 'B' for blasphemer, his tongue bored through with a hot iron, and imprisoned.

Afterwards he became truly humble, and wrote:

'There is a spirit which I feel that delights to do no evil, nor to revenge any wrong; but delights to endure all things in hope to enjoy its own in the end. Its hope is to outlive all wrath and contention, and to weary out all exaltation and cruelty . . . As it bears no evil in itself so it conceives none in thought to any other. If it be betrayed, it bears it, for its ground and spring is the mercies and forgiveness of God, its crown in meekness . . .'

The Nayler episode caused Quakers to check the 'Spirit's leadings' with what Scripture says and by prayerful meetings of the church. Indeed in the eighteenth century they became over-cautious.

The early Quaker preachers sounded rather like the Old Testament prophet Amos: they proclaimed Christ as truth and let that truth stand in judgement over current evils. They wanted people to live by Christ's righteousness, rather than to speculate about his second coming.

Fox once went to Oliver Cromwell to plead for religious freedom. He told the Protector that it wasn't enough for Christians to have the Scriptures; they ought to live them. He commended to him a Christian life-style which rejects military weapons in favour of the armour of the Spirit. Cromwell remarked that in the Quakers he had found a people whom he could not influence, 'either with gifts, honours, offices, or places'.

Quakers were imprisoned, sometimes thousands of them, for such offences as refusing to speak deferentially to judges, meeting in forbidden religious assembly, or refusing the compulsory state church tithe. If they were asked to take the oath in court, they refused on the basis of Jesus' words, 'Swear not at all . . .'

In Boston, New England, a confrontation occurred between the Puritans who had left their homes in England to set up a pure Christian community and Quakers who challenged their religious exclusiveness. When banishment failed to eliminate the Quakers, Governor Endicott ordered the death penalty. Three Quakers were hanged on Boston common (1660–61) because they chose to hold to their convictions rather than obey the authorities. Their deaths raised an outcry against intolerance which helped pave the way for religious liberty.

As early as 1659 the Quaker John Taylor visited the American Indians. He was well received, and stayed in a wigwam as their guest. He urged them to turn from darkness to the light of Christ Jesus in their own hearts.

This began a long and friendly relationship with aboriginal people. The Indians trusted the Quakers and the Quakers trusted the Indians. In subsequent years some of the American Indian people became Quakers. Today aboriginal people who are Friends (from Alaskan Inuit to Andean Aymara) outnumber English Quakers.

John Woolman was a modest New Jersey tailor who became disturbed about slavery. He was convinced it was wrong, in the face of all reasonings and Bible 'proofs'. This patient eighteenth-century prophet campaigned first to get his fellow Quakers to stop keeping slaves. Through the Quakers the conscience of others was reached. If Woolman was guest in a home where a slave served, he would politely pay for their services. His point was well made. It was a non-violent kind of revolution. Woolman also believed that long hours of hard labour led to drunkenness. He calculated that a six-hour day would provide for necessities in society and keep up employment levels.

James Nayler, the English Quaker, was whipped as part of his punishment for riding through Bristol in 1656 as if he were the Messiah.

Some enduring Quaker principles

Jesus Christ is the Light of the world, historically and inwardly—Christ died for all. People are in unbelief and darkness until convicted by Christ and converted to his power. The salvation made possible by Jesus' death and resurrection may be appropriated by obedience to Christ's Spirit. Christ offers victory over sin and calls people to live by the standards of God's kingdom now, not waiting for a better situation or Christ's second coming. Christ baptizes believers with the Holy Spirit, is present with them in worship, and directs their ministry. Hence outward sacraments belong to pre-Christian times. Christ takes away the need for war in support of Christian outreach or the social order. The church means people not buildings. The Spirit who inspired the Scriptures guides the church in understanding them and applying their teachings.

The Unitarians

Ian Sellers

Unitarianism rejects the idea of the Trinity. It questions belief in the divinity of Christ and of the Holy Spirit in favour of the oneness of God. This idea was found in the early church, particularly in the Monarchianist heresy.

The modern movement dates from the early sixteenth century. Renaissance ideas combined with some extreme teaching in the Radical Reformation to produce Unitarian ideas in the minds of many individuals. Notable early Unitarians included Martin Cellarius, Michael Servetus and Bernard Ochino.

The new teaching alarmed both Catholics and Protestants. Servetus was put to death for his heresies by Calvin in 1553. Two prominent centres of early Unitarianism were Poland and Hungary. Blandrata was active in Poland between 1558 and 1563, and was followed by Gregory Paulus. Unitarian congregations sprang up and were known as the 'Polish Brethren'. They were formally organized in 1565, and became known as the Minor Church.

After 1574, when Faustus Socinus became their leader, Unitarianism spread quickly. Its intellectual centre was Racow. There a Polish Unitarian declaration of faith, the *Racovian Catechism,* was published in 1605. During the reign of the Catholic King Sigismund III (1587–1632) a reaction set in. The Unitarian community at Racow was suppressed in 1638. In 1658 the Unitarians were given the choice of conforming or going into exile. Many chose exile and emigrated to Holland, Hungary and England.

In Hungary, Blandrata was also active as a Unitarian. He arrived from Poland to become the court physician.

Unitarianism spread rapidly in Transylvania, the eastern part of the old kingdom. Blandrata had a strong influence on Francis David (1510–79), who, in 1564, became bishop of the Reformed church in Transylvania. David was also court preacher to the king, John Sigismund (1540–71). The king was impressed and at the Diet of Torda (1568) he ordered Unitarianism to be tolerated. In 1571 this faith, along with Catholicism, Lutheranism and Calvinism, was recognized as a 'received religion'.

But when John Sigismund died, severe persecution began. By the later eighteenth century Unitarianism in Hungary had been almost completely suppressed. It only revived in the early nineteenth century, when contacts were resumed with English and American Unitarians. Unitarian theology in Hungary was always compromising and conservative. It did not want to invite persecution by appearing aggressively heretical.

John Biddle (1615–62) is regarded as the founder of English Unitarianism, which emerged in the turbulence of the Civil War period. It remained confined to individual people at first. But in the rationalistic atmosphere of the eighteenth century, very many English Presbyterian and General Baptist churches began to be affected. They adopted first Arian, and then Sabellian, Socinian or full-blown Unitarian ideas. Both became largely Unitarian denominations by the second half of the eighteenth century. The liberal Anglican Theophilus

Lindsey left the Church of England in 1773 and opened the first self-styled Unitarian church, Essex Chapel, in London.

Unitarianism now spread rapidly. This was thanks to active missionaries, the intellectual distinction of the Unitarian-controlled Warrington Academy and the teachings of the well-known Dr Joseph Priestley. Unitarianism was not legally recognized in the Toleration Act of 1689. It was legalized in 1813.

In the first twenty-five years of the nineteenth century, Unitarianism slowly took on the trappings and organization of a separate denomination. The British and Foreign Unitarian Society was founded in 1825. There were a number of legal disputes with orthodox nonconformists. These threatened to deprive the Unitarians of many of their older church buildings, about a third of which claimed a seventeenth-century foundation. An Act of 1844 settled the question, largely in the Unitarians' favour, but left relations with the other nonconformists very bitter.

Meanwhile there were theological changes in Unitarianism, Priestley and his successor, Thomas Belsham, found their source of authority in Scripture. They interpreted the Bible in a rationalistic and optimistic way, to get round those verses which Christians had previously used to support the doctrine of the Trinity and the belief that humanity has a fallen nature.

But in the 1830s James Martineau and some younger Unitarians led a revolt against biblical Unitarianism and its dogmas. They advocated a less argumentative religion. They wanted a more refined, romantic and devotional spirituality. They found religious authority in reason and conscience, rather than in a biassed interpretation of Scripture. Henceforth the Unitarians were rather sharply divided into an older, 'biblical', and newer, 'spiritual', wing. The new group was well on the way to eclipsing the 'biblical' wing by 1850.

In Ireland Thomas Emlyn was prosecuted at Dublin in 1703 for denying the deity of Christ. A Unitarian 'Non-Subscribing Presbytery of Antrim' arose out of a group of liberal Presbyterian congregations in 1726. In 1830

The interior of an eighteenth-century dissenters' meeting-house. The atmosphere is that of the debating hall—far removed from the devotion and mystery of the medieval cathedral.

Dr Joseph Priestley (1733–1804) the English Unitarian minister, chemist and thinker. He rejected the doctrines of atonement and the Trinity. His support for the French Revolution led to his home in Birmingham being wrecked by protesters, and eventually to his emigration to the United States in 1794.

the 'Remonstrant Synod of Ulster' was formed. These two Unitarian groups merged in 1835. They were, and are today, more conservative in their beliefs than English Unitarians.

In North America Unitarian teaching first arose in the later eighteenth century among New England Congregationalists. But the first to take the title 'Unitarian' was an Episcopalian, James Freeman. His King's Chapel, Boston, became in 1785 the first Unitarian church in the New World.

After the Revolution, Unitarianism spread rapidly. It was encouraged by Priestley, who fled from England to North America in 1794. W.E. Channing, from 1803 minister of Federal Street Congregational Church, Boston, also promoted Unitarianism. In 1816 the famous divinity school of Harvard University was founded. It became the centre of Unitarian thought. In 1825 the scattered Unitarian congregations, like their counterparts in England, organized themselves into a denomination. It was known as the American Unitarian Association, and had its headquarters in Boston. A theological revolution similar to Martineau's was brought about in America by Theodore Parker and Ralph Waldo Emerson. In America the radicals used terms such as transcendentalism and anti-supernaturalism to describe their position. In England such labels tended to cause some alarm. Dr Joseph Tuckerman and his Domestic Mission movement took a new direction in charitable work. This was widely admired, and similar missions were promoted in several English cities.

SECTION 7
CITIES AND EMPIRES 1789–1914

EUROPE IN REVOLT

Wayne A. Detzler

Revolution was in the wind during the last quarter of the eighteenth century. In 1776 the North American colonists declared their independence from the British crown. A dozen years later, revolution erupted in France, shattering for ever the tradition of a monarchy ruling by divine right. The events in France set the course for the next century in both the spread of revolutionary ideas and the conservative reaction against them.

A second revolutionary force transformed the economy of much of Europe. This was the Industrial Revolution, which began in Britain late in the eighteenth century, and spread to Germany and France in the nineteenth century. Industry attracted working people into the growing urban centres. As a result many injustices appeared in society.

Napoleon leads the forces of the French nation: a painting by Meissonier. The French Revolution and Napoleon had a lasting effect on Europe in the nineteenth century.

Trade grew in parallel with the growth of industry, and the boundaries of the British Colonial Empire expanded. By about 1850, however, relations between the colonies and the British crown entered an era of change which gave birth to the Commonwealth. During this century of revolution the church had to adapt itself to the many developments occurring around it.

To the Bastille!

On 14 July 1789 a mob of enraged French peasants attacked the Pari prison called the *Bastille*, freeing the prisoners and razing it to the ground. Centuries of oppression had created popular ferment whic was directed against the prison as a symbol of the hated Old Régime.

The government of France under King Louis XVI was extremely unjust. The French parliament, the Estates-General, had not met for parliamentary business since 1614. Most of the land was owned by the clergy and nobility, who also monopolized position of power in the church, army and government. They were remarkably skilful, too, at evading taxation. More than 95 per cent of the French population were peasants, who were frequently exploited by the privileged aristocracy. The middle class was better off financially but equally vulnerable t abuse by the privileged.

Thinkers such as Voltaire (1694–1778) helped to fan the fire of discontent by suggesting social change. They did not suggest the abolition of the monarchy, but either benevolent despotism or a constitutional monarchy. Another Enlightenment thinker was Denis Diderot (1713–84). Together with D'Alembert (1717–83) he edited the *Encyclopédie,* first published secretly in 1759. His early education had been in a esuit school; but Diderot and his collaborators claimed that they based all knowledge on science, and rejected traditional, Catholic hought. A third influential writer of pre-revolutionary France was Jean-Jacques Rousseau (1712–78). But violence such as the attack on he *Bastille* did not form part of Rousseau's plan for social change.

In the event, change came hrough much more practical neans than the philosophers' writings. In June 1789 a National Constituent Assembly was summoned. In August the Old Régime was brought to an end when a Declaration of the Rights of Man' was published. Local government was reorganized, and eighty-three new administrative areas, 'departments', set up. At the suggestion of bishop Talleyrand, church lands were taken into public ownership, in an attempt to finance the evolutionary changes taking place.

The church was dealt with n the *Civil Constitution of the Clergy,* enacted in 1790. Diocesan boundaries were made the same as hose of the new political departments, and the number of bishops educed from 140 to 83. Bishops and priests were to be elected by the people. Clergymen were compelled to swear allegiance to he French constitution rather than o the pope. Many went along with his, others refused; the church split over the issue. In practice, he power of the papacy was abolshed in France. 'Gallicanism'—the movement to assert the sovereigny of the French monarch in temporal matters, the authority of general church councils over the pope and the rejection of papal influence in the affairs of the French nation—had arisen in 1682. In 1791 it won a resounding victory.

The goddess Reason

During the early days of the revolution a party known as Jacobins, because they met in the Jacobin convent in Paris, came into being. They called for freedom and justice for the masses. Their leaders included Jean Paul Marat, George Jacques Danton and Maximilian Robespierre. They

A French anti-religious cartoon. Citizens are invited to watch a magic-lantern show satirizing the religion of their parents.

mustered an army of peasants, called the 'federates', and marched on Paris in 1792. Nobles and clergy who opposed the revolution were summarily executed. King Louis XVI was guillotined on 21 January 1793.

The Jacobins also took religious affairs in their own hands. On 10 November 1793 a group of deputies marched to Notre Dame Cathedral. There they enthroned a dancer of doubtful morals as 'the goddess of Reason'.

Between 1793 and 1815 France was almost continuously at war with other European powers—England, the Netherlands, Prussia, Austria and Spain. The French suffered several early defeats. Meanwhile Paris experienced the horror of the Reign of Terror, 1793–94. The execution of its instigator, Robespierre, brought the excesses to a halt. But France remained ungovernable until Napoleon took control in 1795.

One of the early act of Napoleon Bonaparte (1769–1821) was to restore normal relations with the Vatican. Pope Pius VII (1740–1823) agreed to a new *concordat* with Napoleon in 1801. Under its terms Napoleon received from the pope grudging assent to the revolution. The French clergy were to receive a regular stipend from the state. Although the pope was to appoint bishops, the state could veto his appointments. Similarly the state could veto the appointment of lower clergy made by the bishops. Protestants were granted freedom of religion.

A powerless pope?

In December 1804 Pope Pius VII sat as a pathetic spectator as Napoleon crowned himself Emperor. Immediately the Emperor embarked on an ambitious programme of conquest. In 1808 Napoleon took the Vatican States. The pope was seized and deported to Savona during the following year. Pius VII was finally exiled to Fontainebleau, near Paris. He was not restored to the Vatican until 1814.

When the pope returned to Rome, the restoration of the Jesuits followed quickly. Their activities had been suspended in 1773 by Pope Clement XIV. They had previously been expelled from Portugal, France and Spain. When the pope was restored to Rome there arose a new movement called 'Ultramontanism' (literally, 'beyond the mountains'); this group recognized the authority of the pope in Rome and the southern side of the Alps. The Ultramontanists were militantly loyal to the pope as the supreme authority in matters of faith and practice. Throughout the nineteenth century a struggle persisted in the French church between Ultramontanists and the Gallican nationalists.

In Germany, a Catholic party standing for the German equivalent of Gallicanism was known as Febronianism. It arose as a result of the writings of the bishop of Trier, J.N. von Hontheim (1730–88). Writing in 1763, under the pseudonym of 'Justinius Febronius', he argued that the keys of the kingdom of God had been committed to the entire church, not only to Peter and his successors. The church councils, not the pope, were the primary source of authority. The pope was in fact only first amongst equals. In Febronianism, Germany and Austria both experienced a nationalistic movement similar to Gallicanism.

Whilst the Roman Catholic church endured a buffeting from political revolution, Protestantism faced disruptive theological challenges. Dogmatic and biblical theology was threatened by naturalistic theories or rationalistic reductions of Christian beliefs.

Varied routes to renewal

The Enlightenment and deep confusion of the Napoleonic Wars provoked a new wave of popular pietism. The monarchs of Europe had been seriously threatened by the aggression of Napoleon. They felt that their only hope lay in asserting both the divine right of kings and the hierarchical authority of the Church.

The Congress of Vienna, convened by the European powers in 1815 to establish the security f Europe, immediately restored nost of the previous rulers in atural units with boundaries as hey had been left before Napole-n's campaigns. At Vienna, Czar lexander I of Russia (1777–1825) roposed a Holy Alliance, to con-rol international relations by 'the ublime truths which the Holy Reli-ion teaches'. In September 1815 treaty on this basis was signed Paris by Alexander I, Emperor rancis I of Austria (1768–1835) nd King Friedrich Wilhelm III of russia (1770–1840). Privately it vas conceded that their aims were nore political than pious. They vished to counterbalance British ea power.

Another example of the onservative reaction was the russian Union of 1817. At the ercentenary of the Reformation, riedrich Wilhelm III of Prussia ecreed the union of the Lutheran nd Reformed churches in ermany. The king hoped in this vay to achieve a common front gainst rationalism, the enemy of ith. In fact, he provoked opposi-on from all sides. Both Lutheran nd Reformed reacted against a niform church order and liturgy.

Between 1815 and 1848 a series f popular religious awakenings rose throughout Protestant urope. The awakening (*Réveil*) French-speaking Europe had s origins in Geneva, in the minis-y of the Scot, Robert Haldane 1764–1842). In Denmark, Nicolai .S. Grundtvig (1783–1872) itiated a pietistic movement by penly opposing liberal theology. he revival in Sweden resulted om the ministry in Stockholm f an English preacher, George cott. In Norway the awakening as largely a lay movement, onnected with the name of Hans ielsen Hauge (1771–1824). hese revival movements were ot related to each other, and ey mainly involved ordinary Christians.

In 1802 Chateaubriand's *Génie du Christianisme (The Genius of Christianity)* appeared in France. This immensely popular Romantic writer presented a powerful argument for Christianity, based on the aesthetic values of Christianity.

After Napoleon, Ultramontanism gained ascendancy in Catholic countries. The Ultramontane party in France was eloquently represented by the 'three prophets of traditionalism': de Maistre, de Bonald and Lamennais. Joseph de Maistre (1754–1821) experienced the invasion of Savoy by the revolutionary French, and this awakened in him a strong spirit of conservatism. His Ultramontane ideas are most clearly set out in *Du pape (On the pope)* (1819). De Maistre argued that society required a central authority to achieve cohesion. The two pillars of such authority were the papacy and the monarch by divine right. De Bonald and Lamennais defended a similar standpoint and were close friends of de Maistre.

'God and the people'

Lamennais (1782–1854) gradually moved away from his earlier hopes for an alliance between Ultramontanism and royalism. When he founded the newspaper *L'Avenir* in 1830, he was trying to promote liberty for the church from the state. Accordingly, *L'Avenir* rejected the divine right of kings, and advocated popular sovereignty. Pope Gregory XVI (1765–1846) condemned the teachings of Lamennais and *L'Avenir* in the encyclical *Mirari Vos* (1832). After the French revolution of 1848, Lamennais, who had by that time lost all Christian commitment, became a member of the new republican government until 1852. He remains one of the founders of liberal Catholicism.

"Without the pope there can be no church, without the church no Christianity, and without Christianity no religion and no society . . ."

LAMENNAIS

Despite the existence of Ultramontanism, in the period 1815–48 the Catholic church was never free from conflict with political liberals and republicans. Such conflict was particularly evident in the *Risorgimento* (literally, 'resurrection') period of Italian history, 1815–70.

After the defeat of Napoleon there was a conservative reaction in southern Europe similar to that in the north. Italy was at this time divided into small duchies ruled by rival dynasties. Any moves towards either unity or liberalism in Italy were quickly and thoroughly suppressed by the Austrians and French. About 1820 a force of dedicated democratic revolutionaries, the *Carbonari,* appeared in Italy. Not long after, Giuseppe Mazzini (1805–72) joined them and emerged as one of their leaders. The *Carbonari* stirred up small uprisings in Sardinia, Naples and the Piedmont, but each time the Austrians put them down. Mazzini and his compatriots were aiming to unify Italy on the basis of 'God and the people'.

Pope Gregory XVI (1765–1846) steadfastly opposed the *Risorgimento,* for he feared the loss of his temporal power in the Papal States. When Gregory died, he was succeeded by Pius IX (1792–1878), who was more sympathetic towards liberal democracy. His republican sympathies were, however, short-lived. In 1848 a revolutionary attack on Rome by Mazzini, supported by Giuseppe Garibaldi (1807–82) and his army, resulted in the exile of Pius IX. Not until 1850 was the pope restored to his residence, and then it was by the French. Pius IX struggled with revolutionary republicans throughout most of his time as pope. In the end this led to his loss of the Papal States.

Street-fighting in the Paris quarter of Saint Antoine. In 1830 revolution broke out again in France when the restored Bourbon monarchy was overthrown.

The barricades crumble

1848 saw the outbreak of revolution in France, Germany and Italy. Barricades were thrown up in the streets of Paris during February 1848, and a provisional government proclaimed a republic. King Louis Philippe fled to England.

After some short-lived experiments with republican government, elections for a president at the end of 1848 led to the victory of Napoleon's nephew, Louis Napoleon (1808–73). He soon dissolved the legislature, and by 1852 had declared himself emperor. The Second Republic came to an abrupt end.

Meanwhile, in Prussia, Friedrich Wilhelm IV (1795–1861) had come to the throne. Most expected him to be an enlightened monarch, open to social and political reform, but they were disappointed. When presented with a written constitution in 1847, Friedrich Wilhelm IV declared: 'Neither now or ever will I allow a scribbled sheet of paper to intervene like a second Providence between our God in Heaven and his land of ours.'

In March 1848 street fighting erupted in Berlin. The king lost nis nerve and ordered his army o leave Berlin, so that he could conclude peace with 'his dear Berliners'. The king promised mmediate constitutional concessions. Over 500 representatives rom the German kingdoms, Austria and Bohemia, attended an assembly at Frankfurt 'to create a constitution for Germany, for the whole Empire'.

By December 1848 the Frankfurt Assembly produced a Declaration of the Rights of the German People'. It included a guarantee of religious freedom for dissenters. The 'Old Lutherans', who had rejected the Prussian Jnion (between Lutherans and Reformed) of 1817, were allowed freedom of conscience. Nonconformists who had appeared n Germany as a result of missionary activity by English-speaking nations also gained toleration.

But democratic institutions made little further progress in Germany at this period. By 1850 most republican institutions and eforms, including the Frankfurt Assembly, had either disappeared or lapsed into disuse.

Bless Italy'

n Italy the 1848 revolutionary movements were much more closely related to the church. After becoming pope in 1846, Pius IX had made several significant reforms. He hoped to use he nationalist sentiments of the *Risorgimento* to bind the fragmented Italian states more closely ogether. When Sicily rose against he Bourbon monarchy, and north taly rebelled against Austria, Pius X made an appeal for a united taly. He prayed: Bless Italy, Great God, and preserve her with hy most precious gift of faith.'

The pope stopped short of advocating military action against the Austrian troops, since he feared the loss of Austrian support. By November 1848 the pope was forced to flee from Rome. By the time he returned in 1850, Pius IX had lost any liberal sympathies he had once had. Although his temporal power was doomed, he clung tenaciously to the Papal States until 1870.

As political power ebbed away from him, the pope increasingly emphasized his spiritual power. In 1853 Pius IX issued the papal bull *Ineffabilis Deus*. This set out the doctrine of the immaculate conception of the Virgin Mary: that from the first moment of her conception she was entirely free from original sin. This laid a solid foundation for the veneration of Mary, and at the same time strengthened the spiritual authority of Pius himself.

'Heralds of infidelity'

Ten years later Pius issued the encyclical *Quanta Cura,* with the *Syllabus of Errors* attached to it. This categorically condemned political liberalism as one of an all-inclusive list of modern errors. It had been in preparation since 1852, was approved in 1862 by the synod of bishops, and issued in 1864.

The *Syllabus of Errors* also condemned rationalism in all its forms, liberal theology, freemasonry, and religious toleration. Even the Bible Societies, which had entered the European continent from Britain mainly after 1815, were rejected. In 1816 Pius VII had rebuked the Bible Societies for distributing Scriptures without the comments of the church Fathers. Pope Gregory XVI in the 1830s condemned Bible Society Scripture distributors as 'Daring heralds of infidelity and heresy'. In this respect the *Syllabus* merely

POPE PIUS IX

Wayne A. Detzler

Pius IX (1792–1878), who enjoyed the longest papacy in history, did much to strengthen the doctrinal supremacy of his office. He was born in 1792 as Giovanni Maria Mastai-Ferretti, and ordained to the priesthood in 1819. In 1823–25 he served as papal ambassador (nuncio) in Chile. Consecrated Archbishop of Spoleto in 1827, he also became bishop of Imola (1832) and in 1840 a cardinal. He served as pope from 1846.

While he was pope, the papacy endured a humiliating loss of temporal power. When the Italian nationalists invaded Rome in 1848, Pius IX was forced to flee from the 'Eternal City'. He took refuge at Gaeta, near Naples, and his earlier liberalism soon vanished.

In 1850 the French and Austrians restored Pius IX to his rightful place in Rome. There he remained until 1870, when the triumphant King Victor Emmanuel seized the city. A year later the pope was deprived of church lands by the Law of Guarantees. Of the once extensive papal holdings he retained only the Vatican, Lateran and Castel Gondolfo.

Although he lost ground on the political side, Pius IX strengthened the doctrinal position of the papacy. He was firmly in favour of the view that focussed all power in the Roman Catholic church in the papacy (Ultramontanism).

In 1854 Pius IX proclaimed the immaculate conception of the Virgin Mary. The Virgin was, according to his dogma, purified from original sin before her birth.

The *Syllabus of Errors* was issued in 1864, in connection with the papal encyclical, *Quanta Cura*. This list of heresies and threats to the church was in the main a reaction against political liberalism, democratic ideas, rationalism in theology and anti-clericalism.

On the eve of his political disaster, Pius IX summoned the first Vatican Council to meet in Rome (1869–70). The pope had strengthened his hand by re-establishing Catholic hierarchies in England (1850) and the Netherlands (1853). He had also concluded favourable agreements (concordats) with Russia (1847), Spain (1851) and Austria (1855). At the Vatican Council his position in the church was strengthened by the declaration of papal infallibility when speaking *ex cathedra* on faith and morals. There were 276 Italian bishops and only 265 from *all* the other European countries. There was a built-in majority in favour of Ultramontanism. Pius IX enthroned tradition. He once rebuked a dissenting bishop with the words: 'Tradition; I am tradition.'

Pope Pius IX, one of the most significant popes of the nineteenth century. He is shown here in a specially decorated coach at the first railway station in Rome in 1863.

consolidated earlier opposition.

The pope issued a strong attack on the separation of church and state, fearing the strength of republicanism in France. The *Syllabus of Errors* also prohibited civil marriage and liberal Catholicism as popularized by the Frenchman Lamennais. In response, France prohibited the publication of the *Syllabus of Errors* in 1865.

The peak of papal power under Pius IX was reached in 1869 with the opening of the first Vatican Council. In many ways the Council, which lasted until 1870, was the ultimate confrontation between Ultramontanist and conservative Catholicism on the one hand and Gallicanism, Febronianism and liberal Catholicism on the other hand. Conflict centred on the role of the papacy. The Gallicans insisted that supreme authority within the church was vested in its universal councils, such as Vatican I. The Ultramontanists regarded the pope as the supreme religious power. At Vatican I the Ultramontanists triumphed.

The most immediate result of this victory was the publication on 13 July 1870 of the dogma of papal infallibility. This taught that the pope is infallible when speaking *ex cathedral* on matters of faith and practice. Those who opposed this outright, or as being ill-timed, were in a small minority. Eventually only two voted against the proposal. J. H. Newman (1801–90) in England, and the French bishops Dupanloup (1802–78) were unhappy about the change, but both accepted the view of the majority. The German church historian, J.J.I. Döllinger would not withdraw the arguments he had put against papal infallibility, and was excommunicated. He did not, however, join the 'Old Catholics', who separated from Rome after 1870, partly through the inspiration of his writings.

Vatican I had established the papacy as the primary authority within the Roman Catholic church. But this could not mend the damage caused by the development of modern thought. The pope was also found his political strength permanently weakened. In 1861 Victor Emmanuel (1820–78) was proclaimed king of Italy, though it was not until 1870 that the city of Rome was included. By the end of 1870 Pius IX was left with only the Vatican, the Lateran and Castel Gandolfo. The pope became a 'prisoner of the Vatican' until Pius XI was freed by Mussolini in 1929.

"Tradition; I am tradition."

POPE PIUS IX

The Iron Chancellor

In 1862 Otto von Bismarck (1815–98) became Chancellor of Prussia. This put him at the head of the growing German Confederation of States. Within two years he had commenced a series of campaigns for international power. In 1871, at the end of the Franco-Prussian war, King William of Prussia (1797–1888) was proclaimed Emperor of Germany.

Still pursuing German unity, Bismarck initiated the *Kulturkampf* against the Roman Catholic church. The roots of the *Kulturkampf* reached back of the 1830s when Archbishop Droste-Vischering (1773–1845) of Cologne had refused to sanction marriages between Protestants and Catholics. In 1837 he was imprisoned by Friedrich Wilhelm III. Although he was released after a few months, a lasting rift appeared between the Prussian crown and the papacy.

The pronouncement of papal infallibility by Vatican I disturbed the Prussians further. Döllinger had considerable support within Germany when he opposed and rejected papal infallibility. The dogma appeared a serious affront to both Prussian political leaders and Protestant theologians.

The *Kulturkampf* arose out of this history of conflict. The legal status of Catholics in Germany was seriously weakened in 1871, when Bismarck abolished the Catholic bureau in the Prussian Ministry of Education and Public Worship. A year later Adalbert Falk (1827–1900) was appointed Minister of Public Worship. He restricted Roman Catholic influence by expelling the Jesuits from Germany and taking education wholly under state control.

Falk was also responsible for the enacting of the 'May Laws' of 1873. These claimed absolute supremacy for the state. The bishops' powers of discipline, particularly excommunication, were seriously limited. A supreme church court appointed by the Emperor was set up. Candidates for ordination were required to study at state universities and pass examinations in literature, history and philosophy. Pope Pius IX roundly condemned the laws, but they were not modified until 1886–87, after Leo XIII had become pope.

After 1861 a milder form of the *Kulturkampf* occurred in Austria. German liberals controlled the Austrian government and passed laws restricting the Catholic church. Civil marriage was introduced. Schools were brought under the control of the government, and Protestants were made equal in law. The church would almost certainly have plunged into decline throughout Austria if the ruling Habsburgs had not been loyal Catholics.

France breaks with the church

Meanwhile France was rapidly being secularized. In 1870 Napoleon III had withdrawn his troops from the Papal States to meet the Prussian threat to France. This gave fuel to his Catholic critics. When the Emperor was forced to choose between Catholicism and the national interest, he had to choose the second.

The sharpest critic of Napoleon was Louis Veuillot (1813–83), editor of the strongly Ultramontanist *L'Univers* (1843–60, 1867–74). When he criticized Napoleon in 1860 for deserting the pope, the Emperor suspended publication of *L'Univers*. Veuillot was obsessed with the unrealistic dream of reversing the French Revolution. He wished to bring education under the control of the church once more. He lived in Rome during Vatican I and gave strong support to papal infallibility.

L'Univers was enthusiastically read by rural, conservative clergy. But it did nothing permanent to stem the rising tide of secularism in France. In a gesture of conciliation, Leo XIII urged French Catholics to accept the Republic (1892). He tried unsuccessfully to get the French clergy to disown the royalist cause.

In 1901 the Association Law was passed in France. This defined the legal status of all religious institutions in France. Every religious body was required to register with the state. No member of an unregistered association was allowed to teach in a French school. Any congregation could be closed simply by government decree. About 615 congregations registered, but 215 did not. Among those who refused were the Jesuits and Benedictines. When Emile Combes became Minister of Religious Affairs he used the Act to close 13,904 schools by 1904.

In 1905 came the final break between church and state in France. Gallicanism and its philosophical offspring, anticlericalism, finally triumphed. The socialist Aristide Briand

(1862–1932) introduced the Separation Law which finally repealed the *Concordat* of 1801. All state subsidies to religious institutions were withdrawn. Church buildings became state property, but they would be held in trust by 'associations for public worship'. The law abolished all privileges previously enjoyed by the Catholic church. But it also introduced complete freedom of worship.

Pius X declared the Separation Law null and void, and he called on French Catholics to disobey it. He regarded the 'associations' as heretical, because they brought together lay people and clergy to control church property. But this papal decree stood no chance of success against Georges Clemenceau (1841–1929), the powerful anti-clerical premier of France after 1906.

Meanwhile the Catholic church suffered further restrictions of its temporal power in Rome. In 1871 the Law of Papal Guarantees was passed in Italy. It defined the pope's rights. The pope's person was declared inviolable. He was granted an annual income of £365,000. The properties of the Vatican, the Lateran and Castel Gandolfo were to remain in his hands. Any further general councils of the church would be allowed complete freedom, and papal diplomats would be granted the usual rights. Pope Pius IX categorically rejected this law. He refused the financial offer and withdrew into voluntary exile within the Vatican. The popes remained there until 1929 when Mussolini agreed to the more favourable *Lateran Treaty*.

Into the twentieth century

Pope Leo XIII (1810–1903) succeeded Pius IX in 1878. He strengthened papal diplomatic relations with Washington, Tokyo and Moscow. In his encyclical *Rerum Novarum* (1891) he pleaded for social reform and for trade unionism, to ensure proper income for workers. He encouraged Bible study, and made an approach to the Church of England through his apostolic letter *Ad Anglos* (1895). The commission he appointed to study ecumenical relations declared Anglican orders invalid (1896).

Following the brief liberal interval of Leo XIII, there was a return to conservativism under Pius X (1835–1914). Coming to the papacy in 1903, Pius X was almost immediately confronted with the crisis caused by French anti-clerical laws. In 1904 he broke off diplomatic relations with France. But he made concessions to the constitutional monarchy in Italy in 1906 by allowing Catholics to exercise their vote.

Pius X sought to strengthen the use of the liturgy in the church. In 1904 he launched a revival of the Gregorian chant, and urged a zealous veneration of the Virgin Mary. He revised the breviary of prayers in 1911. A deeply pious person, his example brought new hope to many Catholics perplexed by the difficulties of the modern world.

During the period 1789–1914 democracy achieved ascendancy over most of northern Europe and much of the south. In most cases the Catholic hierarchy sought to withstand this movement of popular government. The Protestant response was very varied, and ranged from the attitude of the Prussian nobleman to that of the British trade unionist.

Although it lost ground temporally, the Roman Catholic church strengthened its spiritual hold on the faithful. The pope was declared infallible, and the Vatican Council ensured wide support for theological developments.

THE FIRST INDUSTRIAL NATION

John Briggs

A schoolboy once despatched the industrial revolution in one sentence when he wrote: 'About 1760 a wave of gadgets swept over England.' The process was much more complicated than that. In the mining industries—iron and coal—important innovations came in the later seventeenth century, whilst in other industries technological change did not come until the twentieth century. In fact the pattern seems to be one of gradual development rather than revolution. Often hesitant and uncertain innovations were introduced into the manufacturing processes at different times in different industries, even in differing parts of the same industry.

An Industrial Revolution?

But the term 'Industrial Revolution' still had much relevance. Contemporaries clearly perceived the revolutionary spirit of the age. Dr Johnson was worried by it all: 'The age is running mad after innovation, all the business of the world is to be done in a new way.' 'By any reckoning,' concludes Professor Hobsbawm, 'this was probably the most important event in world history, at any rate since the innovation of agriculture and cities. And it was initiated by Britain.'

The Industrial Revolution was not a change imposed from above, but something which emerged from below, from the daily work of provincial England. The British Industrial Revolution was revolution by consent. It was stimulated by the expanding market represented by the increasing population of the eighteenth century. But at the same time the early capitalists of the textile industry (first silk and then cotton) were driven to make technical innovations to make up for a scarcity of appropriate labour.

Each industry had its own technical breakthroughs, but of most universal significance was the improved form of steam engine produced at the Boulton and Watt factory in Birmingham. At last the manufacturer had a source of power independent of climate and season, both of which had until this time limited the power available from wind- and watermills. With the development of the canal system and later the railway system the old limitations on the geographical location of industry were also removed.

The use of steam power changed the working situation of many Englishmen. An engine was expensive to purchase, and set a minimum scale and efficiency of enterprise below which it failed to provide the hoped-for profits. It offered little to the small manufacturer, but strengthened the slow movement towards purpose-built factories. The industrial Revolution brought capital, power and labour together under the one roof of the factory.

The tyranny of the machine

British agriculture was unable to employ the expanding population gainfully. Industrialization meant jobs for the victims of bad harvests

and destitution. But they did not often see it in this way. They hated the new factories. It was not the long hours or low wages they objected to. They were used to toiling day after day for a mere pittance. Nor were urban slums much worse than rural slums. And old agriculture depended on the employment of women and children as much as new industry.

'The real tyranny was the substitution of the rhythm of the machine for the rhythm of nature in the daily lives of the people.' Over against the irregularity of life in Old England with its loose discipline, and pace of work determined by night and day, sowing and harvest, had to be set the precision, the discipline, and the regularity of the factory world. God's sun was now hid in the heavens and in its place was the factory clock and bell, symbols of human time as against divine time. Within the factory the emphasis was on precision, scrupulous standards of care and the avoidance of waste. The greatest industrial sin was drunkenness, which so cheerfully challenged all the values of the new capitalist system.

Industrial capitalism then put forward a new morality which had much in common with the social values praised by the Evangelical Revival. The great potter, Josiah Wedgwood, sought a lifestyle for his workers which has much in common with that seriousness of life often attributed to Evangelicalism.

Saved from revolution?

The Evangelical Revival witnessed not only a renewal of evangelistic activity but also renewed concern for Christian morality. The nineteenth-century historian W.E.H. Lecky, although himself a free-thinker, credited it with bringing about: 'a great moral revolution

An artist's impression of the ironworks at Coalbrookdale, in Shropshire, England. It was in this area that the Industrial Revolution made its first impact.

"In the brave new world envisaged by Wedgwood and his friends there was little place for brothels, alehouses, cock-fighting and bull-baiting for the ease and amusement of his workmen. . .In their place there would be schools for their children, hospitals for their sick, homes for their orphans and societies, libraries and institutions for themselves."

in England: it planted a fervid and enduring religious sentiment in the midst of the most brutal and most neglected portions of the population, and whatever may have been its vices or its defects it undoubtedly emancipated great numbers from the fear of death and imparted a warmer tone to the devotion, and a greater energy to the philanthropy of every denomination both in England and the Colonies.'

Lecky went on to suggest that a major reason why Britain was saved from the ravages of a revolution similar to that in France was this new religious commitment. This idea was taken over by the French historian Elie Halèvy: 'We shall explain by (the Evangelical Revival) the extraordinary stability which English society was destined to enjoy throughout a period of revolution and crises; what we may truly term the miracle of modern England, anarchist but orderly, practical and businesslike, but religious, and even pietist.' What Halèvy saw as providential, left wing historians have labelled as a conservative prop for an economically oppressive society. But more recently other historians have suggested that evangelical and Methodist strength in England was too small either to prevent revolution, or to act as a widespread 'opiate'.

There is little firm evidence of the extent and class nature of church attenders in Victorian England. England's first census of church attendance was recorded in 1851. The deduction was made that roughly 30 per cent of those who could have attended service on census Sunday did not do so. Dissenting churches were found to be approximately as strong as the Church of England, in fact stronger in urban England. Church absenteeism was highest in the new industrial towns of the north.

“You saw nothing in Coketown but what was severely workful. If the members of a religious persuasion built a chapel there—as the members of eighteen religious persuasions had done—they made it a pious warehouse of red brick, with sometimes (but this only in highly ornamented examples) a bell in a birdcage on the top of it.”

CHARLES DICKENS,
Hard Times

Churches for industrial England

One consequence of industrialization was the emergence of an urban society in England, particularly in the midlands and the north. Alongside William Blake's 'dark Satanic mills' there emerged towns like Dickens' Coketown, 'a town of machinery and tall chimneys, out of which interminable serpents of smoke trailed themselves for ever and ever, and never got uncoiled'.

The Church of England was particularly slow to respond to the new situation, and found it difficult to do so. An act of Parliament was needed for a new parish to be created. This was both time-consuming and costly. As a consequence the Church of England found itself unable, until the 1840s, to respond to the new industrial England. The new urban masses consequently grew up very often beyond the care of the Church of England. There was no room for them in church, and all too often no clergy to care for their spiritual needs.

Methodism did not face the same difficulties. With its simple, barn-like preaching-places, its itinerant ministers, and its local preachers it was admirably designed to go where the established church was unable to go. Other dissenters, too, expanded into the towns and cities of industrial England, and engaged in missionary work there with some success. But there always remained many more people beyond, in the unreached jungle of 'darkest England', as General Booth described it.

Part of the difficulty was that the churches were dominated by the concept of class. Many congregations became middle-class preserves, though the working classes were not all non-church goers. Different denominations appealed to different classes—the Wesleyans and Congregationalists tended to attract the middle classes, whilst the Baptist 'Tabernacle' and the Primitive Methodist 'Bethel' were more likely to have a largely working-class congregation.

The parish church all too often represented 'the Tory Party at prayer'. In the 1830s, for example, the protest movement called the Chartists found little support in the established church. They frequently marched on the parish church and required the vicar to preach on some congenial text, such as: 'Go to now, ye rich men, weep and howl for your miseries which are coming upon you.' The rebuff they got from all the churches led them to establish separate Chartist churches in certain areas, for many of the Chartist leaders of the thirties and forties were Christians.

'We can't get at the masses'

How to evangelize the working classes was an ongoing problem, partly because the children of working-class Christians tended to join the middle class. There was something bourgeois about Christian ethics in practice: gone was the old expenditure on drink; new priorities included the family, self-improvement, and Sunday School education. So there came to be a distinction between 'chapel working class' and the 'brute working class' of the back alleys.

One organization which attempted to keep in touch with the working classes was the Pleasant Sunday Afternoon (PSA) Movement, formed in the 1880s with the motto 'Brief, Bright and Brotherly'. Its meetings were for men only, and were held on Sunday afternoons, so that men would not feel ashamed to come in their working clothes. The Sunday afternoon programme was part entertainment, part evangelistic and part political, and some of the early Labour leaders were frequent speakers. In the twentieth century the PSAs became the basis of the international Brotherhood Movement. The Salvation Army, too, came into being to serve the working classes. 'We can't get at the masses in the chapels,' claimed Catherine Booth, so in 1865 she and her husband opened their own Christian Mission in a tent in Whitechapel.

Varieties of Methodism

The Booths had found themselves

Part of the close-packed slums of London, pictured from a railway viaduct. This illustration, by the French artist Gustave Doré, dates from the 1870s.

THE SALVATION ARMY

John Briggs

William Booth, founder of the Salvation Army, had a varied previous career. He had preached for the Wesleyans, the Wesleyan Reformers and then the Methodist New Connexion, by whom he was ordained in 1858 after being disciplined the previous year for his irregular itinerant ministry. He stayed within the New Connexion for only three years before again becoming an irregular itinerant.

In 1865 the Booths began their own Christian Mission in a tent in Whitechapel, London. This venture gradually grew into the Salvation Army—to the irritation of many churchmen. Even Lord Shaftesbury, in extreme old age, concluded that the Salvation Army was a trick of the devil, who was trying to make Christianity ridiculous. Others, less Christian, retaliated against this new military presence more violently—in 1882, for example, 642 Salvation Army officers, including women, were assaulted, and sixty army buildings were damaged. Much of this opposition was undertaken by a 'Skeleton Army' which parodied Booth's activities and was supported by brewers who opposed the Army's teetotalism as a threat to their trade.

The Salvation Army was concerned about spiritual rather than material conditions. Booth spoke out against attempts to deal with great social difficulties as though they were simply due to lack of bricks and mortar. The first thing to be done to improve the condition of the wretched was to get at their hearts. The Salvation Army was not engaged in a fight, in the first place, against bad conditions and oppressive political philosophies.

Booth was authoritarian in his attempt to achieve results. He gained control of the Mission in 1877 by what was virtually a military coup. After that, the military emphasis was developed, with uniforms, corps and citadels, and the magazine *The War Cry*.

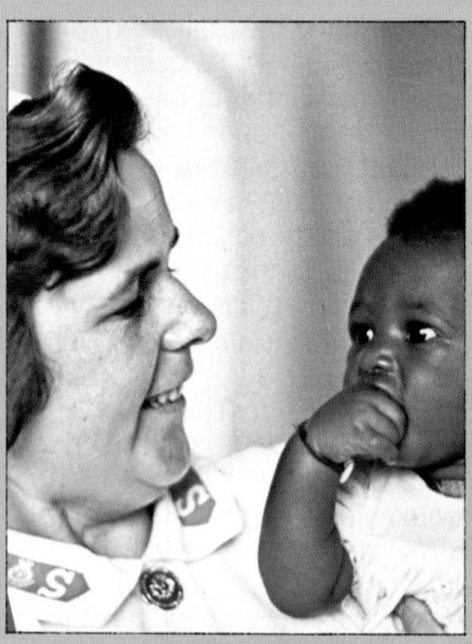

A Salvation Army nurse. The Salvation Army is very active in many countries with its hospitals, hostels and relief work.

The Salvation Army has always been known for its uniforms and music. This Salvation Army band is from Penzance, Cornwall, and was photographed in the 1880s. General Booth can be seen in the middle of the back row, with a long beard and top hat.

But this did not worry ordinary Salvationists, for theirs, too, was an exalted position. Booth remarked that the Salvation Army made 'every soldier in some degree an officer, charged with the responsibility of so many of his townsfolk'. Booth offered his followers not only a force with which they could identify but also a task to which they were committed. The Army was perhaps the only Christian movement to reach the wavelength of the masses in the nineteenth century. They alone understood the principles of mass communication and, in particular, the techniques of religious advertisement.

To begin with the Salvation Army continued the traditional revivalist evangelism, adding its own military slant, which fed the appetites of an increasingly jingoistic nation. But Booth's friendship with J.B.Paton, a Congregationalist theologian concerned with social problems, and W.T.Stead, editor of the *Pall Mall Gazette*, led him to wider concerns. It was widely believed that Stead was the ghost writer for Booth's *In Darkest England and the Way Out* (1890). The *Methodist Times* exclaimed, 'Here is General Booth turning Socialist.' The book was designed to show that 'the submerged tenth' in England were as much in slavery as certain African tribes.

The Salvation Army today is a worldwide movement. At its centenary meeting in London in 1965 General Frederick Coutts outlined its twin aims: 'If we refer to our evangelical work and also to our social work, it is not that these are two distinct entities. . . They are but two activities of the one and the same salvation which is concerned with the total redemption of man.'

Two Salvation Army bandsmen in Germany joke with their audience of children.

The Army is coming—amen, amen!
To conquer this city for Jesus—amen!
We'll shout 'Hallelujah!' and praise his dear name,
Who redeemed us to God through the blood of the Lamb.
The sound of its footsteps is rolling along;
The kingdom of Satan, triumphant so long,
Is shaking and tott'ring, and downward shall fall
For Jesus, the Saviour, shall reign over all.

Salvation is coming—amen, amen!
And Jesus will save all this city—amen!
We'll shout 'Hallelujah' and praise his dear name,
Who redeemed us to God through the blood of the Lamb.
The sound of salvation shall float on the wind—
Through street, court and alley its way shall it find,
The stubborn to break, and the broken to bind,
For Jesus is mighty, yet gentle and kind.

The judgement is coming—amen, amen!
God will judge all this city, amen, amen!
But we'll shout 'Hallelujah!' to Jesus' name
We're redeemed unto God through the blood of the Lamb.
And you to the bar of the Judge must each haste;
Your day of salvation will then have been past;
Take heed to this warning, it may be your last;
Oh, come to the Saviour, to Jesus hold fast.

A Salvation Army song, to the tune of The Campbells are coming

Salvation Army officers file their reports on 'slum work'

"*Mrs W.—of Haggerston slum. Heavy drinker, wrecked home, husband a drunkard, place dirty and filthy, terribly poor. Saved now over two years. Home A1, plenty of employment at cane-chair bottoming; husband now saved also.*

A.M. in the Dials. Was a great drunkard, did not go to the trouble of seeking work. Was in a slum meeting, heard the Captain speak on 'Seek first the kingdom of God!' Called out and said: 'Do you mean that if I ask God for work, he will give it me?' Of course she said 'Yes.' He was converted that night, found work, and is now employed in the gas works, Old Kent Road.

Jimmy is a soldier in the Borough slum. Was starving when he got converted through being out of work. Through joining the Army he was turned out of his home. He found work, and now owns a coffee-stall in Billingsgate Market, and is doing well."

unable to reach the masses from a position within mainstream Methodism. In the nineteenth century the Wesleyan Methodists, led by Jabez Bunting, became a staid, respectable denomination. It had not always been so. Even in the early 1800s the Home Office feared leaving education in industrial areas to Methodists, 'a set of men not only ignorant but of whom I think we have of late too much reason to imagine are inimical to our happy Constitution'.

Wesleyan Methodism imposed upon itself in the nineteenth century a 'no politics' rule, and until the late 1880s it was suspicious of open political discussion. But Methodism had its own nonconformity where this restraint was missing. For example, the Staffordshire Primitive Methodists produced several Chartist leaders. Involvement in chapel affairs made them into natural community leaders. They learnt organization, how to speak in public and how to deal with people. The local preacher could step readily from the pulpit to the political platform.

As a result, the Primitive Methodists had a close connection with the Trade Union movement. John Wilson, the leader of the Durham miners, described his conversion at the age of thirty-one at a Primitive Methodist Class Meeting:

'I took my seat, and when the class leader came to where I was sitting and asked me to tell him how I was getting on (meaning in a spiritual sense), I was speechless. The others, in response to his query, had replied readily but my eloquence was in my tears which I am not ashamed to say flowed freely. . . All was joy, and not the least joyous was myself, even while the tears were chasing down my cheeks. This change made, I began seriously to consider how I could be useful in life.'

This conversion experience led on to a search for education, enrolment as a local preacher, an office within the Miner's Union, and election to Parliament in 1885, as one of the earliest Labour MPs. Many other Labour leaders, especially in the north-east, had a similar story.

This world—or the next?

One of the great debates in the nineteenth century concerned the relationship between a Christian's citizenship in this world and that in the other world. Miranda, a delicate female character in the improving novel *Thornton Abbey*, used the story of Noah to portray her sense of alienness from life in this world. Christ was her ark, but in this present world, like Noah's dove, she could find nowhere to rest. In short, the earth was 'an enemy country, a parched wilderness, a barren desert'.

Lord Shaftesbury, the evangelical social reformer, had an answer for that kind of argument. He told a Social Service Congress at Liverpool in 1859: 'When people say we should think more of the soul and less of the body, my answer is that the same God who made the soul made the body also . . . I maintain that God is worshipped not only by the spiritual but by the material creation. Our bodies, the temples of the Holy Ghost, ought not to be corrupted by preventable disease, degraded by avoidable filth, and disabled for his service by unnecessary suffering.'

Christians with similar views were much offended at the end of the eighteenth century by slavery—that 'odious traffic in human flesh' which William Wilberforce had attacked in a precocious letter to a Hull newspaper in 1773. British trade was reckoned at the time to depend so much on slavery that intense opposition arose to the

Abolition Committee set up in 1787.

So great was the protest that it provoked Wilberforce into developing a new style of political opposition, in the form of pressure-group politics. The Abolition Committee was convinced of the need to acquire information about the operation of slavery in practice. By widespread use of stimulating propaganda a public opinion was created in the country. By means of petitions this sought to influence the judgement of MPs.

This pressure had to be kept up for twenty years before the slave trade was finally abolished in 1807. The emancipation of slaves within the British Empire did not come until 1833, after a long campaign led by Fowell Buxton, who was aided by indignant missionaries on the spot. They described the part played by slavery in dehumanizing the life of blacks in Africa and America.

White slaves

1883 also saw the first effective Factory Act passed by Parliament. It has often been suggestd that Wilberforce and his associates, the 'Clapham Sect', were only concerned with black slaves overseas and not with the white slaves of industrial England. This is unfair. Wilberforce was in fact one of the few to complain that the ineffective Factory Acts of 1802 and 1818 did not go far enough. The specialists in the industrial problem were, however, the Yorkshire evangelicals, such as Wilberforce's friend

THOMAS CHALMERS

W. J. Roxborogh

Thomas Chalmers (1780–1847) was a central figure in Scottish church life in the early nineteenth century. He was ordained a minister of the Church of Scotland in 1803, but his outlook was radically changed after his conversion in 1811. While minister in Glasgow from 1815 to 1823, first at the Tron Church and then at St John's, he insisted that the traditional parish system could cope with the problems of a growing industrial city. Chalmers revived the office of deacon, and was supported by an enthusiastic group of laymen. They visited systematically area by area, and established day and Sunday schools. Chalmers strongly believed that the needs of the parish poor could be met by the parish itself, but this part of his experiment ultimately failed.

In 1823 Chalmers became professor of moral philosophy at St Andrews University, where he also taught political economy. In 1828 he moved to Edinburgh to become professor of divinity. As chairman of the church extension committee of the Church of Scotland in the 1830s he raised over £300,000 for the building of more than 200 new churches. He played a leading part in the disputes over the independence of the church which led to the founding of the Free Church of Scotland in 1843.

Chalmers believed that the church had a mission to all the people and this determined how it should be organized. An energetic supporter of foreign missions, he claimed that they would stimulate the church at home. Above all, Chalmers was a compelling preacher, and his published sermons and other writings sold by the thousand.

Thomas Chalmers, the great Scots minister and thinker. He devised new means to care for his enormous industrial parish in Glasgow, and is regarded as one of the founders of modern sociology.

Thomas Gisborne, Richard Oastler of Huddersfield, Parson Bull of Bierley, Michael Sadler, MP, their parliamentary spokesman, and John Wood, a Bradford textile manufacturer.

Wood put the issue to Oastler in 1830 in terms of the earlier campaign against the slave trade: 'You are very enthusiastic against slavery in the West Indies: and I assure you there are cruelties practised in our mills on little children, which, if you knew, I am sure you would strive to prevent.' Within a few months Oastler had written his famous letter to the *Leeds Mercury* entitled 'Yorkshire Slavery'. These Yorkshire campaigners constantly regretted the lack of support from dissenters and the more pietistic of their fellow evangelical Anglicans, who appeared content to leave the plight of the depressed to the operation of so-called 'natural laws'.

As time went by there emerged a proliferation of philanthropic activity. It was based on a perilously fragile 'social theology'. Some Christians argued that the campaign for social righteousness was essential to a proper gospel ministry, whilst others saw social action as little more than a device for securing a working-class hearing for the gospel.

THE BRETHREN

Harold H. Rowdon

From time to time in the history of Christianity, movements have arisen which refuse any special title and strive to recapture the outlook and beliefs of the church in its earliest days. One such movement which emerged in Britain early in the nineteenth century also arose in Switzerland, Germany and other countries on the continent of Europe. Dubbed 'Plymouth Brethren' because Plymouth was prominent in the early days, Brethren have always tried to avoid any distinctive label.

The founding fathers were mainly Anglican evangelicals who felt that the Evangelical movement was not going far enough. There were also nonconformists who deplored certain features of nonconformity in their day.

The founders shared a deep concern at the divided state of the church. They wanted their simple communion service to be a means of fellowship for Christians irrespective of denomination, expressing the priesthood of all believers and therefore needing no priestly order. They also shared an expectation that Christ would soon return, and an insistent appeal to Scripture. They renounced the possessions, pleasures and status of this world. Their earliest leaders held strongly Calvinistic doctrines, and were often enthusiastic evangelists. Soon they developed a distinctive form of worship and church life.

From the start there were two different emphases. J.N. Darby and others believed that the church was in ruins, as at the end of other 'dispensations' of God's dealings with men and women. The assemblies were not to be set up with elders and deacons, but simply to be groups of people separated from the world awaiting Christ's return. Later these 'exclusive' assemblies declined into authoritarianism.

The other grouping, simply known as Christian Brethren (or 'open' Brethren), developed into a

A Christian social order?

It is doubtful whether the activities of the 'Christian Socialists' added up to very much. The novelist Charles Kingsley set out their responsibilities attractively in *Alton Locke* (1850). The Christian Socialist co-operative workshops were weak in organization and unduly idealistic about the contribution of labour, and only lasted a short while. However, Christian Socialists did good work in securing a better legal framework within which workers' organizations could develop, and in fostering worker's education.

The ideas of F.D. Maurice, their principal thinker, were to have a tremendous influence on Anglican thought about the secular world in the twentieth century. This was partly due to the solid work of the Christian Social Union, founded in 1889 with Brooke Foss Westcott, the Cambridge New Testament scholar, later bishop of Durham, as its first president.

In England this tradition came to its climax in the work of William Temple, Archbishop of Canterbury, 1942–44. Temple had deep insights into the nature of Christian worship, and a commitment to evangelism; he constantly exercised prophetic judgement on the

small but influential nonconformist group. As the result of emigration and a strong missionary emphasis (in Britain something like one per cent of Brethren became missionaries), Brethren are to be found in most parts of the world. They are relatively numerous in Argentina (where they make up the second largest Protestant group), Zaïre, Zambia, southern India, Singapore, and New Zealand.

The most distinctive emphasis of the Brethren is that the ministry and gifts of the church are distributed to all believers. The service of worship and communion is led by different members of the congregation. Full-time pastors are rare, though they are becoming more common; full-time evangelists and Bible teachers travel widely.

What also distinguishes the Brethren from other groups is that there is no church government beyond the local church. Agencies may be set up to cater for particular functions, such as financing missions and church-building, or setting up a Bible college. But there is no hierarchy or centralized organization. Local churches are free to apply the teaching of Scripture in the light of contemporary needs and the local situation—though in practice the inbuilt conservatism of any grouping results in widely-recognized common practice. Conferences and magazines strengthen shared doctrinal and practical viewpoints.

The contribution and experience of the Brethren, particularly in an age concerned for church unity and reorganization, has been out of all proportion to their numbers. They have held to the authority of the Bible during a time when it has been under constant fire. Many of their members have had leading positions in interdenominational agencies. They have been active in evangelism and have drawn attention to the church as the body of Christ, made up of all true believers and equipped with spiritual gifts distributed amongst the members.

Thomas Barnardo helping to feed some of the hungry homeless boys of Victorian London. Barnardo (1845–1905) set up a huge institution to care for the homeless children of England. He belonged to the Brethren.

> *"In many cases, because the children are so destitute that they cannot be taught, we give food—generally soup, occasionally meat, and good wholesome bread, sometimes coffee or cocoa, and bread and cheese. In one school they feed about two hundred twice or thrice a week. . .The children who come to the schools pay nothing; all the Ragged Schools are quite free, being intended only for the destitute.*
>
> *Kindness, Christian love to the children, and teaching them their duty to their neighbours and to their God, and making the Bible the theme of all our instruction. . ."*
>
> *MR WILLIAM LOCKE reports on the English Ragged Schools, 1844*

A detail from *Work*—a painting by Ford Madox Brown. The artist has depicted many of the occupations and skills of his Victorian world.

social situation. William Temple kept both this world and the next in equal focus.

A battery of societies

From the 1790s, the churches began to found overseas missions. At home a whole galaxy of home missionary agencies also sprang up. The sense of crisis in Europe emphasized the urgency of the times, and brought to birth a range of agencies 'making for the prospect of a popular evangelical church'. Accordingly, there developed itinerant societies, the great urban Sunday schools, an undenominational Christian press and a great battery of Bible, tract and missionary societies. These organizations formed a pattern of Christian progress all the way 'from Basle to New York', all seeking to capitalize on the evangelistic opportunities which seemed to be afforded by the turmoil of society. Such a movement, like society, seemed to be getting out of control as the social tensions of the early nineteenth century increased. In consequence the 'undenominational evangelicalism' of the 1780s and 1790s was short-lived, and by the 1800s was challenged by the assertion of 'denominationalism'—new to both the Church of England and to dissent.

The leaders of the Oxford Movement were alarmed at what they took to be the liberal tendencies of modern thought. In particular they were worried by liberal reform of the church by a Parliament whose members, since 1828, did not need to be Anglican, and who, since 1829, did not need to be Protestant. Furthermore, with the first rumblings of biblical criticism in Germany, the Bible appeared to them an uncertain authority. Accordingly they placed their faith in the church itself, as represented by the apostolic succession of the bishops, the sacraments and priestly office.

Nonconformists also felt the tensions involved in the relationship between church and evangelism. Victorian noncomformity blended Puritan tradition and revival evangelism. The revivalist strand was reinforced by the experience of the revival of 1859, and later by the visits of American revivalists such as Moody and Sankey, and Torrey and Alexander.

A chapel culture

From the 1840s onwards most city churches boasted a cluster of satellite missions in the poorer areas of the city. These mission halls were often far more than preaching stations, and provided their respective areas with a kind of all-purpose relief station, complete with clothing societies, penny banks, tontine clubs, soup kitchens and other agencies. They paralleled the many-sided activities of the institutional church of the suburbs which apparently provided a total 'chapel culture' for its adherents.

In church and mission alike it was possible to forget what the true nature of the church really was. Amidst a welter of activity, the idea of the church was increasingly confused and altered. The old Puritan concept of the covenant community gave way to a Christian presence, represented by a range of Christian societies engaged in various aspects of the missionary task. In the late nineteenth century, people's concerns broadened and many agencies of the church became more concerned to offer a social gospel than the old dogmatic one. The Christian minister was becoming an organization man rather than a pastor of the local body of Christ. He was the mechanic who cared for a

"We are living in a new world and evangelicals do not seem to have discovered it. The immense development of the manufacturing industries, the wider separation of classes in great towns. . . the new relations that have grown up between the employers and the employed, the spread of popular education, the growth of a vast popular literature, the increased political power of the masses of the people, the gradual decay of the old aristocratic organization of society, and the advance in many forms of the spirit of democracy have urgently demanded fresh applications of the eternal ideas of the Christian Faith to conduct."

R.W. DALE (1829–95), the Birmingham Congregational leader

THE OXFORD MOVEMENT

Michael Hennell

The Oxford Movement within the Anglican church aimed at making real the clause in the Creed, 'I believe in one holy catholic and apostolic church.' The movement, also known as the Tractarian Revival, had its roots in the High Church movement of the seventeenth century. From this movement the 'Tractarians' derived their interpretation of the doctrine of apostolic succession. They believed that it was wrong to recognize the ministers of non-episcopal churches.

"There seems about the Church of England a want of antiquity, system, fullness, intelligence, order, strength, unity . . ."

HENRY MANNING, later Cardinal Manning, criticizes Anglicanism in 1846

The beauty of holiness

The Oxford Movement also looked back to the church of the first four centuries, which they believed placed more emphasis on the authority of the tradition of the church than on that of the Bible. They shared with seventeenth-century Anglicans a sacramental attitude towards nature and the world, and the belief that only the best is good enough for God. This made them pay careful attention to church furnishings and church services. They were also influenced by the Romantic Movement. Some feared that a second French Revolution might cross the Channel, bringing atheism and democracy with it, and sweeping away the God-given authority of the king and the bishops.

All this is found in John Keble, a country clergyman with poetic gifts, and an early leader of the movement. He firmly believed in tradition, in the catholic, apostolic church and its apostolic ministry. He preached in his assize sermon (1833) that the government had no right to suppress bishoprics in Ireland or England. He opposed the Reform Bill of 1832. But above all he was a sacramentalist. His hymnal, *The Christian Year* (1827), shows that feeling and emotion are central to Tractarianism. In its own way the Oxford Movement was as much a revival as the Evangelical Movement which preceded it.

The Oxford Movement began in Oriel College, Oxford, which had the highest academic reputation among the colleges. Keble was a Fellow from 1811 to 1823. J.H. Newman, E.B. Pusey, Herrell Froude and Robert Wilberforce joined him to form the initial group. Pusey insisted on keeping a little apart from the others.

Events in the late twenties and early thirties made this group determined to declare themselves publicly. In 1828 the restrictive Test and Corporation Acts were repealed which meant a better deal for dissenters. In 1829 Roman Catholic Emancipation became law, which improved the position of Roman Catholics. In 1830 the disestablishment of the church of England seemed a distinct possibility. Keble and his friends asked: 'If the church is disestablished . . . on what grounds has it a right to be heard, over against the Roman Catholics on the one hand and the dissenters on the other?' Their own answer was that the Church of England is nearer the purity of the early church than the corrupt Church of Rome; and that it was a true church because Anglican clergy were episcopally ordained and visibly within the apostolic succession, as dissenting ministers were not.

Soon after Keble's assize sermon on 14 July 1833, the group had set out to show that the church was completely separate from the state. Newman, Keble and Froude published their views in a series of *Tracts* setting out the nature of the church. The first, by Newman himself, claimed that the church's authority was guaranteed by its apostolic descent. The early tracts were brief and pithy, but changed in character when Pusey wrote one on fasting. More important than the tracts were Newman's sermons, Keble's poetry and Pusey's scholarship.

As support for the Reformation grew stronger among evangelicals, a Romeward wing formed among some of the younger Tractarians. Newman's *Tract 90* was an attempt to keep this group in the Church of England, by showing that the Anglican Thirty-Nine Articles could be interpreted in a Catholic sense. This caused a furore. The bishop of Oxford forbade the publication of further tracts. In 1845 Newman was received into the Church of Rome, followed in 1851 by Robert Wilberforce and Henry Manning.

A medieval revival

The original Tractarians showed no special interest in ritual. Two Cambridge undergraduates, J.M. Neale and B. Webb, started a society to revive interest in church architecture, the internal arrangement of churches and medieval ritual. Their magazine, *The Ecclesiologist*, had a wider circulation than the *Tracts* and their society had a large and distinguished membership, including two archbishops and sixteen bishops. A pamphlet of 1844 claimed that Romanism was taught artistically at Cambridge. Whereas it was propagated theoretically in tracts at Oxford, it was *sculptured, painted* and *graven* at Cambridge.

Clergy influenced by the movement went on to work in east London, Leeds and other industrial areas. These 'Anglo-Catholics' believed that to reach scarcely literate congregations Catholic truth required Catholic ritual. Stewart Headlam founded the 'Guild of St Matthew' in 1877 to link Christian Socialists and Anglo-Catholics. Charles Gore edited the critical essays in *Lux Mundi* in 1889, which led an increasing number of Anglo-Catholics to accept biblical criticism. Robert Aitken and G.H. Wilkinson broke away from Keble's restrictions on popular preaching and conducted evangelistic missions. Though no bishop was appointed from the Tractarians until 1854 the successors of the Oxford Movement dominated the Anglican Church in England for the first half of the twentieth century and are predominant in most of the Anglican churches of the British Commonwealth.

Anglo-Catholics have stressed the church, ministry and sacraments. The doctrine of apostolic succession has been a stumbling-block in the way of reunion with non-episcopal churches. Controversy has arisen over the sacraments of baptism and the eucharist, and made the whole Church of England put more emphasis on the sacraments. The Tractarians' main lasting contribution is in worship. They restored a sense of reverence. They restored to Anglicanism such features as religious communities, retreats, pilgrimages, the sacrament of confession, the reading of devotional books, and a pattern of disciplined prayer and regular communion for ordinary Christians.

Part of the richly decorated interior of All Saints, Margaret Street, London. In the wake of the Oxford Movement came a revival of medieval traditions in church architecture and ritual. This church was designed by the architect William Butterfield.

CARDINAL NEWMAN

Michael Hennell

John Henry Newman (1801–90) was a leader of the Oxford Movement, and later a cardinal of the Roman Catholic church. His father, an evangelical banker, sent him to a private school at Ealing. At sixteen he had a conversion experience through the influence of one of the masters. Newman was never a typical evangelical. From his reading he gained 'a zealous faith in the Holy Trinity'. He seems never to have believed in 'justification by faith'.

Newman went up to Trinity College, Oxford, in 1817; in 1822 he was elected a Fellow of Oriel. He was ordained in 1824. In 1828 he was made vicar of St Mary's, Oxford.

His views changed rapidly under the influence of friends. Chief of these was Hurrell Froude who 'made me look with admiration towards Rome and . . . dislike the Reformation'. In the winter of 1832–3 Newman and Froude went on a tour of the Mediterranean, during which Newman wrote his poem *Lead kindly Light.* They were back in Oxford in time for Keble's assize sermon in July 1833.

Newman immediately became the leader of the Oxford Movement by his sermons in St Mary's (*Parochial and plain Sermons*), by the twenty-four *Tracts for the Time* which he wrote, and by his books. Newman tried to show that the Church of England had steered a middle way between Roman Catholicism and Protestantism. He gradually became convinced that the only true successors of the early Christian theologians were in the Roman Catholic church. He wrote *Tract 90* in 1841 to show that the Thirty-Nine Articles can be interpreted in the spirit of the Catholic church. This created an uproar. The bishop of Oxford forbade Newman to publish further tracts. The Anglican-Lutheran alliance, which resulted in setting up a bishopric in Jerusalem, further alarmed Newman about the Protestant leanings of Anglicanism. In 1843 he resigned from St Mary's after preaching a sermon on 'The parting of friends'. Two years later, in 1845, he was received into the Roman church, and almost immediately published his important 'Essay on the Development of Christian Doctrine'.

After ordination in the Roman Catholic church Newman was appointed head of the Oratory of St Philip Neri in Birmingham. From 1854–58 he was rector of the new Catholic university in Dublin. While there he wrote his *Idea of a University.* In 1864 he responded to an attack by Charles Kingsley in his famous *Apologia Pro Vita Sua.* The following year he wrote the poem, *The Dream of Gerontius* which contains 'Firmly I believe and truly' and 'Praise to the Holiest in the height'. In 1870 came the *Grammar of Assent,* which defended religious belief. He was made a cardinal in 1877 and died in 1890.

Cardinal Newman, caricatured for the Victorian magazine *Vanity Fair*.

great streamlined machine, powerfully tooled up for evangelism and social redemption. But sometimes, large congregations, gathered together in great solid temples of middle-class respectability, possessed neither the common life of the meeting-house nor the urgent concern to rescue the lost. Instead they seemed to perpetuate themselves by some self-justifying principle. Church building programmes increased in every decade of the century, and many full churches, both in city centres and in the suburbs, were presided over by the princes of the Victorian pulpit. An impression of progress and advance was often conveyed. In fact the churches were failing to keep pace with the expanding population.

Church v. chapel

The 1810s and 1820s saw the end of the easy eighteenth-century co-existence between church and chapel. The revival of hostility led to the fierce campaign for the repeal of the Test and Corporation Acts, which achieved success in 1828. Even after repeal, many irritants remained for nonconformists: first the need to secure validity for nonconformist marriages and funerals, then the campaign to repeal church rates, which were finally abolished in 1868. The ancient universities were bastions of Anglican power, and a campaign to open them to nonconformists achieved most of its aims by 1871.

The campaign for the outright disestablishment of the English church (shorn first of the minority churches in Ireland, 1869, and Wales, 1920) ceased to concern late Victorian nonconformists. But the fight between church and chapel over the nature and control of primary education festered on until the outbreak of World War I. This campaign did little credit to either side, but deprived several generations of English children of elementary education. All the labours of the Sunday schools of both sides hardly compensated for that.

Early Victorian nonconformist movements tended to concentrate on the negative campaign of disestablishment. But the free church movement of the 1890s was more missionary minded. It did not campaign so much against the Establishment as for the gospel, and employed Gipsy Smith for a time as its full-time evangelist. It also reflected certain solid achievements concerning unity among the free churches. In 1856 a number of Methodist groups came together in the United Methodist Free Church; Presbyterian union was achieved in 1876, and in 1891 the New Connexion of General Baptists finally united with the particular Baptists.

A Victorian family on their way to chapel. In the Victorian period it became 'respectable' for the middle classes to attend church or chapel.

But at the end of the nineteenth century the rift between church and chapel in English society still ran very deep. It was not simply 'the chapels of the industrial revolution confronting the churches of the rural squirarchy'; urban Anglicanism and rural dissent were equally part of the conflict.

'Church' meant not only bishops parishes and the *Book of Common Prayer*, but also deference to 'the Establishment' in both church and state. 'Chapel' stood for two forms of dissent: the older, more loosely organized, congregational Christianity, principally of the Baptists and Congregationalists; and the newer, more centrally organized, evangelicalism of the various brands of Methodism. Chapel religion had made such advances in the early nineteenth century that nonconformists became more and more ambitious to secure equal rights with Anglicans in what was becoming a pluralist and a largely secular state.

Protestant v. Catholic

Only slowly in Victorian England did Catholic–Protestant antipathy decrease. From Stuart times onwards it had been easy to rouse a popular mob to campaign under the banner of 'no popery'. The most dramatic occasion was the Gordon Riots in 1780, when a mob under Lord George Gordon held the city of London in terror, demanding the repeal of a moderate Act of Catholic Relief.

Catholic emancipation increased Protestant suspicions in 1829, and a further anti-Catholic outburst occurred in the 1840s when the British government increased its grant in support of a Roman Catholic seminary in Ireland. The climax of anti-Catholicism came in 1850 when the re-establishment of the Roman Catholic hierarchy in England was regarded as a 'papal aggression' upon Protestant England. John Kensit and the Protestant Truth Society in the 1890s provided a further focus for Protestant feelings, but their concern was initially with the growth of ritualism within the Church of England. The contest was violent and Kensit himself was fatally wounded in a religious riot in Liverpool in 1902.

Throughout the period, anti-catholicism was supported by fictional literature, dating back to M.G. Lewis's *The Monk*, 'the original horror novel—spine-chilling and suspenseful', in 1796. Even in the midst of a most moral society, pornography was permissible as long as the perversity was perpetrated by Catholics—and preferably by monks and nuns. Books in the traditions of *The Female Jesuit or the Spy in the Family* (1851), *The Awful Disclosures of Maria Monk* (1836), and *Geralda, The Demon Nun*, continued to appear up to World War I. Catholicism was portrayed as un-English, priest-ridden and ruled over by a capricious but all-powered pope. The word of a Roman Catholic could not be relied upon, and the work of the Jesuits was a byword for sinister duplicity.

The growth of Catholic sentiment within the English church formed part of the same problem.

C. H. SPURGEON

D. W. Bebbington

Charles Haddon Spurgeon (1834–92) was a celebrated Victorian Baptist preacher. His father and grandfather were independent ministers. Spurgeon was converted while listening to a Primitive Methodist local preacher in January 1850. He was baptized and became a Baptist village-preacher in Cambridgeshire. In 1854, before his twentieth birthday, he became Baptist pastor at New Park Street Chapel, Southwark (London).

Spurgeon quickly gained fame for his directness in preaching, which seemed to some to border on irreverence. But the power of his sermons led to many conversions. He drew vast congregations to the Exeter Hall, and (to the scandal of some) to the Surrey Gardens Music Hall, when his own chapel was being extended.

From 1861 until 1891 Spurgeon preached in the specially-erected Metropolitan Tabernacle, which seated 6000. Associated with the Tabernacle were a Pastors' College which trained nearly 900 men before Spurgeon's death, a Colportage Society for distributing Christian literature, an orphanage and the monthly magazine *The Sword and the Trowel.*

Spurgeon gloried both in being a Calvinist (although he warmly supported Moody and Sankey), and in being a Baptist. But he left the Baptist Union during the 'Downgrade Controversy' of 1887. He claimed that some Baptist ministers were relaxing their grasp of vital doctrines.

Spurgeon injected his playful humour, common sense and gift for epigram into all his numerous works, which included an extended commentary on the Psalms, *The Treasury of David* (1870–85). His sermons were published weekly until 1917. He was the most popular and the greatest preacher of his age.

C.H. Spurgeon, the 'prince of preachers', as a young man of 21. He built up a congregation of over 6,000 people at his Baptist church in London.

It was worriedly discussed in the highest councils of state. Dr Arnold, the headmaster of Rugby School, said: 'I look upon a Roman Catholic as an enemy in his uniform, I look upon a Tractarian as an enemy disguised as a spy.'

Catholic priorities

Part of the problem was that there was a racial question bound up with the religious question. Anti-catholicism thrived on the threat to employment posed by Irish immigrants. This same migration of labour presented problems to the Catholic hierarchy. Should they use their new-found freedom to build splendid cathedrals—or should they first provide for urban migrants? Priority had to be given to pastoral provision for the faithful. Under Cardinal Wiseman, the Catholic hierarchy was successfully re-established and Catholic life in England was accepted as respectable.

Under Cardinal Manning the three distinct strands of English Catholicism—the old Catholic families, the Irish and the converts—were slowly integrated into one community and moved forward to make a positive impact on English society. Manning lent his support to Joseph Arch, a Primitive Methodist, in his agricultural unionism; served on the royal commission on the housing of the poor; and in 1889 mediated in the London dock strike. He did not forget his own evangelical background, and tried to get his clergy to engage in missions, to conduct open-air services, and to be more missionary minded.

Worldwide vision

In 1846 interdenominational co-operation was promoted through the founding of the Evangelical Alliance. In part a rebirth of the popular ecumenism of the 1780s and 1790s, it also sought to promote 'an enlightened Protestantism against the encroachment

GOD'S GRANDEUR

The world is charged with the grandeur of God.
It will flame out, like shining from shook foil;
It gathers to a greatness, like the ooze of oil
Crushed. Why do men then now not reck his rod?
Generations have trod, have trod, have trod;
And all is seared with trade; bleared, smeared with toil;
And wears man's smudge and shares man's smell: the soil
Is bare now, nor can foot feel, being shod.

And for all this, nature is never spent;
There lives the dearest freshness deep down things;
And though the last lights of the black West went
Oh, morning, at the brown brink eastward, springs—
Because the Holy Ghost over the bent
World broods with warm breast and with ah! bright wings.

GERARD MANLEY HOPKINS

of Popery and Puseyism and to promote the interests of a Scriptural Christianity'. It was an international movement, though differences over the issue of slavery prevented the founding of an American branch until 1867.

Two years prior to the founding of the Evangelical Alliance, George Williams, a London draper, had founded the first branch of what was to become the Young Men's Christian Association, an international organization for evangelism amongst young men. Lay, interdenominational and worldwide in character, it represented one of many initiatives bringing Christians of differing traditions closer together.

In 1895, the World Student Christian Federation brought together the various university interdenominational Christian Unions. Under such influences many of the ablest young men of late Victorian Cambridge offered for missionary service overseas. Both their university and their missionary experience argued against the denominational strait-jacket that had emerged in Victorian England. It was in order to produce a strategy to surmount denominational barriers in promoting world evangelization that the delegates came to the first World Missionary Conference at Edinburgh in 1910. Whatever their meaning in Europe and North America, most denominational differences meant little or nothing in the Third World.

The Evangelicals

Michael Hennell

> *"Hundreds were crying for mercy at once. Some remained in great distress of soul for one hour, some for two, some six, some nine, 12 and 15 hours before the Lord spoke peace in their souls—then they would rise, extend their arms and proclaim the wonderful works of God with such energy that bystanders would be struck in a moment and fall to the ground and roar for the disquieture of their souls."*
>
> *The revival at Redruth, Cornwall, which continued for nine successive days in 1814*

Three groups emerged from the Evangelical Revival in the eighteenth century: the Methodists, separated from the Church of England after Wesley's death; the Calvinists, successors of Whitefield and the Countess of Huntingdon; and the Evangelical Anglicans, of whom the key figures were Samuel Walker of Truro, Henry Venn of Huddersfield and John Newton of Olney.

The Methodists believed that Christ died for all, and that some might attain Christian perfection in this life. The Calvinists, led by Thomas Haweis, believed that Christ died only for the elect, and stressed that human nature was fallen in every aspect (total depravity). The Anglican Evangelicals believed that Christ died for the whole world; they also believed in total depravity, and shared with both the other groups the assurance that their sins were forgiven. They also held that, through Christian missions, the whole world would eventually come to faith in Christ. At that time Christ would return and the millennium would begin.

These were the beliefs of the group of influential evangelicals who became known as the Clapham Sect. They became founder members of the Church Missionary Society, the British and Foreign Bible Society and the Religious Tract Society. They drew away from the Calvinists and nearer to the Methodists, as they emphasized that salvation was for the world and not just for the elect. On the other hand, they rejected Wesley's doctrine of Christian perfection. They also strongly supported the parish system and objected to the tendency of Methodists to set up their own churches in evangelical parishes.

A moral revolution

Wesley had begun a revolution in morals and behaviour among the working classes. This revolution spread to other classes at the beginning of the nineteenth century, through the writings of William Wilberforce and his friend, Hannah More. She wrote simple moral tales, in homely English. Her tracts were distributed by door-to-door salesmen, very cheaply. They circulated in huge numbers. Many were read at court and by the upper classes.

For the privileged classes Wilberforce wrote his book, *A Practical View of the Prevailing Religious System of Professed Christians in the Higher and Middle Classes in this Country contrasted with Real Christianity*. In it he commented on the increase of prosperity, the growth of new cities, the splendour and luxury of the age, and the decline of religion, manners and morals. He reminded the rich of their duties to the poor, and claimed that the only remedy for the selfishness that their wealth encouraged was to turn from their nominal Christianity to the real Christianity to be found in personal commitment.

Seven thousand five hundred copies were sold in six months. Few books have been more influential. The 'reformation of manners' for which Wilberforce had campaigned, took place before his eyes. Cock-fighting, bull- and bear-baiting died out through lack of support. Bookshops selling 'dirty books' had to close down for lack of customers.

In fact within the first twenty years of the nineteenth century a complete change came over the social habits of Britain.

'Victorianism' had arrived twenty years before Victoria came to the throne. The old upper classes together with the new wealthy classes became less frivolous and more conscious of their responsibilities. Some of the coarseness and cruelty which had marred eighteenth-century life disappeared. In 1826 one writer mentioned the courtesy of the people of Petticoat Lane. He walked there with his wife without hearing or seeing anything objectionable. Fifteen years earlier he had been 'blackguarded from one end of the lane to the other'.

A cult of respectability

All was not gain. The cult of respectability was not the same as real Christianity and hypocrisy replaced corruption as the typical sin of the age. The evangelical magazine, *The Record,* is full of advertisements such as this one for a coachman: 'High wages not given. A person who values Christian privileges will be preferred' (privileges doubtless meant permission to attend church and family prayers).

Evangelicals believed in neither democracy nor in trade unions. The French Revolution had frightened them away from such radical ideas. The Evangelicals were willing to do all they could for the poor—but not to allow them to do it for themselves.

Most evangelicals observed Sunday strictly, but the Victorian evangelicals were strictest of all. The Lord's Day Observance Society was founded 1831. Numerous letters and articles in *The Record* protested against Sunday opening of parks, museums and zoological gardens. For six years, the evangelical minister at Cheltenham managed to prevent all passenger trains stopping there on a Sunday.

Evangelical societies made it their business to supply evangelical ordinands and endow evangelical parishes where they might serve. The most important patronage trust was that begun by John Thornton and taken over by the Rev. Charles Simeon. When Simeon died the Simeon Trust had the right to nominate the clergy to twenty-one Anglican positions. These were mainly in large towns such as Bradford and Derby. By 1820, one in twenty of the Anglican clergy were evangelical; by 1830 it was one in eight.

New patterns and parties

Evangelicals gained high office only slowly. Henry Ryder became bishop of Gloucester in 1815; Charles Richard Sumner became bishop of Winchester in 1827; and John Bird Sumner, Archbishop of Canterbury in 1848. These three men produced a new style for bishops. They were much simpler in their life-style than their predecessors. They visited all parts of their dioceses, and took more care over confirmations and ordinations. Their example was followed in the fifties by the 'Palmerston bishops', who were mostly appointed on the advice of the evangelical, Lord Shaftesbury.

Evangelical ranks divided from the 1820s. Edward Irving convinced many evangelicals that they were far too optimistic about the conversion of the world; in fact, the day of judgement was at hand. Christ's second coming would precede the millennium. He believed that the missionary societies were deceiving the elect by talking of the conversion of the world. At the

Lord Shaftesbury, the English evangelical social reformer. He supported numerous causes, including improved factory conditions for the working classes, the regulation of child and female labour, and slum schools.

same time the Calvinist, Robert Haldane, won his campaign against Simeon to prevent the apocrypha from being included in Bibles published by the Bible Society.

Haldane's nephew, Alexander, a young London barrister, shared his uncle's views. When the younger Haldane became the chief owner of the twice-weekly *Record* in 1828, he propagated these strong ideas. Haldane gave strict Calvinism a foothold again in Anglican Evangelicalism. *The Record* also adopted Irving's views on biblical prophecy and the millennium.

The policy of *The Record* was ultra-conservative in politics and theology. Its strongest condemnation was for sabbath-breakers and Roman Catholics, but 'The Recordites' were a strident minority within the Evangelical party. 'The mainsteam party' continued the tradition of Simeon and the Clapham Sect. Among their leaders were Edward Bickersteth, John Venn and J.W. Cunningham. Their journal, which stressed loyalty to the church, was the monthly *Christian Observer*, started in 1802. In spite of theological differences there was no open rift. 'May Meetings' were held in Exeter Hall, London, every year, and were able to accommodate every kind of evangelical society and every kind of evangelical.

Hymns and church music after 1800

John S. Andrews

In the Church of England, hymn-singing was long considered to be illegal. In 1819 Thomas Cotterill, a Sheffield vicar, was charged by a church court for using a hymn-book in services. This test case led to hymn-singing being more or less legally accepted in the church of England. Cotterill's book contained many hymns by James Montgomery, a radical Sheffield journalist who wrote 'Prayer is the soul's sincere desire', and 'Stand up and bless the Lord.'

The Victorian collections

In 1827 Bishop Reginald Heber's *Hymns* was published. The collection had the advantage of the advice of the poet Robert Southey and the novelist Sir Walter Scott. Its literary merits and the authorization it secured from the bishops did much to extend the use of hymns in the Church of England. Heber's collection included his own hymn, 'Brightest and best of the sons of the morning', and his classic missionary hymn, 'From Greenland's icy mountains', as well as Dean Milman's 'Ride on! Ride on in majesty.'

The Oxford Movement revived interest in early Greek and Latin hymns. J.N. Neale translated and adapted many early Christian and medieval hymns. Neale also wrote carols, including 'Good King Wenceslas'. *The Christian Year,* an anthology by John Keble, was first published in 1827, and by 1867 had run through over 100 editions. Some of his hymns are still sung today, amongst them 'New every morning', and 'Sun of my soul'. Cardinal Newman, another leader of the Oxford Movement, wrote 'Lead, kindly Light,' and 'Praise to the Holiest in the height'. The Oxford Movement's emphasis on personal devotion comes over in F.W. Faber's hymn. 'Souls of men, why will ye scatter'. But Victorian sentimentality all too easily took over.

Women hymn-writers

There were many women hymn-writers in the nineteenth century. Some of the best-known children's hymns were written by Mrs C.F. Alexander. She set out basic Christian beliefs in such hymns as 'All things bright and beautiful', 'Once in royal David's city', and 'There is a green hill far away'. For adults she wrote hymns for the church's year. Among other women hymn-writers were Charlotte Elliott ('Just as I am without one plea') and Sarah Adams ('Nearer, my God, to thee'). Catherine Winkworth, the finest translator of German hymns after John Wesley, put into English, 'Now thank we all our God.'

Between 1800 and 1880, 220 hymn-books appeared within the Church of England alone. Many of the authors are now almost forgotten. But many of the 600 hymns of the Presbyterian, Horatius Bonar, are still sung. For example, 'Fill thou my life, O Lord my God', and 'I heard the voice of Jesus say'. So are many of over 760 written by Thomas Kelly, a Church of Ireland minister who wrote 'The Head that once was crowned with thorns'.

Hymns Ancient and Modern (1861) came out of the Oxford Movement; but its wide selection

"All things bright and beautiful All creatures great and small All things wise and wonderful The Lord God made them all."

of hymns finally made it popular with Anglicans of all parties. Total sales of all editions are now well over 150 million. It was revised again and again, and by the end of the century far outstripped its main rivals, the *Hymnal Companion* (1870) and *Church Hymns* (1871). The only collection anywhere near as popular was the *Methodist Hymn Book*, which was revised in 1876.

When the saints . . .

American religious music was less inhibited. The folk tradition of the Baptists in the south and the singing-school movement produced simple but distinctive congregational music. The gospel songs had simple repetitive rhythms and harmonies. Rivals in Kentucky in 1797–1805 inspired negro spirituals, full of longing for release from slavery—for example, 'Swing low, sweet chariot'.

Many American hymns of the nineteenth century, however, reflected a literary, but liberal or Unitarian outlook. This is particularly true of *Hymns of the Spirit* (1864), compiled by Samuel Johnson and Samuel Longfellow, brother of the poet. One of Johnson's hymns expressed his opposition to dogma: 'City of God! how broad and far/Outspread thy walls sublime!' Other similar writers were Oliver Wendell Holmes ('Lord of all being, throned afar'); Frederick Hosmer ('Thy kingdom come! on bended knee'); William Merrill ('Rise up, O men of God'); and Edward Sears ('It came upon the midnight clear'). One of the most popular of these hymns still sung today is 'Dear Lord and Father of mankind', taken from a poem by the Quaker, John Greenleaf Whittier. By contrast, Ray Palmer, author of 'Jesus, these eyes have never seen', wrote in a spirit of deep Christ-centred devotion.

In 1870 Dwight L. Moody and Ira D. Sankey began to collect hymns for their evangelistic campaigns. It is said that fewer people listened to the works of Bach during the entire nineteenth century than heard Sankey sing in 1875. Moody and Sankey's *Sacred Songs and Solos* grew from a sixpenny pamphlet (1873) to a book of 1200 pieces (1903). Its restricted subject-matter and mass-appeal were ideal for revival meetings, but less suitable for ordinary congregations. Some of the better hymns, such as Elizabeth Clephane's 'There were ninety and nine,' have been taken into standard hymn-books. This collection introduced the music of the music-hall into the churches, and brought story-telling into the hymns. The most prolific contributors were Fanny Crosby, P.P. Bliss, Frances Ridley Havergal, and David W. Whittle.

'Her second sermon'; detail from a celebrated anecdotal painting of the nineteenth century. Church-going formed part of the weekly activities of most of the middle classes in England and America.

Music in Britain

Many new hymn-tunes were written in the nineteenth century, but they were often too concerned with harmonic part-writing and chord sequences. John Bacchus Dykes and Sir John Stainer wrote many tunes for *Hymns Ancient and Modern*. Dykes wrote *Nicaea* for 'Holy, holy, holy,' and *Lux Benigna* for 'Lead, kindly Light'. He had a remarkable gift for writing memorable and singable melodies. Stainer's compositions, particularly his oratorio, *The Crucifixion*, still remain popular with church choirs. Sir Joseph Barnby, a well-known choral conductor, and editor of five hymnals, wrote over 200 hymn-tunes, including *Laudes Domini* for 'When morning gilds the skies'.

Samuel Sebastian Wesley, Charles Wesley's grandson, was an influential cathedral organist who composed fine anthems, such as *The Wilderness*, and many hymn-tunes, and did much to improve the music of the church. *Ancient and Modern* gave each hymn its own 'proper' tune. It was not the first book to do so; but it made this common practice.

It was the poet, Robert Bridges, who in his *Yattendon Hymnal* (1895–99) set a new high standard in tunes and words for hymns. He reacted against the rather cloying tunes of Dykes and Barnby. German chorales and old psalm-tunes, rediscovered by Bridges and others, were gathered into *The English Hymnal* (1906) by Ralph Vaughan Williams. He contributed strong tunes of his own, such as *Sine Nomine* and *King's Weston*, and also adapted folk melodies for it.

During the second half of the nineteenth century the free churches, though still heavily influenced by Watts and Wesley, shaped their hymn-books along the lines of *Ancient and Modern*. They gave a lead Anglicans could not ignore in getting the entire congregation to sing.

In Scotland only psalms were sung until the mid-nineteenth century. When hymns were introduced, they mainly used English tunes. On the other hand, the Evangelical Revival released a stream of haunting tunes in Wales.

From the second half of the century English Roman Catholics involved their congregations in hymn-singing. F.W.Faber, one of their most prolific authors, aimed at providing the Catholic church with a hymn book which would do for their services what Wesley and Watts had done for Protestant worship. Later in the century there was a revival of authentic plainsong— 'Gregorian chant'. This consisted of a vast repertory of unharmonized music intended for the use of trained choirs singing the Roman liturgy.

Young children sing Sunday school hymns at their church open to the elements.

A crusade among equals

Janette Bohi

When the Frenchman Alexis de Tocqueville visited the United States in the 1830s, the religious life of the country was the first thing that caught his attention. The longer he stayed, the more he understood of how religion influenced the politics of the country.

A Methodist field-preacher gathers a crowd in the United States. Field-preachers made a great contribution to American Protestantism.

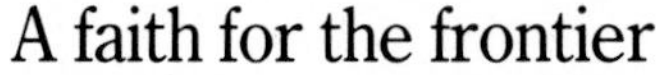

A faith for the frontier

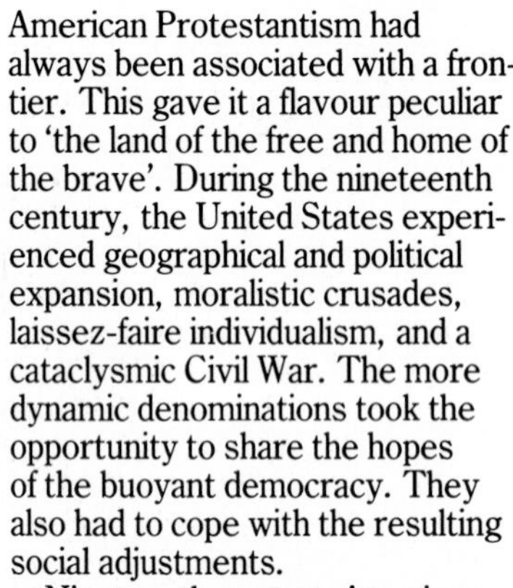

American Protestantism had always been associated with a frontier. This gave it a flavour peculiar to 'the land of the free and home of the brave'. During the nineteenth century, the United States experienced geographical and political expansion, moralistic crusades, laissez-faire individualism, and a cataclysmic Civil War. The more dynamic denominations took the opportunity to share the hopes of the buoyant democracy. They also had to cope with the resulting social adjustments.

Nineteenth-century American Protestantism responded to the geographical and social differences it met across the country. It responded with two merging forces—Christian revivalism and democratic nationalism. The stage was set for 'a crusade among equals', as a second Great Awakening.

By 1800 there were manifestations of a second Awakening. Lyman Beecher, a Congregational-Presbyterian minister, and Timothy Dwight, president of Yale, initiated the crusade that was to continue for seven decades. The Presbyterian James McGready, and the Methodist circuit-rider Peter Cartwright, carried the torch of revival to frontier. There they popularized the idea of holding 'camp meetings'. In 1801 Presbyterians and Methodists staged the Cane Ridge meeting in Kentucky; and Baptists joined Methodists in carrying the Awakening over the mountains into the Old Southwest. They were forming an 'Evangelical United Front'.

These early nineteenth-century revivals put the principle of churches being supported freely by their members (voluntarism) before liturgy, democracy before orthodoxy, and emotion before intellect. By crossing denominational barriers, they enabled the churches to reach the masses. They made the camp meeting a social institution which supported the politics, spirit and mood of American expansion to the West. Revivalism emphasized the work of man in salvation but also stressed the doctrine of the sovereignty of God. It was approved of as a missionary movement both at home and abroad. The idea of a personal encounter with God, preached at revival meetings, gave them a democratic character. The belief that America was being visited by God linked politics and religion. The writer Emerson noted that Europe extended to the Alleghenies but America lay beyond. This was true of American religious history as well as American political history.

Most Protestants were initially sympathetic to the revival movements in the West. But the Methodists and Baptists were more actively involved in this work. Both groups were equally comfortable on the frontier. But they differed about education for the clergy and disagreed on the doctrines of the eternal security of the believer, free will, and grace. Methodist circuit-riders such as

D. L. MOODY

D. J. Tidball

D.L. Moody (1837–99) was the most noted evangelist of his age, though life did not give him a promising start. He was one of nine children born to a Unitarian family in Northfield, Massachusetts. His father died when he was four, leaving the family in a struggling financial position. With little schooling, Moody left home at seventeen to work in his uncle's shoe shop in Boston. There he was converted through his Sunday school teacher, Edward Kimble. But his request for membership of the Mount Vernon Congregational church was turned down for a year because of his ignorance about the Christian faith.

Moving to Chicago in 1865 Moody became a successful businessman and an active worker in Plymouth Congregational church. Every Sunday he filled four pews in the church with those he had recruited. He also successfully recruited members for the Sunday school, and at the age of twenty-three founded his own Sunday school which he served as administrator and recruiter rather than teacher. Soon he devoted himself to Christian work full-time, speaking at Sunday school conventions, preaching to troops, establishing his own church and serving as the president of the YMCA.

But it was Moody's tour of Great Britain (1873–75) which launched his career as a renowned evangelist. It started unpromisingly but by the time he returned to America he was a preacher of international fame. He had already teamed up with Sankey, and Harry Moorehouse had taught him how to preach. When he left England it was to devote his life to conducting revival campaigns. He was never a polished preacher. But the style and organization of his campaigns were to have a long-term influence on mass evangelism.

In his last years Moody established two schools and a regular summer Bible conference at Northfield. In 1886 he founded the Chicago Evangelization Society, known today as the Moody Bible Institute. His death robbed the world of a tireless and colourful evangelist.

Moody and Sankey, the revival leaders, conduct a mass rally at Brooklyn, New York. Ira D. Sankey, the hymnwriter and musician, can be seen sitting at the harmonium on the right.

Francis Asbury inspired many a boy to feel called to preach as he listened to the gospel in a barn or tavern.

By 1855 the Methodist church numbered over a million and a half members, and formed the largest Protestant denomination in the United States. The Baptists appealed particularly to the lower middle class. Their untrained and unpaid farmer-ministers would gather a few families around them, and organize a church, before moving westwards to spread the revival fire. Second in size to the Methodists, the Baptists numbered over a million by 1855.

A camp meeting in America. These open air religious gatherings were frequent in the early nineteenth century. The meeting would take place in the middle of a ring of tents.

This 'crusade among equals', which multiplied the 'sects', alarmed the Unitarian-Universalist Association. Their most illustrious member was the defector from Congregationalism, Ralph Waldo Emerson. But the Methodists and Baptists stoutly defended their orthodoxy—emphasizing their trust in the Bible as the Word of God, and their faithful observance of the sabbath. These unquestioned standards were passed on to their campfire converts.

An army of crusaders

The 'crusade among equals' was conducted in the social arena, too. Every Protestant denomination participated in social action during the twenty-five years before the Civil War. Issues such as women's rights, temperance, prison reform, public education, world peace, and the abolition of slavery thrust American Christians into a multitude of crusades. The evangelistic campaigns of Charles Finney and the founding of hundreds of church-linked parish schools and colleges were other signs of Protestant social concern. Anti-freemasonary, millennialism, spiritualism, Mormonism, and communalism claimed their adherents, while the churches crusaded against sabbath-breaking, the theatre, duelling, prostitution, alcohol, immigration, slums and, most important, Roman Catholicism and slavery. As the century progressed, the denominations became less sophisticated and ordinary Christians played a more important role. There was more emphasis on love and social concern.

The most militant Protestant crusade was against its oldest rival, Roman Catholicism. Hatred of Catholics and of foreigners had been growing steadily in the United States since the seventeenth century. In the nineteenth century popular Protestantism joined with democratic nationalism to produce 'Native Americanism'.

For example, in 1830 the American Bible Society urged Protestants to unite against Catholic influence in the west. The Society pledged to get Bibles into every schoolrooms in the country, to combat the Catholic effort to throw the Word of God out of the classroom. The American Home Missionary Society was dedicated to 'the general welfare of society and the west', and the American and Foreign Christian Union sought to 'diffuse and promote the principles of religious liberty . . . both at home and abroad, wherever a corrupted Christianity exists'. During the American war with Mexico (1846) it was rumoured that there were popish plots to poison US soldiers. In many people's minds, preaching the gospel and purifying the government had come to mean the same thing.

The grapes of wrath

American slavery had always been opposed by humanitarians both inside and outside the church. In

1817 the American Colonization Society put forward a plan to send freed black people to Liberia. Within four years this had won the backing of the leaders of every major Protestant denomination in the USA.

Unfortunately this did not solve the problem. A decade later, Christians from all part of the United States began to use the Bible either to attack or to defend slavery. The churches split over this issue. Northern seminaries became hotbeds of support for the abolition of slavery. The evangelist Charles Finney, though not a radical, supported the abolitionist cause. Southern Methodists declared themselves independent in 1845, in the same year that the Southern Baptist Convention was organized. After 1860 ministers on both the north and south encouraged their young men to serve in their respective armies.

During the American Civil War (1861–65) northern chaplains visited the fields and hospitals, and received $100 a month from Congress. Both sides prayed for victory, the south with more emotion than the north. Julia Ward Howe wrote the 'Battle Hymn of the Republic' in 1861, to explain that God was 'trampling out a vintage where grapes of wrath were stored' and that God's truth (the northern cause) was marching on. The Confederates answered with a prayer to the same God: 'Lay thou their legions low, roll back the ruthless foe; Let the proud spoiler know, God's on our side.'

The surrender of the southern armies brought no reconciliation between the churches of the north and south. Northern churches tended to look upon the Southern churches as needing evangelization, along with the freed slaves. Most Negroes became Baptists or Methodists, because they were freer to express their emotions in those denominations. After the Civil War southern Christians failed to admit the wrong of slavery, and to pledge their loyalty to the Union, because they were committed to the southern cause.

In the post-war decades the 'new frontier' was more urban than rural. American claims to be fulfilling her 'manifest destiny' stretched beyond the continent in imperialism expansion. The day of the crusade among equals was past. John Greenleaf Whittier's 'Centennial Hymn' (1876) aptly expressed that sense of balance towards which the United States had pressed so strenuously for the previous century:

'Our fathers' God! from out whose
  hand
The centuries fall like grains of sand,
We meet today, united, free
And loyal to our land and thee,
To thank thee for the era done,
And trust thee for the opening one.'

A simple church in Dawson City, Yukon, Canada. It was built soon after the gold rush of 1898, for the use of prospectors.

"The state, being democratic in its constitution, and consequently having no religion to which it does or can give any legal sanction, should not and cannot, except by manifest inconsistency, introduce either religious or irreligious teaching into a system of popular education which it authorizes, enforces and for the support of which it taxes all the people in common."

A US Presbyterian defends the American system of secular education in 1870

A WORLD COME OF AGE

Colin Brown

> *"Men find that now they have got rid of an interfering God—a master-magician as I call it—they have to choose between the absolute empire of accident, and a living, immanent, ever-working God."*
>
> CHARLES KINGSLEY *describes the impact of Darwin's theory*

To many people the Victorian age conjures up a picture of church-going, seriousness on Sunday, packed pews and the father of the family questioning his off-spring on the theological points of the morning sermon. The very word 'Victorian' has passed into our language as the epitome of grim, humourless authoritarian-ism, heavy-handed religion and ugliness.

But there is another side to the picture. While the solemn Mr Gladstone was observed to hang on the words of the rawest curate in the pulpit, and volumes of sermons found ready purchasers among the faithful, there were others who were less reverent. The Victorian era *was* an age of authority and conformity. But it was also an age of doubt and of seething discontent. The seeds of doubt that had been sown by the rationalists of the seventeenth century and were nurtured by the sceptics and deists of the eight-eenth century came to full flower in the nineteenth century. The whole fabric of Christianity was called into question. Science, philosophy and history were all called upon to show that the Christian faith no longer had a leg to stand on.

A sophisticated ape?

Were human beings really sophisticated apes? That is what the theory of evolution seemed to be saying. But more important was the reason why it was said. It was bad enough to imply that we were descended from the mon-keys. What made matters worse was that the reasoning behind it suggested that the world was not the work of a wise, loving Creat-or who had planned everything. Instead, all plant and animal life had just evolved naturally, and the fittest had survived. God was an unnecessary hypothesis.

The idea of evolution was not exactly new. It had its advocates from the ancient Greek philoso-pher, Anaximander, right down to Darwin's own grandfather, Erasmus Darwin. In the 1830s, Charles Lyell had published *The Principles of Geology*, in which he argued that the present state of the earth's surface had been brought about by a long and grad-ual development. The chalk cliffs of Dover contained the remains of sea creatures which had been deposited over many centuries. It was claimed that the fossils found at places such as Whitby and Lyme Regis dated back an almost incalculable length of time. In 1844 the idea of evolution was extended from geology to the whole of animal life in *The Vestiges of the Natural History of Creation*, published anonymously by Robert Chambers. But the crisis came to a head with the publication of Darwin's *The Origin of Species* in 1859.

Charles Darwin (1809–82) had studied medicine at Edinburgh and theology at Cambridge—but neith-er with conspicuous success. In the 1830s he sailed as a naturalist on *H.M.S. Beagle* on a survey expedition to South America. For years he pondered his theories. At last he was stung into action, when he received a manuscript from A. R. Wallace outlining ideas similar to his own. They published a joint paper which paved the way for Darwin's masterpiece.

The creation story in Genesis 1 tells how God created the world in six days and rested on the seventh. The evolutionists were now saying that the world had evolved over millions of years, possibly from a single prototype being. To explain how life had developed, Darwin set out the principle of natural selection or, more bluntly, the survival of the fittest. In order to survive, he said, plants and animals have to prey upon each other. To cope with their environment they have to develop new capacities. Where such capacities become a permanent feature, a new species evolves.

Darwin's work met with a mixed reception. Darwin himself was not free from nagging doubts. At the meeting of the British Association in Oxford in 1860, the bishop of Oxford, 'Soapy Sam' Wilberforce, treated his audience to a display of sarcastic wit, ridiculing the new ideas. But the bishop found more than his match in T. H. Huxley. Huxley took the stance of a humble scientist who faced facts rather than indulging in fine speaking and dogma, and persuasively argued the case for evolution. In the following years it was Huxley, as much as anyone, who gave the evolutionary theory the stamp of scientific orthodoxy.

Huxley also coined the word 'agnosticism'. There were many -isms that claimed definite knowledge of all kinds of things. Huxley wanted a word to express the state of not knowing. Rather than adopt the point-blank denial of God of the atheist, Huxley said that he just did not know, and was not in a position to know. In *The Origin of Species* Darwin had left room for belief in the Creator. In its sequel, *The Descent of Man* (1871), he was more openly agnostic. But in spite of everything, when Darwin died, he was duly buried in Westminster Abbey.

Charles Darwin was attacked and ridiculed for his theory of evolution. This cartoon pictured him as an ape himself.

Public reaction to the theory of evolution ranged from outright hostility to wild enthusiasm. All kinds of people tried to jump on the band-wagon, using 'evolution' to justify whatever they happened to believe. Karl Marx declared that Darwin had provided the biological basis for communism. But, equally, capitalists such as Andrew Carnegie and J. D. Rockefeller appealed to 'evolution' to justify the growth of big business.

A monstrous error?

Among Christian leaders, C. H. Spurgeon pronounced the theory of evolution a monstrous error, which would be ridiculed before another twenty years. Others were cautiously in favour. Frederick Temple, who later became Archbishop of Canterbury, was fairly typical of this attitude. He held that the concept of evolution left the argument for an intelligent Creator and Governor

Immanuel Kant, the German philosopher, claimed there were fatal flaws in traditional arguments for the existence of God.

of the earth stronger than ever. The world was not just a series of accidents. The old argument from design to belief in God could be restated in a dynamic way.

The Scottish freechurchman, Henry Drummond, who helped bring the evangelists Sankey and Moody to Britain, applied the idea of the survival of the fittest in a novel way. Even in the animal world, survival is not simply a matter of stealth and strength. Care and compassion play an important part; the gospel of Christ is essential to human survival.

At first sight the idea of evolution seemed flatly to contradict the book of Genesis. For centuries Christians had read Genesis 1 as if it had been a newspaper account of what had happened, step by step. Many Bibles were printed with marginal notes stating that the world was created in the year 4004 BC (the date worked out by Archbishop Ussher).

After Darwin, there were many who continued in these beliefs. But others began to ask whether their reading had not been too rigidly literal. After all, there were two creation narratives in Genesis, both giving a rather different slant. Could it be that we are not intended to take these stories as exact, literal and scientific descriptions of what happened? Do they not rather present profound insights into human relationships with the world and God, in terms which could be understood by pre-scientific people? Could it not be that, in describing the origin of the world, Genesis had to use a certain amount of symbolism, just as the last book of the Bible uses symbolism to describe the cosmic events of the end of the world?

Since the habit of reading Genesis 1 literally (and often at the expense of Genesis 2 which tended to be ignored) was deeply ingrained it was inevitable that the battle should rage over creation *versus* evolution. It was equally inevitable that many people should exchange an uncritical view of creation for an equally uncritical view of evolution. Today we can take a more objective view. For most Christians it is not so much a case of either/or, but of seeing God's creative action in the processes of evolution. To do this requires a right understanding of the Bible and a right understanding of modern science. It means relating Christian belief, not only t[o] an evolutionary time-scale, but als[o] to relativity.

In the past people have thought of God as a God-of-the-gaps. God and nature were quite separate. For most of the time nature functions quite adequately on its own. God comes into the picture only where there is a break in the processes of nature. The trouble with this view is that the more the scientist is able to explain our life in terms of natural processes, the less room there is for God. In the end God is squeezed out altogether.

But God is not a term of scientific explanation. He is not one cause alongside other natural causes. Rather, he is there working in and through all that goes on in the world. The believer knows from the Bible and in his experience that this is so. It is the unfinished task of twentieth-century theology to show us more clearly how we can think of God against the background of a scientific view of the world.

A world come of age

The debates on science and religion occupied the centre of the stage in mid-Victorian England. Meanwhile, a debate of no less significance was taking place in the universities of Germany throughout the nineteenth century

FRIEDRICH SCHLEIERMACHER

Colin Brown

The life of the German theologian Friedrich Schleiermacher (1768–1834) would make a good subject for a wide-screen film with a cast of thousands. Born into a clergy family, he received a strict pietistic upbringing against which he rebelled. In later life he described himself as a pietist again—but a pietist of a higher order. For a time he was a hospital chaplain in Berlin, where he mixed with the brilliant circle of romantic writers.

As a young professor at Halle, Schleiermacher witnessed the Napoleonic invasions. He fell in love with a married woman, who after much heart-searching decided to stay with her boring husband. He returned to Berlin as a preacher, and professor at the newly-founded university.

The work of Schleiermacher's later years has to be seen against the background of the rise of Prussia. With the defeat of Napoleon a new Prussia emerged as the foundation of the new Germany. Schleiermacher was tireless as a patriotic preacher. He also keenly commended uniting the Protestant church in Germany. This would form part of the programme for national renewal.

It has been said that Schleiermacher did not found a school of thought but an era. He was the first great theological thinker after Kant. In effect he accepted Kant's prohibition on metaphysical speculation. Schleiermacher was also a pioneer of biblical criticism. In this approach he steered a middle way between secular philosophy and orthodox Christianity, by taking religious *experience* as his starting-point.

Schleiermacher saw the essence of religion in experience; and the essence of experience in the believer's sense of absolute dependence. He made this in turn the key to every other Christian doctrine. God is that on which we feel dependent. Sin is a failure of our sense of dependence. Christ is the man who was utterly dependent upon God in every thought, word and action. This dependence added up to an existence of God in him. Christ's mission was to communicate this sense of dependence to others.

In saying all this Schleiermacher anticipated by over a century some of the radical views of Paul Tillich and others who base their ideology on human experience. Schleiermacher has been criticized for relying too much on religious experience. The question has also to be asked whether he did not take too narrow a view of it. By reducing it to a single idea, he was rather like Procrustes, of Greek mythology, who stretched those who were too short for his bed to make them fit. And those who were too long he cut down to size.

Already, before the opening of the century, Immanuel Kant (1724–1804) had flung down the gauntlet.

Previously, philosophers had held that God's existence could be proved by various rational arguments. Kant swept all these away—or at least he thought that he had. In addition, he argued that the human mind was only equipped to grapple with the objects that we see around us, which exist in time and space. Once we try to think about any kind of reality which might lie beyond the objects in time and space, we land ourselves in all kinds of contradictions. Therefore it is impossible to think coherently about God. If God is to play any part at all it is in the area of morals. There God is necessary—if there is to be any kind of after-life where virtue can be rewarded. Religion is useful for the simple and uneducated. But it can never be a substitute for philosophy. We should not do good because God says so; we should do good for its own sake. Human reason is our only authority and guide.

Kant regarded his philosophy as a second Copernican revolution. This is rather ironical. Copernicus had inaugurated a new era, by teaching that the earth is not the centre of the universe. Instead, it rotates around the sun. Kant's philosophical revolution took humanity as its starting-point. It began by setting out the scope and limitations of human knowledge. This approach was revolutionary (though Kant was merely completing a process begun by Descartes over a century before). But the irony is that Kant was doing the opposite of Copernicus. He was placing mankind in the centre of his universe and making everything else rotate around him.

Georg Hegel, the philosopher who led the German idealist movement. For Hegel, religion was simply a pictorial and imaginative way of representing the truth of philosophy.

It is often the case with philosophers that what they hand out as a solution is only the old problem in another form. Certainly Kant put his finger on numerous weaknesses in the old approach of philosophy to religion. But to reject the old-fashioned proofs for the existence of God is simply to see the flaws in the logic of particular arguments. It still leaves unanswered the question of whether God can be known in some other way. To say that our minds think in terms of time and space is not the same as saying that we can have no insight into what lies behind our existence in time and space.

If we recognize that God is not an object of time and space, but that our language is geared to think in terms of time and space, it is inevitable that our language about God uses a great deal of symbolism. When Jesus said that the kingdom of God was like this or that, he was drawing on picture language to convey truths that could not be put in any way but by symbols.

The fact is that we do not have direct access to God—not even in the Bible. We do not see God directly as he is in himself. Our knowledge of him is always *mediated* by events, experiences and words. Without the words of the Bible there could be no revelation. The theory of evolution initiated an on-going debate as to how we should think of God in relation to science. In a similar way Kant began a debate on how we should think of God in the light of our existence in time and space, the limitations of the human mind and the nature of our language. The debate is still going on today.

God a 'world-spirit'

In the meantime, the attempt to outflank Kant was a major preoccupation of nineteenth-century thinkers. In theology, Schleiermacher looked for a new approach which accepted Kant's criticisms of the proofs for the existence of God and his strictures on the limitations of human thought. His answer lay in basing theology on religious experience.

The 'Absolute Idealism' of philosophers such as G.W.F. Hegel (1770–1831) was partly an attempt to outflank Kant. But it was also partly an attempt to provide an alternative understanding of God to that of orthodox

Christianity. Instead of starting with the individual 'I', the Idealists began with the absolute 'I'. All reality is the manifestation of the Absolute Spirit. God does not exist over and above the world (as in Christian orthodoxy). God is the 'world-spirit' that is to be found in the depths of the world-processes. The world is a manifestation of God.

The end-product of all this was a dynamic pantheism similar to the radicalism of Paul Tillich and Bishop John Robinson's *Honest to God* (1963) of a century later. These different philosophical approaches left their mark on the way in which Jesus Christ is understood. In the writings of Kant and in liberal Protestant theology, Jesus appears as an enlightened teacher of moral religion. In Schleiermacher and Hegel, Jesus appears as the supreme manifestation of the divine Spirit among men and women, and as the agent of the divine being in achieving the oneness of God and humanity.

When Hegel died in a cholera epidemic his followers split into two camps. The right wing were concerned to preserve the teachings of their master more or less as he had left them. The left wing were revisionists and malcontents who ended up by standing Hegel's philosophy on its head.

Ludwig Feuerbach (1804–72) had studied under Hegel. Hegel had regarded all reality as the outworking of the Absolute Spirit. But Feuerbach coolly told his readers that this 'spirit' was none other than nature. He could agree with Schleiermacher that the essence of all religion is a sense of absolute dependence. But that on which humanity depends and feels dependent is simply nature. God is a projection of our own nature that has been purified and freed from all limitations. Theology is simply anthropology, and the knowledge of God is nothing else but the knowledge of ourselves.

Workers unite!

Feuerbach protested that he was not so much an atheist as an 'antitheist'. But this thought was too subtle. His writings were devoured, not by the masses, but by intellectual cliques. The same could not be said of that other one-time devotee of Hegel, Karl Marx (1818–83). Born in the Rhineland to Jewish parents who became Lutherans, Marx was a student of philosophy. After leaving university he became a journalist, but soon fell foul of the authorities on account of his political views.

Marx was expelled from Germany in the year of revolutions, 1848, and found a haven of refuge in London, and a supporter in Friedrich Engels. In London he divided his time between stirring up agitation and gathering evidence in the British Museum for what he intended to be the grand indictment of the capitalist system, *Das Kapital* (1867).

By this time Marx had rejected not only Hegel but Feuerbach as well. Neither the Absolute Spirit nor nature was the basis of reality. The basis of reality was to be found in matter. The history of the human race, then, is the history of how people are related to material things. According to Marx, history is moving relentlessly forwards in the direction of the communist society. Up to this point, all history is the history of class struggle. When the communist society is reached, private property will be a thing of the past, and the state itself will manage everything.

The political programme had already been announced by Marx and his patron, Engels, in *The Communist Manifesto* (1848). The authors called upon the downtrodden proletariat to unite

---

"The Communists disdain to conceal their views and aims. They openly declare that their ends can be attained only by the forcible overthrow of all existing conditions. Let the ruling classes tremble at a communist revolution. The proletarians have nothing to lose but their chains. They have a world to win. Working men of all countries, unite!"

K. MARX and F. ENGELS, Manifesto of the Communist Party, *1848*

---

in revolution to overthrow the existing order and usher in the new society. Bertrand Russell once remarked that, although Marx claimed to be an atheist, he had an optimism about the outcome of history which only a believer in God could justify.

God is dead

An atheist with a more individualistic approach was Friedrich Nietzsche (1844–1900). Whereas Marx was the prophet of communism, Nietzsche was adopted as a prophet of their new order by the Nazis in the 1930s. Nietzsche regarded himself as a prophet of the death of God, and a spokesman for liberated humanity. Since God is dead, humanity must go it alone. We must make up our own rules and values as we go along. Virtues which were prized by Christianity must be discarded, as they tend to preserve the weak and ailing. What is needed is a reassessment of all values and a will to impose new values on others, whether they want them or not.

> *"The most important of more recent events—that 'God is dead', that the belief in the Christian God has become unworthy of belief—already begins to cast its first shadows over Europe."*
>
> *FRIEDRICH NIETZSCHE*

A thinker who saw clearly the dangerous way in which political and even church systems were developing was the Danish writer Søren Kierkegaard (1813–55). In his lifetime he was little known beyond the borders of his native Denmark. It was only in the twentieth century, as his writings began to be translated, that his real significance came to be appreciated.

Kierkegaard had a horror of systems. He was also acutely aware of the danger of trying to manipulate God. We must never forget that God is *other*. He exists on a different plane and in a different way from ourselves. It is therefore folly to try to prove his existence by rational arguments. To be known directly is the mark of an idol—not the living God.

God is known as he makes himself known. He does so in Jesus Christ. But because he takes on human form and speaks to us in human words, God comes to us in Christ *incognito*. We can know him—but we can only do so in faith. The faith that counts is one which is willing to put all at risk for God and lead a life of personal discipleship. This was Kierkegaard's answer to the totalitarian schemes of idealist philosophy and of church politics. It is an answer which the twentieth century has repeatedly forgotten, but which has to be re-learned in every generation.

The Bible under fire

In the nineteenth century the Christian faith found itself challenged from three directions: from science in the shape of the theory of evolution, from philosophy in the form of alternative world-views intended to make belief in God obsolete, and from history in the guise of biblical criticism. If the truth of the Bible could be shown to be doubtful, then there would be nothing left on which Christian faith could stand.

As the nineteenth century wore on, the Old Testament came increasingly under fire. It was widely assumed that the patriarchs Abraham, Isaac and Jacob were mythical figures, or perhaps titles of tribes associated with particular names. Many questioned whether Moses had ever lived.

The most influential critic of all, Julius Wellhausen (1844–1918), held that Hebrew religion had undergone a development from the primitive stories of nomadic times to the elaborate, institutionalized ritualism of the period of the centuries before the birth of Jesus. He claimed to find various sources behind the Old Testament law, which he dated to different stages of the history of Israel. Scholars of this outlook saw the Old Testament as a patchwork of pieces which owed their shape and texture to outside influences.

But the central issue of biblical criticism concerned the figure of Christ. The quest of the historical Jesus'—the supposed picture of Jesus as he really was, behind the theology of the New Testament—dates back to the English deists in the eighteenth century. Among the early German writers in this tradition was H.S. Reimarus. He saw Jesus as an earnest Galilean teacher, who met an untimely end because he got his earnest moral teaching mixed up with the idea that the kingdom of God meant the setting up of a new political state in which God was King. After the crucifixion, he said, the disciples put out the story that Jesus had risen from the dead and would come again. The whole thing was a fraud, committed for material gain.

Another writer who took a sceptical view was D.F. Strauss. In his famous *Life of Jesus* (1835–36) Strauss dismissed all the supernatural and messianic elements in the Gospels as myth. In Catholic France, J.E. Renan's *Life of Jesus* (1836), and in Protestant England J.R. Seeley's *Ecce Homo* (1865), both took a more positive view of the historical contents of the Gospel stories. But both tried to eliminate the supernatural, and reduced Jesus merely to a magnetic teacher.

Perhaps the most notorious of the nineteenth-century critics was Strauss's former teacher, F.C. Baur (1792–1860). Baur worked on the assumption that there had been a great conflict in the early church between Peter (whose party stood for a strictly Jewish attitude to the law) and Paul (whose party held a more liberal Greek approach, which set little store by the law and Jewish ritual). On this basis Baur set about deciding which books of the New Testament were genuine. Those which did not appear to reflect this supposed conflict were dismissed as later productions. Thus, only four of Paul's letters could be regarded as genuine: Romans, Galatians and 1 and 2 Corinthians. The rest were all later.

New light on the Bible

But not all nineteenth-century biblical scholarship was negative. Among the positive gains was the less spectacular but steady work of reconstructing the text of the Bible from ancient manuscripts such as the *Codex Sinaiticus,* (which was discovered in a monastery on Mount Sinai). The discovery of new texts and the development of the scientific study of manuscripts confirmed the essential accuracy of the texts on which the older translations of the Bible, such as the *King James' Version* (1611) were based. Prominent in New Testament research were the Cambridge scholars B.F. Westcott, F.J.A. Hort and J.B. Lightfoot. Westcott and Hort's Greek text of the New Testament surpassed all earlier versions. In their hands the historical study of the New Testament was not something negative. The exploration of the language and background history of the New Testament threw fresh light on what the Bible was actually saying. Lightfoot's study of early Christian literature after the New Testament period disproved Baur's late dating of the New Testament books. For it showed that the New Testament must already have been written by the end of the first century.

Archaeology too has confirmed the accuracy of a great deal of the information given in the Bible. This can readily be seen from the writings of a scholar such as Sir

Søren Kierkegaard, the Christian thinker from Copenhagen. He emphasized that Christ can only be known by faith, and is one of the fathers of modern existentialist thinking.

> *"Matthew and Mark and Luke and Holy John Evanished all and gone . . ."*
>
> *ARTHUR HUGH CLOUGH, the English poet, reacts to the rise of biblical criticism*

Detail from a Victorian painting entitled *The Doubt—Can these dry bones live?* (1855). Victorian thinkers were increasingly worried by religious doubts and scepticism.

William Ramsay. His study of the geography and archaeology of the Roman Empire supported the picture painted by Luke in the Acts of the Apostles.

The conclusions of such as Strauss and Baur highlight the danger of building a lot on a little—especially when that little happens to be a preconceived idea. But if Christianity is a historical religion based on events which happened in history, these events are open to the historian to investigate. True, these events contain more than history, and the enquirer must not lose sight of this. But they *have* a historical dimension, which is a subject for historical study. The work of scholars such as Westcott, Hort, Lightfoot and Ramsay showed that Christianity has nothing to fear and everything to gain from balanced historical work.

The theory of evolution, philosophy and biblical criticism threw the church on to the defensive. They seemed to many to be saying that humans were only superior apes; that philosophy puts things in a clearer light which shows that there is nothing but the material; that the Bible is based on fancy. But, as so often in the past, opposition brought out the best in the church. What these movements did was to present problems. In the nineteenth century the church included Christians who were prepared to wrestle with them and give good answers. But each generation must give its own answer. It is up to the church in the twentieth century to take up these questions again and bring God's truth to bear on them.

OUTPOSTS OF EMPIRE

A. F. Walls

Of all the transformations of Christianity which have taken lace since 1789, perhaps the nost remarkable is the shift of its eographical and cultural centre of ravity. In 1789, an observer from Mars might well have assumed Christianity to be the tribal religion f the white peoples (Caucasans). With a few exceptions, eadily explained by historical ircumstances, all the Caucasians f Europe and their descendants n the New World professed Christianity. With a few more xceptions, explained by survival r conquest, no-one else did. Such n observer might have doubts bout the survival of Christianity n Europe. Had the recent revival n Protestant areas come too late o stem the tide of rationalism which was producing, in both Catholic and non-Catholic areas, non-religious interpretation of fe? But at least he could not doubt hat Christianity was identified with Europe and the Europeans.

If the Martian next returned to Earth in the 1970s, he would find Christianity a world religion. It had ecome firmly established in every ontinent, among people of the nost diverse and disparate origins nd cultures. It was still growing, nd most rapidly in the southern ontinents (especially tropical Africa and Latin America). It was eceding only amongst the Caucasans—to whom 200 years before t seemed confined.

Between the Martians's two isits fall events which transormed the relations of East and West, and of North and South: the ndustrial Revolution, the rise and fall of the European empires, and the missionary movement. The relation between these is highly complex, and cannot be explained by any single theory. What is certain is that not only the world, but the church, was changed out of recognition as a result.

By 1789, Europeans knew the outline map of the world much as it is today except for some tentativeness about Australasia and the larger Pacific islands. They knew very little of the interior of any of the continents except their own (if we leave the Middle East and India out of account). Scientific concerns (it was a self-consciously investigatory age) and commercial interests (the quest for both raw materials and markets) prompted greater curiosity about these continents. An important minority also wished to spread the gospel.

Motives for mission

On the whole, Protestant thinkers were slower than others to recognize the implications of these discoveries. When Roman Catholic controversialists asked where were the Protestants' missions, a common orthodox reply was that it was presumptuous to apply to oneself Christ's missionary commission addressed only to apostles. Captain Cook believed that it was unlikely that the faith would ever be preached in the islands he discovered, since it could never be worth anyone's while financially. Devout Anglican churchmen, shocked at the prevalence of Presbyterianism and vice in the American colonies,

Eighteenth-century Spanish-style houses in Rio de Janeiro, Brazil. Spain and Portugal had brought Roman Catholicism to their extensive colonies in South America.

had in 1701 formed the Society for the Propagation of the Gospel. Among the founders, committee and clergy there were always those with a vision for evangelizing neighbouring peoples. But, with rare exceptions, the SPG in the eighteenth century was essentially concerned with the English overseas.

It was in North America that the crucial experience came. The line connecting the Puritan missionary endeavours with the Evangelical movement never quite broke.

Two strands led to a new Protestant world vision. One was prophetic: the thought of the earth 'filled with the knowledge of the Lord as the waters cover the sea'. Jonathan Edwards, for instance, believed this biblical prophecy was near fulfilment. The other strand is evangelical: the sense of God's command to preach the gospel, which broke through theological rigidity and habits of sanctified self-interest. In America these impulses led to a renewed concern for the Indians. In Britain, with no neighbouring non-Christian peoples, but now wide awake to regions overseas, the same thoughts (often coming from American sources) produced a concern for the evangelization of the world.

Belief into action

The new organization—the missionary society—turned prophetic conviction into action. A remarkably wide spectrum of churches and denominations was involved. The tiny Moravian community was the acknowledged leader, not only in time, but in numbers of missionaries in proportion to its membership, and the lengths to which they were prepared to go. Moravian missionaries in the West Indies even sold themselves into slavery.

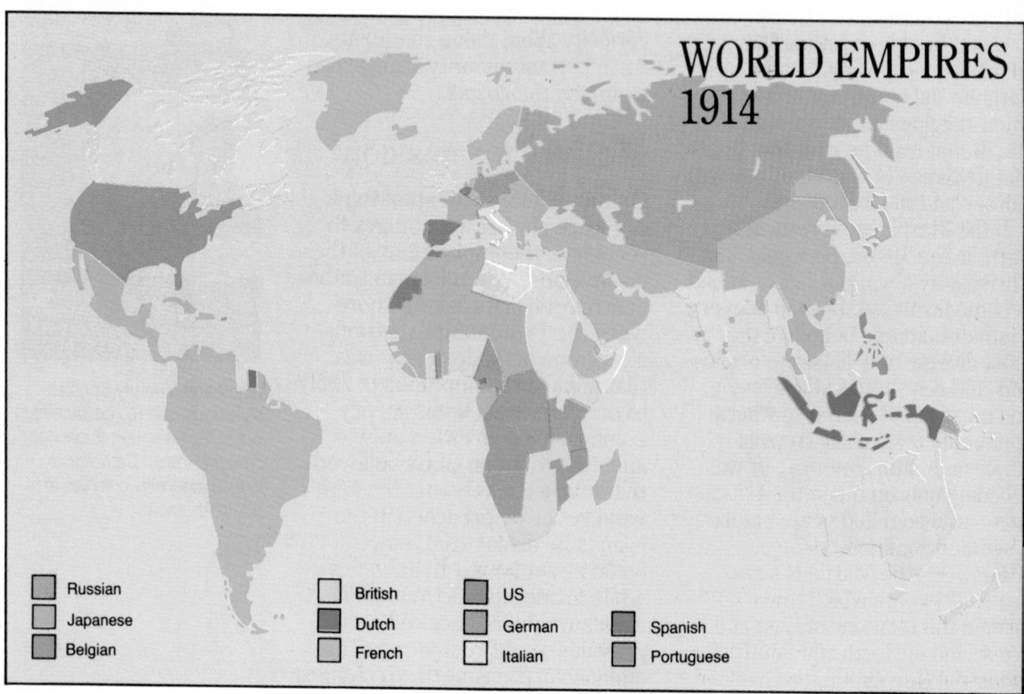

By the 1790s Calvinistic Baptists, Arminian Methodists, impeccable Anglican churchmen and ardent dissenters and seceders in England and Scotland were seeking to 'use means for the conversion of the heathens' (William Carey's phrase). But, with the rarest exceptions, such interests reached only those touched by the Evangelical Revival. For the first two or three decades of the missionary movement, interest in missions was restricted to the Evangelicals.

This is hardly surprising. The Evangelical Revival revolutionized preaching and its objectives. Earnest churchmen, who regarded the clergyman's task as being to nurture the seed of faith planted at baptism in virtually all members of his parish, could not easily adjust to the thought of preaching the gospel in a tribal society. People who inherited a rigid doctrine of predestination, in which God inscrutably made up his elect, saw no reason to concern themselves with why there were evidently no elect in India or China. But the Evangelicals saw preaching as calling sinners to God through faith in Christ. They felt a personal responsibility to do this, and saw no difference in principle between 'baptized heathen' in Britain and in non-Christian peoples overseas.

Only in the 1820s and 1830s did interest in overseas missions become a regular feature of British church life generally. This was due partly to the success of the Evangelicals in influencing English and Scottish life. Many of their values were adopted outside their circle. In particular, the idea of Britain as a Christian nation, with Christian responsibilities overseas, took root.

Bishoprics were established in India and elsewhere (none had ever been established in pre-colonial America). The Society for the Propagation of the Gospel enlarged its operations to those of a genuine missionary society. In Scotland, moderate churchmen joined with evangelicals to promote missions, strongly educational in character, under the umbrella of the General Assembly of the Church of Scotland.

Throughout the Victorian era, and long beyond it, overseas missions were taken for granted in the European churches. They were supported by all sections of the church. The Evangelicals and Anglo-Catholics provided the greater part of the interest, funds and personnel. A small but significant 'liberal' missionary movement developed in the early twentieth century, with a more sympathetic approach to other faiths, and a stress on Christian service. Only rarely did doctrinal differences split missionary societies. Until at least the middle of the twentieth century, children in Christian homes and Sunday schools were reared on stories of 'missionary pioneers'.

Following the flag?

The birth of the missionary societies had nothing to do with the protection of British interests abroad. The earliest missions were in fact associated with traditionally radical groups such as the Baptists and supported by people with known revolutionary sympathies, such as the Haldanes. This caused some to fear that they were basically subversive. To this was added the fear that missionary preaching would offend Hindus and Muslims, upset a volatile situation in India, and harm British trade. The semi-official Honourable East India Company, through which British administration and trade was exercised, was not initially well-disposed towards Carey and his colleagues. They had to sail in a

"Firmly relying ourselves on the truth of Christianity, and acknowledging with gratitude the solaces of religion, We disclaim alike the right and the desire to impose Our convictions on any of Our subjects . . ."

Queen Victoria's proclamation of responsibility for governing India, 1858

Danish ship and work from Danish territory.

The situation altered through the changes in British life brought about by the Evangelicals. Charles Grant, who had been radically converted in India, rose to the highest position in the Company. When the Company's charter came up for renewal in 1813, the Evangelicals of the Clapham Sect, briefed by Grant, denounced some aspects of its policy. Not only did the Company not promote the gospel, not only did it hinder missionary work; it positively profited by means of the temple tax and similar institutions for idolatry. Britain should awake to its Christian responsibilities, abolish the tax and, by appointing a bishop and all other means, stand up for the Christian faith.

The outcome was a qualified victory for the Evangelicals. Temple tax was abandoned, and later administrations felt free to intervene against certain Indian religious customs such as *sati* (widow burning). Bishops were appointed, and the system of government chaplains reformed and enlarged. Missions were, with occasional exceptions, unhindered, and often favoured. But anything approaching an official mission to India was carefully avoided. This attitude towards missions remained characteristic of government policy throughout the nineteenth century.

Grants to missions by colonial governments were tied to specific projects, particularly grants-in-aid for education. The largest extension came after World War I, when the colonial powers, especially the British, came to recognize a wider responsibility for education than previously. The cheapest and most efficient way of putting this into practice was to develop a system of funding education by means of grants to the missions.

Nineteenth-century evangelicals soon stopped asking for 'official' backing for missions. They continued, however, to claim that the British owed a debt to Africa on account of the slave trade, and to India on account of the wealth derived from it. What was require[d] was the best that Britain could giv[e] in return. Apart from India, there was little appetite in Britain in the first half of the nineteenth century to acquire new overseas territories, and in the 1840s there wer[e] plans to abandon as many as possible of such expensive luxuries.

The missionary societies fough[t] to keep overseas concerns before the public and the government. They persuaded a reluctant government to fund a philanthropi[c] expedition to the Niger in 1841 to develop agriculture and undercut the slave trade. They lobbied for British support for the little Africa[n] state of Abeokuta, when it was threatened with destruction by its powerful slave-running neighbour, Dahomey. There was little though[t] of acquiring territory for Britain in all this. It was a call for Britain to use its power and influence on behalf of justice, and freedom fro[m] slavery.

The scramble for Afric[a]

When Britain and other European powers moved into the high imperial period and annexed large sections of territory, the missionary interest on the whole went along with it. Sometimes it seemed the best way to deal with an unsatisfactory situation. For instance, Scottish missionaries in Malawi begged for a British protectorate, lest Portuguese misrule spread from Mozambique and increase war and slavery. (When the protectorate was set up, the same missionaries were soon protesting about British maladministration.) John MacKenzie sought a British protectorate for Botswana to stop Cecil Rhodes' British South Africa Company acquiring it.

Sometimes the factors which influenced the great powers in 'the scramble for Africa' also influenced the missionaries. Protestant missionaries feared annexation by a Catholic power and vice versa. Sometimes annexation was seen as opening up to Christian influences territories closed until then; rightly so—for 'closed' areas knew that to admit one sort of white man would ultimately mean admitting them all. European overrule, in Africa at least, was seen by most people as inevitable. Except for some American missions, there is little sign of missionaries opposing in principle the spread of imperial rule.

But relations between missions and colonial governments were not always smooth. Missions were often critical of government actions. Governments were often nervous of missionary activities. The nervousness sometimes extended to excluding missionaries altogether. The Muslim-ruled provinces taken into Northern Nigeria by the British contained many millions of non-Muslims, who had been conquered in holy wars (*jihads*). The British governed them by 'indirect rule' which insulated some of these provinces from missionary activity. This ensured that they became completely Muslim.

The most notable casualties of the age of imperialism were (especially in Africa) the indigenous educated leaders. Most were Christian, brought up under Christian influences, who under earlier conditions had been trained for responsibility. It is not surprising to find such people—for example, James Africanus Beale Horton, Bishop James Johnson, J.E. Caseley Hayford, and the many-sided Afro-West Indian, E.W. Blyden—leading early nationalist and pan-African thought. They made their case by appealing to the Christian faith.

The nationalist movement evolved into the independence movement. Many of the new leaders not only derived from Christian schools the education which made them effective, but also (even when they were critical of existing missionary institutions) drew their inspiration—and their criticisms—from Christian teaching. In India, where Christians made up only a tiny proportion of the population, the Christian colleges often contributed much to the agitations of the 1920s and 1930s. That many of the missionaries sympathized strongly with the national aspirations of their students is very apparent. In fact, some of the bitterest modern critics of missions have been white settlers.

The relation between missions and colonial expansion is complex. Sometimes missions preceded the flag, sometimes they followed it. But one thing is clear. If missions are associated with the rise

A village in Botswana. The European powers were struggling to gain territories in this part of Africa in the late nineteenth century. Scots missionaries requested a British government protectorate for Botswana, to prevent Cecil Rhodes' British South Africa Company from taking it over.

of imperialism, they are equally associated with the factors which brought about its destruction.

Abolishing slavery

In the 1790s the evangelical was marked out as much by a desire for the abolition of the slave trade as by an interest in missions. Inevitably, the two causes marched together.

William Wilberforce, the man who campaigned against the slave trade. At the age of fourteen he wrote a letter to a local paper attacking the evils of slavery.

The Sierra Leone colony was founded by the enterprise of the evangelical 'Clapham Sect', most of whose members also supported the missionary societies. The colony had three aims: to provide a haven for freed slaves: to prove that economics did not dictate the need for the slave trade; and to be a base for missionary operations in Africa.

After the abolition of the British slave trade in 1807, the colony (its capital significantly called Freetown) became the centre to which intercepted slave-ships from all over West Africa were diverted, and their miserable cargoes of slaves landed. From this source came a people who were to be vital for the spread of Christianity in West Africa. By the time of the emancipation of the slaves in British territories (1834), opposition to slavery had become a normal British reaction, just as interest in mission had become part of church life.

But acts of Parliament did not end the slave trade. In the 1830s abolitionists were still led by an evangelical, Sir Thomas Fowell Buxton. They reflected sadly that more slaves than ever were now crossing the Atlantic, and that West Africa was being depopulated by the trade and the wars it encouraged. Buxton, like Wilberforce before him, believed that an economic institution could only be countered by an economic initiative. It burst upon him one day that the solution for Africa lay in developing its own resources: Africa would be reborn by the Bible and the plough.

A substitute for slaver

So came to birth the doctrine of the 'Three Cs'—Christianity, commerce and civilization. The basic idea was that the interests of all three lay in the same direction. Christianity and slavery were irreconcilably opposed. The most effective way of combating the slave trade was to provide an attractive commercial substitute. The development of the export of raw materials from Africa, instead of the export of labour, would in turn involve developing in Africa commercial agriculture and the appropriate technologies—'civiliz tion', in fact, as Buxton understoc it.

These ideals inspired the Niger Expedition of 1841, which was forced by Buxton on the reluctant British government. Three specially designed ships, with hand-picked crews, sailed up the River Niger with instructions to make anti-slavery treaties, set up model farms, and survey the possibilities for technological and commercial development. Some months later the expeditior limped back, its ranks decimated by fever, and little of significance achieved. Buxton was discreditec Except in the eyes of the missionary representatives all that had been proved was that European residence, and consequently 'civilization', was impossible in inland Africa.

But those with missionary interest continued to argue that 'Christianity, commerce and civilization' stood together. In a modest way, the Church Missionary Society was able to prove the effectiveness of the 'Three Cs' in its Yoruba mission, not many yea

WILLIAM WILBERFORCE

D. W. Bebbington

William Wilberforce (1759–1833) is best known for his campaign against the slave trade. He was educated at St John's College, Cambridge, and became MP for his home town of Hull in 1780. During a continental tour in 1784–85 Wilberforce read Philip Doddridge's *Rise and Progress of Religion in the Soul*, and subsequently underwent a spiritual crisis. He emerged a believer in 'real Christianity' centred on Christ's redeeming work. He later contrasted this with nominal religion in his very influential book *A Practical View of the Prevailing Religious System of Professed Christians* (1797).

In 1784 Wilberforce became MP for Yorkshire, a seat which he retained until 1812, when he moved to a safe seat, held until he retired from Parliament in 1825.

His conversion gave Wilberforce the dynamic to lead the campaign against the slave trade, which he had abominated since the age of fourteen. From 1789 on he frequently moved parliamentary resolutions against the British slave trade. After its formal abolition in 1807, he pressed for the enforcement of the ban and for European agreement to prohibit the trade.

As leader of the 'Clapham Sect' of parliamentary evangelicals, Wilberforce also helped to open India to missionaries in 1813, and to protect popular travelling evangelists in Britain from government interference. Wilberforce supported repressive statutes between 1795 and 1819 in his concern to preserve constitutional order. But he was in favour of such changes as moderate parliamentary reform, relief for boy chimney-sweeps and Jeremy Bentham's 'model' prison.

Wilberforce influenced prominent politicians quietly and persuasively—particularly his friend William Pitt, who was Prime Minister in the periods 1783–1801 and 1804–6. He used his charm, tact and eloquence in a political life to which he was sure he had been called by God.

A model of a slave ship, which shows clearly the inhumane way that hundreds of African slaves were confined below deck for the voyage from Africa to America or the West Indies.

after the Niger Expedition. Old chiefs were soon saying that the mission-sponsored cotton industry brought more benefits than all the slave trade.

The Atlantic slave trade was killed by moral, political and economic factors. Attention next turned to the East African slave trade, which was operated by Arabs and Swahili peoples and sometimes favoured by the Portuguese. The British government directed pressure mainly on the Sultan of Zanzibar. But the doctrine of the 'Three Cs' found its last and great-

DAVID LIVINGSTONE

A. F. Walls

> *"I place no value on anything I have or may possess, except in relation to the kingdom of Christ. If anything will advance the interests of the kingdom, it shall be given away or kept, only as by giving or keeping it I shall most promote the glory of him to whom I owe all my hopes in time and eternity."*
>
> *From David Livingstone's journal*

David Livingstone, the missionary and explorer, was born in Blantyre in the industrial west of Scotland in 1813. His parents were poor and godly, members of an independent church. At ten years of age he began work in a local cotton mill, with a book propped up on the machine. By this means, and through night classes, he built up some general education. Converted and convinced that he had a missionary calling, Livingstone studied medicine in Glasgow and London hospitals and theology in England. He was not a promising student—awkward, dour and heavy.

From 1841 to 1856 Livingstone served under the London Missionary Society, starting in South Africa, under the celebrated Robert Moffat, whose daughter he married. David was soon going into uncharted territory, laying the foundation for missions, building relationships, acquiring a knowledge of the geography, transport possibilities, movement of peoples, and the horrible facts of the slave trade.

Livingstone's remarkable travels between 1851 and 1856 included his walk across Africa from west to east, which was readably recorded in *Missionary Travels and Researches in South Africa* (1857) and first established his now legendary reputation. His committee, however, were not convinced of the missionary relevance of such travels, and when he returned to Africa in 1858 it was to lead a British government expedition to explore the River Zambesi ('God's highway into the interior' he called it). The expedition did not prosper and in 1863 it was recalled. Livingstone had failed in his objects, his wife had died, his enthusiasms were questioned.

But he was soon back, this time without European companions. From his landing in Zanzibar in 1866 he continued his quests in the East African interior with incredible endurance until his death in 1873. His African companions carried his body back to the coast, and he was buried in Westminster Abbey.

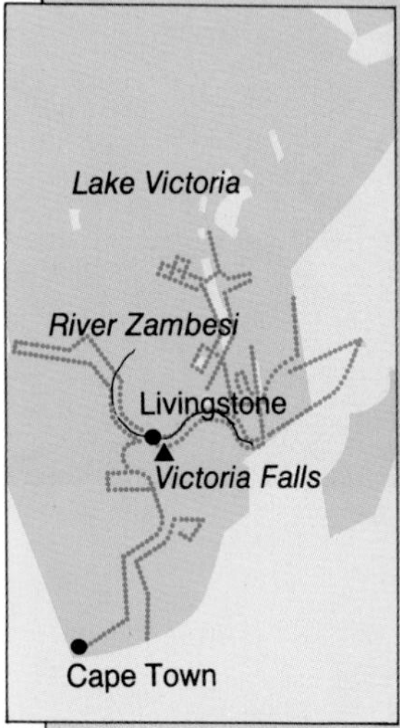

Livingstone's journeys

Livingstone's achievement

As an explorer, Livingstone ranks with the greatest. He walked further—across what is now South Africa, Botswana, Zambia, Mozambique, Malawi, Tanzania and Eastern Zaïre—and recorded better than most of his contemporaries. He held to his early belief in the ultimate unity of all truth, biblical and scientific. But a mastering motive for his journeys was that they could help drain 'the open sore of Africa', the Arab slave trade.

Livingstone came to realize that his early dream that white settlement would cure the ills of the poor of Scotland and of Africa was illusory. But he remained convinced that the slave trade had to be countered with an economic substitute, to lessen its attractiveness. Trade and developed agriculture, accompanying the gospel, could do this. His relations with Africans were excellent; his failures mostly with Europeans. His strategy was not to exploit but to liberate. In this he contrasts with Cecil Rhodes, the other major British figure significant in Central Africa.

Though technically a missionary for only half of his thirty years in Africa, Livingstone saw all his work in the context of a providential plan in which gospel-preaching, the increase of knowledge and the relief of suffering marched together. The Anglican Universities Mission to Central Africa owed its inspiration to this Scots independent (through a speech in Cambridge in 1858). After his death, the Church of Scotland and the Free Church of Scotland opened Central African missions which reflected his ideals and breadth of vision.

David Livingstone, the Scots missionary and explorer, wanted to help drain the 'open sore of Africa'—the Arab slave trade.

The Victoria Falls on the River Zambesi, Zambia. In 1858 Livingstone led a British government expedition to explore the Zambesi—'God's highway into the interior.' Livingstone was the first white man to set eyes on the Victoria Falls. 'No-one can image the beauty of the view from anything witnessed in England. It had never before been seen by European eyes, but scenes so lovely must have been gazed upon by angels in their flight.'

est prophet in David Livingstone. His journeys were based on the conviction that the Arab slave trade could be strangled by alternative commerce.

The other main areas directly affected by slavery were the West Indies and, to a lesser extent, South Africa. The West Indies had been one of the earliest targets for missions. But the slave-owners were deeply hostile to missionary activity, whether evangelistic or educational. Missionaries were generally instructed by their home committees not to attack slavery publicly or to encourage dissidence among the slaves. This did not prevent the prosecution or maltreatment of anti-slavery missionaries such as the Baptist William Knibb in Jamaica or the London Society's John Smith, who died in prison in Demerara while under sentence of death. Missionaries such as Knibb, and stories such as Smith's, provided much of the evidence used by abolitionists in their campaign in Britain.

An encampment on an island on the River Niger, in Mali, West Africa. Sir Thomas Fowell Buxton led an expedition up the Niger in 1841, aiming to set up a Christian culture as an alternative to the slave trade.

The slaves avidly embraced Christianity. They were not always passively obedient: the leaders of the slave revolt of 1831–32 were Jamaican Baptists. When emancipation came in 1834, the chapel bells were rung all through the islands. Only afterwards did the Anglican church, until then on the side of the owners, have a chance to spread in the black community.

'Christianity, commerce and civilization'

By the middle of the century, the belief that the interests of 'Christianity, commerce and civilization' were in harmony brought some missions into actual trading. The Basle Mission developed the idea of trade as a means of self-support in the Gold Coast (modern Ghana) and elsewhere. The Church Missionary Society developed cotton growing in Yorubaland (Nigeria), introduced machinery to process the cotton, provided facilities for training the technologists to maintain the machinery and, with the help of a sympathetic Manchester merchant, arranged an export trade for it. Self-supporting Christian communities emerged in other areas—such as in British Columbia under the extraordinary Henry Duncan.

Later in the century the alliance of Christianity and commerce turned sour. Merchants complained of unfair mission competition, missionaries complained of the evil example of nominally Christian European traders. Alcohol became increasingly important in trade. Travellers reported that the effects of alcohol were just as bad as those of the slave trade in those areas open to trade. They contrasted this with the sober Muslim areas. Mission theory at home was veering away from involvement in trading institutions and towards 'direct' evangelism. The CMS abandoned its institutions associated with trade. However, the 'African churches' which split from the CMS in the 1890s continued to involve themselves in agriculture and trade.

The missions came into direct conflict with trading interests in China. The attempts to force the opium trade on China by Western powers were opposed vigorously by missionaries. Marshall Broomhall of the China Inland Mission constantly wrote against opium trading and government indecision.

Learning and praying

From the first, missions were involved in education. Protestantism was a religion of the Book:

Christian growth without Bible reading would be unthinkable. Also, in many situations, education was the most attractive side of the package on offer. For example, in India, Western education opened up a new intellectual world and, from the 1830s, positions in the administration. In Africa and the Pacific, literacy offered access to the powers which the Europeans displayed. Perhaps no invention has a more revolutionary effect on any society than writing. At any rate, young people came to learn and stayed to pray.

One early result was that peoples in some mission areas became more literate than some levels of Western society. The American mission presses provided the Hawaiians with a wider range of literature than was available in rural America. Freetown, Sierra Leone, had a grammar school in 1845 and a girls' grammar school in 1865. By 1876 Fourah Bay College was affiliated to the University of Durham in England, which made it possible for Africans to take arts and theology degrees in Sierra Leone. The satirical magazine, *Punch,* suggested that Durham would soon affiliate to the London Zoo.

This anecdote illustrates the important fact that on some matters missions were out of step with contemporary Western opinion. From earliest days the missionaries believed that, given the same opportunities, Africans and Pacific islanders would perform equally well with Europeans. In general, this conviction weathered the nineteenth-century theories that the races had different inherent abilities.

Literacy led to a demand for higher education, and in English-speaking areas the English grammar school became the model. Missionary suggestions that subjects such as Greek were unnecessary in Africa were brushed aside: African schools must have all that British schools had. Government officials often suggested that agriculture and technical subjects were as important as the academic, but they could not dim the attractiveness of the grammar school, or seriously modify it. The Scottish missions in central Africa achieved perhaps the most successful marriage of academic, technical and agricultural education.

Only at the end of the nineteenth century did Roman Catholic missions seriously rival Protestants in education. But when they did intervene, it was on a massive scale, using the primary school as an instrument of primary evangelization.

India, with its ancient literary heritage, contrasted strongly with the pre-literate societies. Certainly missionaries from the beginning taught in schools attended by low-caste people. But when Alexander Duff arrived in India in 1830, he decided to work by means of higher education in English. His decision was based on his idea that truth is a unity: the teaching of science, philosophy and Christian doctrine would undermine the foundations of Hinduism.

Duff was assisted by the ferment already proceeding among young Hindu intellectuals, who were disillusioned with old corruptions, rebelling against old institutions, and already influenced by Western rationalists. When the East India Company decided in 1835 to replace Sanskrit and Persian with English as the language of administration, the prospects for his work were further improved. Duff received support from the Hindu liberal Ramohun Roy, and eminent converts such as K.M. Banerjea carried on his work.

The 'Scots colleges' became an important part of missionary operations in India. They offered

The Cinnamon Hall, an old plantation owner's house in Jamaica. The plantation was worked by African slaves until they were emancipated in 1834. This house once belonged to the family of the English writer, Elizabeth Barrett Browning.

West Africa

high academic standards and recruited missionaries of high academic calibre for their staff. But most of their students remained non-Christian, and Hinduism did not crumble, as Duff had hoped. He lived long enough to see the emergence of biblical criticism in Britain and the Bengal Renaissance in India. By the end of the century Western-educated Hindus were turning weapons forged in the West against the Christians.

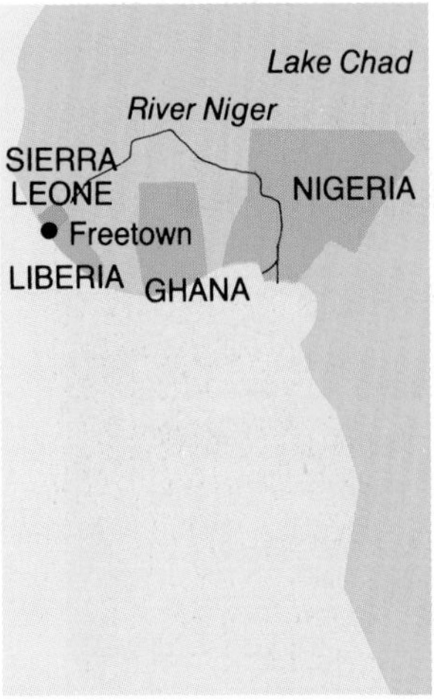

When the modern missionary movement began in the 1790s, its activists had nothing but the prophecies of the Bible and the conversion of a few hundred American Indians to support their endeavour. By 1910 the church had changed out of recognition, and was now rooted in every continent.

The change had come almost imperceptibly. Carey and his colleagues were in India seven years before baptizing their first convert. Disasters abounded. Of more than thirty enthusiastic London missionaries who sailed to the South Seas in 1795, only a handful survived the physical, mental and spiritual strains placed on them.

African missionaries

We have seen how 'Clapham Sect' enterprise founded the Sierra Leone colony. Eleven hundred people of African descent were brought there from America in 1792, to form a 'province of freedom' in Africa. They came as Christians, bringing their own churches and preachers with them. To these people were added the 'recaptives' rescued from slave-ships after 1809—uprooted, disorientated people from all parts of West Africa. It was from these that the first mass movement towards Christianity in modern missionary history took place. Sierra Leone became a self-consciously Christian community, and a literate one. Many missionaries died in the 'White Man's Grave' of Sierra Leone, and as the demand for missions moved to other areas, and particularly to India, fewer missionaries went to Sierra Leone.

But Sierra Leone Christians found their way back to their original homelands as traders. On their initiative the Anglican and Methodist Yoruba missions were begun in Nigeria in the 1840s. When the missionaries arrived, they found the church already there. When most people were deducing from the failure of the Niger Expedition that it was impossible for Europeans to reside in inland Africa, the missionary representatives, J. F. Schön and Samuel Ajayi Crowther, were arguing that Africans must be Africa's evangelists. They pointed to Sierra Leone, where there was a firmly planted church of people who already spoke the various languages of West Africa. Over the next half century, the tiny Christian population of Sierra Leone produced dozens of ministers, missionaries, catechists and agents for the rest of West Africa, and particularly the Niger territories. Dozens more Sierra Leone Christians, as traders, clerks or workmen, first introduced the Christian faith to other places. The United Free Methodists even sent two Sierra Leonean missionaries to Kenya in the 1880s, and Bishop Crowther once planned a Sierra Leone mission to the Congo.

The Sierra Leonean was often regarded as a 'black European'—in dress, speech and customs. If this was true—and in fact Sierra Leone produced a distinctive *African* literary culture—it was a missionary advantage in the period of the 'Three Cs'. African peoples who did not divide life into 'culture' and 'religion', met the Western and Christian way of life as a single

SAMUEL ADJAI CROWTHER

A. F. Walls

Samuel Crowther (about 1806–91) was the outstanding African Christian leader of his time. Adjai (properly Ajayi) was born in the Egba group of the Yoruba people in what is now Nigeria. When he was about 15, he was captured by slave raiders. But the slave ship was intercepted by a British warship, and Adjai was taken to Sierra Leone where he was converted and baptized, taking the name Samuel Crowther.

Outstanding at school (and a foundation pupil of Fourah Bay College) Crowther became a teacher for the Church Missionary Society, and was a pioneer of Yoruba services in Freetown. He was one of two CMS representatives on the 1841 Niger Expedition, and became convinced that the evangelization of inland Africa must be carried out by Africans. Ordained in London in 1843, he was appointed to the new mission in his own Yorubaland. Among the first converts were his long-lost mother and sister.

Crowther achieved much as evangelist, translator and negotiator. He impressed many, including Queen Victoria, when he visited England. He led the new Niger Mission in 1857 and in 1864 became the first African Anglican bishop. His all-African staff operated over hundreds of miles of the Niger territories. His last years were clouded by controversy concerning alleged indiscipline in his staff.

Samuel Crowther, the great African Christian leader. He was the first African Anglican bishop (1864).

ɔackage. The fact that they met t embodied in black people was :rucial. (There were twenty-six nembers in the first CMS mission o Yorubaland; most of them were rom Sierra Leone.) It was often he 'angry young men', impatient vith the old ways of old men, who 'esponded most readily. They took ɔn a total way of life.

The people most likely to listinguish between 'secular' and religious' aspects of missionary ıctivity lived in those areas used o Western traders. The Scottish Calabar mission knew that some of heir African hosts were interested n reading only for trading purɔoses. Here, and elsewhere, a ;ood deal of missionary activity vas aimed at reforming local nstitutions—especially human ;acrifice—at moving the whole :ommunity in a Christian direction, ıs well as forming churches.

At the beginning of the missionary movement there was no reason to expect that one people would respond more readily than another. Practical considerations led missionaries to go first to India, certain Pacific Islands, Sierra Leone, the West Indies and the Cape of Good Hope. China was impenetrable, except for certain ports, until mid-century, and Japan until later still. By mid-century, too, it was plain that in India more Christians came from among Hindus than from among Muslims, and more from among the tribal peoples than from either.

By the end of the century it was clear that, although Christians in India, China and even Japan were a significant part of the world church, it was in Africa and the Pacific that the most dramatic changes had happened. Hinduism and Buddhism (which was hardly recognized at the beginning of the nineteenth century) had not collapsed. Indeed both were adapting to the impact of Western culture. Islam had almost wholly resisted Christian mission. It was from among the world's tribal peoples that most Christians were coming; and in the African grasslands a race with Islam promised to follow.

One other feature of the early missionary societies had proved disappointing: the attempt to work for revival in the ancient churches of the Mediterranean, the Middle East, Ethiopia and India. Despite temporary encouragements in all these places, only in India was effective contact made between Protestant Christians and Orthodox, Nestorian and Monophysite churches.

Pupils from the Catholic school at Cochin, Kerala, India. From an early stage, education has formed an important part of missionary work.

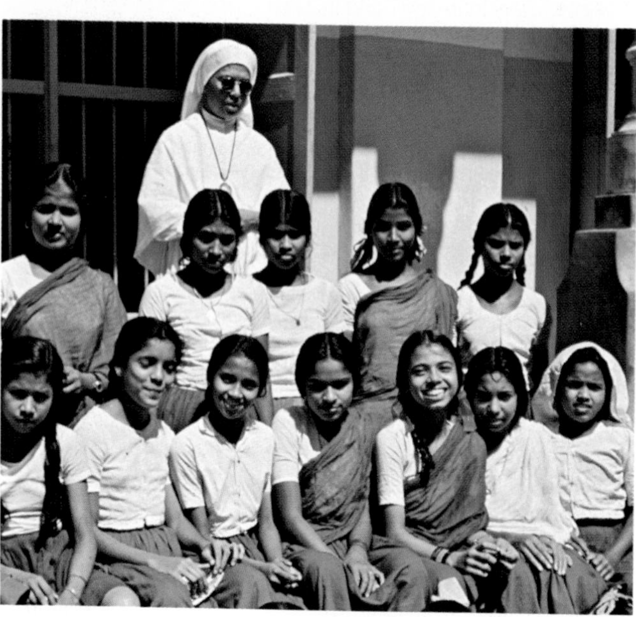

The first Roman Catholic missionary movement had almos burnt out when the Protestant movement began. The second came in imitation of the Protestants. The intellectual centre was in France, the Catholic power wit strongest overseas commitment. New missionary orders were formed: the White Fathers, the Congregation of the Holy Spirit a the Society of the Divine Word. Like the Protestants, the Catholi supporters of missions identified themselves with anti-slavery agitation, in which the great Cardinal Lavigerie was particular prominent. Rivalry with Protestant missions was bitter, and in the period of the 'Scramble for Africa' got entangled with politics Catholic missionaries (who were often French) were assumed to favour French colonial policies an Protestant missionaries those of Britain. In many areas which the French annexed, such as Indo-China, the only important Christi presence was Roman Catholic.

World War I damped the drean of the 1890s of the evangelization of the world in one generation. B when it broke out the church was already more like that 'great mult tude whom no man can number o of all nations and peoples and trib and tongues' than at any previous period of its history.

Societies for mission

A. F. Walls

In the eighteenth century it was taken for granted that there were only three forms of church government: episcopal, presbyterian and independent (or congregational). The supporters of each claimed to be following the Bible, and all the main arguments on each side were well known. Men had suffered much, and shed blood, for each form.

But as the conviction of the responsibility to spread the gospel worldwide began to dawn on British Christians at the end of the century, it became clear that none of these forms of church government enabled the church to embark on a world mission. The Church of England, with its hierarchy of bishops, had at this time no central organization; nor, by definition, did the independent churches. The Church of Scotland, the only large Presbyterian church, did discuss in 1796 whether to appoint a committee or take a collection for missions. But they voted to approve the principle—and prevent anything being done in practice. The friends of world mission were driven to find another form of machinery: the voluntary society.

Organizing for mission

The voluntary society was still a relatively undeveloped type of organization. The Church of England had two well-established societies—the Society for Promoting Christian Knowledge and the Society for the Propagation of the Gospel—but these had royal charters and the approval of the bishops. Political pressure-groups of this time operated through loose 'association' and not societies. In fact, when William Carey wrote his book, *An Enquiry into the Obligations of Christians to use Means for the Conversation of the Heathens*, he asked: what would a trading company do? From this, he proposed the formation of a company of serious Christians, laymen and ministers, with a committee to collect and sift information, and to find funds and suitable men.

The voluntary society, of which the missionary society was one early form, was to transform the nineteenth-century church. It was invented to meet a need rather than for theological reasons, but it undermined all the established forms of church government. In the first place, it made possible ecumenical activity. Churchmen and dissenters or seceders cut off from church business could work together for defined purposes. It also altered the power base in the church by encouraging lay leadership. Ordinary Christian men, and later women, came to hold key positions in the important societies. And again, the best societies made it possible for many people to participate.

All these features appeared early in the history of missionary societies. The London Missionary Society adopted in 1795 its 'fundamental principle that our design is not to send Presbyterianism, Independency, Episcopacy or any other form of church government . . . but the glorious gospel of the blessed God to the heathen'. One of the founders called for 'the funeral of bigotry'. Ordinary Christian people held responsible office in missionary societies at a time when such responsibilities would have been unthinkable elsewhere in the church.

The arrest of Adoniram Judson

"On the eighth of June, just as we were preparing for dinner, in rushed an officer, holding a black book, with a dozen Burmans accompanied by one, whom from his spotted face, we knew to be an executioner, and a 'son of the prison'. 'Where is the teacher?' was the first inquiry. Mr. Judson presented himself. 'You are called by the king,' said the officer; a form of speech always used when about to arrest a criminal. The spotted man instantly seized Mr Judson, threw him on the floor, and produced the small cord, the instrument of torture . . . The hardened executioner, with a hellish joy, drew tight the cords, bound Mr Judson fast, and dragged him off, I knew not whither . . .

Mr. Judson and all the white foreigners were confined in the death prison, with three pairs of iron fetters each, and fastened to a long pole . . ."

ADONIRAM JUDSON was one of the first American missionaries to India.

WILLIAM CAREY

D. W. Bebbington

William Carey (1761–1834), an English Baptist, devoted most of his life to taking the gospel to India. He was born at Paulerspury, Northamptonshire, the son of a parish clerk and schoolmaster. He was converted in 1779 through a fellow apprentice shoemaker, became a dissenter, and was baptized as a believer in 1783. After some local preaching, Carey became pastor of Moulton (1786) and then Harvey Lane, Leicester (1789), Baptist church. He was deeply influenced by the theology of the American Jonathan Edwards, which supplied an impetus to mission.

William Carey's chief object

". . . the forming of our native brethren to usefulness, fostering every kind of genius, and cherishing every gift and grace in them; In this respect we can scarcely be too lavish in our attention to their improvement. It is only by means of native preachers we can hope for the universal spread of the Gospel through this immense Continent."

In 1792 Carey published *An Enquiry into the Obligation of Christians to use Means for the Conversion of the Heathen*. He argued that Christ's great commission to 'preach the gospel to every creature' still applied to all Christians. In the same year in a sermon at Nottingham he urged Christians to 'expect great things from God' and 'attempt great things for God'. As a direct consequence in October 1792, the Baptist Missionary Society was founded. It was the first foreign missionary organization created by the Evangelical Revival.

William Carey, the pioneer English Baptist missionary, baptizing an Indian convert. He preached the importance of mission with the stirring words: 'Expect great things from God; attempt great things for God.'

Carey and his family sailed to India in the following year. He became foreman of an indigo factory in Bengal (1794–99), a post that occupied him for only three months of the year, leaving him free to study oriental languages intensively. In 1799 he was joined at Serampore, near Calcutta, by two fellow-Baptists, Joshua Marshman and William Ward. For the next quarter-century the three men worked together to organize a growing network of mission stations in and beyond Bengal. Carey translated the New Testament into Bengali, and was given a tutorship in languages at Fort William College in 1801. In the years up to 1824, Carey supervised six complete and twenty-four partial translations of the Bible as well as publishing several grammars, dictionaries and translations of eastern books. Although some of his early translations were hurried and stilted, his work was an immense achievement for a largely self-educated pioneer.

Carey achieved much in various areas. He initiated mission schools, conceived the idea of Serampore College, founded the Agricultural Society of India (1820) to promote agricultural improvements, studied botany (being awarded a fellowship of the Linnaean Society in 1823) and took a leading part in the campaign for the abolition of widow-burning (*sati*), which succeeded in 1829. Carey's devotion to India, which he never left, and his practical wisdom are shown in his encouraging Indians to spread the gospel themselves.

The enthusiast who collected a penny a week from members of his local missionary society auxiliary, and distributed the missionary magazine, was fully involved in the work of the society. It was through the work of such people that missionary candidates came forward. The American missionary, Rufus Anderson, wrote in 1834: 'It was not until the present century that the evangelical churches of Christendom were ever really organized with a view to the conversion of the world.' They became organized by means of the voluntary society.

The 'society' is invented

By the 1780s many Christians in all denominations were feeling that the signs of revival in Protestants countries foreshadowed an extension of gospel preaching to the whole world. It was a group of Baptists from the English midlands who first formed an effective organization, as The Particular Baptist Society for the Propagation of the Gospel (later the Baptist Missionary Society).

The London Missionary Society (at first called simply The Missionary Society) also began in regional gatherings for prayer. But the leading figures, men like John Love and David Bogue, were, unlike William Carey, prominent figures in their denominations. Most were Independents, but some were churchmen or Presbyterians: and it was proposed to form a society which would ignore denominations. The scale was vastly greater than that of the Baptists; soon after its formation in 1795 the society sent a party of more than thirty missionaries to the Pacific. Despite its ecumenical intentions the LMS soon became an overwhelmingly Congregational society (partly because other denominational societies were formed).

In Scotland the refusal of the 1796 General Assembly closed the door to any official church mission. This left friends of mission in the Church of Scotland free to join with members of the secession churches in local societies, modelled on the LMS. Societies in the smaller towns could only collect funds; but the Glasgow and Edinburgh (later the Scottish) Missionary Societies sent out their own missionaries. Scotland contributed many missionaries to serve the LMS.

The denominations mobilize

These developments presented strict Anglican evangelicals with a problem. They felt the need for missions just as much as their dissenting brethren, but did not believe the SPG was suited to gospel-preaching. On the other hand, they wanted to keep denominational boundaries, and ruled out participation in the LMS under mainly dissenting leaders. Crucial discussions took place in an evangelical club, the Eclectic Society, and in 1799 the Church Missionary Society for Africa and the East was formed. Its first committee mostly consisted of little-known London clergymen. The Anglican hierarchy acquiesced but gave no approval. Only when the society had proved itself, many years later, did prominent churchmen recognize it.

John Wesley was very conscious of the transatlantic dimension of Methodist work. This included the West Indies, to which preachers were regularly sent, and which by 1790 had been made a separate Methodist province. Thomas Coke, to whom Wesley gave much responsibility in his last

Worshippers at a Buddhist shrine in Rangoon, Burma. Adoniram Judson, the American missionary, was arrested in Rangoon in 1824, suspected of being a British agent.

years, was anxious to extend Methodist missions on a world scale. Coke published a plan for a society as early as 1784, and tried several times after that to get the Methodist Conference to approve an extension. The objections were financial. Coke worked towards forming local auxiliaries and by 1814 these were recognized by the Conference. In 1818 the Methodist Conference brought together the auxiliaries in a Methodist Missionary Society. Eventually every member of the Methodist church was automatically a member of the Society.

It was twenty-eight years after the 1796 Assembly debate that the Church of Scotland took direct responsibility for missions, and commissioned its first missionary, Alexander Duff. By that time evangelical and moderate could agree on this, and possibly the stress on education, which was to be so important for Scottish missions, first arose from their agreement. When the church was split by the 'Disruption' in 1843, the missionaries all joined the Free Church. The Church of Scotland had to begin again recruiting missionaries.

HUDSON TAYLOR

Harold H. Rowdon

A Yorkshireman, converted at seventeen, James Hudson Taylor (1832–1905) went to China in 1853 as a missionary with the Chinese Evangelization Society. The short-comings of the support system of the society (and possibly the influence of Brethren thinking) made him cut his links with the CES. He continued in China as an independent missionary until ill-health forced him home in 1860. He completed his medical training, and in 1865 he founded the China Inland Mission. This was the first truly interdenominational foreign mission, and the prototype of the 'faith' missions that were to play so prominent a part in world evangelization during the nineteenth century.

Hudson Taylor's great concern was to bring the gospel to every unevangelized province of the Chinese Empire, now at last open to westerners. Anxious not to divert funds from other missions he resolved never to appeal for financial support. The example of George Müller made him determined to rely on prayer to bring in supplies, and on careful administration to conserve them. This 'faith principle' did not rule out appeals for prayer and for specific numbers of missionary recruits.

Hudson Taylor introduced several innovations into the general mission practice of his day. He was prepared to accept candidates who had no college training, and he required his missionaries to identify with the national peoples by, amongst other things, wearing Chinese dress. He was determined not to locate ultimate control of mission operations at home, and insisted that the work be directed on the spot. He himself had earlier suffered from the home-controlled system.

At the same time Hudson Taylor saw the need to keep Christians at home fully informed. By his writing and preaching he made a great impact during his lifetime. The biography written by his son and daughter-in-law, Dr and Mrs Howard Taylor, rapidly became a Christian classic.

In North America the presence of a neighbouring non-Christian people, the American Indians, meant that the missionary challenge was always present, if not always taken up. Indian missions had first stimulated British missionary societies. In turn the example of the British Societies led to American societies patterned on the LMS (the first was the New York Missionary Society in 1796). In 1810 the first society specifically designed for worldwide mission was founded: the American Board of Commissioners for Foreign Missionaries.

In Holland the voluntary society began almost as early as in Britain in the inter-denominational Nederlandse Zendeling Genootschap in 1797.

Europe catches the vision

On the rest of the European continent, the missionary seminary came earlier than the missionary society, but in the years following the Napoleonic wars missionary societies sprang up. The religious societies of German Pietism were specially fertile soil: a missionary visit to the Deutsche Christentumsgesellschaft (founded in 1780) produced missionary societies in Bremen (1819), Hamburg (1822) and elsewhere, which merged to form the North German Missionary Society in 1834. Berlin had its missionary society for Prussia from 1824, and the Rhineland its own society from 1828. From 1815 Basle formed the focus of Protestant missionary interest in Switzerland, south Germany, southern France and the Austrian Empire. Its roll of missionary recruits was long and its seminary influential. French Protestants had formed the Paris Mission by 1822.

As in Britain, the ecumenical impulse was strong in early days. But tensions between Lutherans and Reformed eventually split the North German Mission. The Basle Mission in its early days required those of its missionaries who served with the Church Missionary Society to become Anglicans, those serving in the Danish territory, Lutherans, and so on.

Denmark (still a minor maritime power, with interests in West Africa and the West Indies) founded its missionary society in 1821. For various reasons, major societies did not emerge in the other Scandinavian countries until late in the century.

Common-sense missionaries

The founding fathers of the early British societies clearly did not expect many missionary recruits from among ministers—or the normal sources of supply of ministers. Carey—a self-educated cobbler turned minister—is an exception. Most of the early recruits were craftsmen or tradesmen, who would be unlikely to obtain ordination for the home ministry. The first enthusiasm of the LMS—that spirituality and common sense were qualifications enough—was damped by the disasters which overtook too many of their early missionaries. 'Culture shock' took a heavy toll, and a few years' experience was enough to show the importance of preparing missionaries. Though many LMS candidates had little formal education, their training, superintended originally by David Bogue, was impressive. Much early LMS study on languages and tribes is strikingly scholarly.

The greatest recruiting difficulties were met by the CMS, since their principles required the use of ordained men as missionaries—and very few came forward. The difficulty was

The nineteenth-century Scots Kirk in Calcutta is sandwiched between modern office buildings. The Church of England appointed bishops in India during the early nineteenth century.

Women suffering from leprosy in a 'mission compound' at Champa, India, in 1903. It was run by the Mission to Lepers, now known as the Leprosy Mission.

eased by co-operation with the continental seminaries. Many German and other missionaries from continental Europe served the CMS with distinction. Of the first twenty-four CMS missionaries, seventeen were German and only three were ordained Englishmen. Things changed when the English bishops became more favourable to the society, and also as the society became more rooted in the parishes.

By mid-century the importance of 'native ministers' was becoming recognized, and an increasing number were serving on the staffs of missionary societies. The CMS Niger Mission, begun in 1857, was entirely African staffed. In the last third of the century, missionary recruitment expanded enormously. This was largely due to the effects of the 1859 revival, the Keswick Movement and other forces. The universities were particularly affected. The 'Cambridge Seven', ex-Cambridge undergraduates who set out for China in 1885, were only the first of hundreds to follow.

These decades—the period of high imperialism—not only produced many more missionaries, but a different *type* of missionary. The same influences were at work in America, where students had been important in the missionary movement from the beginning. In 1886 the Student Volunteer Movement was founded. This led in turn to the Student Volunteer Missionary Union and later the Student Christian Movement. In the last two decades of the century a series of conferences were held under titles such as, 'Make Jesus King' and 'Students and the Missionary Problem'. The numbers of volunteers, together with the technological and political developments of the age, led to the prospect of 'The evangelization of the world in this generation'. World War I transformed the whole situation: but by the time European manpower was reduced the great African-led mass-movements had begun.

The forces which produced new supplies of candidates produced also new forms of society. These maintained the voluntary society principle, and were directed to particular areas—for example, the China Inland Mission (1865) or the Qua Iboe Mission (1887). Others met particular needs, such as the Mission to Lepers (1874).

The nineteenth-century missionaries, and the societies which called and directed them, were a major factor in transforming Christianity into a world church—perhaps the most important fact about it in the past century.

> *"I am not reaping the harvest; I can scarcely claim to be sowing the seed; I am hardly ploughing the soil; but I am gathering out the stones. That, too, is missionary work; let it be supported by loving sympathy and fervent prayer."*
>
> *ROBERT BRUCE, an Irish missionary, writes of the slow progress of the gospel in Persia (Iran)*

The Bible Societies

Wayne A. Detzler

In December 1802 Thomas Charles, a noted Calvinist minister from Bala, North Wales, attended a committee meeting of the Religious Tract Society (RTS) in London. He was deeply concerned about the unavailability of Bibles in Welsh, and urged the Society to produce a Welsh Bible.

The Tract Society did not regard Bible distribution as part of its job. A separate Bible Society was required. Joseph Hughes, a Baptist from Battersea, urged that an agency be formed to provide Bibles, both for Britain and for other countries throughout the world. The next year Hughes, a secretary of the RTS, prepared an essay, *The Excellence of the Holy Scriptures, An Argument for their More General Dispersion at Home and Abroad.*

A new society

On 7 March 1804, at London Tavern, the British and Foreign Bible Society (BFBS) was established. Most of the well-known evangelicals soon associated themselves with the project. Amongst them were Lord Teignmouth, Charles Grant, Zachary Macaulay, the bishops of London and Salisbury, and William Wilberforce, MP. The purpose of the new organization was: 'to encourage the wider circulation of the Holy Scriptures, without note or comment'.

The governing committee of the BFBS reflected its broad-based character. It was composed of fifteen Anglicans, fifteen nonconformists and six foreign members. Joseph Hughes became the first nonconformist secretary. The Church of England secretary was Josiah Pratt. He was replaced within a year by John Owen, chaplain to the bishop of London. The post of overseas secretary went to C.F.S. Steinkopff, minister of the German Lutheran church in the Savoy.

Sympathetic societies soon appeared throughout the United Kingdom. In 1805 the Glasgow Bible Society was formed; in 1809 came the Edinburgh committee. The Hibernian Bible Society was founded in 1806 at Dublin. Societies proliferated throughout the British Empire: Canada (1807), Australia (1817) and New Zealand (1837).

At the tenth anniversary of the BFBS their agents John Paterson and Robert Pinkerton reported on the founding of the Russian Bible Society (1813). Prince Galitzin, minister for foreign religions, had proposed the establishment of a Bible Society to Czar Alexander I, who readily agreed. The British supporters of the BFBS were so pleased about the Russian Society, that they dispatched Pinkerton and Paterson as their exclusive agents to Europe.

On his way back to Russia, Pinkerton crossed Holland, Germany and Poland. In rapid succession he established committees at Amsterdam, Elberfeld (Rhineland), Hanover, Berlin and Dresden. Meanwhile, John Paterson toured Scandinavia setting up societies in Norway, Sweden and Denmark. Most of these European agencies flourished with generous financial support from the BFBS.

Roman Catholics also enjoyed the support of the BFBS. Soon after its founding, the BFBS sent funds to Bishop Michael Wittmann of Regensburg. When the Bavarian

A Kenyan woman reads a Gospel in her own language in a country marketplace.

priest Johannes Gossner prepared a German translation of the New Testament, he too was supported by the BFBS. The main Catholic agent of the BFBS was, however, Leander van Ess, a priest and professor of theology at Marburg. His German translation of the New Testament was tolerated by Catholic authorities until 1822, when it was condemned, and included in the *Index*. Nevertheless, the energetic van Ess distributed more than 500,000 copies of his New Testament with the aid of the BFBS.

Some growing problems

For its first two decades, the Bible Society's operation was unclouded by conflict. But in 1825 the German Bible societies applied for permission to include in their editions of the Bible the Apocrypha, a collection of books written between the periods covered by the Old and New Testaments. Roman Catholics accepted them as additional to the canon (deuterocanonical), but most Protestants set them apart from the traditionally recognized list of Bible books.

The application by the German societies resulted in a split within the Bible Society movement. The BFBS refused permission to include the Apocrypha in editions for which the British paid. Almost immediately the Germans cut themselves off from the London Committee.

The Scottish societies also separated themselves from the BFBS, but for other reasons. Under the aggressive leadership of the evangelist Robert Haldane, the Edinburgh and Glasgow societies declared their independence. The Scots felt the BFBS had been too slow in refusing to print the Apocrypha. In 1861 the Glasgow and Edinburgh agencies united to form the National Bible Society of Scotland.

A second source of conflict within the BFBS arose from the variety of views represented by individuals co-operating. At the anniversary of the BFBS in May 1831, James Edward Gordon, MP for Dundalk, stood to demand the expulsion of Unitarians from the managing committee. When the BFBS refused to introduce a doctrinal test, the Trinitarian Bible Society was formed.

203,931,768 publications

Despite divisions, the BFBS expanded continuously. By 1906 there were 5,800 auxiliaries and branch societies in the United Kingdom. Australia had 52 auxiliaries and 1,500 branch Bible societies. Outside the United Kingdom there were 2,200 auxiliaries and branch societies. The BFBS reported in 1907 that since its founding, 203,931,768 Bibles, Testaments and portions of Scripture had been put into circulation.

Meanwhile an American

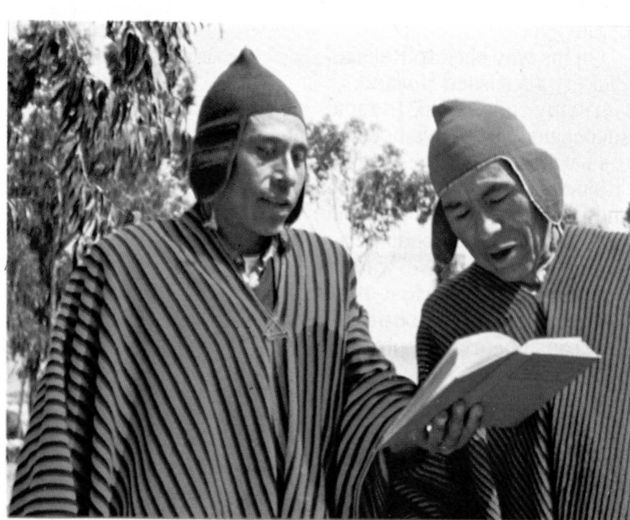

Two Bolivians reading part of the Bible in their own language. The translation was made available through the work of the Bible Societies.

An early Bible distributor in Malagasy, carrying Bibles in two trunks. The Bible Societies have supported Bible distribution in many parts of the world.

Bible Society (ABS) had been formed. The BFBS had formed a central committee which produced branches. By contrast, the ABS was an amalgamation of earlier local committees. In 1808 the Philadelphia Bible Society appeared. A year later similar societies emerged in Connecticut, Massachusetts, New York and Maine.

During 1814 Samuel Mills, an American missionary leader, journeyed throughout the frontier territories of the United States. Like the Welshman, Thomas Charles, Mills saw the place for an organization which could provide Bibles for the spiritually needy. In the western territories of Kentucky, Tennessee and Illinois, Mills calculated that there were at least 70,000 families without a Bible. In all, he estimated that 500,000 copies of the Scriptures could usefully be distributed in the United States.

To provide Bibles for the American west, the American Bible Society was founded on 8 May 1816 in New York. Sixty-one delegates from thirty-one local Bible societies met to set it up. Most of the early effort was devoted to providing Bibles for the pioneers who were opening up the west, for European immigrants who were flooding into the United States and for various tribes of American Indians.

Like the BFBS, the ABS also split. In 1835 the British Baptist missionary, William Pearce, applied to the ABS for aid in printing a Bengali Testament at Calcutta. He asked for permission to put the word 'immerse' for 'baptism' wherever it appeared in the New Testament. When this suggestion, with its denominational interpretation, was refused, the American Baptists withdrew from the ABS. In 1836 they formed the American and Foreign Bible Society.

After the initial period of establishment, the Bible societies thrived and extended their operations. Wherever missionaries worked, Bible societies appeared. Significant aid was given to the young churches by the Bible societies. They supervised the translation of the Bible, produced Scriptures and distributed them to the emerging churches.

During the first half of the twentieth century the life of the church was marked by co-operation. This ecumenical spirit also spread to the Bible societies. During the thirties the possibilities of joint activity were explored. This was interrupted by the 1939–45 war.

Bibles world-wide

The major Bible societies met in 1946 at Haywards Heath, England, and formed a fellowship of Bible Societies, the United Bible Societies (UBS). The next year Oliver Beguin, a Belgian, was appointed general secretary.

Six primary purposes were set out for the United Bible Societies. First, they were to encourage the co-ordination and extension of efforts, and to develop co-operation between societies. Second, the UBS would help exchange information between members and harmonize policies and techniques. Third, the central committee would supply its member agencies with helps and services. Fourth, information would be collected concerning religious trends in the world and the uses of the Bible. Fifth, the UBS would represent the Bible societies in talks with other Christian organizations. Finally, emergency services could be arranged by the UBS.

Anxious to avoid the traditional centres of London and New York, the UBS set up regional offices in Nairobi for Africa, Mexico City for the Americas, Singapore for Asia and Bassersdorf, Switzerland (now Brussels) for Europe. Each office has specialists in Bible translation, production and distribution. The world UBS translation co-ordinator supervises about 62 translations consultants who are currently involved in the translation of 624 languages.

In 1963 at Tokyo the president of the UBS, Dr Donald Coggan, called for a new effort to increase Bible distribution. At that time the annual distribution of Bibles, Testaments and Scripture portions totalled 54.1 million. It was hoped that this could be trebled within three years.

Although this goal was not immediately achieved, within a decade circulation had been increased by more than 400 per cent. In 1992 the Bible Societies sent out 618,185,347 Bibles and portions of scripture. The Bible, or part of the Bible, was available in 2,009 languages. The largest single group of languages was African, accounting for a total of 576 languages or dialects. The complete Bible had been printed in 329 languages.

SECTION 8
PRESENT AND FUTURE

Reason, Revival and Revolution

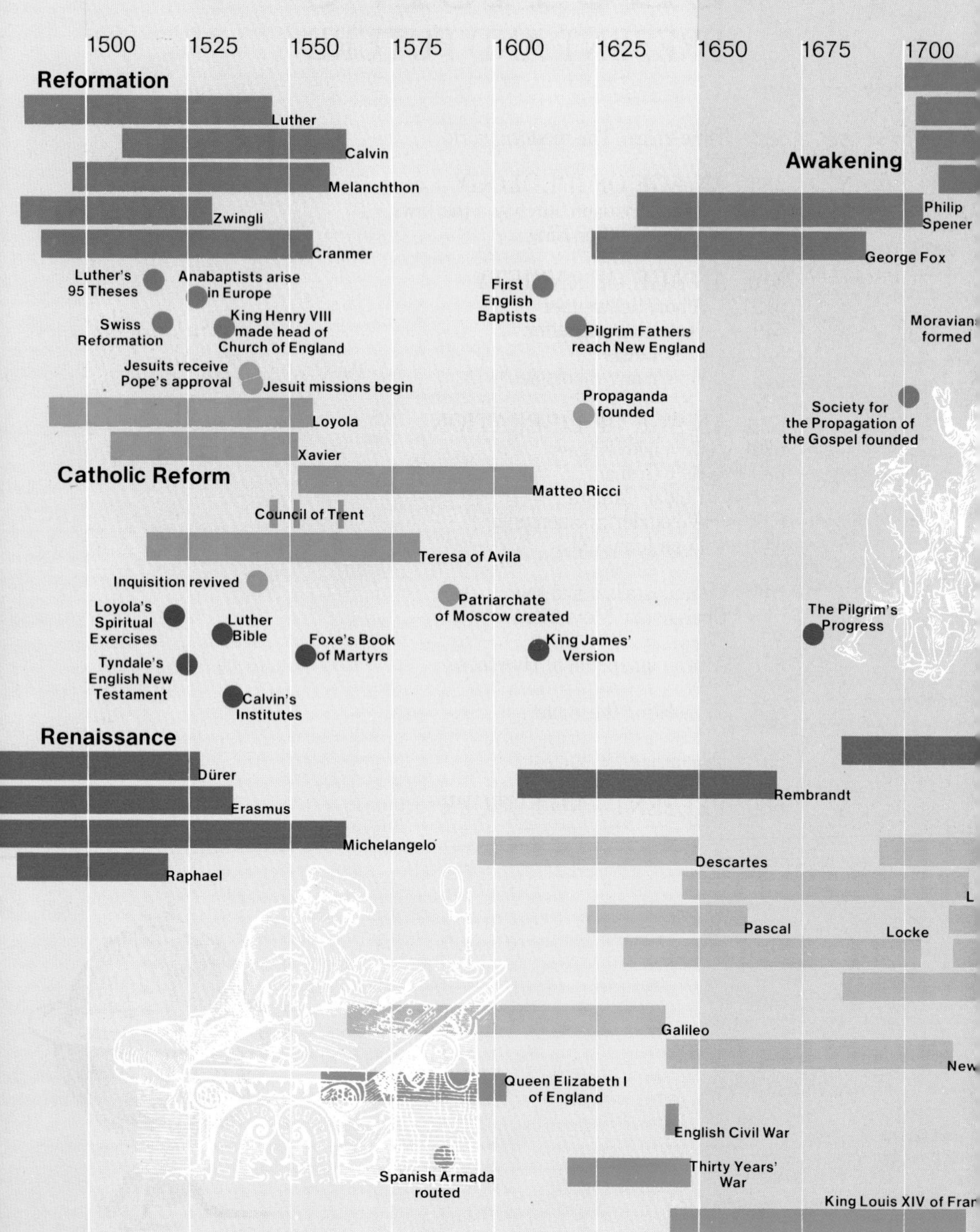
1500
1525
1550
1575
1600
1625
1650
1675
1700
Reformation
Luther
Calvin
Melanchthon
Zwingli
Cranmer
Luther's 95 Theses
Anabaptists arise in Europe
Swiss Reformation
King Henry VIII made head of Church of England
Jesuits receive Pope's approval
Jesuit missions begin
Loyola
Xavier
Catholic Reform
Matteo Ricci
Council of Trent
Teresa of Avila
Inquisition revived
Loyola's Spiritual Exercises
Luther Bible
Tyndale's English New Testament
Calvin's Institutes
Foxe's Book of Martyrs
Patriarchate of Moscow created
First English Baptists
Pilgrim Fathers reach New England
Propaganda founded
King James' Version
Awakening
Philip Spener
George Fox
Moravians formed
Society for the Propagation of the Gospel founded
The Pilgrim's Progress
Renaissance
Dürer
Erasmus
Michelangelo
Raphael
Rembrandt
Descartes
Pascal
Locke
Galileo
Queen Elizabeth I of England
Spanish Armada routed
English Civil War
Thirty Years' War
King Louis XIV of Frar

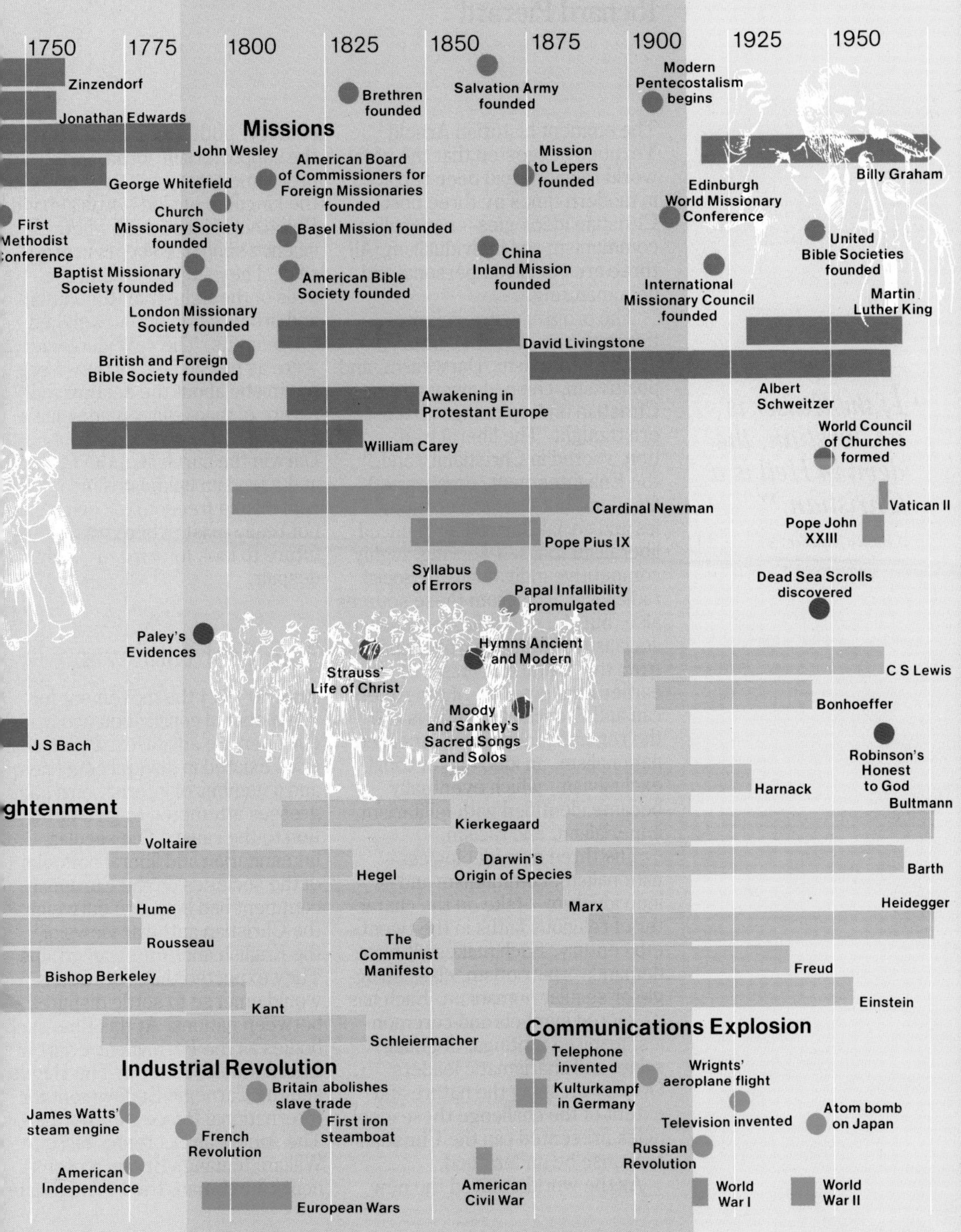
1750
1775
1800
1825
1850
1875
1900
1925
1950
Zinzendorf
Jonathan Edwards
John Wesley
George Whitefield
First Methodist Conference
Church Missionary Society founded
Baptist Missionary Society founded
London Missionary Society founded
British and Foreign Bible Society founded
Missions
Brethren founded
American Board of Commissioners for Foreign Missionaries founded
Basel Mission founded
American Bible Society founded
Salvation Army founded
Mission to Lepers founded
China Inland Mission founded
Modern Pentecostalism begins
Edinburgh World Missionary Conference
International Missionary Council founded
Billy Graham
United Bible Societies founded
Martin Luther King
David Livingstone
Albert Schweitzer
Awakening in Protestant Europe
William Carey
World Council of Churches formed
Cardinal Newman
Vatican II
Pope Pius IX
Pope John XXIII
Syllabus of Errors
Papal Infallibility promulgated
Dead Sea Scrolls discovered
Paley's Evidences
Hymns Ancient and Modern
Strauss' Life of Christ
Moody and Sankey's Sacred Songs and Solos
C S Lewis
Bonhoeffer
J S Bach
Robinson's Honest to God
Harnack
ghtenment
Bultmann
Kierkegaard
Voltaire
Darwin's Origin of Species
Hegel
Barth
Hume
Marx
Heidegger
Rousseau
The Communist Manifesto
Bishop Berkeley
Freud
Kant
Einstein
Schleiermacher
Communications Explosion
Industrial Revolution
Telephone invented
Britain abolishes slave trade
Wrights' aeroplane flight
Kulturkampf in Germany
James Watts' steam engine
First iron steamboat
French Revolution
Television invented
Atom bomb on Japan
Russian Revolution
American Independence
American Civil War
World War I
World War II
European Wars

AN AGE OF IDEOLOGY

Richard Pierard

> *"If the Kaiser is a Christian, the devil in Hell is a Christian."*
>
> *A Boston preacher*

The eminent historian Arnold Toynbee suggested that the great world religions had been replaced in modern times by three post-Christian ideologies—nationalism, communism and individualism. All three are equally impersonal and dehumanizing.

The progress of secularization in the nineteenth century, aided by Marxism, Darwinism, and positivism, chipped away at the Christian underpinnings of Western thought. The liberal tradition, rooted in Christianity and the Enlightenment, emphasized freedom, but classical economics and social Darwinism reduced liberalism to a self-serving, highly competitive individualism. Social radicalism drew from these sources also, but the scientific, materialist socialism of Marx sharply departed from the liberal humanism of earlier thinkers. Out of the American and French Revolutions and the romantic movement emerged nationalism, an ideology of tribal exclusivism, which eventually became identified with militarism, imperialism, and racism.

The three new ideologies—nationalism, communism and individualism—take on the character of religious faiths in the twentieth century. Each makes ultimate demands—patriotism, class struggle or secular humanism. Each has its sacred symbols and ceremonies, inspired writings, dogmas, saints and charismatic leaders. Only by grasping the nature and extent of the challenge these ideologies presented can the Christian response be understood.

As the world entered the new century, both liberal humanists and the supporters of social Christianity proclaimed that a better world—or the kingdom of God—was at hand. But others questioned whether science supported belief in progress. They suggested that the evils of the Industrial Revolution and urbanization far outweighed the benefits. The new ideologies were as pessimistic as they were optimistic about the destiny and nature of man. Marx made man a reflection of property-relations, Darwin the survival of the fittest, and Freud an unknown libido. Self-control and freedom of choice did not really exist. There was no future to look forward to—only despair.

The first total war

Prior to 1914 the movement for international conciliation had made considerable advances. Peace societies existed in several countries, and a number of international congresses attempted to give direction to the cause. The secular, humanitarian and liberal outlooks of the societies on the European continent had begun to outweigh the Christian anti-war views of the English and American groups. They expected that institutions would emerge to settle disputes between nations. At this time such bodies as the Permanent Court of International Justice at The Hague and the Carnegie Endowment for International Peace were formed. The American Secretary of State, William Jennings Bryan, a prominent churchman, tried to negotiate 'cooling-off treaties' to deter countries from rushing hastily into war.

In spite of these well-meaning efforts, international tensions rose steadily, fuelled by an escalating arms race and imperialistic confrontations abroad. It took only a spark to ignite the tinder-box of Europe—and it came with the assassination of the Crown Prince of Austria–Hungary in Sarajevo on 28 June 1914.

The armies marched joyously off to war, naîvely assuming that in a few weeks they would win a glorious victory which would solve all the pressing problems their countries faced. What in fact followed was a stalemate. The so-called civilized peoples of the West engaged in an unparalleled carnage, which annihilated the greater part of a generation of men. The ideals of liberal humanism proved inadequate for the times. The sudden unleashing of the pent-up emotions of war shattered the optimism of the peace advocates.

For the first time, the world knew 'total war'. It was fought on land, sea and air. Industry was regimented to maintain a constant flow of weapons. Governments directed the economic life of their countries, strictly controlling industrial output, food production, and allocation of labour and raw materials. Through naval blockade and submarine warfare each side tried to throttle the economy of the enemy.

Governments restricted the activities of civilians. Civil rights were curtailed to combat subversion at home. Those who had reservations about the war were pressured to conform. Censorship was used to stop the spread of news helpful to the enemy and to strengthen morale. The people were instilled with a sense of solidarity, singleness of purpose, and the conviction that they were engaged in a righteous crusade. This belief was reinforced by church leaders on both sides. British liberal writers, in particular, hammered home the idea that it was a 'holy war' against tyranny, despotism and militarism. On the other hand, Christian groups worked to relieve suffering in the war-torn areas, and to aid prisoners-of-war and wounded soldiers.

Allied propagandists slanted news reports and exploited such German blunders as the sinking of the *Lusitania* and the execution of nurse Edith Cavell. In this way they won the sympathy and co-operation of influential people in the United States, especially in church circles. They took a moralistic and ideological view of the war which ruled out a negotiated peace based on re-establishing the balance of power. When the idealist President Woodrow Wilson, son of a Presbyterian minister, brought the USA into the war, it was clear that the Central Powers had to be totally defeated so that an entirely new world could be created. The overthrow of the Russian autocracy in March 1917 further strengthened the ideas that the war was a struggle between democracy

Western Europe was shattered by the impact of World War I. The picture shows the *Grande Place*, Ypres, in 1916, with the remains of the Cloth Hall and Cathedral, destroyed during the fighting on the Western front.

and authoritarianism. Neither side obtained a breakthrough, but then the radical Marxist Bolshevik faction led by Lenin overthrew the moderates in November and took Russia out of the war. The Germans were poised for a knock-out blow on the western front, but the resources of the USA precluded a German victory. The Central Powers finally collapsed, revolution swept their countries, and Germany surrendered on 11 November 1918.

Peace and punishment

At the Paris Peace Conference which followed, the mood was one of nineteenth-century nationalism—the desire for national self-determination and security against Germany. Some of the statesmen and many churchmen wanted to overcome future conflicts and tensions by supra-national organization and by strengthening international law. But their hopes were dismissed in favour of power politics, nationalist fervour and fear of Bolshevism spreading to Europe.

The delegates felt compelled to settle scores with their principal foe, Germany, and the final Treaty of Versailles had the appearance of a dictated peace. The peacemakers also constructed a dam to contain the Bolshevik menace by permitting the creation of six new states in eastern Europe.

The settlement with Turkey was significant because during the war the Allies had promised independence to the sultan's Arab subjects. However, Britain and France had agreed secretly to a partition of the Ottoman lands among themselves. Britain had also promised in the Balfour Declaration of 1917 to support the establishment of a Jewish national home in Palestine. What followed was the creation of mandates in Palestine and Transjordan, and French ones in Lebanon and Syria. Tensions mounted among Arabs, Jews and Europeans in the Middle East.

A further difficulty facing the peace conference concerned the Orthodox minorities which were almost autonomous in Ottoman Turkey. Massacres of Armenians before, and Greek minorities after, the war had aroused passions in the West. But Turkish nationalists bitterly resented the terms agreed in Paris and, led by Mustafa Kemal, forced a revision of its terms in 1923. Kemal then began to bring Turkey into the twentieth century. He secularized the state, reducing the influence of both Islam and the Christian minorities.

Finally, the peace settlement founded the League of Nations—a world-wide organization for the preservation of peace, proposed by Wilson. He believed that in the new order, openly-arrived-at agreements would guarantee the political independence and territorial integrity of all states. He felt it provided the peace settlement with a moral foundation and the machinery for correcting defects in the treaties.

The inter-war period saw great changes. For one thing, the great 'civil war of the West' had undermined Europe's pre-1914 world position. The new industrial giants, the United States and Japan, were now finding places in the imperial sun. Great Britain was under pressure to relax its hold over Ireland, India and the Middle East, while the Statute of Westminster (1931) accorded the white dominions (Canada, Australia, New Zealand, South Africa, and Ireland) legal equality with Britain in the Commonwealth. Colonial nationalism in North Africa and southeast Asia undermined France's effort to promote cultural assimilation in its possessions.

The economies of the western countries were shattered by

the war, and a whole generation of leaders perished on the battlefield. The democratic nations broadened the base of political participation (including the vote for women), but they were plagued by unemployment and inflation. Socialist agitation and demands for welfare intensified. Left-wing parties (such as the British Labour and German Social Democratic parties) now participated in government. Socialism fitted in well with the rapid advance of secularism in the post-war decade. Protestant and Catholic churches alike proved unable to hold the allegiance of younger people. The more progressively-minded channelled their energies into secular ideologies.

Although it began with high aspirations, the League of Nations failed to prevent aggression and preserve peace. From the outset the United States refused to take part, and Germany and Soviet Russia were excluded. For this reason the Bolsheviks regarded it as a capitalist plot to overthrow communism in Russia, and the Germans saw it as a weapon for keeping Germany down. The member states would not accept infringements on their sovereignty, and the major disarmament and political agreements of the interwar years took place outside its framework. The League did promote co-operation in the technical and economic spheres, and guaranteed religious and missionary freedom in the former German and Turkish territories under its mandatory supervision.

The new menace

The most deadly challenge facing democracy in the interwar period was totalitarianism. A totalitarian order is marked out by such features as an official ideology that covers all vital aspects of human existence and looks towards a perfect state of mankind; a single, mass party led by a dictator or small group who are dedicated to the ideology, and which controls almost every aspect of life; a political police using sophisticated scientific and psychological techniques, directed against all 'enemies' of the regime; a monopoly over the media and education; and the systematic use of propaganda to manipulate and control the public. Totalitarian governments tightly regulate the economy and all means of combat, but also aim at a social revolution which will produce a new type of man, utterly lacking any sense of individual freedom. Only with the coming of universal literacy, modern technology and mass democracy in the twentieth century could a genuinely totalitarian system emerge. Totalitarian governments offered several different challenges to the Christian church, which responded in a variety of ways.

"We entered the war as the disinterested champion of right."

PRESIDENT WILSON

Right-wing versions of totalitarianism are popularly known as 'fascism'. They counter personal frustration and alienation as well as social and economic tensions by stressing class unity and reaffirming traditional values. Fascist movements glorify the national entity—defining it in terms of national mission, imperial greatness, the racial or folk community, or the state itself. Fascism also often features some sort of civil religion, anti-rationalism, elitism, and an emphasis upon the values of struggle, action, violence, courage and self-sacrifice. Private property and capitalist enterprise are permitted, but tightly controlled.

Fascism appeared first in Italy, as a response to the frustrations of the war and ensuing economic crisis. Benito Mussolini, a former socialist journalist and army veteran, founded the Fascist Party in 1919. He obtained power in the mythical 'March on Rome' (1922) which exploited nationalist discontents and the spectre of Bolshevism. Police supervision, terror, censorship, and propaganda characterized his regime. His 'Corporate State' was a facade of economic democracy which mainly benefitted large industrialists and landowners.

Mussolini achieved a reconciliation between the Roman Catholic church and the Italian state which brought to an end the antagonism dating from 1870. Cardinal Achille Ratte, elected Pope Pius XI in 1922, had experienced first-hand the Bolshevik attack on Poland in 1920 and was a bitter foe of communism as well as traditional liberalism. He was willing to wink at the more unsavoury aspects of the fascist regime in Italy in order to solve the 'Roman question'.

Although Mussolini himself was outspokenly anti-clerical, he saw the political advantages of a settlement, and came to terms with the pope in the Lateran Agreements of 1929. The papacy gave up its territorial claims in Italy, recognized the Italian ruling dynasty, agreed to keep out of politics, and accepted that the state should approve nominations to bishoprics. Fascist Italy recognized the Vatican City as an independent, sovereign state and the pope as its ruler, compensated the papacy for revenues lost because of the seizure of Rome in 1870, established Catholicism as the 'sole religion of the state', extended rules of canon law to marriage matters, allowed religious instruction in secondary schools, and gave legal standing to Catholic religious orders and associations.

A 'man sent by providence'

Pius XI praised the Italian dictator as a 'man sent by providence'. But Mussolini's views that the state was superior, and his cynical attitude towards the church soon cooled relations between them. In the encyclical *Quadragesimo anno* (May 1931), Pius XI criticized certain features of the corporate state. A month later, in *Non abbigmo bisogno,* he denounced the fascist crackdown on Catholic Action, a lay organization with social and educational functions. Eventually Mussolini backed off and agreed to permit the continued existence of Catholic Action, but under severe restrictions.

Italian churchmen generally gave their blessing to overseas ventures such as the conquest of Ethiopia and the intervention on Franco's side in the Spanish Civil War. Any criticism of fascism was usually restricted to specific matters where the state competed for the religious loyalty of Catholics, rather than on broad philosophical, humanitarian or theological grounds.

Ties also existed between Roman Catholicism and fascist-type movements in other parts of Europe. Examples include the 'clerical-fascist' state of Engelbert Dollfuss in Austria, the *Falangist* regime in Spain, the 'New State' of the Jesuit-trained Antonio Salazar in Portugal, and the 'Arrow-Cross' party of Ferenc Szálasi in Hungary. The anti-democratic royalist Charles Maurras and his *Action Française* commanded a wide following among Catholics in France and Belgium. But the pope condemned his basically atheist views in 1926, and the group's influence diminished.

German National Socialism (Nazism) also fed upon disillusionment with the war, resentment over the peace, fear of communism, and the economic crisis. Adolf Hitler, the Austrian-born leader of the movement, was named chancellor of the German Republic on 30 January 1933. Within two years he achieved greater control over the state than Mussolini, who remained subordinate in law to the Italian crown.

The basic Nazi organizational idea was the absolute unity of the German people with the leader (*Führer*) and the implementation of the leadership principle in the political, economic and social structures of the country. Through extensive regulation and economic planning, a system of state capitalism replaced the autonomy of capital and industry. By integrating all the various competing classes and interest groups into the nation, the Nazis sought to form an ideal super-community. They set in motion a social revolution of great significance, but were unable to win the full allegiance of the army and churchmen, and the support of workers and rural villagers was only lukewarm.

Ideologically, National Socialism was similar to Italian fascism, but its distinctive trait was a utopian anti-modernism that rejected the assumptions underlying the Enlightenment and industrial revolution and glorified a primitive, idealized past portrayed in Wagnerian operas and ancient Germanic sagas where the complexities of modern life had no place. The concern with race was central to Nazi ideology. The *völkisch* thinkers provided the emphasis on 'people', 'soil' and 'blood'—the idea that Germans possessed a series of traits bound up with their homeland and environment that set them apart from others. Foreign persons, ideas and institutions were considered corrupting, especially those identified with Jews. Pseudo-anthropologists set out the 'science' of race, which distinguished between superior and inferior human types. Social Darwinism supplied the idea of a struggle between groups and nations, in which the stronger peoples would dispossess and destroy the weaker.

A 'culture-destroying race'

Drawing upon these ideas, Nazi theoreticians developed their barbaric doctrine of anti-Semitism. In order to regain the lost innocence of the past, they argued that it was necessary to purge the present of its impurities. The Jew was the source of all modern evils, the 'culture-destroying race' that gave the world both capitalism and Marxism. Hitler declared that even the Christian faith was a Jewish plot: 'The heaviest blow that ever struck humanity was the coming of Christianity. Bolshevism is Christianity's illegitimate child. Both are inventions of the

A Jew in Nuremberg, Germany, in the 1930s, forced to parade with an accusing placard. The Nazis had a sustained policy of anti-semitism.

"The Swastika on our breasts, the Cross in our hearts."

Motto of the 'German Christians'

Jew.' The Nazis argued that the 'culture-creating' Aryan race was engaged in a life-and-death struggle. The eradication of the Jewish race would be the act of social purification necessary to restore the uncorrupt past.

Another key concept was space: the master race needed more room to live (*Lebensraum*). Hitler's aim was to acquire space in Russia and eastern Europe which would end German dependence on imported foodstuffs and raw materials. There German colonists could settle on the land, away from the defiling influence of the cities, and this simple yeomanry would provide an inexhaustible reservoir of warriors for future conflicts. Racial purity supplemented by cultural purity would restore health to Germany.

The Nazis deprived German Jews of their rights as citizens and encouraged them to emigrate by boycotts, expelling them from their jobs, and constantly harassing them. When the German armies overran eastern Europe, which had a much larger Jewish population, anti-Semitism became much more violent. In Russia Nazi death-squads liquidated many thousands of Jews on the spot, while in Poland Jews were herded into urban 'ghettos' and forced to live in horrendous slums. The infamous concentration camps, originally created to break the spirits of Nazism's opponents, had even more ominous overtones for the Jews. In 1940–41 a series of new camps were created in Poland, of which the best known were Auschwitz and Treblinka. Here the Nazis put into operation the 'final solution', the extermination of the entire Jewish population of Europe. Men, women and children were transported to these 'death factories' and in a cold-blooded, calculated manner beaten, starved, shot, worked to death, utilized in medical experiments, and gassed. Reasonable estimates put the number of Jewish deaths in the 'Holocaust' at six million.

The plight of Christians under the Nazi regime was also precarious. Born and reared a Catholic, Hitler abandoned whatever Christian principles he had in favour of the secular philosophies of the day. But he never formally cut his ties with the church, nor was he excommunicated. National Socialism itself was a new faith which appealed to the millions of Germans who longed for national regeneration. Hitler's distaste for the church was primarily political; he envied the power Catholicism had over its adherents, but despised Protestantism for its lack of unity and of authority. However, he courted both Protestant and Catholic support during his rise to power by emphasizing the nationalist aspects of his programme, and by claiming to support the church's position in the state.

The German defeat and revolution in 1918 had stunned the Protestant church leaders. They were cool towards the new republic, which seemed to be dominated by socialist and Roman Catholic politicians. The Weimar Constitution of 1919 provided for separation of church and state, thus removing the threat of government control of the church. But the churches retained a privileged legal status, continued to receive state subsidies, and kept their traditional role in education.

Most churchmen sympathized with the anti-republican right wing, and were won over to the 'national movement' as conditions deteriorated after 1929. Many Protestants, particularly theological conservatives and those in the free churches, overlooked the anti-Semitic and pagan side of Nazism, and praised Hitler's anti-communism and call for 'positive Christianity'. Hitler cleverly held in check the anti-Christian radicals such as Alfred Rosenberg, so as not to alarm church leaders. The three different factions of 'German Christians' which arose in the 1930s even formed a pro-Nazi party within the church.

Regeneration through Nazism?

Conservative churchmen felt that if Nazism were treated with understanding, it would grow out of its faults (such as racialism) and bring about national regeneration. Many protestants welcomed Hitler's overthrow of democracy in 1933 as a first step toward replacing the 'Marxist' republic with 'Christian' rulers. His 'pro-moral, pro-family' stance was also appealing. He emphasized the importance of child bearing and the role of women in the home. He wanted to eliminate pornography, prostitution and homosexuality. Although some of the Catholic hierarchy were uneasy about National Socialism, most of them shared the same outlook as the Protestants.

Hitler's policy toward the churches after January 1933 was purely pragmatic. He realized the power they possessed, and did not want to initiate another *Kulturkampf.* But he assumed that, in time, the outdated Christian faith would die out. The Catholic bishops endorsed the new regime. The Catholic Centre Party voted for the measure which allowed Hitler to rule by decree, and the Centre and Catholic trade unions 'voluntarily' dissolved themselves.

In return the Führer agreed to a concordat with the Vatican which guaranteed Catholics freedom to profess and practise their religion, and the independence of the church. The complicated treaty reaffirmed diplomatic relations with the Vatican and the legal status of the clergy, spelled out matters concerning the appointment of bishops, protected the Catholic educational system, continued public funds for the church, provided pastoral care in the army, prisons and hospitals, permitted non-political religious organizations, and forbade all political activities by the clergy.

The concordat greatly increased the prestige of Hitler's regime. By it the church sanctioned the liquidation of the religious (confessional) political parties, and the barring of the clergy from politics. It formed a milestone in the consolidation of the totalitarian state. Many churchmen feared that open conflict with the regime might jeopardize those privileges still protected by the agreement. The Nazis violated the concordat almost from the very beginning; it gave no protection against attacks, and at the same time it undermined the developing Catholic resistance.

A movement swept the Protestant church in 1933 calling for the unification and 'nationalization' of the twenty-eight provincial churches (*Landeskirchen*) with a single '*Reich*-bishop' at its head. This seemed in line with Hitler's policy of bringing all groups under the total control of the Führer and the state. The 'German Christians' secured the election of Ludwig Müller, a fervent Nazi. They also restructured the church along Nazi lines, by introducing the Führer principle into church government and adopting the 'Aryan paragraph' which provided for dismissal of all people of Jewish origin from church staffs. Hitler, however, took little notice of these steps, and rejected the 'German Christians' idea of a National Socialist state church. He felt that the church's sole function was to cater for benighted people who still had religious needs. Any church, even a Nazified

> "*Silent night, holy night,*
> *All is calm, all is bright,*
> *Only the Chancellor*
> *steadfast in fight,*
> *Watches o'er Germany*
> *by day and night,*
> *Always caring for us.*"
>
> *Nazi version of Silent Night*

> "*Christ has come to us through Adolf Hitler. . . We know today the Saviour has come. . . We have only one task, be German, not be Christian.*"
>
> PASTOR LEUTHEUSER

Pius XII was pope during World War II. His failure to speak out against German aggression attracted much criticism.

one, threatened to divide loyalties; he would tolerate no such limitations to his power.

Hitler listened increasingly to anti-Christian Nazis who called for the elimination of both the 'German Christians' and their opponents in the church. After 1934 Nazi support for the 'German Christians' waned, although many continued to occupy church posts. They became even more extreme in their claims that the Nazi movement represented the true fulfilment of Christianity, but they found that Nazi favour could be gained only by a wholehearted commitment to its racial ideas and the exaltation of the Fürher. With the creation of the Ministry of Church Affairs in 1935, under Hanns Kerrl, they and the *Reich*-Bishop lost all influence.

The German church divides

The increasing encroachment of the Nazi state on religious matters alarmed many Protestants and Catholics, and what followed was the well-known *Kirchenkampf* (church-struggle). In September 1933 Dr Martin Niemöller formed a Pastor's Emergency League to combat 'German Christian' ideas. In the following year his group repudiated Müller and set up an alternative church government structure known as the Confessing Church. Its theological basis was spelled out in the *Barmen Declaration* of May 1934. Largely written by Karl Barth, the *Declaration* called the German church back to the central truths of Christianity and rejected the totalitarian claims of the state in religious and political matters.

The *Barmen Declaration* was not intended as a political protest and the Confessing Church did not plan to spearhead resistance to Nazism. It was a theological document directed against the heretical distortions of the 'German Christians'. In fact the leaders repeatedly affirmed their loyalty to the state and congratulated Hitler on his political and foreign policy moves. Because Luthe traditionally supported the ruling Power, the Confessing Churcl decided not to set itself up as a riv free church, but simply to defend the orthodox Christian faith agains innovations.

Harassed by the Gestapo and repudiated by most Protestant leaders, the Confessing Church le a perilous existence. Its very pres ence was an embarrassment to th Nazis and its witness to Christ's Lordship over the world implicitly challenged Hitler's totalitarianism. A few of its members, such as Dietrich Bonhoeffer, were conscious of their political responsibility and reluctantly became involve in the anti-Hitler resistance. But the conservatism and nationalism most Germans deterred them fro standing up publicly for democrac and individual rights.

After the war, in October 1945, Niemöller and the surviving leaders of the Confessing Church poignantly declared their guilt for failing to speak out against the Nazi regime, especially in its early stages.

Opposing the 'new heathenism'

The German Catholics, too, wanted to uphold the state and keep their privileged status. They remembered the *Kulturkampf* of Bismarck's day. But they, too, were drawn into the church struggle. The Nazis gradually, but methodically, destroyed the network of Catholic organizations in Germany, and clamped down on the Catholic press and schools. In vain churchmen expressed alarm over the spread of 'new heathenism' and increasing restrictions on their work; finally they turned to the Vatican for help.

With the assistance of Eugenio Cardinal Pacelli, the papal secretary of state who was soon to be pope, Pius XI drafted the encyclical *Mit brennender Sorge* (*With deep anxiety*) of 14 March 1937. This was the first major church document to criticize Nazism. Smuggled into Germany, it was read on Palm Sunday from every Catholic pulpit—before a single copy had fallen into Nazi hands. The encyclical protested against the oppression of the church and called upon Catholics to resist the idolatrous cult of race and state, to stand against the perversion of Christian doctrines and morality, and to maintain their loyalty to Christ, his church and Rome. The pope condemned the excesses of Nazi doctrines without denouncing the regime's totalitarianism, keeping the door open for reconciliation.

Hitler reacted furiously at first, but then decided to avoid a break by treating it with complete silence. Knowing that he had the support of the German Catholic lay people, Hitler simply stepped up the pressure on church activities and clergy, to rule out the possibility of organized resistance. The Nazis dealt severely with dissent in the lower ranks, but were reluctant to move against high dignitaries such as Bishop Galen of Münster, whose forthright attack on the euthanasia programme in August 1941 aroused such public indignation that Hitler had it suspended.

The communist challenge

Communism, the left-wing variety of totalitarianism, has generally arisen in poorer, less developed nations. Communist systems are similar to those on the right in many ways: they stress dictatorial, charismatic leadership; a centralized, bureaucratic party whose members form the 'elite' of the new order; rigid discipline and ruthless terror, with a secret police and concentration camps; the use and even glorification of violence to achieve the regime's goals; a stereotyped negative image of the enemy (the Wall Street banker or Yankee imperialist); propaganda and censorship to condition and direct the public mind; indoctrination of youth; strict control of the economy, and hostility to all organized religion.

The ideology emphasizes the working classes, revolution as the means for social change, and the utopian ideal of a classless society. Lenin, the principal theorist of totalitarian communism, regarded his work as a logical development of Marxist historical and dialectical materialism. He formulated a doctrine of the party and the nature of revolution that would ensure the ultimate victory of the proletariat.

According to Lenin, the party is a small, tightly-knit organization that instills political consciousness into the masses and leads in the struggle for power, even to the point of actually seizing power on behalf of the workers. To obtain unity of action, the party is organized on the basis of 'democratic centralism'. The party bodies are elected by the members and represent the masses' interests, but no deviation is permitted from the party 'line'—the tactics and strategy developed by the leadership. Lenin believed the workers and peasants could together overthrow the tsarist regime and establish a revolutionary dictatorship that would direct the country's economic development and create the classless society. His bolsheviks identified with the popularly elected councils (*soviets*) and seized power from the tottering republican regime that replaced tsarist

rule in March 1917. As he began to put his theories into practice, his enemies struck back, leading to a bitter civil war and intervention by the Western Allies. Trotsky saved the day by raising from scratch a 'Red Army', which defeated the 'Whites' after two years. Now the Russian communists were more hostile than ever to the Western capitalist countries, and the memory of this has continued to

THE CHRISTIAN CHURCH AND THE JEWS

H. L. Ellison

At first Christians were regarded as a Jewish sect by both Jews and Gentiles. This led to opposition and persecution of the church by the Jewish authorities, who objected to its doctrines and the admission of Gentiles without their accepting the Law. After the Jewish revolts against Rome (AD 66–74, AD 132–35) most Christians dissociated themselves from the Jews. The Jewish Christians' refusal to support the revolts caused them to be regarded as national enemies. From this time few Jews were converted to Christianity.

Increasingly Christians came to regard Jews as deliberate haters of the good. When the church became recognized by Constantine legal discrimination against Jews increased and they were gradually deprived of all rights. Until the French Revolution no distinction can be made between the attitudes of church and state towards the Jews.

In the Dark Ages and the Middle Ages the Jews were exposed to constant harassment, frequent expulsions, and sometimes massacre. One of the worst examples occurred during the First Crusade (1096–99). The Jews were banished from England in 1290, from France in 1306, 1322 and finally in 1394. Increasingly the Jews were given the choice of accepting Christianity or banishment. In Spain the massacres of 1391 led many 'Marranos' to accept Christianity, though often only in name. The inquisition investigated with its horrors the genuineness of their faith. Eventually all Jews were expelled from Spain in 1492. Throughout this period in Europe, contacts between Christians and Jews were minimal. Jews were forced to wear distinctive dress and to live in special streets or districts (ghettos).

The Renaissance and Reformation brought a few of the more learned and liberal to revise their opinions of Judaism and the Jews. But even such a man as Martin Luther, after earlier more favourable views, made bitter and despicable attacks on them. Jews were allowed to settle in Holland in 1598, in Hamburg in 1612, and in England (unofficially) in 1656.

From 1354 Poland was the chief centre of European Jewry. As the country grew weaker the Jews were increasingly subjected to the hatred of the Roman Catholic church and the hostility of the people. When, after 1772, Poland was partitioned, most Polish Jews found themselves under either Roman Catholic Austria or Orthodox Russia. Economic pressure and the Russian massacres (the 'pogroms' of 1881–1914) sent nearly two million Jews from eastern Europe, mainly as emigrants to the United States.

poison East-West relations.

Proceeding on Leon Trotsky's theory of 'permanent revolution' —that the Russian venture could not succeed unless revolution occurred in other countries as well—the Bolsheviks in 1919 created the Communist International (Comintern) to co-ordinate the world revolutionary movement and obtain support abroad for their regime. In 1919

The Enlightenment of the eighteenth century brought a new attitude towards Jews. In opposing traditional Christianity many thinkers also attacked Christian ideas about Jews. This led to complete emancipation of French Jews during the French Revolution (1790). By 1914 emancipation had occurred all over Europe to the frontiers of Russia and the Balkans.

But political acceptance for Jews did not remove deep-rooted popular prejudice. This came to a head in 1878 in the movement of Antisemitism which soon spread throughout the civilised world. It found its logical expression in Hitler's 'Final Solution', in which about six million Jews, a third of world Jewry, perished. Even in the United States, where the Jews had never been discriminated against, antisemitic feeling increased, especially where Jews were little known.

The first real missionary concern for Jews since the early days of the church was shown by the Moravians and the German pietists in the first half of the eighteenth century. But there was no major advance until Jewish missions were started in the Church of England in 1809, in the Free Churches in 1842, and in Scotland in 1840. From Britain this movement spread rapidly to other Protestant countries, especially to Norway. The Jewish mass exodus from eastern Europe to America resulted in further missionary work there. Some Roman Catholics also sought to evangelize among Jews.

During the Middle Ages the Jews were frequently persecuted and often confined to ghettos. The illustration is of the Eve of Passover service at a Jewish synagogue in fourteenth-century Spain.

Most of the converts, however, belonged to the fringe of Jewry. This was partly because of bitter memories of the past, partly because Jews knew that most Christians did not really support the missionaries.

Since 1939 and the Nazi holocaust Christians have tended to stress understanding, the removal of prejudices, and dialogue rather than a direct missionary approach, although there is little evidence that Antijudaism is disappearing.

communist regimes briefly held sway in Hungary and Bavaria, and popular hysteria (the 'Red Scare') against leftists was whipped up in the United States. But world revolution never got off the ground. When they recognized that the European capitalist states drew much of their strength from their new empires, the communists at once backed the cause of colonial liberation.

When Lenin died in 1924, a bitter struggle for Soviet leadership raged between Trotsky and the ambitious Joseph Stalin, resulting in the latter's victory by 1927. As a boy, Stalin attended the Orthodox seminary in Tiflis, but he abandoned religion for Marxist materialism without completing his studies for the priesthood. Stalin realized that in the immediate future any hope of spreading revolution beyond Russia was futile; he countered the idea of permanent revolution with his doctrine of 'socialism in one country'. He argued that Russia must be transformed into a highly industrialized state on the basis of its own resources so that it could compete with the capitalist nations and resist their aggression.

The First Five Year Plan (1928) laid the basis for the totalitarian control of the country's economic and social life. The collectivization of agriculture was decreed, and those prosperous peasants (the *Kulaks*) who resisted were wiped out as a class. The capital generated in the agricultural sector was diverted to heavy industry, and though wages were depressed and the production of consumer goods low, Russia was transformed into an industrial nation.

Stalin also concentrated heavily on education and youth organizations to win over the younger generation to the new order, and the party exercised a dictatorship over all aspects of life and thought in the Soviet Union, as the country had been renamed in 1922. What resulted was the strengthening, not the withering away, of the state; but Stalin said this was necessary so long as the capitalist encirclement of the country prevailed. An even more brutal and ruthless dictator than his counterpart in Germany, the moody, suspicious Stalin utilized secret police terror and labour camps to suppress even the slightest dissent and to eliminate all potential rivals, including his old Bolshevik comrades who were executed after the spectacular Moscow trials in 1936–38. He had brought into Soviet communism the 'cult of the personality'.

The Orthodox church at Smolensk, Russia, became a factory under the Soviet regime. Other churches in the Soviet Union were converted into museums, cinemas and houses.

Opiate of the people

A hostility to Christianity—and all religion—is a central theme in Marxism-Leninism. Marxists claim that the existing sociopolitical order determines all phenomena—including religious beliefs; atheism is implied in such a claim. Religion is false consciousness, an illusory reflection of the world resulting from class divisions. It will die a natural death when society is restored to a 'normal' state in communism. Until the advent of *glasnost* and *perestroika* in the 1980s, Russian communists actively struggled against religion. The party regarded itself as embodying the ideals of Marxism-Leninism, and could not allow some part of visible reality to remain outside its scope. Institutional religion was a reactionary social force that only impeded progress towards the classless society, and it had to be smashed.

Clearly, Christianity was an alternative world-view that, if tolerated, would threaten the power and prestige of the Communist party. At the same time, Christians could not accept a secularized version of their own understanding of history —that nature is moving humanity towards a final perfect end. Moreover, since Marxism-Leninism stressed the need for violent class struggle, Christians found it difficult, if not impossible, to come to a settlement. The Bolshevik revolution confronted Christianity with an enormous ideological challenge.

The Russian Orthodox church had long been subservient to the state, but pressure for reform was mounting. Although the Tsar was in theory the head of the church, the procurator of the Holy Synod, appointed by the Tsar, actually governed the church. More and more churchmen believed that the conditions of workers and peasants must be improved. Except for a small group of radical priests, Christians rejected socialism as a solution. The Rasputin scandal, interference by the imperial couple in church matters, and ignored pleas for reform so undermined Nicholas II's position among Orthodox leaders that they welcomed the March Revolution of 1917 and sided with the provisional government.

This crude anti-Christian poster was circulated by communist authorities in the USSR. Christianity was branded as superstition, fit only for the senile, to prevent young people becoming interested.

In August 1917 an All-Russian Council (*Sobor*) of the church was convened. This rather conservative body challenged revolutionary public opinion by reintroducing the old patriarchal system of church government. When the Bolsheviks took over, they confiscated church lands, cancelled state subsidies for the church, decreed civil marriage, and nationalized schools.

Patriach Tikhon responded in February 1918 by excommunicating the government leaders. Church officials organized demonstrations and armed resistance, and called for restoration of the monarchy. The Council of People's Commissars immediately ordered the separation of church and state, in a decree which recognized the equality before the law of all religious groups, and permitted them freedom of worship 'so long as they do not disturb public order or interfere with the rights of citizens'. It completely disestablished the Orthodox church, and banished every vestige of religion from state and public schools. All church property was nationalized. That which produced revenue was kept by the state, and church buildings used for worship were leased to their congregations free of charge. Churches and sects were denied the rights of a person in law, which placed them in an extremely vulnerable legal position in the years to come.

The regime moved slowly to implement the law. It surrounded the church with an ever-tightening network of administrative and police controls. When famine spread through Russia in 1922, the government ordered the confiscation of church treasures for humanitarian relief purposes. Patriarch Tikhon denounced this as sacrilege and urged the faithful not to submit, but the authorities quickly quelled resistance and arrested him. But he was freed after recanting his 'anti-Soviet actions' and declaring himself loyal to the regime.

Meanwhile, a schism occurred when a group of parish clergy formed the 'Living Church' (Renovationists), which opposed the monastic-episcopal basis of the patriarchal church, and took up a pro-Soviet position. In 1923 the *Sobor* accepted the reforms of the Living Church, cut all counter-revolutionary links, assured the government of its unconditional loyalty, and recognized the separation of church and state and the nationalization of church property. But neither this surrender, nor later expressions of Soviet patriotism, restored the church to official favour or healed its divisions. The unwritten rule in Soviet church-state relations was that the right to a carefully limited freedom of worship would extend only to groups which could prove their loyalty to the regime.

League of the Godless

From the beginning the Bolsheviks sponsored atheist endeavours. These efforts were eventually concentrated in the League of Militant Godless, formed in 1925. It spread anti-clerical propaganda and promoted cultural enlightenment by stressing science and materialist philosophy. The League produced anti-religious films, plays, radio talks and literature, sponsored lectures and exhibits, and established museums of atheism.

Although the Russian Republic constitutions of 1918 and 1925 guaranteed 'freedom of religious and anti-religious propaganda', the 1929 Law on Religious Associations placed strict limits on the activities of churches. They could not engage in social, charitable or educational work, hold prayer, Bible study, women's or young people's meetings, or even give their members material aid. They were free only to worship, and were deprived of any influence on society.

Meanwhile, the state had unlimited power to control religious bodies. Every congregation had to be registered, and the registering authority could exclude individuals from elected church councils. All extraordinary meetings and religious conferences required special permission, and local officials could close a church if they decided the building was needed for some public purpose. The Russian constitution was amended to exclude the right of religious propaganda, which crippled the evangelistic efforts of the non-Orthodox movements. From this point only public worship was tolerated.

The 1930s were years of intense persecution. Thousands of clergymen were imprisoned or liquidated during the collectivization of agriculture and Stalin's purges.

The new Soviet constitution of 1936 restored voting rights to the clergy (they had been classified as an 'exploiting element', and automatically disfranchised). But the 'servants of religion' continued to be second-class citizens, members of a profession that 'exploited the backwardness and ignorance of the toilers'. They were constantly harassed by the secret police as 'clerico-fascists'.

The Russian Orthodox church as an institution was on the verge of disintegration by 1939. The rigid application of anti-religious laws, atheistic propaganda, and Stalinist terror almost wiped out the Lutheran and ravaged the Baptist and Evangelical Christian denominations. Large numbers of Russian Mennonites emigrated to the Americas in the 1920s, but those staying behind suffered along with other religious groups. Similar treatment was meted out to Roman Catholics, non-Russian minority groups of Christians, Old Believers, Uniate (Greek rite) Catholics, and even Jews and Muslims.

Rome versus Moscow

Soviet persecution of Christians contributed greatly to the revulsion against the Soviet regime in the West. The Roman Catholic church was most alarmed about events there. Moscow in turn regarded Catholicism as the ally of capitalism, reaction and fascism—a major obstacle to world revolution. In 1930 Pope Pius XI called for a world-wide day of prayer, and celebrated a mass of expiation on behalf of suffering Christians in Russia, and the Anglican and German Lutheran churches joined in the protest. The Soviets responded by forming a Militant Atheists International to combat the Vatican. But when Hitler began persecuting Catholics, the Soviets retreated, declared fascism to be the main enemy, and called for a united front with Catholic anti-fascists.

Viewing the Soviet anti-religious campaign with deepening concern, Pius XI issued the encyclical *Divini Redemptoris* on 18 March 1937, condemning the 'errors of communism'. He criticized the spread of communism into Spain and Mexico, expressed sympathy for the Russian people, and offered the doctrines of the Catholic church as the alternative to communism. To counter the current 'popular front' policy of Stalin, the pope declared that 'communism is intrinsically wrong and no one who would save Christian civilization may collaborate with it in any undertaking whatsoever'. Coming only four days after his encyclical criticizing Nazi Germany, this placed the Vatican firmly on the side of persecuted believers in the totalitarian countries.

Christians and World War II

The determination of the German and Italian dictators to engage in expansion brought Europe to the brink of war. A militaristic clique imposed a fascist-style regime in Japan which made common cause with the European Axis powers. In 1939 Stalin concluded a non-aggression pact with Hitler that opened the way for the German invasion of Poland and the formal launching of World War II, but two years later Hitler abruptly turned on his former ally. President Roosevelt prevailed over isolationist sentiments in the United States to undertake preparations for war, and the Japanese attack on the American and European possessions in the Pacific set the stage for the greatest conflict in history.

During the 1930s Christians in the United States were divided in

"To bomb cities as cities, deliberately to attack civilians, quite irrespective of whether or not they are actively contributing to the war effort, is a wrong deed, whether done by the Nazis or by ourselves."

BISHOP GEORGE BELL of Chichester

> *"We shall not rest until we have rooted out Christianity."*
>
> *HIMMLER*

their attitudes toward the totalitarian dictatorships. Some were so staunchly anti-communist that they backed fascist-type movements. Even Hitler found favour with a number of Christians and one leader is reported to have commended him for building 'a front line of defence against the Anti-Christ of Communism'.

On the other hand, the agonies of the depression pushed many clergy towards the left. Liberal Christians denounced the evils of capitalism, called for social reform, and embraced Roosevelt's policy of a 'New Deal'. Some were active socialists—for example Reinhold Niebuhr and Norman Thomas—but very few actually joined the Communist party or approved of events in the Soviet Union.

Although torn by ideological and organizational divisions, the American peace movement grew in numbers during the 1930s and provided considerable support for isolationist policies. Liberal Christians were heavily involved in the peace societies, but some came to see a vast difference between the totalitarian threat and the pre-1914 situation. They began to argue for American participation in the widening struggle. Outraged by what they regarded as short-sighted pacifism, Reinhold Niebuhr and others founded in 1941 the journal *Christianity and Crisis* which challenged church people to reject neutralism and to accept intervention as necessary.

When World War II broke out in 1939, churchmen in the various countries pledged loyalty to their regimes. But in comparison with 1914, the commitment was more tentative, and a crusading air not so evident. In the West the peace movement collapsed. Churches supplied servicemen with the pastoral care of military chaplains. The rights of the tiny minority of religious conscientious objectors were usually (but not always) respected and the historic peace churches and liberal pacifist organizations were left alone. Some clergymen actually opposed the war and worked for a negotiated peace, and others condemned the obliteration-bombing of Germany and Japan.

German Protestant and Catholic leaders alike publicly urged their people to back the war effort, and the Russian churches enthusiastically supported the 'Great Patriotic War'. In 1941 most Christians in Japan had, under government pressure, united into one church, the *Kyodan,* which, after Pearl Harbor, urged believers to 'promote the Great Endeavour'.

German church officials remained conciliatory towards the Nazi state, but this failed to turn aside the suffering of Christians in Germany. Hitler's closest advisers, Bormann, Himmler and Heydrich, systematically worked towards the 'final settlement' in church-state relations. The churches were to be subordinated to the 'new order', the clergy stripped of all privileges and Christianity left to suffer what Hitler called 'a natural death'.

In the occupied areas of eastern Europe priests and pastors, along with devout laymen, were treated as common criminals. Thousands were executed or sent to concentration camps. The exigencies of the war and need for popular support prevented the Nazis from eradicating religion in Germany itself. But what lay ahead was dramatized in the Warthegau, the model territory in Poland, where the institutional church was virtually wiped out by the Nazis.

Germans resist Hitler

However, a small minority of clerics and laymen in both denominations openly opposed the Nazis.

The Kreisau Circle, a group led by Count Helmuth von Moltke, met regularly at his estate to discuss the spiritual and other problems that would confront Germany once Hitler was gone from the scene. Although no evidence was found that directly implicated these men in the assassination attempt of 20 July 1944, they were tried and condemned. Count Klaus von Stauffenberg, who planted the bomb, was a Catholic, but the Catholic hierarchy itself offered no encouragement to him or other conspirators.

The execution of Father Alfred Delp, a Jesuit member of the Kreisau group, and of Dietrich Bonhoeffer revealed the implacable hostility of National Socialism to Christianity. By and large, however, the churches' resistance was meagre. They were exclusively concerned with individualistic personal faith, traditional submission to the state, and a conservative outlook which rejected all left-wing proposals for social and political reform and enabled them to accept the Nazis' claim to be the only alternative to communism.

Two decades later, Christian activists in the United States and other countries drew inspiration and ideas from the German experience in the struggle for social justice in their own lands. In post-war West Germany the memory of the church conflict led to a revitalization of the role of the ordinary Christians, acceptance of political and social responsibility as a Christian duty, and the total rejection of pseudo-religious glorification of the nation. Recognizing that unity in Christ binds together Christians of every nation and race, they now took an active part in the ecumenical movement. Conscious of their own deeply-rooted anti-Semitism, many churchmen openly confessed guilt for the horrors that overtook their Jewish compatriots, and gave their backing to the new state of Israel.

Stalin's unexpected ally

The situation in wartime Soviet Russia was quite different. Stalin realized the value of the church's contribution to public morale in the war, and how it could help integrate the territories acquired during the war and promote Soviet foreign-policy views later on.

Stalin therefore allowed the patriarchal church to revive (the Renovationist rival was dissolved in 1943), reduced the level of atheist propaganda, and relaxed the application of the 1918 and 1929 laws. The church could set up its hierarchical organization again, collect funds, and give some private religious instruction to children. In 1945 the Orthodox church and other religious groups regained status as a legal corporation and with it the right to possess property and produce liturgical objects. The Orthodox church enjoyed the most favourable position since the civil war, but it was still closely supervised by the state. The Council for the Affairs of the Russian Orthodox Church was created in 1943, and a similar one for other religious groups in 1944. These maintained liaison between the government and the churches, drafted regulations on religion and ensured that the laws were enforced.

The Roman Catholic church clearly recognized the difficulties posed by the spreading conflict and, in March 1939, chose an accomplished diplomat, Cardinal Pacelli as pope. As Pius XII he was deeply committed to bringing peace to the world, but held no illusions about either communism or Nazism, both of which he detested. He had personally experienced the communist coup in Munich in 1919 and later, as papal secretary of state, confronted Nazi deceit whenever he tried to uphold the concordat.

But Pius' valiant efforts to avert conflict and lessen suffering in occupied areas were unsuccessful. The problem of how to overcome the sin of war and yet minister to those overwhelmed by the catastrophe seemed insoluble. A forceful denunciation of Nazi crimes might only increase Nazi atrocities and result in still more suffering. If he said nothing, the reputation of the Vatican as the guardian of moral and spiritual values would be shattered.

Why the pope was silent

Why then did Pius remain silent about German aggression, and especially the murder of millions of Jews? Critics argue that if he had spoken out vigorously, and threatened to excommunicate all Catholics involved in carrying out the 'final solution', the Jewish massacre could have been averted. But to have done so would have lost the allegiance of German Catholics, and the institutional church throughout occupied Europe might have been smashed. To preserve that seemed more important than saving Jewish lives. In addition, Pius did not want to undermine the German struggle against Russia; he regarded Bolshevism as a greater evil than National Socialism.

A Russian soldier raises the red flag over the Reichstag building in Berlin at the end of World War II. With the defeat of Nazism, the 'Iron Curtain' fell over Eastern Europe, posing a communist challenge to the capitalist West.

Pius' defenders argue that he took the stance of strict neutrality in order to be in a position to negotiate reconciliation, and to avoid lending any religious support to the conflict. He also realized that most German Catholics supported Hitler and that anti-Semitism had so infected them that they probably would not respond to papal efforts to counteract Nazi Jewish policies. There were also other problems; it was difficult to obtain solid information on crimes against Jews and practically impossible to spread this to a large enough number of Germans. Finally, a Catholic call to action against the central tenet of National Socialism would most certainly be regarded as high treason, and dealt with in a brutal, summary fashion. World War II presented the pope with a crisis of conscience that could not easily be resolved.

The Protestant ecumenical movement also found itself in an awkward position because of the war. The 1938 Madras conference of the International Missionary Council observed that a militant 'new paganism' had arisen which demanded religious devotion from its followers. But, fearful that believers in the Soviet Union, Axis countries, and Japanese-occupied lands in Asia would suffer retaliation, no specific national sins were pinpointed or condemned. After 1939 the council assisted the 'orphaned missions' of Germany and other European countries in Africa and Asia to continue functioning. It demonstrated that a Christian world fellowship, transcending nation and denomination, was possible. Other ecumenical groups concentrated on international relief efforts, caring for war prisoners and refugees, and maintaining contacts between churches on both sides.

World War II had a devastating impact on Christianity, both physically and morally. Thousands of churches were destroyed, clergymen killed, and faithful believers persecuted or uprooted from their homes. The level of violence escalated with the use of armoured vehicles, incendiary bombing, guided missiles, and the atomic bomb, which together snuffed out the lives of millions.

The deliberate direction of war against civilian populations, indifference to the sufferings of Jews and other minorities, development of a military-industrial complex, and the alliance of the Western democracies with the totalitarian Soviet Union were moral issues of paramount concern to Christians. These led many to question whether a 'just war' could any longer be possible. They suggested that Christian endorsement of war only led to its intensification. Although some Christians were involved in attempts to bring nations and churches together in community—the United Nations (1945) and the World Council of Churches (1948)—the coming of the cold war frustrated their work.

Ideologies in conflict

After 1945 a rift opened between the victors, and the United States as leader of the Western democracies took the initiative through the 'containment' policy to counter Soviet expansion. This was, however, confused with communism as a political doctrine, especially after China was 'lost' in 1949. Communism anywhere, whether at home, in Europe, or in the Third World, was viewed as a direct threat to American national security. The 'witch-hunts' of Senator Joseph McCarthy and others were aimed at domestic subversion, while foreign economic and military aid and a string of defensive alliances with independent countries around the world were designed to counter possible communist exploitation of their weakness. The United States was committed to resisting communism almost everywhere, even if this meant military intervention, but eventually the development of the H-bomb and long-range ballistic missiles made armed conflict between the superpowers unthinkable.

An artist's impression of the devastation caused by bombing in London during World War II. Both sides used saturation bombing with terrible effect on such places as Dresden and Coventry.

Although the cold war started as rivalry between the great powers, it rapidly took on an ideological dimension. Both sides in the polarized world received support from their Christian populations. In a messianic manner, the Soviets preached the doctrines of communism and the necessity of freeing peoples oppressed by 'imperialists'. At the same time, by installing friendly regimes on their borders, they secured Mother Russia against another attack from the West, like those in 1914 and 1941.

The Russian Orthodox leaders meanwhile sought to bring churches in other countries under their jurisdiction. Orthodox representatives travelling abroad invariably proclaimed the current Moscow 'line' on world issues and praised conditions in the Soviet Union. They were especially active in the Soviet-sponsored peace campaigns. With the emphasis on 'peaceful co-existence' following Stalin's death in 1953, the Orthodox church participated in ecumenical affairs, and finally joined the World Council of Churches in 1961.

The West reacted with the counter-ideology of anti-communism. The basic assumption was that there was a universal communist conspiracy controlled by Moscow, which masterminded all revolutionary unrest in the world. Anti-communism was, particularly, an American response to the East-West stalemate after World War II, and the frustration resulting from America's inability to spread the virtues of liberal democracy to all nations. It also sprang from the anxieties of people whose traditional values had been uprooted by the social changes of the war years—the extreme mobility of American life that shattered their sense of security, the demands of minorities for equality, and the impersonality of bureaucratized society. Communism, the ideology that seemingly clashed with the basic elements of 'Americanism' as a secular faith, was regarded as the source of these problems. The 'American way' was hard work and rugged individualism, and 'compromise' with this global adversary was an inconceivable alternative to 'victory'.

The Vatican was extremely critical of communism. Pius XII excommunicated Catholics involved in communist activities, openly denounced persecution, backed resistance efforts by East European Catholics, and called upon the faithful in Italy to reject the party. Similarly, most American Catholics (Senator McCarthy was one) were hostile to the 'foreign' ideology.

Even more fervent in its support of anti-communism was the conservative Protestant community in America. Communism was regularly condemned from pulpits of the land. The interdenominational National Association of Evangelicals and American Council of Churches urged forceful action to halt the spread of the red menace. Funds flowed into the coffers of those religious groups of the radical right which exposed alleged conspirators and reaffirmed the traditional values which they regarded as both American and Christian. They singled out for attack internationalist and social-activitist liberal churchmen and ecumenical bodies. Although American Christian anti-communism remained strong well into the 1960s, the easing of the cold war, the liberalizing currents following from the Second Vatican Council, and the quest for East-West *détente* undermined the impact of what had become an outdated ideology.

By the 1960s new forces were shaping world politics. First there was the recovery and growing independence of western Europe. Second, there was the disintegration of the monolithic communist bloc, because of the Sino-Soviet rift and increasing assertiveness of the leaders of Moscow's East-European 'satellites' and communist parties elsewhere. A third major factor was the end of colonialism and the spectacular appearance in the world arena of Africa, Asia and Latin America. World revolution was redefined as the quest for economic and racial equality with the white nations of the northern hemisphere. Finally there was a decline in the importance of nuclear weapons in the world power balance since they were not used in settling political disputes and were of no value in guerrilla wars.

The Marxist challenge

In addition to the resurgence of traditional religions and the rise of new religions, political and social challenges faced Christianity that had enormous religious implications. Among these were Marxism, ethnic and religious strife, and civil religion.

As World War II ended, the Chinese communist leader Mao Ze-dong resumed his struggle for control of China with Chiang Kai-shek's *Kuomintang* (Nationalists). Mao's forces were finally victorious in 1949, and established the People's Republic of China. Believing that Christianity was tied both to Western colonialism and to Vatican and American anti-communism, Mao's government expelled all foreign missionaries, liquidated church organizations and subjected believers to intense persecution. This reached its peak in the 'cultural revolution' of 1966–71.

There was also a resurgence of nationalism which led to a split with its Soviet ally and the end of monolithic communism in the 1960s. However, after China's *rapprochement* with the United States, admission to the United Nations, and the death of Mao, the more stringent aspects of the regime were relaxed.

Out of the Chinese Revolution came a new variant of Marxism known as Maoism. Mao emphasized the peasantry rather than the proletariat as the social basis of the revolution. He regarded the party as a people's democracy, where the peasantry, workers, petty bourgeoisie, and intellectuals would unite in a revolutionary organization. The tactics for obtaining power were those of guerilla warfare and disciplined action which chipped away at the existing order. Finally, Mao stressed Chinese nationalism and blamed feudalism and imperialism for the country's desperate plight.

China was an outstanding example of an underdeveloped country, but under Mao's communist rule it made enormous strides in eliminating hunger, creating an industrial base, and building a military machine. This was a model for revolutionary action that could be imitated and implemented elsewhere.

The Chinese claimed to be the ally of the world's impoverished nations and tried to win their allegiance in a struggle of the poor against the rich, thus making Marxism an instrument of class warfare between rich and poor countries rather than economic classes within nations. Both Maoism, and the recently developed Christian variety of Marxism, the theology of liberation, have appealed to revolutionary leaders in Africa, Asia and Latin America.

However, in the late 1970s China began orienting itself more toward the West. Outside business interests invested heavily, tourists flocked in, teacher and student exchanges multiplied, and the

Chairman Mao, the Chinese communist leader, who died in 1976, presides over a mass rally in Peking. His *Thoughts*, published in pocket-sized books, became a bible for Chinese communists.

MARTIN LUTHER KING

Wesley A. Roberts

Martin Luther King, Jr, the black Civil Rights leader, was born in Atlanta, Georgia, in 1929. Both his father and grandfather had been ministers of the Ebenezer Baptist Church in Atlanta, where he, too, later served as co-pastor with his father. King attended Morehouse College, Crozer Theological Seminary, and Boston University and in 1953 married Coretta Scott.

In 1955, while King was pastor of Dexter Avenue Baptist Church in Montgomery, Alabama, a black woman, Mrs Rosa Parks, refused to move to the black section of a racially-segregated bus and was arrested. The young pastor was suddenly thrust into the leadership of the bus boycott which followed. He achieved the de-segregation of the buses and was propelled into world prominence as a crusader for social justice. As president of the Southern Christian Leadership Conference, King gave dynamic leadership to the Civil Rights movement, which gained more for black people than they had achieved in the previous three centuries.

The key to King's success was his Christian commitment. Brought up in the black evangelical tradition, and influenced by the social gospel movement, he saw Christianity as a force that could transform not only the individual but the whole of society. His unique combination of the message of Jesus (love your enemies) and the method of Gandhi (non-violence) gave both a philosophy and a strategy to the Civil Rights movement. The use of non-violence as a means of achieving social justice in a violent society appealed greatly to both blacks and whites.

During the thirteen years he led the Civil Rights movement King won victory after victory without once resorting to violence. His message to his white opponents was: 'We shall match your capacity to inflict suffering with our capacity to endure suffering. We will meet your physical force with soul force. Do to us what you will, and we shall continue to love you . . .' His message and method became world-famous and in 1964 he was awarded the Nobel Peace Prize.

An assassin's bullet ended the life of Martin Luther King, Jr. in 1968 at the age of 39. In spite of being a victim of hate, he left to the world his conviction and demonstration of the power of Christian love over hate.

Dr Martin Luther King leads a Civil Rights march with other clergymen and activists in Selma, Alabama.

transfer of Hong Kong from British control in 1997 was arranged. Especially noteworthy was the growth of Christianity. Churches had been allowed to re-open after Mao's death and they expanded so rapidly that China seemed to be on the verge of a major revival. The Marxist regime was also moving toward genuine democracy when the brutal supression of the student protest movement in June 1989 put political, economic, and religious progress on hold. Only slowly did the democratization process resume.

Meanwhile, in communist Europe, organized religion was subjected to varying degrees of restriction. In Albania all religion was rooted out, and it professed to be the world's first truly atheistic state. Churches in Bulgaria and Romania worked under severe restraints, while the other bloc countries permitted substantial religious activity, although churches were hardly a welcome feature.

In 1959 the level of persecution in the Soviet Union intensified considerably, and the Russian Baptists were split over whether they should continue to submit to state regulation of religious activity. The determination of Soviet believers to practise their faith, and the pressures of world opinion, made a return to the excesses of the Stalin era impossible.

Although the church laboured under severe constraints, both in the Khrushchev and Brezhnev eras, it was clear by the 1980s that times had changed. The pressure of world opinion produced some moderation, a few outspoken religious figures were permitted to emigrate, and Billy Graham (the prime symbol of western evangelicalism) was allowed to visit and preach. When Mikhail Gorbachev assumed power in 1985, he proclaimed new policies of *perestroika* and *glasnost,* and pressures on the churches were further relaxed. Prisoners in labour camps were freed, Bibles were allowed in the country, closed churches reopened, regulations restricting religious education were modified, and Christian leaders could freely attend international gatherings.

In Poland the level of religious freedom remained extremely high for a communist state. The overwhelming majority of the people identified with the Roman Catholic church, and it provided the spiritual and ideological backing for the Solidarnösc movement which in 1989 formed the first non-communist government in Eastern Europe since the imposition of the Peoples' Republics in the immediate post-war years.

The regime of the (East) German Democratic Republic waxed hot and cold on Christianity. Its construction guaranteed a substantial level of religious freedom, and university theological faculties, religious publishing houses, and a large number of churches existed. But there was subtle discrimination in employment against practising Christians, and the regime provided various substitute rituals and activities to woo young people away from the church. More significantly, in 1978 the head of state and the church leaders reached an understanding which allowed the churches more freedom of action. They, in turn, agreed to function as 'the church within socialism', that is, to minister within the system.

Then, in 1989 when it became clear that the Soviets would not interfere in the internal affairs of the bloc, a wave of grassroots uprisings swept eastern Europe. Following the Polish example, first Hungary and then East Germany, Czechoslovakia, Bulgaria, Romania, and Albania replaced their communist regimes with democratic ones. Christians were visible in all of these, especially in the GDR where churches served as gathering points for those disaffected with the system and the church leadership negotiated with state officials and counselled the populace to moderation and non-violence.

As the Soviet clients now went their own separate ways, East and West Germany reunited, and the demands of the constituent nationalities for freedom forced far-reaching changes in the Soviet Union, leading to the dismantling of the entire communist system and the country's dissolution into over a dozen separate states. Yugoslavia also disintegrated into competing national entities and a bloody civil war ensued, while Czechoslovakia split into two parts. Resurgent nationalism was the source of most conflicts and religion was a central factor in this as well. At the same time, the old anti-religious laws were repealed and the traditional churches sought to regain their former power. They competed with evangelical missionary agencies and new religions from the West, and before long they were pressing for restrictions on the newcomers.

Racial tensions

The second problem, ethnic and racial strife with religious overtones, has been most serious. Both in South Africa and the United States relations between blacks and whites reached a critical stage in the 1960s. The South African apartheid policy was supported by most white church leaders, but their country became an international outcast because of it. The programme consisted of laws requiring racial classification and identity cards, residential separation and remote 'homelands', separate public amenities and accommodation, and racial discrimination in employment. Suffrage was for whites only. The regime had virtually unlimited police and judicial power to enforce these regulations, and imprisoned, tortured and even murdered alleged violators.

South African Christians played the leading role in the struggle against apartheid. Individuals such as Alan Paton, Bishop Desmond Tutu, Beyers Naude, Allan Boesak, Frank Chikane and John de Gruchy; groups such as the South African Council of Churches, the Christian Institute and African Enterprise; theological declarations such as the *Kairos Document* (1985) and the *Kabare Statement* (1987), were acclaimed for their bold criticism of the system. Various churches in the country, especially charismatic ones, provided models of integrated life, and by 1990 even the mainline churches were speaking out against apartheid. As more and more Christians withdrew their support from the system, and international economic and political boycotts left South Africa isolated, apartheid was gradually dismantled and the country move[d] toward multi-racial rule.

In the United States, racial segregation was deeply rooted in the churches. The black church came into existence largely as response to their exclusion from white congregations. However, the Civil Rights movement had a significant Christian dimension. The black church was the one social institution that enabled the ex-slaves to survive in a racist society. Some white Christians became convicted of their own sin of racism and joined with African-Americans in the quest fo[r] justice. The outstanding figure in this movement was the Rev. Martin Luther King, Jr. Many other Civil Rights activists came from the ranks of black and white clergy. Although legal integration was achieved, the social and economic gaps between races still remain as serious as ever.

In the Middle East and Northern Ireland both ethnic and religious differences contributed to tensions. The founding of Israel in 1948 came after thirty years of strife among Palestinian Arabs, Jewish immigrants and the British. Israel received solid support from west European and North American Christians, partly from a sense of guilt over the Holocaust and partly because many saw the return of the Jews to Palestine as the fulfilment of prophecy. On the other hand, Orthodox Christians sided with the Palestinians against Israel, so it was not solely a Muslim-Jewish controversy. As tensions between the Israelis and Palestinians mounted Christian support for Israel weakened, and more and more church leaders called for a political solution. At the same time some Jewish extremists demanded a religious state and the expulsion of the Palestinians. Although violence seemed to be the way of life in the region, the 1978 Camp David accord between Egypt and Israel and the 1993 agreement between Israel and the Palestine Liberation Organization granting the Arabs a measure of autonomy in the occupied areas showed that peace was possible.

In Northern Ireland the differences were more historical and sociological in nature than religious. Protestant and Catholic leaders alike roundly denounced the violence perpetrated in the name of religion: but the continuing crisis sapped the vitality of all Christian groups.

Civil religion

A third threat to Christian vitality was 'civil religion'. Also known as public religion or civic deism, it is a group of commonly accepted religious sentiments, symbols and concepts which serve to undergird the state and help secure popular allegiance. An elaborate matrix of beliefs flowing from a nation's historic experience, it generally blurs religion and patriotism.

Whether or not civil religion is identified with a particular denomination or faith, it is enlisted in the patriotic cause of enhancing national identity. Examples include Japanese Shinto, the white Afrikaner's sense of divine chosenness, the use of Islamic Shi'ism in Iran, and the North American understanding of being a 'nation under God'.

In the American context, the Declaration of Independence and the Constitution were the 'sacred documents' and the president the 'high priest'. The God of civil religion was a unitarian deity whose name was invoked on public occasions. State schools became the vehicles for inculcating and celebrating the national faith. The country's wars were 'righteous conflicts' and the 'American Way of Life' was seen as synonymous with God's way. The extensive use of public religion in recent years reveals how enticing it was, especially to committed Christians who loved their country and who believed it had been set apart by God as a 'Christian nation'.

In spite of these challenges, Christianity has remained vibrant and growing. Old structures have crumbled, traditional approaches been discarded, new ideas accepted, and Western hegemony in the church replaced with a shared responsibility with the peoples of the 'two-thirds world' for proclaiming the gospel. It faces the new century with vigour and optimism.

AN AGE OF ANXIETY

Anthony C. Thiselton

The twentieth century has seen an astonishing diversity of theological thinking, from the speculative thought of Liberalism to radical new approaches and painstaking biblical scholarship.

The most important and influential theologian in the first decade of the twentieth century was Adolf von Harnack of Berlin (1851–1930). Christian doctrine, he believed, developed largely under the influence of Greek thought. The essence of Christianity lay in three central truths which he found in the teaching of Jesus: the fatherhood of God, the brotherhood of man and the infinite value of the individual human soul.

Adolph Harnack, the German theologian and historian, claimed that Christ preached a gospel of the fatherhood of God, and the infinite value of the human soul.

The roots of Harnack's liberalism lay in the theology of Albrecht Ritschl (1822–89). Ritschl was suspicious of the role of doctrine, rather than experience, as an authentic source of truth. Harnack communicated his ideas to a vast readership in his book, *What is Christianity?* He was deeply concerned to commend the teaching of Jesus as something relevant to men of his own day. For this reason he especially stressed the role of Jesus as a liberator who released men from legalism, and showed them the presence of God and the way of love.

Harnack's influence declined when thinkers began to call attention to the basic weakness of liberalism as a whole. The whole teaching of Jesus cannot be reduced to three general truths, nor can the whole gospel be reduced to certain elements in the teaching of Jesus.

America too had many exponents of an optimistic and humanist kind of Christian liberalism. What came to be known as the 'social gospel movement' had theological roots in Ritschl's liberalism. The most famous theologian of the social gospel was Walter Rauschenbusch (1861–1918), whose major work was *A Theology for the Social Gospel* (1919). He claimed that all theology must stem from the central idea of the kingdom of God, believing that when Jesus spoke about the kingdom this meant, not the community of the redeemed, but the transformation of society on earth. It meant social reform and political action. Rauschenbusch himself called on the church to ally with the working class to transform the social order.

Rauschenbusch's approach began to lose momentum when two difficulties were spotlighted. First, it is doubtful whether Jesus himself understood the kingdom of God in this way at all. Second, the gospel contains much more than this one particular aspect. But his emphasis on the social gospel was also a reaction against Pietism, which was growing in the churches.

What is the essence of Christianity?

Harnack's attempt to find the essence of Christianity in the teaching of Jesus was immediately criticized by the French scholar, Alfred Loisy (1857–1940). As a Roman Catholic, Loisy saw the essence of Christianity in the ongoing faith of the church, rather than exclusively in the teaching of Jesus.

But Loisy was also a modernist. He insisted that the truth of

Christianity is something living, and is constantly re-shaped by the present. It is not a once-for-all deposit of truth from the past. He also argued that the Gospels do not report reliably the teaching of Jesus, but express the faith of the early church. He concluded that Harnack's Protestant liberalism could have no historical basis. The Roman Catholic church officially condemned Loisy's work because of its disturbing implications.

In Britain, one notable cause of controversy was R. J. Campbell's *The New Theology* (1907). It almost completely removed any distinction between God and man, and made the incarnation no more than the supreme example of God's indwelling a human being.

The vacuum left by Liberalism is illustrated by the reaction of the Scottish theologian, P. T. Forsyth. Forsyth began as a liberal, but gradually became disillusioned with what he saw as its shallowness. He discovered the truths, emphasized by evangelicals, of the centrality of the cross and the power of grace. He comments, 'I was turned from a Christian to a believer; from a lover of love into an object of grace.'

Is the Bible unique?

One group of scholars began to try to shed light on biblical and Christian thinking by comparing similar or parallel features in other (usually ancient) religions. Many of these scholars, especially in the first two decades of the century, claimed that biblical and Christian thought were by no means as unique as had been supposed. One of the main leaders of this 'history of religions' school was the German, Hermann Gunkel (1862–1932). He examined ancient Babylonian myths in his attempt to shed light on biblical ideas about the beginning and end of the world.

The work of the 'history of religions' school was not simply destructive. For biblical material cannot be viewed in isolation as if there were no cultural interaction between the biblical writers and the wider world of their day.

A startlingly different approach from the prevailing liberal view of the kingdom of God was adopted by Johannes Weiss (1863–1914) and by Albert Schweitzer (1875–1965). Weiss argued that in the teaching of Jesus the kingdom of God referred, not to a human society or to human activity, but to the sovereign rule of God breaking in upon history. It was God's supernatural intervention as King, acting in judgement and grace, in accordance with the expectations of Jewish apocalyptic literature.

Schweitzer developed this idea to argue that Jesus was wholly dominated by an expectation of the imminent end of the present world order, and that he attempted to force the arrival of this end by his death. Schweitzer's approach, although it contained elements of truth, was too extreme to be taken seriously.

In America, the movement protesting against liberal theology became known as 'fundamentalism'. Fundamentalists believed not only in the verbal inspiration and infallibility of the Bible, but also in a whole series of evangelical doctrines published around 1909 under the title of *The Fundamentals*. The writers included such men as B. B. Warfield, H. C. G. Moule and James Orr. They emphasized the substitutionary death of Christ on the cross, the reality of eternal punishment, and the need for personal conversion.

In later years the term 'fundamentalism' came to denote an unduly defensive and obscurantist attitude which was anti-scholarly, anti-intellectual and anti-cultural. For this reason many conservative theologians who might be regarded as heirs of the original fundamentalists disown the label today.

Karl Barth's 'strange new world'

The twentieth century has produced few theologians of greater stature or importance than Karl Barth (1886–1968). For twelve years Barth served as a pastor in Switzerland. During the anguish and suffering of World War I, Barth became increasingly convinced that liberal theology was bankrupt. He saw in the Bible 'a strange new world', which spoke of God and of the 'otherness' of God; a world which is utterly different from our world. His viewpoint owed something to the writings of Luther and Calvin, but much more to the nineteenth-century religious thinker Søren Kierkegaard.

Barth's protest against Liberalism broke upon the world with the publication of his now-famous commentary on Romans, in 1919 and 1922. Its themes were the sovereignty of God, God's grace and revelation, and human finiteness and sinfulness. God is wholly other. Christianity is not 'religion' at all. It is God's sovereign and revealing word, to which people can only respond.

Barth argued that since God cannot be grasped by any single set of human concepts, we can speak about him only by the dialectical method of statement and counter-statement, of 'yes' and 'no'. Barth also taught that God's word stands over against us and judges us. In the tradition of the Reformation, we stand 'under' God's word. Barth also argued that Christianity is a matter of revelation, not of our religious aspirations. Any point of contact between God, who is wholly other, and us lies solely in God's revealing word.

ALBERT SCHWEITZER

F. W. Kantzenbach

Albert Schweitzer (1875–1965) achieved greatness as a theologian, philosopher, musician, and missionary doctor. As a theological scholar he wrote *The Mystery of the Kingdom of God* (1901), an outline of Christ's life, and *In Quest of the Historical Jesus* (1906). From 1915 onwards Schweitzer proposed 'reverence for life' as the solution to the world's problems. 'Being good is to preserve life, to promote life, to raise life to the highest level that it can attain. Being evil is to destroy life, to injure life, to suppress life which could attain a higher level.'

Schweitzer felt compelled to become a doctor and to help preserve life. His medical work at Lambarene in the Cameroons, to which he devoted thirty-five years, broken by only occasional visits to Europe, made his message clear to the whole world, as did his pleas for world peace and his warnings (from 1957 onwards) against the atomic bomb. In 1953 he was awarded the Nobel Peace Prize.

Schweitzer also made an impact as an interpreter of Bach. His tours giving organ recitals led to theoretical discussions of musical problems. Schweitzer's autobiographical writings, *On the Edge of the Primeval Forest* and *Memoirs of Childhood and Youth,* made him and his work internationally famous.

Albert Schweitzer—theologian, musician and medical missionary. He went to found a hospital at Lambarene in the Camaroons in 1913. He was later criticized by some for his paternalistic methods.

After 1945 the influence of Barth's theology began to wane, and to give way to the influence of Rudolf Bultmann. However, even today Barth's theology still has its champions.

Another figure closely associated with Barth is the famous Swiss theologian Emil Brunner of Zurich (1889–1965), who represented a more restrained form of Barthianism. The Swedish bishop Anders Nygren (born in 1890) also shared Barth's emphasis on the distinctiveness of the Christian faith over against other religions.

Moral man and immoral society?

During the 1930s and 1940s the most important theologian in America was probably Reinhold Niebuhr (1893–1971). For thirteen years, until 1928, he was a pastor in Detroit and, like Barth, he found Liberalism and moral idealism inadequate for the pastoral problems that he faced. In the tradition of much American theology, he was particularly concerned with social and political ethics. But he took a more positive approach to the Bible. He was influenced by Kierkegaard and Barth, but criticized their failure to talk adequately about ethics.

In his first major work, *Moral Man and Immoral Society* (1932), Niebuhr made use of Marxist ideas, and reacted against liberal theology and the optimistic humanism of the social gospel movement. He argued that because of the evil in people and in society, Christian political action called not simply for love, but for an attempt to give each group within society enough power to defend itself against exploitation by other groups. Although relations between individuals might be a matter of ethics, relations between groups were a matter of politics. Niebuhr himself took an active part in politics and founded the Fellowship of Socialist Christians.

In his later work Niebuhr criticized equally both the liberal and Marxist views of human nature, and wrote *The Nature and Destiny of Man* (1941–43). He stressed that the final answer to the human problem lay beyond history, in the love of God and the cross of Christ. But Christians must not seek to evade their real human nature and real human tasks by opting out of the politics and power-struggles of the twentieth century.

Reinhold's brother, H. Richard Niebuhr (1894–1962), also criticized liberal theology. According to American liberalism, he ironically remarks: 'A God without wrath brought men without sin into a kingdom without judgement through the ministration of a Christ without a cross.'

Jesus: history or faith?

The German Rudolf Bultmann (1884–1976) has probably had more influence on twentieth-century theology than any other thinker. His early work, *The History of the Synoptic Tradition* (1921), came to very sceptical conclusions about the historical reliability of the Gospels as reports of facts, and was extremely pessimistic about the extent of our historical knowledge of Jesus.

Bultmann was using the method of 'form criticism', which assumes that much of the biblical material circulated in oral forms before it was committed to writing. It also holds that every 'form', or type of material in the Gospels, reflects a typical situation in ancient Israel or the earliest churches. Bultmann argued that the situations behind the 'forms' of the gospel were often those of preaching, argument, or

Karl Barth was one of the most influential theologians of the twentieth century. His commentary on *Romans*, published in 1919, marked a break with liberalism.

“The Gospel falls upon man as God's own mighty Word, questioning him down to the bottom of his being, uprooting him from his securities and satisfactions, and therefore tearing clean asunder all the relations that keep him prisoner within his own ideals in order that he may be genuinely free for God and for his wonderful new work of grace in Jesus Christ.”

KARL BARTH

> *“If we have to choose between making men Christian and making the social order more Christian, we must choose the former. But there is no such antithesis . . . There is no hope of establishing a more Christian social order except through the labour and sacrifice of those in whom the Spirit of Christ is active, and the first necessity for progress is more and better Christians taking full responsibility as citizens for the political, social and economic system under which they and their fellows live.”*
>
> *WILLIAM TEMPLE*

> *“Christ meets us in the preaching as one crucified and risen. He meets us in the word of preaching and nowhere else. The faith of Easter is just this—the faith in the word of preaching.”*
>
> *RUDOLPH BULTMANN*

teaching—but hardly ever that of historical reporting. The Gospels reflected the theology of the earliest churches rather than the facts about Jesus.

Bultmann inherited the liberal belief in the priority of experience and ethics over doctrine. It was easy for him to conceive of the earliest churches as proclaiming the risen Christ of their own experience rather than being concerned mainly with historical facts about Jesus of Nazareth.

It will come as no surprise that in his book *Jesus and the Word* Bultmann wrote, 'We can now know almost nothing about the life and personality of Jesus.' He even argued that this is a positive advantage to genuine Christian faith. Jesus, Bultmann believed, must not be located in the realm of facts and objects, and made to fit in with categories which describe the everyday world. He is not the Jesus of history, but the Christ of faith and present experience.

From the very first, many questioned Bultmann's position. Why is such a sharp division between history and experience necessary? What becomes of the biblical emphasis on Christ's taking flesh and living a real flesh-and-blood life? Was the resurrection of Christ a historical event in the sense of being a factual event? Bultmann rejects this possibility. Finally, many of Bultmann's arguments based on form criticism are also questionable.

A world of myth?

Bultmann's historic essay on myth in the New Testament appeared in 1941. It gave rise to a debate which has still not ended. Bultmann believed that the New Testament embodied a pre-scientific view of the world which he called a 'mythical' outlook. When its message is communicated today it should be translated into non-mythical terms ('demythologized').

Although the gospel must be demythologized, Bultmann insists that this in no way reduces its power to save people. He writes: 'The purpose of demythologizing is not to make religion more acceptable to modern man . . . but to make clearer to modern man what the Christian faith is.' Bultmann is not simply a liberal theologian; on the matter of presenting people with the challenge and offence of the cross, he stands nearer to Barth and Kierkegaard than to Liberalism.

Bultmann's proposals have met with some very hostile criticisms. The United Evangelical Lutheran Church of Germany condemned his whole position. His left-wing and right-wing critics join in making one common criticism. Once Bultmann starts to demythologize, how can he know where to stop? His chosen stopping-point appears to be arbitrary. Bultmann has affected the churches partly by undermining confidence about the right way to use the Bible, and partly by increasing suspicions about the reality of the supernatural in Christianity. J. A. T. Robinson's popular book, *Honest to God* (1963), took up and supported some of Bultmann's claims.

Can we talk about religion?

Positivism is the philosophical doctrine that all valid knowledge comes through the methods of the sciences. The French positivist philosopher, Auguste Comte, claimed that there were three stages in the evolution of human thought. Early mankind thought largely in theological terms, seeing the gods as responsible for events. Next, humanity reached the speculative or metaphysical stage, with better explanations, but still not based entirely on fact. Finally, humanity has arrived at the positive stage, and sees that all claims to knowledge must be tested by scientific fact. This scientific knowledge is positive knowledge, which no longer depends on superstition or speculation.

Replies to positivism came from many philosophers and philosophical theologians. They argued that the decision to restrict all knowledge to scientific observation was a personal decision and not a logical necessity.

The most striking version of positivism in the twentieth century came in the philosophical doctrine known as logical positivism. In Britain, the climate for logical positivism was prepared early in the century by the reaction against philosophical idealism led by G. E. Moore and by Bertrand Russell, and particularly by Moore's defence of 'common sense' realism in philosophy.

In 1936 A. J. Ayer published his famous book, *Language, Truth, and Logic*. He argued that statements which cannot be checked or verified by observation through the physical senses are not so much false or undemonstrable as simply meaningless. Religious statements, such as 'God is love', were held to be 'non-sense'. Ayer stated his arguments so well that his book had an enormous influence.

Replies came from various thinkers, including the philospher F. C. Copleston and the theologian E. L. Mascall. What was the logical status, it was asked, of Ayer's own principle of verification? It was neither a tautology nor could it be checked by scientific observation, so it would exclude itself as a 'meaningless statement'. Partly in response to this criticism the area of debate moved from verification (how can a statement be checked as true?) to falsification (how can it be shown to be false?).

Since the 1920s Marxists in France, Italy, and more recently Latin America and Africa, have increasingly dissociated themselves from the repressive regime of Soviet communism. Stalin's status as an interpreter of Marx is challenged, and increasingly emphasis is laid on Marx's earlier writings, in which Marx was more concerned with human nature and alienation than with materialism as such. Under capitalism, he argued, labour is alien to us because we do not work for ourselves. We are de-personalized into a mere tool of production for someone else's gain. We need to be liberated and restored to true dignity.

This approach of Neo-Marxism, developed by the German Ernst Bloch, has contributed to the Christian theology of hope, and especially to the thinking of Jürgen Moltmann in the 1960s. Neo-Marxism has also inspired much of the theorizing about liberation in the Third World, and is closely connected with recent theologies of revolution in Latin America.

The urge to commitment

It is difficult to define existentialism in general terms, for existentialist philosophers are themselves partly making individual protests against generalization and abstract thinking. The father-figure of existentialist thought is the Danish thinker Søren Kierkegaard (1813–55). Kierkegaard stressed the importance of first-hand practical decision and involvement, as against mere intellectual assent to abstract truths. He attacked nominal Christian orthodoxy which was not personally committed. It is personal decision, rather than abstract reason, which brings a person into relationship with God. This idea was taken up both in

"Man is the product of causes which had no prevision of the end they were achieving; his origin, his growth, his hopes and fears, his loves and his beliefs are but the outcome of accidental collocations of atoms."

BERTRAND RUSSELL

> *“While I believe that there can be an explanation in mundane terms for anything that happens within the world, I do not think it makes sense to ask for an explanation of the existence or the characteristics of the world as a whole. In this sense, it is a matter of brute fact that the universe exhibits the patterns which it does.”*
>
> A.J. AYER

> *“From the Christian point of view faith belongs to the existential; God did not appear in the character of a professor who has some doctrines which must first be believed and then understood.”*
>
> SØREN KIERKEGAARD

Barth's earlier writings and by Bultmann.

German existentialist philosophers include Karl Jaspers (1883–1969) and especially Martin Heidegger (1889–1976). Heidegger stresses the relativity of knowledge. We cannot view reality as a detached observer outside history. Heidegger also declared: 'The person is not a thing, not a substance, not an object.' Whereas 'things' exist, in the sense of having certain fixed properties, people exist in the sense of having intentionality or possibilities for the future. A person can be open to the future and cease to be an 'object', by breaking out of the conventions and mere everydayness of the crowd. In this way he or she may achieve authentic existence. Heidegger had enormous influence in Europe, especially in Germany.

Existentialism is most widely known in France through the writings of Jean-Paul Sartre (born in 1905). Like Kierkegaard and other existentialists, he investigated such experiences as anguish, dread and the prospect of death, and reasserted individualism. He is also known to a wider public for his novels and stories. Sartre's thought is also militantly atheistic; because God is neither (in Sartre's sense) a person nor a thing, 'the idea of God is contradictory'. 'God' is a weapon used by society to impose its moral values on the individual.

But existentialism is not necessarily always anti-Christian. Kierkegaard wrote as a Christian criticizing merely nominal Christianity. Jaspers opposes the exclusive claims of Christianity, but is sympathetic with religious belief.

Martin Buber was born in Vienna in 1878. He wrote from the perspective of a very strong Jewish faith, yet is also regarded as a major existentialist thinker. There is, he said, a sharp contrast between our relationship to objects which we observe (the I-it relation) and our relationship to a personal 'Thou' who addresses us (the I-Thou relation). God must not be changed into an 'it' by being regarded as a mere object of thought or experience. Gabriel Marcel, writing as a Roman Catholic, insists that no human person is to be reduced to a mere 'case' or number.

Language and life

One of the most original thinkers in twentieth-century philosophy is Ludwig Wittgenstein (1889–1951). He was born in Vienna but came to England in 1908. When the war came in 1914, he joined the Austrian army, and carried about with him in his rucksack the notebooks on logic which provided the basis for his great work, The *Tractatus Logico-Philosophicus* (1918). In the first part of this work he sets out statements about the relation between language and the world. The most famous part of this work is his picture theory of meaning: 'A proposition is a picture of reality.' Elements of the world correspond with elements of language in such a way that 'the totality of true thoughts is a picture of the world'. Propositions depict facts, but values are higher than facts. The riddle of life, Wittgenstein believed, went beyond the limits of thought and language; the attempt to *speak* about it resulted in confusion.

After 1929 Wittgenstein became increasingly dissatisfied with this way of looking at the problem and developed a different approach. He examined the relation between uses of language and the particular 'surroundings' which gave them currency and meaning. Wittgenstein used the term 'language-games' to stress that 'only in the stream of thought and life do words have meaning'. Confusions arise when uses of language are examined 'outside a particular language-game'. Wittgenstein therefore aimed to make observations about particular uses of language in their concrete settings in life, not in the abstract. For example, he shed light on language about expecting, intending, understanding and believing.

Wittgenstein's methods inspired the movement known as linguistic philosophy. Some philosophers, including Antony Flew and R. B. Braithwaite, were influenced both by positivism and by the methods of linguistic philosophy, and attacked certain aspects of language in religion. Thinkers such as Copleston and Mascall defended traditional views, claiming that analogy had a valid place in religious language.

Man's obsessional neurosis?

Sigmund Freud (1856–1939) is without doubt one of the most influential figures of the twentieth century. The whole of modern psychology is influenced by his work, even if only certain psychologists still regard themselves as belonging to his school of thought. His influence on popular ideas about religion can hardly be exaggerated.

Psychological disorders, Freud believed, can often be cured by probing the unconscious to release repressed wishes into self-knowledge. One important way of gaining access to the unconscious is through dreams, which are repressed wishes in disguise. Repressed urges often take the form of sexual desires. In psychoanalysis, a patient is encouraged to talk freely about his dreams, feelings, attitudes and mental associations, in the hope that these will bring aspects of the unconscious to light.

Freud was an atheist, and was deeply influenced by the positivism of Comte. His theories about religion rest on the positivist claim that all knowledge comes through the sciences. He described religion as 'the universal obsessional neurosis of humanity'.

Neurosis is a conflict between different parts of the mind which results in stress or anxiety. One part of the mind clamours for the gratification of desires which another part represses. Freud argued that part of the mind (the 'superego') tries to repress by projecting or 'externalizing' the figure of the human father into that of God. The father who gave life and protection, but also enforces laws, becomes the God who creates and sustains, but also gives commands. For Freud 'God' is a device conjured up from the mind to cope with its own inner tensions. This figure also comforts and supports the mind when tensions arise from suffering, guilt, or disappointments in life. 'The face which smiled at us in the cradle, now magnified to infinity, smiles down upon us from heaven.'

Christian thinkers have reacted to Freud's claims in several ways. They have pointed out that Freud's theories about religion owe more to philosophical speculation than to scientific observation. They are theories which cannot be proved. Some have also argued that, on the basis of Freud's theories, his own hatred of his Jewish father might be said to account for his own repression of God into his unconscious.

Some Christian thinkers, especially in America, have been more concerned to apply some of his psychological insights in Christian pastoral counselling. Pastoral psychology and what is sometimes called 'clinical theology' attempt to relate the more positive aspects of modern psychology to questions about Christian growth and maturity.

> *"Dying my death is the one thing no-one else can do for me."*
>
> MARTIN HEIDEGGER

> *"Up till now, man derived his coherence from his Creator. But from the moment that he consecrates his rupture with him, he finds himself delivered over to the fleeting moment, to the passing days, and to wasted sensibility."*
>
> ALBERT CAMUS

Sigmund Freud, whose writings on psychology have greatly influenced ideas and attitudes in the twentieth century. He labelled religion as a neurosis.

> *"Religion is an attempt to get control over the sensory world in which we are placed, by means of the wish-world, which we have developed inside us as a result of biological and psychological necessities."*
>
> SIGMUND FREUD

The difficulty which still faces this movement is that psychiatrists still argue over the value and validity of the different approaches in psychology.

A world come of age

Dietrich Bonhoeffer (1906–45) put forward the idea of religionless or 'worldly' Christianity. In his earliest works he argued that the church is concerned not with religious ideas, but with Christ. In *The Cost of Discipleship* (1937), he argued that the Sermon on the Mount is not to be shelved on the pretext that it sets out an impossible ideal intended only to convict men of sin. The standard way of preaching justification by faith to bourgeois congregations, Bonhoeffer insisted, makes for 'cheap grace'. Grace comes only when people step out and follow Christ in costly discipleship.

In 1945 Bonhoeffer was executed, but after his death passages from his prison letters were published. In them Bonhoeffer attacks that 'religion' which calls God in either as a psychological crutch in moments of need, or to explain otherwise inexplicable phenomena. Too often God is seen as the source of comfort, helping men in moments of stress or insecurity. Evangelists even try to make men feel guilty or insecure in order to make them turn to God. Bonhoeffer called this 'an attempt to put a grown-up man back into adolescence'. The world today has 'come of age'. 'God is teaching us that we must live as men who can get along very well without him.' This does not mean atheism. It means rejecting the way of 'religion'. God's reality is revealed in Christians serving their fellow human beings in a costly and positive way amidst life as it is. The pattern for this, Bonhoeffer believed, was Christ. Jesus Christ was 'there only for others'. 'Being there for others' is what really points to the reality of God.

God and the Ultimate

The main aim of Paul Tillich (1886–1965) was to relate Christian faith to secular thought. In his intellectual autobiography, *On the Boundary*, he writes of how he wished to make connections between theology and philosophy, religion and culture, Lutheranism and socialism, and between German and American thought. He was born in Germany and taught at five German universities; but with the rise of Hitler he moved to the United States.

Tillich's *Systematic Theology* (1951, 1957 and 1963), attempts to offer theological answers to secular questions. Questions about reason, being and existence are matched by answers about revelation, God and Christ. He probed into human anxieties about fear and death, and into experience of emptiness, meaninglessness and guilt. In his attempt to come to grips with the questions asked by secular people, he used the resources and vocabulary of existentialist philosophy and depth-psychology.

Tillich is particularly concerned with the problem of the 'Ultimate', which must be located only in God. Unbelievers may imagine that they have thought about God and rejected him, when all the time they have never encountered the Ultimate at all. 'It is not *he* whom we reject and forget, but some distorted picture of him.' Tillich does not like to say that God 'exists'; for to ascribe ordinary existence to him is to view him as one object among others in the everyday world.

The only way of encountering the Ultimate, Tillich believes, is through experience. His method is to start 'with the experiencing of

DIETRICH BONHOEFFER

Ruth Zerner

Active in the Anti-Hitler resistance movement, the German Lutheran clergyman Dietrich Bonhoeffer was imprisoned in 1943 and hanged by the Nazis at Flossenbürg on 9 April 1945. The son of a Berlin professor of psychiatry, Bonhoeffer studied theology at Tübingen, Berlin and at Union Theological Seminary, New York City. When Hitler came to power in 1933 Bonhoeffer, student chaplain and lecturer at the University of Berlin, joined the anti-Nazi pastors in the German 'church struggle'. In 1935 he was appointed head of the Finkenwalde Confessing Church Seminary, which was closed by the government in 1937.

In 1939 Bonhoeffer rejected the possibility of a job in America, safe from the impending European war. He was convinced that he had to face the difficulties ahead with the Christians in Germany. During World War II Bonhoeffer, forbidden to preach or to publish, served as a double-agent on Admiral Canaris's military intelligence staff. Using his ecumenical contacts, especially his friendship with Bishop George Bell of Chichester, England, Bonhoeffer vainly sought the British government's support for the anti-Hitler conspirators. His arrest in 1943 arose from his involvement in smuggling fourteen Jews to Switzerland.

Although only thirty-nine when killed, Bonhoeffer left a rich legacy of books—*Sanctorum Communio, Act and Being, The Cost of Discipleship* and *Life Together*—as well as letters, papers and notes published after his death by his close friend and biographer, Eberhard Bethge. These include *Letters and Papers from Prison, Ethics,* and six volumes of collected writings.

A seminal thinker who refused to retreat from the harsh realities of his day, Bonhoeffer challenged Christians to reject complacent, undisciplined faith and life. His writings focussed on Jesus Christ, 'the man for others', and on the nature of Christian community. In his prison letters, the most popular of his works, Bonhoeffer explored pathways of future church renewal. Exposing the negative side of institutional religion, Bonhoeffer called for mature faith in the God of weakness and suffering in 'a world come of age'.

Bonhoeffer's thought and example, climaxed by his acceptance of the guilt and responsibility of political conspiracy, continue to influence both conservatives and liberals in Protestant, Catholic, and secular circles, especially in the English-speaking world, and more recently in the Third World. His ideas have sparked and shaped diverse movements, including ecumenism; death of God theology; liberation theology; commentaries in communist countries about the church without privileges and the world; Christian resistance to war and to oppressive political regimes; as well as traditional tributes to Christian discipleship, heroism and martyrdom.

Dietrich Bonhoeffer

"It is infinitely easier to suffer in obedience to a human command than to accept suffering as free, responsible men. It is infinitely easier to suffer with others than to suffer alone. It is infinitely easier to suffer as public heroes than to suffer apart and in ignominy. It is infinitely easier to suffer physical death than to endure spiritual suffering. Christ suffered as a free man alone, apart and in ignominy, in body and in spirit, and since that day many Christians have suffered with him."

DIETRICH BONHOEFFER, Letters and Papers from Prison

> *"Do not seek for anything; do not perform anything; do not intend anything. Simply accept the fact that you are accepted."*
>
> *PAUL TILLICH,* The Shaking of the Foundations

> *"The infinite significance of every moment of time is this: in it we decide, and are decided about, with respect to our eternal future."*
>
> *PAUL TILLICH,* The Shaking of the Foundations

the holy' and advance 'to the idea of God'. 'God' becomes almost a 'feeling of the holy'. Critics comment that in Tillich's thought an ultimate God has become merely any experience which 'feels' ultimate.

Tillich helped to initiate dialogue between theology and secular thought—including existentialist philosophy, depth-psychology and political and cultural movements. But he also led many to challenge the authority of theological creeds and church structures. Tillich also raised questions about what we mean by the personality of God, and whether God may still be conceived of in traditional terms at all. Symbols to describe God effectively, Tillich urged, may well change from age to age.

The Bible and scholarship

Between the early 1940s and the early 1960s the biblical theology movement arose. It stressed that the various books of the Bible proclaimed what was basically a single message, and attempted to single out what was most distinctive to the Hebrew or biblical outlook. The Bible was seen as the continuous unfolding to faith of God's saving acts in the sacred history of Israel and the church.

A great exponent of this salvation-history theme in New Testament studies is Oscar Cullmann (born in 1902). He declared that his aim was 'to determine what is central in the Christian proclamation'. He finds this distinctive theme in the biblical view of time and history. The particular claim of the Bible is that the key to all history lies in the salvation-history of Israel, Christ and the church. It sees history as linear, not cyclical, which points both to the unrepeatable uniqueness of God's acts and to the importance of history's future goal.

Patient and solid work on biblical commentaries also proceeded steadily. Old Testament commentaries were produced by the German scholars Martin Noth, A. Weisser and Gerhard von Rad. Important New Testament commentaries appeared in Britain by Vincent Taylor, C. K. Barrett and F. F. Bruce. In America the biblical theology movement was represented in the fields of Old Testament archaeology and history by G. E. Wright, John Bright and, less directly, W.F. Albright.

All this activity enriched the life of the church, but three kinds of criticism have been levelled against it. First, it was claimed that the variety of the Bible was lost from view. Second, there were sometimes faults in the linguistic methods of the movement. Third, it had often failed to pay attention to the relations between theology and history, and between the ancient text and the modern reader (the questions of interpretation or 'hermeneutics'). What was the relevance of the Bible? By 1970 the biblical theology movement had gone out of favour although its influence was still felt.

The new quest . . .

Criticism has arisen among Bultmann's own former pupils who have attempted to pay more attention to Jesus as a figure of history than Bultmann did. This movement has become known as the 'new quest of the historical Jesus', and its leaders include E. Käsemann of Tübingen, G. Bornkamm of Heidelberg and E. Fuchs of Marburg. Käsemann insisted that the earthly history of Jesus must be taken seriously as part of the truth of the word made flesh.

The stress on the unity of the Bible represented by the biblical theology movement was replaced by a stress on its diversity. In

C. S. LEWIS

Walter Hooper

Clive Staples Lewis (1898–1963) became the most popular defender of orthodox Christianity in the English-speaking world in the mid-twentieth century. Lewis was born in Belfast in 1898 and was brought up in the Christian faith—a faith he lost before he reached his teens. He was educated at Malvern College and then privately under a tutor whose atheism had such an influence on him that by the time Lewis went up to Oxford University in 1917 he described himself as an unbeliever.

Lewis took a triple First at Oxford and was elected to a fellowship in English at Magdalen College, Oxford. He held this post till 1954 when he became the Professor of Medieval and Renaissance English Literature at Cambridge. Over the years he wrote a number of works of literary criticism which are classics in their field, the best known being *The Allegory of Love.*

After a long intellectual battle, Lewis was converted to Christianity in 1931. Gifted with an extraordinary intellect and a reasoning mind, his conversion triggered off a rich variety of creativity. His international best-seller, *The Screwtape Letters* (1942), won him the reputation of being able to 'make righteousness readable'. He wrote many other works of theology and fantasy with theological dimensions. Lewis achieved further fame as a preacher, debater and brilliantly effective 'apostle to the sceptics'. Believing, as he said, that 'all that is not eternal is eternally out of date', he was completely orthodox and is admired by Christians from all branches of the church.

A jovial and saintly man, he could have amassed a fortune, but following his conversion he regularly gave two-thirds of his income to charities. Between 1950 and 1956 C. S. Lewis published seven fairy tales about his invented world of Narnia, beginning with *The Lion, the Witch and the Wardrobe.* These books are his most delightful approach to the word of God, and are probably the most loved. Lewis also wrote an autobiography, *Surprised by Joy,* which traces the story of his conversion.

"God whispers to us in our pleasures, speaks in our conscience, but shouts in our pains: it is his megaphone to rouse a deaf world."

C. S. LEWIS, The Problem of Pain

"A man can't be always defending the truth; there must be a time to feed on it."

C. S. LEWIS, Reflections on the Psalms

research on the Gospels this was linked with a new interest in the technique known as 'redaction criticism'. This is the study of how each individual Gospel-writer or Gospel-editor ('redactor') shaped the material that came to him in such a way as to reveal his own special theological interests.

Redaction criticism of the Gospels has now become widespread. But it still encounters two main difficulties. It is difficult to prove just how free the gospel writers felt themselves to be to re-shape material in their own interests. There are many competing theories about what precisely these interests are. Nonetheless, redaction criticism, form criticism and literary criticism (or theories about sources) remain standard tools in both Old and New Testament studies.

The practical effect of all this is to see the Bible as containing not one theology but many theologies. Israel and the New Testament churches, it is argued, did not simply hand down fixed doctrines which came to them from the past, but interpreted the word and deeds of God afresh for themselves. On this basis some have argued that

> *“‘I’m ready to accept Jesus as a great moral teacher, but I don’t accept his claim to be God.’ That is the one thing we must not say. A man who was merely a man and said the sort of things Jesus said would not be a great moral teacher. He would either be a lunatic—on a level with the man who says he is a poached egg—or else he would be the Devil of Hell. You must make your choice. Either this man was, and is, the Son of God; or else a madman or something worse. You can shut him up for a fool, you can spit at him and kill him as a demon, or you can fall at his feet and call him Lord and God. But let us not come with any patronizing nonsense about his being a great human teacher. He has not left that open to us. He did not intend to.”*
>
> *C. S. LEWIS,* Mere Christianity

it is less ‘biblical’ to look back to a fixed body of doctrine than to state anew what God is for the present. This has opened up new questions about biblical authority, and the relation between the Bible and tradition.

In the 1980s, two further developments occurred in biblical scholarship. First, there was an increasing emphasis on theories of interpretation, or hermeneutics. To explore issues of biblical interpretation, specialists drew on ideas found in the philosophy of language, linguistics and literary theory. Second, new developments underlined the importance of sociology. One example of this approach is the research of Gerd Theissen into the Gospels and Pauline churches.

Behind these two developments—of interpretative models and sociology of knowledge—lies an important conviction. The New Testament message concerns specific situations, people and communities. It is not simply a collection of thoughts or ideas divorced from time and social realities.

Some startling finds

From 1929 onwards a series of vital discoveries was made at Ras Shamra in Syria, the site of the ancient city of Ugarit. The material found shed new light on the myths and religious practices of the Canaanites. In addition, inscriptions from excavations at Mari, on the River Euphrates, shed new light on the history of the Near East from the time of the early patriarchs to the conquest of Canaan. These finds mean that the biblical narratives are generally regarded as more reliable than was fashionable some years earlier. But some archaeological discoveries, such as the excavations at Jericho in the 1950s, posed new problems. Israeli archaeologists particularly have contributed increasingly to our knowledge of biblical times.

The discovery at Nag-Hammadi in Upper Egypt in 1945 of numerous so-called gnostic texts (for example the Gospel of Thomas) raised fresh questions about the religious environment of the New Testament.

The discovery of the famous Dead Sea Scrolls occurred in 1947 by accident. A Bedouin boy was searching for a lost sheep among the caves of Qumran, just northwest of the Dead Sea. He came upon several jars, about two feet tall, which contained leather scrolls wrapped in linen cloth. He had stumbled upon part of an extensive library of scrolls which belonged to a monastic-like community of Jews living in the first century BC and in the time of Christ, which had been hidden at the time when the Romans put down the Jewish rebellion of AD 70.

By 1949 several hundred writings were recovered from this source. What most caught the popular imagination was the find of the copper scrolls, which had become so oxidized that they could only be deciphered by treating them and cutting them into thin strips. For theologians the most important were the scrolls of the Old Testament text and commentaries, 1,000 years older than texts previously known, and scrolls describing the life of the community itself, which shed light on one type of Judaism in the time of Christ.

These and other discoveries all helped to encourage a biblical scholarship which used the Bible itself as a source-document of historical evidence, and used other evidence to shed light on its setting and meaning.

Professors Fuchs of Marburg and Ebeling of Zürich have asked how an ancient writing such as the Bible can come alive for today (the problem of hermeneutics). After a gap of two thousand years, the words will be understood differently from their original thrust. It is not enough to examine the text objectively. The text must actively address modern humanity as its object. Fuchs and Ebeling in some ways go further than Bultmann in their existentialism. Truth, they claim, is what rings a bell with *me*; for example, the truth of the resurrection is what it means to me.

It remains to be seen what consequences, if any, will follow from the new linguistic approaches for the church's attitude to the Bible. They may well lead to fresh account being taken of its literary and symbolic power to open up our understanding of ourselves. But some will feel that the Bible is being viewed as a book about people rather than as a book about God.

Honest to God

In 1963, J. A. T. Robinson, then Bishop of Woolwich, published the paperback, *Honest to God*, asking: 'How does one preach the gospel today?' For his answer he drew on Bultmann's ideas about myth and demythologizing, on Tillich's notion of God as the ground of our being, and on Bonhoeffer's comments about religionless Christianity.

Why did *Honest to God* make such an explosive impact? In simple, often autobiographical, language Robinson succeeded in familiarizing a massive readership (more than a million copies were sold) with ideas which were almost unknown outside the lecture-room. Here was an English bishop expressing what many regarded as radical ideas.

What caught people's imagination was his rejection of the notion of a God 'up there'. Robinson also made it clear that traditional teaching on prayer left him cold. Thousands who for years had never opened a Bible claimed to gain reassurance from finding their doubts and problems shared by a bishop. But Robinson failed to show how the very different ideas which he called into play could be combined together in a consistent and positive way. The book is better at raising questions than at answering them. Robinson's thought has been followed with interest in all parts of the world, including America, Europe and India.

1963 also saw the first published declarations of the Second Vatican Council (1962–65). The Council ushered in a new era in Roman Catholic thought, and showed a new openness to many theological questions, including dialogue with Protestant churches and even with non-Christian religions.

The theologian most associated with the post-Vatican spirit is the Jesuit, Karl Rahner. Rahner, influenced by the existentialism of Heidegger, stresses that divine grace can be fully understood only when it is experienced in practice. But he also endorses traditional Catholic doctrine and its claim to be universal truth.

Rahner's thought is marked by this two-sidedness. He asserts that only through Christ and the church can salvation become real to people. On the other hand, he believes that 'the people of God' extend outside the Roman Catholic church and the other churches to include the whole of humanity. The church, Rahner declares, must be open to the outer world. This means drawing a distinction between nominal church membership and a genuine commitment to Christ.

Hans Küng of Tübingen, another influential Roman Catholic, has published an important work on the doctrine of justification and

Israeli archaeologists uncover a 4,500-year-old building near the Dead Sea. During the twentieth century archaeologists have made discoveries which shed much new light on life and times in the New Testament world.

stresses the priesthood of the whole people of God.

'God is dead'

In the 1960s the headline-catching 'death of God' movement appeared. The slogan 'the death of God' was used in several different ways. In 1963 Paul van Buren declared that the *word* 'God' is dead. Using well-worn arguments of logical positivism and positivist brands of linguistic philosophy, he insisted that language about God had no meaning. He also drew on Bonhoeffer's hints about 'religionless Christianity'.

Jacob Epstein's sculpture of St Michael and Lucifer, commissioned for the new cathedral at Coventry, England, which was built to replace the one destroyed in World War II.

The most uncompromising writer on the death of God is the American, Thomas J. J. Altizer. He draws his inspiration from Nietzsche, Hegel and Blake, and asserts that God died when Christ died on the cross. Altizer ends in an obscure kind of mysticism: God is dead, but somehow he is represented by Jesus.

Harvey Cox's *The Secular City* (1966) has been described as the Bible of post-liberal American theology. The secular city is seen as a fulfilment of God's purposes, since it provides people with fuller lives. 'God comes to us today in the event of social change.' Cox, too, frequently quotes Bonhoeffer.

It would be a mistake to imagine that secular theology entirely dominates the American scene. Conservative writers such as Edward Carnell, Bernard Ramm and G. E. Ladd stress the importance of the Bible as the source of revealed truth, and their outlook speaks for millions of American Christians. Unlike the American fundamentalists of a previous generation, Ladd uses the tools of biblical criticism. This does not mean criticizing the Bible, he insists, but paying attention to the historical particularity of the biblical text.

Conservative scholars have entered into debate with other viewpoints, for example in the volume *Jesus of Nazareth*, edited in 1966 by Carl Henry. The book included contributions from ten Americans, as well as scholars from other countries, including F. F. Bruce from Britain, Leon Morris from Australia and Birger Gerhardsson from Sweden.

God of the whole world

Wolfhard Pannenberg of Munich (born in 1928) is one of the most important theologians of the late twentieth century. He clashes head-on with assumptions held by Bultmann and his followers, enters into serious dialogue with atheism, and raises fundamental questions about almost every aspect of theology. Pannenberg insists that the saving acts of God do not belong exclusively 'in a ghetto of redemptive history'. God's deeds must be understood within the wider context of history as a whole. Theology must take account of history, because its task is 'to understand all being in relation to God'.

Pannenberg's attitude to the resurrection of Jesus Christ is of special interest. He attacks Bultmann's approach. Even from the point of view of impartial historical investigation the resurrection of Christ is ruled out only if we insist in advance that dead men do not rise. 'Try to imagine how Jesus' disciples could proclaim his resurrection if they could constantly be refuted by the evidence of the tomb in which Jesus' corpse lay.'

Jürgen Moltmann of Tübingen is best known for his book, *Theology of Hope* (1965), in which he argued that hope still lies ahead and that the people of God are the pilgrim people—one with the poor and oppressed. Salvation involves a faith that is socially relevant. In the cross, Moltmann argues, Jesus identified himself with those who were abandoned, and challenged the *status quo*. In 1972 he published *The Crucified God*. His more recent work has been concerned to relate the doctrine of the trinity to that of creation.

Revolutionary Christians

The theology of liberation in Latin America is greatly influenced by Marxism, and sees salvation largely in terms of political and economic liberation. Its leading exponents include Gustavo Gutiérrez of Peru (the father of the movement), Juan Luis Segundo of Uruguay, José Porfirio Miranda of Mexico, Enrique Dussel and Severino Croatto of Argentina, Jon Sobrino of El Salvador, and Hugo Assmann and Clovodis and Leonardo Boff of Brazil. The Boff brothers were the subject of papal silencing in 1985. On the protestant side, liberation theology has found an able expositor in the Argentinian Methodist José Miguel Bonino.

Hunger and poverty are serious problems in Latin America. In the 1950s hopes were vainly pinned on what could be achieved by economic aid. Many came to believe that gaps between rich and poor nations could never be closed under the capitalist systems, but that China, and especially Cuba, demonstrated that Marxism held the key to the future for Latin America.

Latin Americans associated the church with existing power structures and European imperialism. Many Roman Catholic priests began to share the revolutionary perspective. One folk-hero of the revolutionary movement, Father Camilo Torres, who was shot in 1966, declared, 'The Catholic who is not a revolutionary is living in mortal sin.'

Gutiérrez argues that we must not begin with theology or with the Bible, but with our own place in the world and our own attempts to change it. The Bible becomes relevant only if or when it speaks on these 'questions derived from the world'. Gutiérrez finds a point of contact in the biblical accounts of the exodus, which he sees as an act of political liberation. Salvation means 'to struggle against misery and exploitation' and involves 'all men and the whole man'.

José Miranda believes that the Old Testament prophets and the teaching of Jesus attack the principle of private property. Western Christians have failed to see this because they have come to the Bible with capitalist presuppositions, and read it theoretically rather than with practical questions (on the basis of 'praxis').

> *"The mystery of the Christ is primarily a matter of recognition, not, Can you believe this individual to be the Son of God? but, Can you see the truth of your humanity given its definition and vindication in him?"*
>
> J. A. T. ROBINSON

> *"The synthesis of the Christian 'God' on high and the Marxist 'God' of the future is the only God we can henceforth adore in spirit and in truth."*
>
> TEILHARD DE CHARDIN

HOW MANY THEOLOGIES?

C. René Padilla

For centuries it was taken for granted that the only Christian theology ever possible was theology written in the context of Christendom in the West. It was also assumed that this theology made in the West (preferably in England, Scotland, Holland, Germany, France and the United States) was truly universal, and should therefore be transplanted (often with no adaptations) to the non-Western world. All this led to the view that theology in the non-Western world had merely to repeat and, at best, imitate the theology brought from abroad.

In recent years the weakness of this position has been made clear. A number of theologians in the Third World (especially in Latin America) have pointed to the failure of Western theology (most of it produced in universities and seminaries) to cope with such problems as poverty, social injustice, racial discrimination, institutionalized violence and economic dependence. This critique has been voiced mainly by Roman Catholics in 'liberation theology' but also in general terms by some evangelical thinkers.

Some critics have objected that we do not need particular theologies, such as 'Black theology' or 'Latin American theology'; *one* theology, namely, *biblical theology*, is enough. But even among conservative theologians in the West theologies range from Dispensationalism to the Reformed position, each claiming to be more biblical than any other. It is now widely recognized that all theology, regardless of the race or culture of its author, bears the imprint of its origin in such matters as language, approach, values and emphasis.

There is a distinction between *gospel*—a message centred on the person and work of Jesus Christ—and *theology*—the human discipline that seeks to understand the gospel and its implications for practical life. If this difference is admitted, the way is open to recognize the need for Christians to make a theology in their own particular situation.

Naturally it is easiest either to repeat previous theologies or to introduce completely new ideas. But the 'ethnic' theologian maintains that the gospel itself demands a constant effort to translate its central claims into cultural categories, in order to obey Christ in a practical way.

The gospel for Africa and India

Two leading African theologians are J. S. Mbiti of Kampala and H. Sawyerr of Sierra Leone. African peoples have a strong oral tradition and a great emphasis upon practical experience in religion. The Bible itself remains a closed book to many, since literacy still ranges between five and fifty per cent of the population, varying from country to country.

Sawyerr argues that Africans can and should build bridges between the Christian gospel and African thought-forms, and African theologians generally agree that the urgent task is to provide a theology which is both true to the gospel and yet free from Western cultural additions. It may be argued that the Bible itself provided the answer to this search. Both the Bible and African experience stress the reality of the spiritual realm, and both reject an undue emphasis on individualism and abstract theory. Both celebrate the great acts of God in story and song passed down from generation to generation.

Indian theologians are also concerned to express the Christian gospel in thought-forms which relate to their own culture. Raymond Pannikar argues that the concepts of Hinduism must be used to expound the doctrine of Christ to Indians. Many aspects of Hindu thought, he argues, are compatible with a Christian understanding of Christ. Indian Christian theologians should try to draw positively on Hindu thought, rather than simply attacking it.

Pannikar's approach does not represent all Indian theologians. Sabapathy Kulandran, for example, compares the Christian and Hindu concepts of divine grace and concludes that they are incompatible; Hindu grace is not really grace at all. Many Indian Christians regard Pannikar's approach as compromising the purity of the gospel.

The theology of liberation pinpoints a question which is likely to remain a live issue for some time: is the starting-point in theology our own present experience of life, or should we begin with the givenness of revealed truth? Many continue to re-assert the classical Christian view that revelation is the starting-point. On the other side stand theologians such as Harvey Cox, along with a growing number of theologians from the Third World, and even certain biblical scholars. Still others believe that these are not exclusive alternatives, since we can still hear the Bible speaking to questions which are genuinely 'ours'.

The relation between Christianity and Marxism has become an urgent matter in the Third World. How does theology relate to political or social action? Other questions are increasingly urgent. Can we still accept traditional formulations about the two natures of Christ as truly God and truly man? How is Christian faith to be related to the claims of non-Christian religions? Is it possible to see Christ as merely one revelation of God among others? Can we still assert that Christ is God's own revelation, in contrast to the merely human aspirations expressed in other religions? Can language about the other-worldly be translated into language about this world? These questions are likely to remain with us for some time.

A Bible study group in Southern Thailand. Christians around the world are concerned to relate the gospel to their own life situations and cultures.

AN AGE OF LIBERATION

C. René Padilla

When we survey the expansion of Christianity in the twentieth century, three historical facts of particular importance emerge. First, the modern missionary movement had its base in the West at a time when, as a result of the Industrial Revolution, the West had become dominant politically and economically. Second, missionaries carried not only Christianity but also values and perspectives typical of Western society and associated with modernity. They brought with them a naturalistic worldview. Finally, missionary work contributed to the disruption of order in the traditional non-Western societies and brought a new desire for development. A revolutionary situation was created which eventually led to liberation.

These facts are basic in understanding the role that Christianity has played in the modern search for national liberation and also the challenge to the church that the current revolutionary mood presents. The church today has to face the demands of an age of liberation that its missionary thrust has been largely responsible for ushering in.

A world-wide church

As a result of the work of the voluntary missionary societies, established first in western Europe and then in the United States, the 'younger churches' in the non-Western world had the hallmarks of their origin, and depended heavily on foreign leaders for many years. Even so, they vividly demonstrated the fact that the Christian faith is for all people.

By the end of the nineteenth century there were only a few regions where the gospel had not been preached, and a few countries (such as Afghanistan, Tibet and Nepal) remained closed to missionaries. A world-wide Christian community had been created.

Four distinct factors contributed to the missionary movement responsible for this dramatic change.

In the first place, Protestant missions were rooted in the Evangelical Awakening of the eighteenth century. The Awakening emphasized personal conversion and holiness of life; this emphasis became in turn one of the characteristics of the 'younger churches' of the non-Western world.

Second, 'the great century' of missions saw amazing achievements both by Protestants and also by the Roman Catholic church. Various countries in Europe, especially France and Belgium, and later Holland and Ireland, became the base of Roman Catholic missions.

Third, missionary advance coincided with the heyday of Western imperialism. The modern mission movement cannot be understood in isolation from political, economic and cultural imperialism.

Finally, the modern missionary movement, particularly in its Protestant form, was initially a revolutionary force. It confronted the traditional societies of the non-Western world with a message of freedom, and a 'modern' outlook which challenged the old values. In many lands missionaries were pioneers in various fields of human endeavour, particularly in higher education and medicine. In some cases their efforts were rewarded by the emergence of an educated Christian *élite* which had an influence out of all proportion to its numbers.

The first World Missionary Conference, held in Edinburgh in 1910, heralded the situation that the church was to attain in the twentieth century. The conference took place at a time when a combination of forces was beginning to threaten to destroy Christianity in the countries of western Europe which until then had been the basis of its expansion. Throughout the nineteenth century, the development of science and technology, followed by industrialization, urbanization and the disruption of traditional patterns of society, had been producing a revolution that was accompanied by a growing secularization of life, with the abandonment of faith by millions of European Christians. Edinburgh marked the end of an epoch, but it also pointed towards a new age—the age of liberation, when the world-wide movement that had taken shape through missionary work was to come into its own. It pointed to the displacement of Christianity from its traditional centre, which was entering a so-called 'post-Christian' era, to a new one in the world beyond Europe.

'The Evangelization of the World in this Generation'

Out of more than 1,200 representatives at Edinburgh, only seventeen came from the 'younger churches' (eight from India, one from Burma, three from China, one from Korea and four from Japan). Latin America was completely omitted, for it was regarded as a Christian continent. Although the church had by then become a global fellowship, it reflected a church colonialism that paralleled the contemporary political colonialism. In line with the recommendations of the organizing committee, each participating missionary society (the delegates represented missionary societies rather than churches) sent some of its 'leading missionaries' and 'if practicable, one or two natives'.

The Edinburgh Conference demonstrated the growing interest in missionary work among Christians in western Europe and the United States, and the remarkable influence of the Student Volunteer Movement. The vision of the SVM was summed up in the watchword, 'The Evangelization of the World in this Generation,' which had helped numerous students to see their responsibility regarding world missions. But it also threw into relief a problem that for many years remained unsolved, at least for a large portion of the missionary movement. This was the great resistance on the part of missions to establishing truly indigenous churches ('self-governing, self-supporting and self-propagating', according to Henry Venn's dictum).

Indian women study the Bible together. The Bible has now been translated into most of the world's major languages, and is available to readers throughout the world, playing a vital part in World evangelization.

The churches multiply

World War I marked a new stage in the modern revolutionary age and in the history of Christianity. Having reached its peak of world power, western Europe began to experience a decline that culminated in the liberation of its colonies. Meanwhile, the process of secularization which had gained ground during the nineteenth century speeded up so greatly that it became doubtful whether Christianity would survive in what was traditionally called Christendom.

Paradoxically, in the non-Western countries where, in 1914, Christians were still very small minorities, the churches (particularly the Protestant churches) began to display an unexpected vitality. But soon they had to face the same revolutionary forces that Christianity had helped to create, and that the West had both faced and also spread to the rest of world during the nineteenth century. After 1914 these revolutionary forces continued to mount until they formed the greatest challenge that Christianity had ever had to face.

Although in Europe many observers claimed that the post-Christian era had arrived, Christianity continued to advance in the rest of the world. In the United States, church membership continued to rise in proportion to the growth in population. Missionary interest grew in such a way that by the time the USA had become

TOYOHIKO KAGAWA

S. Funaki

Toyohiko Kagawa (1888–1960) became well-known in Japan as a Christian social reformer, evangelist and author. The son of a wealthy businessman and one of his many concubines, he lost both parents when he was only four. Kagawa was baptized in his teens after he had come under the influence of Presbyterian missionaries. He received theological training at Kobe Presbyterian Seminary and the Princeton Seminary, USA.

While at Kobe he dedicated his life to the cause of the poor, when his life was spared during a serious illness. Before fully recovering, he moved into a bad slum district in Kobe. He made an attempt to attack the root of social evils by organizing the first labour and peasant unions. He became a leader in the midst of the social unrest which arose out of the rapid development of capitalism during and after World War I.

A shift within the labour movement towards Marxism made Kagawa change his own direction. He started the more church-related 'Kingdom of God Movement' in an effort to combine the church's spiritual mission and his social movement. With the rise of Japanese nationalism in the early thirties this movement came to a halt.

Kagawa interpreted the Bible in a unique and rather dogmatic way. For him, the cross stands for the power of love and the willing acceptance of suffering. The meaning of the cross consists of discovering that power. For example, the Mormons' founding of Salt Lake City is a working out of the love of Christ. Kagawa used the language and ideas of psychological analysis to express the basic facts of the historical Jesus.

a world power, it had also become the main headquarters of the Protestant missionary movement and began to contribute greatly to Roman Catholic missions. In 1973, seventy per cent of all Protestant missionaries in the world and an even higher proportion of the total cost of the missionary operation was estimated to come from North America. Christianity in general terms influenced the institutions of the nation. Each President since Jimmy Carter has claimed to be a Christian, and the Moral Majority Movement tried to make a clear link between Christian values and the American way of life, which President Reagan especially decked in evangelistic terms.

But by far the most amazing numerical growth of the church in the twentieth century took place in the Third World.

Asian expansion

In Japan, where the centenary of the re-launching of Roman Catholic missions, and the beginning of Protestant missions, was celebrated in 1959, the results were not very impressive in terms of numbers. Yet the percentage of Christians, more than half of them Protestant, after 1914 increased faster than the population. At an early stage Christianity appealed to the intelligentsia and then, with the influx of North American missionaries after 1945, it began to attract people of lower income. In 1914 there were more than 100,000 Roman Catholics in Japan growing to 750,000 in 1980. By 1980 there were over 950,000 Japanese Protestants.

In Korea, the 'hermit kingdom', in 1914 there were approximately 80,000 Roman Catholics and 96,000 Protestants. Despite political problems caused by empire-building nations in the years between World War I and World War II, the number of Christians continued to increase in a remarkable way. After World War II and the invasion of South Korea by North Korea in 1950, Christians, like the rest of the population, suffered greatly. But once the armistice was signed, in July 1953, Christianity began to flourish in the South, encouraged by the efforts of North American missionaries. It is estimated that Roman Catholic and Protestant Christians now number fourteen million out of a population of forty-five million, and that this number is increasing at the rate of eight per cent per year—almost four times as fast as the population growth. In the capital, Seoul, alone, there are more than 1,600 churches.

Taiwanese children eagerly read Christian books from a mobile bookstall. In the twentieth century books like these have become a major means of spreading the Christian gospel.

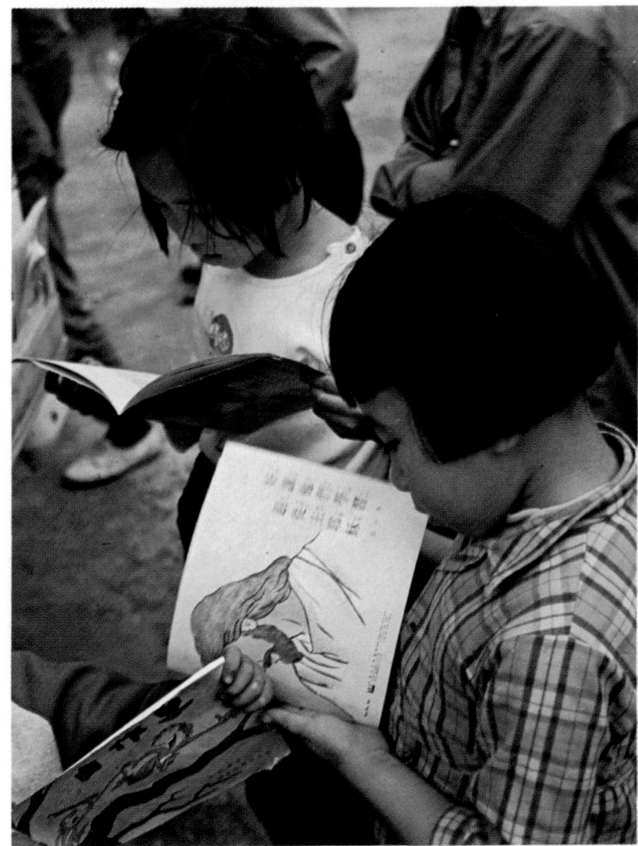

In North Korea, as in China, the organized church has faced great difficulties. However, in 1989 Ko Gi Yun, the general secretary of the [North] Korean Christian Fellowship was able to bring greetings to the meetings of the World Council of Churches in Moscow. By contrast, in a few countries of South-East Asia and the fringing islands the rate of church growth since World War II surpassed that of the population. For instance, in Indonesia, the number of Christians was said to have increased from four million in 1964 to eleven million in 1970, the greatest growth being registered in northern Sumatra, East Java, Kalimantan (Borneo), and the islands of Nias and Timor, where thousands of Muslims were converted to Christianity. In Burma, Buddhism was declared the state religion in 1961 and the 'Burmese way of socialism' (established by a military government in 1965) did not allow the presence of foreigners. In spite of this Christianity was said to be growing in such a way that in 1972 a new church was being organized every week. Ten years later there were over 7,000 congregations, amounting to nearly two million Christians. Since World War II the number of Christians multiplied also in Cambodia, Hong Kong and Taiwan.

Christians from Taiwan leave church after a service.

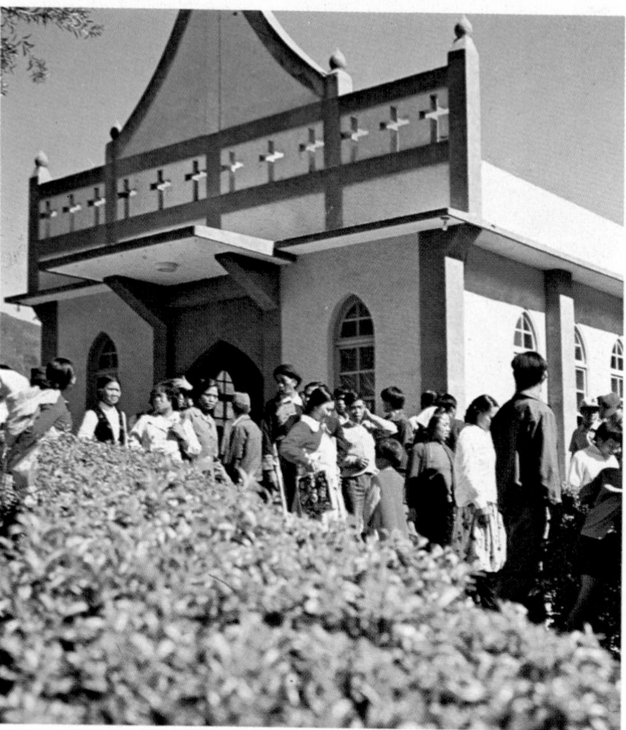

In addition various countries that had traditionally remained closed to missionaries from abroad changed that policy, noticeably the Himalayan kingdoms of Bhutan, Sikkim, Nepal, and the Tibetan refugee kingdom on the Indian border. The first church in Bhutan was organized in 1970, with P.S. Tingbo as its pastor. Meanwhile, in the subcontinent of India, restrictions were placed on the entrance of missionaries in the years that followed independence (1947), but this resulted in an unprecedented growth of the national leadership in the church. Christianity, represented by the Syrian Orthodox church, or Mar Thoma (the oldest Christian community, claiming to have originated with the apostle Thomas), Catholicism and Protestantism, gained ground especially among the underprivileged and the animistic tribes on India's northern frontiers. By 1990 the Christian population was well over thirty million. Afghanistan, perhaps the largest unevangelized nation in the world, remained closed to the gospel.

In the Pacific, some tribes in Papua New Guinea were practically unaware of the existence of the white man until the middle of the present century. But missionaries representing fifteen different Protestant organizations and several Roman Catholic orders entered the island, and within a few years the great majority of the population—ninety-two per

BILLY GRAHAM

Richard V. Pierard

Billy Graham is undoubtedly the most successful Christian mass evangelist in history and his converts number millions. He was born on a farm in North Carolina, USA in 1918, and was converted in an evangelistic campaign in 1934. He graduated from Wheaton College, Illinois, in 1943, married Ruth Bell, daughter of a veteran missionary to China, and became the first evangelist of the Youth for Christ movement. In 1947 Graham was named president of Northwestern College, Minneapolis, and two years later rose to national prominence when he led a Los Angeles Crusade.

In 1950 Billy Graham brought together a talented group to form the Billy Graham Evangelistic Association, and initiated a radio programme, *The Hour of Decision*. Resigning the college presidency in 1952, he devoted his time to holding evangelistic rallies in major cities throughout the world, most of which were televised to widen their impact.

Possessing a warm, winsome personality, Graham uses modern mass communications and organization effectively to put across a simple, Bible-centred gospel message. He emphasizes individual decisions for Christ and careful follow-up to integrate the new believers into churches. Although at one time a strong anti-communist and American nationalist, in his mature years Graham developed an ecumenical vision, global awareness and sense of social concern that gained him world-wide respect. Not only has he preached on all six continents and in the Soviet Union and China, but many presidents and heads of state regard him as a friend and welcome his counsel.

Billy Graham has written several best-selling books. His organization produced numerous evangelistic films and started the magazine *Decision* in 1960. He played a leading role in founding the periodical *Christianity Today* in 1956 and in setting up the World Congresses on Evangelism in Berlin (1966) Lausanne (1974) and Manila (1989), and the Amsterdam Conference for Itinerant Evangelists (1983 and 1986). He also founded a research centre on evangelism and missions at Wheaton College, and a training school for Christian workers in Asheville, North Carolina.

'The Bible says . . .' Billy Graham, the American evangelist, whose mass crusades have been held in many countries around the world.

cent, according to recent estimates—claimed to be Christian, the greater number of them Protestant.

Advance in Africa

The startling advance of Christianity in Africa in the age of liberation led Stephen Neill, a distinguished historian, to state that 'on the most sober estimate . . . by the end of the 20th century Africa south of Sahara will be in the main a Christian continent'. His claim was supported by the increased rate of church growth after World War II, when a large number of African nations were becoming independent.

From the nineteenth century on, thousands of Africans had been educated in mission schools, frequently subsidized by the colonial governments. For both Protestant and Catholic missionaries, education had in fact been such a common method of work that it could be claimed that for most African Christians the mission school was the door to the church. After World War I great stress had been laid, particularly by the Roman Catholics, on building up a complete educational system, from primary to university levels. By the early 1920s, in British Africa alone, there were about six thousand mission schools, compared with a hundred government schools.

With the coming of independence (in the 1950s and 1960s for most African countries), the new governments increasingly took control of mission schools. Yet the number of Christians continued to increase, although growth varied from country to country. In some areas the educated class returned to the churches. A revival movement, which had begun in Ruanda-Urundi in 1935, influenced the life of the churches in Uganda, Kenya and Tanzania. African independent churches proliferated right across the continent south of the Sahara, notably in South Africa, Nigeria, Zaire, Ghana and Kenya. By 1980 there were 17 million Christians in South Africa, 25 million in Zaire, 20 million in Nigeria, 8 million in Uganda and 7 million in Tanzania. By denomination, there were 66 million Roman Catholics, 38 million Protestants, 24 million independent Protestants, 11 million Anglicans, and 23 million Orthodox.

In Latin America, regarded for centuries as a Christian continent, Protestantism grew at an amazing rate during the first three quarters of the twentieth century. By 1914 Protestant Christians were a minority of 500,000, often persecuted by the official church; by 1975 they were over twenty-five million, with nearly fifteen million of these coming from Brazil. Indeed, one Latin American writer claimed that this is 'the only area in the world where a Christian church is growing more rapidly than the population' (Emilio Castro). The greatest growth was among the Pentecostals, who made up over sixty per cent of the Protestant total, and among the Seventh-Day Adventists. Among Roman Catholics, the great new development in the 1980s has been the 'base communities', of which tens of thousands now exist, especially in Brazil. Poor people study the Bible in the light of their own experience of oppression, and find it comes to life.

This summary of the numerical growth of the church outside Europe in the twentieth century provided grounds for optimism about the future of Christianity. The global community that had taken shape during the nineteenth century through the missionary movement grew steadily in many countries and, in some areas of the non-Western world, at a phenomenal rate. By 1975 more than three thousand Third World missionaries (mostly Asian) were at work abroad. One group of Asians was planning to send out ten thousand missionaries by the year 2000! The great new fact of the century was an exploding world-wide Christian movement, advancing mainly among the masses of the non-Western world, and with a growing concern to make disciples among all nations.

Obstacles to growth

The expansion of Christianity outside Europe during the twentieth century is undoubtedly impressive. Never before in history has religion spread so vastly and so rapidly as Christianity has in the last few decades. But there are still many largely unevangelized areas, particularly the Muslim countries of the Near East, the Middle East and North Africa, but also within countries with a growing percentage of Christians. For instance, in the state of Kashmir (India), only one in a thousand persons is a Christian; and in the state of Himachal Pradesh there is only one church for every two thousand villages.

When the communists took over China in 1949, there were under one million Protestants and about two million Roman Catholics. Stories of a persecuted church circulated which, along with government disinformation, led many to believe that the church in China had virtually died out under the strains of the cultural revolution. When, however, in 1979 churches began to open again for worship, they were filled to overflowing. Far from dying out, the church had grown remarkably. In 1983 the China Christian Council estimated there were two million Protestants and three million Roman Catholics. Jonathan Chao of the China Research Centre in Hong Kong estimates there are at least 30 million Christian believers in China. The Roman Catholic Church is split between the government approved Catholic Patriotic Association and a persecuted church loyal to the Vatican. Protestantism embraces both the officially recognized Three-Self Patriotic Movement and the house church movement. In some places the house churches are simply extensions of the Three-Self movement, but elsewhere they embrace those who would not wish to be so associated. In 1989 the Three-Self organization courageously gave vocal support to the students' agitation for greater democracy.

Religion revives world-wide

The phenomenal growth of the church in the last few decades is part of a much wider revival of religion that is taking place all over the world. Evidence of this revival includes the way occultism and Asian religions have come to flourish in the West; the resurgence of Islam in some areas of Africa and in Malaysia and Pakistan; the revival of Buddhism in Thailand, Vietnam, Cambodia, Burma and Sri Lanka, of Hinduism in India and of Shintoism in Japan; the vitality of Spiritism (and especially of *Umbanda*) in Brazil and of the *Sokka Gakkai* in Japan. Fundamentalist movements have flourished: Islamic in Iran, Jewish in the settlement movement, protestant in North America and Roman Catholic in Spain's 'Opus Dei'. If it is true that 'The Industrial Revolution has become a kind of irresistible bulldozer forcing a way for Western civilization into the non-Western areas of the World', it is also true that in this 'one world', bewitched by the achievements of Western civilization, people continue to search for answers to their deep existential questions.

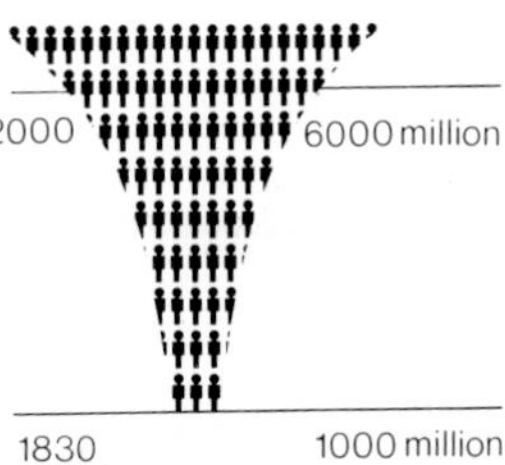

World population mushrooms

It is very significant that the greatest growth of the church in the twentieth century has taken place among animistic peoples, and among the deprived classes in the cities. Contemporary mass movements to Christianity (like other flourishing religious movements) in the Third World seem to be both a result of the impact of Western civilization upon traditional societies, and a reaction against it.

The revolution that the West has brought to the values and lifestyle of millions in the rest of the world can hardly be exaggerated. To cope with this revolution many people are turning to religion, but not mainly to westernized Christianity, with its bad associations from colonial times. They are turning either to a resurgent ancient religion (sometimes championed by nationalistic political leaders, who use it to create a new national identity), or to a 'native' version of Christianity (sometimes strongly nationalistic, and tolerating ancient ideas and customs), that takes into account aspects of human life that the Western church left out. In Africa, for instance, the independent churches are said to attract between 400,000 and 450,000 people a year from the traditional churches, both Roman Catholic and Protestant; in Latin America, Pentecostalism—'The only Christian movement with real indigenous roots,' according to many observers—is the least dependent upon foreign personnel and finance. If the survival of Christianity is not in doubt in the Third World, the survival of those churches founded by Western missionaries and soaked in Western culture certainly is.

In any event the church in the Third World is threatened by a number of problems.

Indian children process with banners during a Sunday school rally. Much Christian work is devoted to bringing the good news to a new generation.

Christianity meets culture

Some Western missionaries have labelled as 'syncretism' legitimate efforts to express Christianity through indigenous cultural patterns. Western missionaries have often all too easily assumed that the new churches will have to pattern themselves on the models imported from abroad. Undoubtedly one reason for the proliferation of 'indigenous' Christian movements is the missionary's lack of cultural sensitivity.

However, some of the mass movements with a high rate of numerical growth may be no more than 'baptized heathenism'. For it is clear that for many people in the Third World Christianity has become a symbol of modernity, alongside which non-Christian views and customs are allowed to survive. For example, in New Guinea and other areas, new Christians followed a 'cargo cult' and constructed installations on the seashore in the hope that God—the 'higher power' whom they supposed had sent the white man and the many material objects that had arrived by sea and air—would make them rich. In

HELDER CAMARA

C. René Padilla

Dom Helder Camara, the courageous Archbishop of Recife, Brazil, has worked strenuously for social justice and on behalf of the oppressed for many years.

Helder Camara has spoken out for the oppressed peoples of South America as the Roman Catholic Archbishop of Olinda and Recife, in north-east Brazil, the most underdeveloped region in that vast country. Born in Fortaleza (in the same region) in 1909, Camara was ordained as a priest in 1931 and became an archbishop in 1964.

Although he held fascist ideas in his youth, the situation of poverty and his growing understanding of the social implications of the gospel led him to take up a radical position. Archbishop Camara has been one of the most influential figures in the Latin American General Episcopal Conference (CELAM) since its inception in 1955.

Helder Camara's greatest achievement has been to defend the rights of the poor through non-violent means. His prophetic stand has been widely recognized, especially abroad, where he has received a number of prizes (including an honorary doctorate from the University of Louvain in 1970). He is the enemy of conservatives in both government and the church, who frequently call him 'the red bishop'. Despite such accusations, he has openly rejected Marxism, and criticized equally the Soviet Union and the United States for their disregard for the needs of the Third World. For 'Dom Helder', as he is familiarly called, both 'superpowers' remain 'enclosed and imprisoned in their egoism.'

Dom Helder has similarly opted for non-violence, believing that it is rooted in the gospel. He believes that the force of truth, justice and love is greater than that of wars, murder and hatred. But he has claimed that the violence of the rich against the poor, and the violence of the developed countries against the under-developed, is more worthy of condemnation than the revolutionary violence that they create.

Africa, the practice of polygamy or witchcraft, and the use of charms and fetishes often co-exist with outward acceptance of the Christian faith. In some areas of Latin America, adherence to Christianity does not necessarily imply a complete break from Spiritism.

Too many denominations?

A more common problem is what may be called the 'over-denominationalism' of the church in the Third World. In Africa alone approximately one hundred new 'independent' groups are founded every year. The same trend is present in both Asia and Latin America. Denominational allegiance is one of the major hindrances to mission in the Third World.

But it must be remembered that in 1900 there were sixty-one Western missions working in China, and that between 1900 and 1913 the number was increased to ninety-two. The church in non-Western countries has been

Times Square, New York, graphically represents some of the values of the West. Many of these values and attitudes have been exported to other parts of the world—as well as the Christian gospel.

split by imported divisions from the beginning. The 'younger churches' of Africa, Asia, and Latin America have in turn produced their own divisions, often brought about by individualistic leaders with little or no concern for the unity of the body of Christ.

Western missionaries took to the Third World not only the gospel but also a Western naturalistic outlook. They carried a world-view in which disease and disaster were explained in terms of the natural law of cause and effect. The supernatural was restricted to a small area of human experience. They stressed technological responsibility for the natural world, rather than interdependence with the environment. They brought with them a sharp division between the sacred and the secular, according to which secular matters lay outside the orbit of religion.

Christian ghettoes

The result of this missionary work conditioned by Western secularism was churches in which a sharp separation between the sacred and the secular (and therefore between the church and the world, faith and works, religion and daily life) was taken for granted. An Asian author states that, as a result, the churches in Asia 'are living spiritually and socially in what are called mission compounds, "Christian ghettoes" of their own creation, inward-looking and concerned with themselves'. An African has said that the church there is 'suffering from a conservatism which makes it look like a relic of medieval European Christianity deposited here and left to rust and rot away'. For such reasons the leaders of the new nations are increasingly rejecting Christianity as 'irrelevant to practical life'. Pentecostalism in Chile, though a vigorous religious movement, is on 'social strike'. The same is true in general terms of Protestantism in the rest of Latin America.

The isolation of the church from society is a matter of deep concern to Christians who see it in the light of the radical social, political and economic changes taking place in the developing countries. They claim that if the churches that have emerged out of the Western missionary enterprise are more interested in their numerical

ALEXANDER SOLZHENITSYN

Paul Bechtel

Alexander Solzhenitsyn (born in 1918), the Russian writer, has been acclaimed for his powerful novels. He was born in Rostov-on-Don to a mother who had lost her husband in a hunting accident six months before. Solzhenitsyn was trained in science but developed an early interest in literature. Drafted into the Red Army in 1941, he was arrested in 1945 and sent to a remote prison camp for criticizing Stalin in letters to a friend.

Solzhenitsyn won wide acclaim for *One Day in the Life of Ivan Denisovich* (1962), which was based on his personal experiences of the brutality of Stalin's prison camps. The book was issued with official approval, but when Kruschev fell from power Solzhenitsyn was silenced and his later books were brought secretly out of Russia for publication abroad. *The First Circle* (1964), in which intellectuals were forced to serve the state, grew out of the author's own experience. *Cancer Ward* (1969), set in a small hospital, similar to the one in which Solzhenitsyn himself had recovered from cancer, describes the way several different people react to the disease. Both novels suggest by allegory the dangers of the Soviet system. *August 1914*, dealing with Russia's role in World War I, appeared in 1971; and *Gulag Archipelago* (1973) documents the terror reign of Lenin and Stalin.

Solzhenitsyn was awarded the Nobel Prize for literature in 1970, but was forbidden by the USSR to accept it at that time. He was later forced into exile. He has clear sympathies with the Russian Orthodox church and several Christians who appear briefly in his books are treated with understanding. In exile, Solzhenitsyn criticized what he regarded as the dangerously degenerate character of life in the West.

Alexander Solzhenitsyn, the Russian writer, who has been forthright in his criticism of both the Soviet Union and the West.

growth as distinctly *religious* institutions than in the meaning and practice of Christian discipleship in a revolutionary situation, the future of Christianity in the Third World is in question.

Such concerns are illustrated by the struggle of the Chinese Church since the Communist take-over of China in 1949 when all foreign missionaries were required to leave the country. By that date a protestant church of something less than a million believers and a Roman Catholic Church some two million strong had developed as the fruit of patient missionary endeavours, but concern was essentially restricted to personal salvation, and thus Chinese Christianity up to that time essentially failed to make any mark upon the structures of Chinese society.

The years of 'The Great Leap Forward', of Mao Ze-dong's Red Guards and of the Cultural Revolution, that followed all put the church under great pressure. In 1951 denominational Christianity was replaced by the Three-Self Patriotic Movement, which, whatever its faults, represented a genuinely Chinese form of church organization, independent of Mission Boards in the West. In 1967 the formation of a Catholic Patriotic Association sought to nurture a continuing Catholicism independent of Vatican control, but not all Roman Catholics accepted this and

POPE JOHN XXIII

John P. Donnelly

Pope John XXIII, elected in 1958, soon gained the love and respect of Christians throughout the world. A man of warm humanity, he was also responsible for calling the revolutionary Second Vatican Council.

"Truth calls for the elimination of every trace of racial discrimination, and the consequent recognition of the inviolable principle that all states are by nature equal in dignity . . ."

POPE JOHN XXIII

John XXIII was born Angelo Giuseppe Roncalli near Bergamo, Italy, in 1881 and died in 1963. His parents were tenant farmers, but scholarships enabled him to attend seminaries at Bergamo and Rome, where he was ordained in 1904. After serving in World War I, he filled administrative posts at Rome until appointed papal nuncio in turn to Bulgaria (1925–34), Turkey (1934–44) and France (1944–53). In 1953 he became Cardinal Patriarch of Venice. His energy, charity and ability to get on with people of all persuasions marked out his early career.

Roncalli's election, at the age of seventy-six, in the difficult conclave which followed the death of Pius XII in 1958, suggested that he would be a caretaker pope. Instead, he began a new age in the Roman Catholic church. He issued eight encyclicals. *Mater et Magistra* (1961) updated papal social teaching. It insisted that co-operation between individuals and social groups, rather than national or class struggle, is the basic principle of social order. It stressed for the first time, the duty of developed nations to aid emerging nations by technological means. *Pacem in Terris* (1963) argued that peace flows from right order, that all nations are equal in dignity, and that co-operation and trust must replace the arms race. John XXIII urged reconciliation during the world political crises over Berlin, Cuba and Algeria. He elevated many clergymen from developing nations to the posts of bishop and cardinal. He sought closer ties with Eastern Orthodoxy, sent representatives to the World Council of Churches, and set up the Vatican Secretariat for Promoting Christian Unity.

The aim of all his work was to update the church (*aggiornamento*). Accordingly he created a commission to revise canon law. The peak of his achievement was the Second Vatican Council (1962–65), which he called to improve the pastoral work of the church. Once the council opened, the pope intervened rarely, but liberal bishops took courage from his stand.

Whether John XXIII was responsible for shaping post-Vatican II Catholicism is doubtful. His actions before and after becoming pope show him swinging between conservativism and liberalism. His personal spiritual notes, published posthumously as *Journal of a Soul*, reveal a deep but traditional piety. His peasant background and appearance tended to obscure his wide learning. Although he deliberately discouraged the cult of personality, his kindliness and wit made him a charismatic and popular pope.

so a split occurred. Similarly not all protestants, and especially some who associated with local house churches, were prepared to work within the Three-Self Movement, with its search for a church which would be self-supporting, self-administering and self-propagating. They judged the movement to be too closely associated with the state, though the Three-Self Movement, along with other Christians, suffered in the years of persecution – a time when many people around the world prayed for the survival of the church in China.

The church, in fact, more than survived. It emerged in 1979 both stronger and more Chinese. A woman who had been a church worker before the Cultural Revolution testifies to how, before the Cultural Revolution, 'my only contact with those outside the Church was as objects of evangelization. It seemed I always assumed a higher status.' But eight years working in a factory enabled her to find a new identity with ordinary factory workers and their needs, providing both opportunities for practical service, and a place to confess her faith from within the community of workers.

Thus, when the churches were reopened in 1979 there were many new believers and seekers anxious to attend. The church had certainly more than doubled in numbers, and some would suggest it had grown even faster. In subsequent years Bishop Ting and other leaders of the China Christian Council began to travel extensively abroad, conferences were held, institutions reopened, and Bibles printed. The constitution of 1982 provided for the rights of religious believers but with the proviso that they should be free of foreign control.

Post-Mao China found itself with a desperate need for modernization, and the need for outside help to aid that process was reluctantly agreed by an ageing leadership. But with economic modernization and the opening up of education overseas to Chinese students, the demand for greater democratization developed. This burst through the system on the occasion of Mr Gorbachev's visit to Beijing in the early summer of 1989 when large numbers of students took the opportunity of defying the security forces by gathering in force in Tienanmen Square. In this they had the courageous support of the leadership of the China Christian Council, and at first it looked as if their peaceful protests might prevail, but the security forces were apparently only biding their time before taking pre-emptive action.

The most urgent question confronting the churches in the Third World today is whether Christianity has anything to say to the millions of people struggling against poverty and social injustice and searching for liberation and development. The tendency to reduce the gospel to a 'spiritual' message, and to fail to be concerned for social righteousness, however, seem to be constant features of Christianity in the Third World, as they have been of Christianity in the West for several centuries.

Bringing a Western gospel

During the heyday of Western political imperialism, which came to a close in 1914, few missionaries could have suspected that their alliance with the world powers would in time become a danger to them and an embarrassment to the 'younger churches' which resulted from their work. Most of them simply took it for granted that Western prestige and power should be used in the service of Christ—as they were. It would be wrong to dismiss the dedication and self-sacrifice with which they undertook the task of spreading the gospel to the ends of the earth, or to fail to see the spiritual motivation behind much of what they did. Further, Western missionaries courageously opposed their own governments in matters related to colonial policies. But it is an indisputable fact that missionary work was done from a position of political and economic power, and with the assumption of Western superiority with regard to cultures and race.

World War I did much damage to the image of 'The Christian West'. The shattering of that image was completed with World War II. Within a few years the age of Western political imperialism was brought to an end, giving way to an age marked by the liberation of 'new nations'. The change resulted immediately in the resurgence of nationalism and traditional values. Several countries, notably India, were closed to foreign missionaries. It looked as if circumstances would force the 'young churches' to depend completely on their own leaders and finance.

But American Protestant Missions (almost wholly dependent on American personnel, leadership and finances) grew in numbers during the same period. For the Western missionary movement, the age of liberation has hardly dawned. In fact, many Christian churches, institutions and movements in the Third World continue to live in a 'colonial' situation, heavily dependent on foreign resources and therefore subject to foreign control. Despite the progress made towards genuine independence, Christians in the developing countries are caught in a situation in which economic and cultural imperialism has hardly been broken, even though its outward appearance has changed.

It is also true that the mentality of colonial dependence lingers in the 'younger churches'. An African writer has said: 'The church in Africa has for too long been very missionary minded, but only in terms of receiving missionaries and depending on them.' The missionary movement has been extremely slow to recognize the importance of a real partnership in Christian work. Even after the 'Retreat of the West' in the Third World, Christianity is still commonly regarded as a Western religion and the Christian mission is still generally identified with a white face. Words written about Latin America are also true of Asia and Africa: 'The most acute problem of the Protestant churches will be the nationalization of the church with its inherent ecclesiastical conflicts with the mission boards, especially in the United States.'

The church in the Third World is faced by problems that reflect its beginnings in a missionary movement largely captive to the West. Its impressive numerical growth provides a basis for optimism, but it must be viewed as the brighter side of a picture in which there are also dark shadows that must be faced realistically.

Partners in mission

The church has become a worldwide community. Its emergence as such coincided with the emergence of a 'global consciousness'—the sense shared by a large part of humanity that they belong to *one world*, that all nations share a common destiny. Christianity is not a Western religion and the community that has been called to witness to it will fulfil its purpose to the extent to which it moves from missionary paternalism to partnership in mission.

The 'parity' between older and younger churches was brought to the fore as never before at the

Second World Missionary Conference held at Jerusalem in 1928. At the next World Missionary Conference (Madras, 1938) the emergence of a world-wide Christian community was reflected by the presence of delegates from nearly fifty countries, many of them from the non-Western world. Madras also insisted that mission and the creation of indigenous churches must be closely linked. But it was at the enlarged meeting of the International Missionary Council held at Whitby (Canada) in 1947, that the church was uniquely confronted with the need to break down the distinction between 'older and younger churches' and to face its global responsibility. 'Whitby's emphasis centred upon missionaries as agents of the church universal whose responsibilities, like those of their national colleagues with whom they should be on a par, would be determined by their training and ability.' But many of its recommendations have still not been put into practice by a number of mission agencies which many years later remain bound by tradition.

Stop the missionaries?

This great reluctance by missions to take to heart the call to partnership, even in the post-colonial situation, explains the 'Call for a Moratorium' issued by the Commission on World Mission and Evangelism of the World Council of Churches at its assembly held at Bangkok in January 1973. The recommendation was that mission agencies consider stopping sending funds and personnel to particular churches for a period of time, as 'a possible strategy of mission in certain situations'. The debate that followed, especially among conservative evangelicals, was characterized by more heat than light. For its part the All-Africa Conference of Churches added heat by adopting the 'Moratorium' at its meeting at Nairobi, in December 1973, and adding: 'Should the moratorium cause missionary agencies to crumble, the African church could have performed a service in redeeming God's people in the Northern

An aerial is erected for the transmitters of a Christian radio station in the Seychelles, which broadcasts to parts of India and Africa. Twentieth-century Christians have used radio, TV and film to communicate the Christian message.

Hemisphere from a distorted view of the mission of the church in the world.' On the other hand, the International Congress on World Evangelism, held at Lausanne in August 1974, added light by recognizing in its Covenant that 'a reduction of foreign missionaries

“Christ calls each of us to be his co-worker by allowing him to radiate and live his life in us and through us in the world today, so that the poor, seeing us, may be drawn to Christ and invite him to enter their homes and their lives; the sick and the suffering may find in us real angels of comfort and consolation; the little ones of the street may cling to us because we remind them of him, the friend of the little ones.”

From the Constitution of the Missionaries of Charity

One of the most famous women of recent history, winner of the coveted Nobel Peace Prize, is an unassuming Albanian nun – Mother Teresa – who has devoted her energies to helping the needy in Calcutta's slums. 'Poverty is necessary because we are working with the poor,' she says. 'It opens the heart of the poor when we can say we live the same way they do.' Others have joined her in her work, forming the order of the Missionaries of Charity, dedicated to the worship of God and care for the sick and dying.

may sometimes be necessary to facilitate the national church's growth in self-reliance and release resources for unevangelized areas.' By the time of the follow-up conference in Manila in 1989, these truths had become common ground throughout the evangelical movement.

After the Lausanne Congress, at which a number of critical issues had been brought up, mainly by Third World speakers, it became increasingly clear that even the most traditional missionary agencies would no longer be able to avoid the issue of world partnership in the Christian mission. The Lausanne Covenant claimed that 'a new missionary era has dawned' and that 'a growing partnership of churches will develop and the universal character of Christ's church will be more clearly exhibited.' At the end of 1976 a group of executives of the North American Evangelical Foreign Missions Association and the International Foreign Missions Association (who together controlled one third of all Protestant missionaries in Latin America) met in Quito (Ecuador) with representatives of the church in Latin America. The frank discussion of such painful realities as 'the ecclesiological crisis, the phenomenon of dependence, and the too-frequent failure to reach true brotherly interdependence' showed that changes were taking place in the relationship between the 'younger churches' and missionary agencies.

Leading their own people

At the same time, parallel progress was made by the Roman Catholic church. Already in his encyclical,

Maximum Illud (1919), Pope Benedict had admitted that in some regions where the Catholic faith had been present for centuries there were no indigenous clergy except those of a lower order; and that nations that had for long been illuminated by the faith had not for centuries produced 'bishops to rule them, or priests capable of making a deep impression on their fellow-citizens'. It took several years, however, for that situation to be altered. The first six Chinese bishops were consecrated there in 1926; their consecration was paralleled by that of an Indian in 1923, a Japanese in 1927, an Annabite and a Sri Lankan in 1933, and a Korean in 1937. The consecration of the first African bishop did not take place until 1939. In the following years, however, a rapid multiplication of bishops, archbishops and even cardinals occurred in the Third World. And the general attitude towards foreign missionaries was expressed by the AMECEA (Association of the Members of the Episcopal Conferences of Eastern Africa) in its 1973 meeting in Nairobi: foreign missionaries were needed to support and to train national leaders, and their presence showed the universality of the church.

The movement from missionary paternalism to partnership in mission was painfully slow; but by the mid-1970s it had become clear that the process was irreversible.

Totality of human life

The greatest challenge that confronts the church in the last decades of the century is to apply Christianity to practical life in a world plagued by poverty, social injustice, racial discrimination and oppression, and ridden by secularism and materialism. This challenge will have to be met in the context of a world in which all the nations (both capitalist and socialist) are slowly being drawn into a new culture characterized by the mythology of *modernity*.

Among Protestants there is evidence of a growing concern to bridge the separation between religion and life, evangelism and social action. A number of missionary strategists will continue to emphasize the numerical growth of the church, applying techniques perfected by North American industry and commerce. But time will show the inadequacy of such tools to face problems created by a common religious revival often void of ethical concerns. Hope for the future lies with movements in the church that are searching for a more biblical understanding of Christian mission which involves the totality of human life in personal, social and public aspects.

Within Roman Catholicism, Vatican II has opened the windows of an old church structure. As a result, the winds of revolution are affecting every aspect of its life and mission. For the first time in centuries, well-established traditions are being questioned and important issues openly debated.

If the present trends continue, it is quite probable that Christianity will again, as on many occasions in the past, play an important role in bringing humanity into a greater experience of freedom. The attempt to turn Christianity into the ideology of the West will be defeated by the recognition that the church is universal; the attempt to reduce Christianity to an individualistic religion will be overcome through a rediscovery of biblical revelation, whose relevance is being forced upon Christians by the revolutionary situation in this age of freedom.

Pentecostalism and the Charismatic Movement

James Dunn

Pentecostalism belongs to that stream within Christianity which places a personal experience of the Holy Spirit high among the marks of a Christian. In contrast, the Catholic has normally tended to 'channel' the Spirit through bishop and sacrament, and the Protestant through the Bible.

The most important figure within that stream in previous centuries was John Wesley. Indeed Wesley —whose own heart was 'strangely warmed', who emphasized the inner 'witness of the Spirit', and taught that sanctification was a second work of grace distinct from and following justification— might well be called the great-grandfather of Pentecostalism. From the early Methodists the stream runs directly through the Holiness movement of the nineteenth century. In camp meetings and 'higher life' conventions, holiness teachers proclaimed the 'second blessing' of sanctification as a cleansing of the heart from all sin, and sometimes called it 'the baptism of the Holy Ghost'.

Ablaze with the Spirit

Towards the end of the nineteenth century, three significant developments in the USA heralded the emergence of Pentecostalism as such. Increasing opposition to holiness teaching within the older denominations, particularly Methodism, resulted in the formation of several distinct holiness churches. Belief in baptism in the Holy Ghost and fire as a *third* blessing became increasingly widespread. And there was also a renewed interest in spiritual gifts, particularly healing.

The decisive step was taken at the turn of the century in Topeka, Kansas. There the doctrine was first formulated that 'speaking with other tongues' was the initial evidence that a person had received the baptism with the Holy Spirit. ('Other tongues' were generally understood as the Holy Spirit speaking through a person's speech organs in a language he had not previously known.) This teaching began to gain scattered support in the southern states of the USA during the early 1900s.

But it was the revival which began in Azusa Street, Los Angeles, in 1906, which really forged the link between Spirit-baptism and tongues. This three-year-long meeting was the launching-pad of twentieth-century Pentecostalism. Many hundreds of Christians from all over North America and then from Europe and the Third World visited Azusa Street and took its message back with them. The fire spread quite rapidly, resulting in the formation of many new churches. Most of the Holiness groupings were also influenced and either split over the new teaching on tongues or else became Pentecostal in doctrine.

A fourth strand in Christianity

In the seventy years since Azusa Street, Pentecostalism has spread throughout the world. It is important to realize that Pentecostalism is not a denomination or a Protestant sect. In fact, it represents a fourth major strand of Christianity—alongside Orthodoxy, Roman Catholicism and Protestantism—and is composed of many denominations.

The largest Pentecostal denominations in the USA include the Assemblies of God, the Church of God in Christ (the largest negro denomination), the Church of God and the Pentecostal Holiness Church. In Europe Pentecostalism is strongest in Scandinavia, and in Italy it has more adherents than all the Protestant groups put together. In Britain it remained a movement within the older denominations for some years. The Apostolic Church, predominantly Welsh, began in 1916, and the Elim Alliance, and Assemblies of God established themselves in the early 1920s. When many people emigrated from the Caribbean in the 1950s West Indian Churches of God organized themselves separately from the more established British groups. Pentecostals claim that Pentecostalism is still growing in Russia and probably China, too. Elsewhere in Asia the most significant advance has taken place in Indonesia.

The most striking spheres of Pentecostal influence, however, are Latin America and Africa. In many Latin American countries Pentecostalism is the largest non-Catholic grouping—a 1973 estimate suggests a total of fourteen or fifteen million Pentecostals in Latin America alone. The most striking examples are Brazil, where Pentecostals have been estimated to number more than four million (about seventy per cent of all non-Catholic Christians), and Chile, where in recent years about one in seven of the population was reckoned to be Pentecostal. In West Africa, Zaïre and southern Africa there are large independent churches which have derived much of their inspiration from Pentecostalism. Pentecostalism's growth in these two continents is, in fact, so great that it is quite probable that the Christians in Africa and Latin America will outnumber those in the rest of the world by the year 2000.

What Pentecostals believe

Pentecostalism is for the most part wholly orthodox in its beliefs as far as the major Christian doctrines are concerned. The one exception is the 'Jesus Only' churches in the USA, who hold a modalist view of God and baptize in the name of Jesus only. The largest of these churches is the United Pentecostal Church, and in all about twenty-

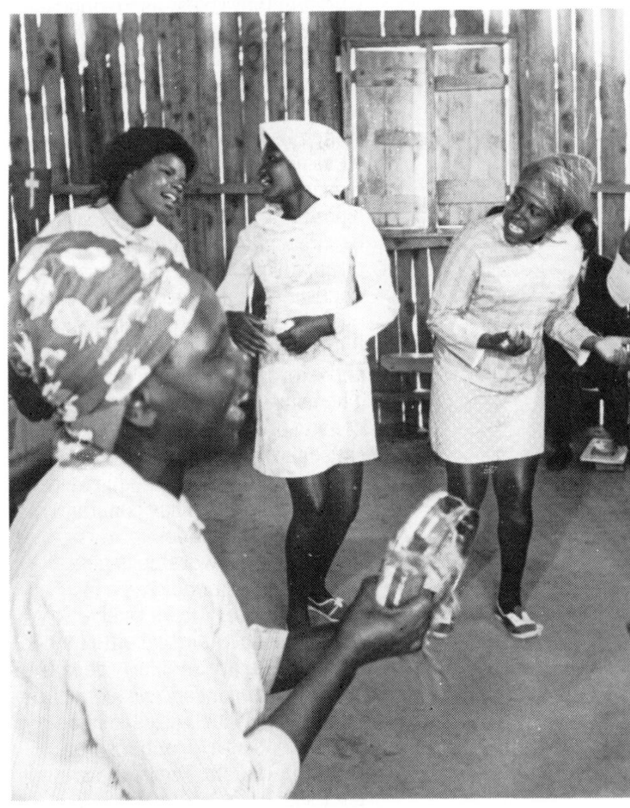

Kenyan Christians celebrate after a family baptism in a remote village.

five per cent of Pentecostals in the USA are unitarian. The one other major theological split within Pentecostalism concerns the question of whether baptism in the Spirit is a second or third work of grace. Almost all the Pentecostal pioneers simply tacked a belief in Spirit-baptism as a third work on to the Holiness belief in sanctification as a second work of grace. But in the years after 1910 there was increasing support for the doctrine that sanctification is part of Christ's 'finished work' on the cross, and so part of conversion. The Pentecostalism that is rooted in North America is split about fifty-fifty on this issue. A number of Pentecostal churches also regard footwashing as being as obligatory as baptism and the Lord's Supper.

Pentecostalists tend to see Christ in four roles: as Saviour, Baptizer in the Spirit, Healer and soon-coming King. A distinctive dogma is that tongues are the initial physical sign of Spirit-baptism (though some of the early pioneers were not so insistent on this). Healing evangelists have played a significant role in Pentecostalism's expansion, and teaching on healing often still includes the unfortunate doctrine that all illness is the result of sin or lack of faith. Belief in demon possession is also general and exorcism regularly practised. The conviction that the second coming of Christ is at hand has caused strains between the generations—but the continued growth of Pentecostalism has constantly revitalized this hope.

Pentecostal worship is patterned on the model given in 1 Corinthians, chapters twelve to fourteen. The spiritual gifts mentioned there are regularly regarded as the norm, and spoken contributions in a service will usually be understood as a 'prophecy', or 'word of wisdom'. Services are not necessarily without a structure and there will usually be a leader or pastor at the front. The attempt is usually made to observe Paul's guidelines in 1 Corinthians, chapter fourteen. Worship in older (white) Pentecostal churches has often become stereotyped and in practice little different from that of many Protestant churches. One result of the increasing importance of a minister has been the formation of the Full Gospel Business Men's Fellowship International, an organization of ordinary Christians which has done much to spread Pentecostal ideas all over the world.

Who are the Pentecostals?

For most of its existence Pentecostalism has been rigidly fundamentalist and anti-intellectual. It was not until the 1950s at the earliest that Pentecostal theological students began to move in significant numbers into non-Pentecostal seminaries in the USA. In the early decades it drew its support almost entirely from the poorer classes of society, and made the sort of impact in the twentieth century that Methodism made in the eighteenth and the Salvation Army in the nineteenth centuries. From the beginning blacks have played a significant role in the development of Pentecostalism and for nearly twenty years Pentecostal churches were among the most interracial organizations in the USA. Pentecostals have generally given little consideration to social issues and have strict ethical standards. But some of the newer churches in Africa and Latin America are developing a concern for social issues.

Their phenomenal growth has been due in large part to the enthusiastic vitality of their experience of the Spirit, the appeal of their spontaneous style of worship, in which all can participate in their own way, the absence of a caste of clergy and of a priestly hierarchy, and the insistence that all members must share their faith with others. For the most part Pentecostals in the Third World have not had to labour under the church structures and forms imposed from North America and Europe. This has made possible an indigenous growth which can hardly be rivalled in the history of Christian expansion. On the other hand, the Pentecostal churches have been remarkably divisive—as is clearly seen in the fragmentation of West Indian Pentecostal sects in Britain.

Pentecostals world-wide

In the past quarter of a century the growing influence of Pentecostalism on world Christianity has been marked by several significant developments.

In the early 1950s leading figures in the World Council of Churches began to recognize Pentecostalism as genuinely Christian—indeed as a 'third force' within Christianity. At about the same time David du Plessis, then Secretary of the Pentecostal World Conference, believed that God was calling him to make contact with the World Council. Following this he was an ambassador extraordinary for Pentecostalism within ecumenical circles and exercised a widespread influence.

In the early 1960s Pentecostal teaching and experiences began to penetrate significantly into the older Protestant denominations, starting with Anglo-Catholics in California. This neo-Pentecostalism caused strains within many congregations, but neo-Pentecostals have for the most part remained within their original

A fresh spontaneity and joy in worship is one of the gifts which Pentecostalism and the Charismatic Movement have brought to the church.

denominations, functioning mainly in prayer groups and conferences.

In the second half of the 1960s this emerging charismatic movement spread rapidly among the drop-out generation, who were disillusioned with a society which justified the Vietnam War. The 'Jesus Movement' caught attention for only a short time, but made a lasting impact on that generation. More significant was the development of Catholic Pentecostalism, which within a few years has become one of the most significant forces within Roman Catholicism, supported by Cardinal Suenens of Belgium and a significant number of bishops.

The acceptance of Pentecostalism by the leaders of the World Council marks the first time that more traditional Christianity has genuinely welcomed this enthusiastic brand of faith and worship as a valid and important expression of Christianity. Previously such forms of Christianity were either persecuted or only able to flourish outside the organized church.

Now the charismatic movement has increasingly broken down many of the barriers and misconceptions on both sides. Initially the charismatic movement operated at a very personal level. But when the first Roman Catholics became involved in 1967 the movement entered into what has been called its corporate phase. As the movement developed its own understanding of the nature of the church, difficulties arose within the mainstream churches. The result was the formation of some new denominations, although the term 'denomination' was denied by the new groups. For example, in Great Britain house churches and the restorationist movement began. By the 1980s the charismatic movement had moved into its global phase, with ever increasing influence in most world communions, particularly in Latin America. By the mid-1980s over 100 Anglican bishops were active in renewal, and in France there were almost one million charismatics within the Roman Catholic Church.

In some places the movement has produced schism and tension, and has fostered an immature intellectualism and an unhealthy emphasis on authority. But, at its best, it has led to a renewal of confidence, a re-energizing of lay authority, an enlivening of worship, a new emphasis upon the church as community, and the offering of a new basis for unity between Christians. It has spread across all the traditional groups in society and church life, and Catholic Pentecostalism, particularly, has drawn in a calibre of scholarship, and a respect for authority, sacraments and tradition which was missing from classic Pentecostalism. In the 1960s neo-Pentecostals were content to take over Pentecostal theology in large measure and gave speaking in tongues a Pentecostal prominence. But the widening of the charismatic movement since the 1960s has brought with it a questioning of the classic Pentecostal categories, a desire to formulate the theology of the 'Pentecostal experience' more carefully and a renewed concern to let the life of the Spirit be expressed in new forms of community.

Those belonging to classic Pentecostalism are still wary of the new developments. But in recent years many leaders of national churches have moved from a cautious 'No comment' to the view that the charismatic movement is the best hope for a renewal of the church in the closing decades of this century.

African independent churches

A. F. Walls

For some centuries Christianity as a world religion has been divided into three main traditions, Protestant, Roman Catholic and Orthodox. To these should now perhaps be added a substantial African development of Christianity. This African strand has been given a variety of titles: indigenous, separatist, prophetic, messianic, millennial, Zionist. These terms were really either too wide or too narrow to describe the movements which, while remaining recognizably Christian in intention, have abandoned any connection with the mission-founded churches. Here we will call them 'African independent churches'.

These African independent churches are a recognizable new form of the Christian tradition. But they are also part of a wider series of new religious movements in tribal societies in Africa, the Americas and the Pacific, which result from Christian and other Western influences interacting with tribal culture to produce something new to both. The African independent churches must not be too sharply distinguished from other forms of African Christianity. Some of the factors which make them popular are common African features which can often be traced within mission-founded African churches.

Independent churches occur widely in West, East, Central and Southern Africa. There are, however, great differences in the *extent* of their influence, both between nations, and between peoples and areas within the same nation. They rarely occur where Christians are few, or where Christianity has only recently arrived.

The independent churches differ widely in style, organization and attitudes. One classification divides between 'Ethiopian' churches (which assert African and reject European leadership, but keep the 'shape' of the church much as before) and 'Zionist' churches (which are charismatic, and seek the fulfilling of a Zion of their own). Perhaps the description 'prophet-healing' would be better for these churches. It is impossible to guess sensibly at total membership (though it must be many millions). Many people belong to both a 'mainline' church, out of loyalty or respectability, and to an independent church, for their deepest needs.

Why independent churches?

In trying to understand the origins of the independent churches we must distinguish between *immediate* causes (events which lead to a break with older churches or missions) and *underlying* causes (which produce conditions where a break becomes likely). Five underlying causes can be isolated:

The desire to be free of foreign domination in the church. Some of the oldest 'Ethiopian' churches arose from such a desire. West African Christians felt in the 1880s and 1890s that the missionary societies were going back on their principles of self-governing, self-supporting, self-propagating churches. As a result they produced the African church, the Native Baptist church and others. Elsewhere, the feeling that missionary leaders did not understand important local institutions such as ancestor veneration or marriage, has encouraged this desire for freedom.

Conditions produced by white dominance. No country has been more marked by the movements than South Africa. There the feeling among Africans of dispossession, the lack of other outlets for leadership, the effects of the migrant labour system in separating men from their families, and the strict controls on black residence and movement have produced the commonwealths of Isaiah Shembe and Ignatius Legkanyane, and other attempts to build 'Zion which is our home'.

The effects of mass movements. Between 1910 and 1930 African evangelists with little or no official church status led mass movements towards Christianity. Many who obeyed the call of Prophet William Wade Harris to abandon fetish joined the 'mainline' churches. But '*Harriste*' churches of the rest are still important in Ivory Coast. Sampson Oppong (an illiterate jail-bird) in Ghana and Walter Matitta in Lesotho were also men whom the missions had to recognize as very influential but who did not meet the missions' formal requirements for 'native ministers'. None of these movements were themselves independent churches, but they produced the conditions for them.

African boys play football in a township in south-west Transvaal. Many independent churches have sprung up in Southern Africa.

Religious revival. Simon Kimbangu, a young Baptist catechist, led a revival movement which in 1921 began to alarm the Belgian Congo government. He ws sent to jail for life; but the church bearing his name now claims three million members in Zaire. Another church of similarly extensive membership is the Church of the Lord (Aladura) found throughout West Africa. Immigrant communities in Europe and North America have brought their church with them. Joseph Babalola, a steamroller driver, received in 1928 a call to preach and gave a new impetus to revival in western Nigeria. The preaching of the catechist Garrick Braide brought thousands into the Anglican church in the Niger delta. His dismissal took thousands out into the Christ Army and other churches.

Quest for a wider salvation. In traditional African society healing is closely linked with religion. Africans asked whether faith in Christ was not equally effective. The 1918 influenza epidemic in particular posed this question acutely for African Christians. Kimbangu, Babalola and Braide were all healers attended by vast crowds. Healing is a feature of many independent churches today.

What distinguishes independent churches?

The movements are usually Bible-centred. They occur most readily where the whole Bible is available in the local language.

The independent churches seek direct continuity with the New Testament period. They claim to display the power and gifts of that period (often prophecy, revelation and healing—less frequently the gift of tongues). They also often continue traditions of healing or the work of mediums from pre-Christian religion and culture.

The movements combine ritualistic elements, such as robes, ceremonies, a hierarchy of apostles and prophets, with charismatic ones such as spontaneity, dancing and ecstasy. In Western Christianity, these two elements are found in different types of religion. But African society is both ordered *and* spontaneous.

The independent churches reflect the concerns most pressing to local people, concerns which were not necessarily those picked out by missionaries. A few have emphasized polygamy, but many do not regard monogamy as essential (except for churches such as the Kimbanguists). But independent churches take witchcraft and the evil produced in the community by hatred (the essence of witchcraft) very seriously. They are frequently accused of being mixtures of Christian and traditional elements (syncretistic) and undoubtedly many of them are. But many of the churches are *radical,* requiring a complete break with features of the old religion—witchcraft, charms, fetish—which are maintained among nominal members of older churches, as well as a break with tobacco, alcohol and gambling.

Like other religious movements, the independent churches have a history. They change and develop. They may move closer to or further from biblical Christianity. They may become inspired less or more by religious, economic or political factors. Some also represent splits from European Catholicism or the ancient Orthodox churches.

The independent churches are immensely diverse. Some have expressed political protest or nationalist sentiment, others are quietist and non-political. Some are large and highly-structured; others small and localized. Some have developed doctrinal peculiarities. The concern with 'power' sometimes makes the Holy Spirit more prominent than the Son. But theology is rarely important for them, and most do not consciously wish to break with the central Christian doctrine. The independent churches want to be part of a wider fellowship of churches (several have joined the World Council of Churches) but fear a take-over.

It is helpful to think of the independent churches as Africa's Anabaptists. Profusion of variety, the eccentricity of their wilder manifestations, and a spirituality and radical Bible-centredness are essential to them at their best. They relate to older Reformed churches as the sixteenth-century Anabaptists did to the Reformed. They are a response to Christianity in African terms, 'a place to feel at home'; and also a witness to the fact that there is here no 'abiding city'.

Translating the Bible

R. W. F. Wootton

Bible translation is one of the success stories of Christian history in this century. In 1900 there were 517 languages into which at least one book of the Bible had been translated; at the beginning of 1975 the figure had reached 1577, and by 1990 it was almost 2,000. The total of complete Bibles translated was 118 in 1900; today it is 310. At the same time there has been a great upsurge of new translations in languages which have long had versions of the Bible. There have been over 45 new versions of the New Testament in English and 16 in French in the twentieth century. Further, interest in translating the Bible has greatly increased in the ancient churches, especially the Roman Catholic church. Seventeen new Spanish New Testaments have appeared since 1945 and seven new Italian Bibles between 1965 and 1971, all translated by Roman Catholics.

The great increase in missionary Bible translation has been largely the result of the work of the Bible Societies associated with the United Bible Societies and the Wycliffe Bible Translators. Other bodies, such as the Scripture Gift Mission and the Trinitarian Bible Society, and Roman Catholic translators, have also contributed.

The founding of the Wycliffe Bible Translators in 1934 by an American translator, Cameron Townsend, was a milestone. Today it is one of the largest missionary societies in the world, with over 4,500 missionaries. The Wycliffe Bible Translators have worked on over 1,200 languages, reducing practically all of them to writing for the first time. Some of the tribes among whom they work number under a hundred people, and many have had no other contact with Western civilization. The great aim of the Wycliffe Bible Translators is to supply part of the Bible to every person in his or her own language in a form that can be understood.

By their study of linguistic principles the Wycliffe Bible Translators have added a fresh dimension to Bible translation. Formerly an academic knowledge of the Bible—preferably in Greek and Hebrew—and a firm grasp of the language into which it was to be translated were regarded as all that was necessary for a Bible translator. But it is generally accepted today that it is also necessary to understand the basic principles which apply to all languages, if the meaning is to be communicated effectively. Two American scholars, who began their work in the 1930s with the Wycliffe Bible Translators, have reached a high rank in international linguistic scholarship. Kenneth Pike has continued to work with the Wycliffe Bible Translators; Eugene Nida, who shaped the translation policies of the American Bible Society in the post-war years, is today the leader in the translation field for the United Bible Societies.

Translating more freely

This new approach to Bible translation has resulted in much greater freedom for the translator. *The Good News Bible* (American Bible Society, 1976) is typical of the new style. Translations such as the GNB are not 'free paraphrases'. They are based on the principle of providing the closest *natural* equivalent of the original. The meaning of the original is carefully analyzed, then the result is reconstructed in the receptor language, according to the principles of that language. A careful study is also made of the components of meaning of particular words. For example, bad behaviour, sorrow and a change of behaviour are the components of 'repentance'. Variations of meaning in different contexts are also noted. Seven different meanings of the Greek word for 'flesh' can be distinguished; in many languages these will be expressed in seven different ways. No attempt is made to make a word-for-word translation or to keep the same translation throughout from the Greek or Hebrew word.

A good deal which is implied in the original is brought out, so as to make the meaning quite clear. The original readers had many clues to the meaning which today's readers lack. For example, 'grace' is translated 'God's grace', 'Jordan', 'the River Jordan', and 'the forgiveness of sins' is expressed by 'God forgives sins'. For easier understanding, long sentences are broken up into short ones. Both these processess involve some lengthening of the text. In the Maya-Mopan language of Guatemala the thirteen Greek words of one verse in Mark's Gospel are rendered by fifty-seven in ten sentences.

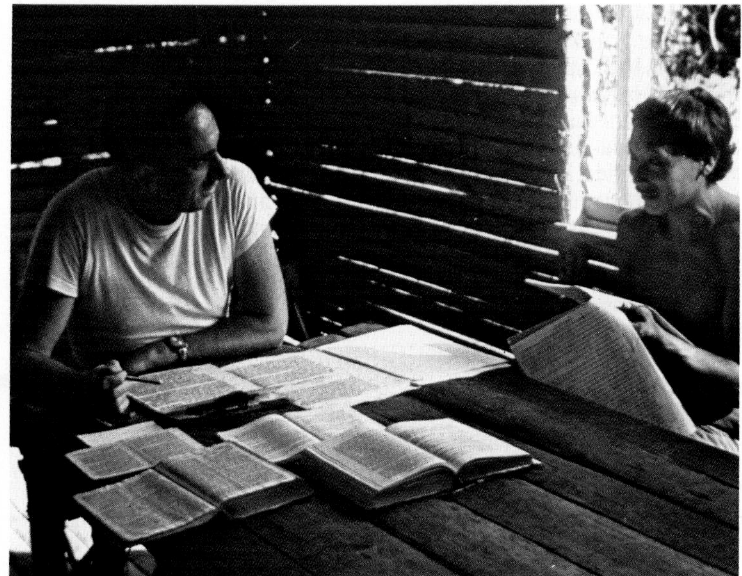

A Brazilian Indian and a missionary work together to translate part of the Bible. Bible translation is now normally undertaken by a local speaker of the language concerned.

Earlier translators faced problems presented by regional dialects. They often united these by a rather artificial language, such as Union Ibo (Nigeria, 1908). Today they are more concerned with the different levels of language arising from social and educational differences. Most new translations are made in 'common language', which spans the ranges of different social dialects, excluding at one extreme scholarly, literary and religious technical terms, and at the other all slang and sub-standard expressions. In European and some Indian languages, where there is a long tradition of Bible translation, up-dated versions of the old translations are still needed for parts of the church.

A third kind of translation is for new literates, generally adults. Once they have mastered the reading primer they need some very simple reading before they can reach the level of the common language translation. The United Bible Societies have selected twenty-five New Testament passages at five ascending levels for the use of new literates. Such selections have appeared in a number of languages, including English, Spanish and Bengali. Bible translation and literacy work go closely together. The Scriptures are very frequently the first words ever to be committed to writing, and translators have the difficult task of adapting an existing script (generally Roman) to the sounds of an unwritten language.

One important aspect of Bible work in the twentieth century is the close involvement of the Roman Catholic church in many parts of the world. The Second Vatican Council (1961–65) greatly encouraged the wide dissemination and study of the Bible. It also insisted on the use of the mother tongue in worship and authorized Roman Catholics to work with other Christians in Bible translation.

In 1968 an agreement between the Roman Catholic church and the United Bible Societies was published which has governed such work since then. Over a hundred projects have resulted from this agreement. For instance one interesting result of this co-operation is that Bible readings are broadcast daily in Malta in a new translation made by Maltese Catholics in association with the United Bible Societies.

Today the Bible Societies have over 100 highly qualified staff engaged in training and guiding translators in hundreds of languages. There is a steady output both of first translations and of up-to-date and intelligible 'common-language' translations. These give great promise both of spiritual growth among Christians and of the spread of the gospel, especially in the Third World where literacy is extending rapidly.

Organizing for unity

Colin Buchanan

Ecumenism, in the twentieth-century sense, began in a shared concern for evangelism in the Student Volunteer Movement, a forerunner of the Student Christian Movement. There was also a concern to recover shared denominational heritage. There had already been reunions in Scotland at the turn of the century, and the merging of two Methodist groups in England to form the United Methodists a few years later. But the new incentive ran across denominations and led to a dynamic discovery of a much wider oneness in Christ. In part this already existed.

Beginning from Edinburgh . . .

The movement was first organized at the International Missionary Conference held at Edinburgh in 1910, under the chairmanship of John R. Mott. Its task was to survey the world mission of the non-Roman churches. Over 1,000 delegates from all over the world encountered each other across the denominational divides. Three main movements arose as a result of this conference.

First, the International Missionary Council was formed in 1921, the result of the work of the Continuation Committee from the Edinburgh Conference. The IMC met at Jerusalem in 1928, and at Madras in 1938. When the World Council of Churches was formed in 1948, the IMC did not participate directly. However, when the IMC met in Ghana in 1958 its Assembly voted to merge with the World Council of Churches, and this occurred at the New Delhi Assembly of the WCC (1961).

The second outcome of the Edinburgh Conference was the 'Faith and Order' Movement. Bishop Brent of the Protestant Episcopal Church in the USA returned from Edinburgh with a vision for the union of the churches, and with a strong desire to see the doctrinal problems faced squarely. He persuaded his own church to issue in 1912 an invitation to 'all churches' to join in this endeavour. Planning was delayed by the war. But from a preliminary meeting in 1920, there grew the first World Conference on Faith and Order at Lausanne in 1927. This had an even wider membership than the original Edinburgh Conference, and included some Eastern Orthodox delegates. The next meeting was held at Edinburgh in 1937, where proposals for a 'World Council of Churches' were received from the Life and Work conference at Oxford. The Faith and Order conference accepted these proposals, and worked towards forming the WCC.

The third strand originating from Edinburgh, Life and Work, took shape in the period after World War I when much reconstruction was needed. Archbishop Soderblom of Uppsala was fired by the concept of churches uniting in service to the world. His initiative led to conferences at Stockholm in 1925 and at Oxford in 1937. At the Oxford conference proposals were drawn up to unite with Faith and Order, and become one 'World Council of Churches'. When this was accepted by Faith and Order, at Edinburgh in the same year, an exploratory meeting was held at Utrecht in

1938. A 'World Council of Churches in process of formation' established Headquarters in Geneva. World War II held up progress, but the WCC was inaugurated in Amsterdam in 1948.

The World Council has now held six full Assemblies: at Amsterdam (1948), Evanston (1954), New Delhi (1961), Uppsala (1968), Nairobi (1975), and Vancouver (1983). The seventh Assembly will meet in Canberra in 1991. At New Delhi the IMC merged with the WCC, and for the first time the Orthodox churches were fully represented. Some Pentecostalist churches were also involved. At Uppsala and Nairobi the Roman Catholic church was represented by 'participating observers'.

Whilst the WCC (and the various national councils of churches) still has a concern with doctrine, it has also assumed a growing political role. This is increased by the addition of non-European members. One particular cause of tension has been the special fund connected with the 'Programme to Combat Racism' which has supported black 'freedom fighters' and guerrilla movements in Southern Africa, though without supplying arms.

Rome changes course

The Roman Catholic church itself has changed completely in its approach to ecumenism. In the first half of the century the nearest it came to treating non-Catholics as anything other than heretics was at the Conversations at Malines (1923–27). These were unofficial talks between a few Anglicans (mostly extreme Anglo-Catholics) and a few Roman Catholics conducted with the knowledge of the pope and the Archbishop of Canterbury. Pius XI finally brought them to a halt.

It was not expected that the Church of Rome would hold an 'Ecumenical Council' of its own. The last, Vatican I (1870), had declared that when speaking *ex cathedra* in his own person, the pope was infallible, even without the backing of a council. This view was confirmed when in 1950 Pius XII, without the backing of a council, defined and enforced the doctrine of the bodily assumption of the blessed Virgin Mary into heaven. This decree both showed that councils were now unnecessary, and also increased the distance between the Church of Rome and other churches.

The surprise came when Pius XII's successor, John XXIII (1958–63), announced that he would call a council. He called on non-Roman Catholics to seek 'that unity for which Jesus Christ prayed'. His council was to bring up to date *(aggiornamento)* the Roman Catholic church itself. The council, Vatican II (1962–65), fully achieved his purpose. There were no infallible pronouncements. Instead the council worked out a whole series of advisory, pastoral, disciplinary and exemplary documents. A new climate of relationships arose, shared worship has followed, and genuine ecumenical dialogue has been joined. Intercommunion is just beginning, along with shared ministerial training, a 'Common Bible', and doctrinal agreements with other denominations reached by joint commissions. It is impossible to predict where it will lead.

The Roman Catholic Church still stands outside the World Council of Churches. The Orthodox are fully involved in ecumenical dialogue, although their doctrine of the church severely limits the recognition they can give to other churches. However, in the last two decades both Roman Catholics and Orthodox have engaged in theological dialogue with other world communions, notably the

Anglicans, Lutherans, Methodists and Reformed. The World Council of Churches has contributed to these bilateral discussions by issuing in 1982 its statement *Baptism, Eucharist and Ministry* (the 'Lima' statement). This text has been under discussion in the subsequent years by more than 200 church bodies and denominations.

Evangelicalism has largely been suspicious of ecumenical dialogue, and even more so of ecumenical action. The call to live in organic unity with all believers has been in tension with a concern for doctrinal purity for the sake of the gospel. Evangelicalism has suffered from a built-in tendency towards separation. This can be traced in history from the Anabaptist and other radical groupings of the Reformation, through the Pilgrim Fathers, puritans and Quakers starting in the seventeenth century, to the Methodists of the eighteenth century and the Brethren movement of the nineteenth century. In the last hundred years the church has seen the formation of the Pentecostals and latterly the 'Restorationist' or house churches.

The charismatic movement and the rise of the house churches have tended to draw adherents away from the historic, mainstream churches into more exciting yet more uniform groupings. The dialogue across this divide has not yet seriously begun. On the other hand, charismatics would claim that a shared *experience* of the Holy Spirit has a uniting power across the denominational divides, and by its very nature exposes a longing for spiritual union without which structural renewal is sterile. Shared conventions and worship which include Roman Catholics alongside house church members have their own attractiveness, and they give some plausibility to the claim. Critics inevitably see this as naive.

There are other divisive tensions within the world's churches. There is the traditional split between those who are doctrinally conservative and those who are more liberal. For some the divide is political—churches differ, for example, over how to confront apartheid or resist dictatorial governments. For others the tension lies in their own organization and structures: for example, some churches do not view the ordination of women as conformable to the Bible or their own tradition. There is also the constant issue of the position of the Christian church on non-Christian religions. These are now found in force in the Western world, as well as in Africa, India and Asia. The issue has become a high priority, creating tension between Christians.

Organic union between denominations has been achieved. Perhaps the most notable have been the creation of the united Churches of South India (1927), North India (1970), Pakistan (1970) and Bangladesh (1971). In 1972 in Great Britain, Congregationalists joined Presbyterians to form the United Reformed Church, and they added the Churches of Christ to their union in 1982. However, such structural unions do not touch those who stand outside the traditional structures, and it is true engagement between the historically structured churches and the newly grown independent or semi-independent fellowships which most urgently needs undertaking.

The concern of the Orthodox Church for Christian unity, the emergence of the Church of Rome as a partner in ecumenical discussions, and the impact of the charismatic movement, has totally changed ecumenical relationships.

PRESENT AND FUTURE

John Briggs

The leaders of the Enlightenment in the eighteenth century, the positivists of the nineteenth century and orthodox Marxist thinkers in the twentieth century all agreed on one thing. They believed that advances in scientific understanding would give birth to a world in which religion would die at the hand of an ever more confident secularism.

With the emergence of the new, almost entirely man-made, environment of the city dwellers of the late twentieth century, old moral landmarks seem to have been supplanted. Society is less conscious of its roots and its direction. It is pluralist in culture, and it operates on essentially pragmatic and empirical considerations: does it work, and how does it fit with our experience? 'Computers,' as a Russian scientist remarked recently, 'know no morality, only mathematics'.

Over against this 'scientific secularization', popular superstitions—such as luck, fate and astrology—continue to command support, even in technological societies. Nonetheless, as this history of Christianity has clearly demonstrated, churches continue to grow and to develop new ways of being relevant to human needs. Alongside this, there is a resurgence of some of the other world faiths, which raises the question of how different religions can live together in the modern world. The Christian church must consider to what extent dialogue is a legitimate aspect of mission, especially if it is made quite clear that dialogue in no way negates the mandate for evangelism.

Western historians, although confident about the inevitability of secularization, nonetheless now have to learn how to spell Ayatollah. Others involved with global politics have to distinguish different traditions within Islam to understand a world that stretches from Nigeria to Indonesia. Students of anthropology stress the similarities between all fundamentalisms, noting the significance for international relations of all such religious intransigence. In fact no one can hope to understand the modern world without a thorough mastery of the nature of religious belief and practice. Religion at the end of the twentieth century is, in fact, very much alive.

Race and nationality

A largely post-colonial world still faces many problems associated with race. In the last decades of the twentieth century this has been clearly focused in the struggle against apartheid in South Africa. There the Dutch Reformed Church abandoned its attempts to underpin the doctrine of apartheid with theological argument. But for many years it failed to use its influence with sufficient urgency to hasten the coming of a government that would effectively reflect the multi-racial nature of South African society. Other Christians and churches have understood the Bible's insistence that all people are God's creatures and require equal respect. They have sought an end to injustice, and accepted the personal cost demanded by their Christian discipleship.

In the changing world of the Soviet Union, ethnic diversity has presented major problems in the southern republics. In the north, old Baltic nationalisms have become vocal. Ethnicity is a worldwide phenomenon. There is Basque separatism in Spain, and the demands of Hungarian and Albanian minorities in Romania and Yugoslavia respectively. In Asia the same ethnic questions strain the peace, with Kurds ill-used by several different states. Tamils revolt in Sri Lanka, and Tibetans continue to resent government from Beijing. Religion has often been at the heart of a people's culture. And so in many places ethnic divisions have been reinforced by credal divisions in a variety of political power struggles: Christian against Muslim in Nigeria and in the Lebanon, Sikh against Hindu in India, Muslim versus Muslim in the Gulf, and Christian versus Christian in Northern Ireland.

Elsewhere the moral issue of racial integrity and ethnic rights is seen in the land-claims of the North and South American Indians, or those of the Maoris and Aborigines in Australasia. Such claims are made by indigenous peoples all round the world, the claims of peoples who have seen their best land taken over by settlers from overseas. This is the mirror image of the plight of the world's refugees. Exiled from their own land, they have increased in number and range in the later twentieth century, though economic migrants are no longer considered genuine refugees.

Although migration may provide the solution for a few individuals, the problems of an unjust international order leave many peoples without hope. Third World debts, the arbitrary pressures of international commodity prices for primary products, and the fact that every year in Third World countries more days' work are needed to secure the same technological necessities, leave many communities without reasonable hope of orderly economic development. In the short term all these factors present problems of survival for the southern poor, but in the longer term they challenge the stability of East and West, North and South.

Archbishop Desmond Tutu, here under arrest in Cape Town, has been one of many Christians involved in the struggle against apartheid in South Africa. In many parts of the world today Christians are deeply involved in issues of peace and justice.

At times the power of the nation state has been questioned. In Eastern Europe, people's power in the late 1980s became a formidable agent for large-scale changes. Elsewhere the elected government has been shown to be the pawn of a well-entrenched military cadre. On the one hand, we witness the inability of the authorities in arguably the most powerful nation on the earth to intervene effectively against the arbitrary action of hostage-takers, hijackers and other terrorists or to force a determined aggressor to implement peace terms. On the other, the weakest nations know full well that many a trans-national company wields more effective power than they could ever dare hope to employ.

At another extreme, the late twentieth century has seen the emergence of extra-national organizations deploying immense influence over sovereign states. The most obvious example is the European Economic Community, though the nature of its powers has been hotly contested. At the same time, central bureaucracies in many countries still do not allow their citizens proper participation in the decision-making crucial to their future welfare.

Glasnost and perestroika

Within Russia, China and the Eastern bloc, questions were raised as to the viability of the Communist system of production. Working for the State or for the future advance of Communism was no guarantee of a well-motivated work force. Given the built-in frailty of human nature, some more immediate incentive to secure adequate effort seemed to be required. This called for basic changes not only in the economic but also in the political sphere, and so, in Russia, Gorbachev advocated both *glasnost* (openness) and *perestroika* (restructuring).

These new strategies not only revolutionized domestic policies but also placed the Soviet Union in the forefront of those advocating drastic reductions in nuclear weaponry. It made Russia a much less certain agent, both in capacity and desire, in exporting her revolution overseas. This suggested that the twenty-first century would be less dominated by the influence of the superpowers than had been the late twentieth century. Success seemed so often to have eluded them, for Russia had its Afghanistan and the USA its Vietnam.

Within the Warsaw pact, economic difficulties secured both economic and political change in Hungary in the late 1980s. In 1989 Poland appointed its first non-Communist prime minister since 1948. Again the dynamics of change need to be heeded: the free trade union, Solidarnösc, was founded in 1980, banned a year later, but by the end of the decade was sharing in government. Dramatic changes at an alarming and unanticipated pace also brought about peaceful revolutions in East Germany, Czechoslovakia and Bulgaria, but in Romania changes were only secured with considerable loss of life. Changes however have not all been in one direction. Moscow has witnessed armed insurrection on its streets and several east European

The last months of 1989 and the start of the new decade brought dramatic change to Eastern Europe. Entrenched regimes fell before the power of the people. This picture from Timisoara in Romania sums up the mood. In many places it was the church which kept hope alive through dark days.

countries have used the ballot box to re-elect governments of the left.

In 1989, *glasnost* and *perestroika* made it possible for the Central Committee of the World Council of Churches to meet in Moscow and to be received at a reception by the Soviet Prime Minister. One of the younger leaders of the Russian church, Archbishop Kirrill of Smolensk, confessed that when he first became involved in the ecumenical movement many of the programmes of the World Council of Churches seemed to be of little relevance. But involvement in them, he said, had provided him with an enviable education, equipping him to understand the critical needs of the Soviet Union today.

The churches in many parts of Eastern Europe have experienced new opportunities for re-establishing themselves: churches have been reopened, seminaries have been re-established and the churches have again developed their own newspapers and radio programmes, while the secular press now carries stories about their charitable works. Opportunities for Christian witness have become widespread in situations of such profound change: the Bible is a much sought-after book and people have found that the Christian conscience speaks powerfully to many contemporary questions in Russian society.

In Poland and the German Democratic Republic, both Roman Catholic and Protestant churches played a significant part in encouraging change: they offered an ideological alternative to a Communism which no longer commanded popular support. But the ending of communism did not remove all difficulties; economic chaos and the exclusiveness of some state churches still made Christian witness difficult,

In November 1989 the unthinkable happened: the Berlin Wall, separating East from West, was opened and demolition began – with everyone joining in.

especially since the authorities did not always find it easy to distinguish between well-established churches with significant national support and highly sectarian external groups, most often financed from North America.

Within the churches

Christian churches themselves have been the focus of changes as radical as those influencing other aspects of society. In many respects the centre of gravity within Christendom is moving from Europe and North America to Latin America and Africa. The phenomenal growth of indigenous Third World churches has almost reversed the situation faced by the European and American missionary societies at the end of the last century: missionaries are now coming from the developing world to Europe and North America.

Even in the West the historical structures of the mainstream denominations have been challenged by a number of movements, variously described as charismatic, restorationist and communitarian. Their emphases are not wholly new, but are a recovery of earlier movements. The new charismatic awareness looks back to earlier revival movements; the house churches find continuity with the impact of the Brethren movement of the nineteenth century; and the focus on community, with Christians sharing together in all aspects of life—and not just worship, evangelism, Christian education and service—has its roots within the Anabaptist tradition.

These new movements have not always been easy for the established churches to accept, especially when they seem to exhibit the spiritual buoyancy that the older churches lack. However, all churches have developed a much greater freedom as they have been forced to accept diversity of outlook, especially those which are more traditionally and more hierarchically organized. This is partly the result of a new pluralism, seen in a diversity of versions of the Bible, varieties of liturgy, and the widespread adoption of new hymns and music.

Where tradition finds itself in conflict with pluralism, difficulties often arise. For example, at the 1988 Lambeth Conference the provinces of the Anglican Communion differed over the ordination of women to priests' orders. The consecration of the Reverend Barbara Harris the following year as the first woman bishop of the Episcopal Church in America was soon followed by the appointment of the first woman diocesan bishop in New Zealand. Both produced predictable reactions. Those opposing this change embraced both extremities of church tradition, including some Anglo-Catholics and some Evangelicals. Questions were asked not only on the role of women in the church, but also on the nature of authority within a world-wide communion.

Votes for women was the issue at the start of the twentieth century. The close of the 1980s saw the consecration of Barbara Harris in Boston: the first woman bishop. But the issue of women's ordination goes deeper than that of sexual equality and the church remains divided.

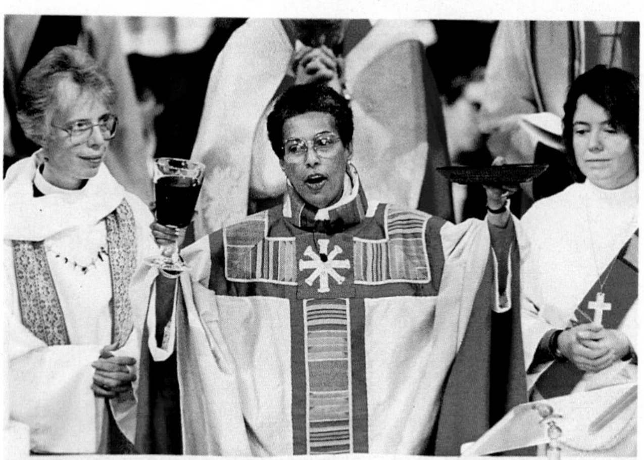

Thus the ordination of women produced widespread theological debate. Churches reacted differently to the issue. For some, a woman cannot be a priest, and they take as their models the Old Testament priesthood and the twelve male disciples of Jesus. Others place no special emphasis on the nature of priesthood, but believe the Bible does not allow women into positions of authority. Yet others have no theological objections. Instead they stress the removal of divisions in Christ, and they have forged ahead for several generations, ordaining suitable candidates and appointing them at all levels of leadership throughout their churches. Concern has also been expressed over the language used in liturgy, and attempts are being made to use more inclusive phrases to remove what many see as an over dependence on male images and words.

The Church of England's 1992 vote in favour of ordaining women was bitterly contested. Whilst some argued for justice and for releasing gifts for mission, others passionately believed the traditional apostolic faith was being compromised. Some left to join the Roman Catholic Church, which in the Papal Encyclical *Veritatis Splendor* reinforced its commitment to traditional teaching.

Church and society

In the United States of America, in the 1980s conservative Christians began to play a major part in politics. They secured the White House for Ronald Reagan on two occasions and for George Bush as Reagan's successor. To this end Jerry Falwell, a fundamentalist Baptist preacher, founded the Moral Majority Movement, which was supposedly concerned to protest against the liberal trend of American politics. However, the definition of what was moral was largely personalist, and did not embrace those issues of structural injustice that concerned many other Christians. High-profile television evangelists secured vast followings which, in some cases, they exploited in a fashion shown to be corrupt in the American courts. Most often they preached an other-worldly gospel that put its silent voice behind support for the *status quo*.

Among Evangelicals, often criticized in the past for caring only for the soul and not the body, there were calls to think seriously about the radical ethical demands made by a biblical faith. Many became actively engaged in combating structural evil within the contemporary world, and their writings and example have been widely influential in changing evangelical attitudes all round the world. Lack of consent as to the nature of Christian ethics (as much as the content of Christian doctrine) has everywhere made Christians less influential in society than they might otherwise have been.

Evangelicals have developed a much more aggressive critique of society and the structural injustices of the international economic order. The Lausanne Congress of 1974 was an important landmark in successfully reintegrating social action and evangelism. At their second Congress in 1989 in Manila, they acknowledged the imperative for 'the whole church to take the whole gospel to the whole world'. Under this heading, Jovito Salonga told those assembled, 'We achieve spirituality when we are out there in the busy streets or in the crowded market place, among the oppressed and the poor, identifying ourselves with the lowliest of them and struggling with them for a free, open society where the weak shall be strong and the strong shall be just.' A similar emphasis has come from Mortimer Arias, a Latin American Bishop who advocates 'holistic' evangelism. At the same time, many agencies with ample funds (often from North America) still preach an other-worldly, sectarian gospel, little related to the day-to-day conditions of their listeners.

Evangelicalism has developed a new confidence since the Second World War. This is partly a reflection of its growing strength of numbers, partly because of the success of its evangelism, and partly through the impact of its scholars, who by their scholarship have won such respect that the movement can no longer be classed as anti-intellectual. In many parts of the world the movement has been much influenced by the church-growth principles emanating from Passadena, California, whose leaders have always stressed the need to perceive growth in more than numerical terms. Evangelicalism must now be distinguished from its right wing, Fundamentalism, which remains exclusive, denying the validity of the faith of other Christians, and pietistic, often opposing the findings of broader theological scholarship.

The future of Christianity is with the young. Conferences and conventions around the world bring young people together, strengthening friendships across the different churches.

Varieties of faith

Pentecostalists are close cousins to Evangelicals, but they now represent a new strand in Christian history. Through the charismatic renewal, the influence of Pentecostalism has extended out beyond traditional Protestant circles to include Anglo-Catholics, Roman Catholics, and some Orthodox. Although some remain suspicious of charismatic influences, many congregations have found their worship enlivened, with a new sense of participation by the whole church membership rather than reliance on just one minister or leader. Together they have discovered a new unity with Christians in traditions which, before now, seemed very distant from their own.

The state churches of Northern Europe remain strong, at least from the viewpoint of official statistics, with impressive budgets largely provided by church taxes. Church buildings are beautifully maintained and ecclesiastical headquarters offer a wide range of services. The activities of the churches continue to make media news. But church attendance is declining. Young people are noticeably absent in many places, regardless of stringent pre-confirmation discipline. Successive *kirchentags* (national church conferences) or meetings at Taizé (the French monastic community whose devotion to liturgical reform and Christian unity has inspired many to renewed commitment) capture the imagination of a wide range of people in the way that the routines of parish life do not. Elsewhere the legacy of various movements of pietistic revival is to be found in the existence of fellowship organizations which exist as a kind of church within the church.

The Second Vatican Council (1962-65) was a watershed in Roman Catholic history. It divided the years of Counter Reformation exclusiveness from the new, more open, co-operative stance legitimized under Pope John XXIII's benign rule. After the Council there was greater emphasis upon the church as the whole body of all the baptized, lay and ordained. The church was seen as God's pilgrim people, commissioned to serve his mission in the world. The liturgy was modernized and offered in the vernacular. The Bible was accorded a more celebrated place in Catholic life. Many, however, regretted the passing of the old order and found the new world threatening and uncertain.

Pope John Paul II, the Polish Pope, and the first non-Italian to sit on Peter's throne since 1523, has given high visibility to the papal office by his world-wide travels. Parts of the church in Europe, North America and Latin America have pressed for further reforms with regard to the role of women in the church and the possibility of ministry by married clergy. Some want to accept new emphases in theology. However, Pope John Paul's personal judgement has for the most part been exercised in a conservative direction. At the same time the pressures of contemporary culture have led to both monks and nuns forsaking their orders, and parish priests leaving the priesthood. Such pressures put strains on recruitment to both the priesthood and to monastic life.

The World Council of Churches

Although there has been a tendency for the Protestant world to divide into Evangelicals and ecumenically-committed Christians, there are significant overlaps between the groups. Hopeful conversations are taking place, but it has to be recognized that many Evangelicals remain opposed to organizational links with non-evangelicals.

The World Council of Churches seeks to be a vehicle to express the common mind and conscience of its member churches yet, at the same time, to give prophetic leadership. These functions are not easy to combine, and tensions have arisen over some aspects of the Council's work. In particular, some have expressed reservations over the Programme to Combat Racism, and more especially that programmme's special fund of separately donated gifts from which grants are made to various protest agencies for their humanitarian activities. When challenged about this, Archbishop Desmond Tutu, himself a Nobel Peace Prize Winner, posed the question as to why Bonhoeffer was

The community at Taizé, in northern France, has played a special part in the wider ecumenical movement, by bringing together young people from many countries and many branches of the Christian church.

In 1989 the World Council of Churches held a World Conference on Mission and Evangelism in Texas, USA. The theme was 'Mission in Christ's way.' In many different ways, in countries all around the world, Christians continue to obey Christ's command to 'make disciples of all nations'.

regarded as a saint for trying to kill Hitler when black South Africans who took up arms against an apartheid-supporting regime were labelled terrorists.

Another area of concern has been the injustices suffered by many women in the modern world, which has led to the coining of the phrase 'the feminization of poverty'. Although many churches are committed to working for a better deal for women in society, others reinforce the prejudices of secular society by their own exclusive structures. Patriarchal traditions, long accepted as the order of things, are now challenged by feminist theology. This theology is sometimes strident, but frequently derives from a clear biblical basis. Many are now aware of the hurts caused by the older exclusiveness, and consequently take far greater care over the wording of hymns, the translation of the Bible and the revision of liturgies. They seek to avoid thought-forms which suggest male dominance, and use inclusive language wherever possible. At the same time, it is important to recognize that the Bible speaks of God as Father, and that the particularity of the Christian revelation comes through the incarnation of the Son of God.

The World Council of Churches' document *Baptism, Eucharist and Ministry* provoked worldwide discussion of these critical issues. At the same time the churches were asked to consider a second document, *Mission and Evangelism, an Ecumenical Affirmation.* Raymond Fung, a Baptist lay person from Hong Kong and WCC Secretary for Evangelism, commented, 'We cannot be serious, and do not deserve to be taken seriously, if we claim to be interested in global evangelization—of Asia, of Africa, of Latin America—and yet refuse to take as central to our evangelistic commitment the masses of the poor in the cities and villages all over the world. A middle-class church in a sea of peasants and industrial workers makes no sense, theologically and statistically.'

Third World churches

A post-colonial world is also in many respects a post-missions world in so far as missionary societies now look to working in partnership with national churches rather than perpetuating any form of missionary imperialism. Ideally this partnership should extend to sharing of resources of all kinds—personnel, finance and education. And where possible the sharing should be in both directions. But, in truth, the imperialism of those who provide the financial support very often still determines which projects are funded and which are not.

Fortunately, there has been an encouraging move from focusing funds on immediate aid to investing resources in long-term development. This has as its aim increased self-dependency, or at least the strengthening of production processes so that the developing country improves its trading position and thereby its bargaining power in the world market.

The national churches of the developing world now enjoy complete autonomy of jurisdiction. However, in many places they are challenged by 'independent' churches which deliberately reject the legacy of western missions and mission culture. African independent churches, for example, are growing fast, claiming a more complete relevance to African culture and thought. In addition, they seem to combine charismatic and ritualist elements, are conservative in their interpretation of the Bible, have a delight in hierarchical titles and exercise a strict discipline over their members.

The independent churches are to be found all over the African continent—some are relatively small and local, while the largest, such as The Church of The Lord Aladura (Praying) and the Kimbanguists, spread across national boundaries in West Africa and have growing branches in the capitals of the western world. Similar movements are to be found in other parts of the world and their theology reaches across a broad spectrum. For example, some indigenous pentecostal churches in Latin America exercise an acute social conscience, while others emphasize millennarian and other-worldly views. The growth of the church in China is part of the same story. It is clear that, after the missionaries had been expelled from the country, the church became far more Chinese. Not only did the church survive in China; it has grown remarkably, though its evangelistic faithfulness and its willingness to criticize the ruling political system still represents costly witness.

Latin America

Latin America has made its greatest impact on Christian thinking as the home of Liberation Theology. This approach was initiated by Catholic theologians such as Gustavo Gutierrez, Juan Luis Segundo, José Miranda and the Boff brothers. Liberation theologians affirm that theology is not something to be isolated in a university or seminary. Rather, theology is 'done' as theory is put into practice, and that practice should then be allowed to inform and revise the theory. In this way the key inter-connecting word for the Latin American theologian becomes *praxis*—that is, theology hammered out in terms of its relevance to the everyday experience of ordinary people and then used to illuminate their situation and provoke significant action.

There is, they say, in the gospel a bias to the poor. In developing countries Protestantism tended to create a modernizing elite, but the liberationists are concerned about justice for the poorest groups in their society. Because of their emphasis on praxis, theological education is undertaken in the community rather than separate from it in some academic ivory tower. More contentiously, the liberation theologians have found Marxism a useful tool for social analysis. Marx helps them to understand the ills of their society. But they make a clear distinction between analysis and cure: Marxist social science provides a valuable diagnostic instrument, but Marxist politics are not necessarily seen as the solution to Latin American problems. Nevertheless, liberation theologians are widely condemned by a middle-class society, which in Latin America is capable of labelling quite centrist democratic programmes as Communist.

These theological emphases have divided the Roman Catholic Church in Latin America. Some leaders have taken up the new thinking, while others have bitterly opposed it and made life difficult for priests who introduce it into their ministry. But the radical reshaping of the Catholic Church in Latin America has shown itself unwilling to be bound by church bureaucracies. New life has broken out at local level in what have been called 'grass-root' or 'base communities'. Here, often without any priestly superintendence, lay people gather around the Bible and seek to apply its guidance to all aspects of their daily living. In so doing the Latin American poor have found a new way of affirming their own dignity. Leonardo Boff describes such groups as 'a resurrection of the church', while others have seen them as critical agencies of change 'from the bottom upwards'. In areas of profound shortages of clergy, lay participation has been further advanced by the widespread appointment of 'Delegates of the Word'. These lay ministers supplement the ordained ministry.

With appropriate amendments and developments, the radicalism of Liberation Theology has been made available to protestant audiences through the writings of José Miguel Bonino, among others. A specifically evangelical response has been found in the work of René Padilla, the late Orlando Costas, and Emilio Nunez, and creative thought within the Latin American Theological Fraternity has been one influence that has led to a renewal of evangelical social thinking all around the world.

Twentieth-century theologies

Liberation theology is but one attempt to relate theology to people's personal circumstances. The vitality of theology in the latter part of the twentieth century is to be seen in the very many attempts to contextualize theological truth to a particular problem or situation. The problem is not new. Many of the so-called classic theologies were in their day contextual theologies, building bridges between biblical revelation and the dominant philosophical culture of the time. But because the world of theological discourse was so much smaller, the divergences of history and the dependency on prevailing cultures were less apparent. Moreover the passing of time has hallowed these statements as classic forms.

The need for theology to become indigenous to many very different specific cultures has produced the variety we see today. There are theologies of liberation, of the poor, of suffering; feminist theology, black theology, African theology, and *minjung* theology (meaning, 'of the mass of the people') from Korea. Even this list is not exhaustive.

The danger is that coherence can be lost in the search for vitality and relevance. And so there is a search today for a way in which to hold all this liveliness within the coherence of the biblical and trinitarian faith of the church. This underlines two basic ways of regarding theology: one way is to see theology as a *task*, which the professional theologian undertakes in order to clarify the mind of the church, the other is to see theology as *something given*, that is, the truth about God and his purposes for creation graciously revealed to those who will receive such a revelation. On this second understanding, to engage in theology is to move on to ground where 'we have to remove our shoes'. We are not present to manipulate words or to display our own academic dexterity, but to open ourselves up to God's given truth. It is God's truth which, if faithfully perceived, secures both vitality and coherence.

Justice, peace and the integrity of creation

In 1990 the World Council of Churches organized a major convocation on Justice, Peace and the Integrity of Creation. It met in Seoul, South Korea. Under this headline it sought to bring together the major aspects of a practical programme of Christian discipleship. They were seeking a commitment to peace over against all that destroys or puts life at risk. But they sought peace with justice, for the biblical concept of peace is not simply an absence of violence but a concern for wholeness of life for all humanity. To these themes of peace and justice they added a third: the integrity of creation. This third dimension is not just a baptism of green politics, but a thoroughgoing working out of God's creation mandate to those created in his image. It is a mandate given in the context of a world which, rather than the fruit of random accident, is God-created and to be respected as such.

God's plan of redemption is not just for the human race but the whole created order, which today seems to be as much under threat from human agency as the weakest members of human society seem to be from their fellows. We now need to add to the traditional list of social injustices. We must move beyond the violation of human rights, the unjust international economic order, the impact of Third World debts, the exploitation of women and the tenacity of racism. To these we now must add our sins against creation: the 'greenhouse effect', the devastation of the world's forests, the production of acid rain, the pollution of the seas, the exhaustion of finite resources, and an unbridled biotechnology

In South America many Roman Catholic priests work for the liberation of the poor, taking both practical and political action that justice may be done in the name of Christ.

which unless subjected to proper disciplines does not always provide the improvement of life it promises. With reduced tension between the superpowers, the threat of nuclear holocaust may have retreated. But the disposal of nuclear waste and the stability of nuclear plants remain major problems awaiting resolution. Chernobyl may yet prove a turning-point in history.

Christians believe that the cause of this crisis is essentially theological. Taken together, the Enlightenment and the experience of industrialization led humanity to believe that material progress was the goal of society. Given this, humanity had a right, and even a duty, to dominate and to exploit creation. Thus a secular world-view was legitimized which made no reference to the creator or his purposes in creation. Creation was instead viewed 'as a receptacle for raw materials which are only given value through exploitation'. Since such a philosophy increasingly puts the world itself at risk, Christian thinkers are properly calling for a reassessment of the exploitative ethic and the world-view that underlies it. Such a task is intellectually necessary to make sense of a world in crisis. This in fact gives new relevance to the biblical theology of creation and human alienation from both the created order and its creator. It is socially urgent because of the appalling destitution suffered by the poor in many parts of the world today. It is also vital in view of coming generations threatened with the legacy of a polluted and denuded cosmos.

Within such a programme lies an evangelistic strategy through which people of all ages and all classes are alerted to the demands and the hope of the Christian gospel. Without the biblical perspective, the world of today is a world without sense or meaning. The Bible speaks of a good creation destroyed by human sin, of a God who is passionately concerned for peace and justice for all his creation, of a world redeemed by the sacrificial death of God's only Son. The death of Jesus can put into reverse the processes of sin, both for creation and for individual men and women. Only this Bible message makes sense out of the non-sense of the human condition as now experienced. Thus, as the structural problems of a threatened creation are positively addressed, the personal needs of individuals to be reconciled to their creator God become revealed.

The next chapter of history

The crucible of history in the last decade of the twentieth century takes on a new dimension. For beyond the history of nations and their citizens, it will now have to embrace a history of the created order itself. Have destructive processes been set in train which mean that its fate is already sealed? Is there time left for a vital change? Can a new sense of responsibility for nature save not only threatened species, and threatened landscapes, but life itself? And where lies the salvation of individual men and women in all this?

These will be the critical issues that must be embraced within the next chapter of history. They are of such a profound nature as to challenge shallow pragmatisms and to drive men and women back to asking fundamental questions about purpose and reality. If the Christian church fails to meet such questioning with answers of sufficient depth and conviction, it will have failed at a vital turning-point of human history.

REFERENCE SECTION

PEOPLE

Page numbers in bold type indicate a special article: page numbers in italic indicate a picture.

PLACES

SUBJECTS, MOVEMENTS AND EVENTS

BIBLE REFERENCES

PICTURES

The photographs in this book are reproduced by permission of the following photographers and organisations.

David Alexander: 23, 28, 57, 58 (both), 59, 60, 61, 62, 64, 68 (both), 71 (all), 76, 82, 83 (with the permission of Izmic Archaeological Museum, Turkey), 84 (below), 94 (below), 97, 102 (with the permission of the Museum of Bible Antiquities, Amsterdam), 121, 130 (right, with the permission of the Bible Society, London) 141, (left), 151, 169, 174, 193, 197, 213, 222, 232, 234, 240, 243, 281, 291, 314, 332, 339, 367, 369, 371, 376, 437, 667
Alitalia: 86
John C. Allen: 142 (below), 181, 195 (all)
Andes Press Agency/Carlos Reyes: 671
Architectural Association: 303
Ashmolean Museum, Oxford: 95, 231
Associated Press: 662, 663, 664

Baptist Missionary Society: 409
Barnaby's Picture Library: 29
Richard Beaton: 27, 44
Benedettine di Priscilla, Rome: 101, 140
Bernisches Historisches Museum: 228
Bible Society: 577, 578, 579, 629
Bildarchiv Foto Marburg, Germany: 160
Billy Graham Evangelistic Association (Russ Busby): 633
Bodleian Library, Oxford: 229
Osvaldo Böhm: 159
Anne Bolt: 567
Bridgeman Art Library: 38 (above right), 487, 528 (below)
John Briggs: 519, 531
British Library Board: 37, 38 (below right), 39, 96, 97 (below) 104, 105, 131, (all), 132, 135 (both), 136, 156, 233, 241, 246, 265, 269 (left), 277, 290, 300 (below), 306, 307, 308, 337, 345, 346, 347, 359, 373, 374, 397, 399, 461 (below) 467, 595,
British Museum: 69 (above), 85, 92, 94 (above), 108, 126, 141 (right), 142 (above), 144 (both), 147, 209, 238, 242, 259, 348, 406, 414, 429, 468
British Tourist Authority: 202
Bulgarian National Tourist Office: 316
Bulloz, Paris: 488

Camera Press: 251, 256, 257, 547, 605, 612, 613, 637, 640
Cephas/Mick Rock: 649, 666
Chester Beatty Library, Dublin: 469
Church Missionary Society: 569
CMS/Camerapix Nairobi: 647
Cliche Musées Nationaux Paris: 415, 431
Combier, Maçon: 158
Corinium Museum, Cirencester: 73
Cowper and Newton Museum, Olney: 460

Daily Telegraph Colour Library: 235, 236–237, 280, 349, 470
Danish Tourist Board: 302
David Livingstone Memorial Trust, Blantyre: 565 (above)
James De Jong: 474, 475
Deutsche Fotothek Dresden: 602
Douglas Dickins: 570, 573, 575
Dover Publications: 394, 430
Tim Dowley: 244, 310, 325, 389, 427, 443, 476, 477 (above), 480, 495
Barry Dunnage: 16, 19

FEBA: 643
Fritz Fankhauser: 627, 631, 632
Fototeca Unione Americana, Rome: 84 (above)
Peter Fraenkel: 561, 565 (below) 566, 652
French Government Tourist Office: 323
Friends' Historical Library of Swarthmore College: 501

Gabinetto Fotografico Nazionale, Rome: 143
German Embassy: 311
Giraudon, Paris: 150
Martin Gostelow: 69 (below), 155, 214, 253, 473, 557
Joy Guy: 72, 139

Sonia Halliday Photographs: 109, 204, 297, 298, 299 Jane Taylor: 171
Sonia Halliday and Laura Lushington Photographs: 46
André Held: 116, 128
Hirmer Fotoarchiv München: 191
Andrew Holder: 293, 331, 335, 356, 638
J. Hutchinson: 78

Imperial War Museum, London: 585, 603
Irish Tourist Board: 217, 218, 219 (P. Tutty)
Italian State Tourist Office: 201, 272, 411

John Rylands University Library, Manchester: 130 (left)

A. F. Kersting: 153, 165, 178, 276
Keston College: 596, 597
Keystone Press: 606, 639

Jean Lassus: 206
Lateran Museum, Rome: 75
Leprosy Mission: 576
London Mennonite Centre: 403

Phil Manning: 32 (*all, with help of the* Rev. A. Medforth), 124 (both, left with help of CMJ)
Mansell Collection: 24, 26, 40, 49, 50 (both), 52, 79, 80, 90, 114, 118, 122, 125, 146, 157, 166–67, 175, 176, 177, 189 (above), 200, 360, 368, 413, 418
Mary Evans Picture Library: 489, 490, 491, 492, 503, 509, 512, 528 (above), 534, 544, 549
Methodist Church, Overseas Division: 183, 543, 636
Tim Miles: 161 (all), 215
Musée Publique et Universitaire, Geneva: 381, 382, 383

National Gallery, London: 38 (above and below left), 266, 353
National Maritime Museum, London: jacket
National Portrait Gallery, London: 300 (above), 387, 391, 454, 539
Netherlands National Tourist Office: 361
Royal Norwegian Embassy: 385
Novosti Press: 41, 42, 317, 318, 319

Pontifica Commissione di Archeologia Sacra, Rome: 117
Pompeii Exhibition, London: 70, 74
Popperfoto: 47, 53, 589, 592, 618, 623, 644, 661

Radio Times Hulton Picture Library: 344, 379 (above), 398, 420, 440, 442 (both), 452, 461 (above), 465, 483, 485, 497, 500, 506, 514, 521, 525, 533, 535, 545, 546, 550, 552, 610
Rheinisches Landesmuseum, Bonn: 190, 194

Salvation Army Information Services: 522 (both), 523
Santa Sabina Basilica, Rome: 145
Scala, Florence: 273, 289, 341, 343
Scottish National Portrait Gallery: 392
Ronald Sheridan: 106, 107, 182, 425
Master and Fellows of Sidney Sussex College, Cambridge: 267, 269 (right), 270, 274
Spanish National Tourist Office: 294
SCM Press: 619
Susan Griggs Agency: 20, 30 (both), 31, 45
Swiss National Tourist Office: 379 (below)
Syndication International: 624

Thames and Hudson: 185
Jim Thornton: 463
Tourist Photo Library: 248, 328
Master and Fellows of Trinity College, Cambridge: 285
Tunisian Tourist Office: 205

USPG: 479
Uppsala University Library, Sweden: 188

Victoria and Albert Museum, London: 33, 258, 354, 364
John White: 22

Wilberforce House, Hull: 562, 563
Paul Williams: 477 (below)
World Council of Churches: 668
Wycliffe Bible Translators: 655

Yale University Art Gallery: 77

Zefa (UK) Ltd: 260, 313, 320, 322, 401, 432, 433, 434, 451

Illustration p 312 by Victor Mitchell